Richard Crashaw
An Annotated Bibliography of Criticism
1632–1980

RICHARD CRASHAW
An Annotated Bibliography of Criticism
1632–1980

John R. Roberts

University of Missouri Press
Columbia, 1985

Library of Congress Cataloging in Publication Data

Roberts, John Richard.
Richard Crashaw: an annotated bibliography of
criticism, 1632–1980.

Bibliography: p.
Includes index.
1. Crashaw, Richard, 1613?–1649—Bibliography.
I. Title.
Z8198.84.R63   1985   [PR3386]   016.821′4   84-52264
ISBN 0-8262-0468-6

For My Wife
Lorraine Margaret Roberts

Contents

Preface   1

Abbreviations of Titles of Journals   5

Bibliography   7

Index of Authors, Editors,
    Translators, and Composers   451

Subject Index   461

Index of Crashaw's Poems
    Mentioned in Annotations   473

Preface

The primary purpose of this study is to provide students, critics, and scholars of seventeenth-century English poetry with a fully annotated, comprehensive enumerative bibliography of criticism on Richard Crashaw that contains, in addition to editions of his poetry, all books; parts of book-length studies; monographs; and critical, biographical, and bibliographical essays on the poet, written in English, as well as in languages other than English, from 1632 (the date of Crashaw's first published poem) to 1980. Although no previous study has attempted to collect and to annotate fully this vast body of criticism and scholarship, my own work has been greatly facilitated by a number of previously published bibliographical essays and checklists and is, in a sense, both an extension of and an elaboration on these earlier studies, especially "The Reputation of Crashaw in the Seventeenth and Eighteenth Centuries" by Austin Warren in *SP* 31 (1934): 385–407; "Crashaw's Reputation in the Nineteenth Century," also by Warren, in *PMLA* 51 (1936): 769–85; *Studies in Metaphysical Poetry: Two Essays and a Bibliography* by Theodore Spencer and Mark Van Doren (New York: Columbia University Press, 1939); *A Bibliography of Studies in Metaphysical Poetry, 1939–1960* by Lloyd E. Berry (Madison: University of Wisconsin Press, 1964); "Richard Crashaw" by P. K. Sundararajan in *BB* 30 (1973): 69–75; "Recent Studies in Crashaw" by Albert R. Cirillo in *ELR* 9 (1979): 183–93; and *Lesser Metaphysical Poets: A Bibliography, 1961–1980* by William McCarron and Robert Shenk (San Antonio: Trinity University Press, 1983).

Although many items in this bibliography (especially the earlier ones) are quite obviously very minor efforts, often inspired more by religious prejudice or denominational zeal than by serious critical thought and objective scholarship, others represent important contributions to our understanding not only of Crashaw's poetry but also of the art and sensibility of the seventeenth century, of so-called metaphysical and baroque poetry and poets as a whole, and, in some cases, of the very nature of poetry itself and of the creative process. Although many critics of the past accused Crashaw's poetry of being "foreign," "grotesque," and even "perverse" and often ridiculed and dismissed it for being "notoriously baroque," more recent literary scholars have become increasingly aware of Crashaw's central importance to an adequate understanding of seventeenth-century poetic theory and aesthetics and, for the most part, agree that his poetry occupies a permanent and significant position in the intellectual, religious, and literary history of his time. As Robert M. Cooper, editor of the first collection of critical essays devoted exclusively to Crashaw, has noted recently, "The problem for critics today is no longer one of defend-

1

ing Crashaw," but "rather it is one of reappraisal—of new approaches both to the unique effects that he produced and to the traditions in which he worked" (*Essays on Richard Crashaw* [Salzburg: Institut für Anglistik und Amerikanistik, Universität Salzburg, 1979], preface). My hope is that this bibliography will serve as an impetus to renewed interest in Crashaw and will facilitate a scholarly reevaluation of his very important contributions to seventeenth-century art and thought.

The annotations in this bibliography are essentially descriptive, not evaluative, because I find that what is significant and/or useful to one scholar may not be equally so to another. Since I have made the annotations quite detailed and often have quoted extensively from the item so that the reader will have some notion of its critical sophistication and tone, the user should be able to judge for himself rather easily whether a particular work will be helpful for his purposes. Also, I have listed each item chronologically so that by glancing through the bibliography the reader will be able to obtain a sense of the various shifts and developments that have occurred in Crashavian criticism during the past three and one-half centuries. Such an arrangement allows the reader to observe that Crashaw and his poetry have been run through many critical sieves (linguistic, stylistic, biographical, psychoanalytic, bibliographic, textual, formalistic, and so on) and that, in a sense, the work done on him represents a kind of microcosm of what has taken place in literary criticism over the years. By means of three detailed indexes (author, subject, and poems of Crashaw cited in the annotations), the user can quickly locate individual studies that interest him.

I have attempted to make the bibliography as complete and as comprehensive as possible. Yet, even from the beginning, I had to impose certain limitations. The basic guiding principle has been to include every book, monograph, and essay specifically on Crashaw published between 1632 and 1980; in addition, I have also included extended discussions of Crashaw that appear in books and essays not centrally concerned with him. Nearly all books and many essays on metaphysical poetry or on individual metaphysical poets contain some comment on or reference to Crashaw, but to have included all items that mention Crashaw in relation to Donne, Herbert, Vaughan, Marvell, Traherne, et al. would have extended the present bibliography far beyond manageable bounds and would have obscured the main directions of Crashavian criticism. Likewise, I have not included all anthologies that contain only selections from his poetry, although I have included those that contain critical discussion and/or notes or that, for one reason or another, seem to have special historical significance, such as Palgrave's *Golden Treasury* (1861). Also, I have included editions of Crashaw's poetry as well as translations into foreign languages, which indicate the popularity and availability of Crashaw's poems to those who do not read English. Except for the pre-1900 period, most book reviews have been excluded, because it is impossible to locate all modern ones and to list only those found would be misleading and not fully representative of a given work's reception. Review articles, however, are included. Also, brief mentions of Crashaw in modern literary histories, encyclopedias, anthologies, and textbooks have been omitted. Unpublished doctoral dissertations have been excluded because many of them are unavailable, especially those in languages other than English, and because a number of them have been published, partially or wholly, in later essays and books. The reader is encouraged, however, to check *Dissertation Abstracts* and *Dissertation Abstracts International* for many of them, most of which have been adequately annotated by their authors. Many items in languages other than English have been included (French, German, Dutch, Italian, Spanish, Portuguese, Japanese, Polish, Czech, and so on), but I have no assurance that I have located all items in these languages or in lesser-known ones. In referring to Crashaw's poems, I have followed George Walton Williams's edition (1970) because the titles are more concise than those in L. C. Martin's edition (1927, rev. ed., 1957). By doing so, I do not intend necessarily to indicate a preference for Williams's text and arrangement of the poems, but simply hope to avoid confusion. Items in this bibliography are entered under the date of their first publication; reprints, revisions, and later editions, when known, have been recorded with the original entry. Letters and journal entries, however, when dated, have been included in the year of their composition, even though they may not have been printed until many years later. I have not included letters, journal entries, and manuscript material that has not been published.

It is a great pleasure to acknowledge and to thank all those who have generously assisted me in this project. Above all, I wish to thank Melissa Poole, my research assistant, who gathered materials, checked numerous details, edited and proofread all the entries several times, solved many of the bibliographical problems that arose with the earlier items, and helped me in sundry ways. Her dedication to the bibliography was second only to mine. I am also indebted to Motosuke Arai, Katharina Brett, James Curtis, Ebion de Lima, Mildred Flynn, John Foley, Karl Klein, M. Bonner Mitchell, Edward Mullen, Joseph F. Nagy, Mary Ricciardi, Robert and Hiroko Somers, and Timothy Stoffregen, who assisted me with foreign-language items, and to Jeaneice Brewer and Marilyn Voegele, librarians, who were most helpful in locating books and essays unavailable at the University of Missouri Ellis Library. Many scholars and friends called my attention to lesser-known items, supplied me with offprints or photocopies of difficult-to-locate items, and/or offered me professional advice and assistance, especially Heather R. Asals, Diana Benet, T. A. Birrell, Robert Burchell, Amy Charles, Thomas Cooke, David Crane, Eugene Cunnar, Dennis Flynn, Sidney Gottlieb, Marshall Grossman, Achsah Guibbory, Dayton Haskin, Thomas Healy, Akira Kawata, Hilton Kelliher, Clayton Lein, Peter Milward, Isamu Muraoka, Paul A. Parrish, C. A. Patrides, Robert H. Ray, Walter D. Reinsdorf, Robert Sattelmeyer, Louise Schleiner, John T. Shawcross, Giuseppe Soldano, John Stubbs, Carroll Viera, Bruno von Lutz, David J. Wallace, Helen Wilcox, Sachiko Yoshida, and Robert V. Young. I wish also to thank Mrs. Valerie Eliot for permission to examine the unpublished manuscript of eight lectures (now at the Houghton Library, Harvard University) by T. S. Eliot.

I should also like to acknowledge with much gratitude the Research Division of the National Endowment for the Humanities for a grant that allowed me to take a sabbatical leave during the 1981–82 academic year and the Research Council of the University of Missouri-Columbia for grants in 1981 and 1982 that enabled me to visit several major libraries in this country and abroad. I wish also to thank the National Endowment for the Humanities, the Development Fund Board of the University of Missouri, and the Weldon Springs Endowment Fund of the University of Missouri for grants that supported my research assistant during the years this volume was in preparation. I am also indebted to Michael Smith, chief bibliographer of the Modern Humanities Research Association (Cambridge), for making his files available to me on several occasions, and I wish to thank members of the staff of numerous libraries, all of whom were gracious with their time and advice, especially of the University of Missouri Ellis Library, the Bodleian Library, the Cambridge University Library, the New York Public Library, the library of Peterhouse (Cambridge), and the British Library. I should also like to express my appreciation to William Shaw, who photographed the Crashaw window at Peterhouse, with the kind permission of the college. I want also to thank the Master, the Fellows, and members of St. Edmund's House (Cambridge), where during the Easter Term of 1982 I was a Visiting Scholar and during the Michaelmas Term of 1984 I was elected into a Visiting Fellowship. And, to my wife, Lorraine, to whom this volume is dedicated, I owe a special note of thanks for having very generously supported me with her love and scholarly advice throughout the years this bibliography was in preparation.

J. R. R.
Columbia, Missouri
24 December 1984

Abbreviations of Titles
of Journals

AI • *American Imago: A Psychoanalytic Journal for Culture, Science, and the Arts*
AL • *American Literature: A Journal of Literary History, Criticism, and Bibliography*
Anglia • *Anglia: Zeitschrift für Englische Philologie*
Arcadia • *Arcadia: Zeitschrift für Vergleichende Literaturwissenschaft*
BB • *Bulletin of Bibliography*
BC • *The Book Collector*
BI • *Books at Iowa*
BlakeN • *Blake Newsletter*
BNYPL • *Bulletin of the New York Public Library*
BSE • *Brno Studies in English*
BuR • *Bucknell Review: A Scholarly Journal of Letters, Arts and Science*
CathW • *Catholic World*
CE • *College English*
Cithara • *Cithara: Essays in the Judaeo-Christian Tradition*
CL • *Comparative Literature* (Eugene, OR)
CollG • *Colloquia Germanica, Internationale Zeitschrift für Germanische Sprach und Literaturwissenschaft*
ContempR • *Contemporary Review* (London)
Costerus • *Costerus: Essays in English and American Language and Literature*
CP • *Concerning Poetry* (Bellingham, WA)
CQR • *Church Quarterly Review*
DubR • *Dublin Review*
DUJ • *Durham University Journal*
E&S • *Essays and Studies by Members of the English Association*
ECS • *Eighteenth-Century Studies* (Davis, CA)
EIC • *Essays in Criticism: A Quarterly Journal of Literary Criticism* (Oxford, England)
EigoS • *Eigo Seinen* (Tokyo, Japan)
ELH • *Journal of English Literary History*
ELLS • *English Literature and Language* (Tokyo, Japan)
ELN • *English Language Notes* (Boulder, CO)
ELR • *English Literary Renaissance*
ES • *English Studies: A Journal of English Language and Literature*
ESRS • *Emporia State Research Studies*
Expl • *Explicator*
GHJ • *George Herbert Journal*
GorR • *Gordian Review*
GRM • *Germanisch-Romanische Monatsschrift*
HJ • *Hibbert Journal*
HLQ • *Huntington Library Quarterly: A Journal for the History and Interpretation of English and American Civilization*
HSL • *University of Hartford Studies in Literature: A Journal of Interdisciplinary Criticism*
HudR • *The Hudson Review*
HUSL • *Hebrew University Studies in Literature*
IER • *Irish Ecclesiastical Record*
JAAC • *Journal of Aesthetics and Art Criticism*
JEGP • *Journal of English and Germanic Philology*
JHI • *Journal of the History of Ideas*
KR • *The Kenyon Review*

L&P • *Literature and Psychology* (Teaneck, NJ)
Lang&L • *Language and Literature* (Copenhagen)
Lang&S • *Language and Style: An International Journal*
LCrit • *The Literary Criterion* (Mysore, India)
Library • *The Library: A Quarterly Journal of Bibliography*
LJGG • *Literaturwissenschaftliches Jahrbuch im Auftrage der Görres-Gesellschaft*
LQHR • *London Quarterly & Holborn Review*
M&L • *Music and Letters*
McNR • *McNeese Review*
Merc • *London Mercury*
MissQ • *Mississippi Quarterly: The Journal of Southern Culture*
MLN • *Modern Language Notes*
MLR • *Modern Language Review*
Mosaic • *Mosaic: A Journal for the Interdisciplinary Study of Literature*
MP • *Modern Philology: A Journal Devoted to Research in Medieval and Modern Literature*
N&Q • *Notes and Queries*
Neophil • *Neophilologus* (Groningen, Netherlands)
NEQ • *The New England Quarterly: A Historical Review of New England Life and Letters*
NS • *Die Neueren Sprachen*
Paragone • *Paragone: Rivista Mensile di Arte Figurativa e Letteratura*
PBA • *Proceedings of the British Academy*
PHum • *Przegląd Humanistyczny*
PLL • *Papers on Language and Literature: A Journal for Scholars and Critics of Language and Literature*
PMLA • *Publications of the Modern Language Association of America*
PoetryR • *The Poetry Review* (London, England)
PQ • *Philological Quarterly* (Iowa City, IA)
PR • *Partisan Review*
QQ • *Queen's Quarterly*
RES • *Review of English Studies: A Quarterly Journal of English Literature and the English Language*
RFH • *Revista de Filologia Hispánica*
RLC • *Revue de Littérature Comparée*
RMS • *Renaissance & Modern Studies*
RSH • *Revue des Sciences Humaines*
SaS • *Slovo a Slovesnost*
SB • *Studies in Bibliography: Papers of the Bibliographical Society of the University of Virginia*
SCN • *Seventeenth-Century News*
SEL • *Studies in English Literature, 1500–1900*
SoR • *The Southern Review* (Baton Rouge, LA)
SoRA • *Southern Review: Literary and Interdisciplinary Essays* (Adelaide, Australia)
SP • *Studies in Philology*
SR • *Sewanee Review*
SRen • *Studies in the Renaissance*
TCBS • *Transactions of the Cambridge Bibliographical Society*
Thought • *Thought: A Review of Culture and Idea*
TLS • [London] *Times Literary Supplement*
TSLL • *Texas Studies in Literature and Language: A Journal of the Humanities*
UTQ • *University of Toronto Quarterly: A Canadian Journal of the Humanities*
UWR • *University of Windsor Review* (Windsor, Ontario)
WCR • *West Coast Review*
Więź • *Więź* (Warsaw, Poland)

1632

ᴥᶴ 1. Crashaw, [Richard]. "In faciem Augustiss. Regis à morbillis integram," in *Anthologia in Regis Exanthemata: Seu Gratulatio Musarum Cantabrigiensium de felicissimè conservata Regis Caroli valetudine*, 33. [Cambridge]: Ex Academiæ Cantabrigiensis typographeo.
STC 4475.
First publication of the poem. Included in the 1646 and 1648 editions of *The Delights of the Muses*. For more information, see Martin, pp. 190–91, and Williams, pp. 554–57.

ᴥᶴ 2. [Crashaw, Richard.] ["Upon Bishop Andrewes his Picture before his Sermons"], in *XCVI. Sermons by The Right Honovrable, and Reverend Father in God*, Lancelot Andrewes, *late Lord Bishop of Winchester*. Published by his Majesties Speciall Command. Second issue of the Second Edition. London: Printed by Richard Badger.
STC 607.
First publication of the poem, untitled and unsigned, beneath the picture of Andrewes (engraved by John Payne), facing the title page. Crashaw's poem appeared in the second issue (1632) of the second edition (1631). Included in the 1646 and 1648 editions of *The Delights of the Muses*. For more information, see Martin, pp. 163–64, and Williams, pp. 490, 672, and plate 3.

1633

ᴥᶴ 3. Crashaw, [Richard]. "Ad Reginam," in *Ducis Eboracensis Fasciæ A Musis Cantabrigiensibus raptim contextæ*, 50–51. Cantabrigiæ: E. Typographeo Th[omas] Buck, & R[oger] Daniel.
STC 4480.
First publication of the poem. Included in the 1646 and 1648 editions of *The Delights of the Muses*. For more information, see Martin, p. 187, and Williams, pp. 558–61.

ᴥᶴ 4. [Crashaw, Richard.] ["The Frontispiece explained"], in *Satvrni Ephemerides Sive Tabvla Historico-Chronologica* . . . by Henry Isaacson, A1ᵛ. London: Printed by B. A[lsop] and T. F[awcet] for Henry Seile and Humphrey Robinson.
STC 14269.
First publication of the poem, unsigned and untitled. Two poems explaining the frontispiece (engraved by William Marshall), one of which is by Crashaw. Included in the 1646 and 1648 editions of *The Delights of the Muses*. For more information, see Martin, pp. 191, 410–11, 463, and Williams, pp. 491–92 and plate 4.

◄§ 5. Crashaw, Rich[ard]. ["Rex Redux"], in *Rex Redux. Sive Musa Cantabrigiensis voti damnas De incolumitate & felici reditu Regis Caroli post receptam Coronam, comitiaq; peracta in Scotia*, 49. [Cambridge]: Ex Academiæ Cantabrigiensis Typographeo.

STC 4491.

First publication of the poem, signed but untitled. Included in the 1646 and 1648 editions of *The Delights of the Muses*. For more information, see Martin, p. 193, and Williams, pp. 556–57.

1634

◄§ 6. C[rashaw], R[ichard]. *Epigrammatum Sacrorum Liber*. Cantabrigiæ: Ex Academiæ celeberrimæ typographeo. 8°. ¶⁸. A-E⁸. Paginated (A1)1–79.

STC 6009.

Another ed., *Richardi Crashawi Poemata et Epigrammata . . . Editio Secunda Auctior & emendatior* (Cambridge, 1670; entry 42); reissued with a new title page (Cambridge, 1674). Wing C 6835.

Selections, with English translations probably by Clement Barksdale, *Epigrammata sacra selecta, Cum Anglica versione* (London, 1682; entry 48).

First edition of Crashaw's Latin epigrams. Contains dedications in Latin to Benjamin Laney (prose and verse), John Tourney (verse), and Robert Brooke (verse) and a preface to readers (verse and prose) (¶2–8), followed by 178 Latin epigrams on New Testament themes (pp. 1–79). For more information, see Martin, pp. xliii–xliv, 1–71; Williams, pp. 258–59, 624–49, 678–79; Allison (entry 1069), pp. 28–29; and Sister Maris Stella Milhaupt, "The Latin Epigrams of Richard Crashaw: With Introduction, English Translation, and Notes," Ph.D. diss., University of Michigan, 1963 (DA, 23:4687).

◄§ 7. Crashaw, R[ichard]. "To the Reader, upon this Books intent," in *Hygiasticon: Or, The right course of preserving Life and Health unto extream old Age: Together with Soundnesse and integritie of the Senses, Judgement, and Memorie*. Written in Latin by *Leonard Lessius*, And now done into English, ¶9-¶9ᵛ. Cambridge: Printed by Roger Daniel, printer to the Universitie of *Cambridge*.

STC 15520.

2d ed., 1634 (STC 15521); 3d ed., 1636 (STC 15522).

First publication of "In praise of Lessius" (lines 15-end). Included in revised form in the 1646 and 1648 editions of *The Delights of the Muses*, under the title "In praise of Lessius his rule of health," and in *Carmen Deo Nostro* (1652) under the title "Temperance. Or the Cheap Physitian Upon the Translation of Lessius." For more information, see Martin, pp. 156–58, 342–44; Williams, pp. 510–13; Hodgkin (entry 405); and Hutchinson (entries 406, 407).

1635

◄§ 8. Crashaw, R[ichard]. "In Serenissimæ Reginæ partum hyemalem," in *Carmen Natalitium Ad cunas Illustrissimæ Principis Elisabethæ decantatum intra Nativitatis Dom. solennia per humiles Cantabrigiæ Musas*, sig. K4ᵛ–L. [Cambridge]: Ex Academiæ Cantabrigiensis Typographeo. STC 4479.

First publication of the poem. Included in the 1646 and 1648 editions of *The Delights of the Muses*. For more information, see Martin, pp. 161–62, and Williams, pp. 560–63.

◄§ 9. Crashaw, Rich[ard]. "Upon the ensuing Treatises," in *Five Piovs and Learned Discourses* . . . by Robert Shelford, A1-A1ᵛ. Cambridge: Printed by the printers to the Universitie of *Cambridge*. STC 22400.

First publication of the poem. Included in the 1646 and 1648 editions of *Steps to the Temple* under the title "On a Treatise of Charity," without the last ten lines. For more information, see Bowes (entry 294), p. 20; Martin, pp. 137–39; and Williams, pp. 69–70.

1637

◄§ 10. Crashaw, Ric[hard]. "Principi recèns natæ omen maternæ indolis," in ΣΥΝΩΔΙΑ, *Sive Musarum Cantabrigiensium Concentus et Congratulatio, Ad Serenissimum Britanniarum Regem Carolum, De quinta sua sobole, clarissima Principe, sibi nuper felicissimè nata*, M3-M3ᵛ. [Cambridge]: Ex Academiæ Cantabrigiensis Typographeo. STC 4492.

First publication of the poem. Included in the 1646 and 1648 editions of *The Delights of the Muses*. For more information, see Martin, pp. 154–55, and Williams, pp. 565–66.

◄§ 11. Holdsworth (Oldsworth), Richard. "Directions for a Student in the Universitie" (circa 1637).

Printed in Harris Francis Fletcher, *The Intellectual Development of John Milton*. Vol. 2: *The Cambridge University Period, 1625–32* (Urbana: University of Illinois Press, 1961), appendix 2, 623–64.

Emmanuel College manuscript (MS 1.2.27. [1]) that contains a course of study for undergraduates at Cambridge designed by Richard Holdsworth (Oldsworth) (1590–1649), Master of Emmanuel College from 1637 to 1639. Includes in a list of suggested readings *Epigrammatum Sacrorum Liber*.

1640

◆§ 12. Cambridge University. *Voces votivæ Ab Academicis Cantabrigiensibus Pro novissimo Caroli & Mariæ Principe Filio emissæ.* Cambridge: Apud Rogerum Daniel. 4°. A3-A4ᵛ, B1-H4ᵛ, a1-b4ᵛ.

STC 4495.

Contains the first publication of (1) "In Reginam, Et sibi & Academiæ semper parturientem" (signed Ri. Crashaw), F2ᵛ, and (2) "A Panegyricke [Upon the Royal Family]" (signed R. Crashaw), The first poem was added to the 1648 edition of *Steps to the Temple*, while the second poem appeared in both the 1646 and 1648 editions (with many revisions in the 1648 edition). For further information, see Martin, pp. 176–81, 214–15; and Williams, pp. 500–509, 566–69.

1641

◆§ 13. Crashaw, Richard. "Wishes to his supposed Mistresse," in *Wits Recreations. Containing 630. epigrams. 160: epitaphs. Variety of fancies and fantasticks good for melancholly humours . . .* [compiled by John Mennes], V8ᵛ–X1ᵛ. London: Printed by Thomas Cotes, for Humphry Blunden.

Wing M 1720.

Later editions published under the title *Recreation for ingenious headpeeces . . .* , 1645, 1650, 1654, 1663, 1665, 1667, 1683.

First publication of the poem (only ten of the final forty-two stanzas). Included in the 1646 and 1648 editions of *The Delights of the Muses*. For more information, see Martin, pp. 195–98, 443–44; Williams, pp. 479–83; and Tom F. Healy (entry 1160).

1643

◆§ 14. C[rashaw], R[ichard]. Letter dated 20 February 1643/44.

A Letter from Leyden (now in the University Library, Cambridge), possibly written to John Ferrar, brother of Nicholas Ferrar, or to John Collet, father of Mary Collet. First published in 1912 by E. Cruwys Sharland (entry 380) and reprinted in Martin (pp. xxvii–xxxi), along with a photocopy (facing p. xxx). Sharland and Martin maintain that the letter is in Crashaw's own hand, a claim that has been disputed by W. W. Greg (entry 532). In the letter Crashaw laments that he is no longer permitted to visit an unidentified lady (likely Mary Collet) by her uncle; suggests a plan to resign his fellowship at Peterhouse in the hope that Ferrar Collet, his former student and friend, may receive it; and describes his emotional state and uncertain future during this difficult time of his life. For more information, see E. Cruwys Sharland (entry 380), Martin (pp. xxv–xxxvi), and W. W. Greg (entry 532).

1646

◆§ 15. Cr[ashaw], Ri[chard]. "Bulla," in *Crepundia Siliana* . . . by Daniel Heynsius [Heinsius]. Cantabrigiæ: R. Daniel.

Wing H 1372.

First publication of "Bulla," found after the index to Heynsius's (Heinsius's) work (six unnumbered pages). For details, see Martin, pp. 216–17, and Williams, pp. 612–21, 677.

◆§ 16. Crashaw, Richard. *Steps to the Temple. Sacred Poems, With other Delights of the Muses.* London: Printed by T. W. for Humphrey Moseley. 12°. A3-A6ᵛB-G11ᵛ. Paginated (B1)1–138.

Wing C 6836

2d ed., 1648 (entry 20); another ed., London, 1670 (entry 43), a reprint of the text of the 1646 edition of *Steps to the Temple* and *The Delights of the Muses* and of the 1652 edition of *Carmen Deo Nostro*, erroneously called the "second" edition; reissued as the "third" edition, London, circa 1690; facsimile reprint of the 1646 edition, 1970 (entry 1003).

First collection of Crashaw's sacred and secular poems, some in Latin and some in English, in two parts: *Sacred Poems* (pp. 1–99) and *Delights of the Muses* (pp. 103–38). In "The Preface to the Reader" (A3-A5ᵛ) the unknown editor calls Crashaw "*Herbert's* second, but equall" (A3ᵛ) and suggests that, on the Judgment Day, Crashaw will "sit above, and looke downe upon poore *Homer, Virgil, Horace, Claudian?* &c. who had amongst them the ill lucke to talke out a great part of their gallant Genius upon Bees, Dung, froggs, and Gnats, &c. and not as himselfe here, upon Scriptures, divine Graces, Martyrs and Angels" (A4). Praises Crashaw's extraordinary abilities as a sacred poet but notes that his secular verses "(though of a more humane mixture) are as sweet as they are innocent" (A4ᵛ). Stresses the nearly mystical quality and power of the sacred poems, suggesting that they "shall lift thee Reader, some yards above the ground" (A3), and advising one to take a poem and "tune thy soule by it, into a heavenly pitch" (A3ᵛ). Says that Crashaw is "now dead to us" (A5ᵛ), meaning that the poet was then in exile. For more information, see Martin, pp. xliv–xlvi, 73–201; Williams, pp. 650–52, 688–89; and Allison (entry 1069), pp. 30–31.

◆§ 17. Henrietta Maria (Queen). Letter to Pope Innocent X, from St. Germaine-in-Laye, Paris. 7 September.

Copied from Archivio Vaticano, *Nunziatura di Francia*, vol. 89, in the *Roman Transcripts* (series I, bundle 93) in the P.R.O. and published in Martin, p. xxxiii.

An English translation appears in *Calendar of State Papers, Domestic Series, of the Reign of Charles I, 1625–49.* Vol. 21: 1645–47, ed. William

Douglas Hamilton (London: Printed for Her Majesty's Stationery Office by Eyre and Spottiswoode, 1891), 467.

Recommends Crashaw to Pope Innocent X. Notes that Crashaw, having been a minister in England and educated in "les Universitez" among people estranged from Catholicism, was converted to Rome by his studies, exiled himself in France to exercise more freely his religion, and has lived near her for almost a year, edifying all who have conversed with him. Notes that Crashaw is "une personne de qui les Catholiques Anglois ont conceu de grandes esperances, et que J'estime beaucoup" and asks the Pope to be generous to him.

1647

◆§ 18. Digby, Kenelm. Memorandum to Pope Innocent X. 20 November.

Public Records Office, series I, bundle 94, p. 251, from *Archivo Vaticano Politicorum*, T. 16.

Translated from the Italian into English in "The Negotiation of the Hon[ble] S[r] Kenelm Digby Resident for y[e] late Queen at Rome. . . . Faithfully translated out of the Italian Manuscript," in the Archives of the See of Westminster, vol. 30, no. 100. Both printed in Martin, pp. xxxiv–xxxv.

Indicates the impoverished state and ill-health of Crashaw at this time and points out to the Pope Crashaw's urgent need for financial assistance.

1648

◆§ 19. Beaumont, Joseph. *Psyche: or Loves Mysteries in XX. Canto's: Displaying the Intercourse Betwixt Christ and the Soule.* London: Printed by John Dawson for George Boddington. 3 p.l., 399, [1]p.

Wing B 1625.

2d ed., Cambridge: Printed at the University Press for Tho[mas] Bennet, 1702.

Praises Crashaw in stanzas 94 and 95 of Canto IV (107 and 108 in the 1702 edition). Suggests that, through *Steps to the Temple*, Crashaw is still present in England, in spite of his travels: "Th'art more in *England*, than when thou wert here" (Stanza 94, line 6). Assembles his favorite poets (Pindar, Horace, Herbert as lyric poets; Homer, Virgil, Tasso, and Spenser as epic poets; Theocritus, Ovid, and Marino as secular poets of a more luxurious sort) and assigns Crashaw to none of these groups but places him under the care of St. Gregory of Nazianzanus, the father of sacred poetry.

◆§ 20. Crashaw, Richard. *Steps to the Temple, Sacred Poems. With the Delights of the Muses . . . The Second Edition wherein are added divers pieces not before extant.* London: Printed for Humphrey Moseley. π1 A⁶ B-F¹² 2A-C¹² Paginated (B1)1–113². (A1)1–71.

Wing C 6837; C 6831 (*The Delights of the Muses* only).
Second edition of Crashaw's sacred and secular poems. Adds several new pieces and amplifies several previously published poems. The unrevised poems are set from the 1646 edition. *The Delights of the Muses* has a special title page and separate signaturing and pagination. For additional information, see Martin, pp. xlvi–xlvii, 203–30; Williams, p. 691; and Allison (entry 1069), p. 31.

1649

≈§ 21. Carier, [Benjamin]. "The names of some who have late been *Ministers, or University men in England and Scotland, and are now converted to the Catholike Faith,*" in A *Missive to His Majesty of Great Britain, King James,* A9-A11ᵛ. First printed at Liege and now re-printed at Paris.
Wing C 572.
A list of English and Scottish ministers or university men recently converted to Catholicism. Lists Crashaw as "Master of Arts of *Peter-house Cambridge,* now Secretary to a Cardinall in *Rome,* well known in England for his excellent and ingenious *Poems.*"

1650

≈§ 22. [Mennes, John], ed. *Recreation for Ingenious Head-peeces. Or, A Pleasant Grove for their wits to walke in* . . . [Popularly known as *Wits Recreations*]. London: Printed by M. Simmons.
Wing M 1713.
Later editions, 1654, 1663, 1665, 1667, 1683.
In addition to "Wishes. To his (supposed) Mistresse," first included in the 1641 edition (entry 13), includes lines 11–12 of "On Mr. G. Herberts booke, The Temple" in the introduction to a selection from Vaughan's "The Resolve" entitled "An Invitation to the Reader" (sig Bb⁸). This piece first appears in this edition of *Wits Recreations* and remains in later editions of the collection.

1651

≈§ 23. [Barksdale, Clement.] "Herbert and Crashaw," in *Nympha libethris: or the Cotswold muse,* 93–94. London: Printed for F. A. at Worcester.
Wing B 804.
A six-line poem that makes a reference to *Steps to the Temple,* beginning, "When into *Herberts Temple* I ascend / By *Crashaws Steps,* I do resolve to mend / My lighter verse, and my low notes to raise. . . ."

24. Leigh, Jo[hn]. "To the Stationer (Mr Moseley) on his Printing Mr Cartwright's Poems," in *Comedies, Tragi-Comedies, with other Poems, by
Mr William Cartwright . . .* , sig. *1-*1ᵛ. London: Printed for Humphrey Moseley.
Wing C 709.
One of fifty-odd panegyrics prefacing the collected edition of Thomas Cartwright's works. Praises Humphrey Moseley for having printed the works of
many of the major poets of the age, including Crashaw: *"Then learned
CRASHAVV'S Muse proves to the eye / Parnassus lower than Mount* Calvary"
(lines 35–36).

25. Stubbe [Stubbs, Stubbes], Henry. *Horæ Subsecivæ: seu Prophetiæ
Jonæ et Historiæ Susannæ Paraphrasis Græca Versibus Heroicis.* London: Typis Du Gardianis. 39p.
Includes "Marc. 10:52. Ad verbum Dei sanatur caecus" and "Luc. 1:18.
Zacharias minùs credens" with Greek translations (pp. 38–39) as well as three
epigrams in both Greek and Latin that Martin claims either were translations
of Crashaw's English epigrams "Act. 8. On the baptized Aethiopian," "Two
went up into the Temple to pray," and "Sampson to his Dalilah" (pp. 36–37),
or were perhaps Crashaw's own Latin versions, which he later suppressed. For
further information, see Martin, p. xliv.

1652

26. [Austin, John.] *The Christian Moderator, Second Part.* London: Printed
by M. H. for W. C. 33,[1]p.
Wing A 4244.
Includes Crashaw in a list of twenty important converts to Roman Catholicism: "Master *Richard Crashaw*, Master of Arts of *Peter*-house *Cambridge*,
well knowne for his excellent Poems" (p. 20).

27. C[rashaw], R[ichard]. *Carmen Deo Nostro, To Decet Hymnvs Sacred
Poems. . . .* Paris: Peter Targa. a⁴A-Q⁴R². Paginated (A1)1–130.
Wing C 6830.
Another edition, London, 1670 (entry 43); reprint of the text of the 1646
edition of *Steps to the Temple* and *The Delights of the Muses* and the 1652
edition of *Carmen Deo Nostro*, erroneously called the "second" edition; reissued, London, circa 1690 and incorrectly called the "third" edition.
Contains thirty-three sacred poems, only one of which is new ("Letter to
the Countess of Denbigh"); the remaining poems are selected (and sometimes
altered) from the 1648 edition. Dedicated to the Countess of Denbigh and
probably seen through the press by Crashaw's friend, Thomas Car [Miles
Pinkney]. Contains two prefatory poems by Car, in one of which he incorrectly suggests that the twelve engravings in the edition are the work of

Crashaw; more likely, only three are by the poet. For additional information on this edition, see Martin, pp. xlvii–xlix, 231–46; Williams, pp. 652–54, 694; and Allison (entry 1069), pp. 31–32.

1653

ᵥᵦ§ 28. Crashaw, Richard. *A Letter from Mr. Crashaw to the Countess of Denbigh, Against Irresolution and Delay in the matters of Religion.* London. A². Paginated (A1ᵛ) 1–3.
Wing C 6833.
A longer version of the poem, with many textual variants, first published in *Carmen Deo Nostro* (1652). For additional information, see Martin, pp. xlix, 347–50; Williams, pp. 146–53; and Allison (entry 1069), p. 28.

ᵥᵦ§ 29. [Prynne, William.] [Crashaw], in *Legenda Lignea: with an Answer to Mr. Birchley's Moderator. (Pleading for a Toleration of Popery.) And a Character of some hopefull Saints Revolted to the Church of Rome . . . ,* 169–71. London.
Reprinted in Martin, pp. xxxv–xxxvi.
Attacks Crashaw for his conversion to Catholicism: "This peevish sillie Seeker glided away from his Principles in a Poetical vein of fancy, and impertinent curiosity; and finding that Verses, and measur'd flattery took, and much pleas'd some female wits, *Crawshaw* crept by degrees into favour and acquaintance with some Court-ladies, with the gross commendations of their parts and beauties (burnisht and varnisht with some other agreeable adulations) he got first the estimation of an innocent harmless Convert; and, a purse being made by some deluded, vain-glorious Ladies, and their friends, the Poet was dispatch'd in a Pilgrimage to *Rome*, where if he had found in the See Pope *Urban* the eighth, instead of Pope *Innocent*, he might possibly have received a greater quantity and a better number of Benedictions" (pp. 169–70). Suggests that, when Crashaw had little success in obtaining money and favor from Pope Innocent, it put him into "a humor of admiring his own raptures: and in this fancy (like *Narcissus*) he is fallen in love with his own shadow, conversing with himself in verse, and admiring the birth of his own brains" (p. 170). Maintains that Crashaw "is onely laughed at, or (at most) but pitied by his new Patrons, who conceiving him unworthy of any preferments in their Church, have given him leave to live (like a lean Swine almost ready to starve) in a poor Mendicant quality; and that favour is granted only because *Crawshawe* can rail as satyrically and bitterly at true Religion in Verse, as others of his grain and complexion can in Prose, and loose discourses" (p. 171–72). Concludes that "this fickle shuttlecock so tost with every changeable puff and blast, is rather to be laughed at, and scorned for his ridiculous levity, than imitated in his sinfull and notorious Apostacy and Revolt" (p. 172).

❧ 30. Thimelby, Edward. Verse letters to Mr. Normington.

First printed in *Tixall Poetry, with Notes and Illustrations* by Arthur Clifford (Edinburgh: Printed by James Ballantyne and Co. for Longman, Hurst, Rees, Orme, and Brown, London; and John Ballantyne and Co., Edinburgh, 1813), 37–42.

Mentions Crashaw in two verse letters that appear in *Poems, collected by the Honourable Herbert Aston* and dated by the editor as 1653: (1) "And thus our soft-pend Crashaw writes above / Thees toyling witts as much, in what should moove, / As in the choice, and obiect of his love" and (2) "I'm yet a libertin in a verse, and write / Both what the spiritt and the flesh indite, / Nor can be yet our Crashaw's convertite." See also Arthur Clifford (entry 121) and N. W. Bawcutt (entry 874).

1656

❧ 31. Cowley, Abraham. "On the Death of Mr. Crashaw," in *Poems: Viz. I. II. The Mistress, or Love Verses. III. Pindarique Odes. And IV. Davideis, or a Sacred Poem on the Troubles of David*, 29–30. London: Printed for Humphrey Moseley.

Wing C 6682.

Modern edition, *Abraham Cowley: Poetry and Prose*, ed. L. C. Martin (Oxford: Clarendon Press, 1949, 1959), 21–23, 116.

Often-quoted elegy on Crashaw in which Cowley praises him as "poet and saint."

1657

❧ 32. B[elasyse], Henry. "An English Traveler's First Curiousity: or The Knowledge of his owne Countrey (April 1657)."

Printed in *Report of Manuscripts in Various Collections*, Historical Manuscripts Commission (London: Printed for Her Majesty's Stationery Office by Mackie & Co., 1903), 2:193–204.

Lists Crashaw, along with Jonson, Shakespeare, Beaumont, Fletcher, Donne, Randolph, Cleveland, Sidney, and Bacon, as examples of the "good witts in England" (p. 194).

❧ 33. [London, William.] A *Catalogue of the most vendible books in England. . . .* London.

Wing L 2849.

Reprinted, 1658 (Wing L 2850).

Lists *Steps to the Temple* under "Romances, Poems, and Playes" (Ee3ʳ).

1658

❧ 34. Anon. "Upon the Death of the Honourable Francis Pierepont, third Son of the late Earl of Kingston," in *The Upright Man And His Happy*

End: Opened and Applyed In A Sermon Preached at the Funerals Of the Honourable Francis Pierrepont, Esq. . . . by John Whitlock, G3ᵛ-G4ᵛ. London: Printed by D. M. for John Russell.

A poem by an anonymous poet on the death of Francis Pierrepont that appropriates, without acknowledgment, forty-eight lines from Crashaw's "Upon the Death of the most desired Mr. Herrys." See also Thomas Shipman's *Carolina: or Loyal Poems*, which contains an attack on the plagiarist (entry 50), and Martin, pp. xl–xli.

1660

⋙ 35. Southwell, Robert. Letter from Rome to his brother-in-law, Sir John Percivale. 23 December.

Printed in *Report on the Manuscripts of the Earl of Egmont*, Historical Manuscripts Commission (London: Printed for His Majesty's Stationery Office by Mackie & Co., 1905), vol. 1, pt. 2, 615–16.

Reports that he was told about the life and death of "your famous Cambridge wit, Crasshaw" (p. 616). Notes that Crashaw was said to have been disappointed with the twenty pistoles offered him by the Pope and was reported to have said that, "certainly if the Roman church be not founded upon a rock, it is at least founded upon something which is as hard as a rock" (p. 616). Notes further that "the English wits do think that if they turn, and come hither, they shall be courted as princes; which is a sad mistake, for it is well if they get a livelihood" (p. 616). See also W. P. Courtney (entry 366).

⋙ 36. Winstanley, William. "The Life of *Lancelot Andrewes* Bishop of Winchester," in *England's Worthies. Select Lives of the most Eminent Persons of the English Nation from Constantine the Great to the death of Cromwell*, 289–98. London: Nathan Brocke.

2d ed., London: Printed by J. C. and F. C. for Obadiah Blagrave, 1684.

Refers to Crashaw as "the second *Herbert* of our late Times" (p. 294) and reproduces two poems on Andrewes, "In Picturam Reverendissimi Episcopi, D. Andrews" and "Upon Bishop Andrewes his Picture before his Sermons" (p. 295).

1662

⋙ 37. Bargrave, John. "Joann. Baptista Tit. S. Petri ad Vincula S.R.E. Pr'br. Card. Pallottus Picenus. XIX Novemb. MDCXXIX."

Printed in *Pope Alexander the Seventh and the College of Cardinals, with a Catalogue of Dr. Bargrave's Museum*, ed. James Craigie Robertson, Camden Society, vol. 92 (Westminster: Printed for the Camden Society by Nichols and Sons, Printers, 1867), 34–37.

Presents a contemporary, often anecdotal biographical sketch of Cardinal Palotto, Crashaw's patron in Rome, calling him "a man of an angellic life"

(p. 36). Notes that Crashaw "infinitely commended his Cardinal, but complained extremely of the wickedness of those of his retinue" and that, when Crashaw pointed out their faults to the Cardinal, "the Italians fell so far out with him that the Cardinal, to secure his life, was fain to put him from his service, and procuring him some small imploy at the Lady's of Loretto; whither he went in pilgrimage in summer time, and, overheating himself, died in four weeks after he came thither, and it was doubtful whether he were not poisoned" (p. 37).

1667

◆§ 38. Worthington, John. Extracts from two letters to Dr. Ingelo. 10 June and 19 October.

Printed in *The Diary and Correspondence of Dr. John Worthington*, ed. James Crossley, Publications of the Chetham Society, 36 (Manchester: Chetham Society, 1855), vol. 2, pt. 1, 229–33, 245–48.

In the first letter (pp. 229–33), Worthington notes that he "met with one to whom Mr. Crashaw delivered (before his going away) his poems, writ with his own hand" (p. 230) and that "I know not where to procure the second, which is the best edition of his poems here; and I gave away my own" (p. 230–31). Requests that Ingelo "send down one or two from London, with some white leaves added" so that he can "both correct the printed ones by the original, and add those not yet printed" (p. 231). The editor, in a note, gives a brief sketch of Crashaw, notes Pope's criticism, praises "Musicks Duell" and "Sospetto d'Herode," and observes that "whether the manuscript of Crashaw's poems, to which Dr. Worthington refers, now exists, does not appear, but it is certain that the additions and alterations in it were not made use of in the subsequent edition of 1670" (p. 231). Notes that Worthington was Crashaw's contemporary at Cambridge and "would take an interest in Crashaw personally, independently of that which he always felt in fine devotional poetry" (p. 231). In the second letter (pp. 245–48), Worthington asks his friend to inquire in London from "some booksellers where [Humphrey] Moseley's widow now keeps shop" since he has heard that "she saved her books from the great fire" (p. 247). Notes that Moseley printed Crashaw's poems, asks again for two copies of the 1648 edition, and promises to return one to Mrs. Moseley "with the printed poems corrected by the author's original copy, and also with the addition of other poems of his, written with his own hand, and not yet printed" (p. 248). Notes that "the original copy is with a neighbour of mine, the author's intimate friend" (p. 248). See also Edwin Greenlaw (entry 486).

1668

◆§ 39. Austin, John. *Devotions in the Ancient Way of Offices: with psalms, hymns, and prayers; for every day in the week, and every Holiday in the Year.* Paris. [14], 555p.

Wing D 1239.

Roman Catholic prayerbook for private devotions, especially noted for its inclusion of hymns in the order of service. Thirty-seven of the hymns are Austin's own compositions; two are adaptations from Crashaw's "Lauda Sion" (pp. 183–85) and "Adoro Te" (pp. 203–4). The *Devotions* went through four Roman Catholic editions (1668, 1672, 1684, 1685) and then was revised to reflect Anglican beliefs and tastes by Theophilus Dorrington in 1686 and by Lady Susanna Hopton under the editorship of George Hickes in 1687. The later edition was reprinted until 1869. Austin does not acknowledge his borrowing from Crashaw, and Dorrington's and Hopton's versions, though much altered, are clearly based upon Austin's adaptations of Crashaw, not upon Crashaw's own translations (or adaptations) of St. Thomas Aquinas.

◄§ 40. Lloyd, Da[vid]. "Mr. Richard Crashaw," in *Memoires of the Lives, Actions, Sufferings & Deaths of Those Noble, Reverend, and Excellent Personages, That Suffered By Death, Sequestration, Decimation, Or Otherwise, for the Protestant Religion, And the great Principle thereof, Allegiance to their Soveraigne, In our late Interstine Wars, From the Year 1637, to the Year 1660 and from thence continued to 1666*, 618–19. London: Printed for Samuel Speed, etc.

Wing L 2642.

Biographical sketch of Crashaw, stressing his educational background, scholarly achievements, and religious sensibility. Notes that "his nature being leisurely advanced by Art, and his own pretty conceits improved by those of the choicest Orators and Poets, which he was not onely taught to understand, but imitate and make, not only their rich sense his own, but to smooth his soul as well as fill it . . . ; the essays Mr. *Brooks* [Robert Brooke] . . . imposed upon him, on the Epistles and Gospels, at School, were the ground of that Divine fancy, so famous in *Pembroke-hall*, which he was Scholar; and *Peterhouse*, where he was Fellow, in Cambridge" (pp. 618–19). Notes that at Cambridge Crashaw "was esteemed the other *Herbert* of our Church" but that later he embraced Catholicism, "chusing rather to live in the Communion of that corrupt Church, in the practise of fundamental truths, confessed to be then mixed with some errors, than to stay here, where was hardly the face of any Church" (p. 619).

◄§ 41. Worthington, John. Extract from a letter to Dr. Ingelo. 3 June.

Printed in *The Diary and Correspondence of Dr. John Worthington*, ed. Richard Copley Christie, Publications of the Chetham Society, 114 (Manchester: Chetham Society, 1886), vol. 3, pt. 2, 275–77.

Notes that he has not yet received a copy of Crashaw's poems from Henry Herringman (printer of the 1670 volume), which he had requested Dr. Ingelo to request of Herringman. See also Edwin Greenlaw (entry 486) and John Worthington (entry 38).

1670

≈§ 42. Crashaw, Richard. *Richardi Crashawi Poemata et Epigrammata . . . Editio Secunda, Auctior et emendatior.* Cambridge: Ex Officina Joan. Hayes. A-F⁸. Paginated (B7) 1–67.

Wing C 6834.

Another issue, Cambridge, 1674 (Wing C 6835).

Contains Latin poems from the 1648 edition of *Steps to the Temple* and the Latin epigrams of 1634. Adds five new Latin epigrams, with Greek versions, and nine Greek versions of previously published Latin epigrams (1634).

≈§ 43. Crashaw, Ric[hard]. *Steps to the Temple, The Delights of the Muses, and Carmen Deo Nostro.* The 2d Edition. In the Savoy: Printed by T. N. for Henry Herringman. 12°, in eights. A-O7ᵛ (omitting a J signature). Paginated (B1)1–208, omitting 113–14; misprinting 180–81 as 182–83; 184–85 as 186–87; 188–89 as 190–91; 192–93 as 194–95.

Wing C 6838, C 6839.

Reissued as the "third" edition, London: Printed for Richard Bently, Jacob Tonson, Francis Saunders, and Tho. Bennet, circa 1690 (Wing C 6840).

Reprint of the 1646 and 1652 editions. Erroneously called the "second" edition. Apparently the printer was unaware of the 1648 edition. For more information, see Martin, pp. liii–liv, and Allison (entry 1069), p. 32.

≈§ 44. Walton, Izaak. *The Life of Mr. George Herbert.* London: Printed by Tho[mas] Newcomb, for Richard Marriott. 146, [2]p.

Reprinted in *The Lives of Dʳ John Donne, Sir Henry Wotton, Mʳ Richard Hooker, Mʳ George Herbert* (London: Printed by Tho[mas] Newcomb for Richard Marriott, 1670).

Numerous later editions.

Includes Crashaw's tribute to Herbert, "On Mr. G. Herberts booke, The Temple" (pp. [147–48]). In the first collected edition of the *Lives*, the poem appears without Crashaw's name; the poem was dropped from several of the later editions.

1675

≈§ 45. Phillips, Edward. "Eminent Poets Among the Moderns," in *Theatrum Poetarum, or a compleat collection of the Poets, especially the most Eminent, of all Ages. The Ancients distinguish'd from the Moderns in their several Alphabets. With some Observations and Reflections upon many of them, particularly those of our own Nation. Together with a Prefatory Discourse of the Poets and Poetry in Generall,* 1–196. London: Printed for Charles Smith.

Wing P 2075.

Abridged edition, *Theatrum Poetarum Anglicanorum*, ed. S. Egerton Bridges (Canterbury, 1800).

Modern reprint, Anglistica & Americana, vol. 61 (Hildesheim: G. Olms, 1970).

Brief account of Crashaw's life and works (pp. 158–59). Calls him "a Devout pourer forth of his Divine Raptures and Meditations, in smooth and Pathetic Verse" (p. 158).

1677

◄§ 46. Herne, Samuel. "The Charter-House," in *Domus Carthusiana: or an Account of the Noble Foundation of the Charter-House near Smithfield in London . . .* , b2-b7ᵛ. London: Printed by T. R. for Richard Marriott and Henry Brome.

Wing H 1578.

An irregular, twenty-one stanza ode on the Charterhouse included in the preface. Stanza fifteen is devoted to Crashaw. Notes that "Crashaw's pious muse" was bred at the Charterhouse, refers to Cowley's elegy on Crashaw, and criticizes Crashaw's defection from the Anglican Church. See also Hilton Kelliher (entry 969).

1679

◄§ 47. S., T. "An Epistle from a Late Roman Catholick To the Very Reverend Dr. Edward Stillingfleet, Dean of St. Pauls, etc.," in *Several Weighty Considerations Humbly Recommended To the Serious Perusal of All, but more especially To the Roman Catholicks of England . . .* , 1–7. London: J. Holford.

Wing S 183.

2d ed., *The Sincere Popish Convert . . .* (London, 1681).

Explains how he was converted to Catholicism but found his way back "into the Bosome of my antient Mother the Church of England." Mentions Crashaw, among several other "learned men, converts of our own nation" (p. 2), whose example contributed to his conversion to Rome.

1682

◄§ 48. [Crashaw, Richard.] *Epigrammata Sacra Selecta, Cum Anglica Versione. Sacred epigrams Englished.* London: Printed for John Barksdale. A⁸. Paginated (A3) 3–13.

Wing C 6832.

Contains selections from *Epigrammatum Sacrorum Liber* (1634), with English translations, probably by Clement Barksdale. For additional information, see Allison (entry 1069), p. 29.

৺১ 49. W[illis], Thomas. "Apples of Gold in Pictures of Silver, for The Use and Delight of Children and Servants: Being A Collection of Certain Verses, from Some of our Divine Poems, more fit to be Imprinted on the memories of Young People, than Prophane Songs," in *The Key of Knowledg, Opening The Principles of Religion; And The Path of Life* . . . , 137–70. London: Printed for Tho[mas] Parkhurst.
Wing W 122.
Includes nine stanzas from "Dies Irae Dies Illa" (pp. 167–68), without notes or commentary.

1683

৺১ 50. Shipman, Tho[mas]. "The Plagiary. 1658. *Upon* S. C. a Presbyterian *Minister, and Captain, stealing* 48 *Lines from* Crashaw's *Poems,*" in *Carolina: or, Loyal Poems,* 29–30. London: Printed for Samuel Heyrick and William Crook.
Wing S 3440.
Facsimile reprint, Westmead, Eng.: Gregg International Publishers, 1971.
Satirical poem by Thomas Shipman on an unidentified Presbyterian minister who appropriated lines from Crashaw's "Upon the Death of the most desired Mr. Herrys" to compose his elegy on Francis Pierrepont. See John Whitlock (entry 34) and Martin, pp. xl–xli.

1684

৺১ 51. Cosin, John. "For my very good and worthy Friend, Mr. *Richard Watson,* Chaplain to my Lord *Hopton,* at *Jersey,*" in *The Right Reverend Doctor John Cosin Late Lord Bishop of Durham, His opinion (when Dean of Peterburgh, and in Exile) for communicating rather with Geneva than Rome,* etc., 10–15. By Ri[chard] Watson, D. D. London: Printed by F. Leach for Nich[olas] Woolfe.
Wing W 1094.
Reprinted in *The Works of the Right Reverend Father in God, John Cosin, Lord Bishop of Durham.* Vol. 4: *Miscellaneous Works* (Oxford: John Henry Parker, 1851), 387–89.
Undated letter from John Cosin (Master of Peterhouse from 1634 until his ejection in 1644) to Richard Watson, in which he states that "of Mr. Crashaw &c. I know too much, but I am more glad to hear you say, that you have no thought of following their ungracious and fond fancies" (p. 15). Cosin congratulates Watson for not leaving the Church of England, in spite of current turmoils, and encourages him in his resolve.

1685

৺১ 52. [Wesley, Samuel.] *Maggots: Or, Poems on Several Subjects, Never before Handled.* London: Printed for John Dunton. 172p.
Wing W 1374.

Makes two references in notes (pp. 6, 170) to Crashaw's "On Nanus mounted upon an Ant" (a translation of Ausonius's Epigram XX, "In Faustulum staturae brevis") and compares lines from Crashaw's translation to his own poem in the collection, "On a Maggot." See also Martin, p. 440.

1687

◄§ 53. Winstanley, William. "Mr. Richard Crashaw," in *The Lives of the most Famous English Poets . . .* , 161–62. London: Printed by H. Clark, for Samuel Manship.
Wing W 3065.
Facsimile edition, with introduction by William Riley Parker (Gainesville, Fla.: Scholars' Facs. & Reprints, 1963).
Calls Crashaw "this devout Poet, the Darling of the *Muses*, whose delight was the fruitful Mount *Sion*, more than the barren Mount Parnassus" and "a religious pourer forth of divine Raptures and Meditations, in smooth and pathetick Verse" (p. 161). Calls *The Delights of the Muses* "such rich pregnant Fancies as shewed his Breast to be filled with Phoebean Fire" (p. 161). Biographical sketch, stressing Crashaw's love of religious solitude and of a recluse's life.

1689

◄§ 54. Selden, John. *Table-Talk: Being the Discourses of John Selden Esq; or His Sence of Various Matters of Weight and High Consequence Relating especially to Religion and State.* London: Printed for E. Smith.
Wing S 2437.
Modern edition, *Table Talk of John Selden,* ed. Frederick Pollock (London: Quaritch, 1927), xxv, 191p.
For more than a century, Selden's comments on Crashaw (pp. 41–42) were thought to refer to Richard Crashaw. Hayley (1789) first perpetrated the error, which was picked up by Chalmers (1810) and Watt (1824) and not corrected until Grosart pointed out in 1873 that the Selden reference was, in fact, to William Crashaw, the poet's father, who, in his *Sermon Preached at the Crosse* (1608) denounced the stage. (See Austin Warren, entry 560, pp. 402–3.) The comment reads: "I never Converted but two, the one was Mr. *Crashaw* from writing against Plays, by telling him a way how to understand that place [of putting on Womens Apparel] which has nothing to do in the business [as neither has it, that the Fathers speak against Plays in their time, with reason enough, for they had real Idolatries mix'd with their Plays, having three Altars perpetually upon the Stage]" (pp. 41–42).

1692

◄§ 55. [Dunton, John]. "An Essay upon all sorts of learning," in *The Young-Students-Library, containing Extracts and Abridgments of the Most*

Valuable Books . . . , i–xviii. London: Printed for John Dunton.
Wing D 2635.
Reprinted (with minor revisions) in A Supplement to the Athenian Oracle:
Being a Collection of the Remaining Questions and Answers in the Old Athenian Mercuries . . . (London: Printed for Andrew Bell, 1710).
Describes the state of learning in such diverse fields as divinity, history, philosophy, physics, law, surgery, mathematics, poetry, painting, geometry, as-
tronomy, navigation, dialing, optics, and geography—with selected bibliographies. Urges would-be poets to read the best authors and critics and lists
Crashaw as one of nineteen best English poets (p. xiii). See also W. G. Day
(entry 1029).

◄§ 56. Wood, Anthony à. Fasti Oxonienses, in Athenæ Oxonienses . . . , vol.
      2, cols. 687–906. London: Printed for Tho[mas] Bennet.
      Wing W 3383A.
      2d ed., 1721; new edition, ed. Philip Bliss (1813–1820) with the Crashaw
entry appearing in vol. 4, in Fasti, second part, p. 4); facsimile reprint, Anglistica & Americana, v. 22 (Hildeshiem: G. Olms, 1969); the Crashaw entry
also appears in Martin, pp. 417–18.
      Notes that Crashaw was incorporated at Oxford in 1641. Observes, how-
ever, "not that it appears so in the publick register, but in the private observations of a certain Master of Arts that was this year living in the University" and
adds that "in what degree he was incorporated those observations mention
not" (col. 688). Presents a biographical sketch of Crashaw and mentions by
name only Steps to the Temple, The Delights of the Muses, and Carmen Deo
Nostro. Stresses Crashaw's deeply religious temperament and suggests that
"at length upon an infallible foresight that the Church of England would be
quite ruined by the unlimited fury of the Presbyterians, he changed his religion and went beyond the Seas" (col. 688). Notes that The Delights of the
Muses, "tho of a more humane mixture, yet they are sweet, as they are innocent" (col. 689).

1693

◄§ 57. [Dunton, John?] Athenian Gazette: or Casuistical Mercury, resolving
      all the most nice and curious questions proposed by the ingenious of
      either sex . . . [sometimes known as the Athenian Mercury] 8, no. 6
      (17 September).
      Includes an original poem in which Crashaw is mentioned: "Crashaw, for
whom our love and grief are paid, / Whom Cowley sung, as he the Sacred
Maid."

◄§ 58. ———. Athenian Gazette: or Causuistical Mercury, resolving all the
      most nice and curious questions proposed by the ingenious of either

sex . . . [sometimes known as the *Athenian Mercury*] 12, no. 1 (24 October).

In response to the question, "What Books of Poetry wou'd you Advise one that's Young, and extreamly delights in it, to read, both Divine and other?" recommends Herbert's and Crashaw's poems, among many other works.

1700

◄§ 59. Oldys, Alexander. *An Ode, By way of Elegy, on The Universally lamented Death Of the incomparable Mr. Dryden.* London: Printed and sold by most Booksellers. 8p.

Wing O 267.

Briefly mentions Crashaw in stanza 7, line 7: "*Herbert* nor *Crashaw*, tho on earth *Divine*, / so sweetly cou'd their Numbers Joyn!" (p. 6).

1705

◄§ 60. Collier, Jer[emy], ed. "Crashaw," in *A Supplement to the Great Historical, Geographical, Genealogical and Practical Dictionary: Being a Curious Miscellany of Sacred and Profane History*, sig. Dd4ᵛ. London: Printed for Henry Rhodes and Thomas Newborough.

Biographical sketch of Crashaw, calling him "a good Linguist" and "an extraordinary Latin and English Poet."

1707

◄§ 61. Bury, Samuel. *A Collection of Psalms, Hymns, and Spiritual Songs, Fitted for Morning and Evening Worship in a Private Family.* London: Printed by Tho[mas] Bunce, for Tho[mas] Parkhurst. 146p.

Includes a twenty-line adaptation of Crashaw's "Dies Irae Dies Illa" (p. 111).

1710

◄§ 62. Pope, Alexander. Letter to Henry Cromwell. 11 November.

Printed in *Letters of Mr. Pope, And Several Eminent Persons. In the Years 1705, &c. to 1717* (London: Printed for J. Roberts, 1735), 136–37.

Modern edition, *The Correspondence of Alexander Pope.* Vol. 1: 1704–1718, ed. George Sherburn (Oxford: Clarendon Press, 1956), 103–4.

Notes that "Musicks Duell" is an imitation of Strada's neo-Latin poem on the nightingale in *Prolusiones Academicae* (1617) and quotes lines 119–22 of Crashaw's poem, calling them "very remarkable" (p. 137).

◄§ 63. ———. Letter to Henry Cromwell. 17 December.

Printed in *Letters of Mr. Pope, And Several Eminent Persons. In the Years 1705, &c. to 1717* (London: Printed for J. Roberts, 1735), 145–48.

Modern edition, *The Correspondence of Alexander Pope.* Vol. 1: 1704–1718, ed. George Sherburn (Oxford: Clarendon Press, 1956), 109–11.

Tells Cromwell that he is sending a copy of Crashaw's poems and notes that they have "held a place among my other books of this nature for some years; in which time having read him twice or thrice, I find him one of those whose works may just deserve reading" (p. 145). States that Crashaw wrote "like a Gentleman, that is, at leisure hours, and more to keep out of idleness, than to establish a reputation: so that nothing regular or just can be expected from him" (p. 145). Notes that "all that regards Design, Form, Fable (which is the Soul of Poetry) all that concerns exactness, or consent of parts, (which is the Body) will probably be wanting; only pretty conceptions, fine metaphors, glitt'ring expressions, and something of a neat cast of Verse, (which are properly the dress, gems, or loose ornaments of Poetry) may be found in these verses (pp. 145–46). Suggests that "since no man can be a true poet, who writes for diversion only," Crashaw, as well as the writers of miscellanies, "should be consider'd as *Versifiers* and *witty Men*, rather than as *Poets*" (p. 146). Notes that Crashaw "form'd himself upon *Petrarch*, or rather upon *Marino*" but that "his thoughts one may observe, in the main, are pretty; but oftentimes far fetch'd, and too often strain'd and stiffned to make them appear the greater" (p. 146). Calls stanzas 2, 4, 6, 14, and 21 of "The Weeper" "sublimely dull" whereas stanzas 7, 8, 9, 16, 17, 20, and 23 are "soft and pleasing," and suggests that "the remaining thoughts in the Poem might have been spared, being either but repetitions, or very trivial and mean." Concludes that Crashaw's poetry is "a mixture of tender gentile thoughts and suitable expressions, of forc'd and inextricable conceits, and of needless fillers-up," and advises the reader to "skim off the froth, and use the clear underneath," warning that he who "goes too deep will meet with a mouthful of dregs" for "either the Top or bottom of him are good for little, but what he did in his *own, natural, middle-way*, is best" (p. 147). Finds Crashaw's versification quite uneven, irregular, and often incorrect but adds that "one may imagine from what it now is, that had he taken more care, it had been musical and pleasing enough, not extreamly majestic, but sweet" (pp. 147–48). Claims that Crashaw's best pieces are "Psalme 23," "In praise of Lessius," "An Epitaph Upon Mr. Ashton," "Wishes. To his (supposed) Mistresse," and "Dies Irae Dies Illa."

1714

◄§ 64. Walker, John. "A List of Some of the Loyal and Episcopal Clergy: As Likewise of the Heads of Houses, Fellows, Scholars, &c. in the Two Universities: who were Sequestred, Harrass'd, and by other Methods of Persecution Kept out, or Dispossessed . . . ," in *An Attempt towards* recovering an account of the numbers and sufferings of the Clergy of the Church of England, Heads of Colleges, Fellows, Scholars, etc., pt. 2, 152. London: Printed by W. S. for J. Nicholson et al.

Includes a biographical sketch of Crashaw. Points out that Crashaw was succeeded in his fellowship by Howard Becher by a warrant from the Earl of Manchester, dated 11 June 1644. Notes that, although Crashaw was an excellent poet, a good linguist, and a man of great piety, his conversion to Rome makes him "a Discredit to this List." Lists twenty-two fellows and scholars of Peterhouse who suffered some form of persecution.

1717

⋰§ 65. Pope, Alexander. "Eloisa to Abelard," in The Works of Mr. Alexander Pope, 398–408. London: Printed by W. Bowyer for Bernard Lintot.

Modern edition, The Poems of Alexander Pope. Vol. 2: The Rape of the Lock and Other Poems, ed. Geoffrey Tillotson, The Twickenham Edition of the Poems of Alexander Pope, gen. ed., John Butt (London: Methuen; New Haven: Yale University Press, 1940), 289–349.

Line 212, "obedient slumbers that can wake and weep" is borrowed from "Description of a Religious House and Condition of Life" (line 16). Pope's note, acknowledging his debt to Crashaw, was first published in Warburton's edition (London: J. and P. Knapton, 1751).

1720

⋰§ 66. Jacob, Giles. "Mr. Richard Crashaw," in An Historical Account of the Lives and Writings of Our most Considerable English Poets . . . , 38. London: Printed for E. Curll.

Biographical sketch and list of Crashaw's works. Notes that Crashaw "delighted in Religious Solitude, and was a Lover of a Recluse Life, which occasioned him to employ much of his Time, and to Lodge many Nights under Tertullian's Roof of Angels, in St. Mary's Church in Cambridge."

1725

⋰§ 67. [Reynolds, John.] "To the Memory of the divine Mr. George Herbert, Author of the Temple," in A View of Death: or the Soul's Departure from the World. A Philosophical Sacred Poem, with a copious body of explanatory notes . . . , 110–18. London: Printed for John Clark and Richard Hett.

Original poem praising Herbert, with a note that erroneously attributes The Synagogue to Crashaw. Castigates Cowley for neglecting Herbert and choosing instead to write an elegy for Crashaw.

1728

≈§ 68. Rowe, Elizabeth Singer. "Letter XV," in *Letters Moral and Entertaining.*

Printed in *Friendship in Death: In Twenty Letters from the Dead to the Living* (London: Thomas Worrall), 78–81; reprinted frequently throughout the eighteenth century.

Modern edition, *Friendship in Death* (New York: Garland, 1972).

Contains a paraphrase of "Hymn to the Name of Jesus," noting that "there is little alteration of any thing, but the language" (p. 78).

1730

≈§ 69. Hearne, Thomas. Entries from the diaries of Thomas Hearne. 12 August and 4 November.

Printed in *Remarks and Collections of Thomas Hearne*, vol. 10, ed. H. E. Salter; Oxford Historical Society, vol. 67 (Oxford: Printed for the Oxford Historical Society at the Clarendon Press, 1915), xi, 496p.

Makes two references to the elegy on Nicholas Ferrar, Junior, "which Archbishop Sancroft thought was by Mr. Crashaw" (p. 316). See also entry 70.

≈§ 70. ———. Notes to *Thomas Caii Vindiciarum Antiquitatis Academiae Oxoniensis contra Joannem Caium, Cantabrigiensem*, 2:809–11. Oxford: E. Theatro Sheldoniano.

Reproduces an epitaph on the death of Nicholas Ferrar, Junior (p. 810), and attributes it to Crashaw on the basis of Archbishop Sancroft's belief that the poem was by Crashaw. For more information, see Martin, p. xxiv.

≈§ 71. [Pope, Alexander.] "Epitaph *On Mr.* Elijah Fenton, *At* Easthamsted *in* Berks, 1730." *Daily Post-Boy*, 22 October.

Modern edition, *Alexander Pope: Minor Poems*. ed. Norman Ault and completed by John Butt, The Twickenham Edition of the Poems of Alexander Pope, gen. ed. John Butt (New Haven: Yale University Press; London: Methuen, 1954), 6:318–19.

In lines 1–2 of his epitaph on Fenton, first published anonymously, Pope closely imitates lines 1–4 of Crashaw's "An Epitaph Upon Mr. Ashton" without acknowledgment.

1731

≈§ 72. S., R. "An Epitaph on Alcander, and Julietta his Wife, who died in one anothers Arms, two Days after Marriage," in *New Miscellaneous Poems, with Five Love-Letters from a Nun to a Cavalier. Done into Verse*, 7th ed., 202–3. London: A. Bettesworth and C. Hitch.

An adaptation of "An Epitaph upon a Young Married Couple."

1732

◄§ 73. Anon. "A Critique on English Poets." *Applebee's Journal*, 3 June.
Printed in *The Gentleman's Magazine* 2 (1732): 786–87.
Refers to *Steps to the Temple* but does not name its author. Notes that "at the same time with Mr *Cowley* flourish'd another Genius, pretty much of the same Turn, as full of Wit, and more harmonious but chiefly on *Divine Subjects*, whence his Poems derive the Title *Steps to the Temple*" (p. 787). For a reply, see A. B. (entry 74).

◄§ 74. B., A. Reply to "A Critique on English Poets." *Applebee's Journal*, 17 June.
Printed in *The Gentleman's Magazine* 2 (1732): 802
Reply to entry 73. Identifies Crashaw as the author of *Steps to the Temple* and presents a biographical sketch. Claims that Crashaw was "so exceedingly Devout that he almost wholly resided in St *Mary's* Church." Suggests that "Musicks Duell" is "a Piece not inferior to any modern Production."

1742

◄§ 75. Dodd, Charles [Hugh Tootell]. "Lives of Clergymen," in *The Church History of England from the 1500, to the year 1668*, 3:285–306. [London]: W. Bowyer.
Reprinted, Farnsborough, Eng.: Gregg International Publishers, 1970.
Biographical sketch of Crashaw (p. 303), noting that he "was much admired for his poetical performances both in *English* and *Latin*; and might dispute a superiority with the best wits of his time, in a way." Suggests that, "as he was a great admirer of mr *Cowley*, he endeavoured to imitate the stile of that incomparable poet; and in some things approach'd near to his excellences."

1750

◄§ 76. Lauder, William. *An Essay on Milton's Use and Imitation of the Moderns in His Paradise Lost*. London: Printed for J. Payne and J. Bouquet. 168p.
Charges Milton with plagiarism and notes cases of unacknowledged borrowing by others. Calls "Musicks Duell" "the best in his [Crashaw's] collection and notes that it is "translated from *Strada* the jesuit, without the least distant hint that it was so" (p. 160).

1751

◄§ 77. Johnson, Samuel. [The criterions of plagiarism.] *The Rambler* no. 143 (Tuesday, 30 July).

Modern edition, *Samuel Johnson: The Rambler*, ed. W. J. Bate and Albrecht B. Strauss, The Yale Edition of the Works of Samuel Johnson (New Haven and London: Yale University Press, 1969), 4:393–401.

Discusses the problem of distinguishing between plagiarism and imitation. Notes that, because of similarity of wording, it is clear that Pope copied lines 1–2 of "Epitaph on Fenton" (entry 71) from Crashaw's "An Epitaph Upon Mr. Ashton" (lines 1–4) and did not simply remember or imitate the thought of the original.

1753

◆§ 78. Carter, Edmund. "Peter-house-College, 1257," in *The History of the University of Cambridge from its Original, to the Year* 1753 . . . , 18–50. London: Printed for the Author.

Lists Crashaw as "a famous Divine, Poet, and Linguist under the heading of "Learned Writers" of Peterhouse (p. 24). Presents a brief biographical account (pp. 41–42), calling him "an Excellent *Poet*, a great *Linguist*, being very exact in the *Hebrew, Greek, Latin, Italian,* and *Spanish Tongues*" but noting that he is "a discredit to this List" because of his conversion to Catholicism.

◆§ 79. [Shiels, Robert?]. "The Life of Richard Crashaw," in *the Lives of the Poets of Great Britain and Ireland, To the Time of Dean Swift. Compiled . . . by Mr. [Theophilus] Cibber,* 1:344–46. London: Printed for R. Griffiths.

Facsimile reprint, Anglistica & Americana, vol. 17 (Hildesheim: G. Olms, 1968).

A biographical sketch of Crashaw, based primarily on Wood's account (entry 56). Disapproves of Crashaw's defection from the Church of England and claims that his motives for converting to Catholicism were not pure: "This conduct of Crashaw can by no means be justified" (p. 345). Suggests, however, that as a poet Crashaw "seems to have been a very delicate and chaste writer; his language is pure, his thoughts natural, and his manner of writing tender" (p. 346). For further information, see Lloyd Mayer (entry 1124).

1754

◆§ 80. [Gambold, John, ed.] A *Collection of Hymns of the Children of God in all Ages, From the Beginning till now.* 2 parts. London: Privately printed. xii, 380; 390, 36p.

First edition of the Moravian hymnbook, which includes ten hymns based on stanzas and lines from eleven poems by Crashaw. For a listing and fuller discussion, see John Sparrow (entry 910).

1755

◄§ 81. Johnson, Samuel. A *Dictionary of the English Language*. . . . London: Printed by W. Strahan, for J. and P. Knapton; T. and T. Longman; C. Hitch and L. Hawes; A. Millar; and R. and J. Dodsley. 2 vols.
Modern reprint, New York: AMS Press, 1967.
Quotes Crashaw 103 times in examples of usage. See also A. D. Atkinson (entry 732), David Perkins (entry 756), and W. B. C. Watkins (entry 590).

1756

◄§ 82. Warton, Joseph. An *Essay on the Writings and Genius of Pope*. London: Printed for M. Cooper. xi, 334p.
2d ed., 1762; 3d ed., 1772; 4th ed., 1782; 5th ed., 1806.
Modern reprint, New York: Garland, 1974. 2 vols.
Notes that Pope was familiar with the poetry of Crashaw and that "The Dying Christian to his Soul" was influenced "from the dregs of Crashaw, of Carew, of Herbert, and others (for it is well known he was a great reader of all those poets)" (pp. 86–87). Claims that Crashaw "has well translated the Dies Irae, to which translation Roscommon is much indebted, in his Poem on the day of Judgment" (p. 87).

1761

◄§ 83. Anon. "Crashaw," in A *New and General Biographical Dictionary: Containing An Historical and Critical Account of the Lives and Writings of the Most Eminent Persons in Every Nation* . . . , 3:505. London: Printed for T. Osborne, J. Whitson, etc.
General biographical account of Crashaw, drawing heavily on Wood (entry 56). Suggests that, "as great a saint as he was, yet the time, manner, and other circumstances of his conversion to popery have left some little blemish upon his holiness, as they certainly give room to suspect the sincerity and uprightness of his motives."

1769

◄§ 84. Granger, J[ames]. "George Herbert," in A *Biographical History of England, from Egbert the Great to the Revolution*, vol. 1, pt. 2, 393–94. London: Printed for T. Davies.
Claims that "the anonymous poems subjoined to Herbert's [*The Synagogue* by Christopher Harvey] were written by Crashaw" (p. 394). For corrections, see Thomas Zouch (entry 105) and Alexander Chalmers (entry 119).

✒ 85. Ruffhead, Owen. *The Life of Alexander Pope, Esq., Compiled from Original Manuscripts; with a Critical Essay on His Writings and Genius.* London: C. Bathurst et al. 578p.

Notes that Pope "once had a purpose to pen a discourse on the rise and progress of English poetry, as it came from the Provincial poets, and had classed the English poets, according to their several schools and successions" (pp. 424–25). Crashaw is listed under "The School of Donne."

1770

✒ 86. Gray, Thomas. Letter to Thomas Warton. 15 April.

Printed in *Gentleman's Magazine* 53, pt. 1(1783):100–101.

Sent to the journal by "a gentleman of Oxford." Outlines a projected history of English poetry that will include Crashaw: "A Third Italian School, full of conceits, begun in Queen Elizabeth's reign, continued under James and Charles the first, by Donne, Crashaw, Cleveland, carried to its height by Cowley, and ending perhaps in Sprat" (p. 101). For a variant text of the letter, see Alexander Chalmers (entry 119). For a collation of the two texts and commentary, see *Correspondence of Thomas Gray*, ed. Paget Toynbee and Leonard Whibley (Oxford: Clarendon Press, 1935), 3:1122–25; reprinted, 1971.

1779

✒ 87. Johnson, Samuel. "Life of Cowley," in *Prefaces, Biographical and Critical, to the Works of the English Poets.* Vol. 1: *Prefaces to Cowley and Waller.* London: J. Nichols. 168p. (Each "Life" has separate pagination.)

Modern edition, *Dr. Johnson's Works. Lives of the Poets.* Oxford English Classics, The Works of Samuel Johnson, LL.D., vol. 7 (New York: AMS Press, 1970; reprinted from the 1825 Oxford edition), 1:1–56.

Maintains that the metaphysical poets "were men of learning, and to shew their learning was their whole endeavor; but, unluckily resolving to show it in rhyme, instead of poetry, they only wrote verses, and very often such verses as stood the trial of the finger better than of the ear; for the modulation was so imperfect, that they were only found to be verses by counting the syllables" (pp. 39–40). Calls the wit of the metaphysical poets "a kind of *discordia concors*; a combination of dissimilar images, or discovery of occult resemblances in things apparently unlike" (p. 42). Argues that in their poems "the most heterogeneous ideas are yoked by violence together; nature and art are ransacked for illustrations, comparisons, and allusions" and that "their learning instructs, and their subtilty surprises; but the reader commonly thinks his improvement dearly bought, and though he sometimes admires, is seldom pleased" (p. 43). No specific mention of Crashaw.

1781

◄§ 88. Johnson, Samuel. "Life of West," in *Prefaces, Biographical and Critical to the Works of the English Poets*. Vol. 10: *Prefaces to Young, Dyer, Mallet, Shenstone, Akenside, Lyttleton, West, and Gray*. London: J. Nichols. 15p. (Each "Life" has separate pagination.)
Modern edition, *Dr. Johnson's Works. Lives of the Poets*, Oxford English Classics, The Works of Samuel Johnson, LL.D., vol. 8 (New York: AMS Press, 1970, reprinted from the 1825 Oxford edition), 2:397–99.
In discussing the religious inclinations of Gilbert West, claims that "Crashaw is now not the only maker of verses to whom may be give the two venerable names of *poet and saint*" (pp. 3–4).

◄§ 89. Nichols, J[ohn]. A *Select Collection of Poems: with Notes, Biographical and Historical*. 8 vols. London: Printed by and for J. Nichols.
Modern reprint, New York: AMS Press, 1969.
Reprints "Principi recèns natae omen maternae indolis" under the title "On the Birth of a Princess, the Fifth Child of Charles I" (7:103–5). Presents in the footnotes (7:103–4) a biographical sketch of Crashaw. Notes his friendship with Cowley and points out that he was honored "by the praise of Mr. Pope, who condescended both to read his poems and to borrow from them" (7:103). In "Additional Remarks on the Seventh Volume" (8:313–14) notes that he is unfamiliar with any editions earlier than the second (1670) and quotes selections from "The Preface to the Reader."

1785

◄§ 90. Anon. Review of *Poetry by Richard Crashaw*, edited by Peregrine Phillips. *The Critical Review: or Annals of Literature* 59:255–58.
Focuses on Phillips's charge that both Milton and Pope borrowed without acknowledgment from Crashaw. Argues that Crashaw's description of Satan in "Sospetto d'Herode" is "turgid, bombast, and ridiculous, yet there are many lines which are truly sublime, and of which Milton has made that justifiable use which one poet has ever made of another" (p. 256). Maintains that Pope's borrowings, while "more pointed and particular" (p. 256), are also not a serious crime. Quotes Pope's evaluation of Crashaw and considers it fair and just.

◄§ 91. ———. Review of *Poetry by Richard Crashaw*, edited by Peregrine Phillips. *European Magazine and London Review* 7 (May): 346–47.
Praises Phillips's attempt to rescue Crashaw's poetry from neglect. Challenges his notion that Milton borrowed from "Sospetto d'Herode" in *Paradise Lost* but agrees with Phillips's charge against Pope. Reprints "To the Morning. Satisfaction for sleepe" and gives a brief biographical account of Phillips.

◆§ 92. ————. Review of *Poetry by Richard Crashaw*, edited by Peregrine Phillips. *The Gentleman's Magazine* 66:630–31.

Expresses reserved admiration for Crashaw but challenges Phillips's suggestion that *Paradise Lost* was influenced by "Sospetto d'Herode." Maintains that one of the best pieces in the collection is "An Epitaph Upon Mr. Ashton" and reprints it, noting that Pope "made some uses" of it in his verses on Elijah Fenton (entry 71).

◆§ 93. Crashaw, Richard. *Poetry by Richard Crashaw, with Some Account of the Author; and an Introductory Address to the Reader*, by Peregrine Phillips. London: Printed by Rickaby for the Editor. xxiv, 158p.

Discusses the alleged, unacknowledged borrowings and imitations of Crashaw by Pope, Milton, Young, and Gray and notes that "whatever relates to Theological controversy, has been carefully omitted [from this edition], which makes the work comparatively small" (p. viii). Reproduces Wood's account of Crashaw's life (entry 56) and two letters by Pope to H. Cromwell (entries 62 and 63). Contents (pp. xxiii–xxiv) and selections from the English and Latin poems (p. 1–158), with no notes or additional commentary.

◆§ 94. Maty, Henry. Review of *Poetry, by Richard Crashaw*, edited by Peregrine Phillips. *New Review* 7:185–92.

Quotes extensively from Phillips and agrees with him that "Sospetto d'Herode" "is such a poem as Pope, with all his merit, could not have written; and that Milton certainly had seen it, and taken from it" (p. 186) Reproduces twenty-two stanzas from the poem and marks in italics "what appears to me palpably to have been imitated by Milton" (p. 187). Suggests that "perhaps antiquity cannot produce finer imagery than the last stanza contains" (p. 191). Asserts, however, that "of the other poems, I think Mr. Phillips speaks rather too highly, the wishes, but for an indelicate expression or two, are very good; and the *charitas nimia* contains some very good lines" (p. 192). Recommends also "In Serenissimae Reginae partum hyemalem." For a reply, see William Bagshaw Stevens (entry 95).

◆§ 95. [Stevens, William Bagshaw.] "A farther Account of the Poem called the *Sospetto d'Herode*, the first Canto of which was translated by Crashaw." *New Review* 7:251–59.

Reply to Henry Maty (entry 94). Notes that the whole of "Sospetto d'Herode" was translated into English verse and entitled "The Slaughter of the Innocents Herod; written in Italian by the famous poet the Cavalier Marino, in four books, newly Englished" in 1675 by T. R., but adds "to whom the initials T. R. belong I know not" (p. 251). Suggests that the translation is superior to Crashaw's and agrees with Maty that "there can be no doubt that Milton had condescended to adopt many beauties from Marino, although the circumstance is not mentioned by any of Milton's critics" (p. 251).

1786

◄§ 96. [Headley, Henry.] Letter to the Editor. *Gentleman's Magazine* 56: 311–13.

Discusses the influence of Crashaw on Pope and compares selected passages from both poets to demonstrate his point. Suggests that Pope borrowed from or at least was inspired by "Description of a Religious House and Condition of Life" and "Alexias" in several instances in "Eloisa to Abelard." Regrets that Phillips omitted the "theological poems" of Crashaw and suggests that thereby many of Crashaw's beauties were passed by.

1787

◄§ 97. Headley, Henry. *Select Beauties of Ancient English Poetry*. With Remarks by Henry Headley. London: Printed for T. Cadell. 2 vols. in one. xiv, 113; lxvi, 192p.

List Crashaw, along with Fairfax and Sandys, as a translator of extraordinary merit (2:xv) and presents a biographical sketch and critical evaluation of him (2:xli). Notes that Crashaw "deserves preservation for better reasons that his having accidentally attracted the notice of Pope" and claims that Crashaw "has originality in many parts, and as a translator is entitled to the highest applause" (2:xli). Praises "Sospetto d'Herode" and notes that Milton was aware of it. Claims that Crashaw "possessed one of those ineffable minds which border on enthusiasm, and when fortunately directed, occasionally produce great things" but adds that Crashaw "had too much religion to devote his whole strength to poetry; he trifled for amusement, and never wrote for fame" (2:xli). Concludes, however, that "to his attainments, which were numerous and elegant, all his biographers have borne witness" and that he died, "to use the words of Cowley, both a 'poet and saint'" (2:xli). Notes in the entry on George Herbert (2:lvi) that Herbert is "infinitely inferior to both Quarles and Crashaw" and rejects Granger's suggestion that Crashaw added "The Synagogue" to *The Temple*, noting that the poems are "unworthy of him." Reprints parts of "Sospetto d'Herode"(1:49–64) and entitles it "The Alarm of Satan, with the Instigation of Herod." In notes (2:142–44) comments on the possible indebtedness of Milton and Pope to Crashaw and observes that "the particular relation that the whole of this Piece bears to many passages in Milton's *Paradise Lost*, and the great sublimity of the Poetry, are reasons sufficient to make it acceptable to every reader of taste, notwithstanding its being a translation" (2:142). Suggests that the 1675 translation of Marino by T. R., noted by Henry Maty (entry 94), "would be highly worth republishing, particularly if executed in a superior style [as claimed by Maty] to Crashaw, which seems to me hardly possible" (2:142).

1788

◄§ 98. Anon. Review of *Select Beauties of Ancient English Poetry*, edited by Henry Headley (1787). *Critical Review* 65:49–53.

Notes that Crashaw's "Sospetto d'Herode" is in "the same grand style" as Sackville's "Induction" to the *Mirror for Magistrates* and suggests that "a new edition of the translation of Marino would be a valuable acquisition to the public" (p. 52).

1789

◄§ 99. Hayley, William. "Crashaw," in *Biographia Britannica: or the Lives of the Most Eminent Persons who have flourished in Great Britain and Ireland . . .* , edited by Andrew Kippis et al., 4:427–32. 2d ed. London: Rivington and Marshall.

Notes that Crashaw was omitted from the first edition. Offers a biographical sketch, based on Wood (entry 56). Maintains that Crashaw's conversion was motivated by his piety and his enthusiastic admiration for St. Teresa. Calls "Sospetto d'Herode" "one of the most striking performances of Crashaw" (pp. 429–30). Reprints passages from Crashaw's poems as well as criticism by Cowley, Selden, Pope, Peregrine Phillips, and Thomas Car. Notes Pope's borrowings and defends Pope against Phillips's charges. Parallels stanzas from Marino with Crashaw's "Sospetto d'Herode." Observes that Crashaw's poems have been neglected "not merely because they are devotional, but because their author has frequently fallen into the worst defects of style, in his mode of treating subjects that peculiarly require a chaste dignity of expression" (p. 431). Notes Herbert's influence on Crashaw and says that "the anonymous poems subjoined to the works of that very religious and once popular bard, are said, by Mr. Granger, to have been written by Crashaw" (p. 431). Quotes lines from "To the Infant Martyrs" and calls it "a striking example of the deplorable conceits by which pious poetry was sometimes debased" (p. 431). Notes that Crashaw, "neglected in later days, was the companion of Selden, and the idol of Cowley" (p. 432). For a reply, see M. Green (entry 103).

◄§ 100. Walpole, Horace. Letter to Samuel Lysons. 17 September.

Printed in *Bentley's Miscellany* 27(1850):524–25.

Modern edition, *The Yale Edition of Horace Walpole's Correspondence*, ed. W. S. Lewis (New Haven: Yale University Press; London: Geoffrey Cumberlege, Oxford University Press, 1951), 15:200–202.

Discussing William Hayley's life of Crashaw in *Biographia Britannica* (entry 99), Walpole refers to Crashaw as "that mad, and yet indifferent poet" and suggests that, in order to expand his biographical sketch of Crashaw, Hayley "has been forced to reprint a most wretched poem on his [Crashaw's] death, by Cowley" (p. 524). Quotes lines from Cowley's elegy on Crashaw and concludes that there are things in the last two stanzas, "of which a modern bell-man would be ashamed" (p. 525). See also the editor's comments on the letter in *Bentley's Miscellany* (entry 177).

1790

ᴥᴥ§ 101. Peckard, P[eter]. *Memoirs of the Life of Mr. Nicholas Ferrar.* Cambridge: J. Archdeacon Printer to the University. xvi, 316p.

Abridged, London: Printed and sold by Joseph Masters and Co., 1852. 155p.

Contains a life of Nicholas Ferrar that describes the vigils held at Little Gidding, noting that "several religious persons both in the neighbourhood, and from distant places, attended these watchings: and amongst these the celebrated Mr. Rich Crashaw, Fellow of Peterhouse, who was very intimate in the family, and frequently came from Cambridge for this purpose, and at his return often watched in Little St. Mary's Church near Peterhouse" (p. 243). An attached sequel to the memoirs, which gives an account of Nicholas Ferrar, Jr., and his part in the Harmonies of Little Gidding, reproduces the epitaph on Nicholas Ferrar, Jr., sometimes attributed to Crashaw. Notes that Crashaw had a "familiar and friendly intimacy with the family, and knew every circumstance relative to them" and spent a "great part of his time at Gidding, and was a man of that established virtue and integrity" (p. 275).

1793

ᴥᴥ§ 102. Anderson, Robert. "The Poetical Works of Richard Crashaw," in *A Complete Edition of the Poets of Great Britain*, 4:699–754. Edinburgh: Printed by Mundell and Sons.

Presents a biographical sketch of Crashaw (pp. 701–6), reproduces Cowley's "On the Death of Mr. Crashaw" (p. 699), and reprints poems from the 1648 edition. Calls Crashaw "an accomplished scholar" and a "devout poet" and notes that his "writings have not, hitherto, received so much attention as they deserve" (p. 702). Points out that, in his elegy, Cowley "has sometimes fallen into the principal defect of the poet whom he praises" and "now and then speaks of sacred things, with a vulgar and ludicrous familiarity of language" (p. 702). Claims that Crashaw's "whole works reprinted from the edition of 1648, are now, for the first time, received into a collection of classical English poetry" (p. 702). Links Crashaw with Herbert and Quarles but notes that he was "infinitely superior to the former in sublimity and imagination, and to the latter in beauty and tenderness" (p. 703). Maintains that Crashaw's poetry "bears the marks of a fervid mind, and a poetical imagination; it has strength, warmth, and originality; but it is sometimes debased by the deplorable conceits which characterise the pious poetry of Herbert" (p. 703). Praises "Sospetto d'Herode" and suggests specific passages borrowed by Milton in

Paradise Lost. Notes also Pope's borrowings from Crashaw and reproduces and evaluates Pope's criticism of Crashaw. Praises Crashaw's Latin poetry: "his pieces display uncommon powers of invention and sentiment; and are valuable, as much for their fancy and genius, as for their style and expression" (p. 705). Maintains that Crashaw's English poems are "sometimes tender and beautiful, and sometimes absurd and disgusting" and are "a compound of piety and enthusiasm, sublimity and vulgarity, elegance and affectation, pathos and extravagance" (p. 703); and thus "he is an unequal writer; but his compositions are chiefly characterised by tenderness of sentiment, beauty of expression, and harmony of numbers" (p. 703).

103. Green, M. Letter to the Editor. *Gentleman's Magazine* 63: 1001 – 3.
Challenges certain facts and assumptions about Crashaw's life and works in William Hayley's account in *Biographia Britannica* (entry 99), in particular noting the publication of *Richardi Crashawi Poemata et Epigrammata* (1670).

104. P., T. Letter to the Editor. *Gentleman's Magazine* 63: 1166.
In addition to the 1670 edition of Crashaw mentioned by M. Green (entry 103), calls attention to the 1652 publication of *Carmen Deo Nostro* in Paris "with a number of very neat emblematic vignettes, said to have been executed by Crashaw himself." Rejects the notion that Crashaw wrote the anonymous poems often attached to Herbert's *The Temple*. Points out that in the *Essay on Man*, Pope imitated a couplet from Cowley's lines on the death of Crashaw.

1796

105. Zouch, Thomas. "The Life of Mr. Isaac Walton," in *The Lives of Dr. John Donne; Sir Henry Wotton; Mr. Richard Hooker; Mr. George Herbert; and Dr. Robert Anderson*, with notes and a life of the author by Thomas Zouch, ix–liv. York: Printed by Wilson, Spence, and Mawman.
Points out that *The Synagogue*, often attached to Herbert's *The Temple*, is the work of Christopher Harvey, not Crashaw, as sometimes suggested (pp. l–li). See also Alexander Chalmers (entry 119) and J. Granger (entry 84).

1797

106. Anon. "Crashaw," in *The Encyclopaedia Britannica*, 3d ed., 5: 511 – 12. Edinburgh: Printed for A. Bell and C. MacFarquhar.
Crashaw does not appear in the 1st ed. (1768–1771) or in the 2d (1784). Biographical sketch noting that "by catholic artifices" Crashaw was "perverted to the church of Rome" (p. 511). Repeats the comments of Pope on Crashaw's conversion. Briefly mentions *Steps to the Temple, The Delights of the Muses*, and *Carmen Deo Nostro*.

◄§ 107. Warton, Joseph, ed. Notes to Letter XXVI in *Works, complete* [of Alexander Pope]; *with notes and illustrations by Joseph Warton and others*, 7:142–45. London: Printed for B. Law.

In notes to Pope's letter to Henry Cromwell concerning Crashaw (entry 63), Warton claims that Crashaw "was so fond of *Marino*, a writer of fine imagination but little judgment, as to translate the whole first book of his *Strage de gli Innocenti* (published 1633), which *Marino* himself preferred to his *Il Adone*, and to which *Milton* was indebted for many hints, which, however, he greatly improved" (p. 143). Pope suggests that Crashaw's best pieces are "Psalme 23," "In praise of Lessius," "An Epitaph Upon Mr. Ashton," "Wishes. To his (supposed) Mistresse," and "Dies Irae Dies Illa," to which Warton adds "a translation from *Moschus* ["Out of the Greeke Cupid's Cryer"] and another from *Catullus* ["Out of Catullus" (?)]" (p. 144). Maintains also that "Psalme 23" is inferior to Sandys's version and points out that Roscommon borrowed many lines from "Dies Irae Dies Illa," particularly stanza 17.

1798

◄§ 108. Drake, Nathan. "On the Poetry of the Ages of Elizabeth and the Charles's and of the Present Reign," in *Literary Hours, or Sketches Critical and Narrative*, 441–54. London: Sudbury.

2d ed., corrected and enlarged (2 vols.), 1800; 3d ed. (3 vols.), 1804; 4th ed., 1820; 2d ed. reprinted, New York: Garland, 1970.

Comments on Henry Headley's list of major poets in *Select Beauties of Ancient English Poetry* (entry 97). Notes that, except for Spenser, Milton, and Shakespeare, "though they occasionally exhibit very brilliant passages, yet are they mingled with such a mass of obscurity, vulgarity, obscenity and colloquial barbarism, that he must be a very hardy critic indeed, who can venture to station them on a level with the modern votaries of the muse" (p. 443). Notes, concerning Crashaw, that he "possessed the requisites of a genuine poet, enthusiasm and sublimity, but he never undertook any grand or original work" (p. 454). Maintains that Crashaw's choice of imitating Marino "was injudicious, and though his translation has several passages which challenge admiration, yet as a whole it is far from being pleasing" (p. 454). Asserts that many of Crashaw's images are "disgusting and absurdly gigantic, and tend to call up ludicrous than terrible ideas" (p. 454).

1800

◄§ 109. Southey, Robert. Letter to Lieutenant Southey, H.M.S. Bellona. 23 May.

Printed in *The Life and Correspondence of Robert Southey*, ed. Charles

Cuthbert Southey (London: Longman, Brown, Green and Longmans, 1850), 2:68–74.

Letter written from Lisbon, commenting on the Catholic devotional life of the city, noting that pious Portuguese often "mingle the feelings of earthly and spiritual love, as strangely as our Bible has mixed the language in Solomon's Song" and pointing out that "we have an instance in Crashaw the poet's hymn to St. Theresa" (pp. 72–73).

◄§ 110. Watkins, John. "Crashaw," in *An Universal Biographical and Historical Dictionary*, sig. Qq1. London: Printed by T. Davison and T. Gillet for R. Phillips.

Biographical sketch of Crashaw, noting that he was "inveigled" into "popery" and that "it is to his honour that Pope condescended not only to praise, but to borrow" from his poems.

1801

◄§ 111. Ellis, George. "Richard Crashaw," in *Specimens of the Early English Poets* . . . , 2d ed., 3:197–201. London: Printed for W. Bulmer and Co. for G. and W. Nicol and J. Wright.

1st ed. (1 vol.) of 1790 does not include Crashaw; 3d corrected ed., 1803.

Biographical sketch and headnote and three selections: "Out of Catullus," "Loves Horoscope," and "An Epitaph upon a Young Married Couple." Suggests that Crashaw resembles Herbert "in his turn of mind, but possessed more fancy and genius" (p. 197). Maintains that Crashaw's translations "have considerable merit, but his original poetry is full of conceit," and notes that the Latin poems "have been much admired, though liable to the same objection as his English" (p. 197).

◄§ 112. Todd, Henry John. "An Inquiry into the Origin of Paradise Lost," in *The Poetical Works of John Milton* . . . , edited by John Henry Todd, 1:248–303. London: J. Johnson [et al.] by Bye and Law.

2d ed., 1809.

Modern reprint, New York: AMS Press, 1970.

Discusses Milton's indebtedness to Crashaw, calling attention to parallels between Milton's description of Satan in *Paradise Lost* and Crashaw's "Sospetto d'Herode." Suggests that, although Milton, "no doubt, had read Crashaw's translation [of Marino]" (p. 284), his description is far more complex and rich than Crashaw's. Notes, however, that Crashaw "is entitled to the merit of suggesting the combination and form of several happy phrases to Pope" (p. 284). Calls Crashaw a "distinguished" poet and presents Bargrave's biographical sketch of Crashaw (entry 37).

1802

•§ 113. Anon. Review of George Ellis's *Specimens of English Poets* (1801). *British Critic* 19:217–24, 615–23.

States that "we shall not vindicate the taste of *Crashaw*; but, surely Mr. Ellis has spoken of him with too undistinguished severity" and notes that "it would be difficult to name a versifier, except *Cowley*, who has shown so much genius in a vicious style" (p. 621).

•§ 114. A[ikin, John.] "Crashaw, Richard," in *General Biography; or, Lives, Critical and Historical, of the Most Eminent Persons of All Countries, Conditions, and Professions,* composed by John Aikin, Thomas Morgan, Nicholson, and others, 3:213. London: Printed for J. Johnson, St. Paul's Churchyard; G. and J. Robinson, Pater-Noster Row; and G. Kearsley, Fleet-Street—also for Bell and Bradfute, Edinburgh; and Colbert, Capel Street, Dublin.

Biographical sketch of Crashaw, who is listed as "an English poet, distinguished for devotional enthusiasm." Notes that Crashaw "was indeed formed to sympathise in all the rapturous and seraphic ardours which have distinguished the devotees of the catholic communion, especially those of the female sex," and suggests that his poems on St. Teresa have "the spirit of pious enthusiasm which could only be inspired by kindred feelings." Points out that "posterity has not confirmed, the opinion of Cowley and other contemporaries, of the poetical excellence of Crashaw; though, like Cowley, himself, he possessed true genius, but perverted by bad models." Find Pope's comments on Crashaw in his letter to Cromwell essentially just, "notwithstanding that letter has been adduced as proving a mean purpose in him of depressing the fame of one from whom he has copied a few striking lines." Acknowledges that, although Crashaw "has many truly poetical thoughts, expressed in glowing language, and sometimes smooth and correct versification," his poetry also "abounds in conceits and extravagances, and is often prosaic in matter, and defective in measure." Cites the last line of "Joann. 2. Aquae in vinum versae" as Crashaw's best-known line.

1807

•§ 115. Coleridge, Samuel Taylor. Notebook entries, 1807–1819.

Printed in *The Notebooks of Samuel Taylor Coleridge*, ed. Kathleen Coburn (Bollingen Series 50), vols. 2 & 3, text and notes (New York: Pantheon Books, 1961; Princeton: Princeton University Press, 1973).

(1) Entry 3100 from notebook 19, dated 1807. Contains a line penned by Coleridge ("Sun-rise / As all the Trees of Paradise reblossoming in the East"). Coburn points out that all the elements of the line are in Crashaw's "Sospetto

d'Herode" (Bk. 1, stanza 17) and notes that Coleridge knew Crashaw's poetry from the selections contained in Anderson (1793).

(2) Entry 3102 from notebook 19, dated 1807. Quotes two lines from "A Hymn to Sainte Teresa" with acknowledgment. Coburn points out Coleridge's marginal notes in two sets of Anderson.

(3) Entry 3103 from notebook 19, dated 1807. Quotes two lines from "An Apologie for the fore-going Hymne" with acknowledgment.

(4) Entry 3104 from notebook 19, dated 1807. Quotes two lines from "Upon the ensuing Treatises [of Mr. Shelford]" without acknowledgment.

(5) Entry 3105 from notebook 19, dated 1807. Contains the phrase "a supernumerary excellence." Coburn suggests that Crashaw's phrase "sweet supernumerary star" in "To the Queen, Upon her numerous Progenie. A Panegyrick" may be Coleridge's source.

(6) Entry 3107 from notebook 19, dated 1807. Coburn suggests a parallel between Coleridge's line "The Heavens one large black letter" and lines from "Hymn in the Glorious Epiphanie."

(7) Entry 3911 from notebook 18, dated June 1810. In a passage of Coleridge's notes on St. Teresa's *Works* appears the line "all her thirsts, and Lives, and Deaths of Love." Coburn suggests that Coleridge is misremembering lines 95–98 of "The Flaming Heart."

(8) Entry 4098 from notebook 18, dated May-August 1811. Quotes from "Sospetto d'Herode" (Bk. 1, stanza 4, line 3) without acknowledgment. Coburn points out a similarity in line 18 of *Kubla Khan*.

(9) Entry 4099 from notebook 18, dated May-August 1811. Quotes two lines from "Wishes. To his (supposed) Mistresse" with acknowledgment.

(10) Entry 4100 from notebook 18, dated May-August 1811. Quotes lines from "Wishes. To his (supposed) Mistresse" with acknowledgment.

(11) Entry 4497 from notebook 29, dated March 1819. In notes for Lecture XI in his philosophical lecture series (entry 124), discusses converts drawn to Catholicism by pietism, pointing to Crashaw's having been "captivated" by St. Teresa as an example.

◆§ 116. ———. Notes on Crashaw [circa 1807].

Printed in *Coleridge's Miscellaneous Criticism*, ed. Thomas Middleton Raysor (Cambridge: Harvard University Press; London: Constable, 1936), 277–79.

Reprinted in *Coleridge on the Seventeenth Century*, ed. Roberta Florence Brinkley (entry 773), 613–14.

Collection of Coleridge's critical comments on Crashaw, taken from marginal notes in two sets of Robert Anderson's *British Poets* (entry 102). Commenting on "Ode on a Prayer-book" (1648), Coleridge notes that, except for lines 75–76, he recollects "few poems of equal length so perfect *in suo genere*, so passionately supported, and closing with so grand a swell" (p. 278). Commenting on *Steps to the Temple* in general, he writes, "Who but must regret that the gift of selection and, of course, rejection, had not been bestowed on this sweet poet in some proportion to his power and opulence of invention" (p. 278) and notes that he has "ventured throughout to mark the stanzas by the mere omission of which the [finer] poem[s] would have increased in weight, no less than in polish" (p. 279). Calls "A Hymn to Sainte Teresa" "an admirable poem," especially the first two metrical paragraphs, and notes, concerning "Hymn in the Glorious Epiphanie," that Crashaw "is too apt to weary out a thought" (p. 279).

1808

◄§ 117. Lamb, Charles. "The Lovers Melancholy. By John Ford," in *Specimens of English Dramatic Poets, Who Lived About the Time of Shakespeare: With Notes by Charles Lamb*, 235–36. London: Longman, Hurst, Rees, and Orme.
Reproduces Ford's translation from Strada and maintains that it is superior to all other translations, including "Musicks Duell." Notes that Ford's rendering "is as fine as any thing in Beaumont and Fletcher; and almost equals the strife which it celebrates" (p. 236).

1809

◄§ 118. Campbell, Thomas. Letter to John Richardson. 21 January.
Printed in *Life and Letters of Thomas Campbell*, ed. William Beattie (London: E. Moxon, 1849), 2:161–64.
2d ed., London: Hall, Virtue & Co., 1850.
1849 edition reprinted, New York: AMS Press, 1973.
Discusses his plans for compiling *Specimens of the British Poets* (entry 123). Maintains that there is much excellent poetry that has been neglected by the general public and points to Crashaw as an example. Cites several passages from Crashaw that, he maintains, "it is obvious Milton had warmed his genius with, before he wrote his Paradise Lost" (p. 162).

1810

◄§ 119. Chalmers, Alexander. "The Poems of Richard Crashaw," in *The Works of the English Poets, from Chaucer to Cowper* . . . , 4:549–99.
London: Printed for J. Johnson et al.
Biographical sketch reprinted, with minor alterations and condensation, in *The General Biographical Dictionary* (London: J. Nicols and Sons et al., 1813), 10:482–85.
Biographical sketch of Crashaw (pp. 551–54). Notes that, even before Crashaw left England, "he appears to have practiced many of the austerities of a mistaken piety" (p. 552) and repeats William Hayley's error (entry 99), de-

rived from John Selden (entry 54), that Crashaw wrote against the stage. Observes that the many publications and editions "within a short period, and that period not very favourable to poetry, sufficiently mark the estimation in which this devotional enthusiast was held, notwithstanding his having relinquished the church in which he had been educated" (p. 553). Points out that Crashaw belonged to "the school which produced Herbert and Quarles" (p. 553) and notes that, although Herbert served as a model for him, Crashaw did not, as Granger suggested, write the anonymous poems at the end of The Temple. Mentions Peregrine Phillips's edition (entry 93) and his attack on Pope "for having availed himself of the beauties of Crashaw, while he endeavoured to injure his fame" (p. 553). Agrees with Hayley's vindication of Pope and charges that the attack "is an absurdity scarcely worthy of refutation" (p. 553). Points out the criticism on Crashaw by Phillips, Warton, Pope, Headley, Ellis, and others. Selections from the poems (pp. 555–99).

1811

◄§ 120. [Aston, Walter Hutchinson], ed. Select Psalms in Verse, with Critical Remarks, by Bishop Lowth, and Others, Illustrative of the Beauties of Sacred Poetry. London: Printed for J. Hatchard. xx, 288p.

Includes Crashaw's "Psalme 137" with a selection from Henry Headley's praise of the merits of Crashaw's poetry (entry 97).

1813

◄§ 121. Clifford, Arthur, ed. Tixall Poetry, with Notes and Illustrations. Edinburgh: Printed for James Ballantyne and Co. for Longman, Hurst, Rees, Orme, and Brown, London; and John Ballantyne and Co., Edinburgh. xl, 409p.

In the preface to this collection of poems by a group of seventeenth-century Catholics, presents a biographical sketch of Edward Thimelby (died circa 1690), who in two of his verse letters included in the collection mentions Crashaw (see entry 30). Suggests that Thimelby was a close friend of Crashaw and reproduces Pope's letter to Cromwell on Crashaw (p. xxix). In the notes on Thimelby's verse, refers to Crashaw as a "tender, mystical, enthusiastic poet" (p. 343). See also N. W. Bawcutt (entry 874).

1817

◄§ 122. Anon. [signed Digamma]. "On the Original of Milton's Satan, with Extracts from Crashaw's 'Suspicion of Herod.'" Blackwood's Edinburgh Magazine 1:140–42.

Notes that Milton's portrayal of Satan in Paradise Lost may have been influenced by Marino or by Crashaw's "Sospetto d'Herode," admitting that the suggestion "is not new, but has been little attended to" (p. 140). Reproduces extracts from Crashaw's poem and points out to the editor that, "owing to the general bad taste of Crashaw, it is probable few of your readers are acquainted with [this translation]; and those who are, will readily pardon you for reprinting some of the finest lines our poetry can boast of" (p. 140).

1819

◄§ 123. Campbell, Thomas. "Richard Crashaw," in *Specimens of the British Poets; with Biographical and Critical Notices, and an Essay on English Poetry*, 3:357–64. London: John Murray.
New edition, ed. Peter Cunningham (London: John Murray, 1841), 198–200.
Biographical sketch reprinted in *An Essay on English Poetry; with Notices of the British Poets*, ed. Peter Cunningham (London: John Murray, 1848), 223–24; and in *The Works of the British Poets with Lives of the Authors* by Ezekiel Sanford (Philadelphia: Mitchell, Ames, and White, 1819), 5: 191–92, along with the full version of "Sospetto d'Herode," 193–212.
Presents a biographical sketch, noting that "the little that is known of Crashaw's life exhibits enthusiasm, but it is not that of a weak or selfish mind" (p. 357). Attributes Crashaw's conversion to "his abhorrence of the religious innovations he had witnessed" (p. 358) and notes his admiration of the works of St. Teresa. Points out that Crashaw "fell into neglect in his own age" but was "one of the first of our minor poets that was rescued from oblivion in the following century" (p. 357). Notes Crashaw's dependence on Marino and suggests that "there is a prevalent harshness and strained expression in his verses but there are also many touches of beauty and solemnity, and the strength of his thoughts sometimes appears even in their distortion" (p. 357). Notes similarities between "Sospetto d'Herode" and *Paradise Lost*, especially Satan's address to the sun. Reprints nineteen stanzas from "Sospetto d'Herode" (p. 359–64).

◄§ 124. Coleridge, Samuel Taylor. "Lecture XI, 8 March 1819."
Printed in *The Philosophical Lectures of Samuel Taylor Coleridge*, ed. Kathleen Coburn (London: The Pilot Press, 1949), 312–38.
Comments on the life and mysticism of St. Teresa and twice quotes from "The Flaming Heart."

◄§ 125. Hazlitt, William. "Lecture III: On Cowley, Butler, Suckling, Etherege, etc.," in *Lectures on English Comic Writers*. Delivered at the Surrey Institution, 92–132. London: Printed for Taylor and Hessey.
Modern edition, *The Complete works of William Hazlitt*, ed. P. P. Howe, after the edition by A. R. Waller and Arnold Glover (London and Toronto: J. M. Dent and Sons, 1931), 6:49–69.

Lecture delivered at the Surrey Institution in 1818. Suggests that the metaphysical poets, including Crashaw, "not merely mistook learning for poetry—
they thought any thing was poetry that differed from ordinary prose and the
natural impression of things, by being intricate, far-fetched, and improbable"
(p. 93). Presents a negative estimate of metaphysical poetry. Calls Crashaw "a
writer of the same ambitious stamp [as Sir John Davies], whose imagination
was rendered still more inflammable by the fervors of fanaticism, and who
having been converted from Protestantism to Popery (a weakness to which the
'seething brains' of the poets of this period were prone) by some visionary appearance of the Virgin Mary, poured out his devout raptures and zealous enthusiasm in a torrent of poetical hyperboles" (pp. 100–101). Calls Crashaw
"hectic" and suggests that "Musicks Duell" is "the best specimen of his powers" (p. 101).

126. Sanford, Ezekiel. "Crashaw," in *The Works of the British Poets. With
   Lives of the Authors*, 5:191–212. Philadelphia: Mitchell, Ames, and
   White.

Reproduces Thomas Campbell's biographical sketch of Crashaw (entry 123)
and the full version of "Sospetto d'Herode," without notes or commentary.

1820

127. Hazlitt, William. "Lecture VI: On Miscellaneous Poems, F. Beaumont, P. Fletcher, Drayton, Daniel, &c, Sir P. Sidney's Arcadia, and
   Sonnets," in *Lectures Chiefly on the Dramatic Literature of the Age
   of Elizabeth, Delivered at the Surrey Institution*, 224–78. London:
   Stodart and Steuart.

Modern edition, *The Complete Works of William Hazlitt*, ed. P. P. Howe,
after the edition by A. R. Waller and Arnold Glover (London and Toronto: J.
M. Dent and Sons, 1931), 6:295–326.

Calls Crashaw "A hectic enthusiast in religion and poetry, and erroneous in
both" (p. 251). Quotes several stanzas from "Sospetto d'Herode," noting that
Crashaw's portrayal of Satan is a "portrait of monkish superstition" that "does
not equal the grandeur of Milton's description" (p. 259). Notes Milton's possible debt to both the ideas and expression in Crashaw's translation but concludes that a comparison will show "how much more he added to it than he
has taken from it" (p. 262). Calls "Musicks Duell" "elaborate and spirited" (p.
262) but finds it inferior to Ford's version in *The Lover's Melancholy*. Quotes
one line from the poem to show "the delicate quaintness" (p. 262) of Crashaw's
style.

128. [Hazlitt, William.] Review of Samuel Weller Singer's edition of
   Spence's *Anecdotes* (1820). *Edinburgh Review* 33 (May): 302–30.

Modern edition, *The Complete Works of William Hazlitt*, ed. P. P. Howe after the edition of A. R. Waller and Arnold Glover (London and Toronto: J. M. Dent and Sons, 1933), 16:152–81.

Describes Protestantism as "the religion of philosophy, and of faith chastised by a more sober reason" and suggests that Catholicism, on the other hand, is "in its essence, and by its very constitution, a religion of outward form and ceremony, full of sound and show, recommending itself by the charm of music, the solemnity of pictures, the pomp of dress, the magnificence of buildings, by the dread of power, and the allurements of pleasure" (p. 309). Notes that a number of seventeenth-century poets "were found to waver between the two, or were often led away by that which flattered their love of the marvellous and the splendid" (p. 309). Mentions, in this context, Garth, Wycherley, Pope, Dryden, and Crashaw—men "without much religion" who were "fascinated by the glittering bait of Popery" (p. 309).

✎§ 129. [Hunt, Leigh]. "Retrospective Review—Men Wedded to Books— The Contest Between the Nightingale and the Musician." *The Indicator* no. 32 (17 May): 249–56.

Reproduces "Musicks Duell" and agrees with the reviewer in *The Retrospective Review* (entry 130) that the poem is remarkable for "a wonderful power over the resources of our language" (p. 251). Suggests that part of the translation "is in a false and overcharged taste" but concludes that "in general the exuberance is as true as it is surprising" (p. 252). Suggests that Crashaw's translation is superior to Ford's.

✎§ 130. [Southern, Henry]. "Richard Crashaw's Poems." *Retrospective Review* 1:225–50.

A biographical sketch of Crashaw, a highly qualified evaluation of his poetry, and selections from his verse. Notes that Crashaw "belongs to that class of poets which has been absurdly enough entitled the metaphysical school," that the salient feature of this poetry "is the exuberance of its ingenuity, exerted on every possible subject in every possible form," and that for the metaphysical poets "the highest beauty with them is the beauty of ingenuity, the exquisiteness of workmanship,—and the more recondite, unobvious, or intrinsically worthless the matter might be which was so inwrought, the greater the praise of the poetical mechanic" (p. 225). Admits that "the greater part of Crashaw's poems, it must be confessed, largely partake of the vice of the age; they are, it is true, full of conceits, but yet not cold conceits; and in this consists the superiority of the poet" (p. 226). Maintains that had Crashaw lived in a different age he might have attained a higher status. Notes that he is "never dull; and, in despite of the perverted taste which he had, in common with Cowley and others, there are many of his poems which contain passages of natural tenderness, and of great beauty of sentiment and imagery" and observes that his versification "is nearly always melodious, and his expressions have frequently a delicate and luxurious fullness about them, which makes us lament the strained and unnatural images upon which they are lavished" (p. 226). Comments on Crashaw's devotional and mystical temperament and suggests that "no lover ever depicted the charms of his fair enslaver with greater warmth and animation, than fill the verses addressed to St. Teresa" (p. 227). Calls the sacred epigrams "completely worthless" (p. 228); suggests that "The Weeper" "would very completely illustrate the few remarks we have above made on the conceits of this writer and of the taste of his age" (p. 228), and yet even it has "some tender images and expressions" (p. 229); and states that often Crashaw "dresses up a sacred topic in a painted vest, so gaudy and flowery, as to be disgusting to the simpler taste of a good protestant" (p. 230). Finds numerous praiseworthy passages in *The Delights of the Muses* and calls the poem on Lessius "the best of the productions of Crashaw's muse" and a poem "written with a masterly power over his native language" (p. 235). Praises Crashaw's translations and claims that they "are among the finest specimens of versification in the language" (p. 241). Singles out "Sospetto d'Herode" and "Musicks Duell" for special admiration. Says that in the first "our language gains an accession of new strength in his hands, and breathes a spirit of majesty, by no means unworthy of the study and imitation, as it probably was, of Milton himself" (p. 241).

≼§ 131. Spence, Joseph. *Anecdotes, Observations, and Characters, of Books and Men. Collected from the Conversation of Mr. Pope, and other Eminent Persons of His Time.* With Notes, and a Life of the Author by Samuel Weller Singer. London: W. H. Carpenter; Edinburgh: Archibald Constable and Co. xxxix, 501p.

2d ed., London: John Russell Smith, 1858.

Modern edition, *Observations, Anecdotes, and Characters of Books and Men. Collected from Conversation,* ed. James M. Osborn, 2 vols. (entry 940).

Records Pope's comments on Crashaw (p. 22). Notes that Pope reputedly said that Crashaw "is a worse sort of Cowley; he was a follower too of Petrarch and Marino, but most of Marino" and notes that Pope observed that "Herbert is lower than Crashaw, Sir John Beaumont higher, and Donne, a good deal so."

1821

≼§ 132. Byron, George Gordon (Lord). *Don Juan, Cantos III, IV, and V.* London: Thomas Davison. iv, 218p.

For a modern standard edition, see *Byron's "Don Juan": A Variorum Edition.* Vol. 2: *Cantos I–V,* ed. Truman Guy Steffan and Willis W. Pratt (Austin: University of Texas Press, 1957).

Mentions Crashaw by name in canto III, stanza 79, line 8. See also Frederick L. Beaty (entry 1050).

1823

⋙ 133. Anon. "Selections from the Poetry of Crashaw." *Christian Disciple* n.s. 5, no. 26 (March-April): 81–92.

Gives a biographical sketch and suggests that neither George Ellis (entry 111) nor Thomas Campbell (entry 123) has done justice to Crashaw in selecting from his poems. Points out that Crashaw's poetry "abounds with the faults of his age" and is "full of extravagances, forced thoughts, and harshness of expression" but that "the charm of his finer poems consists partly in the fresh and bright colours of their language, and in the happy turns of expression which now and then occur, and still more in the purity and holiness of feeling which they discover, sometimes calm and deep, and sometimes exalted to enthusiasm" (p. 82). Quotes from "Upon the ensuing Treatises [of Mr. Shelford]" to show "how much good sense was mingled with Crashaw's somewhat erroneous and perverted feelings of religion" (p. 85). Comments briefly on a number of poems and praises "A Hymn to Sainte Teresa" and "Ode on a Prayerbook," which are "glowing with dazzling conceptions of mystic devotion" and admirable for their "continued play of brilliant coruscations" (p. 86). Calls "In praise of Lessius" a very awkward poem but "rich in strong and poetical thoughts and language" (p. 89) and claims that "Sospetto d'Herode" is "on the whole an uninteresting poem" (p. 92).

1824

⋙ 134. Anon. "Richard Crashaw," in *Specimens of the Earlier English Poets*, 135–82. London: Printed for S. W. Simpson.

Popular anthology that includes "Sospetto d'Herode," "Musicks Duell," "Psalme 137," and "Death's Lecture," without notes or commentary.

⋙ 135. Dibdin, T[homas] F[rognall]. "Poetry," in *The Library Companion: or, The Young Man's Guide, and The Old Man's Comfort, in the Choice of a Library*. Part Second, 613–773. London: Printed for Harding, Triphook, and Lepard and J. Major.

Refers to "gentle Crashaw" as one among several minor poets "upon whose works, unknown to posterity, Milton might have silently fed" (pp. 706–7). Briefly discusses Crashaw's poetry in a bibliographical footnote (p. 712), calling attention to Pope's borrowing from Crashaw and referring to the critical essay on Crashaw in the *Retrospective Review* (entry 130). In a further footnote (pp. 712–13) gives a brief summary of Crashaw's life, based largely upon Thomas Campbell (entry 123).

⋙ 136. Watt, Robert. "Crashaw, Richard," in *Bibliotheca Britannica; or General Index to British and Foreign Literature*, 1:268. Edinburgh:

Printed for Archibald Constable and Co.; London: Longman, Hurst, Rees, Orme, Brown, and Green.

Biographical note that perpetuates the notion that Selden was Crashaw's companion, calls Crashaw a "Poet of considerable talent," and suggests that "from this Poet Pope has borrowed not only expressions, but entire lines, particularly in Eloisa to Abelard." Notes Phillips's edition of 1785.

1825

◄§ 137. [Keble, John]. "Sacred Poetry." *Quarterly Review* 32:211–32.

Ostensibly a review of Josiah Conder's *The Star in the East, and other Poems* (London: Taylor and Hessey, 1824) that surveys sacred poetry in English. Briefly notes that current neglect of Crashaw, Quarles, and even Herbert is undeserved, maintaining that "their quaintness of manner and constrained imagery, adopted perhaps in compliance with the taste of their age, should hardly suffice to overbalance their sterling merits," and calls attention to Crashaw's "plaintive tenderness" (p. 230).

◄§ 138. [Procter, Bryan Waller.] "English Poetry." *Edinburgh Review* 42: 31–64.

Reprinted (except for last two paragraphs) in *Essays and Tales in Prose*, by Barry Cornwall (pseud.) (Boston: Ticknor, Reed and Fields), 2:125–72.

Comments briefly on Crashaw's imagery. Notes that "Petrarch, Donne, Cowley, and Crashaw, all men of genius, . . . trusted often to their ingenuity instead of their feeling" (p. 42). Cites lines 57–59 of "Musicks Duell" and suggests that "the idea is overloaded, and extended beyond our sympathy." Points out that "there are four distinct epithets made use of to express a single idea," and maintains that "this argues poverty in the writer, at least as much as a superabundance of imagery" (p. 42).

1826

◄§ 139. [Gorton, John.] "Crashaw, Richard," in *A General Biographical Dictionary, containing a Summary Account of the Lives of Eminent Persons of All Nations, Previous to the Present Generation*, 1:566–67. London: Hunt and Clarke.

Biographical sketch, calling Crashaw a "neglected bard," singling out his translation of Marino, and noting that Milton borrowed from Crashaw's poem.

1827

◄§ 140. Johnstone, John, ed. "Richard Crashaw," in *Specimens of Sacred and Serious Poetry from Chaucer to the Present Day; including Grahame's*

Sabbath and Other Poems, and Blair's Grave. With Biographical Notices and Critical Remarks, 270–81. Edinburgh: Oliver & Boyd.

Biographical sketch (p. 270), noting that, "though the poetical writings of Crashaw do not suffer the reader to forget that he was of the same church as Pascal and Fenelon, they cannot fail to please with their reverential fervour and genuine warmth of devotion" (p. 270). Anthologizes lines from eleven poems.

➳ 141. Mitford, John, ed. "From the *Steps to the Temple* by Richard Crashaw (1646)," in *Sacred Specimens: Selected from the Early English Poets*, with Prefatory Verses by the Rev. John Mitford, 139–43. London: Baldwin, Cradock, and John. T. Cadell; J. Loder, Woodbridge.

Contains "Hymn for New Year's Day" and stanzas from "Dies Irae Dies Illa," without notes or commentary.

➳ 142. Montgomery, James, ed. "Richard Crashaw," in *The Christian Poet; or Selections in Verse on Sacred Subjects* (with an introductory essay), 174–80. Glasgow: William Collins.

Includes five selections from the sacred epigrams; lines from "Hymn to the Name of Jesus," and nine stanzas from "Dies Irae Dies Illa," without notes or commentary, preceded by a brief headnote.

➳ 143. Moore, Thomas. Diary entry. 2 July.

Printed in *Memoirs, Journals & Correspondence of Thomas Moore*, ed. Lord John Russell (London: Longman, Brown, Green, & Longmans, 1852), 5:184.

Mentions that he had considered using lines 23–24 of "A Hymn to Sainte Teresa" as the motto of his *Lalla Rookh* (1817). Notes also that he and friends dined at Lansdowne House and spoke of Crashaw's poetry, commending especially "On Hope."

1828

➳ 144. Johnstone, John, ed. "Richard Crashaw," in *Specimens of the Lyrical, Descriptive, and Narrative Poets of Great Britain, from Chaucer to the Present Day*. With a Preliminary Sketch of the History of Early English Poetry, and Biographical and Critical Notes, by John Johnstone, 252–55. Edinburgh: Oliver & Boyd.

Calls Crashaw "a Catholic priest" and suggests that he is "the most purely poetical of all the devotional lyricists" (p. 252). Reproduces "Out of Catullus," three stanzas from "The Teare," and five stanzas from "The Weeper," without notes or commentary.

1831

◄§ 145. Hunt, Leigh. Review of *Poems, Chiefly Lyrical* by Alfred Tennyson and *Sonnets and Fugitive Pieces* by Charles Tennyson. *The Tatler* 2 (24 and 26 February, 1 and 3 March): 591–94, 601–2, 609–10, 617–18.

Reprinted in *Leigh Hunt's Literary Criticism*, ed. Lawrence Huston and Carolyn Washburn Houtchens, with an essay of evaluation by Clarence DeWitt Thorpe (New York: Columbia University Press, 1956), 344–71.

Suggests that Alfred Lord Tennyson's "Supposed Confessions of a Second-Rate Sensitive Mind Not in Unity with Itself" is a poem "such as Crashaw might have written in a moment of scepticism, had he possessed vigor enough" (p. 601).

1833

◄§ 146. Alford, Henry. "Sonnet, Written in an Interval of Melancholy foreboding respecting the church," in *Poems and Poetical Fragments*, 97. Cambridge: Printed for J. & J. J. Deighton, and C. J. G. & F. Rivington, London.

Reprinted in *The Poetical Works of Henry Alford* (London: James Burns, 1845), 1:107.

An original poem on the English Church that mentions both Crashaw and Herbert.

1834

◄§ 147. Anon., ed. *The Suspicion of Herod, being the First Book of the Murder of the Innocents.* Translated from the Italian by Richard Crashaw. Kensington: Bournes Jun, Brothers. iv, 34p.

Brief critical introduction to Marino and Crashaw (pp. iii–iv). Suggests that Marino wrote his poem as a penance for his earlier, licentious works. Notes that Crashaw wrote "a number of short poems, in which, in spite of much false taste, it is impossible not to admire a true feeling of poetry" and that "added to these qualities he possesses great felicity of expression, and uses his native language in a manner worthy of one living in the same age with Milton" (p. iv). Crashaw's translation follows (pp. 1–34).

◄§ 148. Willmott, Robert Aris. "Richard Crashaw," in *Lives of Sacred Poets*, 295–325, 359–61; London: John W. Parker.

2d ed., corrected and expanded, 1839, 1:301–29.

Biographical sketch of Crashaw, noting that, "after an anxious search in all accessible sources of information, I am able to tell little of one whom every lover of poetry must desire to know so much" (p. 295). Disagrees with Pope's estimation of Crashaw's poetry and suggests that "it may be doubted whether his tastes and prejudices did not unfit him to deliver an impartial judgment on the merits of Crashaw" (p. 307). Notes the influence of Marino on Crashaw and parallels passages from Marino and Crashaw to show that "Sospetto d'Herode" is not merely a translation but "many parts of it are enriched by the fancy of Crashaw" (p. 308). Calls "Musicks Duell" "one of the most remarkable in the language, for its felicity of diction and pictorial effect" (p. 316), shows that Strada was only a starting point for the poem, and maintains that, in richness and fervor, Crashaw's poem is superior to Ford's version. Notes that Crashaw's poetry is called metaphysical and suggests that it "offers an admirable exemplification of this corrupt system" (p. 320). Claims that "the faults of Crashaw are those of his school" (p. 321). Surveys briefly and appreciatively a number of poems and notes that Crashaw "was not always the stringer of pretty beads" (p. 323). Comments also on the relationship between Crashaw and Cowley and notes that the former "was considered an imitator of Cowley, but they resembled each other only in their love of conceits" (p. 324).

1836

✑ 149. Cattermole, R[ichard], ed. "Richard Crashaw," in *Sacred Poetry of the Seventeenth Century*, 1:329–51; 2:219–44. London: Joseph Rickerby.

Each volume has a separate biographical and critical introduction to Crashaw, with selections from his poems. Notes in volume one that Crashaw "sought a refuge upon the barren rock of papal infallibility" and that after his conversion, his writings "contain evident traces of the change; for which an enthusiastic disposition, not unlike that of the ancient anchorites, combined with his misfortunes to prepare him" (1:329). Observes that "Musicks Duell" "is scarcely surpassed by any composition in the language for ease, variety, and richness of diction" but concludes that, although Crashaw is "a genuine and glowing poet," his works are "all more or less vitiated by that tendency to conceit, which, in his friend Cowley, and others, was carried to so extravagant a length, that it finally debased the whole literary character of the age" (1:329). Notes in volume two the critical approval given Crashaw by Coleridge and Pope. Suggests that Crashaw is a poet "whose delicate fancy, tenderness, and singular beauty of diction are alike admirable" but maintains that "Sospetto d'Herode" is "superior to the greater part of Crashaw's original compositions" (2:219).

✑ 150. Coleridge, Samuel Taylor. *Letters, Conversation and Recollections of S. T. Coleridge*, edited by Thomas Alsop, 1:194–96. London: Edward Moxon.

2d ed., 1858; 3d ed., 1864.

Reprinted in *The Table Talk and Omniana of Samuel Taylor Coleridge*, arr. and ed. T. Ashe (London: George Bell and Sons, 1884), 321–22; in *Inquiring Spirit: A New Presentation of Coleridge from his Published and Unpublished Prose Writings*, ed. Kathleen Coburn (New York: Pantheon Books, 1951), 179–81; and in *Coleridge on the Seventeenth Century*, ed. Roberta Florence Brinkley (entry 773), 612–13.

Presents Coleridge's comments on Crashaw, pointing out his admiration for lines 43–68 of "A Hymn to Sainte Teresa," which, he said, "were ever present to my mind whilst writing the second part of Christabel; if, indeed, by some subtle process of the mind they did not suggest the first thought of the whole poem" (p. 196). Coleridge further observes that "On Hope" is superior to Cowley's poem on the same subject and suggests that "where he does combine richness of thought and diction nothing can excel" (p. 195), as evident in "A Hymn to Sainte Teresa," which Coleridge calls Crashaw's "finest" lines.

⚜ 151. ———. Table Talk on Richard Blackmore published in "S. T. Coleridge at Trinity, with Specimens of his *Table-Talk*" in *Conversations at Cambridge* [by Robert Aris Willmott], 7–8. London: John W. Parker.

Reprinted in *Coleridge on the Seventeenth Century*, ed. Roberta Florence Brinkley (entry 773), 634.

Maintains that "no man who, during his life-time has obtained a very large share of applause, is deserving of total oblivion" (p. 7) and suggests that this is emphatically true for such poets as Cowley, Herbert, Crashaw, and even Blackmore.

⚜ 152. Cunningham, George Godfrey. "Richard Crashaw," in *The Lives of Eminent and Illustrious Englishmen, from Alfred the Great to the Latest Times*, edited by George Godfrey Cunningham, 3:369–71. Glasgow: A. Fullarton & Co.

Calls Crashaw "an accomplished scholar" and a "pious poet" but notes that his poems "are but little known, nor can it be said that the neglect into which they have fallen is altogether unmerited" (p. 269). Suggests that, although the poems are "scattered with flowers of exquisite beauty, which Pope thought worth transplanting, the inappropriate expressions, figures, and similes which abound, and the occasional vulgar and ludicrous familiarity of language are so offensive to the reader as nearly to destroy the pleasure derived from his beauties" (p. 269–70). Presents a biographical sketch of Crashaw and sees his conversion to Catholicism as a sincere and natural outcome of his religious temper, which was formed in part by his devotion to St. Teresa. Suggests that Crashaw's original poems are mostly on religious topics and notes that his translations "are considered far superior to his original compositions" (p. 271), especially his translation of Marino. Quotes "Joann. 2. Aquae in vinum versae" and gives a translation "because it contains a celebrated line, the credit of which is frequently not attributed to its real author" (p. 271).

✍ 153. Hall, S[amuel] C[arter], ed. "Crashaw," in *The Book of Gems: The Poets and Artists of Great Britain*, 1:242–47. London: Saunders and Otley.

Biographical sketch and critical evaluation of Crashaw's poetry. Notes that he "is by no means free from affectation—the vice of his age" but adds that "even his conceits, unlike those of most of his contemporaries, are redeemed by fancy and ingenuity" (p. 242). Asserts that Crashaw "is never either tame or dull"; his poems are full of tenderness; his descriptive powers are large; and his versification is exceedingly harmonious" (p. 242). Notes that it is "as a translator that his merit has been chiefly acknowledged" and claims that "Sospetto d'Herode" and "Musicks Duell" are "among the finest specimens of versification in our language" (p. 242). Notes critical remarks on Crashaw by Wood, Selden, Winstanley, Car, Cowley, and Coleridge. Reprints "O Gloriosa Domina" and "Ode on a Prayer-book" (pp. 243–47), without notes or commentary.

1837

✍ 154. Anon. "The Character and Progress of Religious Poetry." *Church of England Quarterly Review* 1 (January): 171–229.

Surveys the development of English religious poetry. Suggests that "of the writers to whom the popularity of Herbert gave birth, the most eminent in every respect was Richard Crashaw" (p. 186). Calls Crashaw a "gifted and poetical enthusiast." Suggests that Spenser's heart "would have rejoiced, could he have known the student of his own Pembroke," and points out that, although Pope's criticism contributed to Crashaw's reputation, "never was a colder eulogy pronounced where it was so little deserved" (p. 187). Maintains that, although Crashaw "possessed all the qualities of a great writer" and although "his fancy was vivid and lively" and "his ear peculiarly attuned to numbers," he failed as an artist "because he forsook nature, and instead of trusting to his own heart, set up Herbert and Marino for his models: "his aim is to glitter and to surprise; to keep the mind constantly awake with novelty" (p. 187). Notes that Crashaw's poetry "is not descriptive but picturesque" and that he "contemplates nature through a painted window, from which every object takes its particular hue" (p. 187). Praises "Hymn in the Holy Nativity," "Sospetto d'Herode," and "Psalme 23" but cites "Hymn to the Name of Jesus" as a poem in which "his faults are strikingly manifest" (p. 187). Suggests that Crashaw's major defect "springs from the want of selection in his imagery" and points out that his poetry lacks that "calm and majestic unity of sentiment which distinguishes the great intellects of an age" (p. 188).

✍ 155. ———. "Crashaw, Richard," in *The Penny Cyclopaedia of the Society for the Diffusion of Useful Knowledge*, 8:140–41. London: Charles Knight; New York: William Jackson; Boston: Joseph H. Francis; Philadelphia: Orrin Rogers; Baltimore: W. N. Harrison.

Biographical sketch of Crashaw and a brief description of his publications. Notes that Pope "occasionally borrowed thoughts from Crashaw, but improved them" and suggests that Crashaw resembled Herbert "in his turn of mind, but possessed more fancy and genius" (p. 141).

1838

◄§ 156. Emerson, Ralph Waldo. Entries in the journals and miscellaneous notebooks of Ralph Waldo Emerson (1838–1877).

Entry 2 (below) was first published in *Journals of Ralph Waldo Emerson, with annotations*, ed. Edward Waldo Emerson and Waldo Emerson Forbes (Boston and New York: Houghton Mifflin Co., 1909–1914), 10 vols; modern edition (containing all 8 entries below), *Journals and Miscellaneous Notebooks of Ralph Waldo Emerson*, ed. William H. Gilman et al. 16 vols. (Cambridge: Belknap Press of Harvard University Press, 1960–1982).

(1) From Journal D, 1838–1839. Undated entry. Copies out Pope's opinion of Crashaw ("Crashaw is a worse sort of Cowley . . .") from Spence's *Anecdotes* (entry 131), without comment. (Gilman edition, 7:163.)

(2) From Journal D, 20 July 1839. Quotes a phrase from "Sospetto d'Herode" (line 240). (Emerson edition, 5:240; Gilman edition, 7:230.)

(3) From Notebook Books Small [II], 1840(?)–1856(?). Undated note to himself to "see if Strada wrote the original of Crashaw's Music's Duel." (Gilman edition, 8:562.)

(4) From Journal U, 1843–1844. Undated entry. Includes "Musicks Duell," which he calls "Crashaw's Musician & Nightingale" in a list of works that he would include in "a true course of English literary history." (Gilman edition, 9:61.)

(5) From Journal 10, 1854. Undated entry. Mentions Crashaw in a paragraph on the subject of quotations. Notes that, although Henry Hallam (entry 160) is a fair-minded critic, he lacks a proper appreciation of "imaginative and analogy-loving souls" such as Crashaw. Later included the paragraph in an essay entitled "Quotation and originality" read at Freeman Place Chapel in Boston in March 1859 (printed in *Letters and Social Aims*, Emerson's Complete Works, Riverside Edition [Boston and New York: Houghton, Mifflin and Co., 1884], 8:167–94). (Gilman edition, 13:353.)

(6) From Journal ST, 1870–1877. Two undated entries. (a) Makes a note to himself to insert verses from the "Sospetto d'Herode" into his collection *Parnassus* (entry 241). (b) Makes a note to himself to check for Crashaw and "Sospetto d'Herode" in *Retrospective Review*, 1820 (entry 130). (Gilman edition, 16:268, 269.)

(7) From Pocket Diary 20, 1869. Undated entry. Copies out the line "Nympha pudica Deum videt et erubuit" from "Joann. 2. Aquae in vinum versae" and notes that it is from "Richard Crashaw 1634." (Gilman edition, 16:389).

(8) From Pocket Diary 22, 1871. Undated entry. Copies out the line

"Nympha pudica Deum videt et erubuit" from "Joann. 2. Aquae in vinum versae" along with the translation "The modest water saw its God & blushed." (Gilman edition 16:411.)

❦ 157. [Longfellow, Henry Wadsworth.] "A Psalm of Life." *The Knicker-bocker, or New York Monthly Magazine* 12:189.
Modern edition, *The Poetical Works of Longfellow*, Cambridge edition, with a new introduction by George Monteiro (Boston: Houghton Mifflin Co., 1975), 2–3.
Quotes (without acknowledgment) stanza 29 of "Wishes. To his (supposed) Mistresse" as a motto to his poem "A Psalm of Life."

1839

❦ 158. Anon. "The Elder Sacred poets." *Fraser's Magazine* 20:400–414.
Essentially a review of Robert Aris Willmott's *Lives of Sacred Poets* (entry 148). Favorably evaluates Crashaw's poetry (pp. 411–13). Notes that "the writings of this poet are some of them remarkable for a power and vitality not excelled by any of our first poets" and suggests that "there are passages which Milton might covet, and Shakespeare not be ashamed of" (p. 411). Agrees with Willmott that "Sospetto d'Herode" is superior to the original, parallels passages from both poems to demonstrate his point, and notes Milton's indebtedness to Crashaw's version. Suggests that Pope plagiarized Crashaw "without conscience" (p. 413). Quotes passages from "Hymn in the Holy Nativity" and "To the Morning. Satisfaction for sleepe" to illustrate Crashaw's poetic ability. Claims that Crashaw's only character flaw was "his change from the faith of Scripture, of truth, of common sense, to the drivelling superstition of the Roman heresy" (p. 413) and reproduces John Bargrave's account of Crashaw in Italy (entry 37) to show that Crashaw's conversion did not bring him happiness.

❦ 159. Bell, Robert. "Abraham Cowley," in *Lives of the Most Eminent Literary and Scientific Men of Great Britain: English Poets*, 1:38–90. London: Longman, Orme, Brown, Green, & Longmans.
Includes a biographical sketch of Crashaw (pp. 57–58). Maintains that Crashaw is a devotional poet, "blamed by some persons for blending with his pious aspirations too much of the heat and fervour of imagination, and apt to run into excesses in the chace of images; but regarding these faults of temperament and judgment in a tolerant spirit, Crashaw must be admitted to a distinguished place among the few poets who have elevated the tone of this class of lyrics, and inspired it with a spiritual beauty the height and delicacy of which no other writer has attained" (p. 58). Points out Cowley's friendship with Crashaw and Pope's borrowings from him, noting that Pope "was so deficient

in magnanimity as not only not to acknowledge them, but even to depreciate the excellence of the poet he surreptitiously copied" (p. 58).

➥ 160. Hallam, Henry. "History of Poetry from 1600 to 1650" in *Introduction to the Literature of Europe in the Fifteenth, Sixteenth, and Seventeenth Centuries*, 3:260–303. London: John Murray.
    Generally unfavorable discussion of Crashaw. Calls him "a man of some imagination and great piety, but whose softness of heart, united with feeble judgment, led him to admire and imitate whatever was most extravagant in the mystic writings of Saint Teresa" (p. 284). Points out that "he was more than Donne a follower of Marino, one of whose poems, The Massacre of the Innocents, he translated with success" (p. 284). Concludes that "it is difficult, in general, to find any thing in Crashaw that bad taste has not deformed" (pp. 284–85). For a response by Ralph Waldo Emerson, see entry 156.

1841

➥ 161. [Cattermole, Richard.] "Richard Crashaw," in *Gems of Sacred Poetry*, 1:200–213. London: John W. Parker.
    Biographical sketch and brief critical evaluation of Crashaw, noting that his poems are not generally known, even though "they display delicate fancy, great tenderness, and singular beauty of diction" (p. 200). Notes that Coleridge considered "Ode on a Prayer-book" one of the greatest poems in the language. Reproduces "Dies Irae Dies Illa," "Ode on a Prayer-book," and selections from "Hymn to the Name of Jesus."

➥ 162. M. "The Hymn—'Dies Irae, Dies Illa.'" *The Congregational Magazine*, n.s. 5:167–75.
    Briefly discusses the history and development of the *Dies Irae* and suggests that Crashaw was the first to paraphrase the hymn in English, "soon after his secession from the Protestant Church" (p. 171). Notes that Pope considered the paraphrase one of Crashaw's best pieces and that Warton "praises it as a translation, which, without considerable latitude, it can hardly be called" (p. 171). Reproduces seven stanzas of the poem without additional notes or commentary.

1842

➥ 163. Anon. *Book of the Poets: Chaucer to Beattie*. London: Scott, Webster, & Geary. xxxii, 458p.
    Includes seven stanzas from "Hymn in the Holy Nativity," twenty-two lines from "Hymn in the Assumption," "To the Morning. Satisfaction for sleepe," and fourteen lines from "Hymn to the Name of Jesus," with a headnote containing a biographical sketch and a general introduction to Crashaw's poetry

(pp. 69–73). Notes that, although there is "a richness and melody in the poetry of Crashaw to which we can scarcely find a parallel among the religious poets of the period," it is very unfortunate that "his fancy was so unconstrained, and his taste so perverted, that he is seldom equal throughout any of his poems" (p. 69). Suggests that "even the most beautiful of his ideas frequently terminates in a perplexing maze, or sinks into absolute bathos" (p. 69). Points out that the lines given from "Hymn in the Assumption" reflect Crashaw's zeal for Catholicism and "the fanciful application which he could make of the Song of Solomon to sanction one of the most untenable dogmas of his church" (p. 69). Observes, however, that in some of his descriptions Crashaw "seems to have caught the very spirit in which Milton conceived the brightest passages of his Paradise Lost" (p. 69). Notes in the general introduction that Crashaw, Herbert, Wither, Marvell, and Quarles are among the most important religious poets of the period and claims that "the most talented and imaginative was Crashaw, whose translations, or rather paraphrases, from the Italian of Strada, are splendid improvements upon the original; while his own poems breathe, in many instances, the very spirit of harmony, imagination, and feeling" (p. xxiv). See also Elizabeth Barrett Browning's review of this collection (entry 164).

◄§ 164. [Browning, Elizabeth Barrett.] "The Book of the Poets." *The Athenaeum* no. 762 (4 June): 497–99; no. 763 (11 June): 520–23; no. 765 (25 June): 558–60; no. 771 (6 August): 706–8; and no. 772 (13 August): 728–29.
Reprinted in *The Greek Christian Poets and the English Poets* (London: Chapman and Hall, 1863), 105–211.
Review of *Book of the Poets: Chaucer to Beattie* (1842; entry 163). Suggests that the treatment of the devotional poets of the seventeenth century, including Crashaw, in this collection is better than Thomas Campbell's estimate of them (entry 123). Notes Crashaw's "fine rapture, holy as a summer sense of silence" (p. 560).

1843

◄§ 165. Chambers, Robert, ed., "Richard Crashaw," in *Cyclopedia of English Literature; A History, Critical and Biographical, of British Authors, From the Earliest to the Present Times*, 1:149–53. Edinburgh: William and Robert Chambers.
Frequently revised and reprinted.
Briefly surveys Crashaw's life and assesses his poetry. Reprints "Musicks Duell," "In praise of Lessius," and "Hymn to the Name of Jesus" (pp. 150–53). Maintains that Crashaw's "devotional strains and 'lyric raptures' evince the highest genius" (p. 149). Claims that he was "of an enthusiastic disposition" and was "an eloquent and powerful preacher" and praises Crashaw's transla-

tions from Latin and Italian as possessing "great freedom, force, and beauty" (p. 149). Quotes lines from "Sospetto d'Herode" and suggests they are "not unworthy of Milton," who had evidently seen the work (p. 149). Notes Crashaw's admiration for St. Teresa, "which seems to have had a bad effect on his own taste, naturally prone, from his enthusiastic temperament, to carry any favourite object, feeling, or passion, to excess" (p. 150). Points out that, although his "musical style of thought and fancy naturally led to exaggeration and to conceits," Crashaw "is seldom tedious," quoting Coleridge's statement of Crashaw's "power and opulence of invention" (p. 150). Claims that Crashaw would have outstripped his contemporaries had he lived longer.

᪐ 166. Holland, John. "Richard Crashaw," in *The Psalmists of Britain* . . . , 2:12–15. London: Groombridge; Sheffield: Ridge and Jackson.

Biographical sketch and brief critical evaluation of Crashaw's verse, suggesting that "his thoughts, in the main, are pretty, but sometimes far-fetched, and often strained and stiffened to make them appear the greater" (p. 13). Reproduces "Psalme 23," noting only that it contains "decided traces of the general character of the poetry of Crashaw" (p. 14).

1844

᪐ 167. Lowell, James Russell. "Third Conversation: The Old Dramatists," in *Conversations on Some of the Old Poets*, 212–63. Cambridge, Mass.: John Owen, 1844.

Reprinted, London: Henry G. Clarke & Co., 1845; 2d ed., Cambridge, Mass.: John Owen, 1845; 3d ed., Philadelphia: David McKay, 1893; "Handy Volume Classics" ed., New York: Crowell, 1901.

Briefly compares Ford's *The Lover's Melancholy* with "Musicks Duell," calling Crashaw's version of Strada "a poem which for exquisite rhythm and diction can hardly be paralleled in the language" (pp. 258–59).

1845

᪐ 168. Browning, Robert. Letter to Elizabeth Barrett Browning. Postmarked 19 December.

Printed in *The Letters of Robert Browning and Elizabeth Barrett Browning 1845–46* (New York and London: Harper & Brothers, 1899), 1:334–36.

Mentions "Musicks Duell," referring to "Ford's and Crashaw's rival Nightingales," and notes that Wordsworth, Coleridge, Lamb, and Hazlitt have "dissertated" on them, and they were "worked to death by Hunt, who printed them entire and quoted them to pieces again, in every periodical he was ever engaged upon" (pp. 335–36).

✑ 169. Craik, George L. "Other Religious Poets.—Quarles.—Herbert.—Herrick.—Crashaw," in *Sketches of the History of Literature and Learning in England. With Specimens of the Principal Writers.* Series second (in two volumes). *From the Accession of Elizabeth to the Revolution of 1688,* 4:16–18. London: Charles Knight & Co.

Suggests that, after Donne, Crashaw is the greatest religious poet of the early seventeenth century. Notes that he belongs to the "school" of Donne and Herrick and "in his lighter pieces has much of their lyrical sweetness and delicacy" (p. 18). Claims, however, that in Crashaw "there is a force and even occasionally what may be called a grandeur of imagination in his more solemn poetry which Herrick never either reaches or aspires to" (p. 18).

1846

✑ 170. Hunt, Leigh. "An Illustrative Essay on Wit and Humour," in *Wit and Humour, selected from the English Poets; with an Illustrative Essay, and Critical Comments,* 1–72. London: Smith, Elder and Co.

Reprinted, New York: Wiley and Putnam, 1846, 1847; 2d ed., 1846, 1848; new ed., 1871, 1882, 1890, 1910.

Modern edition, Norwood, Pa.: Norwood Editions, 1977.

In a discussion of epigrammatic wit, quotes (inaccurately) from memory "On Nanus mounted upon an Ant" and calls the poem "the best mock-heroical epigram I am acquainted with" (p. 46). Does not attribute the poem to Crashaw.

✑ 171. J. "Religious Poetry (English) of the Seventeenth Century." *The American Review: A Whig Journal of Politics, Literature, Arts and Science* 3:250–58.

Primarily a critical evaluation of the poetry of Crashaw and Quarles, noting that Donne, Herbert, the Fletchers, and Vaughan have already received much attention. Comments on the nineteenth-century neglect of Crashaw's poetry and maintains that "a larger proportion of really admirable poetry still remains of Crashaw, amidst all his conceits and crudities, than can be furnished out of any popular poet in England of the present day, except Wordsworth" (pp. 255–56). Praises Crashaw for "tenderness, fancy, occasional sublimity, frequent eloquence, considerable selection in phrases, and a fine ear for harmony" (p. 258). Finds Crashaw's translation of Marino superior to the original; praises "Ode on a Prayer-book," "Musicks Duell," "An Epitaph Upon Mr. Ashton," "Upon the Death of a Gentleman [Mr. Chambers]," "In praise of Lessius," and "Sospetto d'Herode"; and quotes lines from "Dies Irae Dies Illa" and "Hymn in the Holy Nativity" to illustrate Crashaw's poetic mastery. Notes borrowings from Crashaw in the poetry of Milton, Roscommon, and Pope; comments on critical estimates of Crashaw by Pope, Cowley, Coleridge, and Hazlitt; and briefly contrasts Crashaw to James Montgomery, Leigh Hunt, Bryan W. Procter, Milton, Pope, and Keble.

1847

✍§ 172. Cleveland, Charles Dexter. "Richard Crashaw,—1650," in *A Compendium of English Literature* . . . , 169–71. Philadelphia: E. C. and J. Biddle.

Contains a biographical sketch of Crashaw and brief comments, mostly from Headley, on his poems. Notes Pope's possible borrowings in "Eloisa to Abelard." Reproduces the first version of "Ode on a Prayer-book," mentioning that Coleridge considered the poem one of the best in the language.

✍§ 173. Coleridge, Sara. Letter to Mrs. Richard Townsend. September.

Printed in *Memoir and Letters of Sara Coleridge*, ed. her daughter [Edith Coleridge] (London: Henry S. King & Co., 1873), 2:129–31.

Notes that, "though sacred poetry abounds, good sacred poetry is more scarce than poetry of any other sort" (p. 129). Recommends Crashaw, "whose sacred poetry I think more truly poetical than any other, except Milton and Dante" (p. 130). Notes that, when she asked Wordsworth about Crashaw, "he responded very warmly," and adds that her father (Samuel Taylor Coleridge) "admired Crashaw" (p. 131). Concludes, however, that "neither Quarles nor Crashaw would be much liked by the modern general reader" for "they would be thought queer and extravagant" (p. 131).

✍§ 174. R., F. Untitled article. *Newark Daily Advertiser* 16, no. 66 (19 March): [2].

Reproduces seven stanzas of Crashaw's "Dies Irae Dies Illa" and notes that the poem is "filled up with a simplicity and power scarcely found in the original." Notes Roscommon's indebtedness to Crashaw. Laments that Crashaw is not better known and suggests that, although Crashaw "was not a great writer, yet he combined much strength with a sweetness and purity which justly entitles him to our admiration." Cites several lines from "Hymn in the Holy Nativity" and maintains that "we know of nothing finer in the language."

1849

✍§ 175. Griswold, Rufus W[ilmot], ed. "Richard Crashaw," in *The Sacred Poets of England and America, for Three Centuries* . . . , 146–53. New York: D. Appleton & Co.; Philadelphia: Geo. S. Appleton, 1850.

Reprinted, 1853, 1857, 1859, 1866, 1886.

Biographical sketch and brief critical introduction to Crashaw, noting that his poems "display delicate fancy, great tenderness, and singular beauty of diction" (p. 146). Anthologizes "Dies Irae Dies Illa" (pp. 146–48), six stanzas from "Hymn in the Holy Nativity" (pp. 148–49), the conclusion of "Hymn in the Name of Jesus" (pp. 149–50), and "Ode on a Prayer-book" (pp. 150–53), without notes or additional commentary.

◆§ 176. Trench, Richard Chenevix. "De Novissimo Judico," in *Sacred Latin Poetry, Chiefly Lyrical*, 272–77. London: John W. Parker.
2d ed., corrected and improved (entry 209).
In a footnote that discusses various translations of *Dies Irae*, a poem that has "continually allured, and continually defied translators," refers to Crashaw's translation as "noble" and as "rather a reproduction than a translation" (p. 277).

1850

◆§ 177. [Bentley, Richard.] "Inedited Letters of Celebrated Persons." *Bentley's Miscellany* 27:521–26.
Comments on Horace Walpole's letter to Samuel Lysons (entry 100). Notes that Walpole "was not always very happy in his literary criticisms, especially when he was amongst the poets" and that "it was often a matter of mere fashion with him, and his judgment in some cases appears to have been governed by the reigning mode of the hour" (p. 524). Notes that "it is curious enough to find so staunch a collector and admirer of odds and ends and relics of antiquity decrying the old English poets, dismissing Crashaw to the contempt of Mr. Lysons, whose prosaic faculties must have held all such matters in profound indifference" (p. 524). Points out that "the superficial flippancy of this letter is thoroughly characteristic of the writer, and most readers will be content to be amused by its vivacity, without caring much about its critical heresies," noting that "the best critics hold a very different opinion" (p. 524) of Crashaw.

◆§ 178. Gilfillan, George. "Richard Crashaw," in *The Book of British Poesy, Ancient and Modern* . . . , 210–12. London: Published for John Walker, by D. Bogue; Johnstone & Hunter; Hamilton, Adams & Co.; H. Washbourne; Edinburgh: Oliver & Boyd; Johnstone & Hunter; Dublin: James McGlashan.
Anthologizes lines 31–54 of "Upon the Death of the most desired Mr. Herrys" and "In praise of Lessius," without notes or commentary.

◆§ 179. Scrymgeour, Daniel. "Richard Crashaw (——1650)," in *The Poetry and Poets of Britain, from Chaucer to Tennyson, with Biographical Sketches, and a Rapid View of the Characteristic Attributes of Each*, 173–74. Edinburgh: Adam and Charles Black.
Brief introduction to Crashaw's life and poetry. Describes the poetry as having "a fervid religious character" (p. 173) and sees Crashaw's chief strength as

that of translator. Maintains that, although Crashaw's poetry is "never tedious, but full of the strained and exaggerated conceits of the school of Donne," it rises above "the ever-recurring bathos of Quarles" (p. 173). Attributes the neglect of Crashaw to the Catholic attitudes expressed in his poetry. Anthologizes "In praise of Lessius" and "Marke 12. (Give to Caesar—) (And to God—)" with two brief notes on the latter.

1852

◆§ 180. Anon. [signed Rt]. "Lines on the Miracle of Turning the Water into Wine." *N&Q* 1st series, 6:358–59.
Notes that Thomas Campbell (entry 123) traces the image of water blushing and turning into wine to Crashaw's "Joann. 2. Aquae in vinum versae." Gives another example of its use in one of Aaron Hill's poems (*Works* [London, 1754], 3:241). Notes also the occurrence of the image in Vida's *Christiad* (Lib. III, 9984; Lib. II, 431), in St. Ambrose's hymn beginning "Vel Hydriis plennis aquae," and in Psalm 77:16. For a reply, see F. W. J. (entry 182).

1853

◆§ 181. Bede, Cuthbert. "Poetical Epithets of the Nightingale." *N&Q* 1st series, 7:397–99.
Briefly discusses poetical treatments of the nightingale and its song in British poetry and gives in tabular form the great variety of adjectives that have been used to describe the bird and its song. Notes that the list "sufficiently demonstrates the popularity of the nightingale as a poetical embellishment, and would, perhaps, tend to prove that a greater diversity of epithets have been bestowed upon the nightingale than have been given to any other song-bird" (p. 399). Points out that Crashaw calls the nightingale and its song "dainty," "delicious," "enthusiast," "harmless," "hopeful," "light-footed," "listening," "little," "panting," "shrill," "soft," "supple," "sweet," "syren," "tender," "and "Music's best seed-plot."

◆§ 182. J., F. W. "Aquae in Vinum conversae. Vidit et erubuit lympha pudica Deum." *N&Q* 1st series, 8:242.
In part a reply to Rt. (entry 180). Asks if an epigram containing the imagery of water blushing and becoming wine in *Poemata Anglorum Latina* is by Crashaw. Observes that, until he saw the note in *N&Q*, he had supposed the line was "the happy *ex tempore* produce of Dryden's early genius, when a boy at Westminster School."

1855

᠊ᢌᢒ 183. B., G. "Crashaw," in *Nouvelle Biographie Générale depuis les temps les plus reculés jusqu'à nos jours*, 12:354. Paris: Firmin Didot Frères, éditeurs.

Biographical sketch of Crashaw. Suggests that, as a poet, he "n'est jamais plat, jamais lourd et pesant," that "il offre des passages inspirés par un tendresse fervente, des images et des sentiments d'une grande beauté." Notes also that his versification "est presque toujours mélodieuse" but that "il manque parfois de goût . . . un vice général à cette époque." Singles out "Sospetto d'Herode" for its extraordinary beauty and regrets that Crashaw did not translate the whole of Marino's poem. Refers the reader to the article in *Retrospective Review* (entry 130).

᠊ᢌᢒ 184. M., J. "Marino's 'Slaughter of the Innocents.'" *N&Q* 1st series, 11:265.

Asks the identity of the translator (T. R.) of Marino's *Le Strage degl'Innocenti* (Newly Englished, London: Printed for Andrew Clerk, &c., 1675) and for information on a letter by a certain W. B. Stevens (entry 95) that is on the subject of the translation. The editor notes that the article is attributed to the Rev. Dr. William Bagshaw Stevens and appears in Maty's *New Review* 7:251. See also William Bates (entry 213) and J. H. C. (entry 215).

᠊ᢌᢒ 185. Mayor, J[ohn] E[yton] B[ickersteth], ed. *Nicholas Ferrar. Two Lives by His Brother John and by Doctor Jebb*. Now first edited with illustrations, by J. E. B. Mayor. (Cambridge in the Seventeenth Century, pt. 1.) Cambridge: Printed for the editor at the University Press and sold by Macmillan & Co.

In the preface, reprints Crashaw's first version of "In praise of Lessius" (pp. vi–vii). Notes that the epitaph on Nicholas Ferrar, Jr., attributed to Crashaw by Peckard, on the authority of Sancroft, is actually by Mark Frank, once fellow of Pembroke (p. 144). Describes the vigils held at Little Gidding (pp. 46–47) and in a note points out that Crashaw often joined in these vigils.

1857

᠊ᢌᢒ 186. Crashaw, Richard. *The Poetical Works of Richard Crashaw and Quarles' Emblems*. With Memoir and Critical Dissertation, by the Rev. George Gilfillan. (Library Edition of the British Poets.) Edinburgh: James Nichol. xxi, 368p.

Reissued, with the text edited by Charles Cowden Clarke, Cassell's Library Edition of British Poets, parts 122, 123 (London, Paris, New York: Cassell, Petter, Galpin & Co., [1888]).

"The Life and Poetry of Richard Crashaw" (pp. v–xviii); contents (pp. xix–xxi); "The Poetical Works of Richard Crashaw, with a preface to the reader" (pp. 1–179). "The Life and Poetry of Francis Quarles" (pp. 183–97); "Quarles *Emblems*" (pp. 201–368), preceded by preliminary poems and letters (pp. 199–200). Calls Crashaw a "true and transcendent genius" (p. v) and presents a biographical sketch. Laments Crashaw's conversion to Catholicism "less for the sake of that Church [of England] than for the sake of Crashaw himself" (p. vii) and suggests that, "in deploring his secession, we are in fact only mourning the supra-superstitious tendencies of his nature" (p. vii). Notes that, "from the beginning of his being, Crashaw was a Catholic; and in saying so, we deem that we have stated at once the source of his poetic weakness and strength" (p. viii). Attacks Catholicism as "not Christianity" and maintains that Crashaw's "spirit is generally that of a true Christian poet, although considerably perverted by a false and bad form of religion" (p. viii). Asserts, however, that, "in soaring imagination, in gorgeous languages, in ardent enthusiasm, and in exstasy of lyrical movement, Crashaw very much resembles Shelley, and may be called indeed the Christian Shelley" (p. viii). Finds Crashaw often excessive in emotion and in expression. Notes that he is "most at home in the field of sacred poetry" (p. xi) and claims that perhaps no man ever "better appreciated the poetical elements which abound in the Roman Catholic faith" (p. xii), "unnerved by perfumes and lulled with unhealthy opiates" (p. xiii). Notes Crashaw's uses of "that quaint and tricky conceit" (p. xiv) that Dr. Johnson called metaphysical and admits that "here and there he is as fantastic as Donne or Cowley" (p. xiv). Challenges Dr. Johnson's criticism of the metaphysical poets. Calls "Musicks Duell" Crashaw's "finest effort" and the "most deliciously-true and incredibly-sustained piece of poetry in probably the whole compass of the language" (p. xviii).

᪥ 187. Mayor, J[ohn] E[yton] B[ickersteth]. "Richard Crashaw." *N&Q* 2d series, 4:286.

Suggests that of the two poems entitled "On the Frontispiece of Isaacsons Chronologie explained" ascribed to Crashaw, only the one beginning "Let hoary TIME's vast Bowels be the Grave" is actually his and the other, beginning "If with distinctive Eye, and Mind, you look," is the work of Edward Rainbow, who, in 1633, became Fellow of Magdalene College, Cambridge. Bases his information on a biography of Rainbow by Jonathan Banks (London, 1688).

1858

᪥ 188. Anon. "Notes on Books and Book Sales." *N&Q* 2d series, 5:24648.

Notes the publication of Turnbull's edition (1858) and observes that it is "somewhat remarkable, considering the acknowledged merits and widespread reputation" of the poet, that a "full reprint of Crashaw's works should be left to the present day." Notes that Turnbull "deeply sympathises with the feelings of the Poet" (p. 247).

◄§ 189. Allibone, S[amuel] Austin. "Crashaw, Richard," in *A Critical Dictionary of English Literature and British and American Authors, Living and Deceased, from the Earliest Accounts to the Latter Half of the Nineteenth Century*, 1:447. Philadelphia: J. B. Lippincott.

Briefly surveys the life and works of Crashaw. Suggests that his poetry "consists principally of religious invocations and translations of uncommon merit from the Latin and Italian" and that "his luxuriance of imagination and exquisite facility in the expression of his poetical visions have seldom been surpassed." Notes the borrowings of Milton and Pope; maintains that Crashaw was an intimate friend of Selden; and quotes passages of critical evaluation from Pope, Hayley, Phillips, Headley, and Ellis, as well as noting Dr. Johnson's praise of Cowley's elegy on Crashaw.

◄§ 190. B., A. "[Crashaw and Shelley.]" *N&Q* 2d series, 5:518.

Replies to D. F. McCarthy's assertion (entry 194) that Shelley probably had no knowledge of Crashaw. Notes that in Leigh Hunt's *Indicator* for May 1820 (entry 129) "Musicks Duell" is quoted and praised and that a reference is given to a critique of Crashaw that appeared in the *Retrospective Review* (entry 130). Argues that, since Hunt, Keats, and Shelley were intimate acquaintances, "it is therefore highly probable that the merits of Crashaw had been discussed between them, and that his poems were admired by each." See also A. A. W. (entry 198).

◄§ 191. Crashaw, Richard. *The Complete Works of Richard Crashaw, Canon of Loretto*, edited by William B. Turnbull. (Library of Old Authors.) London: John Russell Smith. xxxii, 340p.

Preliminary observations (pp. vii–xvii); a note on additional lines to be included in "Upon the ensuing Treatises [of Mr. Shelford]" (p. xviii); preface to the original edition (pp. xix–xxii); and contents (pp. xxiii–xxxii), followed by the poems, divided into *Steps to the Temple, The Delights of the Muses, Sacred Poems, Poemata Latina*, and *Epigrammata Sacra*, without critical notes or commentary. In "Preliminary Observations," presents a biographical sketch of Crashaw, based primarily on Wood, Hayley, and Willmott, and erroneously suggests that he was born in 1616 and died in 1650. Comments briefly on textual problems, lists and describes Crashaw's supposed engravings, and reproduces Cowley's elegy.

◄§ 192. Dana, Charles A[nderson], ed. *The Household Book of Poetry*. New York: D. Appleton and Co. xxvi, 798p.

Popular anthology (eleven editions by 1866; reprinted almost annually thereafter until 1919) that contains three poems by Crashaw: "Out of the Italian. A Song ('To thy Lover')," "In praise of Lessius," and "Ode on a Prayer-book," without notes or commentary.

◄§ 193. de Vere, Aubrey, ed. *Select Specimens of the English Poets,* with biographical notices, &c. London: Burns and Lambert. xii, 276p.

Includes "In praise of Lessius" and "Hymn to the Name of Jesus" along with a biographical sketch and general introductory comments on Crashaw (pp. 80–85). Erroneously notes that Crashaw was born in 1615 and died in 1650. Suggests that religion is one cause of the modern neglect of Crashaw but adds that "another may be found in the occasional quaintness and conceits that he shared with Herbert, and which were increased by his admiration for the writings of the Italian poet Marino" (p. 80). Claims, however, that "there is an exquisite beauty, richness, and tenderness in the poetry of Crashaw, as well as a noble devotional fervour, and an occasional sublimity" (p. 80). Praises the vigor and exuberance of language in "Sospetto d'Herode" and suggests that in it Crashaw "anticipates a modern poet of a very different school—the unhappy Shelley" (p. 80).

◄§ 194. McCarthy, D. F. "Crashaw and Shelley." *N&Q* 2d series, 5:449–52.

Briefly reviews Turnbull's edition (1858) and suggests that line 2 of "The Weeper" should read "Weeping is the ease of woe," not "the case of woe." Claims that since all previous editions have "case of woe," Turnbull "was perfectly correct in retaining it, either in the text or in a note" (p. 448). Points out resemblances between Crashaw and Shelley and compares lines and passages from their poems to show similarities in structure, rhyme, rhythm, meter, expression, and sentiment. Notes that, although Shelley had probably not read Crashaw, there are many lines and phrases in his poems "which had no prototypes in the whole range of British poesy, except in the hitherto obscure pages" (p. 448) of Crashaw. Notes also a resemblance between a passage in "Upon the ensuing Treatises [of Mr. Shelford]" and Keats's description of Madeline in "Eve of St. Agnes." Maintains that the object of these comparisons is to suggest "the existence of a certain kindred spirit between modern poets whose fame is *now* established, and an elder one whose fame is yet to be won" (p. 452). For replies, see A. B. (entry 190), T. C. Smith (entry 196), W. B. Turnbull (entry 197), and A. A. W. (entry 198).

◄§ 195. ———. "Crashaw and Shelley." *N&Q* 2d series, 6:94–95.

Replies to A.A.W.'s response (entry 198) to his previously published note (entry 194). Maintains his position that there are striking resemblances between the poetry of Crashaw and Shelley and observes that his intention in pointing out these similarities was "to awaken a stronger interest in the works of the elder poet . . . by showing that he was not deficient in some of the characteristics which have rendered the poetry of the younger so attractive"

(p. 95). Argues also for retaining "Weeping is the case of woe" in line 2 of "The Weeper," not as A.A.W. maintains, "the ease of woe." See also, A. B. (entry 190), T. C. Smith (entry 196), and W. B. Turnbull (entry 197).

ᴥᶋ 196. Smith, T. C. "Crashaw." *N&Q* 2d series, 6:234–35.
Reply to D. F. McCarthy (entries 194, 195) and to A.A.W. (entry 198). Quotes from the tenth stanza of "The Weeper" in the 1652 edition of *Carmen Deo Nostro* to show that line 2 reads "Weeping is the ease of woe," not "the case of woe," as McCarthy suggests, and to point out a difference in the last line of the stanza between McCarthy's quotation and the 1652 edition. Asks for information on Crashaw as an artist and comments briefly on the engravings in the 1652 edition. See also A. B. (entry 190) and W. B. Turnbull (entry 197).

ᴥᶋ 197. Turnbull, W. B. "Crashaw and Shelley." *N&Q* 2d series, 6:54.
Reply to D. F. McCarthy (entry 194) and A. A. W. (entry 198). Acknowledges a typographical error in line 2 of "The Weeper" in his edition (1858) and agrees that the line should read "Weeping is the ease of woe," not "the case of woe."

ᴥᶋ 198. W., A.A. "Crashaw and Shelley, and Their Poetical Coincidences with Each Other." *N&Q* 2d series, 5:516–18.
Replies to D. F. McCarthy's suggestion (entry 194) that there are close resemblances between the poems of Crashaw and Shelley and argues that the comparisons are false and misleading: "The mere common-places of poetry, like the notes of music or the seven primitive colours, are at the service of whosoever may think proper to make use of them" (p. 516). Maintains that the two poets "present strong *contrasts*, with but little if any resemblance, to each other," except that "extravagance of sentiment, and wildness of imagination, sometimes carried them both to the very verge of insanity" (p. 517). Challenges McCarthy's assertion that line 2 of "The Weeper" reads "Weeping that is the case of woe" in all earlier editions of the poem. Points out that, "with the single exception of that of 1646, in which one *e*, evidently broken by the press, has been converted into a *c*, all the early editions have given the passage correctly" (p. 516). Notes that only Chalmers among modern editors repeated the error. See also A. B. (entry 190), D. F. McCarthy (entry 194), T. C. Smith (entry 196), and W. B. Turnbull (entry 197).

1859

ᴥᶋ 199. Coles, Abraham. *Dies Irae in Thirteen Original Versions.* New York: D. Appleton and Co. xxxiv, 65p.
Discusses Crashaw briefly in "Translations of the Hymn" (pp. xxvii–xxxiv), but does not include his translation. Calls Crashaw's version "one of the

oldest and noblest of the English translations" (p. xxviii); agrees with Richard Chenevix Trench (entry 176) that, because of the freeness of the rendering, it might be called "a reproduction" rather than a translation; and points out the Earl of Roscommon's indebtedness to Crashaw's version.

◄§ 200. Masson, David. "Survey of British Literature: 1632," in *The Life of John Milton: Narrated in Connexion with the Political, Ecclesiastical, and Literary History of His Time*, 1:387–514. Cambridge: Macmillan and Co.

Revised edition, 1881; reprinted, New York: Peter Smith, 1948.

Cites lines from "Ode on a Prayer-book" as representative of "a kind of introversion of the sensual into the spiritual" found in some devotional poets of the seventeenth century and notes how the language of these poets "was tinged by its deliquescence" (p. 458). Observes that Crashaw's early poetry suggests he should be ranked among the young Spenserians rather than among the devotional poets and speculates that had Milton read "Musicks Duell," the elegies on Mr. Herrys, and other early translations and original pieces, "he would have found in them a sensuous beauty of style and sweetness of rhythm quite to his taste" (p. 459). Suggests that *Steps to the Temple* is "a kind of sequel to Herbert's poems" but maintains that, on the whole, "there is a richer vein of pietical genius in Crashaw than in Herbert," although it is marred by a "spiritualized voluptuousness" (p. 460) and effeminacy of expression. Attributes some of Crashaw's idiosyncrasy to his Catholicism.

1861

◄§ 201. Anon. "The Growth of English Poetry." *Quarterly Review* 110: 435–59.

Essay occasioned by the publication of Bell's *Annotated Edition of the English Poets* (London: J. W. Parker and Son, 1854–1856). Points out that Crashaw and Vaughan, "in style so dissimilar, have alike failed to obtain their due share of study" and includes lines from "On Mr. G. Herberts book, The Temple" as "one pleasing specimen" (p. 455) of Crashaw's poetry.

◄§ 202. Collier, William Francis. "Richard Crashaw," in *A History of English Literature in a Series of Biographical Sketches*, 171–72. London: T. Nelson and Sons.

Includes a biographical sketch of Crashaw and notes that "his religious poetry, and his translations from Latin and Italian, are of the first order, though somewhat marred by the affectations of the time" (p. 172).

◄§ 203. Palgrave, Francis Turner. *The Golden Treasury of Best Songs and Lyrical Poems in the English Language*, edited and arranged with notes by Francis Turner Palgrave. Cambridge and London: Macmillan and Co.

Revised and reprinted frequently.

Crashaw is represented in this important anthology by twenty-one stanzas from "Wishes. To his (supposed) Mistresse" (pp. 66–68). Brief explanatory note (p. 314).

1862

204. Arnold, Thomas. A *Manual of English Literature: Historical and Critical, With an Appendix on English Metres*. London: Longman, Green, Longman, Roberts, & Green. x, 423p.

Notes that Milton alone withstood the fashion for conceited poetry, while the most popular poets of the day, including Donne, Cowley, Crashaw, Waller, Cleveland, and Dryden (in his early poems), "gave in to the prevailing fashion, and, instead of simple, natural images, studded their poems with *conceits* (concetti)" (p. 116). Suggests that Crashaw's devotional lyrics "are often beautiful, though their effect is injured by the conceits in which he, as a writer of the fantastic school, was wont to indulge" (p. 316), and that his "predilection for conceits . . . greatly dimmed a poetical reputation, which force of thought and depth of feeling might otherwise have rendered a very high one" (p. 119). Gives a biographical sketch, mentions Crashaw's friendship with Cowley, and points out his translation of Marino (pp. 118–19).

205. [Findlater, Andrew, ed.] "Crashaw, Richard," in *Chambers's Encyclopaedia: A Dictionary of Universal Knowledge for the People illustrated with Maps and Numerous Wood Engravings*, 3:306. London: W[illiam] and R[obert] Chambers.

Modern edition, London: International Learning Systems, 1975.

Biographical sketch of Crashaw, noting that his "devotional strains exhibit imagination of a high order, with great copiousness and beauty of language." Suggests that Crashaw entered the church in 1641 and became "an earnest and eloquent preacher." Quotes "Joann. 2. Aquae in vinum versae" and notes that the poem has often been attributed to Dryden. Claims that all of Crashaw's poems appeared in 1646. Describes Crashaw as greatly resembling Herbert "in his cast of thought" and notes that Crashaw "is not inferior to him in richness of fancy, though we find in him more exaggeration and conceit."

206. Swinburne, Algernon Charles. *Théophile*.

First printed, edited by Edmund Gosse (London: Printed for private circulation, 1915), 35p. Limited to 20 copies.

Reprinted in *The Complete Works of Algernon Charles Swinburne*, ed. Edmund Gosse and Thomas James Wise, Bonchurch edition, vol. 13 (London: William Heinemann; New York: Gabriel Wells, 1926), 399–414.

Presumably written in 1862 but not published until 1915. Compares and contrasts the poetry of Théophile de Viau and that of Crashaw. Describes Crashaw as "a Christianised Théophile, steeped in Catholic sentiment and deformed by fantastic devotion" (p. 21). Notes, however, that Crashaw "is a far smaller figure, a much weaker and perverser man; but in fancy and melody, in grace and charm of exquisite words and notes, he may rank next and near him" (pp. 21–22). Suggests that Théophile's bad taste "is less monstrous, less violent, less excessive than his religious rival's" but adds that Crashaw "has now and then touched a chord of music too rich and deep for any other trained hand in the same school" (p. 22). Maintains that Théophile's faults are those of "over-careless health" while Crashaw's are "the faults of overstudious disease" (p. 22).

207. Willmott, Robert Aris, ed. *English Sacred Poetry of the Sixteenth, Seventeenth, Eighteenth, and Nineteenth Centuries.* Selected and edited by Robert Aris Willmott. London and New York: Routledge, Warne, & Routledge. xix, 387p.
New ed., 1863, 1877.
Includes the 1652 version of "Hymn in the Holy Nativity" (pp. 113–16), without notes or commentary. In the introduction, briefly notes "the fervour and exultation which inflame the songs of CRASHAW and HERBERT" (p. v).

1864

208. Lowell, James Russell. Review of Hazlitt's edition of Lovelace. *North American Review* 99:310–17.
Later incorporated into "Library of Old Authors," a collection of reviews of volumes in the series of that title (London: John Russell Smith, 1856–1872), printed in *My Study Windows* (Boston: James R. Osgood and Co., 1871), 290–374.
Reprinted in *Literary Essays*, The Riverside Edition of James Russell Lowell in Prose and Poetry, vol. 1 (Boston and New York: Houghton, Mifflin and Co.; Cambridge, Mass.: Riverside Press, 1890), 247–348.
Briefly mentions Crashaw in a discussion of seventeenth-century conceits. Notes that for poets such as Donne, Fuller, Butler, Marvell, and even Quarles, "conceit means wit; they could carve the merest cherrystone of thought in the quaintest and delicatest fashion," whereas in "duller and more painful writers," such as Gascoigne, Marston, Felltham, and others, as well as in the "cleverer ones," such as Waller, Crashaw, and Suckling, "where they insisted on being fine, their wit is conceit" (p. 336).

209. Trench, Richard Chenevix. *Sacred Latin Poetry, Chiefly Lyrical.* 2d ed., corrected and improved. London and Cambridge: Macmillan and Co.
To the note on Crashaw's version of *Dies Irae* included in the first edition (entry 176), adds a note on "Bulla," calling it "one of the most gorgeous pieces of painting in verse" and "more poetical than any of his English poetry" (p. 271).

1866

◆§ 210. Longfellow, Henry Wadsworth. Letter to Bernard Rölker. 8 April.
Printed in *The Letters of Henry Wadsworth Longfellow*, ed. Andrew Hilen
(London and Cambridge, Mass.: The Belknap Press of Harvard University
Press, 1982), 5:45–46.
Quotes the phrase "the not impossible she" from line 2 of "Wishes. To his
(supposed) Mistresse" ("That not impossible shee"), apparently to console his
friend over a broken engagement.

◆§ 211. [Nott, Charles Cooper.] "The Dies Irae," in *The Seven Great Hymns
of the Medieval Church*, 44–83. New York: Anson D. F. Randolph.
Discusses the composition, historical reception, translations, and poetical
features of the *Dies Irae*. Claims that Crashaw's translation "is the oldest in
our language (1646), though there is a weak paraphrase by Drummond of
Hawthornden" (p. 53). Notes that "no translation surpasses Crashaw's in
strength, but the form of his stanza and the measure of his verse are least like
those of the original" (p. 53). Reproduces Crashaw's poem (pp. 75–83), paral-
leling it, stanza by stanza, to the Earl of Roscommon's translation.

1868

◆§ 212. Addis, John, Jun. "Richard Crashaw." *N&Q* 4th series, 1:280.
In part a reply to J. H. C. (entry 215). Calls attention to Crashaw's "beautiful translation" of Strada, "Musicks Duell," and suggests that readers compare it to Ford's rendition in *The Lover's Melancholy*. Notes also the critical
article on Crashaw that appeared in the *Retrospective Review* (entry 130). For
a reply, see Hermann Kindt (entry 216).

◆§ 213. Bates, William. "Slaughter of the Innocents." *N&Q* 4th series,
1:125.
Asks the identity of the translator (T. R.) of Marino's *La Strage degl'Innocenti* (London: Printed by Andrew Clerk, &c., 1675). Notes that the high
quality of the translation would suggest Crashaw as the possible author. Observes that "we know that Crashaw formed his style in great measure upon that
of Marino, whose *Sospetto d'Herode*, included in Mr. Turnbull's edition, he
did translate; but I do not know any evidence to justify the connection of his
name with this other work of the great Italian poet, to which, as a religious
poem, we had no fitting rival to oppose before the appearance of *Paradise
Lost*, the author of which is indebted to the *Adamo* of his southern precursor."
For a reply, see J. H. C. (entry 215). See also J. M. (entry 184).

◆§ 214. Bellew, J[ohn] C[hippendale] M[ontesquieu]. "Richard Crashaw," in
Poet's Corner: A Manual for Students in English Poetry, with biographi-

cal sketches of the authors, 342–50. London: George Routledge and Sons.

Biographical sketch of Crashaw, brief comments on his religious sensibility, several lines from Pope's evaluation of his poetry, and selections from "Sospetto d'Herode," "Wishes. To his (supposed) Mistresse," "On the Blessed Virgins bashfulnesse," and "Two went up into the Temple to pray." Maintains that line 4 of "Joann. 2. Aquae in vinum versae" ("Nympha pudica Deum vidit, et erubuit") "alone would preserve his name in English literature" (p. 343).

⊷§ 215. C., J. H. "Marino's 'Slaughter of the Innocents' and Richard Crashaw." *N&Q* 4th series, 1:208.

Replies to J. M. (entry 184) and William Bates (entry 213). Acknowledges that he does not know the identity of the translator (T. R.) of Marino's *La Strage degl'Innocenti* (1675) but questions the remark of the editor attached to J. M.'s note that the 1675 translation "seems superior to Crashaw's." Points out Crashaw's ability as a translator by quoting stanza 28 of "Sospetto d'Herode" and notes that it "seems to me to be of such surpassing excellence that you will perhaps think it worthy to be placed before your readers." See also John Addis, Jun. (entry 212) and Hermann Kindt (entries 216, 217).

⊷§ 216. Kindt, Hermann. "Richard Crashaw: His Translations, Etc." *N&Q* 4th series, 1:416–17.

In part, a reply to John Addis, Jun. (entry 212) and to J. H. C. (entry 215). Calls attention to and praises Robert Aris Willmott's "exquisite biography" (p. 416) of Crashaw in *Lives of the English Sacred Poets* (entry 148). Comments on Pope's criticism of and borrowing from Crashaw and parallels passages from Crashaw's translations (from Marino, Strada, the *Dies Irae*) with their sources to demonstrate that Crashaw's translations are original, creative works in themselves. Quotes from "Hymn in the Holy Nativity" to show that "not alone as a *translator* ought Crashaw to be studied and appreciated" (p. 417). See also entry 217.

⊷§ 217. ———. "Richard Crashaw: His Translations, Etc." *N&Q* 4th series, 2:134.

Continuation of his earlier article (entry 216); in part a reply to John Addis, Jun. (entry 212) and to J. H. C. (entry 215). Notes that Robert Aris Willmott (entry 148) claims that the translation of Marino's *La Strage degl'Innocenti* by T. R. (1675) is inferior to Crashaw's "Sospetto d'Herode." Presents information on Marino drawn from Willmott and from Campbell (entry 123).

⊷§ 218. Macdonald, George. "Crashaw and Marvell," in *England's Antiphon*, 238–50. London: Macmillan & Co.

Calls Crashaw "one of the loveliest of our angel-birds" (p. 238) and suggests that the "word-music" in his poems reminds one of Shelley and Keats. Offers a biographical sketch. Stresses Crashaw's "sentimentalism" in such poems as "The Weeper" but calls that poem "radiant of delicate fancy" and "fantastically beautiful" (p. 240). Comments on "Easter day," noting its "strangeness," "oddity," and inadequate expression, but urging his readers "to compensate the deficiency by adding more vision" (pp. 243–44). Quotes part of "Hymn in the Holy Nativity," calling it the "most musical and most graceful, therefore most lyrical of his poems" (p. 243) but noting its "peculiarities" and "sentimentalism." Concludes that the hymn is "exquisite" but wishes that it "looked less heathenish" and notes that "its decorations are certainly meretricious" (p. 246).

◆§ 219. Massey, Gerald. "The 'Miltonic' Epitaph." *Pall Mall Gazette*, 11 August, p. 4.
Reprinted in *The Era*, 12 October 1868, and in *N&Q* 4th series, 3(1869): 4–5.
Points out parallels and echoes between several of Crashaw's poems and an epitaph wrongly attributed to Milton. Maintains that, in spite of these similarities, the epitaph in question is not by Crashaw: "Poets do not steal from themselves in that way, whether consciously or unconsciously; nor would Crashawe, a man of fertile, quick fancy, have scattered a dozen ideas over half a dozen poems, and then collected them again to twist them into one poem precisely of the same nature." Suggests that the epitaph may be plagiarized from Crashaw's several poems. See also Brinsley Nicholson (entry 230).

◆§ 220. Schaff, Philip. "Translations of Dies Irae." *Hours at Home*, July, pp. 261–68.
Second of two essays on the *Dies Irae*, the first of which does not mention Crashaw. Discusses the origin and history of the great medieval hymn and presents specimens from a number of the best German and English translations, including one stanza from Crashaw's rendition (p. 264). Calls Crashaw's version "free and vigorous" (p. 261). Both essays are reprinted together in a revised form in Schaff's *Literature and Poetry* (New York: Charles Scribner's Sons, 1890), pp. 134–86.

1869

◆§ 221. Anon. [signed Hic et Ubique]. "Miracle at Cana." *N&Q* 4th series, 4:198.
Asks for information on the lines "Lympha Deum vidit, vidit et erubuit" translated as "The water saw its God, and blushed." Editor notes that "the celebrated epigram on the miracle at the marriage in Cana is by Richard Crashaw" and refers the reader to Turnbull's edition (1858). Notes that Dryden has been credited with writing a similar line during his schoolboy days at Westminster but suggests that, "if so, he was probably indebted to Crashaw for the thought." For a reply, see Grosart (entry 225).

222. Anon. [signed Juxta-Turrim]. "William Crashaw." *N&Q* 4th series, 3:314–15.

Presents biographical information on William Crashaw, the poet's father, and his wife in reply to a query by Wessex (*N&Q* 4th series 3 [1869]: 219). Suggests inaccurately that Mrs. Crashaw "would have appeared to have died whilst giving birth to her first child, at the age of twenty-four, on October 8, 1620" and concludes that "the child thus unhappily deprived of a mother's care was Richard, the poet" (p. 314). Notes that Richard became a "violent anti-Protestant" and points out that the reference in Selden's *Table-Talk* is to William, not Richard Crashaw. Presents a partial list of William Crashaw's publications. For a reply, see James Delano (*N&Q* 4th series, 3 [1869]: 440) and Grosart (*N&Q* 4th series, 3 [1869]: 370–71).

223. Alcott, A[mos] Bronson. Journal entries. 20 May and 8 June.

Printed in *Concord Days* (Boston: Roberts Brothers, 1873), vii, 276p.

Under 20 May, in an entry that discusses Margaret Fuller, reproduces "Wishes. To his (supposed) Mistresse" (pp. 79–82) and under 8 June reproduces the 1646 version of "Ode on a Prayer-book," calling it "exquisite" (pp. 140–42).

224. Grosart, Alexander B. "Additional Notes and Illustrations," in *The Poems of Phineas Fletcher . . .* , edited by Alexander B. Grosart, 2:201–32. (The Fuller Worthies' Library.) Blackburn: Printed for Private Circulation by Charles Tiplady.

Small paper edition limited to 156 copies; large paper edition limited to 106 copies.

Suggests that Crashaw must have had before him Fletcher's "The Locustae" and "The Apollyonists" when he translated the first book of Marino's *La Strage degl'Innocenti*. Notes the possible echoes from Fletcher in Crashaw's description of Satan and observes that "it is exactly in those supreme touches that have no counterpart in the original of Marino, we most clearly trace—as in Milton—the influence of Phineas Fletcher" (p. 201).

225. ———. "Crashaw: Miracle at Cana." *N&Q* 4th series, 4:244.

In part a reply to entry 221. Notes that in *Victor Hugo: A Life* (2 vols., London: Wm H. Allen & Co., 1863) there appears what the author terms "a whimsical explanation" of the miracle at Cana: "La nymphe de ces eaux aperçut Jésus-Christ, / Et son pudique front de rougeur se couvrit."

226. ———. "Richard Crashaw." *N&Q* 4th series, 3:334–35.

Describes a newly acquired, undated quarto, signed R. C. and ascribed to Crashaw by Mr. Corser of the Strand, a bookseller. Asks for information on the subject of the elegy, Margaret Lady Smith. The editor notes that W. Carew

Hazlitt (*Hand-Book to the Popular, Poetical, and Dramatic Literature of Great Britain*, 1876) attributes the work to Robert Codrington.

◆§ 227. ———. "Richard Crashaw and His Patrons, Etc." *N&Q* 4th series, 4:450.

Asks for information on Cardinal Palotto, Thomas Car, and Peter Targa, the printer of the 1652 edition of *Carmen Deo Nostro*. Notes that he possesses a large paper copy of *Carmen Deo Nostro* (with blank pages for the engravings) and asks if there are any other copies in this early state.

◆§ 228. ———. "W. Crashaw." *N&Q* 4th series, 3:511–23.

In part a reply to entry 222 and to J. H. (*N&Q* 4th series, 3 [1869]: 440). Notes that the register of Handsworth, near Sheffield, indicates that William Crashaw was baptized on 26 October 1572 and promises to include in his forthcoming edition of Richard Crashaw's poems "a considerable amount of altogether new information on the numerous clan of the Crashaws" (p. 511). Points out that the wife of William Crashaw who died in childbirth in 1620 was his second wife, not the mother of Richard, as Juxta-Turrim suggests (entry 222). Following this entry are three brief notes on William Crashaw by W. D., Juxta-Turrim, and Upthorpe, none of which refers specifically to Richard Crashaw.

◆§ 229. H., J. W. "Crashaw and Constable." *N&Q* 4th series, 3:581.

Asks for information on the best modern editions of Crashaw and Constable. The editor suggests Turnbull's edition (1858) but notes that Crashaw's poetry is soon to appear in the Fuller Worthies' Library.

◆§ 230. Nicholson, Brinsley. "The Supposed Miltonic Epitaphs." *N&Q* 4th series, 3:37.

Continues his discussion of some Latin epitaphs falsely ascribed to Milton (*N&Q* 4th series, 3 [1869]: 4–5) and suggests that Crashaw may be the author. See also Gerald Massey (entry 219).

1870

◆§ 231. Brown, Gulielmi [William] Haig, ed. *Sertum Carthusianum Floribus Trium Seculorum Contextum*. Canterbury: Deighton, Bell, et Soc.; London: Bell and Daldy. xxi, 397p.

Includes a biographical note on Crashaw (p. xv) and four of the Latin epigrams, without notes or commentary (pp. 145–46).

◆§ 232. Dodd, Henry Philip. "Richard Crashaw," in *The Epigrammatists: A Selection from the Epigrammatic Literature of Ancient, Mediaeval, and*

Modern Times. With Notes, Observations, Illustrations, and an Introduction, 251–53. London: Bell and Daldy.

A biographical sketch of Crashaw followed by "To Pontius washing his hands," "On the Blessed Virgins bashfulnesse," a translation by Aaron Hill of "Joann. 2. Aquae in vinum versae," "To our Lord, upon the Water made Wine," and "An Epitaph upon a Young Married Couple." Calls the translation by Hill "masterful" (p. 252) and suggests that, after reading "An Epitaph upon a Young Married Couple," "all others on the same subject must suffer by comparison" (p. 253).

꘠ 233. Grosart, Alexander B. "Richard Crashaw and His Italian Songs." *N&Q* 4th series, 5:173–74.

Asks for information on the originals of three of Crashaw's translations of Italian songs: "Out of the Italian. A Song," "Out of the Italian ('Love now no fire hath left him')," and "Out of the Italian ('Would any one the true cause find')."

꘠ 234. [Rowley, James.] "The So-Called Metaphysical Poets," in *A Smaller History of English and American Literature*, edited by William Smith and Henry T. Tuckerman, 125–31. New York: Sheldon & Co.

Briefly discusses Crashaw's life and poetry and notes that "the mystical tendency of his mind was increased by his misfortunes and by his change of religion" (p. 127). Maintains that Crashaw "possessed an exquisite fancy, great melody of verse, and that power over the reader which nothing can replace, and which springs from a deep earnestness, no one can deny" (p. 127). Suggests that "the most favourable specimens" of his poetry are to be found in *Steps to the Temple* and singles out "Musicks Duell" as a "beautiful description" (p. 127).

1871

꘠ 235. Beeton, S[amuel] O[rchart], ed. *Beeton's Great Book of Poetry: From Caedmon and King Alfred's Boethius to Browning and Tennyson* . . . . 2 vols. London: Ward, Lock & Tyler; Philadelphia: George Gebbie.

Reissued as *Encyclopaedie of English and American Poetry: From Caedman and King Alfred's Boethius to Browning and Tennyson* (London: Ward, Lock and Tyler; Philadelphia: Geo[rge] Gebbie, 1873).

Includes a biographical sketch of Crashaw and a short critical evaluation of his poetry. Suggests that "it is chiefly in translation that the strength of Crashaw is visible" and points out that "his pieces are never tedious, but full of the strained and exaggerated conceits of the school of Donne" and that "he had a rich warm fancy, and a delicate ear for music." Anthologizes selections from "Sospetto d'Herode," "Hymn to the Name of Jesus," "Upon the Death of

the most desired Mr. Herrys," "Musicks Duell," and "Marke 12. (Give to Caesar—) (and to God—)."

1872

◄§ 236. Anon. Review of Grosart's first volume of *The Complete Works of
Richard Crashaw* (1872). *The Month* 17:327–33.
Surveys Crashaw's life for those "who may appreciate his poems and desire
to become better acquainted with the author" (p. 327) and reproduces stanzas
from "Hymn in the Holy Nativity" as an example of his art.

◄§ 237. Crashaw, Richard. *The Complete Works of Richard Crashaw*, For the
   first time collected and collated with the original and early editions, and
   much enlarged . . . , edited by Alexander B. Grosart. (The Fuller
   Worthies' Library.) 2 vols. Printed for private circulation [London: Rob-
   son and Sons, Printers], 1872–1873. xlviii, 303; xc, 387p.
Large paper edition (with illustrations) limited to 100 copies; small paper
edition (without illustrations) limited to 156 copies.
Reprinted, New York: AMS Press, 1983, with Grosart's supplement (entry
274) included as part of vol. 1.
Selections from "Essay on the Life and Poetry of Crashaw" reprinted in *The
Metaphysical Poets: A Selection of Critical Essays*, ed. Gerald Hammond (entry 1085), 75–76.
Dedicated to John Henry Cardinal Newman, noting that this is an edition
"of a poet he loves as Englishman and Catholic." Vol. 1 contains contents and
list of illustrations (pp. vii–x); preface (pp. xi–xxv); memorial-introduction
(pp. xxvii–xxxviii); note on title pages (pp. xl–xliv); and preface to the reader
(pp. xlv–xlviii), followed by Sacred Poetry: I. *Steps to the Temple* and *Carmen
Deo Nostro* (pp. 1–181); Sacred Poetry: II. *Airelles* (poems from unpublished
manuscripts; pp. 183–94); Secular Poetry: I. *The Delights of the Muses* (pp.
195–276); Secular Poetry: II. *Airelles* (pp. 277–94) and "Letter to the Countess of Denbigh" (pp. 295–303), with notes and illustrations. Presents in the
preface a detailed bibliographical discussion of known manuscripts and early
editions, two poems by Thomas Car, and a description of the engravings.
Notes in the memorial-introduction that Crashaw is "one of the richest of the
minor Poets of England" (p. xxvii), offers a biographical sketch, and reprints
Cowley's "On the Death of Mr. Crashaw." Vol. 2 contains a preface (pp. v–
ix); contents (pp. xi–xx); "Essay on the Life and Poetry of Crashaw" (pp. xxi–
xc); note on *Epigrammatum Sacorum Liber* (1634) and *Richardi Crashawi
Poemata et Epigrammata* (1670) (pp. 2–6); Latin dedication to Benjamin
Laney, with translation (pp. 7–15), Lectori, with translation (pp. 16–33), followed by 1. Sacred Epigrams (1634–1670) (pp. 35–164), and Secular Epigrams (pp. 165–66); 2. Sacred Epigrams. Never Before Printed (pp. 167–

205); 3. Latin Poems. Part First. Sacred. Hitherto Uncollected (pp. 207–18); 4. Latin Poems. Part First. Sacred. Never Before Printed (pp. 219–42); Latin Poems. Part Second. Secular (pp. 243–92); Latin Poems. Part Second Secular. Never Before Printed (pp. 293–330); Latin Poems. Part Second. Secular (pp. 331–84); and a glossorial index (pp. 384–87). "Essay on the Life and Poetry of Crashaw" contains a memoir of the poet's father, William Crashaw, along with comments on his polemical works and verse translations from Latin (pp. xxii–xxxix) and a biographical sketch of the poet, concentrating on his conversion to Catholicism, his friends and associates celebrated in his works, and the general characteristics of his poetry (pp. xxxix–xc). Attributes Crashaw's conversion to Catholicism primarily to his mystical temperament and his reading of the Catholic mystics, especially St. Teresa, as well as to the ritualistic revival in the Church of the period and the turmoil created by the Commonwealth. Discusses Crashaw's "imaginative sensuousness," his thought "surcharged with emotion," and his "subtlety of emotion" and comments on the excellences of the epigrams (which are translated) and of Crashaw's own translations, noting that "the genius of Crashaw shines with its fullest splendour in his Translations" (p. lxxviii) and praising "Sospetto d'Herode" and "Musicks Duell," both of which are compared to the originals.

1873

238. Anketell, John. "The 'Dies Irae.'" *American Church Review* 25: 203–14.

Reproduces Crashaw's version of the *Dies Irae* and calls it "the most forcible and vigorous English translation of the hymn, noting that it is also "one of the oldest" (p. 211). Points out that the translation "is not in the metre of the original" and is thus "far from being a literal version" but that "as a sacred lyric, it is worthy of the highest praise" (p. 211).

239. Grosart, A[lexander] B. Letter to Robert Browning. 14 May.

Printed in *Intimate Glimpses from Browning's Letter File*, ed. A. Joseph Armstrong with an introduction by Roland A. Young, Baylor University's Browning Interests, series 8; *The Baylor Bulletin* 37, nos. 3 & 4 (Waco, Tex.: Baylor University, 1934), 60–61.

Asks Browning to assist him in getting fifteen remaining sets of his Fuller Worthies' Library editions of Crashaw, Southwell, and Donne "into appreciative hands" (p. 61).

240. Morley, Henry. "From Elizabeth to the Commonwealth," in *A First Sketch of English Literature*, 491–594. London, Paris, New York: Cassell, Petter, & Galpin.

Presents a biographical sketch and surveys Crashaw's work (pp. 547–48).

Suggests that Crashaw's lyrics are more "euphuistic" than those of the Cavalier poets and that his religious poems "are not less purely devotional, though they have less beauty and force than those of Herbert" (p. 548).

1874

•§ 241. Emerson, Ralph Waldo, ed. *Parnassus*. Boston and New York: Houghton Mifflin Co. xxxiv, 534p.

Reprinted, Boston: J. R. Osgood & Co., 1875, 1876, 1878; Boston: Houghton Mifflin, 1880, 1881, 1882.

Modern reprint, Freeport, N.Y.: Books for Libraries Press, 1970.

Notes in the preface Spence's report that Pope said that "Crashaw is a worse sort of Cowley: Herbert is lower than Crashaw" and points out that it is "an opinion which no reader of their books at this time will justify" (p. vi). Suggests that Crashaw's translation of Marino "has masterly verses never learned from Cowley" (p. vi). Includes lines from the description of Satan in "Sospetto d'Herode" (p. 179) and the epigram "Two went up into the Temple to pray" (p. 180).

•§ 242. Finlayson, John. "Richard Crashaw and John Henry Newman, Their Poetic Kinship." *Owens College* [Manchester] *Magazine* 6:137–48, 174–88.

Biographical sketch of Crashaw based primarily on Grosart's account (entry 237). Suggests that the most important influence on Crashaw's religious and poetic sensibilities was St. Teresa, "who was to him in his poetic mood all that Beatrice was to Dante" (p. 139) and notes also that John Henry Newman assigns to the Spanish saint a position of preeminence among modern saints. Surveys essential characteristics of Crashaw's poetry, such as sensuous imagery, a tone of grief, mystical intensity, and the infusion of the human into the divine, and notes that, "if the phrase is allowable, he is the most facial in imagery of the fantastic poets; every verse, often every line, as it were, glistens with eyes, tears freely flowing down lily cheeks, and from his fantastic cornucopia he draws a wealth of imagery seemingly inexhaustible" (p. 140). Argues that if Crashaw had remained an Anglican, his life and poetry would be more widely known and appreciated and maintains that his poetry cannot be judged by "Protestant canons of criticism" (p. 147). Compares the religious and poetic sensibilities of Crashaw and Newman and finds several parallels as well as significant differences. Suggests that Crashaw's poetical influence on Newman is "more sympathetically felt in the 'Dream of Gerontius' (not to dwell upon the undertone of grief and many suggestive passages in his earlier poems), in the structure of the poem, in the name it bears, and in the similarity of Catholic sentiment throughout; but is nowhere so observable as in the passages of real grandeur, which are none the less essentially Dr. Newman's, in thought, experience, and expression" (p. 187). Briefly compares and contrasts Crashaw with Southwell, Herbert, Rossetti, Thomas Ken, Keble, and Coleridge.

◄§ 243. Knowles, R. B. "The Manuscripts of the Right Honourable the Earl of Denbigh at Newnham Paddox," in *Fourth Report of The Royal Commission on Historical Manuscripts. Part I: Report and Appendix*, 254–76. London: Printed by George Edward Eyre and William Spottiswoode . . . for HMSO.

In a note, questions whether Crashaw's "Letter to the Countess of Denbigh" was written to her or perhaps was addressed to Elizabeth Bouchier, the second Earl of Denbigh's third wife.

1875

◄§ 244. Swinburne, Algernon Charles. "John Ford," in *Essays and Studies*, 276–313. London: Chatto and Windus.

Briefly comments on "Musicks Duell," comparing and contrasting it to Ford's *The Lover's Melancholy*: "Between the two beautiful versions of Strada's pretty fable by Ford and Crashaw there will always be a diversity of judgment among readers; some must naturally prefer the tender fluency and limpid sweetness of Ford, others the dazzling intricacy and affluence in refinements, the supple and cunning implication, the choiceness and subtlety of Crashaw" (p. 296).

1876

◄§ 245. Brooke, Stopford [Augustus]. "From Elizabeth's Death to the Restoration, 1603–1660," in *English Literature* (Literature Primers, ed. John Richard Green), 94–107. London: Macmillan and Co.

Expanded and revised (entry 301).

Lists Crashaw among the religious poets of the earlier seventeenth century and notes that his "rich inventiveness was not made less rich by the religious mysticism which finally led him to become a Roman Catholic" (p. 100).

◄§ 246. Marshall, Ed. "Tertullian's Roofe of Angels." *N&Q* 5th series, 6:233.

In part, a reply to Christopher Wordsworth's inquiry (entry 248) concerning references in early biographical notices of Crashaw to his having "lodged under Tertullian's roofe of angels." Cites several passages from Tertullian to show that the phrase may simply refer to Little St. Mary's Church and notes that in his "Votiva Domus Petrensis Pro Domo Dei" Crashaw himself calls the church "heaven."

◆§ 247. Whittier, John Greenleaf, ed. *Songs of Three Centuries*. Boston: James R. Osgood & Co. xxviii, 352p.

Includes twenty-one stanzas of "Wishes. To his (supposed) Mistresse" (pp. 29–30), without notes or commentary.

◆§ 248. Wordsworth, Chr[istopher]. "Crashaw and Tertullian." *N&Q* 5th series, 6:169.

Notes that in several early biographical notices of Crashaw it is said that in Little St. Mary's Church "he lodged under Tertullian's roofe of angels" and asks for information on the reference to Tertullian. Points out that Crashaw often visited Little Gidding and imitated the nocturns observed there when he returned to Peterhouse, which has a passage linking it to the church of Little St. Mary's. For a reply, see Ed Marshall (entry 246).

1877

◆§ 249. Anon. "Richard Crashaw," in *Gleanings from the Sacred Poets, with Biographical Notices of the Authors*, 58–59. Edinburgh and London: Gall & Inglis.

Anthologizes ten stanzas from "Dies Irae Dies Illa," claiming that it is the first translation of the hymn into English. Presents in a headnote a partially inaccurate biographical sketch, noting, for example, that Crashaw "became a popular clergyman at Oxford, and was expelled by the Parliamentarians in 1644" and that "in order to obtain the patronage of Charles the First's Popish Queen, he turned a Papist by her recommendation" (p. 58).

1880

◆§ 250. Egan, Maurice F[rancis]. "Three Catholic Poets: A Sketch." *Catholic World* 32:121–40.

Reprinted, without the first six paragraphs, as "Lecture IV: Southwell, Crashaw, and Habington," in *Lectures on English Literature* (New York: William H. Sadlier, 1889), 61–87.

Presents a brief survey of Crashaw's life and poetry, especially its Catholic elements, and claims that "it is plain that Crashaw was always a Catholic at heart" (p. 140). Notes that "The Flaming Heart" is marred by "exasperating conceits" but praises its "intense fervor" (p. 138) and its "mystical fire," which is "characteristic of all Crashaw's religious verses" (p. 139). Suggests that in "Wishes. To his (supposed) Mistresse" Crashaw "plays with one idea, fantastically twisting it and repeating it until the reader grows weary" (p. 139). Notes the influence of Crashaw on Pope and compares him, as a Catholic poet, to Southwell and Habington: "Crashaw had the softened fire of Southwell with the placid sweetness of Habington" (p. 140).

*§ 251. Foley, Henry. *Records of the English Province of the Society of Jesus.*
Vol. 6. London: Burns and Oates. xxxiv, 796p.

Presents a biographical sketch of Crashaw in the introduction to the volume (pp. xxxiii–xxxiv) and notes that four entries in the *Pilgrim-Book* of the
English Hospice (later the English College) in Rome mention Crashaw. The
first entry, dated 28 November 1646, indicates that Crashaw stayed "fifteen
days and frequently afterwards" (p. 634). Notes later that Crashaw dined at the
hospice on 18 and 27 December 1646 (p. 634) and again on 4 April 1649 (p.
639). See also P. G. Stanwood (entry 943) and Kenneth Larsen (entry 1039).

*§ 252. Shorthouse, Joseph Henry. *John Inglesant: A Romance.* Bir-
mingham: Cornish Brothers. 577p.

100 copies printed privately.

First 2 volume ed., London: Macmillan, 1881; numerous editions and
reprints.

Modern reprint, ed. Robert L. Wolff (New York: Garland Press, 1975).

A historical romance set during the English Civil War in which Crashaw
briefly appears as a character and in which his poems are mentioned. Presents
a fictionalized account of John Inglesant, the protagonist, meeting Crashaw at
Little Gidding, where the poet expresses his Catholic sentiments and joins
Inglesant and others in the late-night vigils held in the church there. In another episode, Inglesant reads aloud Crashaw's poems in the company of
Mary Collet; and, when visiting the English College in Rome, Inglesant is
reminded of "Description of a Religious House and Condition of Life" and
quotes five lines from the poem.

*§ 253. Simcox, G. A. "Sandys, Herbert, Crashaw, Vaughan," in *The
English Poets: Selections with Critical Introductions by Various Writers
and a General Introduction by Matthew Arnold,* edited by Thomas
Humphrey Ward. Vol. 2: *Ben Johnson to Dryden,* 192–98. London and
New York: Macmillan and Co.

Suggests that Herbert's direct influence on Crashaw's poetry is slight and
claims that Crashaw's "glowing impetuosity" makes "the laboured crabbed ingenuity of Herbert seem tame" (p. 195). Contrasts Crashaw's "diffuseness and
repetition" with Herbert's careful organization and structure. Suggests that
"Wishes. To his (supposed) Mistresse" is so filled with insignificant variations
that Crashaw "can hardly have read the poem through before sending it to
press" (p. 195). Claims, however, that Crashaw's translation of Marino is superior to the original and says that line 16 of "Description of a Religious
House and Condition of Life" is "worthy of Pope" (p. 198). Suggests that,
unlike Herbert and Vaughan, Crashaw "seems to have no inner struggles; he
passes from Peterhouse to Loretto as pilgrims pass from one chapel to another
in the Church of the Holy Sepulchre" (p. 197). Calls Crashaw a "devotee,"
Vaughan a "mystic," and Herbert an "ascetic" (p. 197). Includes selections

from "Wishes. To his (supposed) Mistresse" and "The Flaming Heart" as well as the whole of "Description of a Religious House and the Condition of Life" (pp. 206–9), without notes.

1881

◄§ 254. Nolan, Joseph A. "Richard Crashaw." *American Catholic Quarterly Review* 6:445–81.

Presents a biographical sketch of Crashaw, whom he calls a minor but inspired poet; a survey of Crashaw's poetry; and a discussion of the political and religious unrest in seventeenth-century England. Notes that until Grosart's edition, Crashaw "suffered greatly from the misleading blunders and careless work of his editors" (p. 446). Praises Crashaw's "creative imagination, natural tenderness, refined sentiment, and delicate imagery; the "masterly melody of his versification and the luxuriousness of his expression"; and his power to awaken "noble feeling, high resolves, and deep-felt veneration" (p. 453). Singles out "Hymn in the Holy Nativity" and "Hymn in the Glorious Epiphanie" to illustrate Crashaw's "grandeur, power, originality, and tenderness" (p. 454), calling the latter "a work of genius" (p. 458). Also comments appreciatively on the three Teresian poems, "Hymn in the Assumption," "Hymn to the Name of Jesus," "On a foule Morning, being then to take a journey," "To the Morning. Satisfaction for sleepe," "Wishes. To his (supposed) Mistresse," and several of the epigrams and epitaphs. Maintains that "even the weakest of the epigrams show forth the beauty of the man" while "the strongest are resplendent with the genius of the poet" (p. 469) and stresses the originality of Crashaw's translations by commenting on "Sospetto d'Herode," "Musicks Duell," "Adoro Te," and "Dies Irae Dies Illa," suggesting that the first two are superior to their originals. Claims that Crashaw's "great power as a poet lies in his perfect insight into nature" (p. 466). Notes his influence on Coleridge, Milton, Dryden, Pope, Edward Young, Aaron Hill, Rev. J. H. Clark, Thomas Ashe, and perhaps Shelley.

◄§ 255. Patmore, Coventry. Letter to Edmund Gosse. 21 June.

Printed in *Memoirs and Correspondence of Coventry Patmore*, by Basil Champneys (London: George Bell and Sons, 1900), 2:253.

Thanks Gosse for his essay on Crashaw, "with most of whose poems I was unacquainted." Adds that he has "not yet found anything equal to 'Music's Duel,' which is perhaps the most wonderful piece of word-craft ever done."

1882

◄§ 256. Schaff, Philip, ed. "Crashaw, Richard," in *A Religious Encyclopedia: or Dictionary of Biblical, Historical, Doctrinal, and Practical Theology*, 1:567. New York: Funk & Wagnalls, Publishers.

A biographical and critical sketch of Crashaw that points out that "there is no religious poetry in English so full at once of gross and awkward images and imaginative touches of the most ethereal beauty." Suggests that "the faults and beauties of his very peculiar style can be studied best in the *Hymn to St. Theresa.*"

1883

✎§ 257. Gosse, Edmund. "Richard Crashaw." *Cornhill Magazine* 47: 424–38.

Reprinted in *The Living Age* 157(1883):195–204; and in *Seventeenth Century Studies: A Contribution to the History of English Poetry* (London: Kegan, Paul, Trench & Co., 1883), 143–67; and in subsequent editions.

General biographical sketch and introduction to Crashaw's poetry. Maintains that Crashaw's works "present the only important contribution to English literature made by a pronounced Catholic, embodying Catholic doctrine, during the whole of the seventeenth century" and that "while as a poet, although extremely unequal, he rises, at his best to a mounting fervour which is quite electrical, and hardly rivalled in its kind before or since" (p. 424). Stresses that Crashaw's poems "are not poems of experience, but of ecstasy, not of meditation, but of devotion" and notes that the life and works of St. Teresa inspired some of his "loveliest and most faultless verses" (p. 430). Compares Crashaw to Friedrich von Spee and argues that Crashaw "is by far the greater and more varied of the two as regards poetical gifts" and was an adept in every refinement of metrical structure which had been invented by the poet artists of England, Spain, and Italy" (p. 432). Comments briefly on Crashaw's resemblance to Góngora and his indebtedness to Marino, suggesting that Crashaw was "a genuine Marinist, the happiest specimen that we possess in English" (p. 432). Thoroughly dislikes "The Weeper" and notes, that, "if language be ever liable to abuse in the hands of a clever poet, it is surely outraged here" (p. 432–33). Calls "Two walking baths; two weeping motions; / Portable, & compendious oceans" "the worst lines in Crashaw" and "perhaps the worst in all English poetry" (p. 433). Praises both "Musicks Duell" and "Wishes. To his (supposed) Mistresse" but maintains that "the sweetest and most modern of all Crashaw's secular lyrics is that entitled 'Loves Horoscope'" and suggests that it "contains some of the most delicately musical cadences to be found in the poetry of the age" (p. 436). Maintains that Crashaw reminds the reader of Shelley and Swinburne and that, "in spite of his conceits and his romantic colouring, he points the way for Pope, who did not disdain to borrow from him freely" (pp. 436–37). Complains that "it would scarcely be unjust to say that Crashaw was the first poet who allowed himself to use a splendid phrase when a simple one would have better expressed his meaning" but acknowledges that "his style has hectic beauties that delight us" (p. 437).

◄§ 258. Linton, W. J., ed. *Rare Poems of the Sixteenth and Seventeenth Centuries: A Supplement to the Anthologies.* Collected and edited with notes by W. J. Linton. Boston: Roberts Brothers. xvii, 264p.

Includes "Wishes. To his (supposed) Mistresse" (pp. 124–28). Observes in the notes (p. 247) that the poem is often "mutilated" by anthologists, pointing out in particular the editorial liberties taken by Ward (entry 253), who omitted twenty-six stanzas without indicating omissions (except in two cases), and by Palgrave (entry 203), who not only arbitrarily transposed stanzas but also omitted twenty-one in order to create "lyrical unity" in the poem.

◄§ 259. [Shipley, Orby.] "Fifty Versions of 'Dies Irae' I. Ancient Versions and Paraphrases." *DubR* series 3, 9:48–77.

Surveys the history and development of the *Dies Irae* and presents a comparative study of fifty English translations and paraphrases of the hymn by both Catholics and Protestants. Calls Crashaw's version "the earliest rendering of *Dies Irae* from the devotion of a Catholic" (p. 72). Suggests, however, that the version is "rugged in character and irregular in metre, and is more an imitation of the original than a translation; at least in some of its stanzas" (p. 73). Points out, nonetheless, that Crashaw's poem contains "much delicate play of thought and expression, in language and idea, and in certain parts is touchingly beautiful" (p. 73). Compares lines from Crashaw's version with lines from versions by Joshua Sylvester (1621), Roscommon (1721), "O" in the *Christian Rememberancer* (1825), John Hoskyns-Abrahall (1868), Macaulay (1826), and Arthur P. Stanley (1868).

◄§ 260. Shorthouse, J[oseph] H[enry]. Letter to Edmund Gosse. 3 April.

Printed in *Life and Letters of J. H. Shorthouse*, ed. his wife (London: Macmillan and Co.; New York: Macmillan, 1905), 1:194.

Laments the lack of a fuller biography of Crashaw and acknowledges that he was perhaps unconsciously influenced by Crashaw's life in *John Inglesant*. Suggests that "Musicks Duell" is "the most successful attempt with which I am acquainted to perform a most difficult feat—that of reproducing in *words* the nameless delight of music and song" (p. 194). Finds Crashaw's poem superior to Ford's *The Lover's Melancholy*.

◄§ 261. Swinburne, Algernon Charles. Letter to Edmund Gosse. 28 March.

Printed in *The Letters of Algernon Charles Swinburne*, ed. Edmund Gosse and Thomas James Wise (London: William Heinemann, 1918), 2:131–32. Also printed in *The Swinburne Letters*. Vol. 5: 1883–1890, ed. Cecil Y. Lang (New Haven: Yale University Press, 1962), 11.

Thanks Gosse for sending his article on Crashaw. Notes that he had written an essay on Crashaw when he was nineteen; "but it never saw the light, and long since probably fed the fire" (p. 131). Acknowledges Crashaw's influence: "Of course you are right in supposing that my *Song in Season* was suggested or instigated by his shorter attempt in the same metre, which always greatly took my fancy; as did also *Love's Horoscope*—one of the most nearly blameless among his poems" (p. 131).

≈§ 262. Ward, C. A. "Crashaw and Aaron Hill." *N&Q* 6th series, 8:294.

In part, a reply to Edmund Waterton (entry 264). Notes that he has seen the image of water blushing and becoming wine from Crashaw's "Joann. 2. Aquae in vinum versae" attributed to Addison: "A poem was required upon the marriage in Cana, and he, not having prepared one, jotted down hastily four lines, of which this was the last:—'The conscious water saw its Lord and blushed.'" Suggests that in Crashaw's epigram "there ought to be no comma after *vidit*, as it spoils the caesure or accent upon *um* in *Deum*." Notes that Aaron Hill's rendering of Crashaw's lines is poor and "evidently done with the intention of appropriation as an original." Points out Pope's borrowing in his epitaph on Fenton and maintains that Crashaw's lines on Ashton are superior. Challenges William Hayley's defense of Pope and suggests that Pope's poetry contains other passages borrowed from Crashaw that have as yet been undetected. Briefly compares Crashaw to Haydn.

≈§ 263. ———. "Richard Crashaw." *N&Q* 6th series, 8:447.

Asks for information about Crashaw's early life and especially about the exact dates of his birth and death, pointing out that both Alexander Chalmers (entry 119) and Peregrine Phillips (entry 93) were apparently uncertain. Notes that Sir Henry Yelverton and Sir Randolph Crew were in charge of Crashaw's education and got him into the Charterhouse school and asks if Crashaw's father was dead at the time. Editor notes that Grosart states that Crashaw was born in 1612 and that Gosse says that William Crashaw died in 1626 and that Richard died at Loreto, "not without suspicion of being poisoned."

≈§ 264. Waterton, Edmund. "Crashaw and Aaron Hill." *N&Q* 6th series, 8:165–66.

Maintains that Crashaw, not Dryden or "an Eton boy," originated the conceit of water blushing and becoming wine in his "Joann. 2. Aquae in vinum versae." Points out that Reginald Heber appropriates the lines in one of his poems and that the epigram was translated, without acknowledgment, and included in Aaron Hill's *Works* (London, 1753), 3:241, under the title "The Miracle at Cana." For a reply, see C. A. Ward (entry 262).

1884

≈§ 265. Hughes, T. Cann. "Richard Crashaw." *N&Q* 6th series, 10:447.

Asks for information on critical articles, pamphlets, and other literature on Crashaw as well as for information on portraits of him. For replies, see

G. F. R. B. (entry 266), J. P. H. (entry 268), J. E. Thompson (entry 269), and C. A. Ward (entry 270).

1885

◄§ 266. B., G. F. R. "Richard Crashaw." *N&Q* 6th series, 11 : 14.
Reply to T. Cann Hughes (entry 265). Notes four critical articles on Crashaw listed in Poole's *Index to Periodical Literature*.

◄§ 267. Bullen, A[rthur] H[enry], ed. *A Christmas Garland: Carols and Poems from the Fifteenth Century to the Present Time*. With seven illustrations newly designed by Henry G. Wells. London: John C. Nimmo. xxxii, 278p.
Reissued in 1886 without illustrations.
Includes the 1648 text of "Hymn in the Holy Nativity" (pp. 120–25) and the opening lines of "Hymn in the Glorious Epiphanie" (pp. 126–27) with notes (p. 262). Points out in the preface that only the opening lines of the Epiphany ode were included because "the latter part abounds with the most violent conceits" (p. xxx). In the notes suggests that the Nativity poem "strikingly exhibits Crashaw's power and weakness" and notes that "thrice-refined golden speech, a subtle sense of melody, fervid richness of imagination,— these great gifts were marred by a constant indulgence in violent conceits, by diffuseness, and occasionally by studied harshness of phrase and rhythm" (p. 262). Biographical note (p. 262).

◄§ 268. H., J. P. "Richard Crashaw." *N&Q* 6th series, 11 : 14.
Reply to T. Cann Hughes (entry 265). Notes an article on Crashaw in the *Cornhill Magazine* (entry 257).

◄§ 269. Thompson, J. E. "Richard Crashaw." *N&Q* 6th series, 11 : 14.
Reply to T. Cann Hughes (entry 265). Calls attention to an essay in *Gentleman's Magazine* (88, pt. 1[1818]: 201) in which Crashaw is mentioned as belonging to Peterhouse, Cambridge. Notes that he can find no references to portraits of Crashaw.

◄§ 270. Ward, C. A. "Richard Crashaw." *N&Q* 6th series, 11 : 14.
Reply to T. Cann Hughes (entry 265). Calls attention to the biographical sketch in Phillips's edition (entry 93). Notes that Crashaw is "very unequal, but when he has expressed anything at his best neither Pope nor anybody else could much improve upon him" and suggests that his style, though uneven, "is much better, purer, and more direct than the Frenchified Augustan Watteauism of Pope."

1886

⋙ 271. Swinburne, Algernon Charles. Letter to the editor. 24 January. Printed in *Pall Mall Gazette*, 27 January 1886, p. 2. Modern edition, *The Swinburne Letters*. Vol. 5: 1883–1890, ed. Cecil Y. Lang (New Haven: Yale University Press, 1962), 134–35.

Lists Crashaw among the one hundred authors that he would recommend.

1887

⋙ 272. Crashaw, Richard. *Poems of Richard Crashaw*. Selected and arranged, with notes, by J. R. Tutin. [Edinburgh]: Printed for private circulation by Turnball & Spears, Printers. xi, 85p.

Limited to 250 copies.

Preface reprinted in *The Magazine of Poetry and Literary Review* (entry 285).

Preface (pp. vii–ix); contents (pp. xi–xii); Sacred Poems (from *Steps to the Temple, Carmen Deo Nostro*, and the divine epigrams; pp. 1–48); Secular Poems (from *The Delights of the Muses*; pp. 49–72); notes (pp. 73–83); and bibliography of Crashaw's works and of modern editions (pp. 84–85). Modernized spelling of the text. In the preface calls Crashaw "a neglected genius of a high order" and comments briefly on his critical reception since his own time. Maintains that Crashaw "has strong affinities to two of our great nineteenth-century poets; he has the rich imagination and sensuousness of Keats, and the subtlety of thought and exquisite lyrical flow of Shelley" (p. viii). Suggests that, as a sacred poet, Crashaw is superior to Herbert, "judged from the purely poetic standpoint" (p. viii). Maintains that Crashaw has never been popular, in part, because of the later seventeenth- and eighteenth-century "taste for artificial poetry of the school of Waller, Dryden, Pope, &c" (p. viii) and, in part, because of his Catholicism. In the notes presents a biographical sketch (p. 75); points out numerous parallels between Crashaw and Milton, Shelley, Sir Henry Wotton, Roscommon, Spenser, Pope, David Gray, Shakespeare, and Ford; and quotes earlier critics on specific lines and/or poems.

⋙ 273. Gosse, Edmund. "Crashaw, Richard," in *The Encyclopaedia Britannica*. 9th ed., 6:553. Edinburgh: Adam and Charles Black.

Biographical sketch and evaluation of Crashaw's poetry. Argues that the poetry "will be best appreciated by those who can with most success free themselves from the bondage of a traditional sense of the dignity of language." Notes the "most rococo excess" of the verse and maintains that "at the same time his verse is studded with fiery beauties and sudden felicities of language, unsurpassed by an lyrist between his own time and Shelley's." Claims that "there is no religious poetry in English so full at once of gross and awkward images and imaginative touches of the most etherial beauty" and suggests that "the faults and beauties of his very peculiar style can be studied nowhere to more advantage than in the *Hymn to Saint Theresa.*" Lists "Musicks Duell" and "Wishes. To his (supposed) Mistresse" as Crashaw's best secular pieces and stresses the resemblances between Crashaw and Shelley.

◄§ 274. Grosart, Alexander B., ed. *Supplement to Complete Works of Richard Crashaw (1873).* Blackburn: Privately printed, 1887–1888. [304]–20 pp.

Reprinted, New York: AMS, 1983, along with Grosart's two-volume Fuller Worthies' Library edition.

Describes a newly discovered manuscript containing Crashaw's poems (British Library, Add. MS 33219) and claims that the manuscript is in Crashaw's own hand. Reports some variants between readings in this manuscript and those in his edition and claims that the manuscript contains five hitherto unprinted and unknown poems by Crashaw and gives the texts of these poems. In fact, the manuscript contains only three previously unknown poems: "[With Some Poems sent to a Gentlewoman. I.]," "[With Some Poems sent to a Gentlewoman. II.]," and "Out of Grotius his Tragedy of Christes sufferinges." In a postscript, points out that "Bulla" first appeared in Heynsius's *Crepundia Siliana . . .* (entry 15). Notes that he has reprinted pp. ix–x of contents and p. 303 of his edition (vol. 1) in order that the supplement may be added to the volume and that the supplement is paginated accordingly. See also Martin, p. lxxxiv.

◄§ 275. King, W[illia]m Francis Henry, ed. "Nympha pudica Deum vidit, et erubuit," in *Classical and Foreign Quotations . . . ,* 383. London: Whitaker and Sons.

Reprinted, 1888; new rev. ed., 1889; 3d ed., 1904.

Reprinted, New York: Frederick Ungar 1958, 1965; Detroit: Gale Research Co., 1968.

Attributes to Crashaw the English translation ("The conscious water saw its God, and blushed") of this famous line from "Joann. 2. Aquae in vinum versae." In the third edition notes Milton's and Dryden's borrowing of the line.

◄§ 276. Lyte, H. C. Maxwell, and F. H. Blackburne Daniell, eds. "Manuscripts of Lord Braye, at Stanford Hall, Rugby," in *Historical Manuscripts Commission. Tenth Report, Appendix, Part VI: The Manuscripts of the Marquess of Abergavenny, Lord Braye, G. F. Luttrell, Esq., &c.,* 104–252. London: Printed for Her Majesty's Stationery Office.

Notes under 27 November 1627 (p. 128) that a number of persons, including "Richard Crashaw, the poet," were given gowns on the occasion of a London funeral, the deceased apparently being connected with the Merchant Taylors. Burton Confrey (entry 426) notes this reference and suggests that it indicates the precocity of Crashaw as a poet.

✥ 277. Saintsbury, George. "Caroline Poetry," in *A History of Elizabethan Literature*, 354–93. London and New York: Macmillan and Co.

Surveys Crashaw's life and poetry (pp. 364–70). Praises the concluding lines of "The Flaming Heart" and calls them Crashaw's "masterpiece" and "one of the most astonishing things in English" (p. 364). Points out, however, that throughout the whole of Crashaw's work there is an "extraordinary inequality" and an "exasperating lack of self-criticism" (p. 367). Finds "A Hymn to Sainte Teresa," "for uniform exaltation, far the best of Crashaw's poems" (p. 368). Maintains that Crashaw's poetry "has an unearthly delicacy and witchery which only Blake, in a few snatches, has ever equalled; while at other times the poet seems to invent, in the most casual and unthinking fashion, new metrical effects and new jewelries of diction which the greatest lyric poets since—Coleridge, Shelley, Lord Tennyson, Mr. Swinburne—have rather deliberately imitated than spontaneously recovered" (p. 369). Notes, however, that "the very maddest and most methodless of the 'Metaphysicals' cannot touch Crashaw in his tasteless use of conceits" and at times, noting in particular conceits in "The Weeper," "it is almost difficult to know whether to feel most contempt or indignation for a man who could so write" (p. 369). Claims that no other English poet has expressed religious passion so fully and that "none in his expression of any sentiment, sacred or profane, has dropped such notes of ethereal music" (p. 369). Concludes that "at his best he is far above singing, at his worst he is below a very childish prattle" but notes that "even then he is never coarse, never offensive, not very often dull; and everywhere he makes amends by flowers of the divinest poetry" (p. 369). Notes Pope's borrowings and compares Crashaw to Carew and Herrick.

1888

✥ 278. Anon. "New Poems by Crashaw." *Saturday Review* (London) 65, no. 1690:323–24.

Essentially a review of Grosart's *Supplement to Complete Works of Richard Crashaw* (entry 274). Suggests that Brit. Mus. Add. MS 33219 is in Crashaw's handwriting. Comments briefly on "[With Some Poems sent to a Gentlewoman. I.]" and calls "[With Some Poems Sent to a Gentlewoman. II.]" an exquisite lyric, characteristic of Crashaw's "most transcendental manner" (p. 323). Observes that the remainder of the newly discovered poems are religious and "are not in Crashaw's very finest manner," noting that "To Pontius washing his blood-stained hands" is typical "of the monstrous chains of conceits which these most unequal poets were at any moment liable to produce" (p. 323). Concludes that "the new readings of old poems which the MS gives are neither, it would seem, very numerous nor very important," noting that

"The Weeper" "is such a distressing, indeed such a humiliating, poem that we receive a new stanza of it with indifference" (p. 324). Notes that Grosart points out that "Bulla" first appeared in a very rare Cambridge volume, *Crepundia Siliana* by Heynsius (1646), two years after Crashaw's ejection from Peterhouse and the same year that it appeared in *The Delights of the Muses*, "with a considerable number of variations of the text" (p. 324).

◄§ 279. ———. "Richard Crashaw." *The Spectator* 61:144–45.
Reviews Tutin's edition (1887). Notes the possibility that Crashaw influenced Pope, Coleridge, Browning, and Swinburne. Praises Crashaw as a translator and suggests that his poems are often superior to the originals of Strada and Marino. Disagrees with Grosart's description of Crashaw's manner as "imaginative-sensuousness" and argues that any description that does not take into account the deeply religious and mystical quality of the poetry is somewhat defective.

◄§ 280. Buckley, W. E. "Crashaw and Aaron Hill." *N&Q* 7th series, 5:301.
Notes the discovery of an alleged autograph of some of Crashaw's poems (now in the British Library) and its publication by Grosart as a supplement to his edition (entry 274). Notes that Grosart points out that the "preludium" of "Joann. 2. Aquae in vinum versae" can be found in lines 49–54 of Crashaw's fragmentary translation "Out of Grotius his Tragedy of Christes sufferinges." Calls attention to another epigram Crashaw wrote on the subject, "To our Lord, upon the Water made Wine" and points out Grosart's change in the second line, replacing *arts* with *acts*.

◄§ 281. L[ee], S[idney] L. "Crashaw, Richard," in *The Dictionary of National Biography*, edited by Leslie Stephen [and Sidney Lee], 13: 33–36. London: Smith, Elder & Co.; New York: Macmillan.
Modern edition, Oxford: Oxford University Press, 1973.
A biographical sketch of Crashaw along with a critical summary and evaluation of his poetry. Claims that Crashaw's Latin epigrams "denote marvellous capacity" and suggests that, although their conceits "are often very whimsical," they contain "many signs of fine classical taste, and very few of immaturity" (p. 33). Maintains that Crashaw's sacred poems "breathe a passionate fervour of devotion, which finds its outlet in imagery of a richness seldom surpassed in our language" (p. 35). Suggests that the major defect in Crashaw's poetry is his diffuse and overly intricate conceits and that "his metrical effects, often magnificent, are very unequal" (p. 36). Notes that Crashaw has little of the "simple tenderness" found in Herbert but suggests that, as a translator of Marino, Crashaw "leaves his original far behind" (p. 36). Briefly surveys critical commentary on Crashaw and mentions the possible indebtedness of Milton, Pope, Coleridge, Shelley, and Swinburne. Brief bibliography.

ᵉᵍ 282. Torry, A[lfred] F[reer]. *Founders and Benefactors of St. John's College, Cambridge, with notes, chiefly biographical.* Cambridge: W. Metcalfe & Son. vii, 112p.

Briefly notes (pp. 23–24) that the account books of St. John's College (Cambridge) indicate that in 1634 Crashaw was paid thirteen pounds, six shillings, eight pence for three pictures, portraits of Lady Margaret, King Charles I, and Archbishop Williams, made from copies of portraits already in the possession of St. John's, used to decorate the *Liber Memorialis*, a manuscript volume prepared to record and honor benefactors of the newly erected library. Notes also that the *Liber Memorialis* indicates that Henry Wriothesley, Earl of Southampton, purchased about two hundred manuscripts and two thousand printed books from the library of William Crashaw as a gift for the new library. For further details, see Austin Warren (entry 547).

1889

ᵉᵍ 283. Palgrave, Francis T. ed., *The Treasury of Sacred Song: Selected from the English Lyrical Poetry of Four Centuries* with notes explanatory and biographical, by Francis T. Palgrave. Oxford: Clarendon Press. ix, 374p.

Includes four stanzas from "Hymn in the Holy Nativity," "A Song ('Lord, when the sense of thy sweet grace')," and "Psalme 23" (pp. 111–12). In the notes (p. 341–42) presents a biographical sketch and suggests that Crashaw represents "sensuous Mysticism" (p. 342). Maintains that, on the whole, Crashaw's poetry "is incomplete and irregular" but concludes that he "has a charm so unique, an imagination so nimble and subtle, phrases of such sweet and passionate felicity, that readers . . . will find themselves surprised and delighted, in proportion to their sympathetic sense of Poetry, when touched to its rarer and finer issues" (p. 342).

ᵉᵍ 284. Thompson, Francis. "Crashaw." *Merry England* 13:44–59.

Reprinted in *A Renegade Poet and Other Essays* by Francis Thompson, with an introduction by Edward J. O'Brien (Boston: Ball Publishing Co., 1910), 129–60.

Notes that Crashaw is essentially an unpopular poet, who "has written no perfect poems, though some perfect poetry" (p. 45) but who has, nonetheless, "won the warm admiration of many eminent men, prominent among whom is said to be Cardinal Newman" (p. 44). Calls Crashaw "a poet of much higher flight" (p. 44) than Herbert and compares and contrasts him with Shelley and Coleridge. Claims that, although Crashaw writes with ecstatic devotion on religious themes, he, like Milton and Rossetti, is "essentially a secular genius . . . allured, not by religious lessons, but by the poetical grandeur or beauty of their subject" (p. 45), and will appeal, therefore, only to serious students of poetry. Suggests that Crashaw's most pronounced fault is his use of ingenious conceits, in, for example, "The Weeper," which, he says, is "essentially fantastic in its fancy" (p. 47). Argues that "fancy, expression, lofty ideal sentiment—these sum sufficiently fairly the qualities which we claim for him at his best" (p. 48) and praises his metrical ability, especially the "cunning originality with which he manipulates established forms" (p. 55), such as the meter of "A Hymn to Sainte Teresa." Reprints stanzas from "The Weeper," "Wishes. To his (supposed) Mistresse," "Hymn in the Holy Nativity," and "Loves Horoscope" with critical commentary.

◄§ 285. T[utin], J[ohn] R[amsden]. "Richard Crashaw." *The Magazine of Poetry and Literary Review* 1:91–94.
Reproduces the preface to his 1887 edition of Crashaw (entry 272), along with "Musicks Duell," "An Epitaph Upon Mr. Ashton," passages from "Sospetto d'Herode," "The Weeper," "Wishes. To his (supposed) Mistresse," "In praise of Lessius," "To the Morning. Satisfaction for sleepe," "Upon Ford's two Tragedyes," "On Hope," and six of the divine epigrams.

1891

◄§ 286. Anon. "Crashaw and Shelley." *Lyceum* 4, no. 47:249–51, 273–75.
Finds it curious that "modern criticism is singularly agreed in connecting two poets together, who differ so widely in aim and in age as Crashaw and Shelley" (p. 249). Argues that, although both poets were "equal in mental gifts, alike in 'ecstasy of lyrical movement,' and rich imagination" (pp. 249–50), Crashaw directed his talents toward loftier ideals and worthier objects than Shelley and is thus a superior poet. Maintains that, because of their subject matter, for instance, the Teresian poems are superior to Shelley's *Epipsychidion*: "Crashaw is more sure of his object, and of his whole moral and logical position" (p. 251). Suggests that Shakespeare in *Venus and Adonis* reintroduced into poetry pagan sentiment and a lowering of Christian ideals that many Caroline poets imitated, whereas Crashaw, even in his secular poems, "was amongst the few, at the time when he lived, who dedicated a rich poetic talent to the praise of the Ideal of Christianity, and thereby to the work of handing on its undying power" (p. 274). For a reply, see Francis Thompson (entry 290).

◄§ 287. Editor. "Notes to Correspondents." *N&Q* 7th series, 12:420.
Reply to J. C. J., whose query was not published. Points out that the line "Nympha pudica Deum vidit, et erubuit" comes from Crashaw's "Joann. 2. Aquae in vinum versae" and reprints the entire poem, noting that it is an "exquisite epigram."

◄§ 288. Gibbons, A[lfred W.] *Ely Episcopal Records: A Calendar and Concise View of the Episcopal Records preserved in the Muniment Room of the Palace at Ely.* Lincoln: James Williamson. xiv, 558p.
Printed for private circulation.

Notes that in 1639 Crashaw was appointed curate of Little St. Mary's Church (p. 274).

❧ 289. Julian, John, ed. A *Dictionary of Hymnology.* . . . London: John Murray; New York: Charles Scribner's Sons. vii, 1504p.
Several later editions.
Contains a brief encyclopedic account of Crashaw's life and works (p. 268). Notes under "English Hymnology, Early" that Crashaw's hymns "belong more to the hymns of Latin origin, and are useless in their present shape" (p. 348). Briefly mentions Crashaw as a translator of the psalms (p. 918), the *Dies Irae* (p. 299), and "Lauda Sion" (p. 663).

❧ 290. [Thompson, Francis.] "Crashaw and Shelley." *The Weekly Register,* 18 July, p. 92.
Disagrees with the reviewer in *The Lyceum* (entry 286) who considers that Shelley's *Epipsychidion* is inferior to Crashaw's Teresian poems simply because of its subject matter. Maintains that Crashaw is an excellent poet and points out that there are many affinities between his poetry and Shelley's. Suggests, however, that in Crashaw's poetry "numerous passages have an exquisite fineness and deftness of turn quite alien to the impetuous Shelley." Maintains that Crashaw "was, by flashes, a genuine precursor of Shelley, a Shelley fitfully realized," and regrets that "to his co-religionists least of all is Crashaw known."

1892

❧ 291. [Carter, Jane Frances Mary.] *Nicholas Ferrar: His Household and His Friends,* edited by T. T. Carter. London: Longmans, Green, & Co. xxvi, 331p.
Discusses briefly Crashaw's acquaintance with the Ferrar family and his attraction to the devotional life at Little Gidding. Suggests that Crashaw may have been introduced to Herbert's poetry though his association with Little Gidding, where Herbert was greatly admired, and speculates that "Ode on a Prayer-book" and "To [Mrs. M. R.] Councel Concerning her Choise" may have been originally addressed to members of the Ferrar family. Notes that during his fellowship at Peterhouse Crashaw was the tutor of Ferrar Collet and comments briefly on Crashaw's conversion to Catholicism.

❧ 292. Choate, Isaac Bassett. "Richard Crashaw," in *Wells of English,* 258–65. Boston: Roberts Brothers.
Biographical sketch of Crashaw and general critical survey of his poetry. Suggests that, because of Crashaw's conversion to Catholicism, his poems, "though breathing a spirit of true piety and fervent devotion—were received with so little favor at first, and have since found so small space open to them

in the collected works of British poets" (p. 260). Calls the poems in the *Steps to the Temple* "devotional poems, glowing with intense feeling, such as marks Italian and Spanish ecclesiastical literature and art of the preceding century" (p. 261). Cites lines from "To the Morning. Satisfaction for sleepe" as an example of Crashaw's genius in secular verse, noting that it "cannot fail to please as long as English poetry shall continue to be read" (p. 264). Predicts that "the world will slowly, but yet surely, come to own Crashawe as a true child of nature, with a strong filial love for the mother who bore him" (p. 265).

1893

293. Renton, William. "The Serious Age," in *Outlines of English Literature*, 115–40. New York: Charles Scribner's Sons.

Briefly comments on Crashaw's artistry (pp. 123–25). Suggests that Crashaw is "most successful in his religious subjects when he approaches them from the side of the amorous" and maintains that "at his best Crashaw is as rich, original, and impassioned as any poet of his time" (p. 124). Praises "the complex structure, the rush and rhythm, the alliteration, [and] the visionary exaltation" of "Hymn to the Name of Jesus" and calls "Musicks Duell" a remarkable feat that renders "in words the intricacies of a bird's vocalization" (p. 124). Suggests that the major conceit in "Joann. 2. Aquae in vinum versae" is "entirely in the style of Donne" (p. 123). Briefly compares and contrasts Crashaw to Donne, Vaughan, Quarles, John Ford, Shelley, and Swinburne.

1894

294. Bowes, Robert. A *Catalogue of Books Printed at or Relating to the University Town and County of Cambridge from 1521 to 1893 with Bibliographical and Biographical Notes*. Cambridge: Macmillan and Bowes. xxxi, 516 + 67p.

Lists and gives brief bibliographical descriptions of Crashaw's works printed at Cambridge. In addition to *Epigrammata Sacrorum Liber* (1634) and *Richardi Crashawi Poemata et Epigrammata* (1670), lists various collections and anthologies printed at Cambridge in which individual early poems appeared. Biographical note (p. 19), erroneously suggesting that Crashaw was born in 1616 and died in 1650.

295. Patmore, Coventry. "Mr. F. Thompson, A New Poet." *The Fortnightly Review* 61:19–24.

Reprinted in *Courage in Politics and Other Essays, 1885–1896*, ed. Frederick Page (London, New York: Oxford University Press, 1921), 157–66.

Essentially an appreciative review of Francis Thompson's *Poems* (London: E. Matthews, 1893). Suggests that Thompson should be ranked with Cowley and Crashaw as an important poet. Singles out "Musicks Duell" as Crashaw's best poem and states that Thompson never achieved anything as technically beautiful. Maintains, however, that "Crashaw himself never did anything else approaching it; and, for the rest of his work, it has all been equalled, if not excelled, in its peculiar beauties as well as its peculiar defects, by this new poet" (p. 20). Suggests that the masculine intellect is "as conspicuous and, alas, as predominant in Mr. Thompson's poetry as it is in that of Crashaw and Cowley" (p. 20) and maintains that the feminine element is often lacking in all three poets.

◆§ 296. Traill, H[enry] D[uff]. "Noticeable Books: Mr. Thompson's Poems." *The Nineteenth Century* 35:229–33.
A review of Francis Thompson's *Poems* (London: E. Matthews, 1893). Calls Thompson "a seventeenth-century rhapsodist born out of due time" (p. 230) and compares his poems to those of Crashaw: "It is not only the religious ecstasy of Crashaw that they recall; for all the daringly fantastic imagery, all the love-lyrical hyperbole, all that strange mixture of simplicity and artifice, of spontaneous passion and studied conceit which were so characteristic of the age of Crashaw are with the same astonishing fidelity reproduced" (p. 231).

◆§ 297. Tynan, Katharine. "Mr. Francis Thompson's Poems." *The Bookman*, January, pp. 117–18.
Suggests that Francis Thompson is "like Crashaw, but a Crashaw of a wider range" and maintains that "The Hound of Heaven" is "worthy in its thought of Crashaw, but Crashaw would have fallen short of the splendour of its execution" (p. 117).

1895

◆§ 298. Anderson, G. F. Reynolds. "Richard Crashaw," in *The White Book of the Muses*, 45. Edinburgh: George P. Johnston.
An original poem on Crashaw.

◆§ 299. Beeching, H. C., ed. *Lyra Sacra: A Book of Religious Verse*. London: Methuen & Co. xx, 364p.
Reprinted, 1903.
Includes selections from eight of Crashaw's poems (pp. 109–24) and notes that "the passages here chosen, while they exhibit his genius, as it has never before been exhibited, in an anthology, are as free as possible from the worst defects of his manner" (p. 345). Presents in the notes a biographical sketch of Crashaw and observes that he "is so fine a poet that it is a pity he took so sentimental a view of religion" (p. 345). Suggests that, "if Herbert with his restrained passion represents the spirit of the Anglican communion, Crashaw with his fervour and want of taste may well stand for the Roman" (p. 345).

Remarks that "the highwater mark of the religious lyric in England is fixed by Herbert; Vaughan in one or two pieces reaches as high; so in another style do Crashaw and Marvell" (p. vi). Claims that, "certain of the brighter luminaries, Donne, Giles Fletcher, and Crashaw, are here for the first time exhibited to the public in their proper greatness" (p. vii).

◄§ 300. Gillow, Joseph. "Crashaw, Richard," in A *Literary and Biographical History, or Bibliographical Dictionary of the English Catholics from the Breach with Rome, in 1534, to the Present Time*, 1:584–86. London: Burns and Oates.
  Biographical sketch of Crashaw claiming that he was born in 1615 and died in 1650. Agrees with Aubrey de Vere (entry 193) that Crashaw's conversion to Catholicism contributed to his later neglect but notes that another cause was "the occasional quaintness and conceits which he shared with Herbert, and which were increased by admiration of the writing of the Italian poet Marini" (p. 584). Maintains, however, that "his luxuriance of imagination and exquisite facility in the expression of his poetical visions have seldom been surpassed" and that, in spite of "a redundant fancy, and the *dulcia vitia* into which it betrayed him, there is a charming beauty, richness, and tenderness in the poetry of Crashaw, as well as a noble devotional fervour, and an occasional sublimity" (p. 584–85). Notes Crashaw's admiration for St. Teresa and suggests he addressed some of his finest poetry to her memory. Praises also "Sospetto d'Herode," suggesting that, in his exuberant uses of language, Crashaw anticipates Shelley. Lists major works, some later editions, and several critical works.

1896

◄§ 301. Brooke, Stopford [Augustus]. "From Elizabeth's Death to the Restoration, 1603–1660," in *English Literature from AD 670 to AD 1832* (Literature Primers, ed. John Richard Green), 150–69. New York, London: Macmillan Co.
  Expanded and revised version of *English Literature* (entry 245), pp. 94–107.
  Suggests that Crashaw's poems, though greater in imagination, are more uneven than Carew's: "He does not burn with a steady fire, he flames to heaven; and when he does, he is divine in music and in passion" but "at other times he is one of the worst of the fantasticals" (p. 158). Singles out "The Flaming Heart" as expressing "in its name his religious nature and his art" (p. 158).

◄§ 302. Corser, Thomas. "Crashaw," in *Collectanea Anglo-Poetica; or A Bibliographical and Descriptive Catalogue of a Portion of a Collection of Early English Poetry, with occasional Extracts and Remarks Biographi-*

cal and Critical, part 4 (Publications of the Chetham Society, 77), II, pt. 2:508–23. Manchester: Printed by Charles Simms and Co. for the Chetham Society.

Biographical sketch of Crashaw, noting that, although he "was of a warm and enthusiastic imagination, a soft and amiable disposition, and of fervent piety" he was also "debased by a spirit of superstition and mystical devotion, which led him away to the Church of his choice" (p. 509). Praises the beauty of Crashaw's images, his felicity of language, his tenderness, the beauty of his thought, and the correctness of his versification but notes that often his poetry, like that of Donne and Cowley, is "full of laboured conceits and false tastes, and a continual straining after unnatural display and effect" (p. 509). Describes and comments on the 1648 and 1670 editions of *Steps to the Temple*, the 1652 edition of *Carmen Deo Nostro*, the 1670 edition of *Richardi Crashawi Poemata et Epigrammata*, and Phillips's edition of 1785. Quotes five stanzas from "The Weeper" to show the merits and weaknesses of Crashaw's verse; quotes "Two went up into the Temple to pray" to show that the epigrams "are without any point or merit" (p. 511); quotes five stanzas from "Sospetto d'Herode" and praises it for its "power and solemnity" (p. 512). Quotes extensively from "Musicks Duell" and calls it "one of the finest and most brilliant efforts of Crashaw's poetical genius" and says that few poems "exceed it in fluency and ease of expression" (p. 513). Comments briefly on the engravings in the 1652 edition of *Carmen Deo Nostro*. Maintains that Phillips's charge that Pope, Milton, Young, Gray, and others borrowed without acknowledgment from Crashaw is too violent and injudicious.

≈§ 303. Scott, Mary Augusta. "Elizabethan Translations from the Italian: The Titles of Such Works Now First Collected and Arranged, with Annotations. II. Translations of Poetry, Plays, and Metrical Romances." *PMLA* 11:377–484.

Revised version included in *Elizabethan Translations from the Italian*, Vassar Semi-Centennial Series (Boston and New York: Houghton Mifflin Co.; Cambridge: Riverside Press, 1916), 188–89; reprinted, New York: B. Franklin, 1969 (Burt Franklin bibliography and reference series).

Describes the Italian poems and translations in *Steps to the Temple* (pp. 429–30). Calls "Sospetto d'Herode" "an interpretive expansion" of Marino's original and notes that the presence of three love lyrics in Italian "show how deeply the mystic poet of *The Flaming Heart* had drunk at the fountain-head of Italian inspiration" (p. 429). Notes also Crashaw's paraphrase of Strada in "Musicks Duell" and points out that John Ford likewise used the fable in *The Lover's Melancholy* (1629).

≈§ 304. [Taylor, Una.] "Italian Influence on English Poetry." *Edinburgh Review* 183:28–54.

Suggests that Milton's sonnets and Crashaw's translations of Italian songs "represent no less than Lodge's verse the facile and often delicate extravagance of the school of Dolce and Marino" (p. 52). Points out that Crashaw's life has many corresponding points with that of his co-religionist, Robert Southwell," and notes that in Crashaw's poems divine emotions again borrow the fire of earth's passions, and by just equipoise earth's passions assume the vesture of spirituality" (p. 53). Briefly contrasts Crashaw to Milton, especially their nativity odes, and notes the "equal fascination with which the Italy of the past magnetized the minds of men so widely parted in sympathy and intelligence, in affections and imagination" (p. 53).

1897

◆§ 305. Crashaw, Richard. *Carmen Deo Nostro, Te Decet Hymnus: Sacred Poems by Richard Crashaw*. Edited, with an introduction by J. R. Tutin. London: William Andrews & Co. xvii, 124p.
Introduction divided into four parts: (1) Biographical (pp. v–vii)—a sketch of Crashaw's life, in which several factual errors are repeated, along with Cowley's "On the Death of Mr. Crashaw"; (2) Critical (pp. vii–x)—a brief review of Crashaw's critical reputation. Notes that "his worst defects are his conceits—often outrageous, and highly offensive to good nineteenth-century taste—and his poetic extravagancies, repulsive to the calm and philosophic mind of the thoughtful student of poetry in this our day" (p. ix). Finds Crashaw's strengths to be "an imagination subtle and sweet," "a harmony and delicacy of language," "a sensuous enjoyment of all good and lofty nature, whether in man, woman, or the outward universe," and "the rare and precious poetic gift in a high degree" (p. ix). Suggests that, like Spenser, Crashaw could be thought of as "the poet's poet" and laments that "he too often let his feelings run away from him, indulging . . . in extravagances of both language and idea, as in S. *Mary Magdalene*" (p. ix). Suggests that had he not been restrained by his religion, Crashaw would have been a sensualist and notes affinities between Crashaw and Keats and Shelley. Notes Coleridge's appreciation and Francis Thompson's indebtedness. (3) Bibliographical (pp. x–xiii)—lists fifteen editions of Crashaw's work, from 1634 to 1887, and expresses a hope that a complete, scholarly edition of the poems will soon appear. (4) Editorial (pp. xiii–xiv)—notes that the present edition is a reprint of the 1652 edition in modern spelling with corrections and, in a few cases, with versions of poems that appeared in the editions of 1646 or 1648 (for example, "The Weeper" is from 1646). Contents (pp. xv–xvii); the poems (pp. 1–120); glossary (p. 121); and index of first lines (p. 123–24).

◆§ 306. Gosse, Edmund. "The Decline (1620–1660)," in *A Short History of Modern English Literature*, 129–60. (Short Histories of the Literatures of the World: III, ed. Edmund Gosse.) London: William Heinemann. Reprinted several times.

Very brief comments on Crashaw's life and poetry (p. 156). Suggests that Crashaw's "religious ecstasy and anguish take the most bewildering forms, sometimes plunging him into Gongorism of the worst description (he translated Marino and eclipsed him), but sometimes lifting him to transcendental heights of audacious, fiery lyricism not approached elsewhere in English" (p. 156).

◆§ 307. Masterman, J[ohn] Howard B[ertram]. "Caroline Lyrical Poets," in *The Age of Milton*, with an introduction, etc. by J. Bass Mullinger, 94–121. (Handbooks of English Literature, ed. Professor Hales.) London: George Bell & Sons.

2d ed., 1900; reprinted frequently until 1937.

Offers a biographical sketch of Crashaw, calling him "the mouthpiece" of the "most fervent aspirations and emotions" of the Arminian movement (p. 109). Notes that "Wishes. To his (supposed) Mistresse" is Crashaw's best known secular poem and suggests that, although it is "pretty," it is also "rather tedious" (p. 110). Finds "Musicks Duell" notable and "Sospetto d'Herode" full of "dignity and grandeur" (p. 112) but argues that Crashaw achieves his mark primarily in religious poems: "Then his mystical piety transforms that sensuous passion, which at times degenerates into sensuality in the lyrics of Carew and Herrick, into an intensity of ecstatic devotion, that is unsurpassed among English poets" (p. 111), quoting by way of example the conclusion of "The Flaming Heart." Maintains that "The Weeper," though "delicately beautiful," is marred by artificial and elaborate conceits and that the lines "Two walking baths; two weeping motions; / Portable, and compendious oceans" represent "perhaps the lowest depth of bathos ever reached by any of the 'metaphysical' poets" (p. 112). Concludes that Crashaw "is remarkable among poets for the extraordinary inequality of his work" (p. 113). Notes the influence of Marino and Góngora and the indebtedness of Pope, Coleridge, Shelley, and Swinburne.

◆§ 308. [Meynell, Alice.] "Abraham Cowley." *Pall Mall Gazette* (London), 28 April, p. 3.

Reprinted in *The Wares of Autolycus: Selected Literary Essays of Alice Meynell*, ed. P. M. Fraser (London: Oxford University Press, 1965), 32–35.

Notes that Crashaw uses the Alexandrine skillfully: "he took precisely the same care as Cowley that the long wand of that line should not give way in the middle—should be strong and supple and should last." Gives four examples of Alexandrines from Crashaw's poems and suggests that Coventry Patmore writes the longest of possible lines, "speeding with a more celestial movement than Cowley or Crashaw heard with the ear of dreams." Notes that Cowley's elegy on Crashaw is one of his finest, most tender achievements.

◆§ 309. ———. "'Fair and Flagrant Things.'" *Pall Mall Gazette* (London), 14 April, p. 6.

Reprinted in *The Wares of Autolycus: Selected Literary Essays of Alice Meynell*, ed. P. M. Fraser (London: Oxford University Press, 1965), 24–28.

Challenges earlier poets who claim that Herbert, Lovelace, and Crashaw lacked taste: "A better opinion on the men of the seventeenth century is that they had a taste extraordinarily liberal, generous, and elastic, but not essentially lax: taste that gave now and then too much room to play, but anon closed with the purest and exactest laws of temperance and measure." Argues that "the extravagance of Crashaw is a far more lawful thing than the extravagance of Addison, whom some believe to have committed none," and maintains that "of sheer voluntary extremes it is not in the seventeenth-century conceit that we should seek examples, but in an eighteenth-century 'rage.'" Calls "The Weeper" "flagrant" but notes that "its follies are all sweet-humored" and "its beauties are a quick and abundant shower." Calls "To the Morning. Satisfaction for sleepe" "luminous," praises "Loves Horoscope" as equal to the best Elizabethan lyrics, and notes the mastery of economy in "A Hymn to Sainte Teresa."

◄§ 310. Meynell, Alice, ed. *The Flower of the Mind: A Choice Among the Best Poems*, made by Alice Meynell. London: Grant Richards. xxiv, 347p.

Includes eight poems by Crashaw (pp. 131–57): "Ode on a Prayer-book," "To the Morning. Satisfaction for sleepe," "Loves Horoscope," "On Mr. G. Herberts Book. The Temple," "Wishes. To his (supposed) Mistresse," "Hymn in the Holy Nativity," "Musicks Duell," and "The Flaming Heart," with notes (pp. 336–38) taken, for the most part, from her essay, "'Fair and Flagrant Things'" (entry 309).

◄§ 311. Thompson, Francis. "Excursions in Criticism: VI.—Crashaw." *Academy* 52 (20 November): 427–28.

Reprinted, in slightly revised form, in *The Works of Francis Thompson*, ed. Wilfred Meynell (London: Burns and Oates; New York: Charles Scribner's Sons, 1913), 3:175–80.

Welcomes Tutin's selected edition of Crashaw's sacred poems (entry 305) but laments the lack of a readily accessible, inexpensive complete edition of both the sacred and secular poems. Praises Crashaw's odes and notes that "he marks an epoch, a turn of the tide in English lyric." Acknowledges Crashaw's "plenteous infelicities" and "deforming conceits" but praises his "brilliant imagery," "rapturous ethereality," "extraordinary cunning of diction," and tenderness. Says that "Musicks Duell" is "the feat of an amazing gymnast in words rather than of an unpremeditating angel" but recognizes it as an "extraordinary verbal achievement" (p. 427). Points out lyrical qualities in "Hymn in the Holy Nativity," "The Weeper," "A Hymn to Sainte Teresa," "Wishes. To his (supposed) Mistresse," "Loves Horoscope," "Upon the Death of a Gentleman [Mr. Chambers]," and "The Flaming Heart." Suggests that the last "has all the ardour and brave-soaring transport of the highest lyrical inspiration" (p. 428). Notes Crashaw's influence on Coleridge and observes that, although "two more alien poets could not be conceived than Crashaw and Browning" (p. 427), there is a similarity between a line in "The Weeper" and one of Browning's well-known lines.

◄§ 312. [Thompson, Francis.] "A New Anthology." *Academy* 52(13 November): 391–92.

Essentially a review of Alice Meynell's *The Flower of the Mind* (entry 310). Points out that Crashaw is more liberally represented in this anthology than in most and suggests that the 1646 version of "Hymn in the Holy Nativity" is superior to the later version that Meynell chose to include.

◄§ 313. Warren, C[harles] F[rere] S[topford]. *The Dies Irae. On This Hymn and Its English Versions. Part I. The Hymn.* London: Skeffington & Son. xxxviii, 170p.

Reissued as *The Authorship, Text, and History of the Hymn Dies Irae . . .* (London: T. Baker, 1902).

Comments in several places on Crashaw's version of the *Dies Irae*, calling it "an exceedingly fine poem" (p. 18) and suggesting that the text Crashaw used for his translation was that of the Roman Missal. Points out the superiority of Crashaw's rendering to those of other English translators.

1898

◄§ 314. Saintsbury, George. "The Metaphysicals—The Lyric Poets—The Miscellanists, Etc.," in *A Short History of English Literature*, 411–31. New York: Macmillan.

Reprinted frequently.

Surveys Crashaw's life and poetry (pp. 411–14). Maintains that Crashaw's poetry, "more almost than any other in English, must underlie different and nearly irreconcilable judgments, according as the judge insists upon measure, order and steady working out of central ideas in poetry, or prefers casual and irregular bursts of expression and fancy" (p. 413). Suggests that, although the bulk of Crashaw's best work treats sacred subjects, "some of his best and prettiest, if not his most sublime, pieces are secular" (p. 413), the two best of these being "Wishes. To his (supposed) Mistresse" and "Out of the Italian. A Song." Notes that "his worst things—things as bad as can be found in the wide and various range of metaphysical absurdity—occur in the poem *The Weeper*" and, commenting on the conceits in the poem, suggests that "common sense may almost be excused if it is indignant and disgusted at these frigid ardours, these fustian imitations of brocade" (p. 414). Praises, however, "The Flaming Heart" and "A Hymn to Sainte Teresa" as poems of "an ever growing and glowing splendour of sentiment and diction, which culminates, in the first named of the two pieces in the most unerring explosion of passionate feeling to be found in English, perhaps in all poetry" (p. 414).

1899

◆§ 315. McBryde, John McLaren, Jr. "A Study of Cowley's Davideis." *JGP* [*JEGP*] 2:454–527.

Reprinted under separate cover, Bloomington, Ind., 1899, iv, 85p. Discusses the relationship between *Davideis* and "Sospetto d'Herode" (pp. 503–12) and finds the treatment of hell in both poems "wonderfully similar" (p. 503) to Virgil's description in the *Aeneid* (book VII). Notes that the rage of Crashaw's Satan "exceeds even that of Cowley's devil" (p. 505) and points out numerous similarities between the two poems, especially "striking verbal correspondences" (p. 527). Suggests that Cowley's poem is much closer to Crashaw's than it is to the first book of Marino's *La Strage degl'Innocenti.* Concludes that, although no definite proof can be had, it is likely that Cowley borrowed from Crashaw, not directly from Marino.

◆§ 316. Schelling, Felix E. *A Book of Seventeenth Century Lyrics.* Selected and edited with an introduction by Felix Schelling. (The Athenaeum Press Series.) Boston: Ginn & Co. lxix, 314p.

Explicates lines 65–70 of the 1646 version of "Hymn in the Holy Nativity" to show that the stanza "is inspired, not by the intellect, which clears and distinguishes objects, but by passion, which blends and confuses them" and maintains that the language of the stanza "is one mass of involved and tangled figure, in which similarity suggests similarity in objects contemplated and intensely visualized—not in abstractions incapable of visualization" (p. xxxii). Suggests that, whereas difficulties arise in Donne because of the subtlety of his thought, those in Crashaw come from too much feeling, "a striving after original effect, an ingenious pursuit of similitudes in things repugnant, that amounts to a notorious vice of style" (p. xxxii). Anthologizes "Wishes. To his (supposed) Mistresse" (pp. 99–103), "Hymn in the Holy Nativity" (pp. 113–17), "Hymn in the Assumption" (pp. 117–20), "Loves Horoscope" (pp. 120–22), and "A Song ('Lord, when the sense of thy sweet grace')" (p. 140). Biographical note (p. 258) and explanatory notes on the selected poems (pp. 258–59, 260–63, 268).

1900

◆§ 317. Alexander, William. "Crashaw's Poems," in *The Finding of the Book and Other Poems*, 295–97. London: Hodder and Stoughton.

Three original sonnets extolling the merits of Crashaw's poetry by William Alexander (Bishop of Armagh and Primate of all Ireland). First sonnet stresses that Crashaw belongs to that number of poets "Unpraised, unprized, unlaurell'd of their peers. / Yet in time's patient light their work shows true" and calls him a "poet of the poets" (p. 295), imitated by Pope and Milton. Second poem denies that Crashaw is simply "a feebler Keats"; maintains that readers "must love thee who love the love of Christ"; refers to Crashaw's sensuousness, his mystical qualities, and the influence of Saint Teresa; and makes oblique allusions to "Musicks Duell" and the literature of tears. Third sonnet notes that Crashaw used ottava rima in "Sospetto d'Herode," a measure later employed by Byron in *Don Juan*.

◄§ 318. Crashaw, Richard. *The Delights of the Muses: Secular Poems by Richard Crashaw*. Edited by J[ohn] R[amsden] Tutin. Published by the editor at Great Fencote, Yorks.: [The Hull Press]. x, 64p. Limited to 250 copies.

Contents (pp. v–vi); introductory note (pp. vii–x); a reproduction of the title page from the 1648 edition (p. xi); selections from the secular poems, divided into three categories: *The Delights of the Muses*; Translations; and Epigrams (pp. 1–56); an appendix of "familiar quotations and felicitous passages from the poems of Richard Crashaw" (pp. 57–61); and an index to the appendix (pp. 62–64). Omits the Latin and Greek pieces from the 1648 edition and modernizes spellings. In the introductory note praises "the ardours and sweetnesses" (p. vii) of Crashaw's secular verse and comments specifically on: (1) "Musicks Duell"—"a marvel of sustained vigour, beauty, and music" (p. viii); (2) "To the Morning. Satisfaction for sleepe" and "On a foule Morning, being then to take a journey"—"he is more picturesque than descriptive" (p. viii); (3) "Wishes. To his (supposed) Mistresse"—"Crashaw's best love poem" (p. ix); (4) "Loves Horoscope"—"the last two stanzas of which are a perfect marvel of verbal melody" (p. ix); (5) the elegiac poems and epitaphs, the poems on Herrys—which "display true feeling, grace, fancy, and truth" (p. ix); (6) the translations—"worthy of the Poet of *Music's Duel*, and that is no small praise" (p. ix); and (7) the epigrams, especially "Upon Ford's two Tragedyes"— "pointed and excellent" (p. ix).

◄§ 319. ———. *English Poems, by Richard Crashaw*. Edited, with introduction, a guide to the study of the poet, etc., by J[ohn] R[amsden] Tutin. 2 vols. in 1. Great Fencote, Yorks.: The editor. xxvii, 109; xvii, 124p. Limited to 500 copies.

Volume 1, *The Delights of the Muses* and *Steps the the Temple*, consists of contents (pp. v–viii); introduction (pp. ix–xii); a guide to the study of Richard Crashaw (pp. xii–xxii); reproductions of the original title pages to the 1648 edition of *Steps to the Temple* and *The Delights of the Muses* (pp. xxiii–xxiv); the 1648 preface to the reader (pp.xxv–xxvii); the English poems from the 1648 edition of *The Delights of the Muses* and *Steps to the Temple* (pp. 1–104), with a translation of "Joann. 2. Aquae in vinum versae" by H. Kelsey White (p. 105); glossary (pp. 107–8); and index to the first lines (p. 109). In the introduction, calls Crashaw "a genuine singer of the seventeenth century" and "our great and neglected Poet" (p. ix). Points out that the poems are ordered in "a natural and sequential arrangement (p. ix) and that spellings have been modernized. Volume 2, *Carmen Deo Nostro*, consists of a biographical, critical, bibliographical, and editorial introduction (pp. v–xiv), reproduced from his 1897 edition of *Carmen Deo Nostro* (entry 305); contents (pp. xv–xvii); a reproduction of the original title page of the first edition of *Carmen Deo Nostro* (p. xix); poems from *Carmen Deo Nostro* (pp. 1–120); a glossary (p. 121); and an index of first lines (pp. 123–24). Often tipped into this volume is Tutin's *Notes and Illustrations to Richard Crashaw's "The Delights of the Muses" "Steps to the Temple," and "Carmen Deo Nostro" ('English Poems')* (entry 327).

◄§ 320. Crouch, Cha[rle]s H. "Richard Crashaw." *N&Q* 9th series 6:237.
"Corrects" Ita Testor's reference (entry 322) concerning information about the will of Richard Crashaw, the poet's godfather, by citing the pages for the information from the 1829 edition of Stephen Glover's *History of the County of Derby* (Derby: Henry Mozely & Son) rather than the 1833 edition that Testor used. Also quotes from Glover the description of the cenotaph erected to the memory of Crashaw's godfather in All Saints Church, Derby.

◄§ 321. Dowden, Edward. "Anglo-Catholic Poets: Herbert, Vaughan," in *Puritan and Anglican: Studies in Literature*, 97–132. London: Kegan Paul, Trench, Trübner, & Co.
2d ed., London: Kegan Paul, Trench, Trübner; New York: Henry Holt and Co., 1901; 3d ed., 1910.
Discusses Crashaw's life and poetry (pp. 128–32), primarily by contrasting his poetry and religious sensibility to those of Herbert and Vaughan. Suggests that, although "neither Vaughan nor Herbert equalled Crashaw in his greatest lines" (p. 130) and "there is something to admire in almost every poem of Crashaw," nevertheless, "there is hardly a single poem that we can admire with good conscience, for his lyrical ardour was too intermittent to enable him often to achieve a beautiful whole" (pp. 131–32). Points out that Crashaw "is always alert for dazzling legerdemain of pious fancy, and so little trusts his theme that he must bedizen it with every paltry bead and spangle of cheap religious merchandize" (p. 132) and wonders why "the fire of Crashaw's ardour did not burn away the tinsel ornament of the school of Marino" (p. 130). Notes that "the word 'nest' can never be resisted by Crashaw; it nestles in nearly every poem" (p. 128).

◄§ 322. Testor, Ita. "Richard Crashaw." *N&Q* 9th series, 6:64–65.
Comments on the will of Richard Crashaw, the poet's godfather. Notes that in the will, dated 26 April 1631, he left to his godson three houses, two gardens, and twenty pounds "to buie him bookes or other things needfull" (p. 64). Points out that the young Richard Crashaw was still at Charterhouse at this time. Gives a brief biography of the elder Richard Crashaw and notes that his executors erected a cenotaph to his memory in All Saints Church, Derby, in 1636. Observes that his nephew, John, had a son also named Richard Cra-

shaw, who in 1640 published a booklet, Visions, or Hels Kingdome . . . , a translation of Quevedo's *Visions*.

1901

◄§ 323. Crashaw, Richard. *The English Poems of Richard Crashaw*. Edited, with an introduction and notes by Edward Hutton. London: Methuen & Co. xxi, 218p.
   Dedicated to Nicholas Ferrar. Contents (pp. vii–x); introduction (pp. xi–xxi); selections from the poems (with notes), divided into five categories: *Steps to the Temple*, Divine Epigrams, *The Delights of the Muses*, Translations, and Epigrams (pp. 1–214); and an index of first lines (pp. 215–18). Introduction presents a biographical sketch and an evaluation of Crashaw's poetry, maintaining "there are few men in all literature more lovable" (p. xix). Stresses the unevenness of Crashaw's imagination and style, pointing, for example, to "The Flaming Heart," in which he is "involved, difficult, full of conceits for two-thirds of the poem, breaking out at last, however, into one of the most glorious lyrical passages in the language" (p. xvii). Suggests that "A Hymn to Sainte Teresa" is Crashaw's finest poem and that "The Weeper" is his most fantastic, yet finds much in it that is "so marvellously delicate" (p. xix). Praises in particular Crashaw's sincerity and his "intellectual imagination" (p. xix).

◄§ 324. Moulton, Charles Wells, ed. "Richard Crashaw," in *The Library of Literary Criticism of English and American Authors*. Vol. 2: 1639–1729, 110–14. Buffalo, N.Y.: Moulton Publishing Co.
   Reprinted, 1935.
   A brief introduction to Crashaw's life and works, followed by a collection of critical comments by poets and critics from Cowley to Francis Thompson.

◄§ 325. S[cott], R. F. "Notes from the College Records." *The Eagle: A Magazine Supported by Members of St. John's College* (Cambridge) 23(December): 22–25.
   Reproduces four letters by the poet's father, William Crashaw, concerning his books and manuscripts (dated 23 March 1614, 5 May 1615, 30 June 1615, and 11 June 1618) addressed to Dr. Gwinn, master of St. John's. Notes that William Crashaw was admitted to St. John's on 19 January 1593/94 and that many of his books and manuscripts were bought by Henry Wriothesley, third earl of Southampton, and later deposited in the St. John's College library. Notes that William Crashaw was "a Puritan divine and a notable man of letters in his day" (p. 22). Suggests that the elder Crashaw's books came to St. John's "at least ten years after the date of these letters" (p. 22). See also P. J. Wallis (entry 802).

◄§ 326. [Thompson, Francis.] "A Great Minor Poet." *Academy* 61(21 December): 607–8.

Reprinted in *Literary Criticism by Francis Thompson*, ed. Terence Connolly (New York: E. P. Dutton and Co., 1948), 62–67.
   In part, a review of Hutton's edition (1901). Calls Crashaw a minor poet, "one of those lesser jewels half-obscured in the opulent English crown of poets," but acknowledges that he is "an artist to the finger-tips, one of the forerunners of that elaborate modern art which diversely blossoms in Shelley and Coleridge" (p. 607). Regrets that Crashaw did not more effectively control his genius, for "his great moments are unsurpassed": "His sins are virtues which have overshot their mark" (p.607). Praises Crashaw's fervor and sincerity even in those poems when "his taste is more than doubtful" (p. 607). Praises "Musicks Duell," "Wishes. To his (supposed) Mistresse," and "Upon the Death of a Gentleman [Mr. Chambers]" but maintains that "the supreme Crashaw is in those ardorous and sensuous religious poems in which he put all his strength—and weakness" (p. 607). Praises in particular "Hymn in the Holy Nativity," in which "for once there are no intrusive absurdities," "The Flaming Heart," and even lines from "The Weeper," which he calls "his most fantastic poem" (p. 608). Suggests that there are analogies between Crashaw and Botticelli and briefly compares and contrasts Crashaw with Donne, Herbert, Vaughan, and Dryden.

◄§ 327. [Tutin, John Ramsden.] *Notes and Illustrations to Crashaw's "The Delights of the Muses," "Steps to the Temple," and "Carmen Deo Nostro" ('English Poems').* [Great Fencote, Yorks.: The author.] 20p.
   Intended as a supplement to (and often tipped in with) Tutin's *English Poems, by Richard Crashaw* (entry 319). Contains brief selections of critical evaluations of Crashaw's poetry by Cowley, Coleridge, George L. Craik, Elizabeth Barrett Browning, George Gilfillan, George Macdonald, F. T. Palgrave, and Stopford Brooke (pp. 1–2), followed by notes on a number of the English poems (pp. 2–20). Maintains that, in spite of the favorable notice that Crashaw has received by important poets and critics of the past and present, his achievements have not been generally recognized and fully appreciated. Notes some of the inaccuracies and prejudices of several earlier editors and anthologists. Points out similarities between Crashaw's poems and those of Marino, Shakespeare, Cowley, Wotton, Milton, Pope, Keats, Shelley, Byron, David Young, Longfellow, Robert Burns, and Francis Thompson.

1903

◄§ 328. Bensly, Edward. "Crashaw: A Recent Edition." *N&Q* 9th series, 12:86–87.
   Points out several "remarkable errors" (p. 86) in Hutton's edition (1901), especially inaccurate classical and historical references, and argues that, "for the satisfactory elucidation of a modern poet whose thought or expression or subject-matter depends to any appreciable extent on ancient authors, some acquaintance with Greek and Latin literature can hardly be dispensed with"

(p. 87). Observes that, although the introduction is sympathetic, the notes "can scarcely be called scholarly" (p. 87).

◄§ 329. [Clutton-Brock, Arthur.] "Crashaw's Christmas Poems." *TLS*, 25 December, p. 373.
  Reprinted in *More Essays on Religion* (London: Methuen & Co.; New York: E. P. Dutton, 1927), 1–10.
  Suggests that Crashaw has an even deeper religious imagination than does Milton and calls him "the most neglected of our greater poets." Attributes this neglect, in part, to Crashaw's Catholicism: he "wrote of sacred subjects rather like an Italian than an Englishman." Points out a number of infelicities in Crashaw's poetry, such as "fantastic Italian conceits," uncontrolled emotion, tasteless sensuousness, and extravagant uses of wit, yet forgives him for these lapses. Suggests that "the great mass of his religious poetry is wholesome enough, though its splendours are remote from our interest." Comments especially on Crashaw's use of "dazzling images" and "rapt expressions" that are "almost pictorial in their vividness, of heavenly magnificence" and finds in them a "certain definiteness . . . that gives substance to his most exalted raptures." Claims that Crashaw at his best is "our greatest master of imaginative epigram" and finds "Hymn to the Name of Jesus" his finest poem. Recommends "Hymn in the Holy Nativity" in spite of its artificial form and its frequent "monstrous conceits": "Half the verses, at least, one could wish away; but the rest have a swift lyrical beauty, a richness and lightness of sound, not heard in our poets before, and not to be heard again until the nineteenth century." Comments briefly on "Hymn in the Glorious Epiphanie," "Hymn for New Year's Day," and "To the Queen's Majesty" and suggests that these "Christmas" poems ought "to be placed among the curiosities rather than the beauties of literature." For a reply, see H. C. Beeching (entry 335).

◄§ 330. Courthope, W. J. "Schools of Poetical 'Wit' in the Reign of Charles I," in *A History of English Poetry*, 3:200–284. London: Macmillan and Co.; New York: The Macmillan Co.
  Biographical sketch of Crashaw and survey of his poetry (pp. 219–30). Stresses the sensuousness, richness, and materialism of Crashaw's imagery and his "admirable faculty of imitating style" (p. 222). Contrasts Crashaw and Herbert: "The author of *The Temple* uses words and images as imperfect vehicles for the expression of things that the heart of man cannot fully conceive; the author of *The Flaming Heart* seems to float on them as on clouds of incense above the limits of ordinary sensation" (p. 223). Comments on the criticism of Coleridge and Pope, noting that, although Pope seems somewhat ungenerous in his evaluation of Crashaw, his judgment "is fundamentally just" (p. 226). Suggests that, "in most of Crashaw's poems, the inspiring motive comes from the thought of others, rather than from his own," and that "his imagination was swayed more through his senses than through his intellect"

(p. 226). Expresses particular dislike for Crashaw's uses of imagery and asserts that "no metrical composition in the English language of the same length contains so much imagery and so little thought" as "The Weeper," a poem in which Crashaw is said to have "lost all sense of proportion" (pp. 227–28). Concludes that "the poems of Crashaw exhibit on the one hand the fruits of a religious mysticism resulting from monastic seclusion, on the other the materialism arising out of the union between the ceremonial of the Jesuits and the traditions of pagan literature" (p. 230).

⋘ 331. Gosse, Edmund. "Richard Crashaw," in *English Literature: An Illustrated Record*, by Richard Garnett and Edmund Gosse. Vol. 3: *From Milton to Johnson*, 61–64. London: William Heinemann; New York: The Macmillan Co.

Reissued, New York: Grosset and Dunlap, 1908, 1910; reprinted, New York: Macmillan, 1912, 1923, 1926, 1931; new ed., 1935.

Presents a biographical and critical sketch of Crashaw, calling him "the one great Catholic mystic in the English literature of the seventeenth century" (p. 63). Maintains that he is "in his genius and his mental proclivities strangely isolated among his fellows" (p. 63). Suggests that Crashaw "has left behind him some of the most splendid verses of the age" but notes that "it is only fair to add that they are embedded in others of the most monstrous flatness and vapidity" (p. 63). Reprints four of the divine epigrams and lines from "A Hymn to Sainte Teresa" as well as two illustrations—a manuscript copy of four of the epigrams and an engraving by Crashaw from the 1652 edition of *Carmen Deo Nostro*.

⋘ 332. Harrison, John Smith. "Theory of Love," in *Platonism in English Poetry of the Sixteenth and Seventeenth Centuries*, 67–166. (Columbia University Studies in Comparative Literature.) London and New York: Macmillan.

Reprinted, New York: Russell and Russell, 1965.

Maintains that in "Hymn in the Glorious Epiphanie" Crashaw's "elevation of the subject from a sensuous image into an object of pure contemplation is effected by conceiving of Christ's nature as that of true being according to the Platonic notion" (pp. 97–98). Observes that the poem begins with a recognition of the beauty of the Christ child's eyes and "ends in a desire not to know what may be seen with the eyes, but to press on, upward to a purely intellectual object,—Christ in heaven" (pp. 98–99). Asserts that "Wishes. To his (supposed) Mistresse" is addressed to an idea, not to a woman (p. 138).

1904

⋘ 333. Anon. "Notes on Books, &c." *N&Q* 10th series, 2:120.

Praises Waller's edition (1904), calling it "by far the best and the most serviceable edition that has yet appeared." Maintains that Crashaw's epigrams, "in spite of their conceits, are admirable" and cites in particular "Joann. 2. Aquae in vinum versae" (and Aaron Hill's well-known translation of it). Calls Crashaw "a true and fine poet" and points out that he inspired both Milton and Pope and was praised by Cowley and Joseph Beaumont.

◄§ 334. ———. "Richard Crashaw." *TLS*, 5 August, p. 241.

Essentially a review of Waller's edition (1904). Calls it "an excellent edition for students and a worthy though a late memorial to the work of the most neglected of our great poets." Compares Crashaw to Donne, Herbert, and Vaughan and notes that "he often tried to be homely, imitated the worst excesses of Donne, and would let any doggerel pass if only its aim was to edify." Maintains that Crashaw's "homely absurdities" seem "wantonly perverse, and nothing comes of them" and calls him "a poet of the vague emotions." Claims, however, that Crashaw's poetry is full of "surprises and anticipations" and that he is a "great poet born out of due time and mistaken about the bent of his mind." Briefly compares him to Keats, Shelley, and Swinburne.

◄§ 335. Beeching, H. C. "Crashaw's Christmas Poems." *TLS*, 1 January, p. 383.

Reply to Arthur Clutton-Brock (entry 329). Disagrees that anthologists have included only Crashaw's inferior poems in their collections and that he is "the most neglected of our greater poets." Points out several lines on the Nativity from "Letter to the Countess of Denbigh" and notes that they are included in his anthology of religious verse, *Lyra Sacra* (entry 299).

◄§ 336. Crashaw, Richard. *Steps to the Temple, Delights of the Muses, and Other Poems*, text edited by A[lfred] R[ayney] Waller. (Cambridge English Classics.) Cambridge: University Press. x, 401, [1]p.

Bibliographical notes by Waller (pp. v–x); *Epigrammatum Sacrorum Liber* (1634) (pp. 1–64); *Steps to the Temple* (1648) (pp. 65–115); *The Delights of the Muses* (1648) (pp. 117–84); *Carmen Deo Nostro* (1652) (pp. 185–298); *Poemata et Epigrammata* (1670) (pp. 299–306); poems from the Sancroft manuscript (pp. 307–63); poems from the British Museum manuscript (Add. MS 33219) (pp. 364–67); appendix (notes) (pp. 369–86); index of titles (pp. 387–93); index of first lines (pp. 394–401 + [1]). Twelve pages of engravings from *Carmen Deo Nostro* tipped in. States that this edition "contains the whole of Crashaw's Poems, English and Latin, now for the first time collected in one volume" (p. v) and notes that "no attempt has been made to 'improve' Crashaw's spelling or punctuation save in the one or two trifling instances mentioned in the notes, and save in the use of the modern type-form for *j*, *s*, *u*, *m̃*, etc." (p. v).

◆§ 337. Jusserand, J. J. "L'arrière saison," in *Histoire littéraire du peuple an-glaise.* Vol. 2: *De la renaissance à la guerre civile,* 843–932. Paris: Li-brairie de Paris, Firmin-Didot.
Translated into English, *A Literary History of the English People.* Vol. 3: *From the Renaissance to the Civil War,* pt. 2 (New York and London: G. P. Putnam, 1909), 464–84.
Briefly discusses Crashaw, along with Quarles, Herbert, and Sandys, as a devotional poet (pp. 852–53). Calls Crashaw's religious poems primarily "effusions sincère, mais associées au plus horrible mauvais goût" (p. 853). Suggests that Crashaw's best religious poem is "The Flaming Heart," a piece that reminds one "pour un instant seulement" of Shelley and claims that Crashaw's Latin poems also "sont déparés, comme les autres, par un effroy-able mauvais goût" (p. 853). Notes, however, that, in addition to pious poems, Crashaw wrote several "très élégants et charmants poèmes mondains" (p. 853), citing in particular "Wishes. To his (supposed) Mistresse."

◆§ 338. Selvage, Watson Bartemus. "Richard Crashaw." *American Catholic Quarterly Review* 29:61–74.
Presents a biographical sketch of Crashaw and survey of his sacred poetry, calling him "a Catholic poet who is to-day unfortunately almost unknown except to literary scholars " (p. 62). Praises Crashaw's translation from sacred verse and claims that "Vexilla Regis" is "the first really literary English transla-tion of that grand old hymn" (p. 65) and that Crashaw's translation of Psalm 137 is "one of the best, if not *the* best, metrical translation of a psalm in our language" (p. 66). Suggests that, although they are often "delicate and musi-cal," the translations from secular verse are "neither better nor worse than a vast quantity of similar work" (p. 68). Finds mysticism and the uses of the conceit Crashaw's most striking and often misunderstood characteristics and attempts to explain them. Cites "A Hymn to Sainte Teresa" as representative of Crashaw's rich imagery and (using Swinburne's term) his "dazzling intri-cacy" (p. 71). Comments on Crashaw's uses of color, rhetorical figures, and music in his sacred poems and stresses that Crashaw "lives and breathes in a sanctified world of sense which the Catholic Christian regards as normal, but in which the Puritan can see no good thing" (p. 72). Finds noteworthy "Mu-sicks Duell," "Wishes. To his (supposed) Mistresse," and "An Epitaph upon a Young Married Couple." Concludes that Crashaw's position is "command-ing" among devotional poets and that his "strong mystical tendencies, his sen-sitiveness and his whole mental constitution are almost unique to our liter-ature" (p. 74).

◆§ 339. [Thompson, Francis.] "Two English Reprints." *The Athenaeum* no. 4103(24 September): 412–13.
Reprint of the review of Waller's edition appears in *The Real Robert Louis*

Stevenson and Other Critical Essays by Francis Thompson, ed. Terence L. Connolly. New York: University Publishers, 1959), 66–69.

Essentially a review of Waller's edition (1904) and the Unicorn Press edition of Sidney's *Defence of Poesie.* Welcomes a complete, inexpensive edition of Crashaw's poems and regrets that readers "should have had to wait till now for it, while Herbert has long been in the hands of the public, while Vaughan, and even the newly discovered Traherne, have appeared in good, complete, and not too expensive editions" (p. 412). Notes that the English poems have been reprinted more than once but claims "this was not enough for a poet now generally recognized and deservedly esteemed by critics" (p. 412). Laments that Waller did not correct the punctuation in his edition. Observes that Crashaw, "even now, is a literary luxury, caviare to the general" and points out that readers who prefer direct and restrained expression and correctness "will recoil from Crashaw" (p. 413). Recognizes some faults and unevenness in Crashaw's poetry, especially "conceits of the most extravagant kind," but notes that his "music is exquisite and original as his substance and diction" and that his diction "is marvellously close and felicitous" (p. 413). Praises the finish and delicacy of the epitaphs and the "triumphant ardour" of the longer poems, especially "A Hymn to Sainte Teresa."

⋑ 340. Wright, Edward. Introduction to *The Poems and Some Satires of Andrew Marvell,* pp. ix–xxxviii. (Methuen's Little Library.) London: Methuen.

Suggests that Marvell may have known Crashaw personally at Cambridge and that Crashaw's poetry exercised much influence on the young Marvell, even though, as poets, the two were quite dissimilar. Notes, in particular, Marvell's debt in "Eyes and Tears" and calls it "scarcely more than a variation" on "The Weeper" and "The Teare," noting that "many of the metaphors are even identical" (p. xxxvi). Points out that, even as a young poet, Marvell "had a manner of his own" and that, "instead of the intensity and extravagance in feeling and expression that distinguish Crashaw," Marvell's poetry has "a kind of waywardness and natural charm" (p. xxxvi). Claims that Milton borrowed more from Crashaw than Marvell borrowed from Milton.

1905

⋑ 341. Brégy, Katherine. "Richard Crashaw." *CathW* 80 (March): 756–66. Reprinted in *The Poets' Chantry* (London: Herbert and Daniel; St. Louis, B. Herder, 1912), 36–51.

Almost unqualified praise of Crashaw as "the Catholic laureate" (p. 765) who "need fear comparison with no English writer before or since" (p. 756). Presents a biographical sketch, suggesting that Crashaw did not take Anglican holy orders and that he became a Catholic before leaving England. Finds

Crashaw superior to Herbert: "In Herbert's work we have the piously beautiful fancies of a poetic English clergyman; in Crashaw's, the burning dreams of a genius and a mystic" (p. 763). Notes also the influence of Marino, Donne, Southwell, and especially Saint Teresa. Agrees with Gilfillan that Crashaw is the "Christian Shelley" and asserts that, in fact, there is no English poet, except perhaps Rossetti, "at all comparable to Crashaw in the enchanting beauty of his religious emotion" (p. 764). Focuses primarily on Crashaw's spirituality, his ingenuity, and his ability to render strong emotion into great poetry. Observes that in his religious poems Crashaw "rises altogether above terrestrial limits, and bequeaths us half-intoxicating draughts of fiery, tender beauties" (p. 764). Finds some excesses in Crashaw's conceits and diction but dismisses them as "flashes of a mind rushed on by the whirlwind of a boundless imagination—never the mock-heroics of a mere rhetorician" (p. 766).

≈§ 342. Crashaw, Richard. *The Poems of Richard Crashaw*, edited by J[ohn] R[amsden] Tutin, with an introduction by Canon Beeching. (The Muses' Library.) London: George Routledge & Sons; New York: E. P. Dutton & Co. lv, 301p.

Editor's note (pp. vii–ix); contents (pp. xi–xx); introduction by Canon Beeching (pp. xxi–lvi); the English Poems, based on the editions of 1648 and 1652 (pp. 1–238); notes, a number of which are by Gordon Goodwin (pp. 239–61); various readings from the earlier editions (pp. 262–97); and index of first lines (pp. 298–301). Calls this edition "the first complete and popular edition of the whole of the poet's English poems in the orthography of the present day" (p. vii). The introduction presents a biographical sketch, surveys the early editions of the poems, and comments on the strengths and weaknesses of Crashaw's poems. Discusses such elements as Crashaw's uses of conceits, his ability to achieve musical effects in verse, and his uses of verse forms, especially the heroic couplet. Finds that, although Crashaw "has occasionally fine poetry which is not religious, and too often ardent religious verse which is not poetry, yet his most exalted verse is that in which both influences meet" (p. lv). Maintains that "Charitas Nimia" is "one of the few religious poems of Crashaw in which no critic could wish for an excision" and observes that "it is perhaps also the only one that shows any influence of George Herbert" (p. xli). Recognizes excesses in "The Weeper" but maintains that it "should give nothing but delight to the lover of poetry" (p. xlv). Compares Crashaw to Coleridge, notes Coleridge's admiration for the earlier poet, and disagrees with Coleridge's suggestion that Crashaw is superior to Cowley (see entry 150). Comments briefly on the Crashavian criticism of Pope, Grosart, Gosse, Saintsbury, and Swinburne. In the notes, Tutin points out parallels between Crashaw's poems and those by Shakespeare, Milton, Giles and Phineas Fletcher, Henry Wotton, Vaughan, John Ford, William Browne, Lovelace, and Shelley.

▪ 343. Grolier Club. *Catalogue of Original and Early Editions of Some of the Poetical and Prose Works of English Writers from Wither to Prior.* Vol. 1. New York: Grolier Club. xiii, 271p.

Reprinted, New York: Cooper Square Publishers, 1963.

Includes a catalogue of seventeenth-century editions of Crashaw's poems (with bibliographical descriptions and a facsimile reprint of the title page of the 1648 edition of *Steps to the Temple*) from the libraries of the members of the Grolier Club (pp. 202–7).

▪ 344. Hall, William C. "Richard Crashaw." *The Manchester Quarterly* 24:322–46.

Praises Cowley's elegy on Crashaw as well as the work of Grosart, Tutin, and Waller and notes the recent revival of interest in Crashaw. Presents a biographical sketch, emphasizing Crashaw's religious temperament, and surveys his poetry. Finds the early Latin epigrams "much better than their counterparts in *Steps to the Temple*" (p. 330) and notes *Steps to the Temple* has some parts that "are excellent, others are 'all right,' as we vulgarly say, the rest are not to be swallowed" (p. 330). Maintains that "The Teare" has "just those conceits that blemish work otherwise well-conceived, an unserviceable redundancy of words, and imagery which is kaleidoscopic rather than panoramic" (pp. 331–32). Finds the English epigrams maudlin and calls them "wearisome, jaded things" but adds that "they are sincere; and sincerity is a quality which, as much as versical finish, makes for poetry" (p. 332). Calls "Sospetto d'Herode" magnificent, poetical, and masterly, argues that the best poem in *The Delights of the Muses* "is indisputably 'Music's Duel,'" and calls it "one of the most beautiful pieces of imaginative verse in our language" (p. 340). Dismisses "The Weeper" as "hopelessly marred and defaced by the crowding of incongruous metaphors and similes, too numerous to contrast, of which the worst, possibly the worst in our literature, is the likening of the tearful eyes of St. Mary Magdalene to 'Two walking baths; two weeping motions; / Portable and compendious oceans'" (p. 341). In *Carmen Deo Nostro* prefers "Hymn to the Name of Jesus," "Hymn in the Holy Nativity," "Charitas Nimia," "Sancta Maria Dolorum," "A Hymn to Sainte Teresa," and "The Flaming Heart"—all of which "have wonderful fluency" (p. 345). Laments Crashaw's unevenness and, while recognizing his excesses, suggests that his poetry is "a body of verse which does not shame, but honours our literature, by representing it at the best" (p. 345). Followed by John Swann's bibliography of Crashaw (entry 346).

▪ 345. Hutton, Edward. *A Book of English Love Poems, chosen out of poets from Wyatt to Arnold.* London: Methuen. xxxv, 230p.

Refers to Crashaw in the preface as "perhaps the greatest religious poet in the language," a poet whose "beautiful and passionate work is among the rarest treasures of English poetry" (p. xiv). Notes that Crashaw's religious poetry "is never commonplace, often indeed it rises to the height of great poetry, while Vaughan and Herbert in Wales and at Oxford and Bemerton sang very sweetly of immortal things, but without the passion or the strength of Crashaw" (p. xiv). Includes "Wishes. To his (supposed) Mistresse" (pp. 112–17) without notes or commentary.

৳ 346. Swann, John H. "A Bibliography of Richard Crashaw." *The Manchester Quarterly* 24:346–48.
Appended to William C. Hall's "Richard Crashaw" (entry 344). Lists chronologically twenty-four editions of Crashaw's works, from 1633 ("Rex Redux" in *Rex Redux, Sive Musa Cantabrigiensis . . .*) to Waller's edition (1904).

৳ 347. [Thompson, Francis]. "Crashaw, Richard," in *Nelson's Encyclopaedia: Everybody's Book of References Containing 50,000 Articles, profusely illustrated.* Part XI: *Cooley to Curio,* 1687. New York: Thomas Nelson & Sons.
Presents a brief biographical account and suggests that Crashaw's fame rests chiefly on *Epigrammatum Sacrorum Liber,* "which, though often whimsical, shows maturity and classical taste," and on his sacred poems, "which exercised great influence on Milton, Coleridge, Shelley, and other poets."

1906

৳ 348. Anon. "Notes on Books, &c." *N&Q* 10th series, 5:160.
Notes the publication of Tutin's *The Poems of Richard Crashaw* (1905). Observes that "editions of Crashaw [continue to] multiply" and claims that Tutin's edition "is cheaper than any, and better than most."

৳ 349. Clutton-Brock, A. "The Fantastic School of English Poetry," in *The Cambridge Modern History,* edited by A. W. Ward, G. W. Prothero, and Stanley Leathes. Vol. 4: *The Thirty Years' War,* 760–75. London and New York: Macmillan; Cambridge: University Press.
2d ed., 1924; reprinted (without bibliography), 1934.
Presents a biographical sketch of Crashaw. Notes that "there is something in all Crashaw's poetry more congruous with Roman Catholicism than with Anglicanism" and calls him "one of the least English of our great poets" (p. 772). Suggests that Crashaw, like Shelley, is "one of those purely lyrical poets whom English literature produces now and then, and who are always rebels against the current English ideas of their day" (p. 772). Calls Crashaw "the poet of saints and martyrs" and maintains that, inspired "by Spanish and Italian extremes of faith," his chief aim was "to express the raptures of a faith which he assumes as an instinct" (p. 772). Calls "A Hymn to Sainte Teresa" "one of the greatest pieces of lyrical poetry in our literature" but notes that "Sospetto d'Herode" is "alternately splendid and absurd" (p. 772). Suggests that, more

than any other metaphysical poet, Crashaw "was infected with the conceits of
the Fantastic Poets of Italy, especially Marino," and that Crashaw's conceits
are often "mere ornaments," the result of "aiming at a wit unnatural to his
way of thinking" (p. 773). Argues that basically Crashaw was "a poet of pure
emotion" and that "his natural means of expression were a lyrical beauty of
rhythm and sound, and not any novelty or profundity of thought" (p. 773).
Compares Crashaw briefly to Donne, Herbert, Vaughan, Traherne, and
Cowley.

◄§ 350. Grierson, Herbert J. C. "English Poetry," in *The First Half of the
Seventeenth Century*, 135–201. (Periods of European Literature, ed.
George Saintsbury, vol. 7.) Edinburgh and London: William Black-
wood and Sons; New York: C. Scribner's Sons.
   A biographical sketch of Crashaw and a general critical evaluation of his
poetry (pp. 169–71). Suggests that Crashaw has "a more ardent temperament" and a "more soaring and glowing lyrical genius" than either Herbert or
Vaughan and notes his love for "religious confectionery of which Marino's
poems are full" (p. 169). Maintains that Crashaw's conceits, often "worse than
Marino's," are "of the physical and luscious character, to which the Italian
tended always, the English poet never" (p. 170). Concludes, however, that
there is "more of Vondel than Marino in the atmosphere" of Crashaw's religious poetry, noting that "Hymn in the Assumption" is "in the same exalted
strain" as Vondel's "Brieven der Heilige Maeghden" but that Vondel's style "is
simpler and more masculine" (p. 171). Notes that Crashaw's epithet, "happy
fireworks," applied to Saint Teresa, is not an inappropriate description of
many of his own poems.

◄§ 351. Seccombe, Thomas, and W. Robertson Nicoll. "Religious Poetry," in
The Bookman Illustrated History of English Literature. Vol. l: *Chaucer
to Dryden*, 161–64. London: Hodder and Stoughton.
   Reprinted in *A History of English Literature*. Vol. l: *Caxton (1422) to Walton (1593)* (New York: Dodd, Mead & Co., 1907), 377–85.
   A sketch of Crashaw's life and poetry (pp. 162–63). Calls him an "erratic
and ecstatic genius" and "the most mystical and perhaps the most unequal of
English poets" (p. 162). Praises "Wishes. To his (supposed) Mistresse" and
"Musicks Duell" but claims that Crashaw's genius "soars to real ecstasy only at
the touch of religious emotion" (p. 163). Calls "Hymn to the Name of Jesus"
"an extraordinary concatenation of inspirational flashes and fantastic conceits" and suggests that in "A Hymn to Sainte Teresa" and in the concluding
couplets of "The Flaming Heart" Crashaw attains the summit of "lyrical exaltation" (p. 163). Maintains that of all the poets of his time, Crashaw "was
perhaps the most conceited," noting that "he sank deeper, and in brief momentary flights it is possible that he fluttered higher than any of his contemporaries" (p. 163). Briefly points out that Coleridge, Swinburne, George Mac-

donald, and Edward Dowden "do reverence to his raptures, and have perhaps successfully vindicated his claim to be regarded as the poets' poet" (p. 163).

◦§ 352. Walker, Thomas Alfred. "Puritans and Cavaliers," in *Peterhouse*, 98–130. (University of Cambridge: College Histories.) London: Hutchinson & Co.
Reprinted, Cambridge: W. Heffer & Sons, 1935.
Presents a historical sketch of the College and briefly outlines Crashaw's career there. Notes that Crashaw signed the loyalist document, dated 2 July 1642, granting a loan to King Charles I.

1907

◦§ 353. Crashaw, Richard. *Wishes*. London: Arnold Fairbanks and Co. [12]p.
Reprints twenty-one stanzas of "Wishes. To his (supposed) Mistresse" without notes or commentary.

◦§ 354. Skipton, H. P. K. "Some Friendships of Nicholas Ferrar," in *The Life and Times of Nicholas Ferrar*, 110–23. London: A. R. Mowbray & Co.; New York: Thomas Whittaker.
Presents a biographical sketch of Crashaw and discusses in particular his friendship with Nicholas Ferrar and his involvement with the community at Little Gidding. Calls Crashaw "the unhappy poet and mystic who was swept away to destruction in the turbid flood of the Puritan domination" (p. 118). Notes that, because of William Crashaw's connection with the Virginia Company, it is likely that the Ferrars knew the poet's father. Suggests that "Ode on a Prayer-book" was written for Mary Collet and that Crashaw had in mind Little Gidding when he wrote "Description of a Religious House and Condition of Life." Notes that, because of Crashaw's conversion to Catholicism, "Protestant writers, incapable of understanding the man or sympathising with the tragedy of his life, wrote cruelly and scurrilously of him" (p. 123).

◦§ 355. Stebbing, William. "Richard Crashaw," in *The Poets: Geoffrey Chaucer to Alfred Tennyson, 1340–1892*. Vol. 1: *Chaucer to Burns*, 89–97. London, New York, Toronto: Henry Frowde, Oxford University Press.
Reprinted in *Five Centuries of English Verse* (London, New York, Toronto, Melbourne: Henry Frowde, Oxford University Press, 1910), 1:89–97. Rev. ed., 1913.
Offers a critical survey of Crashaw's poetry. Calls him "a Christian poet-recluse" (p. 89) and stresses that "his genius was made for suffering, not for doing; not for profound thought, but for tender feeling" (p. 90). Praises Crashaw's "irresistible ingenuousness, blissful resignation, dreaming abstraction, incapability of imagining wrong" and regrets his "lack of a due sense of proportion" in certain poems, his sometimes grotesque images, and his "ex-

traordinary incompetence to bridle fancy" (p. 90). Especially praises "Hymn in the Holy Nativity," "Hymn in the Assumption," "Hymn to the Name of Jesus," "The Flaming Heart," "Musicks Duell," "Wishes. To his (supposed) Mistresse" and "Sancta Maria Dolorum," calling the last Crashaw's "furthest, his highest, effort in the region of sacred song," a poem that is "incomparable in hymnology" (p. 93). Finds "Sospetto d'Herode," however, "a jumble of tiresome exaggeration" and a "poor anticipation of Milton" (p. 90).

1908

◄§ 356. Bailey-Kempling, W. "Coleridge on the Origin of 'Christabel.'" *N&Q* 10th series, 9:27.

Suggests that E. H. Coleridge, in his 1907 edition of his grandfather's poems, failed to point out that Coleridge confessed that he was greatly influenced by "A Hymn to Sainte Teresa" while he was writing "Christabel." For a reply, see S. Butterworth (entry 359).

◄§ 357. Bensly, Edward. "Crashaw and Maximilian Sandaeus." *N&Q* 10th series, 10:307.

Points out that the well-known last line of "Joann. 2. Aquae in vinum versae" may have been suggested by a distich composed by the Jesuit Maximilianus Sandaeus (van der Sandt, 1578–1656). Notes that, opposite the first oration in Sandaeus's *Maria Flos mysticus siue Orationes Ad Sodales in festivitatibus deiparae Habitae desumpta materia a floribus cum figuris Erei* (Mainz, 1629), there is an emblem (a rose in the center of which is depicted the Presentation of Christ in the Temple) and under it the following lines: "Vin' scire unde suum rosa candida traxerit ostrum? / Purgantem vidit Virginem, et erubuit."

◄§ 358. Bliss, Geoffrey. "Francis Thompson and Richard Crashaw." *The Month* 111:1–12.

Compares and contrasts Crashaw and Thompson, traces Crashaw's influence on the later poet, and remarks on their mysticism and religious sensibilities. Calls Crashaw "a poet's poet," admired by such notables as Cowley, Coleridge, and Elizabeth Barrett Browning, and suggests that his influence "has probably been far more considerable than is yet acknowledged" (p. 2). Suggests that what delighted Thompson was the "happy daring" of Crashaw's style (p. 3) and finds many similarities between the two poets in both matter and style. Stresses that both were Catholic mystics but finds Thompson the more profound of the two. Recognizes also that Crashaw and Thompson differ often more in degree than in kind. Notes, for example, that Crashaw's poetry is less obscure and contains more strained and excessive metaphors. Suggests that Thompson's poems on childhood "are things that Crashaw could not have done at all" (p. 12). Maintains that Crashaw's Teresian poems are the ones most likely to offend modern readers, who are unable to understand the kind of transcendent love that motivated the saints portrayed in Crashaw's poems.

◆§ 359. Butterworth, S. "Coleridge on the Origin of 'Christabel.'" *N&Q* 10th series, 9:112–13.

Reply to W. Bailey-Kempling (entry 356). Points out that on page 18 of his 1907 edition of his grandfather's poems, E. H. Coleridge does, in fact, note Coleridge's debt to "A Hymn to Sainte Teresa" while writing "Christabel." Further points out that J. Dykes Campbell notes the debt also in his 1893 edition of Coleridge's poems. Maintains, however, that "if Coleridge were in any way indebted to Crashaw's poem, it would seem to be more to the 'beautiful delicacies of language and metre' than to the subject, between which and that of 'Christabel' it is difficult to trace any resemblance" (p. 113).

◆§ 360. Clifford, Cornelius. "Crashaw," in *The Catholic Encyclopedia*, edited by Charles Herbermann et al., 4:467–68. New York: Robert Appleton Co.

Reprinted several times.

Offers a biographical sketch with brief critical comments on Crashaw's poetry. Notes that Crashaw's "feeling for the remote and more learned sense of words" perhaps accounts for "the defects as well as for the felicities of his poetic style" (p. 467). Suggests that the line "Nympha pudica Deum vidit, et erubuit" "will probably be quoted as long as the Latin tongue retains its spell over Western Christianity" (p. 467). Maintains that Crashaw's place in English literature "may be said to be fixed now for all time" and claims that, "if he is not the most important, he is at any rate not the least distinguished" (p. 468) of the metaphysical poets. Suggests that, like Donne, Herbert, and Cowley, Crashaw "is in love with the smaller graces of life and the profounder truths of religion, while he seems forever preoccupied with the secret architecture of things" (p. 468). Singles out "An Apologie for the fore-going Hymne" and "Wishes. To his (supposed) Mistresse" to illustrate Crashaw's "rare and singularly felicitous gift of epithet and phrase" and suggests that, "if his predilection is for those wanton arabesques of rhythm in which fancy seems suddenly to become crystallized as wit, on the other hand his lyric gift too often becomes merely elaborate and flags because he is forever in quest of a surprise" (p. 468). Highly selected bibliography.

◆§ 361. Saintsbury, George. "Caroline Lyric, Pindaric, and Stanza," in *A History of English Prosody from the Twelfth Century to the Present Day.* Vol. 2: *From Shakespeare to Crabbe*, 321–43. London and New York: Macmillan.

2d ed., London: Macmillan, 1923.

Briefly comments on Crashaw's prosody, pointing out the "'rocket'-like" quality of "A Hymn to Sainte Teresa," the prosodic playfulness of "Wishes. To his (supposed) Mistresse," the noteworthy octave of "Sospetto d'Herode," and the prosodic ambiguities of "On the still surviving markes of our Saviours wounds." Suggests that Crashaw's "constant and very felicitous practice, sometimes in Latin and sometimes even in Greek verse, no doubt helped his English prosody" (p. 331). Compares Crashaw briefly to Cowley, Carew, Herrick, and Suckling. Concludes that Crashaw "has little prosodic mannerism, or rather he has it in so many kinds that it is difficult to isolate" (p. 331).

◄§ 362. Thompson, Francis. "Shelley." *DubR* 143 (July): 25–49.
Reprinted under separate cover with an introduction by George Wyndam and notes by W. M. (London: Burns and Oates, 1909). 91p.
Claims that, as poets, Crashaw and Shelley "sprang from the same seed; but in the one case the seed was choked with thorns, and in the other case it fell on good ground" (p. 39). Notes that "to most people the Metaphysical School means Donne, whereas it ought to mean Crashaw," and argues that "the highest product of the Metaphysical School was Crashaw, and Crashaw was a Shelley *manqué*; he never reached the Promised Land, but he had fervid visions of it" (p. 39). Exclaims that Crashaw, William Collins, and Shelley are "three ricochets of the one pebble, three jets from three bounds of the one Pegasus" (p. 41).

1909

◄§ 363. Cook, Albert S. "Notes on Milton's Ode on the Morning of Christ's Nativity." *Transactions of the Connecticut Academy of Arts and Sciences* 15:307–68.
Points out briefly two parallels between Milton's Nativity Ode and Crashaw's "Hymn in the Holy Nativity": (1) Milton's description of "winter wild" (line 29) and Crashaw's depiction of winter in lines 35–38 of the 1646 edition (p. 318), and (2) Milton's reference to the earthly and heavenly sun (line 83) and Crashaw's use of the same notion (p. 334).

◄§ 364. Crashaw, Richard. *A hymn of the nativity, by Richard Crashaw.* [New York]: Privately printed [by the De Vinne Press], Christmas.
Reproduces "Hymn in the Holy Nativity." Paper, folded leaves in paper cover. Printed for Fitzroy and Charlotte Carrington and their friends. (Only known copy in the New York Public Library.)

◄§ 365. Mabie, Hamilton Wright. "A Hymn of the Nativity by Richard Crashaw." *The Outlook* 93:863–66.
Reprinted in *Introductions to Notable Poems* (New York: Dodd, Mead, and Co., 1909), 147–61.
A biographical sketch of Crashaw and a general introduction to his poetry.

Praises his sincerity and imagination but deplores his "gross absurdities and far-fetched conceits" (p. 864). Suggests that "when he escaped from 'fustian imitation of brocade,' he was capable of a certain nobility and even splendor of thought and diction, and rose in a few passages to the heights of passionate eloquence of style" (p. 864). Reproduces "Hymn in the Holy Nativity," observing that the poem "is quaint after the manner of its time and not free from conceits, but it has touches of tenderness and beauty which entitle it to a place among the true Christmas Hymns of English poetry" (p. 864).

1910

366. Courtney, W. P. "Richard Crashaw at Rome." *N&Q* 11th series, 2:205.

Points out an anecdote related by Sir Robert Southwell in a letter written from Rome at the close of 1660 (entry 35), in which Southwell recounts being told that Crashaw was disappointed by the twenty pistoles offered to him by the Pope and reportedly said that "certainly if the Roman church be not founded upon a rock, it is at least founded upon something which is as hard as a rock."

367. Crashaw, Richard. *The Cradle of the King: A Christmas Anthology.* By Richard Crashaw, John Banister Tabb, Robert Stephen Hawker, Coventry Patmore, Alice Meynell, Katharine Tynan & Francis Thompson. London: Burns & Oates; St. Louis: B. Herder. 24p.

Reproduces, with modern spellings, part of "The Hymn" from "Hymn in the Holy Nativity" (pp. 5–11), without notes or commentary.

368. Fitzmaurice-Kelly, James. *The Relations between Spanish and English Literature.* Liverpool: University Press of Liverpool. 32p.

Suggests that there are clear indications that Crashaw "knew Marino too well" but "of direct Spanish influence there is no such unequivocal sign, though it is hard to believe that Crashaw read Sainte Theresa in translations only" (pp. 16–17). Points out that nothing resembling Crashaw's use of conceits can be found in the works of the Spanish mystic. Notes the influence of "A Hymn to Sainte Teresa" on Coleridge's "Christabel" and suggests that that link "might enable us to bring Coleridge into some distant relation with Spanish literature" (pp. 16–17).

369. O'Brien, Edward J. "The Inspiration of Crashaw." *Poet Lore* 21:397–400.

Notes that Crashaw's poetry is not likely ever to be widely popular, primarily because of his use of excessive conceits. Cites as an example "The Weeper," a poem that reflects Crashaw's "habit of diluting a thought or line until all its force is lost" (p. 398). Surveys selectively the English poems and discusses elements that have attracted the admiration of such poets as Milton, Pope, Coleridge, Shelley, Francis Thompson, and Coventry Patmore. Finds in the sacred poems a "passionate fervor of devotion," "melodious rapture," "choice subtlety," a "mastery of supple and cunning implication," and a "sweetness of diction and purity of fancy which is equalled by few and excelled by none" (pp. 397–98). Claims that Crashaw's metrical effects, "though often magnificent, are very unequal" and that he sometimes "produces a grotesque diffuseness" (p. 398). Suggests, however, that a major characteristic of Crashaw's verse is dignity: "no matter how profuse his ornament may be, it is nearly always subordinate to the moral effect," as reflected, for instance, in "A Hymn to Sainte Teresa," an "exquisite composition, full of real vision and music of the most delicate order" (p. 398). Praises also "Musicks Duell," "Loves Horoscope," and especially "Wishes. To his (supposed) Mistresse," calling the latter "one of the loveliest lyrics of this lyric century" (p. 399). Comments on the general unevenness of Crashaw's canon but claims that at times he is "the Botticelli of poetry" (p. 399) and the "Christian Shelley" (p. 400). Compares Crashaw to Southwell in his "blending of emotional tenderness with ascetic mysticism" and praises Crashaw's musicality and his ability to find words "to clothe a subtle and ravishing emotion" (p. 400). Concludes that, although Crashaw's poems are rarely autobiographical, they bear the stamp of his unique individuality: "We must love the man a little in order to appreciate his poetry" (p. 400).

⋙ 370. Thomas, [Philip] Edward. "The Tenth Muse," in *Feminine Influence on the Poets*, 228–331. London: Martin Secker; New York: John Lane.
This chapter reprinted under separate cover, *The Tenth Muse* (London: Martin Secker, 1911, 1912, 1917, 1918).
Comments on Crashaw's attitudes toward women and on their influence on his life and poetry. Calls his Teresian poems genuine love poems, noting that he "makes much play with words and phrases of amorous association, and then cries out with a wild note for the same religious ecstasy as the saint knew" (p. 262). Notes "the profusion of his physical suggestions of human love" (p. 264) in "Ode on a Prayer-book" and in "To [Mrs. M. R.] Councel Concerning her Choise." Suggests that in "Wishes. To his (supposed) Mistresse" it is characteristic of Crashaw "to enumerate the rich and splendid things which she can do without, just as he enhances the heavenly love by depreciating the earthly" (p. 264), and calls the poem "remarkable for its grave original beauty" (p. 264).

1911

⋙ 371. Crashaw, Richard. *Qvem Vidistis Pastores? A Hymn of the Nativity*. Letchworth: Newly Printed by B[ernard] H. N[ewdigate] and M. N. [7]p.
Reproduces "Hymn in the Holy Nativity" without notes or commentary.

✑§ 372. Holliday, Carl. "Richard Crashaw," in *The Cavalier Poets: Their Lives, Their Day, and Their Poetry,* 109–23, 233–42. New York and Washington: Neale Publishing Co.

Reprinted, Plainview, N.Y.: Books for Libraries Press, 1974.

Biographical sketch and critical introduction to Crashaw's poetry. Praises the "height of feeling," the "rush of emotion," the novelty of poetic structure," and the masterful use of words in Crashaw's poetry, but disapproves of his straining for effect and his use of "most tasteless" conceits (pp. 115–16). Notes that "sister baths" and "portable oceans" in "The Weeper" "have long been considered unpardonable, and other examples equally bad might easily be found" (p. 116) and suggests that the images in "Hymn in the Holy Nativity" "confuse and bewilder him [Crashaw], leaving him no tongue for his onrushing thoughts" (p. 117). Maintains, however, that in "The Flaming Heart" Crashaw "bursts forth with a torrent of ringing words that in their passionate spiritedness are scarcely equalled in the literature of England" (p. 117). Argues that, "in spite of exaggerations, far-fetched metaphors, and wild ecstasies," Crashaw is "seldom tiresome" (p. 117). Compares and contrasts Crashaw with Herbert, Shelley, Keats, Wordsworth, and Robert Burns; surveys critical commentary on him by Pope, Coleridge, Sara Coleridge, Hazlitt, Swinburne, Palgrave, and Gosse; and comments on reasons for Crashaw's being nearly forgotten in the twentieth century. Selections from the poems (pp. 233–42), with brief notes.

✑§ 373. Hutchinson, F. E. "The Sacred Poets," in *The Cambridge History of English Literature,* edited by A. W. Ward and A. R. Waller. Vol. 7: *Cavalier and Puritan,* 3–54. New York: G. P. Putnam's Sons; Cambridge: University Press.

Reprinted several times.

A biographical sketch and a general survey of Crashaw's poetry. Notes that, although Crashaw knew Herbert's poetry, "there is hardly a poem by Crashaw which recalls Herbert," for "the two men are widely different in temperament and genius" (p. 37). Suggests that Crashaw's knowledge of Spanish and Italian "affected both the matter and the manner of his poetry," for "not only did it bring the writings of the Spanish mystics within his reach, but, also, it infected him with the hyperboles and luscious sweetness of the Neopolitan poet, Marino" (p. 40). Finds Crashaw's poetry extremely uneven but praises the "airy metre" and "graceful humour" of "Wishes. To his (supposed) Mistresse" and regards "A Hymn to Sainte Teresa" as Crashaw's most successful sacred poem. Asserts that "Crashaw's passionate outbursts, with their flaming brilliancy, and their quick-moving lines, are hard to parallel in the language" but suggests that many of Crashaw's poems give "positive offense by an outrageous conceit, by gaudy colour, by cloying sweetness or by straining an idea which has been squeezed dry" (p. 42). Concludes that "his defective powers of self-criticism make Crashaw the most unequal of our poets" (p. 42).

◄§ 374. Mullinger, James Bass. *The University of Cambridge*. Vol. 3: *From the Election of Buckingham to the Chancellorship in 1626 to the Decline of the Platonist Movement*. Cambridge: University Press. lx, 743p.

Cites Crashaw throughout. Notes that Crashaw contributed to *Voces Votivæ Ab Academicis Cantabrigiensibus* . . . , 1640 (p. 147); points out that John Bargrave (entry 37) lists Crashaw as one of four "revolters to the Roman Church" from Peterhouse (p. 208); comments on the circumstances surrounding Crashaw's expulsion from Peterhouse in 1644 (p. 282); suggests that Crashaw inherited his literary tastes from his father; notes that as an undergraduate he "distinguished himself by his love of art, his deeply devotional spirit, and not less by his fine poetic taste," and comments briefly on his life (pp. 284–86). Notes Crashaw's admiration of his master at Charterhouse, Brooke; of his tutor at Pembroke, Tourney; and of the master of Pembroke, Laney—pointing out that he dedicated *Epigrammatum Sacrorum Liber* to all three (p. 318).

1912

◄§ 375. Crashaw, Richard. "A Hymn of the Nativity," in *Ode on the Morning of Christ's Nativity by John Milton and A Hymn of the Nativity by Richard Crashaw*, 21–28. (The Arden Books, no. 11.) London: St. Catherine Press.

Reproduces "Hymn in the Holy Nativity" without notes or commentary.

◄§ 376. ———. *Quem vidistis pastores? A Hymn of the Nativity Sung by the Shepherds*. Written by Richard Crashaw. London: Burns and Oates; New York: Benziger. [4]p.

Reproduces "Hymn in the Holy Nativity" without notes or commentary. Frontispiece designed by Paul Woodoffe.

◄§ 377. Haynes, Henrietta. *Henrietta Maria*. London: Methuen & Co. xv, 335p.

Comments on Crashaw's introduction to and friendship with Queen Henrietta Maria and her court in Paris, noting his exhortation to the Countess of Denbigh to follow his example of converting to Catholicism (pp. 221–22). Suggests that, although the Queen probably was unable to understand "the highly difficult poems of the Cambridge mystic" (p. 221), perhaps she talked with him about one of her favorite saints, St. Teresa. Reproduces the Queen's letter introducing Crashaw to Pope Innocent X (entry 17), p. 328.

◄§ 378. Lang, Andrew. "Caroline Poets," in *History of English Literature from "Beowulf" to Swinburne*, 328–57. London, New York, Bombay, and Calcutta: Longmans, Green and Co.

2d ed., 1912; 3d ed., 1913; reprinted, 1914, 1921, 1928.

A biographical sketch of Crashaw and a brief survey of his poetry. Suggests that "a fiery vehemence, an overloaded ornament are his quality and his defect" and maintains that, "save for the Hymn to St. Teresa, with 'That not Impossible She,' 'The Flaming Heart,' and some pretty translations, Crashaw, like all the Cavalier poets, except Carew, is usually on a low poetic level" (p. 329). Disparages Pope's evaluation of Crashaw and compares Crashaw to Herbert, maintaining that Herbert "has not the extravagances that mar the work of Donne and Crashaw" (p. 331), and to Milton, noting that Crashaw's "Hymn in the Holy Nativity" is "a '*fade*' thing, compared with Milton's" (p. 329).

◀§ 379. Reed, Edward Bliss. "The Jacobean and Caroline Lyric," in *English Lyrical Poetry from Its Origins to the Present Time*, 233–301. New Haven: Yale University Press; London: Humphrey Milford, Oxford University Press.
Reprinted, 1914.
Surveys briefly the works of twenty seventeenth-century poets, including Crashaw (pp. 283–87). Maintains that Crashaw's "life history is a series of spiritual experiences to be read in his poems" for "his sensitive and emotional temperament is disclosed in every page of his writings" (p. 283). Finds Crashaw's religious sensibility un-English and to some degree "somewhat incomprehensible" (p. 284). Stresses the influence of Spanish mysticism, especially that of St. Teresa, on Crashaw's life and poetry, asserting that many of his religious lyrics "are not songs, but the impassioned cry of his soul" and that his hymns "are too glowing and mystical to be hymns of the church" (p. 283). Claims, however, that from an artistic viewpoint his religious poems are "brilliant in color, musical in their expression, and thrilling in an emotional power" and cites the concluding lines of "The Flaming Heart" as "unequalled in all the range of the religious lyric" (p. 285). Finds the secular poems lacking in enthusiasm but rich in "music and color" and suggests that "Wishes. To his (supposed) Mistresse" exhibits some of his defects as well as his strengths, those defects being a too facile and versatile handling of language, a kind of diffuseness, a lack of proper restraint, and a general unevenness. Calls Crashaw "a romanticist born out of due time" and concludes that, while "he seems more truly inspired than any of his contemporaries, always excepting Milton, "he stands absolutely alone" (p. 287). Comments on Crashaw's influence on Milton, Pope, and Coleridge and briefly compares him to Herbert, Jonson, Richard Rolle, Quarles, Vaughan, Spenser, Newman, Shelley, and Swinburne.

◀§ 380. Sharland, E. Cruwys. "Richard Crashaw and Mary Collet." *CQR* 73:358–85.
Biographical sketch of Crashaw, stressing his friendship with Mary Collet and his involvement with the community at Little Gidding. Suggests that

Crashaw first met Mary Collet in 1632 and that she was an important influence on his religious life. Discusses a newly discovered letter (now in the University Library, Cambridge), said to be in Crashaw's hand, dated 20 February 1643 (O.S.), and sent from Leyden to perhaps either John Ferrar or John Collet, Mary's father (entry 14). Points out that in the letter Crashaw laments being forbidden to visit Mary Collet by her uncle, in whose house she was residing at the time, and that he proposes to resign from his fellowship at Peterhouse in the hope that Ferrar Collet may receive it. Notes that the letter throws light on Crashaw's temperament and feelings during this difficult time in his life. Calls him "one of the greatest religious poets of the Seventeenth Century" (p. 381), briefly surveys his poetry, and comments on his influence on later poets. Suggests, in a parenthetical remark, that Crashaw's mother was Helen Routh, daughter of John Routh (p. 359). Attributes this information to T. A. Walker, librarian at Peterhouse. For further information on Crashaw's letter, see Martin (pp. xxv–xxxi) and W. W. Greg (entry 532).

✒ 381. Walker, Thomas Alfred, comp. *Admissions to Peterhouse or S. Peter's College in the University of Cambridge: A Biographical Register . . .* Cambridge: University Press. xi, 760p.

Notes that Symon Smethe was succeeded in his fellowship by Crashaw in 1636 (p. 6) and that Crashaw was the tutor of Ferrar Collet, who was admitted to Peterhouse on 16–17 May 1636. Gives a biographical sketch of Crashaw (pp. 56, 691), calling him "the famous Poet" and listing his major volumes of poetry.

1913

✒ 382. Crashaw, Richard. *Qvem vidistis pastores?: A Hymn of the Nativity Svng by the Shepherds vpon their retvrn.* Written by Richard Crashaw. [Cleveland: Printed by Charles Clinch Bubb at his private press.] 8p. 126 copies printed.

Reproduces "Hymn in the Holy Nativity" without notes or commentary.

✒ 383. Fleming, W[illiam] K[aye]. "Post-Reformation Mysticism in England: The Caroline Poets and the Cambridge Platonists," in *Mysticism in Christianity,* 194–212. (Library of Historic Theology, ed. W. C. Piercy.) New York and Chicago: Fleming H. Revell; London: R. Scott.

A biographical sketch and a survey of Crashaw's poetry, describing his mysticism as "the warmly coloured Latin type" (p. 201) and noting that his favorite subjects are the life and sufferings of Christ, the glory of the Virgin Mary, and the praise of St. Teresa. Contrasts Crashaw to Vaughan and Donne and claims that he "was far more a craftsman, and had a far juster ear for music" but that "his art runs away with him, at times, until the art becomes artificiality" (p. 202). Complains that Crashaw "places his gems of thought amid rows of decorative glass beads, and seems really to leave the task of discrimination to his reader without any idea that all is not of the same value" (p. 202). Postulates that if St. Teresa had read the poems addressed to her "she would probably have loved them and laughed at them at the same time" (p. 202). Maintains that Crashaw's finest pieces are "Hymn in the Holy Nativity," "Psalme 23," and "Dies Irae Dies Illa."

◆§ 384. Marsh, Bower, and Frederick Arthur Crisp, eds. *Alumni Carthusiani: A Record of the Foundation Scholars of Charterhouse, 1614–1872.* [London]: Privately printed. xviii, 363p.
Limited to 150 copies.
Lists Crashaw (spelled "Crosshow" and "Crasshow") as being admitted to Charterhouse on 2 July 1629 and presents a biographical sketch (p. 9).

◆§ 385. Osmond, Percy H[erbert]. "With His Back to the Wall," in *A Life of John Cosin, Bishop of Durham, 1660–1672,* 79–110. London: A. R. Mowbray & Co.: Milwaukee: The Young Churchman Co.
Briefly notes Crashaw's support for the ornate ceremonies that Cosin introduced at Peterhouse in the mid 1640s. Suggests that Cosin's influence may have set Crashaw "on the road which (when the Church of England seemed quite defunct) led him finally to Rome" but notes that, in a letter written during Crashaw's exile in Paris, Cosin spoke bitterly of the poet's conversion (entry 51).

◆§ 386. Rhys, Ernest. "The Later Amorists—the Fashionable Lyric—The Herbert Group," in *Lyric Poetry,* 210–21. (The Channels of English Literature.) London and Toronto: J. M. Dent & Sons; New York: E. P. Dutton & Co.
Suggests that Crashaw chose Marino as a model and that the result was "a fanciful extravagance of diction and a flow of conceits which spoil many of his pages" (p. 220). Notes, however, that "even amid his worst trifling, and sentimental bad taste, we come upon verse of superb passion" (p. 221), pointing to lines from "The Flaming Heart" and "Upon the Death of the most desired Mr. Herrys."

◆§ 387. Schelling, Felix E. "The Lyric in the Reigns of the First Two Stuart Monarchs," in *The English Lyric,* 73–111. (The Types of English Literature; ed. William Allan Neilson.) Boston and New York: Houghton Mifflin Co.
Presents a brief sketch of Crashaw's life and poetry (pp. 96–97). Notes that Crashaw, like Herbert, "is a concettist and a follower of Donne; but where Donne sees things oddly from the innate originality of his mind and Herbert dwells with loving ingenuity on every curious detail of his art, Crashaw is carried away in a storm of imagery, confused and incoherent at times from the

very force of his eloquence" (pp. 96–97). Suggests that, although Crashaw's conceits are extravagant and often tasteless, "it is easier to find in him passages of glowing religious emotion, sustained lyrical art, music of words, and splendor of diction, than it is to seek out his inequalities and lapses into excesses of imaginative conceits wherein he has been time out of mind the example and warning of the critics" (p. 97). Concludes that, until Shelley and Swinburne, no English poet "is so dithyrambic as Crashaw, and few have matched the ease and music of his lines and the atmosphere of light and radiance that pervades the best of his poetry" (p. 97).

≪§ 388. Spurgeon, Caroline F. E. "Devotional and Religious Mystics," in *Mysticism in English Literature* (The Cambridge Manuals of Science and Literature), 111–58. Cambridge: University Press; New York: G. P. Putnam's Sons.
   Reprinted, 1922.
   Claims that Crashaw describes the love of the soul for God in terms of human love "with an ardour which has never been surpassed" (p. 126) and "in terms only matched by his spiritual descendant, Francis Thompson" (p. 127). Briefly compares and contrasts Crashaw with Herbert and Christopher Harvey but suggests that Crashaw alone "shares in fullest measure the passion of the great Catholic mystics, and more especially St. Teresa, whom he seems almost to have worshipped" (p. 128). Calls "A Hymn to Sainte Teresa" "one of the great English poems" that "burns with spiritual flame" and "soars with noble desire" (p. 128) and suggests that "spiritual love has never been more rapturously sung than in this marvellous hymn" (p. 129). Notes Crashaw's influence on Coleridge, Coventry Patmore, and Francis Thompson.

1914

≪§ 389. Crashaw, Richard. *The Religious Poems of Richard Crashaw*, with an introductory study by R. A. Eric Shepherd. (The Catholic Library, 10.) St. Louis: B. Herder; London: Manresa Press. viii, 136p.
   Introduction (pp. 1–26) followed by poems from *Carmen Deo Nostro* (pp. 27–131), from *Steps to the Temple* (pp. 132–34), and "Luc. 2. Quaerit Jesum suum beata Virgo" (pp. 135–36). Calls Crashaw "one of the greatest and most sublime of Catholic poets" (p. 9). Presents a biographical sketch and comments on Crashaw's religious development, especially his conversion to Catholicism, suggesting that the writings of St. Teresa were "the determining factor" (p. 7) in his case. Offers a critical analysis of the poetry and suggests that the key to understanding it is "simply this, Crashaw was a convert" (p. 10), an ecstatic, who "does not preach" (p. 11) but rather sings hymns because of the joy of his religious discovery. Observes that it is the note of ecstasy in the poems that alienates his readers, especially his English readers, and argues that the poems, on the whole, have "a spirit that rejoices in the poetic gran-

deur of his themes," which are "deeply and passionately and tenderly full at the same time of love and faith" (p. 14). Defends Crashaw's poetry against those who claim that it is too hyperbolic, too inclined toward emotional exaggeration, and too conceited. Challenges, in particular, the criticism of Francis Thompson and compares Crashaw repeatedly with St. Francis of Assisi. Considers the Teresian poems as Crashaw's best, exemplifying "in small compass the quintessential juice of what I am accustomed to understand by religious poetry" (pp. 23–24). Calls Crashaw's translation of "Dies Irae Dies Illa" "the very radium of religious poetry" (p. 23); sees "The Weeper" as Crashaw's least effective poem; and singles out "Sancta Maria Dolorum" as "the most typical of everything that I have said about the poet" (p. 25).

⊷§ 390. ⸻. "Upon Easter Day," in *Easter Poems: A Religious Anthology by George Herbert, Richard Crashaw, Henry Vaughan, John Banister Tabb, Edward Caswall, Alfred Noyes, Frederick William Faber, Katharine Tynan and Francis Thompson,* 8–9. London: Burns & Oates; St. Louis: B. Herder.
Reproduces "Easter day" (p. 8) and "Mat. 28. Come see the place where the Lord lay" (p. 9) without notes or commentary.

⊷§ 391. O'Neill, George. "Crashaw, Shelley and Thompson: A Tercentenary Paper." *IER*, series 5, 4:1–25.
Compares and contrasts the personalities, lives, and works of Crashaw, Shelley, and Francis Thompson. Suggests that, among the three, "Crashaw excels as a mystic, Shelley as a poet, Thompson, in his best pages, happily blends both characters" (p. 9). Calls Crashaw "the greatest English religious poet" (p. 9) and a "singer *par excellence* of genuine Catholic mysticism" (p. 13). Suggests that Crashaw's lack of popularity results in part from his descriptions of mystical experience, which, to the average Englishman, "will seem to belong to the same category as the fictions of a fairy tale" (p. 13), but notes also Crashaw's too elaborate and overly ingenious uses of conceits and his occasional "eccentric and tasteless conjuring with ideas and words" (pp. 15–16).

⊷§ 392. Robinson, Eloise, ed. Introduction to *The Minor Poems of Joseph Beaumont, D.D., 1616–1699,* edited from the autograph manuscript with introduction and notes by Eloise Robinson, xiii–xliii. London: Constable and Co.
Tentatively suggests that those poems in the manuscript of Beaumont's poems marked R. C. may have been set to music by Crashaw and points out Beaumont's friendship at Peterhouse with Crashaw to whom he paid tribute in *Psyche* (canto 4, st. 107–8). Briefly compares and contrasts Beaumont's poetry with Crashaw's and suggests that he is much more akin to Crashaw than to the other metaphysical poets, noting several parallels and direct borrow-

ings. Points out, however, that Beaumont is an inferior poet who lacks the "vivid mysticism" of Crashaw (p. xli).

◄§ 393. Seth-Smith, E[lsie] K[athleen]. *The Way of Little Gidding.* London: H. R. Allenson. 242p.
Fictionalized account of life at Little Gidding in the 1640s. Mentions Crashaw throughout, especially in chapter 8, "Introduces Mr. Richard Crashaw" (pp. 82–90), and in chapter 21, "Mr. Crashaw Soliloquises" (pp. 207–18).

◄§ 394. Yeats, W[illiam] B[utler]. "Art and Ideas." *The New Weekly* 20,27 June, pp. 6–7, 38–40.
Reprinted in *Essays* (London and New York: Macmillan, 1924), 429–41. In a general essay on art and literature, briefly notes that "Crashaw could hymn St. Theresa in the most impersonal of ecstasies and seem no sedentary man out of reach of common sympathy, no disembodied mind, and yet in his day the life that appeared most rich and stirring was already half forgotten with Villon and Dante" (p. 6).

1915

◄§ 395. Denbigh, Countess of [Cecilia Mary Clifford Feilding]. *Royalist Father and Roundhead Son; Being the Memoirs of the First and Second Earls of Denbigh, 1600–1675.* London: Methuen and Co. 323p.
Briefly notes (pp. 287–88) the Countess of Denbigh's patronage of Crashaw in Paris and his efforts to persuade her to convert to Catholicism. Suggests that Crashaw was secretary to Lord Jermyn in Paris.

◄§ 396. Heide, Anna von der. "Die religiösen Lyriker," in *Das Naturgefühl in der englischen Dichtung im Zeitalter Miltons,* 61–89. (Anglistische Forschungen, 45.) Heidelberg: Carl Winters Universitätsbuchhandlung.
Sees Crashaw as unique in English literature for his spirit of exaltation, visionary ecstasy, and uses of decorative language. Focuses on Crashaw's response to and uses of nature in his early poetry. Suggests that his poetry, like his life, is characterized by a blend of ecstatic vision and platitude and commonplace observations. Points out Crashaw's great interest in nature in his early secular poems, as indicated, for example, in his translations of Virgil. Discusses in some detail the funereal, commemorative poems on Mr. Herrys, noting Crashaw's uses of nature imagery, and suggests that the poems belong to a period in Crashaw's life before he dedicated himself totally to Christ. Maintains that Crashaw at first responded to the inherent beauty of nature but later saw it as a reflection of God's beauty, a symbolic representation of eternal verities. Comments briefly on Crashaw's Christology and concludes that once he turned to religion, under the influence of the members of Little Gidding,

he turned away from the beauties and intricacies of nature and viewed it as secondary to the spiritual order and beauty of creation. Briefly compares Crashaw to Shelley and Swinburne, noting that the ardor and fervor of the nineteenth-century poets, although no less sincere, are less unearthly and less "krankhaften" (sickly). Further suggests that Crashaw appeals to readers of a "nervös" disposition (p. 62).

◄§ 397. Inge, William Ralph. "English Religious Poetry." *Transactions of the Royal Society of Literature* 2d series, 33:177–203.
Reprinted in *More Lay Thoughts of a Dean* (New York and London: Putnam, 1932), 225–54.
Surveys English religious poetry and compares and contrasts poets influenced by different religious traditions and beliefs. Notes that, after the Reformation in England, religious poetry, both Catholic and Protestant, "becomes more didactic, personal, introspective, and meditative" (p. 186). Maintains that, although Crashaw is an uneven poet, he enriched the tradition of religious poetry in the seventeenth century: "if we take him at his best, as every poet has a right to be taken, he must be given a high rank" (p. 186). Calls Pope's comments on Crashaw "one of the curiosities of criticism" (p. 187) and cites lines 79–108 of "The Flaming Heart" and "An Epitaph upon a Young Married Couple" as examples of Crashaw's poetic excellence.

◄§ 398. Martin, L. C. "Crashaw's Translation of Marino's 'La Strage degli Innocenti' ('Sospetto d'Herode')." *MLR* 10:378–80.
Discusses two copies of the text of "Sospetto d'Herode" in MS Tanner 466 (fas. 154–63 and 164–73) that contain several important variants from the printed editions. Notes that the two copies "were not, apparently, made independently from the original, since both agree in certain errors which are not found in the printed editions and which can hardly all have stood in Crashaw's 'own Copie'" and points out that in one copy "most of these errors are corrected in another hand" (p. 379).

◄§ 399. Sears, Clara Endicott, comp. "Appendix: Catalogue of the Original Fruitlands Library," in *Bronson Alcott's Fruitlands*, compiled by Clara Endicott Sears, with *Transcendental Wild Oats* by Louisa M. Alcott, 175–85. Boston and New York: Houghton Mifflin Co.; Cambridge: Riverside Press.
Lists the 1670 edition of *Steps to the Temple* among books in the library of the nineteenth-century transcendentalist community of Fruitlands (Harvard, Mass.).

◄§ 400. Waugh, Arthur. "Richard Crashaw," in *Reticence in Literature and Other Papers*, 125–29. London: J. G. Wilson; New York: E. P. Dutton.
Considers Crashaw as a mystic, an ascetic, and a pioneer of Catholic po-

etry: "He stands, as it were, lonely in a crowd; the forerunner of movements, literary and religious, which have since grown into dimensions he could never have conceived" (p. 125). Calls Crashaw "the first deliberate 'stylist'" among the poets of the seventeenth century and notes the indebtedness of Milton, Pope, Edward Young, Coleridge, and Francis Thompson. Suggests that the faults in Crashaw's poetry, though often serious, are "the faults rather of its artistic isolation than of any radical defect in the poet himself" and argues that, since he was breaking new ground, he "was by stress of influence forced out of simplicity, and the natural result was that his style became vitiated with conceits" (p. 127). Explains Crashaw's "vagaries" as "an effort towards originality of literary expression" (p. 128) that, though well intentioned, sometimes fails in practice. Praises lines from "A Hymn to Sainte Teresa," "Wishes. To his (supposed) Mistresse," and "Loves Horoscope," calling the latter "one of the finest love-poems in the language" (p. 128). Concludes that Crashaw is "the forerunner of that small but devoted body of English Churchmen who roused religion from the apathy of the eighteenth century into the strenuous and sincere anxieties of the last fifty years" (p. 129).

1916

◄§ 401. Gerould, Gordon Hall. "The Reformation and Since," in *Saints' Legends*, 313–48. (The Types of English Literature, ed. William Allan Neilson.) Boston and New York: Houghton Mifflin Co.

Briefly compares "The Weeper" to Thomas Robinson's *The Life and Death of Mary Magdalene* (circa 1620), noting that both poems do not primarily narrate the life of the saint but rather "use her figure as a theme for allegorical interpretation" (p. 328). Points out that, unlike Robinson, Crashaw "merely descanted upon her tears and did not weave into his stanzas an account of her life" (p. 328). Notes that both "A Hymn to Sainte Teresa" and "Alexias" show that Crashaw "was never so much interested in the succession of events as in the significance of them" and that "in dealing with saints' lives, as always, he was a lyrical poet" (p. 328). Calls Crashaw's poems on saints "very subtle" and "very noble" and sees them as a reaction to Puritanism. Maintains, however, that they "were less a contribution to hagiography than to the literature of religious ecstasy" (p. 328).

◄§ 402. Martin, L. C. "A Crashaw and Shelley Parallel." *MLR* 11:217.

Points out parallels in both thought and diction between lines 10–20 of "Death's Lecture" and stanza 47 of Shelley's *Adonais*, suggesting that the resemblances are "an unconscious reminiscence." Notes a further parallel to Crashaw in *Prometheus Unbound* (act 1, 417–22).

◄§ 403. Ramsay, Mary Paton. "Introduction," in *Les doctrines médiévales chez Donne, le poète métaphysicien de l'Angleterre (1573–1631)*, 1–33. London and New York: Oxford University Press.

Reprinted, 1917; 2d ed., 1924.

Briefly discusses Crashaw as one of Donne's better disciples. Suggests that Crashaw "suit Donne plus particulièrement dans ses incursions à travers le domaine de la littérature espagnole, pour en rapporter des inspirations mystiques" and notes that "il a la subtilité d'un Donne dont la passion religieuse s'est de plus en plus exaltée, mais dont la force intellectuelle a dimunué" (p. 32). Observes also that Crashaw "aime à developper l'idée de l'incarnation de Dieu, à contempler le Tout-Puissant fait petit enfant" and that "il rappelle en cela quelques-uns des plus beaux d'entre des sermons de Donne, ses sermons sur la Nativité" (p. 32).

1917

◄§ 404. Candy, Hugh C. H. "Note on an Adapted Copy of Crashaw's Poems (Steps to the Temple, The Delights of the Muses, and Carmen Deo Nostro) 1670." *Library* series 3, 8:77–78.

Describes a copy of the 1670 volume belonging to John Lidyat now at the William Andrews Clark Memorial Library. Notes that that volume has no frontispiece but that the format, watermark, and text are identical with the 1670 edition, except in two minor particulars: (1) the title page to *Carmen Deo Nostro* is missing and (2) the original title page has been replaced by a specially printed one. Suggests that Lidyat had the title page altered for presentation purposes.

◄§ 405. Hodgkin, John. "Luigi Cornaro and Nicholas Ferrar." *TLS*, 28 June, pp. 309–10.

Reply to Francis Hutchinson (entry 407). Denies that Nicholas Ferrar had any literary part to play in the publication of the translation of Lessius's *Hygiasticon* and that Herbert translated Lessius. Claims that the prefatory poem to the translation is by William Crashaw, not Richard. For a reply, see Francis Hutchinson (entry 406).

◄§ 406. Hutchinson, Francis. "Luigi Cornaro and Nicholas Ferrar." *TLS*, 6 July, pp. 321–22.

Reply to John Hodgkin (entry 405). Agrees with Hodgkin that Nicholas Ferrar should not be associated with the translation of Lessius's *Hygiasticon*; notes that he originally claimed that Herbert had translated only the first treatise of Cornaro, not Lessius; and corrects Hodgkin, who falsely suggested that William Crashaw, not Richard, was the author of the prefatory poem.

◄§ 407. ———. "Luigi Cornaro." *TLS*, 7 June, p. 273.

Points out that the first of Cornaro's *Discorsi della vita sobria* was introduced to English readers in a small volume of 1634 "which had Nicholas Ferrar for editor, George Herbert for translator, and Richard Crashaw to commend its theme with his prefatory verses." States that Ferrar consulted Herbert about printing a treatise by Lessius of Louvain (*The Right Course of Preserving Health to Extream Old Age*) and that Herbert approved and suggested Cornaro's tract be added. A third treatise by an anonymous Italian on dieting was added, thus making up the volume *Hygiasticon*. See also John Hodgkin (entry 405) and Francis Hutchinson (entry 406).

1918

◄§ 408. Anon. "Crashaw's 'The Invitation.'" *DubR* 162 (January):130–33.

Reproduces the 1652 version of "Letter to the Countess of Denbigh," without notes or commentary, and a Latin version of the poem by R. K. at Farnborough Abbey "in retreat for his own reconciliation" to the Catholic Church (p. 132).

◄§ 409. Olivero, Federico. "Richard Crashaw," in *Nuovi saggi di letteratura inglese*, 277–82. Turin: Libreria Editrice Internazionale.

Presents an appreciative evaluation of Crashaw's poetry. Suggests that "la grande primavera poetica del secolo XVII vide sbocciare uno de' suoi ultimi e più ardenti fiori nella lirica di Richard Crashaw" and claims that "nè George Herbert, nè Henry Vaughan, e neppur il Milton nelle sue liriche religiose, raggiunge il suo slancio lirico e la sua sfolgorante fantasia" (p. 277). Praises "The Flaming Heart" and suggests that "A Hymn to Sainte Teresa" "si svolge come una stola di sontuoso tessuto, di broccato purpureo a grandi fiorami d'oro; ed un vivo sentimento irradia della sua luce pura ed intensa questa ricca messe di immagini" (p. 279). Suggests that Crashaw's poetry could be compared to the paintings of Fra Angelico and Taddeo Gaddi. Applaudes Crashaw's abilities as a translator of both Italian and Latin and notes his skill as a Latin poet. Points out Crashaw's influence on Coleridge, Shelley, Tennyson, Francis Thompson, Swinburne, Coventry Patmore, and Lionel Johnson.

◄§ 410. Quiller-Couch, Arthur. "Some Seventeenth Century Poets," in *Studies in Literature*, 96–167. New York: G. P. Putnam's Sons; Cambridge: University Press.

Reprinted, 1922, 1926.

Notes Crashaw's "excesses of verbal conceit" and some of the "flagrancies" of "The Weeper" yet maintains that "too much has been made of them" (p. 164). As proof of Crashaw's poetic excellence, points to stanza 8 of "The Weeper" ("The deaw no more will weep"), lines 57–65 of "A Hymn to Sainte Teresa," and several stanzas from "Hymn in the Holy Nativity."

◄§ 411. Shafer, Robert. "Free Verse in Crashaw," in *The English Ode to 1660: An Essay in Literary History*, 145–49. Princeton: Princeton University Press; London: Humphrey Milford, Oxford University Press.

Reprinted, New York: Haskell House; New York: Gordian Press, 1966.
Denies the notion that Crashaw's use of irregular verse was influenced by
Cowley and maintains that, "in view of the friendship existing between the
two men, it appears certain that Cowley knew Crashaw's poetry and that, in
respect of irregular verse, any influence between the two must have been from
Crashaw to Cowley" (p. 146). Discusses Crashaw's uses of irregular verse in
"The Flaming Heart," "Hymn to the Name of Jesus," "Hymn in the Glorious
Epiphanie," "Charitas Nimia," "Sancta Maria Dolorum," "Adoro Te," "Hymn
in the Assumption," "Ode on a Prayer-book," and "To [Mrs. M. R.] Councel
Concerning her Choise."

1919

◄§ 412. Lowes, John Livingston. "The Hardening of Conventions, and Revolt," in *Convention and Revolt in Poetry*, 134–79. Boston and New
York: Houghton Mifflin Co.
Reprinted frequently.
Attacks "The Weeper" as "merely originality gone astray, seduced and obsessed by the mania for novelty at any cost" (p. 155) and suggests that Crashaw
"lets himself go in a wild flight after new images" (p. 153) so that the total
effect is "as if a lunatic had propounded a series of conundrums" (p. 154).
Praises, however, the "splendid lines" of the closing of "The Flaming Heart"
(p. 155).

◄§ 413. [Margoliouth, H. M.] "Marvell and Other Contemporaries." *Saturday Review* (London) 128 (19 July): 55–56.
Notes the "boom in publication" (p. 55) that occurred immediately following the English Civil War, including much of the work of Crashaw. Suggests
that Crashaw had little influence on Marvell, except perhaps "a hint of phraseology" (p. 55) in "Eyes and Tears."

◄§ 414. Massingham, H[arold] J., ed. A *Treasury of Seventeenth-Century
English Verse from the Death of Shakespeare to the Restoration (1616–
1660)*. Chosen and edited by H. J. Massingham. (Golden Treasury Series.) London: Macmillan. xxiii, 399p.
Reprinted, with slight revisions, 1920.
In the introduction surveys English poetry from 1616 to 1660, a period said
to contain "the largest collection of mystical verse in the language" (p. xiii),
and asserts that Crashaw was "so haunted by the feminine spirit that he fuses
heavenly ecstasy and spiritual adoration with erotic passion" (p. xviii). Includes, completely or in part, six secular and five sacred poems by Crashaw
(pp. 52–68) with notes (pp. 330–32). Suggests that Crashaw is as "liable to
lapses into 'slippery blisses,' as Keats is" and that the "foreign, Southern voluptuous element in him . . . is totally unlike the Elizabethan and Caroline tem-

per, masculine (except in the pastoral) at its best and worst" (p. 330). Observes that Crashaw's faults are "a gawdy colouring, an indirect over-consciousness of sex and teazing out an idea until it crumbles to dust" but that "colour and heat are the twin glories of Crashaw" (p. 331). Maintains that Crashaw is "rarely tender . . . not because he is too harsh, but too soft and rich" (p. 331). Suggests that the "simple majesty" of "Charitas Nimia" "is all pure light" but claims that "one can grow tired of Crashaw simply because he is always letting one down" (p. 331).

◄§ 415. Osmond, Percy H. "Crashaw and Beaumont," in *The Mystical Poets of the English Church*, 112–40. London: SPCK; New York: Macmillan Co.

Presents a biographical sketch of Crashaw, calling him the "devoutest of poets" (p. 114). Suggests that in his poetry two key words predominate—*blood* and *fire*. Maintains that his pleas for mystical "inebriation" turned some of Crashaw's poems into "spiritual drinking-songs, which find a more exact counterpart in the bacchanalian lays of Mohammedan mysticism," and suggests that for Crashaw the main attraction of Catholicism was the "sensuous splendour of her ceremonial, which not infrequently induces an emotional intoxication" (pp. 119–20). Finds that Crashaw's "piety, his whole cast of mind was essentially Latin" and "it had none of the frigid decorum of Anglicanism" but rather "palpitated with the warmth of more Southern natures" (p. 122). Enumerates the flaws he finds in Crashaw's poetry—its intensity of emotion, the "cheap glitter" of his diction, his "intolerable" conceits, his "meretricious emotionalism" his "convulsive hysteria," and his "limitless hyperbole" but concludes that, in spite of these defects, at its best Crashaw's poetry has "supreme merit" and reflects "the utterance of a pure and unfeigned sanctity" (p. 125). Notes Crashaw's influence on Coleridge, Shelley, Swinburne, Coventry Patmore, and Francis Thompson as well as on his contemporary, Joseph Beaumont.

◄§ 416. Spender, Constance. "Richard Crashaw, 1613–1648. *ContempR* 116:210–15.

Praises Crashaw as "a visionary and a mystic, who possessed the rare gift of translating his ecstasies and flights into a language which can be understood and appreciated by ordinary mortals" (p. 210). Suggests that his "true poetry of the spirit" makes him seem to "belong far more to the nineteenth and twentieth centuries than to the seventeenth century" (p. 210) and sees him as "the most neglected of our really great poets" (p. 212). Suggests that occasionally Crashaw adopts "some of Donne's absurdities of style and language" but claims "they are *not* Crashaw really, and that they fit him very badly, for they are quite unnatural to him" (p. 210). Lauds Crashaw's deep convictions, sincerity, and intensity, "equalled only by Francis Thompson at his best" (p. 211). Expresses particular appreciation of "Hymn in the Holy Nativity,"

"Hymn to the Name of Jesus," and "A Hymn to Sainte Teresa" and notes the influence of St. Teresa and Marino on Crashaw's poetry. Draws attention to Crashaw's incarnational sense, especially reflected in his poems on Christ's birth and epiphany, and his ability as an epigrammatist. Recognizes Crashaw's unevenness, his "grotesque and almost wanton absurdities" (p. 214), but maintains that "nobody could deny to him an extraordinary command of metre and verse" (p. 215). Compares and contrasts Crashaw to Herbert, Vaughan, Cowley, and Browning.

1921

◄§ 417. [Eliot, T. S.] "The Metaphysical Poets." *TLS*, 20 October, pp. 669–70.

Reprinted in *Selected Essays, 1917–1932* (London: Faber & Faber; New York: Harcourt, Brace, and Co., 1932) and in several other collections.

Review of Grierson's *Metaphysical Lyrics & Poems of the Seventeenth Century: Donne to Butler* (entry 420) and response to his discussion of the nature of metaphysical poetry. Argues that "the poets of the seventeenth century, the successors of the dramatists of the sixteenth century, possessed a mechanism of sensibility which could devour any kind of experience" and that "in the seventeenth century a dissociation of sensibility set in, from which we have never recovered; and this dissociation, as is natural, was due to the influence of the two most powerful poets of the century, Milton and Dryden" (p. 669). Maintains that the metaphysical poets were "engaged in the task of trying to find the verbal equivalent for states of mind and feeling" (p. 670). Notes briefly that the devotional poetry of Herbert, Vaughan, and Crashaw was "echoed long after by Christina Rossetti and Francis Thompson" and claims that Crashaw, "sometimes more profound and less sectarian than the others, has a quality which returns through the Elizabethan period to the early Italians" (p. 669). Contrasts Crashaw and Marvell, claiming that it is doubtful if, in the eighteenth century, "could be found two poems in nominally the same metre so dissimilar as Marvell's 'Coy Mistress' and Crashaw's 'Sainte Teresa'; the one producing an effect of great speed by the use of short syllables, and the other an ecclesiastical solemnity by the use of long ones" (p. 669). Concludes that Crashaw, along with Donne, Herbert, Vaughan, Lord Herbert of Cherbury, Marvell, Henry King, and Cowley at his best, is "in the direct current of English poetry" (p. 670). For a reply, see George Saintsbury (entry 421).

◄§ 418. Eliot, T. S. "The Metaphysical Poets." *TLS*, 3 November, p. 716.

Reply to George Saintsbury (entry 421). Suggests that Saintsbury "appears to believe that these poets represent not merely a generation, but almost a particular theory of poetry." Argues that "the 'second thoughts' to which he alludes are, I think, and as I tried to point out, frequent in the work of many other poets besides, of other times and other languages" and notes that he mentioned Chapman and the contemporaries of Dante. Concludes that he does not believe that Shakespeare "was invariably satisfied with 'the first simple, obvious, natural thought and expression of thought.'" For a reply, see George Saintsbury (entry 422).

◄§ 419. Gosse, Edmund. "Metaphysical Poetry." *Sunday Times* (London), 4 December, p. 8.

Reprinted in *More Books on the Table* (London: William Heinemann, 1923), 307–13.

Review of Grierson (entry 420) that mentions Crashaw only briefly, calling him "the transcendental Catholic [who] flings his soul like so much nard and cassia on the altar-flame." Suggests that a feature of religious metaphysical poetry is the application of intense passion to serious meditation and observes that, although "we meet it in all our serious verse, of course, since even the theological aspirations of Herbert and Crashaw may be paralleled in Wither on the one hand and in Charles Wesley and Christina Rossetti on the other," it is primarily "in the poets from Donne to Traherne, covering a space of nearly one hundred years, that we find it expressed with an intensity and a unity of style that we look for in vain elsewhere." Quotes the opening lines of "A Hymn to Sainte Teresa" to illustrate the "passion of piety" found in metaphysical verse.

◄§ 420. Grierson, Herbert J. C., ed. *Metaphysical Lyrics & Poems of The Seventeenth Century: Donne to Butler.* Selected and edited, with an essay by Herbert J. C. Grierson. Oxford: Clarendon Press. lviii, 244p.

Reprinted many times.

Introduction reprinted in *The Background of English Literature* (London: Chatto and Windus, 1925), 115–66.

Pages xiii–xxxviii reprinted in *Seventeenth Century English Poetry: Modern Essays in Criticism*, ed. William Keast (entry 879).

Critical introduction (pp. xiii–lviii); selections from twenty-six poets divided into three major categories: love poems, divine poems, and miscellanies (pp. 1–215); notes (pp. 217–40); and index of first lines (pp. 241–44). By the introduction and the selection of poems, Grierson, in effect, defines the metaphysical school, although he uses the term itself with caution. Maintains, however, that *metaphysical* "lays stress on the right things—the survival, one might say the reaccentuation, of the metaphysical strain, the *concetti metafisici ed ideali* as Testi calls them, in contrast to the simpler imagery of classical poetry, of mediaeval Italian poetry; the more intellectual, less verbal, character of their wit compared with the conceits of the Elizabethans; the finer psychology of which their conceits are often the expression; their learned imagery; the argumentative, subtle evolution of their lyrics; above all the peculiar blend of passion and thought, feeling and ratiocination which is their greatest achievement" (pp. xv–xvi). Focuses the critical discussion on Donne's poetry, considering the other poets primarily in contrast with or in comparison to Donne. Yet warns that "to call these poets the 'school of Donne' or 'metaphysical' poets may easily mislead if one takes either phrase in too full a sense" (p. xxx). Regards English seventeenth-century religious poetry as a high point in the history and development of sacred poetry. Includes from Crashaw "Loves Horoscope," "Wishes. To his (supposed) Mistresse," "Letter to the Countess of Denbigh," "Hymn in the Holy Nativity," "Adoro Te," "The Weeper," and "A Hymn to Sainte Teresa." Notes Crashaw's familiarity with Italian and Spanish poetry, especially that of Marino; suggests the influence of Southwell on his art; and compares and contrasts Crashaw to Herbert, Vaughan, Donne, Vondel, Shelley, and Swinburne. Calls attention to the "radiant spirit" of Crashaw's odes and suggests that they "give the impression at first reading of soaring rockets scattering balls of coloured fire, the 'happy fireworks,' to which he compares Sainte Teresa's writings" (p. xlvi). Maintains that Crashaw's conceits are "more after the confectionery manner of the Italians than the scholastic or homely manner of the followers of Donne" and asserts that "neither spiritual conflict controlled and directed by Christian inhibitions and aspirations, nor mystical yearning for a closer communion with the divine, is the burden of his religious song, but love, tenderness, and joy" (p. xlvi). Suggests that, unlike Herbert, Crashaw is free from self-analysis of his moods and spiritual state and argues that "it is this *opus operatum* in one or other of its aspects or symbols, the Cross, the name of Christ, the Incarnation, the Eucharist, the life of the saint or the death of the martyr, which is the theme of all Crashaw's ardent and coloured, sensuous and conceited odes, composed in irregular rhythms which rise and fall like a sparkling fountain" (p. xlvii). Claims that Crashaw's poetry "has a limited compass of moods" and that his supreme qualities as a lyric poet are "ardour and music" (p. xlvii).

◆§ 421. Saintsbury, George. "The Metaphysical Poets." *TLS*, 27 October, p. 698.

Reply to T. S. Eliot (entry 417). Suggests that when Dryden used the term *metaphysical* in connection with Donne's poetry, he did not equate it with philosophy but rather opposed it to nature. Notes that, in Greek, the word means "second thoughts, things that come *after* the natural first," and suggests that "this definition would . . . fit all the poetry commonly called 'metaphysical,' whether it be amatory, religious, satirical, panegyric, or merely trifling; while 'philosophical,' though of course not seldom suitable enough, sometimes has no relevance whatever," for "these poets always 'go behind' the first, simple, obvious, natural thought and expression of thought." For a reply, see T. S. Eliot (entry 418).

◆§ 422. ———. "The Metaphysical Poets." *TLS*, 10 November, p. 734.

Reply to T. S. Eliot (entry 418). Notes briefly that he agrees with Eliot that, "in the great examples he quotes, and perhaps in all similar things, there *is* 'second thought'" and that he would even go so far as to say that "all true poetry must be in a way second thought, though much second thought is not in any way poetry." Maintains that his main point had been to suggest that in the seventeenth century "the quest of the second thought became direct, deliberate, a business, almost itself a *first* thought."

◄§ 423. Skipton, H. P. K. "Little Gidding and the Nonjurors." CQR 93: 52–67.

Reproduces and briefly comments on an epitaph presumably written for the tomb of Nicholas Ferrar, Jr., found in a seventeenth-century notebook belonging to Edward Almack, and suggests that it may have been written by Crashaw (pp. 59–61). Notes that if the epitaph "was ever inscribed upon the tomb (as it would seem to have been) it was probably torn down by the Puritan desecrators of the church in 1646" (p. 61).

◄§ 424. Thompson, Elbert N. S. "Mysticism in Seventeenth-Century English Literature." SP 18:170–231.

Comments on the enormous popularity of sacred poetry during the seventeenth century and discusses the elements of mysticism in a number of poets and prose writers of the period as well as in a number of their predecessors. Refers to Crashaw only in passing. Notes the Platonic strain in his mysticism, suggests that the mystics' usual attitude toward reason can be discerned in Crashaw's translation of St. Thomas's "Adoro Te," points out his use of the symbolism of human love to define spiritual love, and notes his love of and uses of nature, observing, however, that "his all-absorbing religious passion raised his thought as a rule above such things" (p. 206). Calls "A Hymn to Sainte Teresa" Crashaw's finest poem and "Hymn in the Assumption" his most mystical, offering a brief analysis of the latter. Points out briefly the influence of Crashaw on Coleridge, Pope, Coventry Patmore, and Francis Thompson.

◄§ 425. Woodberry, George Edward. "Notes on the Seventeenth Century Poets: A College Syllabus," in *Studies of a Litterateur*, 137–48. New York: Harcourt, Brace and Co.

Comments on major characteristics of Crashaw's poetry, suggesting that "one should notice in all the verse the spring, the abundance, the unceasing and voluble melody, together with the heat, the suffusion of warmth of passion, the color and clear tone of color throughout, showing the temperament of his genius—all qualities of richness, fluency, beauty, the sensuous side of life subdued to an expression of the ardors of religious emotion and expressing joyousness (in opposition to Puritan and reformers' modes of religious emotion generally)" (pp. 144–45). Suggests that Crashaw is "more the born poet" than any of the other metaphysical poets and "is nearer to the Fletchers and to Milton than they are" (p. 145).

1922

᪂ 426. Confrey, Burton. "A Note on Richard Crashaw." *MLN* 37:250–51.
Presents evidence, primarily from records of the Historical Manuscript Commission and the *Calendar of State Papers* (entries 17, 32, 35, and 276), that supports the claims "of Crashaw's precocity as a poet, of contemporary appreciation of him, of his taking Anglican orders, and an earlier date for his departure for Rome" (p. 250) than heretofore believed.

᪂ 427. Hodgson, Geraldine Emma. "Anglo-Catholic Mystics and Others," in *English Mystics*, 208–72. London: A. R. Mowbray & Co.; Milwaukee: Morehouse Publishing Co.
Suggests that in "A Hymn to Sainte Teresa" and "The Flaming Heart" Crashaw writes "more about a mystic than of a mystic pouring out his own actual experience" (p. 239) and that the two poems seem "no more than the apostrophe of a man, acquainted with mystical literature, contemplating the life of a great mystic" (p. 240). Suggests that in Crashaw's rendering of St. Thomas's "Adoro Te" there is "more resemblance of personal experience" but "that is at least as much due to S. Thomas Aquinas as to Crashaw" (p. 240). Finds in "Ode on a Prayer-book" and "Letter to the Countess of Denbigh" indications that Crashaw had "real direct knowledge, mystical intuition" (p. 240). Briefly compares Crashaw to Vaughan and Traherne, noting that his claims as a mystic "do not lie so near the surface as those of Vaughan and Traherne" (p. 239).

᪂ 428. Loudon, K. M. "Two Mystic Poets: Crashaw and Vaughan," in *Two Mystic Poets and Others Essays*, 1–29. Oxford: Basil Blackwell.
Summarizes Crashaw's life and works and compares and contrasts him with Vaughan as a mystical poet. Finds Crashaw's "extraordinary conceits, far-fetched fancies, and startling paradoxes" so characteristic of the period that "one comes to have a certain liking for them" (p. 13). Praises, in particular, the three Teresian poems, especially the last lines of "The Flaming Heart," and notes Crashaw's "romantic devotion" (p. 14) to the Spanish mystic. Finds several of the epigrams noteworthy, calls "Wishes. To his (supposed) Mistresse" a poem in which Crashaw "shows a very pretty wit," but concludes that "it is as a religious poet that he is best known" (p. 17). Prefers "Hymn in the Holy Nativity" to Milton's "On the Morning of Christ's Nativity," compares Crashaw to Francis Thompson, and contrasts and compares him with Herbert and Marino.

᪂ 429. Massingham, H. J., ed. *Poems About Birds: From the Middle Ages to the Present Day.* Chosen and edited, with an introduction and notes by H. J. Massingham; with a preface by J. C. Squire. New York: E. P. Dutton and Co.; London: T. F. Unwin. 415p.

Includes "Musicks Duell" (pp. 81–86) with notes (p. 372). Calls it "one of the most extraordinary poems in all English literature" and suggests that "for brilliance of execution, intricate handling, and scattered felicities of phrase, it is almost without a rival, and the strategic mastery over masses of raw levies of words is astonishing" (p. 372). Suggests, however, that the poem strikes one as a "display of coloured lights" and that "one feels the artistry, and coldness, the wonder, and the artificiality of it all at once" (p. 372).

◄§ 430. Nethercot, Arthur H. "The Term 'Metaphysical Poets' before Johnson." *MLN* 37:11–17.

Points out that "the use of the term 'metaphysical' in connection with certain poets or with certain types and styles of poetry was far from uncommon in the seventeenth and eighteenth centuries, and that therefore there were various sources from which Johnson might have got the suggestion for his phrase, altho probably the responsibility was mainly Dryden's" (pp. 12–13). Suggests that the earliest use of the term, as applied to poetry, was made by the Italian poet Testi (1593–1646), who, "with Marino especially in mind, defended his preference of classical to Italian models" and referred to "concetti metaphysici" (p. 13). No specific reference to Crashaw.

◄§ 431. Newbolt, Henry. "Richard Crashaw," in *An English Anthology of Prose and Poetry (14th Century-19th Century). Part 2: Notes and Indices,* 33. London and Toronto: J. M. Dent & Sons; New York: E. P. Dutton & Co.

Notes and indexes to Newbolt's *An English Anthology of Prose and Poetry* (London and Toronto: J. M. Dent & Sons; New York: E. P. Dutton, 1921). Maintains that Crashaw "is more definitely inspired at one moment and uninspired at another, than any writer in our collection" and suggests that, although "he has a music and an intensity of religious imagination" that has influenced other poets, "a considerable part of his verse has long since died stifled by its own tawdry verbiage" (p. 33).

◄§ 432. Quinn, John F[rancis], ed. "Richard Crashaw," in *Loyola Book of Verse: With Biographical, Explanatory and Critical Notes,* 85. Chicago: Loyola University Press.

Reprinted, 1925, 1933, 1936.

Anthologizes "Upon Lazarus his Teares" and the conclusion of "The Weeper." In a headnote calls Crashaw "the first great religious poet" but acknowledges that his "striving for effect sometimes mars the beauty of his verse." Claims that Crashaw "gave up prospects of wealth to enter the Catholic church."

◄§ 433. Thompson, A. Hamilton. "The Mystical Element in English Poetry." *E&S* 8:90–108.

Defines mystical poetry and surveys English mystical poets. Calls Crashaw an exception to the English distrust of the contemplative life and mysticism in general that has existed since the Reformation and maintains that "he belonged to the communion in which the mystical habit of mind finds peculiar encouragement" and that "his most enduring verse was inspired by contact with foreign mysticism" (pp. 93–94). Observes that in "The Flaming Heart," Crashaw, like Cowley, toys with "scholastic argument decked out with artificial metaphor" but that, "when at last he strays into the right key, his melody frees itself of all superfluous intricacy, and his expression is direct and noble" (p. 94). Compares Crashaw to Herbert, asserting that, "while Herbert's verse takes its origin from the suggestion of its natural surroundings, Crashaw uses imagery from nature to express an adoration to which time and place are merely an afterthought" (p. 95).

1923

⊸§ 434. Albert, Edward. "The Age of Milton," in A *History of English Literature: A Practical Text-Book*, 159–89. New York: Thomas Y. Crowell Co.

Revised and reprinted many times.

Offers a brief biographical and critical introduction to Crashaw. Maintains that Crashaw represents "the best and the worst" of the metaphysical poets and suggests that "his style at its best is harmonious, precise, and nobly elevated; at its worst it is disfigured by obscurity, perversity, and unseemly images" (p. 171). Quotes lines from "The Flaming Heart" to show "the exalted mood to which his poetry can ascend" and concludes that "at his best he has an energy and triumphant rapture that, outside the poems of Shelley, are rarely equaled in English," but that "at his worst he is shrill, frothy, and conceited" (p. 171).

⊸§ 435. Barker, Francis E. "The Religious Poetry of Richard Crashaw." *CQR* 96:39–65.

Surveys Crashaw's life and religious poetry and points out some of the major influences on his art, especially Marino, St. Teresa, St. John of the Cross, and possibly Southwell. Notes two major reasons for modern neglect of Crashaw—the unevenness of his poetry and the difficulty of his art—and admits that "to read Crashaw for the first time needs an effort" (p. 41). Maintains that the reason for Crashaw's lack of popularity is that "his attitude of mind was one which is rare among Englishmen, including devout Englishmen" (p. 43). Praises Crashaw's epigrams, for the most part, but suggests that their characteristic feature is cleverness. Points out that erotic mysticism and his attraction for the Magdalene and for the more emotional aspects of Christ's Passion are characteristics of the early poems that become more dominant in the later verse. Argues that, since more or perhaps all of the poems in the

1646 volume were written while Crashaw was yet an Anglican, they should be considered apart from his other works, noting, however, that Crashaw's "muse reveals no very marked change on his submission to the Apostolic See" (pp. 46–47). Sees "Sospetto d'Herode" as an improvement on Marino's poem in some respects but argues that "sometimes by plying a brush too full of colour he strayed into the grotesque or the repulsive which Marino had successfully avoided" (p. 49). Suggests that the greatest weakness in "The Weeper" is not its conceits but its lack of unity and maintains that "nowhere else is the reader confronted in anything like the same degree with a mixture of what is exquisitely good and what is appallingly bad" (p. 51). Claims that "Hymn in the Holy Nativity" is "among Crashaw's most successful poems" (p. 52) and praises its tenderness: "Not here are the chill conceits, the meretricious paradoxes which . . . sometimes disfigure his pages" (p. 52). Calls "A Hymn to Sainte Teresa" "unquestionably Crashaw's highest achievement" (p. 57) and suggests some possible sources for the poem, including the autobiography of St. Teresa and the first two verses of the hymn in the Breviary for vespers and lauds for her feast day, the work of Pope Urban VIII. Notes Crashaw's skill in translating the well-known Latin hymns and suggests that, in fact, "they are really more than translations, they are interpretations of the old hymns in the terms of the Seventeenth century" (p. 58). Claims that Crashaw's translation of "Dies Irae Dies Illa" is the earliest translation of the poem into English. Finds "Hymn to the Name of Jesus" too lavish, overly luscious, and too repetitive but notes that it contains many fine images that recall the Spanish mystics. Discusses the mystical elements in Crashaw's poetry but rejects the notion that the poet was, in fact, a mystic. Observes that, on the whole, Crashaw preferred "warm, rich colours, red and purple, to colder shades, and gold to silver" and that "blood and fire were his favourite metaphors" (p. 53).

◆§ 436. Bax, Arnold Edward Trevor. *To the name above every name*, words by Richard Crashaw, composed by Arnold Bax. London: Murdoch. 36p.
Musical setting for "Hymn to the Name of Jesus."

◆§ 437. Crosse, Gordon, ed. *Every Man's Book of Sacred Verse*. London and Oxford: A. R. Mowbray & Co. xi, 265p.
Anthologizes selections from "Charitas Nimia," "To [Mrs. M. R.] Councel Concerning her Choise," and "On St. Peter cutting of Malchus his eare" (pp. 75–81) with brief notes (pp. 233–34). Points out that poems less widely known, but nonetheless characteristic of Crashaw's art, were chosen for inclusion. Reproduces comments by Meynell and Dr. Johnson concerning the use of conceits in seventeenth-century religious verse and gives a biographical note on Crashaw.

◆§ 438. Falls, Cyril [Bentham]. "The Divine Poet." *The Nineteenth Century and After* 93:225–33.

Reprinted in *The Critic's Armoury* (London: Cobden-Sanderson, 1924), 23–28.

Contrasts Crashaw to George Crabbe and maintains that Crashaw "fulfills the conception of the poet as an ethereal being, whose eyes are fixed upon a world that those of grosser vision see not, whose feet scarce touch the clay of this in his passage through it, who shines with a light reflected from divine fires" (p. 225) and sees ecstasy as his foremost characteristic. Notes that Crashaw's mysticism is "not typically English—is, in fact, most un-English," and that therefore he "stands alone, not only among English poets, but among English Catholic mystics" (p. 226). Presents a biographical sketch, surveys Crashaw's poems, and calls him the "most 'metaphysical'" (p. 227) and most "fantastical" (p. 229) of all the metaphysical poets, suggesting that he "appears to owe rather less than these others to Donne and less still to Ben [Jonson]" (p. 227). Comments on foreign influences on Crashaw's art, primarily St. Teresa and the Spanish and Marino and the Italians, from which come "his religious ardour, wherein the divine mingles so strangely with the half-animal, and also that ultra-refinement of 'wit,' that wealth of extravagant metaphor" (pp. 227–28). Suggests that Crashaw's conceits "are more highly coloured than those of Donne" (p. 228), yet praises Crashaw's wit, flamboyancy, subtlety, and sophistication. Presents a brief analysis of "A Hymn to Sainte Teresa," calls it his most famous poem, and suggests that it is interesting "because it contains instances of all Crashaw's qualities without the exaggeration of those qualities displayed in *The Weeper* and other poems" (p. 229). Finds "Wishes. To his (supposed) Mistresse," "Musicks Duell," and "Out of the Italian. A Song (To thy Lover)" fine poems but maintains that these secular pieces are "the mere diversions of a religious mystic" (p. 232). Notes that Crashaw has two types of admirers: religious mystics like him, and those in whom Crashaw arouses "a more tempered and reasoned delight" and that these latter recognize his unevenness, admire his best lines, and rank him among the second order of poets. Compares Crashaw to Strada, John Ford, Ambrose Phillips, Coleridge, and Francis Thompson and suggests that "at his greatest, when borne along by that lyric flood, he becomes for an instant Shelley's kinsman" (p. 233).

⮑ 439. Fausset, Hugh I'Anson. "Idealism and Puritanism," in *Studies in Idealism*, 87–116. London and Toronto: J. M. Dent & Co.; New York: E. P. Dutton & Co.

Considers Crashaw, Herbert, Vaughan, and Traherne as mystical poets and comments on their religious sensibilities. Maintains that they have "all the vision and blindness of saintliness" (p. 99) and should be seen as "pioneers, questing after some region made after the spirit of nature, but not the letter" (p. 101). Mentions Crashaw only in passing, noting that "both Crashaw and Herbert more often improvise intricately on conventional themes or scriptural formulas than express their 'Flaming Hearts,' as Crashaw can, for example, in his 'Nativity Hymn,' entangling the Saviour whom he addresses in an inspired naturalism" (p. 99). Maintains that religious poetry of the period has often "been debased by the composers of hymns," that "it has given many a religious soul comfort and satisfaction," but that "over the development of poetry itself, over the consciousness of educated men, it has exercised but little influence" (p. 112). Concludes that "not until the end of the nineteenth century was the same tone of religious ecstasy to be enriched by the 'still sad music of humanity' in the person of one who had suffered as an outcast, and walked the pavements of the world in want—by Francis Thompson" (p. 112).

❧ 440. Kobinata, Teijiro. *Eibungaku-shi* [A History of English Literature]. Kyoto: Bunken shoin.
Discusses Crashaw's religious poetry and sensibility (pp. 454–57). Praises in particular "Hymn in the Holy Nativity" and briefly compares it to Milton's Nativity Ode. Quotes lines from "The Weeper" as an example of excellent religious verse. Finds Crashaw's sensual imagery and elaborate conceits somewhat excessive but attributes these extravagances to Crashaw's unusually keen sensibility.

❧ 441. Martin, L. C. "An Hitherto Unpublished Poem by (?) Richard Crashaw." *Merc* 8:159–66.
Suggests that a twelve-stanza poem entitled "Epithalamium" found in the British Library (MS Harleian 6917) is by Crashaw, basing his proof primarily upon internal evidence, and presents an edition of the poem with footnotes. Speculates that the poem was written by Crashaw on the occasion of the marriage of Sir John Bramston the younger (1611–1700) to Alice Abdy in 1635 and notes many parallels in the uses of prosody, phraseology, images, abstract plurals, and so on, between the poem and other known works by Crashaw.

❧ 442. ———. "Richard Crashaw." *Merc* 7:417.
Announces that he is preparing an edition of Crashaw's poems and asks for information on early manuscripts relevant to Crashaw's poems or biography. Specifically asks for information on copies of *Richardi Crashawi Poemata et Epigrammata* (1674) and *Steps to the Temple* (3d ed.), London: Printed for Richard Bentley et al. For a reply see S. C. Roberts (entry 445).

❧ 443. ———. "Richard Crashaw." *Merc* 8:414.
Reply to S. C. Roberts (entry 445). Notes that the copy of *Richardi Crashawi Poemata et Epigrammata* (1674) that Roberts points out "has only just been presented to the University Library at Cambridge, in view of the attention which was called to its rarity."

❧ 444. Monaghan, John. "Two Poets Went Over to Bethlehem." *CathW* 118:381–83.
Contrasts the Catholic vision and sensibility of "Hymn in the Holy Nativity"

with the Puritan temperament reflected in Milton's Nativity Ode and suggests that there is in Crashaw's poem "a warmth of feeling that is utterly absent from Milton" (p. 382). Claims that "the Protestant goes over to Bethlehem to visit a poor relation who happens to be God" whereas "the Catholic is abashed in Bethlehem that he has so impoverished God" (p. 381) and sees this difference in attitude reflected in the two poems. Suggests that Milton's poem, though a magnificent work of art, centers its attention on the poet and his reflections, whereas Crashaw's hymn focuses almost exclusively on the person of Christ. Concludes that "the pagans would have understood Milton" but "only a Catholic comprehends Crashaw" (p. 383).

◀§ 445. Roberts, S[ydney] C. "Richard Crashaw." *Merc* 8:187.
Reply to L. C. Martin (entry 442). Calls attention to a copy of *Richardi Crashawi Poemata et Epigrammata* in the University Library, Cambridge. Notes that the copy is described as "'Editio secunda, auctior et emendator' and would appear to be the edition of 1670 with a cancel title-page." For a reply, see L. C. Martin (entry 443).

◀§ 446. Scott, Cyril Meir. *Nativity hymn (Crashaw), for chorus, soli, and orchestra.* London: Stainer and Bell. 67p.
Musical setting of "Hymn in the Holy Nativity."

◀§ 447. Williams, I. A. "Bibliographical Notes and News." *Merc* 7:411–414.
Calls attention to a version of Crashaw's "An Epitaph upon a Young Married Couple" found in a collection entitled *New Miscellaneous Poems*, published in 1731 by A. Bettesworth and C. Hitch (entry 72). The poem, entitled "An Epitaph on Alcander, and Julietta his Wife who died in one another's Arms, two Days after Marriage," is ascribed to an unidentified "R. S." Suggests that, on the whole, the revised version of the poem is better than Crashaw's original and questions if the second poem might be a revision made by Crashaw himself.

1924

◀§ 448. Chalmers, [Robert]. "Richard Crashaw: 'Poet and Saint,' Fellow of Peterhouse from 22 Nov. 1635 to 8 April 1644," in *In Memoriam Adolphus William Ward, Master of Peterhouse (1900–1924)*, 47–67. Cambridge: University Press.
Presents a biographical sketch of Crashaw, noting especially his connections with Peterhouse and describing his life as "the faithful counterpart of his verse" (p. 47). Briefly surveys his poetry. Notes that all of Crashaw's epigrams are based on the New Testament and "practically all on the Gospels or Acts,— none being derived from Pauline sources" (p. 51) and suggests that his Latin epigrams are not particularly distinguished but are superior to his Greek ones.

Finds his Latin secular poems only "good," points out that in time Crashaw abandoned both Latin poetry and secular verse for sacred poetry, but claims that "his secular muse has proved the more enduring supporter of his poetic fame" and that many lovers of poetry "deplore the undivided allegiance finally bestowed on religious poetry" (p. 58). Maintains that it is hopeless to determine the exact date of individual religious poems but notes that, "intrinsically, they all form a single series; the same thought and the same feeling, though with varying success of workmanship, run through the whole of them and stamp them with a unity unbroken by change of creed and unwavering in outlook" (p. 57). Cites several secular and religious poems "to let Crashaw illustrate himself" (p. 65). Suggests that, "marred though it is by the grotesque imagery of stanzas 19 and 21, 'The Weeper' remains, alike in its exuberance of expression and in its delicacy of spiritual aspiration, perhaps the most typical poem Crashaw ever wrote" (p. 63). Suggests that today, "without either apologetics or condemnation, Crashaw's passage to Rome is seen to have been—for him—an inevitable development" (p. 67).

◄§ 449. Legouis, É[mile], and L[ouis] Cazamian. "La poésie de 1625 à 1660," in *Histoire de la littèrature anglaise*, 531–57. Paris: Librairie Hachette.

Translated into English by Helen Douglas Irvine (New York: Macmillan, 1926).

Surveys Crashaw's life and poetry (pp. 542–44). Notes that, in addition to being influenced by classical models, Crashaw added those of Spain and Italy "dont la couleur, l'exaltation, la mélodie l'enchantment, et, non moins que ces chaudes qualités du Midi, les extravagantes préciosités d'un Marini ou les ardeurs des mystiques espagnols" (p. 542). Praises "Musicks Duell," claiming that "jamais le vers anglais ne montra plus grande virtuosité que dans l'analyse que fait Crashaw des trilles de l'oiseau" (p. 542). Praises "Wishes. To his (supposed) Mistresse" as having "un rhythme unique et d'une verve verbale prestigiouse" but maintains that is it in his sacred verse that Crashaw achieves his mark. Comments specifically on "The Weeper" and, while recognizing its excesses, claims that "les plus cruels affronts au goût alternent avec d'admirables visions de poète" (p. 543). Suggests that Crashaw's most magnificent hymn is "The Flaming Heart," observing that "l'élan d'amour sacré qui termine cet hymne est peut-être ce qu'a produit de plus ardent la poésie religieuse anglaise" (p. 543). Compares Crashaw briefly to Herbert and notes that "moins intellectuel que Herbert, moins simple et précis de langage, il a plus de chaleur, de couleur et d'harmonie" (pp. 543–44). Concludes that "pour l'élan lyrique il n'a d'éqal que Shelley" and that "par l'etangeté, l'obscuritié, les lueurs qui les traversent, l'imprécision parfois charmante et toujours mélodieuse du style, ses poésie ont une analogie curieuse avec celles des meilleurs symbolistes" (p. 544).

◆§ 450. Nethercot, Arthur H. "The Reputation of the 'Metaphysical Poets' During the Seventeenth Century." *JEGP* 23:173–98.

Considers separately the reputations of Donne, Cowley, Cleveland, Carew, Herbert, Crashaw, Vaughan, and Quarles during the seventeenth century. Also discusses Dryden's critical comments on the metaphysicals and gives a brief account of the shifting literary tastes of the Restoration, which account, in part, for the decline of interest in the metaphysical poets. Notes that, in the seventeenth century, "it was always Crashaw the religious poet who was admired or blamed (altho usually the blame was represented merely by silence)" and that his secular poems "were seldom mentioned" (p. 188). Mentions specifically the critical comments of John Bargrave, William Prynne, Clement Barksdale, Edward Phillips, and William Winstanley. Concludes that "to some Anglican readers Crashaw was thus notorious because of his conversion to Roman Catholicism" and that he "was not so widely known as Herbert, altho often linked with him, but was usually praised for his religious fervor, his wit, and his smoothness" (p. 189). Suggests that the decline of interest in Crashaw as the century progressed is evidenced in the dwindling number of editions that appeared after the Restoration.

◆§ 451. Reeves, Jeremiah Bascom. *The Hymn as Literature.* New York and London: Century Co. 369p.

Comments briefly on "A Song ('Lord, when the sense of thy sweet grace')," noting that "however devout its aim, its style is too fulsome for a hymn," and on "Hymn to the Name of Jesus," calling it "an example of personal particularization the like of which is not possible in a good hymn" (p. 104) and suggesting that "probably not one other person would either feel or have any interest in the doubt as to whether one might address his soul by the name of soul" (p. 105).

◆§ 452. Schirmer, Walter F[ranz]. *Antike, Renaissance und Puritanismus: Eine Studie zur englischen Literaturgeschichte des 16. und 17. Jahrhunderts.* Munich: Max Hueber. ix, 233p.

2d ed., 1933.

Briefly discusses the element of erotic mysticism in the metaphysical poets and finds this spirit completely antithetical to Puritan sensibility. Notes that Crashaw saw ritual and liturgy as vehicles for approaching God more closely and points out the mystical element in his love of religious ceremony. Notes that Crashaw "sah mit Verachtung auf Homer und Horaz" (pp. 182–83).

1925

᪥ 453. Duckett, Eleanor Shipley. *Catullus in English Poetry*. (Smith College Classical Studies, no. 6.) Northampton, Mass.: Smith College. 199p.

Suggests that two of Crashaw's poems echo or are adaptations of Catullus's *Carmina*: "Out of Catullus" (*Carmina*, 5) and "The Teare" (*Carmina*, 66, lines 1–14).

᪥ 454. [Eliot, T. S.]. "An Italian Critic on Donne and Crashaw." *TLS*, 17 December, p. 878.

Essentially a favorable review of Mario Praz's *Secentismo e Marinismo in Inghilterra* (1925). Calls Crashaw "one of our poets who is the most deeply saturated in Italian and Spanish influences." Suggests that Praz is "better fitted than most of our English critics to appreciate the enormous influence during the first half of the seventeenth century of the Society of Jesus" and maintains that Crashaw had read the Jesuit poets. Notes Praz's high estimate of Crashaw and his view that, "as Italy expressed the period supremely in architecture, in the Baroque, so Crashaw expresses the Baroque supremely in verse." Notes that Praz translated numerous passages from both Crashaw and Donne in his study but points out that "it is notable how much more stoutly Donne survives translation into Italian than does the more feminine virtue of Crashaw."

᪥ 455. Lea, Kathleen M. "Conceits." *MLR* 20:389–406.

Discusses the nature and development of the conceit and contrasts the Elizabethans and the metaphysicals. Maintains that "for the most part we may say that the besetting sin of the Elizabethans was the over-emphasis of the simile, the tendency to digress upon the comparisons," while "the 'metaphysical' poet regarded the simile as useful, not as an ornamental, device: and the conceits of their poetry were due to under-emphasis" (p. 398). Calls Crashaw "a poet of extravagance" (p. 402) and "the last martyr for the poetical heresy of the conceit" (p. 406). Sees in Crashaw "an irregular, dangerous energy that set fire to the smouldering conceits of his contemporaries" and suggests that "he gave spiritual advice with the exaggeration of worldly compliment" and "made songs not to his Mistress' eye-brow, but to the tears of the Magdalene, in which as he exceeded the sonneteers in fervour, so he outstripped them in conceit" (p. 402). Calls "The Weeper" "beyond disgust" and claims that "it moves us to laughter" (p. 402). Sees Crashaw's genius as "a startling blend of Elizabethan exuberance, Jacobean mysticism, and that love of compression and intellectual point which distinguishes the poets of the Restoration" and maintains that "there is no question of following his thought: we see his meaning on the instant or not at all" (p. 403). Asserts that "from first to last he was an Epigrammatist" and "was gripped by certain conceits" (p. 403). Stresses Crashaw's tendency to contract metaphors until the sense is "barely intelligible" (p. 403) and insists that "he was hardly content with a thought until he had found that angle from which its paradox might be seen; nor was he satisfied with that expression of this thought which did not pack pun and metaphor into an antithetical couplet as neatly as possible" (p. 404). Regards Crashaw's use of "contracted conceits" as something new and shows how he extended this technique even to his use of words, such as *star-paved*, *sweet-lip'd*, and *silver-guarded*. Maintains that Crashaw used words almost "ritualistically and in a colourless sense of his own" (p. 405). Briefly compares and contrasts him with Herbert, Dryden, Webster, and Meredith.

◈§ 456. Leslie, [John Randolph] Shane, comp. *An Anthology of Catholic Poets*. London: Burns, Oates & Washbourne; New York: Macmillan. xv, 371p.
Anthologizes "Luke 2. Quaerit Jesum Suum Maria," "A Hymn to Sainte Teresa," "Hymn in the Holy Nativity," and six epigrams (pp. 217–28), without notes or commentary. Briefly mentions in the introduction that "Catholic royalism was lit by the seraphic Crashaw" (p. 9). Points out that Crashaw "touched Catholic imagery at its best and its worst," calling his image of St. Teresa "chyrselephantine in its beauty of ivory and gold" and noting that his weeping Mary Magdalene is "worse than maudlin" (pp. 9–10).

◈§ 457. Nethercot, Arthur H. "The Reputation of the 'Metaphysical Poets' During the Age of Johnson and the 'Romantic Revival.'" *SP* 22:81–132.
Surveys critical attitudes toward the metaphysical poets (especially Crashaw, Donne, Carew, Cowley, Cleveland, Vaughan, and Quarles) during the eighteenth century (1744–1800) and the early nineteenth century. Notes that in the eighteenth century the center of discussion was Cowley, rather than Donne, Herbert, Crashaw, or the others, and that the notion of a "school of metaphysical poets" was not generally recognized before Johnson. Points out that Johnson does not classify either Crashaw or Herbert as a metaphysical poet and surveys Johnson's comments and discusses his importance in shaping critical opinion during the remainder of the eighteenth century. Treats briefly the interest of the early Romantics in the metaphysical poets.

◈§ 458. ———. "The Reputation of the 'Metaphysical Poets' During the Age of Pope." *PQ* 4:161–79.
Summarizes early eighteenth-century attitudes toward the metaphysical poets. Suggests that, "in spite of the wide and continued diffusion of the Metaphysical taste through the early decades of the eighteenth century, readers and critics soon developed the reaction which had been indicated by the later seventeenth century, so that before many years scarcely any one dared admit himself an unswerving admirer of the Metaphysical writers," and that many of the metaphysical poets "were becoming neglected or else forgotten, although the more important ones still retained a reputation for certain qualities or

types of work" (p. 176). Points out that Cowley was the best known of the metaphysical poets, "thus showing that the populace does not always follow the verdict of the professional critics" (p. 177). Notes in particular Pope's comments on Crashaw and erroneously claims that there were no editions of Crashaw published in the eighteenth century.

⋘ 459. Praz, Mario. *Secentismo e Marinismo in Inghilterra: John Donne— Richard Crashaw*. Florence: Società An. Editrice «La Voce.» xii, 294p.
  Crashaw section issued under separate cover, with revisions, as *Richard Crashaw* (entry 669).
  Richard Crashaw reprinted with a selection of Crashaw's poems in English as an appendix (Rome: Mario Bulzoni—Editore Libreria «Richerche», 1964), 231p.
  Abridged English version, "The Flaming Heart: Richard Crashaw and the Baroque," in *The Flaming Heart: Essays on Crashaw, Machiavelli, and Other Studies in the Relations between Italian and English Literature from Chaucer to T. S. Eliot*, Doubleday Anchor Books (Garden City: Doubleday & Co., 1958; reprinted, New York: Norton, 1973), 204–63.
  Two separate studies in one volume: "John Donne" (pp. 3–141) and "Richard Crashaw" (pp. 145–283), with a preface (pp. ix–xii) and a bibliography of primary and secondary sources (pp. 287–94). Traces the biography of each poet, analyzes and translates into Italian several of the major poems, and shows how each poet is related to the general European movement variously known as Marinism, Gongorism, or the secentismo. Contrasts Donne and Crashaw: "in John Donne nervosa virile passionalità, attitudini speculative e metafisiche, sete d'azione e di sapere che cerca tormentosamente di placarsi in una fede fatta più d'introspezione e di timore, che di spontanea devozione, culminando in drammatici sermoni; in Richard Crashaw entusiasmo contemplativo, estatico e femmineo, tutto pervaso da una sensuale morbidezza, attitudini spiccatamente artistiche, che fanno di questo poeta un musico e un pittore in potenza, e una religione di sentimento ingenua e adorante, che esplode in inni festosi" (pp. xi–xii). Regards Donne as an example of "Seicento ingegnoso" and Crashaw as "uno dei più caratteristici esponenti del Seicento sensuale" (p. xii). Surveys the flamboyant, triumphal spirituality and erotic, mystical religious sensibility of the Counter-Reformation, especially as exemplified in devotion to female saints, the Virgin Mary, and the martyrs, as background for the religious sympathies of Crashaw, suggesting that, although he was the son of a Puritan, antipapist father, his soul was that of a "naturaliter catholica" (p. 151). The first part of the study (pp. 151–217) presents a detailed biography of Crashaw, outlines the political and religious climate of England in the early seventeenth century, and broadly surveys Crashaw's poetry and influences on his art, primarily from a biographical viewpoint. The second part (pp. 219–83) surveys prevalent aesthetical attitudes and mental processes of seventeenth-century European poets, discuss-

ing in some detail the uses of wit and the conceit. Comments on Crashaw's epigrams and "The Weeper" to show the influence of various Continental poets on Crashaw's art, especially the Jesuit and Marinist poets. Argues that "The Weeper" "non è infatti altro che un rosario di epigrammi o di madrigali malamente legati assieme, senza sviluppo" and maintains that "l'unità non è il poema, ma la stanza: il madrigali, l'epigramma; come accade nella collana di madrigali sulla *Maddalena ai piedi di Cristo* del Marino, che forse suggeri lo schema e qualche particolarità del movimento" (pp. 231–32). Suggests that "The Teare" was a first sketch of "The Weeper"; notes the influence of several Latin poets on the poem, especially Rémond, Cabilliau, and John Owen; and maintains that the poem lacks "il senso di un punto centrale attorno à cui il poema graviti in un armonia di parti" (p. 237). Sees "The Weeper," however, as fully representative of secentismo poetry as reflected not only in the works of the poets themselves but also in the theorists of the time, especially Tesauro and Pierfrancesco Minozzi. Praises Crashaw's translations from Latin and Italian as well as his paraphrases of the psalms; compares "Sospetto d'Herode" to Marino's *La Strage degli'Innocenti* to show that often Crashaw's version is more dramatic and contains more effective images than the original; and discusses a number of poems, especially "Musicks Duell" and "Bulla" to show how Crashaw's poems reflect a baroque sensibility. Finds Crashaw more baroque than Marino, suggests that Crashaw's poetry "rappresenta in letteratura, in minore proporzioni, quello che le apoteosi di un Rubens, i languori di un Murillo e le estasti di un Greco rappresentano in pittura" (p. 271), and gives examples of similarities between Crashaw's poetry and the work of these artists. Concludes by praising the mystical rapture in Crashaw's Teresian poems and says of "The Flaming Heart" "non v'è in tutta la letteratura del Seicento espressione più alta di quello spiritualizzamento del senso che qui si compendia in un miracoloso e vertiginoso ascendere d'immagini travolte e infocate" and that the concluding lines of the poem "sembrano contenere *in nuce* l'essenza di tutto il Seicento" (p. 283). Throughout compares Crashaw to his contemporaries as well as to certain nineteenth-century poets, especially Shelley and Swinburne.

1926

◄§ 460. Carver, George, ed. "Richard Crashaw," in *The Catholic Tradition in English Literature*, 110–36. Garden City: Doubleday, Page, & Co.

A biographical sketch of Crashaw followed by selections from his poems, without notes or commentary, including "Hymn to the Name of Jesus," "Hymn in the Glorious Epiphanie," "Dies Irae Dies Illa," "The Weeper," "A Hymn to Sainte Teresa," and "The Flaming Heart." Suggests that the writings of St. Teresa were "one of the most powerful agencies in his final adoption of Catholicism" (p. 110). Claims that Crashaw's place "is an honored one in English literature" and concludes, "mystical, intense, learned in the scholarship

of his day, destined to a life of suffering, it was inevitable that when he turned
to poetry for surcease he should achieve distinction" (p. 111).

✥§ 461. Eleanore, Sister M. "Crashaw the Mystic." *Commonweal* 4:243.
    Defines mysticism as "the intercourse of the Christlike soul with God" and
suggests that it is not to be confused, therefore, with "ecstasy and miraculous
power and other things supernatural." Finds Crashaw's presentation of St.
Teresa in his poems a "perfect expression of mysticism" and commends
Crashaw's vision of spiritual reality, which is briefly contrasted with the perspective of the imagist poets. Notes Francis Thompson's charge that Crashaw
lacks "the human and household emotions" and explains, partly through
Crashaw's biography, that he "had little opportunity to acquire the human and
household emotions" but that "with a heart burning with unsatisfied desires
for sympathetic and understanding love, the poet could but throw himself
wildly and abandonly into the Arms and upon the Heart that always responds
to the feeblest love." Notes that Crashaw, though a contemplative, cannot be
charged with quietism and stresses that his mysticism is "sane and true" because it is grounded in the Gospels. Calls the closing lines of "The Flaming
Heart" "the distilled essence of Crashaw's mysticism."

✥§ 462. [Eliot, T. S.] "The Author of 'The Burning Babe.'" *TLS*, 29 July,
    p. 508.
    Review of Christobel Hood's *The Book of Robert Southwell* (Oxford: Black-
well, 1926). Suggests that, although different as men, Southwell's poetry fore-
shadows to some extent Crashaw's but observes that he "never has the intensity nor the perversity of metaphor of Crashaw." Points out that Southwell's
translation of "Lauda Sion" is "more faithful to the spirit of the medieval
Latin verse" than is Crashaw's rendering in "Vexilla Regis." Observes that, in
general, the reader of Southwell's verse feels "that fusion or confusion of feeling of human and divine, that transposition of human sentiment to divine
objects which characterizes the religious verse of the sixteenth and seventeenth centuries, in contrast to that of the thirteenth century, in which the
distinctions of feeling towards human objects and divine objects are preserved," citing Crashaw's treatment of St. Teresa and Mary Magdelene as the
best examples in English of the fusion or confusion.

✥§ 463. Eliot, T. S. "Lectures on the Metaphysical Poetry of the Seventeenth
    Century With Special Reference to Donne, Crashaw, and Cowley De-
    livered at Trinity College, Cambridge."
    Unpublished manuscripts of eight lectures (now at Houghton Library, Har-
vard University). In Lecture 1 notes that many poets of the 1920s are often
compared to Donne or to Crashaw and points out that Dr. Johnson did not
include Crashaw in his well-known *Lives of the Poets*. In Lecture 2 notes the
influence of St. Teresa on Crashaw as well as Crashaw's influence on Pope,

especially on "Heloise to Abelard." In Lecture 3 distinguishes between two kinds of mysticism, Artistotelian (classic or ontological) and Spanish (romantic or psychological) and sees Crashaw as participating in the latter tradition, along with the Jesuits: In Lecture 4 discusses the language and wit of metaphysical poetry, especially the use of conceits, and notes that Crashaw is Italianate and thus different from Donne. Lecture 5 is devoted to Donne, while Lecture 6 is devoted to Crashaw. Contrasts Donne and Crashaw, finding Crashaw less parochial and more European than Donne, and notes the influences of St. Teresa and the Spanish mystics, the Jesuits, and the Italian poets, especially Marino. Suggests that Crashaw's poetry has more feeling than thought and contrasts his feminine devotional spirit with Donne's more masculine, theological spirit. Also contrasts the blending of human and divine love in both Crashaw and St. Teresa with Dante's awareness that the two kinds of love are distinct and cannot be exchanged without distortion of both. Contrasts Dante's intellectual order with Crashaw's intellectual disorder, regards Crashaw as a voluptuary of religious emotion, and notes his piling of emotions one on top of another, a kind of sensationalism that simply allows one emotion to follow another, rather than a structuring of emotions, one building on another. Compares and contrasts "The Weeper" and "The Teare" and finds "The Teare" somewhat grotesque and hideous but with a strange beauty about it. Compares and contrasts Crashaw with Shelley and Swinburne, poets who often failed to observe the natural connection between thought and feeling. Notes that, typical of Crashaw, "Wishes. To his (supposed) Mistresse" is to a "supposed," not a real, mistress. Sees "A Hymn to Sainte Teresa" and "The Flaming Heart" as Crashaw's most distinguished and least artificial poems and praises their rhythm, unaffected diction, and sensual religious intensity. Suggests that Crashaw's conceits are less extended, more rhythmical, less intellectual, and yet more violent and artificial than Donne's. Argues that Crashaw, for all his differences from Donne, is a genuine metaphysical poet and maintains that even more than Herbert, Vaughan, or Traherne he unifies thought and feeling, although he achieves this union in a way far different from Dante or Donne. Lecture 7 is devoted primarily to Cowley but comments in passing on Crashaw. Notes that Crashaw, unlike Donne, had little influence on the style of later seventeenth-century poets but did introduce a Spanish mood into English poetry that degenerated into sentimentality in the later eighteenth century. Repeats his earlier observations that Crashaw is a genuine metaphysical poet and that he applies human emotion to religious objects. Lecture 8 deals with LaForgue and Corbiere. Briefly compares and contrasts Crashaw with both, noting that whereas Donne essentially expresses thought that is finally apprehended by the emotion, Crashaw primarily expresses feeling that is transformed into thought.

◄§ 464. Hamilton, George Rostrevor. "Wit and Beauty: A Study of Metaphysical Poetry." *Merc* 14:606–20.

Points out that "conditions were in some ways more favourable to meta-physical poetry in the last decades of the Victorian age than in the early seventeenth century" (p. 620). Discusses Francis Thompson's work as a more perfect realization of metaphysical poetry than the poetry of either Crashaw or Donne. Calls "Upon two greene Apricockes sent to Cowley by Sir Crashaw" "a metaphysical play on the idea of autumn," simple "complimentary wit" (p. 607), and "trivial lines" (p. 613). Compares and contrasts Crashaw to Donne and, disagreeing with Francis Thompson's suggestion that Crashaw, not Donne, is most representative of metaphysical poetry, finds that Donne had "by far the more powerful metaphysical wit, and the wider range of imagination" (p. 613). Maintains that Crashaw's imagery "is lacking both in variety and subtlety" and that his distinctive excellence is "a lyrical fervour which is not a metaphysical quality at all" (p. 613), a kind of fervor that anticipates Shelley.

◆§ 465. Newbolt, Henry. "Some Devotional Poets in the Seventeenth Century," in *Studies in Green and Gray*, 277–88. London, Edinburgh, New York: Thomas Nelson.

Reprinted as the introduction to *Devotional Poets of the Seventeenth Century* (London and Edinburgh: Thomas Nelson & Sons, 1929), xi–xxi.

Very general essay on devotional poetry of the seventeenth century. Offers a biographical sketch of Crashaw, calls his taste for conceits "unfortunate," and suggests that his temperament was "wholly alien from Herbert's" (p. 282). Maintains that in "The Weeper" Crashaw "uses images with such crude and puerile absurdity as to combine lack of reverence with lack of humour" (p. 282) and finds it incredible that the same poet wrote "Hymn in the Holy Nativity" and "Dies Irae Dies Illa," the latter of which "inspired the music of Blake's most original lyric" ["The Tyger"] and Cust's "ardently sincere poem "Non Nobis" (p. 283). Concludes that Herbert, Vaughan, Traherne, and Crashaw "are none of them men of our time: we love their sincerity and the beauty of their voices, but we receive a part only of their devotional spirit, because they are speaking of religion, and religion is everywhere and under all forms a unique and individual relation" (p. 287).

◆§ 466. O'Neill, George. "Catholic Activity in English Literature," in *Representative Catholic Essays*, edited by George Carver and Ellen M. Geyer, 91–122. New York: Macmillan.

A lecture given at the Cathedral Hall, Melbourne, 28 July 1924. Calls Crashaw, in contrast to Milton, "a genuinely religious poet" and maintains that, although Crashaw's poems are uneven, they are "so full of beautiful things that choice among them is not easy" (p. 104). Reproduces fifty "rapturous lines" from "Hymn to the Name of Jesus," praises the poem for "its fervor, its intensity, its sweet familiarity with heavenly things and heavenly thoughts," and suggests that "such things we may seek for almost in vain, at least, until we find it awakened again by the Catholic muse of Francis Thompson" (p. 106).

◆§ 467. Porter, Alan. "Richard Crashaw, 1613?-1649," in *Great Names*, edited by Walter J. Turner, 43–44. New York: Lincoln Mac Veagh, Dial Press.

Presents a biographical sketch of Crashaw, a short evaluation of his poetry, and selections from "Hymn in the Holy Nativity," "Song upon the Bleeding Crucifix," and "Wishes. To his (supposed) Mistresse." Suggests that "Wishes. To his (supposed) Mistresse" shows him "master of a debonair sweetness and grace not excelled even in his own time" and that Crashaw is "an individual among the fantastics, though he can bid as fair for absurdity as any" (p. 43). Maintains that "unlike most he had simple, sensuous, and ardent emotion, and when he gave rein to his feeling he burst into pure, direct poetry," observing that "his conceits are the habit, not the body of the man" (p. 43). Insists also that Crashaw, unlike other of the metaphysical poets, was "a true Catholic," who was "free from all turbulence" (p. 44). Notes his faults—a luxuriance and looseness that can result in bad taste—but maintains that, "for all his outward semblance, he ranges really with Spenser, the earlier Keats, and Swinburne, as poets of sound and imagery" (p. 44). Concludes that "the clearness of his spirit and the ardour of his religion place him alone in our poetry" and maintains that Crashaw was a mystic—"with a mysticism lucid, wholesome, and clean," freed from "transcendental vagueness" (p. 44).

1927

◆§ 468. Anon. [sometimes ascribed to T. S. Eliot]. "Crashaw's Poetical Works." *TLS*, 15 September, p. 620.

Review of Martin's edition, a work of "scrupulous completeness and exactitude." Calls Crashaw "a master of luxurious ornament" but "among our minor poets, because decoration distracts him." Maintains that "Wishes. To his (supposed) Mistresse," "runs into every kind of artificiality and extravagance" and that all the "cosmetics with which Crashaw later larded and disfigured its natural daintiness, were the work of the traitorous hand of the self-conscious artist." Finds in several poems, especially "Hymn in the Holy Nativity" and "Hymn in the Assumption," a "sustaining glow which, entering into the music as well as into the diction of his verse, gives it at its best moments such sweetness and sonority as are not elsewhere found mingled in all our poetry." Disagrees with Martin's view that Crashaw's poetic powers were developing to the end, suggesting that, "young as he was when he died, Crashaw had already over-reached himself" and "had indulged in a luxurious expression of the sternest of emotions, and the retort upon him had been a withdrawal of his sense of the realities of which he was professing to speak."

◄§ 469. Confrey, Burton. "Crashaw's Religious Background." *Thought* 2: 392–402.

Reprinted in *The Moral Mission of Literature and Other Essays* (Manchester, N.H.: Magnificat Press, 1939), 63–71.

Asserts that, "although the excesses of the early seventeenth century religious poets mar the work of Richard Crashaw, at times he shows an ability which, if uniform, would give him a place among writers of the greatest English verses" and suggests that "the fact that he did not write for an audience may have prevented any attempt to edify," and that "therein lies his appeal to readers today" (p. 392). Presents a biographical sketch of Crashaw, stressing his religious temperament and development, "a most intricate nexus of Platonic and mystical elements" (p. 396). Mentions new biographical information that has come to light—that Crashaw was known as a poet by the time he was fifteen; that he became an Anglican minister; that he went to Rome in 1646, earlier than previously thought; and that he had a more noteworthy contemporary reputation than hitherto recognized (see Confrey, entry 426). Points out that the reader of Crashaw's poetry must differentiate "between imagery, which serves to clothe the sense with color and goes no further, and the very different imagery which is symbolic and appeals to the analytic sense," noting that the latter "does not rest upon pictorial effects" but rather "opens a door to the arcana of the spirit" (p. 401). Notes the influence of other poets, of mystics such as St. Teresa and St. John of the Cross, and of the Bible, especially the parables, the symbolic teachings, and the "oriental imagery, the impassioned diction, and splendid rhythm of the "Book of Canticles'" (p. 399). Suggests that Crashaw had much in common with Habington, Southwell, Donne, Herbert, Vaughan, Traherne, the Cambridge Platonists, and Sir Thomas Browne.

◄§ 470. Crashaw, Richard. *The Poems, English, Latin, and Greek, of Richard Crashaw*, edited by L. C. Martin. Oxford: Clarendon Press. xcii, 473p. 2d ed., 1957, xcv, 476p., reprinted, 1966.

Preface (pp. vi–xii); biographical introduction: (1) 1612–1631, London and Yorkshire (pp. xv–xxi), (2) 1631–1643, Cambridge (pp. xxi–xxv), (3) 1643–1649, Leyden (?), Oxford, Paris, Rome, Loreto (pp. xxv–xxxviii), and (4) contemporary and posthumous fame (pp. xxxviii–xlii); textual introduction: (1) early printed editions (pp. xliii–liv), (2) manuscripts (pp. liv–lxxxi), and (3) modern editions (pp. lxxxii–lxxxv); list of principal sigla used in footnotes, in numerical and alphabetical order (p. lxxxvi); chronological order of Crashaw's poems (pp. lxxxvii–xcii); *Epigrammatum Sacrorum Liber* (pp. 1–71), with the manuscript dedication (pp. 2–3), the title page of the 1634 edition (p. 5), and the title page of *Richardi Crashawi Poemata et Epigrammata* of 1670 (p. 65); *Steps to the Temple* (1646) with title page (pp. 73–145); *The Delights of the Muses* (1646) with title page (pp. 147–98) and an index to the poems of 1646 (pp. 199–201); poems added in 1648 and not included in

1652, with title pages of the 1648 edition of *Steps to the Temple* and *The Delights of the Muses*, with tables of contents for each (pp. 203–30); *Carmen Deo Nostro* (1652) with title page (pp. 231–346); *A Letter from Mr. Crashaw to the Countess of Denbigh* (1653), with title page (pp. 347–50); poems from manuscripts: (1) poems from manuscripts included in previous modern editions (pp. 352–400)—Bodl. MS Tanner 465 and Brit. Mus. Add. MS 33219; and (2) supplementary poems from manuscripts, not included in previous modern editions (pp. 401–9)—Bodl. MS Tanner 465 and Brit. Mus. MS Harl. 6917; appendix 1: poems probably spurious (pp. 410–14); appendix 2: biographical documents: (1) selection from Lloyd's *Memoires* (entry 40) (pp. 415–16), (2) selection from Wood's *Fasti Oxonienses* (entry 56) (pp. 417–18), (3) documents from Peterhouse (pp. 418–20), and documents from the archives of the Santa Casa concerning Crashaw's appointment and death at Loreto (pp. 415–24); commentary (pp. 425–63); and an index of first lines (pp. 465–73). Three plates: (1) Susan, Countess of Denbigh, from the painting by Gerbier now owned by the present Earl of Denbigh (frontispiece); (2) the letter written at Leyden 20 February 1643/44 (to face p. xxx); and (3) Loreto, an engraving published in 1853 and lent by the authorities of the Santa Casa (to face p. xxxiii).

In the second edition, makes corrections and additions in the light of new information on Crashaw's life and poems. Notes that "some parts of the introduction have been rewritten" and that "nearly all the rest of the new material is in the form of additional notes on pp. xciii–xcv" (preface to the second edition). Adds an index of titles (pp. 475–76) and rearranges plates and adds one plate, Title of the Hymn in Honour of St. Teresa (from a manuscript in the Pierpont Morgan Library, New York).

◄§ 471. Eliot, T. S. "A Note on Poetry and Belief." *The Enemy: A Review of Art and Literature* 1 : 15–17.

Appears in a reprint of *The Enemy* (English Little Magazines, no. 2; London: Frank Cass and Company, 1968).

Rejects the notion that poetry can be separated from belief and disagrees with the idea that people have believed the same things in the same way throughout the ages. Points out that "it would be rash to say that the *belief* of Christina Rosetti was not as strong as that of Crashaw, or that of Crashaw as strong as that of Dante; and among the propositions believed by these persons there must be a number of dogmas, expressed in substantially the same words, believed heartily by all three; nevertheless they are all as different from each other as they are from myself" (p. 16).

◄§ 472. Gillman, Frederick John. *The Evolution of the English Hymn: An Historical Survey of the Origins and Development of the Hymns of the Christian Church.* With a foreword by Sir H. Walford Davies. London: George Allen & Unwin; New York: Macmillan. 312p.

Briefly discusses Crashaw as a member of the Herbert group, "a family party, linked together by ties of blood or friendship or literary tastes, and presided over by the genial and kindly fisherman, Izaak Walton" (p. 164). Includes in the group Crashaw, Donne, Henry Wotton, Henry King, Nicholas Ferrar, Thomas Ken, Vaughan, and Richard Baxter. Suggests that, although Crashaw was not a close associate of Herbert, he was "a personal friend of Izaak Walton" (p. 165) and had close associations with Little Gidding. Observes that Crashaw "hardly finds a niche in our modern hymn books" (p. 167). Praises Crashaw's epigrams as "dainty" and "worshipful" and calls his Teresian verses, especially "The Flaming Heart," his "most brilliant poems" (p. 168). Suggests that perhaps only Crashaw's "The Flaming Heart" "rises to the almost uncontrollable ardour of love" (p. 110) of Jacopone da Todi's "The Soul's Complaint."

◄§ 473. Judson, Alexander Corbin. *Seventeenth-Century Lyrics*. Edited with short biographies, bibliographies, and notes by Alexander Corbin Judson. Chicago: University of Chicago Press. xix, 412p.
Reprinted, 1928, 1932.
Anthology containing 275 poems by fourteen seventeenth-century poets with modernized spellings. Crashaw is represented by selections from nine poems (pp. 144–62), followed by a biographical sketch (pp. 350–52), a highly selected bibliography (pp. 352–53), and notes on individual poems (pp. 353–556).

◄§ 474. Mégroz, R[odolphe] L[ouis]. "Crashaw," in *Francis Thompson: The Poet of Earth in Heaven: A Study in Poetic Mysticism and the Evolution of Love-Poetry*, 108–24. London: Faber & Gwyer; New York: C. Scribner's Sons.
Calls Crashaw "the last English Roman Catholic poet until Thompson arrived to make his faith lyrical with a like ardent beauty" (p. 108) and points out affinities and parallels between the two poets in their uses of images, symbols, metaphors, "metaphysical conceptions" (p. 118), tone, and imagination. Claims that the "subtle differences" between Crashaw and Thompson are due "not to the poetic art, nor to the theology, but to the personalities of the poets" (pp. 122–23). Contends that Crashaw took a more direct and familiar approach to divine subjects: "Crashaw's Blessed Lady was human; Thompson's is strictly a divinity" (p. 123). Professes also that Crashaw's secular poetry is "as good as his 'sacred' poetry" (p. 124). Suggests that Thompson knew Grosart's edition of Crashaw's poems and that not only his early attraction for Donne and Cowley but perhaps also his admiration of Coleridge led him to Crashaw.

◄§ 475. Praz, Mario. Review of *The Poems, English, Latin, and Greek of Richard Crashaw*, edited by L. C. Martin. *ES* 9:202–7.

Praises Martin's editorial work but faults him for not supplying a critical introduction and a more extensive biography. Contrasts it with Grierson's edition of Donne, maintaining that it was Grierson's introduction to Donne's poems that aroused critical interest in Donne's work and suggesting that Martin missed the opportunity to do the same for Crashaw. Disagrees with Martin's suggestion that Crashaw returned to England after his visit to Leyden and dates Crashaw's conversion to Catholicism before 1646. Calls attention to the important influences on Crashaw of Jesuit verse, especially the emblem books, and the devotional poetry of Italy and Spain, and notes parallels between Crashaw and the Church Fathers in order to show that Crashaw had at his disposal "the continental stock-in-trade of religious conceits" (p. 205).

❧ 476. Pulling, Alexander. "Crashaw the Poet: His Pedigree." *N&Q* 152:135.

Asks for information on the forebears of William Crashaw, the poet's father. Specifically wonders whether he was of the Crashaw family of Bentley or that of Woodhouse, Yorks. Notes that the name *Crashaw* "seems peculiar to Yorkshire."

❧ 477. Saito, Takeshi *Eibungaku-shi* [A History of English Literature]. Tokyo: Kenkyusha.

2d ed., revised, 1929; 3d ed., revised, 1938; 4th ed., revised, 1957; 5th ed., revised, 1974.

Collection of lectures originally delivered at Tokyo Imperial University and revised and enlarged over the years. Later editions show no change of attitude toward Crashaw. Briefly discusses Crashaw as a poet of passion, elaborate conceits, and enthusiasm (p. 186) and suggests that he had little influence on English thought of the seventeenth century. Briefly contrasts Crashaw to Donne, Herbert, and Vaughan.

❧ 478. Sawyer, Charles J. and F. J. Harvey Darton. *English Books, 1475– 1900: A Signpost for Collectors*. Vol. I: *Caxton to Johnson*. Westminster: Charles Sawyer; New York: E. P. Dutton. xvi, 367p.

Discusses types of English books that are considered most desirable by modern book collectors. Briefly notes (p. 202) that, for some unknown reason, early editions of Crashaw's poems are not considered as valuable as editions of Herbert and Vaughan and therefore do not have an equal pecuniary value.

❧ 479. Schelling, Felix E. "Devotional Poetry in the Reign of Charles I," in *Shakespeare and "Demi-Science": Papers on Elizabethan Topics*, 138–57. Philadelphia: University of Pennsylvania Press; London: Oxford University Press.

Contrasts the moral poetry of the Elizabethans with the devotional poetry of the Caroline period and surveys the religious verse of Crashaw, Quarles,

Herbert, Wither, Sandys, Herrick, Marvell, and Vaughan. Contrasts Crashaw primarily with Herbert: "Crashaw turns the passion of earth to worship and identifies the spiritual and the material in his devotion; Herbert with all his love of ritual, has somewhat of the Puritan spirit in him, which is troubled in the contemplation of earthly vanities and struggles to rise above and beyond them" (p. 149). Suggests that Herbert is more restrained than Crashaw, more of the craftsman: "But if Herbert has never fallen into Crashaw's extravagances, he is equally incapable of his inspired, rhapsodic flights" (p. 149). Concludes that the fundamental difference between the two poets is "the antithesis of Protestantism and Roman Catholicism" (p. 149). Calls Crashaw "a creature of light and atmosphere," one who "revels in color and the gorgeousness thereof" (p. 149), and notes that he often "rhapsodizes without bridle, and is open at times to grave criticism on the score of taste" (p. 150). Warns, however, that by focusing too much on these "distortions of fancy" (such as images in "The Weeper"), one can forget "the luminousness and radiance, the uncommon imaginative power and volatility of mind of this devout Shelley of the reign of Charles I" (p. 150). Mentions the influence of the Laudian movement and Little Gidding on Crashaw's religious sensibilities and development. Briefly contrasts him to Wither, Vaughan, and Herrick, asserting that even the best of Herrick's religious poems "are as ripples on a shallow lake to the crested waves of Crashaw" (pp. 150–51).

◄§ 480. Walsh, Thomas, ed. *The Catholic Anthology.* New York: Macmillan. ix, 552p.

Rev. ed., 1932, 1939, 1940, 1942, 1943, 1947.

Includes four selections of verse from Crashaw (p. 199–207): "Luke 2. Quaerit Jesum Suum Maria" and selections from "The Flaming Heart," "Hymn to the Name of Jesus," and "Hymn in the Holy Nativity." Offers a biographical sketch of Crashaw (pp. 493–94), calling him "one of the greatest of modern Catholic poets, the inspiration of all who have succeeded him in religious lyrical fields" (p. 494).

1928

◄§ 481. Confrey, Burton. "Crashaw's Divine Epigrams." *Placidian: Journal of the Benedictine Foundation* 5 (October):329–33.

Calls Crashaw "the most considerable Catholic doctrinal poet in the England of his time" (p. 329). Surveys the themes of Crashaw's divine epigrams, noting that, "in his selection of texts from the Gospels, he draws from Matthew, Luke, and John in about equal numbers" (p. 329) and suggests that the parables and the symbolic teachings of the Bible and Christ's uses of nature symbolism to explain spiritual truths especially interested Crashaw. Notes the influence of St. Teresa on Crashaw's poetry and claims that the two "had many inherent and temperamental qualities in common" (p. 330).

◄§ 482. Dearmer, Percy, R[alph] Vaughan Williams, and Martin Shaw, eds. "Summer in Winter (Nativity)," in *The Oxford Book of Carols*, 250–51. London: Oxford University Press, Humphrey Milford.

Reprinted many times.

Includes a carol based upon four stanzas from Crashaw's "Hymn in the Holy Nativity" set to music from a melody found in *Cantiques de Strasbourg* (1697).

◄§ 483. Eliot, T. S. Review of *The Poems, English, Latin, and Greek, of Richard Crashaw*, edited by L. C. Martin. *The Dial* 84:246–50.

Reprinted as "Note on Richard Crashaw," in *For Lancelot Andrewes: Essays on Style and Order* (London: Faber & Gwyer, [1928]), 117–25.

Praises Martin's editorial work but expresses disappointment with the introduction and claims that "we are still left with no first-rate criticism of Crashaw in English" (p. 246). Suggests that Crashaw is "a much greater poet than he is usually supposed to be" whereas Keats and Shelley are, "in their actual accomplishment, not nearly such great poets as they are supposed to be," yet maintains that both of the later poets "would *probably* have become greater poets, poets on a much greater scale, than Crashaw," for "Crashaw was a finished master, and Keats and Shelley were apprentices with immense possibilities before them" (p. 247). Compares and contrasts Crashaw and Shelley and finds that, in spite of some superficial and obvious resemblances, the two are quite different. Contrasts Crashaw briefly to Dante, maintaining that Crashaw's erotic passion "is not impure, but it is incomplete" (p. 250). Sees Crashaw as being "quite alone in his peculiar kind of greatness" and as a European poet, "saturated still more in Italian and Latin poetry than English." Agrees with Praz that he is "the *representative* of the baroque spirit in literature" (p. 250), even more so than Marino or Góngora. (In the preface to a later collection of essays, *Essays Ancient and Modern* [London: Faber and Faber, 1936], Eliot explains that he has omitted this essay "with which I was dissatisfied.")

◄§ 484. Emperor, John Bernard. "Richard Crashaw (1613?–1649)" in *The Catullian Influence in English Lyric Poetry, Circa 1600–1650*, 84–85. (University of Missouri Studies, vol. 3, no. 3.) Columbia: University of Missouri.

Notes that "the body of Crashaw's secular poetry is comparatively small, but, in what little of it there is, the influence of Catullus is rather considerable" (p. 84). Maintains that Crashaw's verse "pours forth from him, as Catullus's did, in a fiery, passionate burst; and, vitiated though it may be by its occasional monstrous conceits and far-drawn fancies, it is always lyrical, always passionate, always the utterance of the heart rather than the lucubration of the brain" (p. 84). Finds Crashaw's translation of "Carmen V. Ad Lesbia" ("Out of Catullus") inferior to the rendition of Alexander Brome. Finds likenesses to Catullus in the following poems by Crashaw: (1) "Upon the Duke of York his Birth. A Panegyricke" (*Carmina* lxii, 49–50, 54, and *Carmina* lxi, 106–9); (2) "Out of Catullus" (*Carmina* v); (3) "Hymn in the Holy Nativity" (*Veneres Cupidinesque, Carmina* iii, 1); (4) "Alexias. (The First Elegie)" (*Coma Berenices, Carmina* lxvi); and (5) "Alexias. (The Second Elegie)" (*Carmina*, lxiv, 164–66).

◆§ 485. Fehr, Bernhard. "Die englische Literatur des 17. und 18. Jahrhunderts," in *Die englische Literatur von der Renaissance bis zur Aufklärung* by Wolfgang Keller and Bernhard Fehr, 117–272. (Handbuch der Literaturwissenschaft, ed. by Oskar Walzel.) Wildpark-Potsdam: Akademische Verlagsgesellschaft Athenaion.

Places Crashaw, along with Herbert, Vaughan, and Traherne, in the mystical tradition (pp. 135–37) and suggests that all four poets are precursors of the religious enthusiasm of the later seventeenth century. Notes that, as a result of his Catholicism and the influence of the Spanish mystics as well as Marino and Góngora, Crashaw is outside the tradition of English poetry. Describes his style as overly emphatic, tortured, and elaborate, yet maintains that "zu seinen besten Momenten kann er Idee und Gefühl in Tongebilde von einer Pracht ausbrechen lassen, die schon an einen Shelley gemahnen" (p. 137). Points out that Crashaw could be called an example of the baroque in English poetry, suggests that he reminds one of Swinburne, and cites "The Flaming Heart" as an example of his finest poetry.

◆§ 486. Greenlaw, Edwin. Review of Evelyn M. Simpson's *A Study of the Prose Works of John Donne* (1924), Mario Praz's *Secentismo e Marinismo in Inghilterra* (1925), and L. C. Martin's edition of *The Poems English, Latin, and Greek, of Richard Crashaw* (1927). MLN 43: 275–76.

Suggests that Praz's study and Martin's edition supplement each other but maintains that Praz's contrast between Crashaw's youth and later life is too dramatically drawn. Praises Martin's edition but notes that he missed "the interesting fact that John Worthington planned to supply materials for a third edition of the poems in 1667" (p. 277). Notes that the letter by John Worthington to his friend Dr. Ingelo (entry 38) indicates "the survival, at least until the date of the letter, of a copy of the poems corrected by Crashaw himself" (pp. 227–28) and asks for additional information on the whereabouts of this copy of the poems.

◆§ 487. Hutchinson, F. E. "Richard Crashaw, 'Poet and Saint.'" CQR 106:140–55.

Review of Martin's edition. Summarizes the facts about Crashaw's life, noting that authentic information on the poet is difficult to find, and comments on the bibliographical difficulties that a modern editor of his poems encounters. Suggests that a few of the engravings in *Carmen Deo Nostro* are by Crashaw and that evidence does not support the notion that Crashaw was a master at the art. Stresses that, in spite of the bulk of poems in Martin's edition, Crashaw's credit will still rest mainly on those few poems which are known to every reader of anthologies" (p. 146). Suggests that Crashaw's Latin poems and the rather large collection of juvenilia will not attract the modern reader. Maintains that several of Crashaw's secular poems are highly successful, such as "Wishes. To his (supposed) Mistresse" and the newly discovered "Epithalamium" but that, "in spite of a few happy examples of secular verse, Crashaw's ardent aspiring nature found its truest outlet in poems of religious ecstasy" (p. 149). Suggests that "English reticence may at times be shocked by his exuberance and cloying sweetness, no less than by his most outrageous 'conceits,' but we may well believe his ardours to be wholly sincere and characteristic of a man of almost feminine sensibility" (p. 149). Finds fault in Crashaw's rendering of the great hymns of the Church and maintains that, "on the whole . . . in spite of many happy phrases and tender graces, Crashaw's versions seldom preserve the tone of the originals, especially when that tone is one of awe" (p. 151). Cites "A Hymn to Sainte Teresa" as Crashaw's greatest poem, noting that it "seldom offends by extravagance or oversweetness" and has "a lightness of touch, a swiftness of movement and a beauty of phrase" (p. 152), and contends that, by comparison, "The Flaming Heart" is inferior, marred by "tiresome conceit" and "artificial strain" (p. 153). Praises both "Letter to the Countess of Denbigh," which shows Crashaw "at his simplest and most moving" (p. 154), and "Hymn in the Holy Nativity."

◆§ 488. Kane, Elisha K. "Meretricious Verse in Other Literatures," in *Gongorism and the Golden Age: A Study of Exuberance and Unrestraint in the Arts*, 128–68. Chapel Hill: University of North Carolina Press.

Discusses the influence of Gongorism on English poetry and prose and asserts that "the poet who approaches closest to Góngora in the use of extraordinary tropes, is, unquestionably, Richard Crashawe," a poet noted for "his lachrymose and treacly verses on religious subjects" (p. 150). Maintains that, in Crashaw, "the extreme of the grotesque and repulsive, however, is reached in a poem describing our Lord's circumcision, the metaphors of which are really beyond citation" and quotes "Luke 11. Blessed be the paps which Thou hast sucked" "only to exhibit it as a literary curiosity" (p. 151).

◆§ 489. Kemp, Violet I. "Mystic Utterance in Certain English Poets." *HJ* 26:474–83.

Discusses the nature of mysticism and the methods of mystical poets. Argues that "poetry can only be mystical to a certain degree" since "pure mysticism, when the state of union is reached, is mute" (p. 475). Denies that Crashaw "was more than an ardent spirit using the marinist style in religious poetry to express the satisfaction of a convert to Rome" and asserts that "A Hymn to Sainte Teresa" illustrates that Crashaw's ardour and music react on each other, producing an ecstasy of mood, but not of thought" (p. 480). Calls "Ode on a Prayer-book" an example of personal devotion, a dramatization of "the self's thoughts and hopes" (p. 477).

◄§ 490. Lee, A. H. E. "English Mystical Poetry." *PoetryR* 19 (October): 321–34.

Discusses the nature of mysticism and its relation to mystical poetry and surveys English mystical poets, including Crashaw. Calls the seventeenth century "the golden age of English mystical poetry" (p. 323) and maintains that, together with Herbert, Crashaw can be regarded as "the father of English devotional poetry" (p. 326). Contends that all of Crashaw's poems are "one long sustained cry for God in lyric after lyric of flaming passion" and that in his verses "he has no other theme, no other thought" (p. 326). Commenting on the concluding lines of "A Hymn to Sainte Teresa," points out that "it is curious to notice that the symbols of Blood and Fire attracted this English Romanist mystic as strongly as they do modern Salvationists" (p. 326). Briefly compares and contrasts Crashaw with Traherne, Herbert, and Milton.

◄§ 491. Read, Herbert. "Poetry and Religion," in *Phases of English Poetry*, 57–82. (Hogarth Lectures on Literature.) London: Hogarth Press.

Reprinted, New York: Harcourt Brace and Co., 1929; revised, London: Faber and Faber, 1950.

Argues that the difference between two Catholic poets, such as Dante and Crashaw, "is a difference which we can only account for by those very factors which explain the Reformation" and claims that Crashaw, unlike Dante, "was an ardent convert to Catholicism, but in his conversion he did not lose the introspective habits of his age, nor its subjective methods of expression" (p. 62). Calls Crashaw "the true type of the divine poet" (p. 67) in comparison to Donne and finds him "more passionate and more complex than either Herbert or Vaughan," suggesting that "he is more complex just because he is more passionate" (p. 72). Maintains that in Crashaw's poetry "the ecstasy of religion and of poetry became identified" (p. 80). Quotes lines 93–108 of "The Flaming Heart" and states that "it may be doubted whether there are any lines so sincere and so passionate, and yet so direct and impressive, in the whole of English poetry" (p. 73). Points out, however, that, even in this poem, "when instead of a particular object or a symbol, passion is directed to ideas and essences, all the intangible universals of thought and meditation, then the passion drives the poet to the expression of innermost opacities and obscurities" (p. 73). Cites lines from "Hymn in the Glorious Epiphanie" and calls it "one of the most beautiful of all Crashaw's poems," in which "the emotional apprehension of ideas infects the whole phraseology" (p. 74). Maintains that in the poem, as well as in many others, Crashaw betrays "a personal idiom of a peculiar intensity," an "inventive originality" (p. 77). Cites "Adoro Te" as fully reflecting Crashaw's mode of thought, noting that "in the act of writing his poem the poet enters on a state in which feeling and reasoning are for the moment suspended, and only intuition is operative" (p. 78).

&§ 492. Tholen, Wilhelm. "Richard Crashaw: ein englischer Dichter und Mystiker der Barockzeit." *Das neue Ufer* 48.
Cited in *YWES* 9(1928): 206. Not located.

&§ 493. Walsh, Thomas. "Crashaw, Poet and Saint." *Commonweal* 7: 1211–12.
Critical discussion of Crashaw's life and poetry, occasioned as a review of Martin's edition. Suggests that "in the entire realm of Catholic poetry, that field which throughout the middle-ages and the days of the Renaissance was practically a Catholic medium of art, there is no figure that may be even compared to Crashaw in English with the exception of Milton" and that "with Crashaw we may go further and declare that through all the ages of our English literature he is the one poet, par excellence, inspired by the Catholic muse" (p. 1211). Presents a biographical sketch of Crashaw. Suggests that "in Crashaw we find a splendid emblazonment of the liturgical page" and therefore "it is necessary to possess a full knowledge of Catholicity, its faith and practice, to appreciate properly the value and the beauty of much of his work" (p. 1212). Notes the praise given to Crashaw by Francis Thompson, Cowley, Pope, Shelley, and Coleridge and claims that "the undeclared debt of all religious poets to his muse can never be fully appraised" (p. 1211). Concludes by calling Crashaw "the seraph voice of our English poetry; the norm of the sublime for every religious author; the herald of the Italian, French and Spanish devotional literature into our native tongue; and the model for future writers when the heights of the sublime shall once more attract them" (p. 1212).

&§ 494. Warren, Austin. "No Apology, Please." *SR* 36:499–500.
Essentially a review of Martin's edition. Notes that Martin feels no need to apologize for Crashaw as earlier editors and critics often did. Suggests that the emergence of certain contemporary "neo-metaphysical" poets, such as Eliot, Elinor Wylie, Laura Riding Gottschalk, and Archibald MacLeish, may in part explain a kind of modern "acclimating of the original manner and idiom" (p. 499) of these once ridiculed seventeenth-century poets. Observes, however, that, although the art and manner of the metaphysicals has been refurbished by modern poets, "the passion, the fire, have disappeared" (p. 500). Claims that, "though learned and subtle, Crashaw was neither pedantic nor coolly intellectual" but was, "like St. Teresa, whom he so magnificently celebrated, a *Flaming Heart*," and stresses that "his poetry is not merely sensuous: it is passionate" (p. 500).

1929

❧ 495. Bernardin, Brother. "Richard Crashaw: A Catholic Poet." *IER*, series 5, 34:164–72.

General biographical sketch and survey of Crashaw's poetry from a Catholic point of view. Defends Crashaw and Catholicism against George Gilfillan's anti-Catholic remarks (entry 186). Praises "Hymn to the Name of Jesus" as "one of the most beautiful of his poems" (p. 167), briefly describes the merits of the Teresian poems, and calls "Description of a Religious House and Condition of Life" a "beautiful and well-wrought poem, which is at once stately and sincere" (p. 170). Suggests that the secular poems are inferior to the sacred because Crashaw's temperament was "so truly devotional" (p. 170). Singles out, however, "Musicks Duell" and "Wishes. To his (supposed) Mistresse" for special notice. Suggests that the defects in Crashaw's poetry "are those which arise from his time and school" but argues that "much can be forgiven to the poet who so sympathized with the wave of mystical love, in sharp contrast to the pagan tenets of the so-called Reformation" (p. 172). Concludes that Crashaw's poetry "makes healthy reading, gives pleasure, and is a true tonic against the pernicious influence exerted by the poetry of some of our present-day poets" and maintains that Crashaw's poems should be studied in Irish colleges: "They would be more suitable for the youth of a Catholic nation, such as ours, than the poems of Tennyson, Swinburne or Arnold" (p. 172).

❧ 496. Clark, Evert Mordecai, ed. "Richard Crashaw," in *English Literature: The Seventeenth Century*, 106–17, 552–53. (English Literature Series of Anthologies.) New York and Chicago: Charles Scribner's Sons. Reprinted, 1930.

Anthologizes "The Authors Motto," "On Mr. G. Herberts booke, The Temple," "Hymn in the Holy Nativity," "The Flaming Heart," "On a foule Morning, being then to take a journey," and "An Epitaph upon a Young Married Couple" (pp. 106–17), with notes and a biographical sketch (pp. 552–53). Maintains that "Hymn in the Holy Nativity" is "notable for its fervor, tenderness, and extravagant conceits" (p. 553).

❧ 497. Draper, John W. *The Funeral Elegy and the Rise of English Romanticism*. New York: New York University Press. xv, 358p.

Refers throughout to Crashaw's funeral elegies. Claims that fundamentally Crashaw's elegies "furnish but little mortuary material" (p. 35). Maintains, however, that his translation of "Dies Irae Dies Illa," "although not strictly elegiac, could hardly omit some such details; but his elegy on Dr. Porter is a mere extension through forty-four lines of the pathetic fallacy; his *Elegy on Mr. Stanninow* is similar; his three poems *Upon the Death of Mr. Herrys* are given over to devout contemplation occasionally pointed by *outré* metaphors;

and the three 'elegies' of his *Alexias* combine religious edification with an occasional Classical allusion" (pp. 35–36). Asserts that Crashaw elegizes in "Upon the Death of a Gentleman [Mr. Chambers]" "somewhat in the tone of Hamlet's graveyard musings; but his usual attitude toward death is epitomized rather in a few exquisite lines from his *Epitaph upon a Young Married Couple*" (p. 36). Briefly compares and contrasts Crashaw to Southwell, Habington, Herbert, Donne, the Calvinists, and Dryden.

◄§ 498. Garrod, H. W. "The Nightingale in Poetry," in *The Profession of Poetry and Other Lectures*, 131–59. Oxford: Clarendon Press.
Discusses poems about nightingales from the middle ages to the nineteenth century. Suggests that "ingenious elaboration is everything" (p. 155) in "Musicks Duell" but believes that "in the kind to which it belongs it deserves a high place" (p. 155). Finds little nature in the poem but admires its uses of heroic meter. Suggests that it is "the kind of poem which Keats, in his early period, was for ever trying to write" and that, "if Keats had not written the Ode, and if ingenuity were truth, and truth beauty, this would be our best Nightingale poem" (p. 155).

◄§ 499. Grierson, Herbert J. C. "Humanism and the Churches," in *Cross Currents in English Literature of the XVIIth Century*, 166–231. London: Chatto & Windus.
Reprinted, New York: Harper Torchbooks, 1959; Gloucester, Mass.: Peter Smith, 1965; Harmondsworth, Eng., and Baltimore: Penguin, 1966.
Suggests that the poetry of Crashaw, like that of Vondel, was greatly influenced by the spirit of Post-Tridentine Catholicism; comments on baroque art, especially its appeal to popular taste and its emphasis on "the pretty, the voluptuous, the sentimental" (p. 177); and contrasts counter-reformation poetry with Protestant sentiment, noting the emphasis of the former on the humanity and physical life of Christ. Calls Crashaw "the chief representative of the Catholic reaction, of the temper of the new Catholicism," and suggests that in his poetry "one hears the voice of the poet who has found his way back to Rome and cannot give too passionate utterance to his sense of regained security, his emotional, sensuous delight in sacraments and ritual and cults, his complete surrender to an unquestioning faith and obedience" (p. 180). Points out that Crashaw's favorite themes are the life and death of Christ, the saints, and the martyrs and the cultic devotions to the heart, wounds, and name of Christ, as well as "all the antitheses of God and man, strength and weakness, life and death, in which the whole subject of Christian faith abounds" (p. 181). Contends that even Crashaw's raptures "are at least as sensuous as they are spiritual" (p. 180), noting that the images in "The Weeper," for instance, are "at once voluptuous and pious" (p. 181). Claims that one can hardly call the ecstasies of Crashaw "an expression of the humanist spirit of Montaigne and Erasmus, the spirit which loves reason, moderation, balance, culture, and

dreads extravagance and other-worldly aspirations and ardours" and denies that Crashaw was a true mystic, for "mysticism implies thought—and Crashaw does not think, he accepts" (p. 182). Briefly compares Crashaw to Southwell and contrasts him to Herbert.

⚜ 500. Hebel, J[ohn] William, and Hoyt H. Hudson, eds. "Richard Crashaw," in *Poetry of the English Renaissance, 1509–1660*, 758–81, 1024–25. New York: Printed for F. S. Crofts & Co.

Reprinted several times.

Anthologizes selections from *Steps to the Temple, Sacred Poems*, and *The Delights of the Muses* (1648), including part of "The Preface to the Reader," and from *Carmen Deo Nostro* (1652) (pp. 758–81). Presents a biographical introduction to Crashaw and notes to poems (pp. 1024–25). Suggests that "the comely restraint of the middle way of Anglicanism, so loved by Herbert, was foreign to the warmer ecstasies of Crashaw's devotions" and that "in his poetry, too, he tumultuously sweeps aside all restraint and piles exclamation upon exclamation, and metaphor upon metaphor" so that "the very excess sometimes obscures the high imaginative quality of many of his lines" (p. 1024). Notes the influence of St. Teresa on Crashaw's religious temper.

⚜ 501. Quiller-Couch, Arthur. "The English Elegy (II)," in *Studies in Literature*, 3d ser., 25–53. New York: G. P. Putnam's Sons; Cambridge: University Press.

Reprinted, 1930, 1933, 1948.

Surveys the history and development of the classical elegy in English poetry from the sixteenth century. Briefly compares Crashaw with William Cartwright. Maintains that Crashaw, "a true poet," abounds in conceits "which we condemn not so much because they are conceits as because they miss 'coming off,' the occasion being too serious for them, or at least too intimate" (p. 33). Cites as an illustration lines 1–4 of "Death's Lecture."

⚜ 502. Reed, John Curtis. "Humphrey Moseley, Publisher." *Oxford Bibliographical Society* (Proceedings for 1928) 2, pt. 2:57–142.

Gives an account of Humphrey Moseley, publisher of the 1646 and 1648 editions of *Steps to the Temple*. Includes prefaces and dedicatory epistles to several works Moseley published, a chronological list of books (with index) he published from 1627 to 1661, a note on Moseley's lists and catalogues, a list of books entered or advertized by Moseley but not issued by him, a list of books entered or advertized but not traced, a list of works sold by Moseley in 1640/41, extracts from the Court Book of the Stationers's Company, extracts from Parish Registers, and Moseley's will.

⚜ 503. Taggard, Genevieve, ed. *Circumference: Varieties of Metaphysical Verse, 1456–1928*. New York: Covici Friede Publishers. xiii, 236p.

Limited to 1,050 copies.
Anthologizes "Wishes. To his (supposed) Mistresse" and "Letter to the Countess of Denbigh" (pp. 76–83), without notes or commentary. Part 1 (pp. 3–13) broadly defines metaphysical poetry as primarily reflecting a "state of mind." Suggests that Donne and Emily Dickinson are the most genuine metaphysical poets in English and that Keats is "the clearest possible example of what a metaphysical poet is not" (p. 7). No specific comments on Crashaw.

1930

◄§ 504. Blakeney, Edward Henry. *Twenty-Four Hymns of the Western Church.* London: Eric Partridge at the Scholartis Press. xvii, 103p.
Limited to 260 copies.
Includes Crashaw's translation of "Dies Irae Dies Illa" (pp. 66–67), notes that the choice was suggested by A. E. Taylor, and maintains that Crashaw's translation "deserves to be better known" (p. 77). Points out the praise accorded Crashaw's translation by F. E. Hutchinson in *The Cambridge History of English Literature* as well as Hutchinson's complaint that Crashaw fails to render the masculine rhythm of the Latin original, but concludes that "every English version of *Dies* necessarily falls short of its august original" (p. 77).

◄§ 505. Crashaw, Richard. *Three Poems from Carmen Deo Nostro: In the holy Nativity of Our Lord God, Near Year's Day, In the Glorious Epiphanie.* Haarlem: Joh. Enschedé en Zonen. [23]p.
Limited to 200 copies.
Includes, in addition to the three poems indicated in the title, "To the Queen's Majesty," without notes or commentary.

◄§ 506. Daly, M. "An Unlooked-For Parallel." *Irish Monthly* (Dublin) 58 (February): 100–109.
Finds certain parallels between the "preposterous tropes" (p. 103) in Crashaw's poetry and those in the verses of an Indian poet, A. S. Hosain (*Priceless Pearls* [Calcutta, 1890]), and suggests that the similarity results from a poverty "in emotionally imaginative expression" (p. 108) in both. Presents a generally negative evaluation of metaphysical poetry but calls Crashaw "the best and (I venture to say) best-known of the Metaphysical poets" (p. 103). Briefly discusses the "absurd figures" in "The Weeper," calling them "monstrously incongruous" (pp. 103–4). Suggests that Hosain's poem "Cuckoo" "has all the Crashavian bombast and puerility and bathos at its very worst" and indulges in "peculiar images drawn from the worn-out language of every-day use" (p. 104). Stresses, however, that Crashaw's "delinquencies, serious though they undoubtedly are," do not "drag him down to or below Mr. Hosain's very low poetic plane" and notes that, "though Crashaw's verse contains all the poetic monstrosities of the age in which he lived, these are more than atoned

for by the singular felicity of epithet, strange beauty of phrase, spontaneous symbolism, rare music, sheer lyric loveliness, winged, aspiring exaltation, and spiritually ecstatic vision of his really inspired moments" (p. 104). Cites "A Hymn to Sainte Teresa" as Crashaw's finest and best-known sacred poem and maintains that in it "the inspiration is ever present and never flags" (p. 105). Finds "The Flaming Heart" uneven and calls "Hymn to the Name of Jesus" Crashaw's "most ambitious" sacred poem, a "splendid religious poem starred with passages of exquisitely accurate expression and enchanting sound" (p. 106). Cites "Wishes. To his (supposed) Mistresse" as the best of the secular pieces but maintains that it is "really a religious poem," filled with "beautiful thoughts and happy phrases" as well as "hackneyed images" (p. 107). Praises "Musicks Duell" because in it Crashaw "shows his genius for musical imitation" (p. 108).

◄§ 507. Eliot, T. S. "The Devotional Poets of the Seventeenth Century: Donne, Herbert, and Crashaw." *The Listener* 3: 552–53.

Distinguishes between religious and devotional poetry: "I call 'religious' what is inspired by religious feeling of some kind; and 'devotional' that which is directly about some subject connected with revealed religion" (p. 552). Calls both Crashaw and Herbert "devotional" poets but sees Vaughan as a "religious" poet. Stresses the variety of the sacred poetry of the period, noting that "all of these men are very different from each other, and from Donne" (p. 552). Contrasts Crashaw and Herbert: "Where Herbert seems simple and austere, Crashaw seems almost vulgarly opulent and decorated," but suggests that the major difference between them is that Crashaw "absorbed many more, and more direct, continental influences than Herbert: he is definitely baroque" (p. 553). Notes that it is strange that "the finest baroque poetry should have been written by an Englishman in English, in a country outside the direct current" (p. 553). Contends that Crashaw is "more complicated" in his religious feeling than Herbert and less easily appreciated by Englishmen, thus "in Crashaw we encounter a fine English poet who is at the same time a little alien," in part because, unlike Herbert, he is "soaked in the Counter-Reformation" (p. 553). Cites "The Teare" as Crashaw's worst poem, notes how in it he pushes the conceit to its farthest limits, and claims that Crashaw even "outdoes Donne"; but cites "The Weeper" as an example of how "wit and torturous ingenuity becomes poetry" (p. 553). Suggests that "The Weeper" reminds one of Shelley's "Skylark" "in its melody, and apparently in its succession of images" but notes that Shelley's images "are a straight succession of plain similes, with none of the delight in intellectual ingenuity" (p. 553) found in Crashaw's poem. Concludes that this kind of intellectual ingenuity, "when combined with emotional intensity, gives the peculiar character of this poetry of the first half of the seventeenth century" (p. 553).

◄§ 508. ———. "Thinking in Verse: A Survey of Early Seventeenth-Century Poetry." *The Listener* 3: 441–43.

Maintains that "the profoundest thought and feeling" of the Elizabethan Age "went into its dramatic blank verse" (p. 441) and thus suggests that "the Elizabethans in their drama are forerunners of the Jacobean and Caroline poets in their lyrical verses" (p. 442). Argues that playwrights, like Chapman, "*think* in verse, rather than *sing* in verse" (p. 441). Comments on the religious sensibility of the seventeenth century and calls that period "the third most interesting period in the history of Christianity; the others being the early period which saw the development of dogma in the Greek and Latin churches, and the thirteenth century" (p. 442). Comments briefly on the influence of the Counter-Reformation on the arts and literature, especially the importance of St. Ignatius Loyola and the Jesuits, of St. Teresa and St. John of the Cross. Briefly suggests that "Donne is more affected by Ignatius; Crashaw more by Theresa" (p. 443).

ᴥ§ 509. Empson, William. *Seven Types of Ambiguity*. London: Chatto & Windus. 325p.
Reprinted several times.
Italian edition, *Sette tipi di ambiguità*, Edizione italiana a cura de Giorgio Melchiori (Turin: Einaudi, 1965).
Defines ambiguity as that which "adds some nuance to the direct statement of prose" (p. 1). Later expands the definition and maintains that ambiguity is "any verbal nuance, however slight, which gives room for alternative reactions to the same piece of language" (p. 1, 2d ed.). Quotes lines from "A Hymn to Sainte Teresa" to show that Crashaw's poetry "often has two interpretations, religious and sexual; two situations on which he draws for imagery and detail" (p. 276). Argues, however, that, although Crashaw puts the religious and sexual side by side and discusses them both, "the two forms of experience are as different as possible; one is good, the other evil" (p. 276). Points out that in the poem the saint is "adored for her chastity" but that "the metaphors about her are veiled references to copulation" (p. 276). Suggests that Crashaw "certainly conceived the bliss of saints as extremely like the bliss which on earth he could not obtain without sin; and this certainty was a supply of energy to him and freed his virtue from the Puritan sense of shame" (p. 278). Argues, however, that Crashaw, does not describe "a sensual form of mysticism" but was "content to use sexual terms for his mystical experiences, because they were the best terms that he could find" (p. 279). Maintains that most of Crashaw's poetry is not particularly ambiguous but that "the ideas involved are so unfamiliar, are used in his judgements with such complexity, that to think of it as ambiguous may be the right mode of approach" (p. 280). Presents a possible Freudian analysis of "Luke 11. Blessed be the paps which Thou hast sucked," finding a range of possible sexual references that includes perversion and cannibalism, but suggests that finally the imagery may be simply a "grotesque seventeenth-century simile" (p. 280). Also finds "curious" references and a "primitive system of ideas" in stanza 12 of "Dies Irae Dies Illa" ("O let thine own soft bowells pay / Thy self; And so discharge that day").

Asserts, however, that "the metaphor was only intended to give a sort of wit and point to the pun on *discharge*" (p. 283), in which case it would reflect the "third type" of ambiguity. Concludes that there are numerous examples in Crashaw's poetry of "wholesale use of sexual metaphor and of the condensation of complex theological ideas into an obscurity of language" but that probably seventeenth-century readers "just thought it curious and Biblical and let it go at that" (p. 284).

◆§ 510. Jones, Richard Foster, ed. "Richard Crashaw," in *Seventeenth Century Literature*, 106–13, 396–97. (Nelson's English Readings, vol. 3.) New York: Thomas Nelson and Sons.
Reprinted, 1935.
Offers a biographical sketch of Crashaw and anthologizes "Letter to the Countess of Denbigh" and "Hymn in the Holy Nativity" from *Carmen Deo Nostro* (pp. 106–13), with notes (pp. 396–97). Suggests that in Crashaw's poetry "the flame of religious ecstasy reaches its greatest intensity" and that, although Herbert is devotional and Vaughan is mystical, Crashaw "expresses his ecstatic religion in glowing sensuous images" and, more than any of the other religious poets, expresses "a complete abandonment to the flaming emotions inspired by spiritual experiences" (p. 106).

◆§ 511. Lee, Kathleen. "Richard Crashaw." *Carmina* 1:19–21.
Presents an appreciative evaluation of Crashaw's life and poetry. Sees him as a "natural" Catholic, suggests that he "carried on to the full the tradition of the old Catholic mystics" (p. 20), and stresses the influence of St. Teresa on his religious sensibility. Suggests that "spiritual love has never been more rapturously sung" (p. 17) than in "A Hymn to Sainte Teresa" and calls it Crashaw's finest poem. Maintains that "The Flaming Heart," "with its intricacies and typical conceits, would be somewhat an anticlimax were it not saved by the magnificent finale" (p. 20).

◆§ 512. Nethercot, Arthur H. "The Reputation of Native Versus Foreign 'Metaphysical Poets' in England." *MLR* 25:152–64.
Discusses the reputation of Marino, Du Bartas, and Góngora in England. Notes that "in the seventeenth century all three continental poets had considerable weight and authority" and "were read, translated, and imitated" but that during the Restoration "all were being severely attacked for excesses of style—whereas the English metaphysicals were yet fairly well entrenched in popular regard" (p. 164). Observes that during the age of Pope these Continental poets "were held in even more contempt than the English, for whom some readers and critics still had a good word to say" and that during the age of Dr. Johnson "that dictator's criticisms of the English would seem fulsome encomiums compared to what was being generally said about the foreigners" (p. 164). Concludes that, although there was a minor revival of interest in the

metaphysical poets during the Romantic period, "there was no such revival for Marino, Du Bartas and Góngora" (p. 164). Notes that Marino "was the only one of these foreign poets whom early English critics and readers regarded as having had an influence on native writers," but that, even then, "the first period of his reputation was marked chiefly by translation and imitation rather than by criticism" (p. 153). Points out that Marino was best known by Englishmen of the period as an epic poet, not as a lyricist, and that Crashaw's translation of the first book of *La Strage degli'Innocenti* "was chiefly responsible for accomplishing this result" (p. 153). Suggests that the inclusion of the translation in the 1646 edition contributed to the popularity of that volume and notes that Marino's influence on Crashaw has been generally acknowledged. Observes that the "most interesting result" of Crashaw's translation was the controversy, begun by Peregrine Phillips in his 1785 edition, that Milton "had pilfered extensively" from *Sospetto d'Herode*, especially in *Paradise Lost*, and notes that the controversy "drew in many of the leading critics of the later eighteenth century" (p. 154).

≈§ 513. Ōjima, Shōtaro. "Richard Crashaw." *Waseda Eibungaku.*
Cited in Yoshihisa Aizawa's "A Bibliography of Writings about Metaphysical Poetry in Japan" (entry 1118). Not located.

≈§ 514. Townsend, Anselm. "A Forgotten English Version of the Adoro Te and the Lauda Sion of Saint Thomas." *Dominicana* (Washington, D.C.) 15 (May):5–11.
Suggests that Crashaw is a better poet than Southwell and perhaps the greatest religious lyricist of the seventeenth century. Gives a sketch of Crashaw's life. Claims that, although Crashaw was completely a poet of his age, he excelled both Herbert and Vaughan, maintaining that he "has the same niceness of diction, the same liking for quaint conceits, and, above all, though in this he far transcends them, the same mystic note, rising with him to rare heights of ecstasy, to heights probably never attained, at least so frequently, by any other English poet" (p. 7). Reproduces Crashaw's renderings of "Adoro Te" and "Lauda Sion" and suggests that his expanded paraphrases reflect "a long and meditative acquaintance with the words and thoughts of the Angelic Doctor" (p. 8). Suggests that, in some respects, Crashaw improved on St. Thomas and, through his interpretations and style, drew out the mystical implications that "the Italian poet placed there, half concealed" (p. 8).

≈§ 515. Ueda, Bin. *Eibungaku-Gairon* [A Survey of English Literature]. (Complete Works of Ueda Bin, vol. 7.)
Collection of lectures originally delivered at Kyoto Imperial University in 1913. General commentary on Crashaw's poetry (pp. 219–21) and notes (pp. 135–36). Singles out "Wishes. To his (supposed) Mistresse" as Crashaw's most famous poem but considers "The Flaming Heart" as most representative of his

art and sensibility. Praises the richness and passion of Crashaw's poetry but regards his use of elaborate conceits as a defect. Comments briefly on Crashaw's influence on the Romantic poets. Considers Crashaw superior to Herbert and suggests that "Hymn in the Holy Nativity" is superior to Milton's Nativity Ode.

⋙ 516. Williamson, George. *The Donne Tradition: A Study in English Poetry from Donne to the Death of Cowley.* Cambridge: Harvard University Press; Oxford: University Press. x, 264p.

Reprinted, New York: Noonday Press, 1958 (paperback) and 1961; New York: Noonday Press, ed. bound by Peter Smith, 1958.

Contends that, while the metaphysical poets did not regard themselves as belonging to a particular school of poetry, there was a Donne tradition, although perhaps not sharply defined: "There was no sealed tribe of Donne," but "his influence was the most profound and pervasive of any in the first half of his century" (p. 229). Chapter 4 discusses two major aspects of the tradition—the conceit and *metaphysical shudder*, a term used to describe the emotional quality of the poems. Places Crashaw in the Donne tradition, noting that his conceits often differ from those of Donne, but points out that, like Donne, Crashaw, "with the modification of his more erotic mind" (p. 95), is fully capable of producing the metaphysical shudder in his readers. Chapter 5 traces the sacred line of the tradition in the poetry of Herbert, Crashaw, and Vaughan. Discusses Crashaw's poetry primarily by comparing and contrasting it to that of Donne and Herbert, noting also the influence of the Italians and Jesuit literature. Suggests that Crashaw has "more of Donne's ecstasy" than Herbert and claims that Crashaw's "voluptuous mysticism" suggests "a mixture of two powerful qualities of Donne's mind in a feminine way that is alien to Donne's masculine sensuality and to Herbert's chaste love" (p. 112). Notes that Crashaw's poetry lacks intellectual analysis and "the searching introspection and anxious personality that distinguishes that of Herbert, and even more that of Donne," resulting in "a poetry of religious states more outward than intimate in its passion for heavenly objects" (p. 113). Stresses that the emotions presented in Crashaw's poetry "lack the precise outline of the emotions of Herbert" and contends that Crashaw has a greater musical sensibility, which "doubtless explains some of the vague mingling of emotion and emotion" (p. 114). Observes that Crashaw's poems lack the structural precision one finds in Donne and Herbert and suggests that such poems as "The Weeper" and "Wishes. To his (supposed) Mistresse" "have only the structure that is given by the string in a rosary" (p. 114). Points out, however, that the structure of Crashaw's sentences "is often more complex than that of Herbert, though generally simpler than Donne's" but that the poems have a "more lyric flow, because the burden of thought is not so great as to steal from grace for the sake of nervy strength" (p. 114). Argues, however, that, on the whole, Crashaw's poems do not lack the precision one finds in Swinburne "because of the analytic strain which the conceit induces" (p. 115). Suggests that the Italians and Jesuit literature "turned Crashaw into the most baroque of the English Metaphysicals" (p. 116). Sees the influence of Cowley on Crashaw as a disciplining force that reasserted and renewed in his poetry the Donne tradition and suggests that "Letter to the Countess of Denbigh" "is closer to Donne in its complex metaphorical utterance than any other poem Crashaw wrote" (p. 119). Finds Donne's influence in a number of the secular poems as well as in "A Hymn to Sainte Teresa" and in "The Flaming Heart" and concludes that "the conceit after the manner of Donne brings an intellectual element which fetters and locks up fast in a powerful precision the subtle and mystical emotions of Crashaw, at the same time releasing their affective power, like a magnifying glass by bringing them to a focus" (p. 121). Concludes that Crashaw is "a true representative of the European, contrasting with Donne therein," and "the most European poet in the sacred line of the Metaphysicals," claiming that his ability "to make his mysticism at least as tangible as incense is an ability which he shares with Donne" (p. 123). Compares and contrasts Crashaw also with Cowley, Vaughan, and Marvell.

1931

◄§ 517. Beachcroft, T. O. "Mysticism as Criticism: A Conversation at the School for Critics." *The Symposium: A Critical Review* 2:208–25.

Dialogue between two fictitious disputants, "Sophister" and "Senior," about the nature of mystical poetry and the relationship between poetic intuition and true mysticism. Contrasts briefly the emblematic habit of Crashaw and other seventeenth-century poets with the Romantic imaginative symbol. Comments on "The Weeper" as a reflection of the tension that arises in the language of the mystic poet: Crashaw "seems constantly on the verge of some dazzling passage which he knew well how to write, and yet again and again the mystic checks him," and thus the images in "The Weeper" "are not to be conceived in the usual view of poetry, and are to be judged rather as a form of Allegory" (p. 220). Notes that at rare times Crashaw seems to resolve the intuitions of the poet and mystic and to fuse them together. Briefly compares and contrasts Crashaw with Southwell, Richard Rolle, and Gerard Manley Hopkins.

◄§ 518. ———. "Quarles—and the Emblem Habit." *DubR* 188:80–96.

Discusses the nature and function of the emblem and the symbolic habit of mind that it reflected and produced. Notes that Quarles "was perhaps the first writer of the Theological school to introduce those multiplied images in illustration of a single thought that are so freely used in Crashaw, Herbert, and Donne" (p. 94). Points out that Crashaw "has many emblem thoughts in his pages" but, "more than that, he produced veritable emblems in the technical sense of the word" (p. 96), noting that the first edition of *Carmen Deo Nostro* contained emblems drawn by the poet himself. Suggests that "the oddity" of "The Weeper" can be partially explained if the poem is related to the emblem tradition and notes how Crashaw "returned verse after verse to a stationary picture that could not change" and thus the poem "could only take the form of a number of descants upon a central theme of inflexible rigidity" (p. 96). Maintains that "whatever is said of 'The Weeper,' and a good deal of wit has been vouchsafed concerning its details, the criticism is not very apt unless it predeclares the modality of the poem-as-style" and concludes that "it is the form in every one of its details that is the quintessence of the thought" (p. 96). Sees such emblematic images, therefore, as "not merely grotesque word-juggling" and the "outward symptom of a fortuitous and unfortunate literary fashion" but rather as "the natural outcome of the highly evolved self-conscious mind, seeking not to play with words, but to find words for spiritual experience" (p. 96).

◄§ 519. Loiseau, Jean. *Abraham Cowley: Sa vie et son oeuvre*. Paris: Henri Didier. xvii, 715p.

Compares and contrasts Cowley with Crashaw throughout. Suggests, however, that "les rapports des deux jeunes poètes semblent avoir surtout été littéraires" and that even in Cowley's elegy on Crashaw "nous y chercherions en vain une note d'intimité personnelle" (pp. 61–62), noting that "cet hommage public rendu par un protestant à un catholique nous permet de classer Cowley au nombre des rares partisans de la tolérance au dix-septième siècle" (p. 213). Mentions Cowley's kind assistance to Crashaw in Paris and Cowley's debt to "Sospetto d'Herode" in *Davideis*. Calls Crashaw "le fougueux et sensuel mystique" (p. 193) and "foncièrement élisabéthain" (p. 625). Points out that Crashaw "chante la joie de l'amour divin, mais a l'air de penser, encore plus que de sentir, sa passion mystique faisant pour les émotions ce que Donne avait fait pour les idées" (p. 619).

◄§ 520. Macaulay, Rose, "Anglican and Puritan," in *Some Religious Elements in English Literature*, 84–126. (Hogarth Lectures on Literature Series, no 14.) London: Leonard and Virginia Woolf at The Hogarth Press; New York: Harcourt, Brace, and Co.

Contrasts the voluptuousness, the religious eroticism in thought and image, and the familiarity of tone of Catholic devotional poetry of the seventeenth century, exemplified by Crashaw, with the restraint, dignity, and reserve of Anglican poetry of the period. Mentions Crashaw's "macabre dwelling" on the wounds of Christ, the tears of the Virgin Mary and the Madgalene, and "most distressing of all . . . on God's thirst for the blood of his son," as seen in "Our Lord in his Circumcision to his Father," and calls this tendency an "unfortunate orgy of sentimental materialism" (p. 93). Suggests that Crashaw, although always temperamentally a Catholic, "threw himself more and more into the voluptuous, ecstatic, sensuous, and erotic piety which has, in art, produced modern Italian Church statuary and Carlo Dolci, in religion the Cult of the Sacred Heart and the sentimentalities of which the Cult of the Little Flower of Lisieux is typical, in literature Marino's poetry, the hymns of Faber, and much beside" (p. 94). Sees such tendencies as "anti-humanist, anti-intellectual, and sometimes anti-spiritual" (p. 94). Contrasts Crashaw briefly with Pope and notes that, although Pope perhaps "underestimated Crashaw, who has splendid passages (notably in the *Hymn to St. Theresa)*" (pp. 94–95), we still agree with his conclusions about Crashaw. Finds Crashaw's secular poems "much easier to enjoy than most of his religious" (p. 95).

◄§ 521. Nethercot, Arthur H. *Abraham Cowley: The Muse's Hannibal.* London: Oxford University Press, Humphrey Milford. vii, 367p.
Reprinted (with additional notes), New York: Russell & Russell, 1967.
Mentions Crashaw throughout this study of the life and works of Cowley. Notes, in particular, Cowley's friendship with and affection for Crashaw during their Cambridge days and gives a sketch of Crashaw's life at the university. Mentions "Upon Two Apricockes sent to Cowley by Sir Crashaw" and "On Hope" and suggests that the two poets were "drawn together by their similarly shy and contemplative natures" (p. 44). Notes Cowley's debt to "Sospetto d'Herode" in *Davideis* and his likely familiarity with Crashaw's elegies on Mr. Herrys. Describes Cowley's friendship and help during Crashaw's stay in Paris. Comments on Crashaw's admiration for Queen Henrietta Maria, especially her intense piety and devotion and their mutual interest in the works of St. Teresa, pointing out, however, that Crashaw's mysticism probably "was as foreign to her temperament as it was to Cowley's" (p. 99). Briefly discusses Cowley's elegy on Crashaw, calling him "poor Dick Crashaw" (p. 133) and giving a brief account of Crashaw's last days in Italy. Suggests that Cowley's elegy is "more interesting as a landmark in Cowley's spiritual biography than as a lyric" and sees the poem as "a plea for sacred poetry such as Crashaw had written" (p. 134).

◄§ 522. Pr[az], M[ario]. "Crashaw, Richard," in *Enciclopedia italiana di scienze, lettere ed arti,* 11:800. Milan: Istituto Giovanni Treccani.
Sketch of Crashaw's life and works, stressing the influence of the Laudian movement, Little Gidding, and St. Teresa on his religious development as well as the influence of Herbert, Marino, and the Jesuit Latin epigrammatists on his poetry. Notes that Crashaw "inizia la sua carriera poetica con poesie piene di concetti, ma anche di ardite freschissime immagini che sembrano precorrere certi moderni come lo Shelley e lo Swinburne." Maintains that in his most mature religious poems Crashaw attains "l'expressione più alta di quella spiritualizzazione del senso a cui tende la migliore arte barocca" and that "col suo miracoloso e vertiginioso ascendere d'immagini travolte e infocate, la lirica del C., in ciò che ha di più peculiare, rappresenta in letteratura,

in minori proporzioni, quello che le apoteosi di un Rubens, i languori di un Murillo, e le estasi di un Greco rappresentano in pittura."

✏ 523. Schirmer, Walter F. "Die geistesgeschichtlichen Grundlagen der englischen Barockliteratur." *GRM* 19:273–84.

Discusses the philosophical background of the English baroque. Places Crashaw, along with Donne, Herbert, and Vaughan, in the mystic current as opposed to the Puritan stream. Studies baroque contributions to drama, epic, and lyric. Briefly compares Crashaw to Bernini in his ability to express mystical ecstasy and suggests that Crashaw is closer to classicism and more polished and refined than Donne.

✏ 524. Warren, Austin. "Crashaw and Peterhouse." *TLS*, 13 August, p. 621.

Discusses Crashaw's associates, both fellows and students, at Peterhouse and comments on conflicting information concerning such matters as the number and exact dates of the ejection of certain fellows, the number of those who converted to Catholicism, and the number of students that Crashaw tutored at Peterhouse. Notes that, in spite of constant charges that the Master of Peterhouse, John Cosin, was inclined to "Popery," a letter Cosin wrote to Richard Watson (entry 51) expresses his joy that Watson and he have remained faithful to "the old ways of Truth."

✏ 525. White, Helen C. *English Devotional Literature (Prose) 1600–1640.* (University of Wisconsin Studies in Language and Literature, no. 29.) Madison: University of Wisconsin Press. 307p.

Reprinted, New York: Haskell House, 1966.

Critically surveys Catholic and Protestant books of devotion published between 1600 and 1640 and discusses the historical circumstances from which they arose and were shaped. Brief references to Crashaw. Calls him "one of the greatest poets of the England of his time and a genuine mystic" (p. 117) and suggests that he "may conceivably have started his Romeward journey in his Puritan father's library" (p. 141), which contained many Catholic books.

1932

✏ 526. Albertson, Charles Carroll, ed. *Lyra Mystica: An Anthology of Mystical Verse*, edited by Charles Carroll Albertson; introduction by William Ralph Inge. New York: Macmillan. lvi, 496p.

Briefly mentions Crashaw in the introduction (pp. xxv–xxxix), calling him a "mystical poet" and "an unequal writer, with flashes of genuine inspiration, as in his noble 'Hymn to the Name and Honor of the Admirable Saint Teresa'" (p. xxxi). Anthologizes "A Song ('Lord, when the sense of thy sweet grace')" (p. 78) and lines 75–108 of "The Flaming Heart" (pp. 78–79), without notes or commentary.

◄§ 527. Bald, R. C. *Donne's Influence in English Literature*. Morpeth: St. John's College Press. 62p.

Reprinted, Gloucester, Mass.: Peter Smith, 1965.

Discusses Donne's influence from his own time to the 1930s, maintaining that Crashaw, Carew, Lovelace, Suckling, Herbert, Vaughan, and Traherne "turned to Donne as their Master" and "reproduced his gestures and his mannerisms freely, even if they did not always catch his spirit" and even if "certain of them, perhaps, missed altogether some of the things that seem most vital to us" (p. 62). Maintains that Donne's influence on Crashaw was mainly through Herbert and suggests that the influence of Herbert's style can be seen in many of Crashaw's poems, as, for instance, the opening lines of "The Weeper." Claims that Crashaw is best described by the word *luxuriant*, for "his conceits are strewn through his pages with reckless profusion" (p. 33). Calls Crashaw "the most sensuous of the metaphysical school" and notes how "images of taste and smell abound in his works" (p. 33), citing lines from "Hymn to the Name of Jesus." Maintains that Crashaw had "little constructive power, and, though he revised and rewrote his poems, many of them one feels, are no more than variations upon a theme" and suggests that the reader "is apt to become cloyed with sweets" (pp. 33–34). Finds that Crashaw's "indiscriminate use of conceits is responsible for some startling lapses of taste" (noting examples from "The Weeper," "Sancta Maria Dolorum" and "Hymn in the Glorious Epiphanie) and claims that "there is only one successful piece among Crashaw's religious poems, *Charitas Nimia*, that is not thickly studded with conceits" (p. 34). Suggests, however, that Crashaw's great quality is "his ability to soar rapidly to ecstasy," which he does "in nearly all his religious poems" (p. 35). Calls "Hymn in the Holy Nativity" a "beautiful" poem in parts but concludes that it is in the conclusion of "The Flaming Heart" that "this power finds its supreme utterance, and his fervidly passionate yearning to be merged into the object of his adoration achieves a mystical note which, frequent though it may be in devotional writings, is almost unique in English poetry before Francis Thompson" (pp. 35–36). Briefly compares Crashaw also to Cowley and Swinburne. Calls Crashaw Marino's "principal English admirer" (p. 9) and contrasts the uses of conceits in "Musicks Duell" with those in the seventh canto of Marino's *Adone*, stressing that, whereas Marino's use of conceits in describing the song of the nightingale is somewhat incidental, "Crashaw's mind passes from one to the other with no intermission; he thinks in conceits" (p. 10). Concludes that the difference between the two poets is fundamental, not merely one of degree: "In Marino, one feels, the conceits, however effective they may sometimes be, are primarily ornaments put on here and there," but "with Crashaw they are the very life and soul of the poem" (p. 11).

◄§ 528. Daly, James J. "Crashaw." *America* 47 (13 August): 453.

An original sonnet in praise of Crashaw.

⊷§ 529. Eliot, T. S. "Studies in Sanctity: VIII—George Herbert." *Spectator*
148:360–61.

Disagrees with those who suggest that "we go to Donne for poetry and to
Crashaw for religious poetry: but that Herbert deserves to be remembered as
the representative lyricist of a mild and tepid Church" (p. 361). Contends that
in Crashaw one is aware "of a passionate fancy and a metrical ability which
might also have employed themselves upon other than religious themes" and
maintains that "Crashaw (or so I believe) had he remained in the world, might
still have been the great poet that he is" but that Herbert "would (I think) at
most have produced a few elegant anthology pieces like those of Herbert of
Cherbury" (p. 361).

⊷§ 530. Elton, Oliver. *The English Muse: A Sketch.* London: G. Bell &
Sons. xiv, 464p.

Reprinted, 1933, 1936, 1937, 1950.

Briefly surveys Crashaw's life and poetry (pp. 219–20). Asserts that, although the poems contain "new and wonderful felicities," "nothing could
eradicate the no less surprising inequality of handiwork" and that "continually
Crashaw drops from a strain of exalted beauty into images too grotesque to
quote" (p. 219). Suggests, however, that at times he can write "as simply and
purely as Herrick," as, for example, in "Wishes. To his (supposed) Mistresse"
and points out that "Hymn in the Assumption" "echoes, in a rhythm hard to
surpass, the language of the *Song of Songs*" (p. 219). Maintains that "it is obvious to compare Crashaw with Francis Thompson; with both of them it is hit
or miss; the lapses are of the sort that is impossible to the born artist; but we
wait, not in vain, for the lightning" (p. 220). Claims also that Coventry Patmore "can be as abstruse and wiredrawn as Crashaw" (p. 378).

⊷§ 531. Friederich, Werner P. *Spiritualismus und Sensualismus in der englischen Barocklyrik.* (Wiener Beiträge zur englischen Philologie, vol.
57.) Vienna and Leipzig: Wilhelm Braumüller. 303p.

Demonstrates that the term *baroque* is applicable to English lyrical poetry
of the seventeenth century. Views the age as one of polarization, disharmony,
and contrasts. Comments on the sensuality and spirituality of the period and
on the effects of the conflict between the two. Briefly suggests that Crashaw
has a Latin mentality in his poems, not an Anglican sensibility. Calls him
"einen der ekstatischsten Mystiker deiser Periode" (p. 203) and notes the influence of Spanish mysticism on his poetry. Contrasts the religious temperament of Crashaw and Herbert. Suggests that Mary Magdalene became an
almost indispensable symbol of the age—the union of the erotic and the spiritual—and notes Crashaw's devotion to her.

⊷§ 532. Greg, W[alter] W[ilson], ed. "William & Richard Crashaw," in *English Literary Autographs, 1550–1650.* Selected for reproduction and

edited by W. W. Greg, in collaboration with J. P. Gilson, Hilary Jenkinson, R. B. McKerrow, A. W. Pollard, pt. 3, XCIX. Oxford: Oxford University Press.

Reprinted, Nendeln: Kraus Reprint, 1968.

Presents a biographical sketch of Crashaw and his father, discusses known manuscripts that contain Crashaw's signature, and presents a summary of bibliographical information on printed works. Briefly comments on the following items: (1) an entry, signed by Crashaw, in the Admission Books of Peterhouse, dated 20 and 22 November 1636, which was probably made a year after his actual election; (2) an entry in the Treasury Records of Peterhouse, dated 2 July 1642, containing signatures of the Master and fellows, including Crashaw, that guarantees a loan to the king; (3) a collection of Latin poems, with an autograph dedicatory epistle, now in the British Library (Add. MS 40176, fols. 2a, 3b) that "seems a yet earlier form" of *Epigrammatum Sacrorum Liber*, and (4) Crashaw's letter from Leyden, dated 20 February 1643/44 and signed "R. C." (entry 14), said to be at the time "in private hands" in Ireland. Maintains that the letter is Crashaw's but is a contemporary copy, not autograph, since the hand is clearly different from the other sources. See also E. Cruwys Sharland (entry 380) and Martin (pp. xxv–xxxi). Reproduces (with transcriptions) items 1, 2, and the beginning and subscription of 3.

◄§ 533. Harvey, Paul, ed. "Crashaw, Richard," in *The Oxford Companion to English Literature*, 193–94. Oxford: Clarendon Press.

Reprinted and revised many times.

Brief account of Crashaw's life and poetry. Notes some of the major themes of his poetry and certain influences on his art, especially Marino, the Spanish mystics, and Strada.

◄§ 534. Huxley, Aldous. *Texts and Pretexts: An Anthology with Commentaries*. London: Chatto & Windus. viii, 312p.

Reprinted several times.

Quotes lines from "Ode on a Prayer-book" to illustrate the quality of physical passion in poetry and claims that the lines "require no comment; they are almost embarrassingly explicit" (p. 108). Reproduces lines from "Musicks Duell," calling the poem "a mine of such purely sensuous images" (p. 239). Notes that Crashaw uses sensuous images "to render the quality of the immediate experience of music," but, finding them inadequate when he wishes "to express the significances and values of music," he turns to other kinds of images—"images of Nature and images of the Supernatural" (p. 240).

◄§ 535. Kurth, Paula. "Crashaw and the Passion." *Ave Maria* 35(19 March): 353–55.

Discusses Crashaw's saintly, personal love for Christ and his ability to express this devotion in poetry. Stresses that, since "nothing grieves a lover more than the sorrow of his beloved" (p. 353), so Crashaw's "tenderest syllables" of devotion were "inspired by the sufferings of the Passion" (p. 354). Cites "Song upon the Bleeding Crucifix," "On our crucified Lord Naked, and bloody," "Upon the Thornes taken downe from our Lords head bloody," "On the wounds of our crucified Lord," "Charitas Nimia," "Office of the Holy Crosse," and other poems in which Crashaw meditates on the Virgin Mary's share in the Passion, especially "Sancta Maria Dolorum." Points out that Herbert and Vaughan, with whom Crashaw is often classified, wrote relatively little on the Passion and claims that Crashaw at his best "soars far above them in an ecstasy of fiery white lyricism" (p. 355).

536. Macaulay, Rose. *They Were Defeated.* London: William Collins. 382p.

Published in the United States as *The Shadow Flies* (New York: Harper & Brothers, 1932); new ed., 1966.

A historical novel set in 1640/41 that attempts to present the political, literary, and philosophical temper of the times. Presents Crashaw as a character in the scenes at Cambridge and mentions him frequently. Portrays Crashaw as an ascetical, saintly man of discriminating literary tastes and papist leanings: "A pale, thin, dreamy young man, with visionary eyes" who sometimes "watches and prays in the church all night" (p. 161).

537. Matsuura, Kaichi. "Crashaw no Ode to the Holy Nativity" [Crashaw's Ode to the Holy Nativity]. *EigoS* 66, no. 8: 11–13; 67, no. 9:9–11.

Comments on "Hymn in the Holy Nativity," offering a summation of its thematic content.

538. Phare, E[lsie] E[lizabeth]. "The Conversion of Crashaw's Countess of Denbigh." *The Cambridge Review* 54:147–49.

Comments on Crashaw's acquaintance with the Countess of Denbigh and discusses her conversion to Catholicism in 1651, a year before her death. Describes the situation of Anglican exiles in Paris during the 1640s and 1650s and the efforts of Anglican divines, especially Cosin and Richard Stewart, to persuade them to remain loyal to the Church of England. Speculates that Cosin, formerly Master of Peterhouse, must have known Crashaw and perhaps attempted to dissuade Crashaw from embracing Catholicism.

539. Warren, Austin. "Crashaw and St. Teresa." *TLS*, 25 August, p. 593.

Notes that Joseph Beaumont in a Latin oration delivered "in Scholis pub. Cantab. an. D. 1638" singles out for special praise the works of St. Teresa and makes it clear that he "or his circle of 'Arminian' and mystically-minded friends had just discovered the Saint." Observes that, "whether it was Beaumont who shared his proud discovery with Crashaw, or Crashaw with Beaumont, I see no reason whatever of doubting that, if Beaumont knew St. Teresa in 1638, Crashaw did so as well." Recalls Beaumont's close friendship with Crashaw and notes that "no poet exhibits so close a resemblance to Crashaw's particular religious temper and poetic idiom as Beaumont." Points out that Beaumont was Master of Peterhouse after the Restoration and that the oration referred to is found in a manuscript volume inscribed "A Collection of my R[evd] Father's Latin Speeches," which was presented to the College library by Charles Beaumont, the Master's son.

◄§ 540. ————. "Crashaw's Residence at Peterhouse." *TLS*, 3 November, p. 815.

Attempts to establish "beyond reasonable doubt" the dates of Crashaw's entry into and exit from Peterhouse by use of entries made in the Peterhouse Buttery books, aided by notes in the Bursar's Book (made by Samuel Baron, Bursar of the College in 1625/26 and 1634/36). Notes that the first charges made against Crashaw's name were for the week of 10 November 1635 and that the last charge that implied he was in residence was made in the week of 20 January 1642/43. Also mentions that the account book in the Peterhouse Treasury has six entries, under the date 12 March 1643, for payment made to Crashaw's friend and former pupil, Ferrar Collet, "for ecclesiastical services rendered by Crashaw." Suggests that the fact that Collet signed for these payments lends further proof that Crashaw left Peterhouse early in 1643, earlier than Martin conjectured.

1933

◄§ 541. Foy, Thomas. *Richard Crashaw: "Poet and Saint."* Dublin: Powell Press. 128p.

Reprinted, Folcroft, Pa.: Folcroft Library Editions, 1971, 1974, 1976, 1977; Norwood, Pa.: Norwood Editions, 1976.

A general survey of Crashaw's life and poetry that relies on quotations from previous criticism and emphasizes the mystical and Catholic dimensions of his temperament and art. The table of contents is divided into nine chapters, but in the text, chapters 2 and 3 are incorporated into Chapter 2, with no chapter 3 appearing. Chapter 1, "Richard Crashaw" (pp. 7–14), offers a biographical sketch and comments on Crashaw's personality and religious sensibilities. Chapter 2, "Crashaw's Latin Poems" (pp. 15–33), surveys Crashaw's translations and secular verse; calls "Musicks Duell" more a *tour de force* than a pleasing poem; claims that Crashaw's greatest failings as an artist are his uses of extravagant imagery, repetition, lack of structure, and too facile use of language; and essentially regards the secular verse as felicitous and embued with a very sincere love of nature but not particularly outstanding. Chapter 4, "Crashaw, the Mystic; Crashaw, the Metaphysical" (pp. 34–49), comments on mysticism in Crashaw's religious poetry; stresses his familiarity "with the spiritual realities of the universe" (p. 36) and his sense of the "nearness of time to eternity, of heaven to earth" (p. 38); accounts for his lack of popularity among English readers and yet claims that certain of his exalted verses have "something which many of the most sublime passages in Shakespeare do not possess" (p. 40); and surveys the "metaphysical" qualities of Crashaw's verse, such as his uses of conceits and his ability to combine thought with feeling. Chapter 5, "Crashaw's Religious Poetry" (pp. 50–89), broadly surveys the religious poems; praises the thought, passion, and language of "A Hymn to Sainte Teresa"; calls the concluding lines of "The Flaming Heart" "the highest achievement of the muse of Religious Poetry" (p. 59); finds "Hymn to the Name of Jesus" too repetitive, too facile, and too long; notes that "Charitas Nimia" "is perhaps the only religious poem of Crashaw which is not spoiled either by glaring conceits or by being too long" (p. 62); prefers the tenderness and simplicity of "Hymn in the Holy Nativity" to the more turgid and artificial "Hymn in the Glorious Epiphanie"; notes that the paraphrases of the Latin hymns lack the merits of the originals; finds the portrayal of Satan in "Sospetto d'Herode" not necessarily inferior to Milton's Satan; calls "The Weeper" the "most typical poem ever Crashaw wrote" (p. 73); and comments on the great unevenness of the religious poetry. Chapter 6, "Crashaw, Shelley and Thompson" (pp. 90–100), compares and contrasts Crashaw to the two nineteenth-century poets, concluding that "for the modern reader these three names will always remain associated—Crashaw, the great mystic; Shelley, the great poet; and Thompson, who is both" (p. 100). Chapter 7, "Crashaw's Place Among the Poets" (pp. 101–8), comments on the influence of Donne and contrasts the two poets; points out similarities and differences between Crashaw and other seventeenth-century poets, especially Herbert, Vaughan, Herrick, and Traherne; and stresses the "Italian strain" (p. 105) in much of Crashaw's poetry, noting the influence especially of Marino. Chapter 8, "Modern Criticism" (pp. 109–13), surveys briefly modern critical attitudes toward Crashaw's art and mysticism. Chapter 9, "Conclusion" (pp. 114–25), points out the wide range of often contradictory criticism about Crashaw's achievement; suggests that his works deserve more sympathetic attention; urges readers "to overlook his failings" and focus "on his worth as a writer" (p. 123); but concludes that few non-Catholic readers are likely to appreciate Crashaw thoroughly since they cannot understand and appreciate his religious sensibility. Highly selected bibliography (pp. 128–29).

≈§ 542. Greene, Graham. "Henry James—An Aspect," in *Contemporary Essays*, 1933, edited with an introduction by Sylva Norman, 65–75. London: Elkin Matthews and Marrot.
    Reprinted, Freeport, N.Y.: Books for Libraries Press, 1968.
    Essay reprinted under the title "Henry James: The Religious Aspect" in *The Lost Childhood and Other Essays* (New York: Viking Press, 1952, 1962, 1966), 31–39.
    Mentions Crashaw briefly in a discussion of the aesthetic appeal that Henry

James found in Catholicism: "Crashaw's style, if it occasionally has the beauty of those 'marble plains' [the pavement of St. Peter's in Rome], is more often the poetical equivalent of the shop for holy statues; it has neither the purity nor the emotional integrity of Herbert's and Vaughan's" (p. 67).

◄§ 543. Patterson, Richard Ferrar. "Richard Crashaw," in *Six Centuries of English Literature: Passages Selected from the Chief Writers and Short Biographies*. Vol. 3: *Herrick to Locke*, with introductory essay by L. C. Martin, 49–55. London and Glasgow: Blackie & Son.

Revised version included in *The Story of English Literature* by R. F. Patterson (New York: Philosophical Library, 1947).

Presents a brief introduction to Crashaw's life and poetry and reproduces "Wishes. To his (supposed) Mistresse" and "The Teare," without notes or commentary. Claims that Crashaw "was a much greater poet than Herbert, and is also far more irritating" and notes that he is "one of the most unequal of poets" and that he "just missed being very great" (p. 50). Maintains that "at his best he soars far above his contemporaries, and is the peer of Shelley" but that "at his worst he is the most ridiculous of all the metaphysicals, and can be taken as an example of the meanest puerilities and the most vapid and grotesque absurdities of his school" (p. 50). Praises Crashaw's sincerity but suggests that in extravagance he outdid his Spanish and Italian models. Concludes that Crashaw "stands an isolated figure among the poets of his time, isolated by his fervent Catholicism and by his great gifts, which he did not always use to the full" (p. 50).

◄§ 544. Phare, Elsie Elizabeth. *The Poetry of Gerard Manley Hopkins: A Survey and Commentary*. Cambridge: University Press. viii, 149p.

Reprinted, New York: Russell and Russell, 1967.

Briefly compares Hopkins and Crashaw and suggests that "it is not only by his ingenious, exaggeratedly logical intellect that Hopkins resembles Crashaw" but "there is also a likeness of tone, more easily caught than defined" (p. 8). Compares, in particular, one stanza from Hopkins's "St. Dorothea" to a stanza from "Hymn in the Assumption" and maintains that both poets are similar in their uses of the conceit. Calls Crashaw "the most baroque poet of all seventeenth-century poets" (p. 9) and points out that Hopkins's "The Blessed Virgin Compared to the Air We Breathe" reflects his baroque mentality.

◄§ 545. Quennell, Peter. "Metaphysical Verse" and "Devotional Verse," in *Aspects of Seventeenth Century Verse*, selected and prefaced by Peter Quennell, 169–224, 225–79. London: Jonathan Cape.

Rev. ed., London: Home & Van Thal, 1947; reprinted, Folcroft, Pa.: Folcroft Library Editions, 1970; Norwood, Pa.: Norwood Editions, 1975; Philadelphia, R. West, 1978.

Mentions the "bold haphazard brilliance of Crashaw and Marvell" (p. 169) and suggests that "not all the extravagances of modern poetry can reconcile us to Crashaw's weeping Magdalen who follows her Lord's footsteps with lachrymose zeal" (p. 171). Comments on Crashaw's "baroque exuberance" and suggests that it is "at its best in the incomparable 'Music's Duel'" (p. 176). Briefly compares Crashaw and Cowley and reproduces "Musicks Duell" without notes or commentary. Comments briefly on Crashaw's life and personality (pp. 227–33) and suggests that "the spirit of the Counter Reformation, as it is expressed by the great monuments of Baroque architecture, gives his poems their exuberance and *brio*" (p. 233). Notes that "something of that sensuous and aspiring richness . . . breathes in the wonderful 'Hymn to Saint Theresa'" (p. 233). Reproduces selections from "The Flaming Heart" and "A Hymn to Sainte Teresa" (pp. 236–38) without notes or commentary.

◆§ 546. Smith, James. "On Metaphysical Poetry." *Scrutiny* 2:222–39.
Reprinted in *Determinations*, ed. F. R. Leavis (London: Chatto & Windus, 1934, rpt., 1970); *A Selection from Scrutiny*, ed. F. R. Leavis (Cambridge: University Press, 1968); and *Shakespearian and Other Essays* (Cambridge: University Press, 1974).
Presents an extended definition of metaphysical poetry that attempts to show precisely how it differs from other kinds of poetry sometimes closely associated with it. Argues that the "verse properly called metaphysical is that to which the impulse is given by an overwhelming concern with metaphysical problems; with problems either deriving from, or closely resembling in the nature of their difficulty, the problem of the Many and the One" (p. 228). Discusses metaphysical poetry primarily in terms of Donne's poetry and argues that a distinguishing feature of metaphysical poetry is its use of the conceit, in which "tension between the elements continues" (p. 234), yet the two elements "can enter into a solid union and, at the same time, maintain their separate and warring identity" (p. 234), thereby effecting a union "of things that, though hostile, in reality cry out for association with each other" (p. 235). Never specifically mentions Crashaw but perhaps has him in mind when commenting on the baroque conceit, which "tends to fall apart like trumpery" (p. 236).

◆§ 547. Warren, Austin, "Crashaw's Paintings at Cambridge." *MLN* 48: 365–66.
Calls attention to three paintings "undeniably from the poet's hand" (p. 365) in the *Liber Memorialis* of St. John's College (Cambridge), a manuscript volume prepared in 1628 (with additions continuing throughout the seventeenth century) to record and commemorate benefactors and gifts to the newly erected library. Notes that the college account book for 11 July 1635, under the heading "Expensae Bibliothecae," records that Crashaw was paid thirteen pounds, six shillings, eight pence for the pictures. Points out that the full-page pictures are copies of portraits belonging to the College of King Charles,

Archbishop John Williams, and Lady Margaret Beaufort and that "the colors of Crashaw's pictures are still fresh and warm" (p. 366). Observes that the paintings do not show "a hand of extraordinary skill or even delicacy" but "are the work of an amateur of talent" (p. 366). Suggests that Crashaw was asked to do the paintings because his talent was generally recognized in Cambridge but speculates also that Crashaw was invited to contribute to the volume because of his father's connections with St. John's.

◄§ 548. ———. "The Mysticism of Richard Crashaw." *The Symposium: A Critical Review* 4:135–55.
Printed also in *CQR* 116 (1933): 75–92.
Discusses the issue of whether Crashaw was himself a mystic or merely a reader of mystical literature who used its language in his own poetry. Wonders whether Crashaw's facility and rhetorical ingenuity negate genuine emotion and acknowledges that there is "ground for suspicion that Crashaw is a mere literary man playing with mysticism in the fact that he deals little if at all with the earlier states and stages of the mystical journey, little if at all with the penitential and the purgatorial, little with *aridity* and the Dark Night" (pp. 139–40). Answers these suspicions with biographical accounts that characterize Crashaw's life as ascetic, austere, and contemplative. Suggests that Crashaw's conversion to Catholicism resulted from an absence of a strong devotional life in Anglicanism rather than from doctrinal dissatisfaction. Comments on Crashaw's knowledge of the mystics and observes that he mentions only two of them in his poetry—St. Teresa and Dionysius the Areopagite. Concludes that, although Crashaw's imagination was fired by the Wound of Love experienced by St. Teresa, only five or six of his poems can be called mystical.

◄§ 549. Watkin, E[dward] I. "Richard Crashaw (1612–1649)," in *The English Way*, edited by Maisie Ward, 268–96. London and New York: Sheed & Ward.
Essay reprinted in *Poets and Mystics* (New York and London: Sheed & Ward, 1953), 136–63; reprinted, Freeport, N.Y.: Books for Libraries Press, 1968.
Calls Crashaw "the singer of Catholic devotion in its most exotic and Latin form" (p. 268) and "the baroque poet *par excellence*" (p. 279). Presents a biographical sketch of the poet and a sympathetic account of his religious sensibility, stressing the role of women in his psychological and spiritual development—Mary Collet, St. Teresa, "Mother" Church, and the Virgin Mary. Surveys Crashaw's poetry, primarily his religious verse, and agrees with Praz that, although many of his poems were written before he was formally a Catholic, the devotion that inspired him "is not the moderate and cautious piety of Anglicanism" but rather "the flaming passion, the mystic fervour, of counter-reformation Catholicism" (pp. 275–76). Registers surprise that Crashaw's poems were openly published during the height of Puritan rule,

perhaps "another proof that English devotional life, even when Catholicism was most hated, was being fed from Catholic sources" (p. 276). Maintains that "prayer, passion, poetry—their unison is the formula of Crashaw's religious art" and that "his entire writing is steeped in a spiritualised sensuousness . . . and in a diffused passion, ardent, tender, and delicate, an indefinable all-pervading atmosphere of fragrance and sweetness" (p. 280). Stresses that in his poetry Crashaw "does not preach; he does not torment himself over his sins; he does not worry about his prospects of salvation; he simply adores,—adoration is the quintessence of religion—contemplates, exalts, dances, fiddles, plays"; thus "he can carry off the most preposterous conceits . . . for they are not frigid exhibitions of ingenuity, but the toys with which he plays before the shrine" (p. 282). Considers Crashaw's treatment of such themes as death, martyrdom, spiritual love, and the saints and comments on his uses of symbols, images, emblems, music, and form. Maintains that Crashaw lacks "the indispensable mastery of architectonic form" (p. 292) and that "his sense of form is so inferior to his sense of colour that his poems possess little structure" (p. 290). Sees the omnipotence of love as the fundamental message in Crashaw's life and poetry. Compares and contrasts him with Coventry Patmore, Bernini, St. Philip Neri, Henry King, Donne, Vaughan, Swinburne, Rubens, Francis Thompson, Keats, Milton, Shakespeare, and Julian of Norwich.

1934

 550. Anon. "Seventeenth-Century Verse." *TLS*, 1 November, pp. 741–42.

Lead article that is ostensibly a review of *The Oxford Book of Seventeenth Century Verse*, edited by Grierson and Bullough (Oxford: Clarendon Press, 1934), Joan Bennett's *Four Metaphysical Poets* (entry 552), and J. B. Leishman's *The Metaphysical Poets* (Oxford: Clarendon Press, 1934); these books, however, serve primarily as a basis for the reviewer's own comments on the metaphysical poets. Suggests that the seventeenth century was fortunate to be a period between "fashionable" and "professional" poetry: "Poetry had stepped down from Court and out into a wider world" (p. 741), and yet it had not become a profession as it would after the Restoration. Points out that, although Crashaw, Vaughan, and Traherne have much in common, they also have readily distinguishable voices in their poetry. Notes that Alice Meynell "found in the use of 'conceits' a satisfying means of expressing a religious emotion comparable with that of Crashaw" but stresses that "the true note" of metaphysical poetry is "rarely recaptured" (p. 741) by its modern imitators. Observes that the reader of the *Oxford Book of Seventeenth Century Verse* "will be surprised to find not how much, but how little, of the best verse of the seventeenth century recalls Donne to their minds" (p. 742).

◄§ 551. Beachcroft. T. O. "Crashaw—and the Baroque Style." *Criterion* 13:407–25.

Maintains that criticism of Crashaw's poetry is often flawed by the denominational allegiance of critics and by the frequent, misleading comparison of his poetry to that of Keats and Shelley. Argues that, if Crashaw's poetry is read "on its own merits, without preconceived notions, it must soon occur to the mind that he is not very much like any English poet" (pp. 408–9) but shares much of the sensibility and techniques of the Continental baroque poets, especially Marino. Discusses the baroque in art, architecture, and poetry and calls Crashaw "the most highly conscious baroque poet of the period" (p. 411). Compares "Musicks Duell" with versions of Strada's original by Ambrose Phillips and John Ford and calls Crashaw's poem "the height of the baroque style in English poetry . . . a style at once formal yet enthusiastic, extravagant yet reasonable, fanciful yet systematic" (p. 415). Suggests that a special character of Crashaw's style is his ability to use sense images in such ways as to create "a kind of *ideal* image, abstracted from the object," and claims that "only a considerable poet could dwell so apart from things and so much with words with such a vivid effect" (p. 417). Contends that the baroque artist "is more absorbed in what he is making than what he is meaning" (p. 419). Discusses the emblematic habit of mind in Crashaw's poetry and suggests that the images of "The Weeper" can only be fully understood if they are read in an anagogical manner. Sees "The Weeper" as "simply a series of descants upon a central theme—when one verse is closed there is nothing to do save to begin another" (p. 423)—but argues that Crashaw is using methods very familiar and approved by baroque theorists and poets and that the poem is carefully constructed. Concludes that Crashaw, "in spite of any ignorance on the part of his readers, knows what devotion in poetry is," that his style, "though luxuriant in detail is abstract in tendency, in which vivid words are curiously remote from object and sensation," and that the emblem habit "prompts a choice of illustration very different from that which romantic poetry has found suitable" (p. 424). Briefly compares and contrasts Crashaw with Herbert, Swinburne, Donne, and the Cambridge Platonists.

◄§ 552. Bennett, Joan. *Four Metaphysical Poets: Donne, Herbert, Vaughan, Crashaw*. Cambridge: University Press. 135p.

2d ed., 1953; rpt. with corrections, 1957.

Selection (pp. 104–5) reprinted in *The Critical Temper: A Survey of Modern Criticism on English and American Literature from the Beginnings to the Twentieth Century*, gen. ed., Martin Tucker. Vol. 1, *From Old English to Shakespeare* (New York: Frederick Ungar, 1969), 299.

3d ed., with a new chapter on Marvell and title changed to *Five Metaphysical Poets: Donne, Herbert, Vaughan, Crashaw, Marvell*, 1963; rpt. 1966, 1971, 1979.

Vintage edition of *Four Metaphysical Poets, with an Anthology of Their Poetry* (see entry 837).

First edition contains seven chapters: (1) Introduction, (2) John Donne, 1573–1631, (3) Donne's Technical Originality, (4) George Herbert, 1593–1633, (5) Henry Vaughan, 1622–1695, (6) Richard Crashaw, 1613?–1649, and (7) Religious Poetry, a Postscript. Short bibliography. In the introduction surveys some of the major features of metaphysical poetry and maintains that the word *metaphysical* "refers to style, not to subject matter; but style reflects an attitude to experience" (p. 3). Suggests that "the peculiarity of the metaphysical poets is not that they relate, but that the relations they perceive are more often logical than sensuous or emotional, and that they constantly connect the abstract with the concrete, the remote with the near, and the sublime with the commonplace" (p. 4). In chapter 6, presents a biographical sketch of Crashaw and comments on the autobiographical dimensions of his poetry, noting that, although little is known about his life, "that little helps us to envisage the man who wrote the poems" (p. 94). Surveys some major characteristics of Crashaw's individual talent: his uses of the conceit, his sensationalism, his proclivity "to elaborate sensations," many of which are "peculiar and repellent" (p. 99), his lack of logical form and focus on the particular rather than the general, and his uses of nesting and sexual imagery. Finds in "The Weeper," as well as in other poems, a "mercilessly minute dwelling on sensations, unrelated to thought" and an "unnecessarily concrete development of an image" (p. 107), yet claims that Crashaw's conceits are metaphysical "in so far as they depend upon logical connections" (p. 111) and create "an unusual collocation of the sensations" (p. 112). Suggests that "A Hymn to Sainte Teresa" is one of his most successful poems and that the closing lines of "The Flaming Heart" "are perhaps the loveliest lines Crashaw ever wrote and the lines in which he most easily and fully expressed himself" (p. 113). Notes the influence of St. Teresa, the Spanish mystics, and Marino on Crashaw's art and sensibility. Contrasts Crashaw's conceits with Donne's and stresses that Crashaw and Herbert "were so different in temperament that, although both wrote love poems to God and both were influenced in some degree by the prevailing poetic fashion, their poetry has little in common" (p. 95).

553. Meissner, Paul. *Die geistesgeschichtlichen Grundlagen des englischen Literaturbarocks.* Munich: Max Hueber Verlag. 292p.

Discusses the influence of Spanish mysticism on Crashaw's religious sensibility and comments on the effect of his religious devotion on the themes and the style of his poetry. Maintains that Crashaw's poems often reflect an unconditional subjection of eroticism to "heisse, beseligende Liebe zu den Heiligen und zu Gott" (p. 148) that leads to spiritual perfection, as evidenced in the lives of his two favorite saints, Mary Magdalene and Teresa. Analyzes "The Flaming Heart" as representative of Crashaw's art and suggests that it reflects the very heights of his ecstatic style. Notes the great tension often present between form and content in Crashaw's poetry. Briefly compares and contrasts him to Marino, Góngora, Vaughan, and the Spanish mystics and suggests that Nathaniel Lee is to drama what Crashaw is to lyric poetry.

≈§ 554. Praz, Mario. "The English Emblem Literature." *ES* 16:129–40.
Comments on Crashaw are expanded and incorporated into Praz's *Studies in Seventeenth-Century Imagery* (entry 616), 1:150–51, 205. Discusses the history and development of emblem books, particularly English emblem books. Suggests that Henry Hawkins's *Partheneia Sacra, or the mysterious and delicious garden of the sacred Parthenes*, published in France in 1633, reminds the reader of Crashaw and notes, in particular, that, "in the essay on the Iris, the wealth of imagery seems to anticipate the luxuriant similes of Crashaw's *Bulla*" and that the display of musical terms in *Musicks Duell* finds a counterpart only in Hawkins" (p. 139), who must have known Strada's poem on the nightingale in *Prolusiones Academicae* (1617). Points out that the volume *Carmen Deo Nostro* contains emblems and suggests that the emblem accompanying "The Weeper" is very similar to those found in certain Jesuit emblem books of the period, especially in Hugo's *Pia Desideria* and in *Amoris Divini et Humani Antipathia*.

≈§ 555. Roberts, Michael [William Edward Roberts]. "Symbolism," in *The Critique of Poetry*, 30–44. London: Jonathan Cape.
Quotes stanza 19 of the 1652 version of "The Weeper" and notes that the lines "have been more often ridiculed than any others in the language" (pp. 36–37). Points out that, as Martin makes clear, the basic metaphor in the stanza was common in English poetry of the period and notes examples of it in the poetry of Southwell, Gervase Markham, Robert Greene, and even Marlowe. Suggests that, as modern readers, "we have been taught that common things are not poetic" and, therefore, the use of the word *bath* "seems out of place and our sense of humour makes us giggle" (p. 37).

≈§ 556. Smith, W. Bradford. "What Is Metaphysical Poetry?" *SR* 42: 261–72.
Argues that metaphysical poetry is "a paradoxical inquiry, imaginative and intellectual, which exhausts, by its use of antithesis and contradiction and unusual imagery, all the possibilities in a given idea" and that "this idea will predominantly be a psychological probing of love, death, or religion as the more important matters of experience in the life of the poet, and will be embodied in striking metaphorical utterance or in the use of the common (familiar) or scientific word" (p. 263). Cites Donne primarily and suggests that Marvell's "To his Coy Mistress" is the perfect example of a metaphysical poem. Mentions Emily Dickinson several times as one who "more than any other except Donne, has faithfully followed the metaphysical muse" (p. 267). No direct mention of Crashaw.

◆§ 557. Turmann, Margaritha. *Farbenbezeichnungen in der Dichtung der englische Renaissance*. Reval: Estlandische Druckerei Akt.-Ges. x, 98p. (Published dissertation.)

Discusses the uses of colors in English Renaissance poetry and comments on their importance and significance in imagery of the period. Points out Crashaw's tendency to use silver, gold, and purple—the colors of royalty and precious metals. Notes also his inclination to employ the spectrum of colors rather than using nuances of shades, with red being a notable exception.

◆§ 558. Walsh, Michael. "Christmas from Crashaw to Chesterton." *CathW* 140:292–96.

Suggests that the Christmas lyric "found its loftiest expression" in Crashaw's "Hymn in the Holy Nativity" "just as in our own day the best Yuletide poem is Chesterton's 'House of Christmas'" (p. 292). Claims that in the full chorus of the shepherds in the ode Crashaw "achieved something that has not been achieved before or since in poetry of the Nativity" and that in his lines there is "something which many of the sublime passages of Shakespeare do not possess" (p. 293). Contrasts Crashaw's ode with Milton's Nativity Ode. Suggests that the fundamental difference is that Crashaw was a Catholic (and perhaps a mystic and saint) whereas Milton was an austere Puritan and concludes that "without reflecting on the accepted majesty and loveliness of Milton's poem it must be admitted that Crashaw is nearer to the true heart and spirit of Christmas" (p. 294). Notes that the time between Crashaw and Milton and modern Catholic poets is an arid era for nativity poems of the highest quality. Praises other nativity poems by Francis Thompson, Thomas Hardy, Nancy Campbell, Katharine Tynan, Joyce Kilmer, Theodore Maynard, Eileen Duggan, and others.

◆§ 559. Warren, Austin. "Crashaw's Epigrammata Sacra." *JEGP* 33:233–39.

Suggests that the majority of Crashaw's epigrams in the 1634 edition were composed as pious exercises over a three-year period while he was a student at Pembroke, a continuation of his practice begun at the Charterhouse. Points out three "fairly regular sequences" (p. 237) of poems that observe the chronological order of the Anglican liturgical year, each of which includes a number of poems centering about the Nativity and some of the Sundays of the Epiphany cycle. Notes, however, that not all of the epigrams follow with regularity the liturgical calendar; rather there are "series of sequences of varying length and completeness, interspersed with groups or units which form no such sequence" (p. 237). Points out also that one of these shorter Trinity-tide sequences allows one to date it as 1632. Notes that 133 of the 178 poems in the 1634 edition are written in quatrains, sixteen in the octave, thirteen in the sextet, six in the decade, nine of "ampler dimensions," and only one in the distich (p. 235). Points out also that most have a set reference exclusively from the New Testament (93 from the Gospels of the Prayer Book), 133 of which come from the Evangelists, 20 from the Book of Acts, and 3 from Revelation; and the remainder, except a distich on the Gunpowder Plot, are "always meditations on subjects drawn from the Gospels and suggested by one of the Festivals of the Church Year" (p. 235). Discusses similar poetic exercises, especially one by a Peterhouse man (BM Add. MS 29241), and notes how High Anglicans and Catholics of the period were inclined to stress New Testament topics whereas the more Puritan practitioners tended to write poems on the whole of the Bible. Observes·that, "in general, Crashaw's epigrams celebrate the life of Christ, the Miracles, and the Saints, the historical and devotional aspects of religion, rather than the doctrinal; just as Crashaw's religion is always of the sacramental type, never the ethical of prophetic; and it is therefore natural that he should neglect the Sermon on the Mount for the Manger, the Cross, and the Empty Tomb, and draw the inspiration for his verses far less from the *words* than from the *works* of his Incarnate Lord" (pp. 238–39). (Mentions in a note that Aubrey L. Attwater, librarian at Pembroke, pointed out that Crashaw held the Greek Scholarship at Pembroke, a fact heretofore unknown to biographers.) See also Sister Maris Stella Milhaupt, "The Latin Epigrams of Richard Crashaw: With Introduction, English Translation, and Notes," Ph.D. diss., University of Michigan, 1963 (*DA*, 23:4687) and Kenneth Larsen (entry 1088).

◄§ 560. ———. "The Reputation of Crashaw in the Seventeenth and Eighteenth Centuries." *SP* 31:385–407.
Surveys critical comment on Crashaw during the seventeenth and eighteenth centuries. All references in this essay have been included as separate items in this bibliography. Notes that Pope "was the first critic to give more than passing mention to Crashaw" (p. 389) and that throughout the eighteenth century "Pope's name persists in Crashaw criticism" (p. 393). Shows that much neoclassical criticism of Crashaw revolved about the controversy over borrowings and imitation, especially purported debts of Pope and Milton to Crashaw. Observes that the eighteenth century often selected "Sospetto d'Herode" for particular acclaim and often preferred Crashaw's translations to his original poems. Concludes that "the prejudice against Crashaw's type of aesthetic was to linger on well-nigh through the nineteenth century, as was the prejudice against his type of religion" (p. 407).

1935

◄§ 561. Brooks, Cleanth. "Three Revolutions in Poetry: I. Metaphor and the Tradition." *SoR* 1(1935–1936): 151–63.
First in a series of three essays (see also entries 562 and 563). Challenges certain modern conservative critics who maintain "the division of the world into poetic and nonpoetic, and the segregation of the intellect from the emotions" (p. 152). Views the modern conceit in a historical perspective. Argues

that modern poets are "the restorers of orthodoxy, attempting to bring back
into poetry some of the virtues of the School of Donne" (p. 162): "The relation of our moderns to the School of Donne is of the same type as the relation
of Wordsworth and Coleridge to the folk ballad. Just as an appreciation of the
folk ballad went hand in hand with appreciation of Romantic poetry, so an
appreciation of our own radicals demands an ability to enjoy the metaphysicals, and involves a revision of our whole conception of poetry, a revision certainly no less radical than that sponsored by the *Lyrical Ballads* in
1798" (pp. 162–63). Stresses in particular the importance of the so-called
radical metaphor and argues that Donne's images (such as the compass) are
functional, whereas Milton's metaphors and similes are primarily decorative.
No specific mention of Crashaw.

◄§ 562. ———. "Three Revolutions in Poetry: II. Wit and High Serious-
        ness." *SoR* 1(1935–1936): 328–38.
    Second in a series of three essays (see also entries 561 and 563). Argues that
"the play of the intellect and the play of wit are not intrinsically incompatible
with the poet's seriousness, or with his sincerity in implying to the reader that
he means to be taken seriously" (p. 329). States that, in fact, much metaphysical poetry occupies a "shadowy borderline between frankly playful *vers de
société* and deeply serious lyric poetry" and that "it is more important to notice
that the deepening seriousness, when it occurs, is not accompanied by a cor-
respondent lessening of the play of wit" (p. 330). Points out that Crashaw and
Herbert, "even when they fail, always impress the reader as being serious"
and that "they succeed often enough to make their poetry, with that of Donne
and Vaughan, the greatest religious poetry which England can claim" (p. 331).

◄§ 563. ———. "Three Revolutions in Poetry: III. Metaphysical Poetry and
        the Ivory Tower." *SoR* 1(1935–1936): 568–83.
    Third in a series of essays (see also entries 561 and 562). Defines meta-
physical poetry as "a poetry in which the heterogeneity of the materials and
the opposition of the impulses united is extreme. Or if one prefers to base
himself directly on Coleridge: it is a poetry in which the poet attempts the
reconciliation of opposite or discordant qualities" (p. 570). Calls the metaphysical poet a "desperate poet" who "has confidence in his own power—in
the power of the imagination" and also "an ambitious poet" who is "constantly remaking his world by relating into an organic whole the amorphous
and heterogeneous and contradictory" (p. 570). Notes that, "as a desperate
poet, as a poet who gambles on an all-or-nothing basis, he is capable of griev-
ous error" but "one must never forget, however, that the roads which lead to
absurdity are many and various: if Crashaw's description of the Magdalene's
eyes as 'walking baths' is absurd, so is Wordsworth's 'Idiot Boy'" (p. 570).
Challenges those who insist on the didactic function of poetry or on the scientific validity of the poetic statement, especially the Marxists. Agrees with I. A.
Richards that "it is never what a poem says that matters, but what it is"

(p. 573). Sees a number of modern poets returning to the orthodoxy of the past, especially to the seventeenth century, in an attempt to repair the damage caused by the Age of Reason and the Romantic Movement. Considers, in particular, Eliot, Tate, Ransom, Crane, Warren, and even Hardy and Yeats in this light.

◅§ 564. Crashaw, Richard. *Musicks Duell* From *The Delights of the Muses; or Other Poems written on severall occasions*. London: Printed and published by Edward Walters. [8]p.

Limited to 250 handprinted copies on handmade paper; 250 additional copies printed by John Hagreen at Ditching Common, Sussex, in 1938.

Contains (1) wood engravings by Philip Hagreen, (2) "Musicks Duell" (1646), and (3) a biographical sketch of Crashaw with a note that calls Crashaw's poem a "free translation" and "expansion of Strada's Latin poem" and points out that the poem has also been translated by such notables as John Ford and Ambrose Phillips.

◅§ 565. Eliot, T. S. "Religion and Literature," in *Faith That Illuminates*, edited by V. A. Demant, 29–54. London: The Centenary Press.

Reprinted in *Essays Ancient and Modern* (London: Faber and Faber, 1936), 93–112.

In an essay that argues for the broad application of ethical and theological standards to all literature, not simply literature with religious subject matter, discusses briefly the response of most modern readers to "devotional" poetry. Maintains that, for the great majority of people who love poetry, '*religious po-etry*' is a variety of *minor* poetry: the religious poet is not a poet who is treating the whole subject matter of poetry in a religious spirit, but a poet who is dealing with a confined part of this subject matter: who is leaving out what men consider their major passions, and thereby confessing his ignorance of them" (p. 35), adding that "this is the real attitude of most poetry lovers towards such poets as Vaughan, or Southwell, or Crashaw, or George Herbert, or Gerard Hopkins" (p. 36). Explains that "devotional" poetry is, in fact, often the prod-uct of limited of special religious awareness and maintains that none of the above-mentioned poets "are great religious poets in the sense in which Dante, or Corneille, or Racine, even in those of their plays which do not touch upon Christian themes, are great Christian religious poets" (p. 36), adding "or even in the sense in which Villon and Baudelaire, with all their imperfections and delinquencies are Christian poets" (pp. 36–37). Concludes that, "since the time of Chaucer, Christian poetry (in the sense in which I shall mean it) has been limited in England almost exclusively to minor poetry" (p. 37).

◅§ 566. Empson, William. "Double Plots: Heroic and Pastoral in the Main Plot and Sub-Plot," in *Some Versions of the Pastoral*, 25–86. London: Chatto and Windus.

Published in the United States as *English Pastoral Poetry* (New York: W. W. Norton, 1938). Reprinted several times.

Suggests that Crashaw in "The Weeper" treats Mary Magdalene "as a sort of rival Christ" or at least makes her "a second atonement, between Christ and the world" (pp. 82–83). Maintains that in the poem it is she, not Christ, "who underlies the order of nature" and is "*the* waterclock by which Nature measures time" (p. 83). Claims that critics have often thought the phrase "Portable and compendious oceans" was absurd "merely because it puts specially clearly what such critics would call the absurdity of the whole conception of the poem; her tears are the idea of water, all water, and make water do whatever it does" (p. 83). Agrees that Protestants were quite right to see this kind of portrayal of a saint as heretical "because it destroys the uniqueness of Christ," but points out that "for literary purposes they continued to do it themselves" (p. 83).

◄§ 567. Musser, Benjamin [Francis], ed. *The House of Bread: a book of Incarnate Love, of the God-Man of Christmass.* Manchester, N.H.: Magnificat Press. x, 306p.

Anthologizes fourteen lines from "O Gloriosa Domina" (p. 41), thirteen stanzas from "Hymn in the Holy Nativity" (pp. 126–29), and "Our Lord in his Circumcision to his Father" (pp. 226–27). Briefly compares Crashaw's Nativity ode to that of Milton (p. 129), suggesting that the fundamental difference is between the temperaments of the mystical and saintly Catholic and the austere Puritan.

◄§ 568. Newdigate, B[ernard] H. "An Overlooked Poem by Richard Crashaw." *Merc* 32:265.

Reproduces an unsigned poem entitled "On the Translation of the House of Loretto," first published in 1813 in *Tixall Poetry* (entry 121), and claims that it was written by Crashaw and may be the last poem he wrote. Maintains that "no poet but Crashaw would have so linked classical myth with pious tradition, paganism with Christian faith, earth with heaven itself, as the writer of these lines has done." Notes that the figure of the Eastern Sun in the poem is one that Crashaw used repeatedly in his sacred verse.

◄§ 569. Osgood, Charles Grosvenor. "Cavaliers," in *The Voice of England*: A *History of English Literature*, 229–36. London and New York: Harper & Brothers.

Reprinted, 1936, 1937; 2d ed., 1952.

Brief introduction to Crashaw's life and poetry. Praises "A Hymn to Sainte Teresa" and "The Flaming Heart" as poems "in which grandeur of idea, power of phrase, and vibrant music all coincide under the heat of his strong ecstasy" but admits that "this happy coincidence is rare, for he is often commonplace, and sometimes sinks to depths of 'conceit' which are ludicrous or disgusting" (p. 234).

⋘ 570. Praz, Mario. Review of *The Oxford Book of Seventeenth Century Verse* edited by H. J. C. Grierson and G. Bullough, *The Metaphysical Poets* by J. B. Leishman, and *Four Metaphysical Poets: Donne, Herbert, Vaughan, Crashaw* by Joan Bennett. *ES* 17:101–5.

Suggests that, once neglected, the metaphysical poets "now risk becoming too popular," notes that the market for additional critical studies of them "has now reached the point of saturation," and asks if, in fact, the metaphysicals "lend themselves to endless investigation like geniuses of the first magnitude" (p. 101). Finds the studies of Leishman and Bennett highly derivative and excessively repetitive of the criticism of Eliot and of Praz himself. Chides Bennett for her failure to study the Jesuit poets of the period, suggesting that, had she done so, she would not have concluded that Crashaw is in some way peculiar for having combined physical torture with sensual love in religious poems. Points out that "this conjunction was universally proclaimed by Continental art, which the Council of Trent had instructed to exalt martyrdom" (p. 104). Claims that Bernini, Rubens, and Crashaw reflect the widespread sensibility of their time.

⋘ 571. Ricci, Seymour de, comp. "The Folger Shakespeare Library, Washington," in *Census of Medieval and Renaissance Manuscripts in the United States and Canada*, compiled by Seymour de Ricci, with the assistance of W. J. Wilson, 1:267–450. New York: H. W. Wilson.

Notes in entry 267.1 a poetical commonplace book (compiled about 1650) in the Folger Shakespeare Library that contains extracts from Shakespeare's sonnets, sixty-five epigrams by Thomas Fuller, and poems by Crashaw, Benlowes, Ravenshaw, Sherburne, Hooke, Llewellan, and others. (The Folger Shakespeare Library indicates thirteen poems attributed to Crashaw in the collection [V.a.148].)

⋘ 572. Sharp, Robert Lathrop. "Observations on Metaphysical Imagery." *SR* 43:464–78.

Stresses the "organic growth of figurative language and the capacity of poets to adjust their imaginations to the resultant new levels of the poetic idiom" (p. 464) and cautions that, although we may balk at certain of the similes in "The Weeper," "the delights of poetry for Donne and the metaphysicals were not wholly what they are for us" (p. 465). Points out that, "because the poetic idiom of the Elizabethans was already a welter of metaphors, with countless variations on the same notion, the poetic necessity of being new and different led the metaphysicals to sensitize their perception" and notes that, "whereas the Elizabethans began with an idiom on a lower figurative level, the metaphysicals began with the figures of a Shakespeare" (p. 470). Notes that the abstract phrase "weeping motions" in "The Weeper" has "a power of suggestion far beyond any of the Elizabethans," warns against visualizing such conceits, and suggests that it may be "a slipshod habit of visualizing all imagery that interferes with the proper appreciation of much metaphysical poetry"

(p. 471). Notes that both Crashaw and Donne were fond of the conceit of spring as a cradle.

◄§ 573. Smith, Chard Powers. *Annals of the Poets: Their Origins, Backgrounds, Private Lives, Habits of Composition, Characters, and Personal Peculiarities.* New York and London: Charles Scribner's Sons. xxv, 523p.

Catalogs miscellaneous information about English poets—their hobbies, pets, friendships, formal education, early domestic attachments, looks and manners, and so on. Mentions Crashaw throughout. Notes, for instance, that Crashaw was the son of an upper-middle-class divine, received degrees from Cambridge, knew Latin and Italian, died young, and that, like Herbert and Vaughan, he had a "negligible" contemporary reputation but has a "modest" permanent fame.

◄§ 574. Thompson, W. Meredith. *Der Tod in der englischen Lyrik des siebzehnten Jahrhunderts.* (Sprache und Kultur der germanischen und romanischen Völker . . . A. Anglistische Reihe. . . . Vol. 20.) Breslau: Verlag Priebatschbuchhandlung. viii, 97p.

Discusses various attitudes toward death as reflected in the works of selected seventeenth-century English poets. Points out that Crashaw expresses his love for God in terms of human love and claims that Crashaw believes that true love can only be perfected through death. Notes Crashaw's strong devotion to the crucified Christ, who in His suffering and death manifests the greatest expression of divine love. Maintains that, although Crashaw seems uncommonly receptive to the beauty of this world, he is, in fact, only using it as a vehicle to express spiritual truths. Suggests that Crashaw's love of baroque word play often draws him from serious presentation of his subject to a more elaborate and overly witty extravagance.

◄§ 575. Wallerstein, Ruth C. *Richard Crashaw: A Study in Style and Poetic Development,* (University of Wisconsin Studies in Language and Literature, no. 37.) Madison: University of Wisconsin Press. 160p.

Reprinted (with a foreword by Helen C. White), 1959, 1962; New York: Lemma Pub. Co., 1972.

Selections (pp. 114, 125–26) reprinted in *The Critical Temper: A Survey of Modern Criticism on English and American Literature from the Beginnings to the Twentieth Century,* gen. ed. Martin Tucker. Vol. 1: *From Old English to Shakespeare* (New York: Frederick Ungar, 1969), 298–99.

Traces the development of Crashaw's style, considering the influences of classical rhetoric, Spenserianism, Jesuit epigrammatists, Marinism, and emblem literature and *impresa.* In chapter 1, "Introductory" (pp. 9–15), maintains that it is only when Crashaw's "inner life lays hold upon us that we can understand how the ingenious, theatrical, often trivial and barbarous elements" of his style "become at last fused and transmuted into poetic utterance" (p. 9). Contends that in Crashaw's poetry there are "two strangely mingled elements, an exceptionally rich sensuous and emotional endowment, and a high degree of stylization within conventional and rigidly mechanized modes of expression" and maintains that Crashaw sought from this mixture "the revelation of a world behind the world of the senses" (p. 14). In chapter 2, "Crashaw's Life and Inner Growth" (pp. 16–55), demonstrates how the poet's life and intellectual development molded his imagination, noting especially the influence of his father, Nicholas Ferrar, Little Gidding, and the Laudian movement. Considers Crashaw's early poetry, especially "Musicks Duell," in the light of Marinism and his interest in music. Discusses the influence of St. Teresa and other Continental religious writers on Crashaw's religious and artistic sensibility and assesses to what degree he was un-English. Argues that "the ardent feeling bound up within intense sensuousness which distinguishes Crashaw from Marino" is central to his development but that "it is an individual thing and yet broadly English" (p. 35). Analyzes "Hymn to the Name of Jesus" to demonstrate the influence of religious music on Crashaw's poetry and discusses religious ecstasy and its development in his poetry, noting that his later poems reflect "an ecstasy rooted in profounder meditation than the ecstasy of the earlier poems" (p. 55). In chapter 3, "School-Work: The Latin Epigrams and the Pattern of the Rhetorics" (pp. 56–72), discusses two primary influences on Crashaw's epigrams—Marino and the Jesuits—and defines their differences: Marino's poetry is "worldly and sophisticated" while the Jesuit epigrams are "resonant of moral purpose" (p. 58). Maintains that the Latin epigrams are mostly school exercises that "translate the Bible into Ovid" (p. 60). Suggests that his dependence upon rhetoric handbooks, phrase books, and poetical guides led Crashaw "to emphasize ingenuity in figure, gaudy decoration, and externality" and "to develop the figure at the expense of the whole" (p. 69). In chapter 4, "The Translations" (pp. 73–113), surveys Crashaw's translations from Latin and Italian. Contrasts "Sospetto d'Herode" with its source and concludes that Crashaw's poem "is far more dramatic, more imaginative and intense, more concrete and rich in imagery than its original" (p. 74). Suggests that divergences from Marino are essentially elements of Spenserianism. Discusses the relation of "The Weeper" and "The Teare" to their Jesuit and Marinist sources, emphasizing that in both poems Crashaw's sensuousness becomes symbolic. Comments also on the influence of Marinism on "Sancta Maria Dolorum," "Song upon the Bleeding Crucifix," and "Hymn in the Holy Nativity." Suggests that Marinism is most evident in Crashaw's use of ingenious figures for their own sake rather than for the idea or emotion. Calls attention to his insistence on sensational, physical details and his analysis of emotions by using a dialectic of violent contrasts. Compares the English translations of the epigrams to the Latin and finds the former more florid and sensuous, more explicitly moral, and more ingenious and colloquial. Briefly compares and contrasts "Musicks Duell,"

"Alexias," and "Out of Grotius his Tragedy of Christes sufferinges" to their originals. In chapter 5, "Emblems and Impresa: The Maturing of Crashaw's Imagery" (pp. 114–35), maintains that Crashaw's mingling of the highly symbolic with homely realism evidences the influence of emblems on his imagery and claims that the high degree of concentration and abstraction of his images and symbolic adjectives make them seem more like *impresa* than emblems. Argues that "imagery is of supreme significance with Crashaw" and that "in a very special sense his imagery is his meaning" (p. 126). Compares and contrasts Crashaw's use of imagery with that of Shelley and Swinburne and demonstrates his growth in poetic intensity by tracing the development of his use of the phoenix and the blush as images, showing how they develop from mere ingenuity to mature symbol. In chapter 6, "Style and Spirit Fused" (pp. 136–47), demonstrates the fusion of the sensuous and the abstract in Crashaw's poetry and compares his poetic temper with that of Spenser and Donne. Cites "Office of the Holy Crosse" and several of his translations of medieval hymns as examples of imperfect fusion of style and spirit. Regards "O Gloriosa Domina" as the finest of the hymns; "Hymn in the Holy Nativity" as the most tender of the poems; and the Teresian poems, "Hymn in the Glorious Epiphanie," and "Hymn to the Name of Jesus" as the most grand and splendid. Concludes by discussing the symbolic content of "Hymn in the Glorious Epiphanie," the relation of "Hymn to the Name of Jesus" to ecstasy, and the fusion of technique with meaning and statement in the Teresian poems. Bibliography (pp. 148–58) and index (pp. 159–60).

◄§ 576. Warren, Austin. "Crashaw's 'Apologie.'" *TLS*, 16 November, p. 746.

Argues that "An Apologie for the fore-going Hymne" is not an "ecclesiastical argument" but rather "an apology for the poet's 'weak and worthlesse song,' for his attempt to laud in English a saint already highly exalted in other tongues" and chiefly is "an apology to his countrymen for having eulogized a foreigner," especially a Spaniard, when "to hate her had been, as recently as 1630, a patriotic duty." Maintains that Crashaw asserts that one must "transcend political rivalries" and, "since no patriotism prevents Englishmen from getting drunk on Spanish sack, then at least Englishmen of piety may freely be permitted to drink, with St. Teresa, the 'strong wine of love,' to experience with her divine inebriation." Stresses that, since Crashaw's sensibility was thoroughly Catholic during his years at Peterhouse, "it is impossible, on a theological basis, to date his poetry *ante* or *post conversionem*."

◄§ 577. ———. "Richard Crashaw, 'Catechist and Curate.'" *MP* 32: 261–69.

Discusses Crashaw's ecclesiastical career during his Anglican years. Argues that, although no definite record survives of his ordination to the priesthood, he was probably ordained as early as 1637 and certainly by late spring or early summer 1639, when he was made curate of Little St. Mary's, a post that he held until January 1643 (see entry 288). Points out also that Crashaw was elected "catechist," that is, "theological tutor or lecturer" (p. 267), of Peterhouse on 31 March 1640. Notes that, although Crashaw is said to have been an outstanding preacher, none of his sermons has survived and speculates that perhaps he burned them before departing from Cambridge, perhaps the Puritan fellows burned them after his departure, or perhaps they were extemporized. Maintains that, "for all their virtuosity, Crashaw's poems generally seem improvisations" and that it is reasonable to think that his sermons "displayed much of the same imaginative exuberance, the same torrential rhetoric, the same breathless ardor" (p. 269). Suggests further that his sermons, like his epigrams, were likely based on the gospels and epistles.

◄§ 578. Wild, Friedrich. "Zum Problem des Barocks in der englischen Dichtung." *Anglia* 59:414–22.

Defines the concept of the baroque for English literature and gives examples of poets and aspects of poetry that might be called baroque. Points out that concepts of the baroque were derived from art history and only later adopted by literary critics and that the baroque is fundamentally a Continental movement, not English. Cites Crashaw's description of Satan in "Sospetto d'Herode" as representative of the extravagance of baroque style, which often stresses the shocking, the terrifying, and the repulsive, and contrasts Crashaw's portrayal of Satan with Milton's more classical description. Notes the predominant influence of the Spanish mystics and Jesuit poets on Crashaw and compares and contrasts his art with that of Southwell. Briefly discusses Crashaw's erotic mysticism, especially in the Teresian poems and in "Hymn in the Assumption," and comments on his attraction to Counter-Reformation themes, especially the Virgin Mary and the saints.

1936

◄§ 579. Barrett, Alfred. "The Tradition of Wit." *Spirit* (January): 183–86.

Reprinted in *Return to Poetry: Critical Essays from Spirit*, ed. John Gilland Brunini, Francis X. Connolly, and Joseph G. E. Hopkins (New York: Declan C. McMullen Co., 1947), 76–80.

Urges contemporary Catholic poets to reject "a vague and wordy pseudo-mysticism" and "a placid, conventional 'piosity'" (p. 183) and to return to the tradition of wit exemplified by the seventeenth-century poets, including Crashaw. Suggests that, although the poetry of G. M. Hopkins shows affinities to the poetry of Southwell, Quarles, Herbert, Vaughan, and others, "much of his work is closest to Crashaw" (p. 186).

◄§ 580. Brinkley, Roberta Florence, ed. "Richard Crashaw," in *English Poetry of the Seventeenth Century*, 353–76. New York: W. W. Norton & Co.

Expanded edition, 1942.

Presents a brief introduction to Crashaw's life and poetry (pp. 353–57), followed by six selections (pp. 357–76). Claims that "Musicks Duell" "exquisitely imitates the sound of the lute and the voice of the nightingale" and calls "Wishes. To his (supposed) Mistresse" "quaintly original" (p. 355). Comments primarily on the mystical temper of Crashaw's sacred poems, maintaining that his poems on the Virgin or the saints "glow with the warmth of human love and his phraseology often becomes that of a lover" (p. 355). Points out Crashaw's vivid presentation of the senses, calling him "a Keats with Catholicism added," but notes also his unevenness, his tendency to pile up conceits, and his careless craftsmanship. Claims that Crashaw "enjoys the questionable distinction of being the author of two of the worst lines in English literature and probably of the most distasteful poem *The Weeper*" (p. 356). Briefly notes the influence of Herbert, and Crashaw's influence on Pope and Coleridge.

◄§ 581. Brittin, Norman A. "Emerson and the Metaphysical Poets." *AL* 8:1–21.

Discusses Emerson's appreciation of the metaphysical poets and the influence they may have had in his own verse. Notes two references to Crashaw in reading lists in Emerson's journal: (1) "Musicks Duell" (under title of "Musician and Nightingale") in 1843 and (2) "Sospetto d'Herode" in 1870 (see entry 156). Perceives little resemblance or discernible affinity between Emerson's poetry and that of Crashaw but points out that the concluding lines of "The World-Soul" may have been suggested by lines from Crashaw's "In praise of Lessius." Challenges Bliss Perry's comment in *Emerson Today* (Princeton: Princeton University Press, 1931) that Emerson read too much metaphysical poetry. Concludes that Emerson's poetry, "not in general, but in numerous individual passages, resembles slightly that of Donne and Cowley, and strongly, that of Herbert and Marvell" (pp. 20–21).

◄§ 582. Colby, Elbridge. "Two Religious Poets: Southwell and Crashaw," in
    English Catholic Poets: Chaucer to Dryden, 137–58. Milwaukee: Bruce
    Publishing Co.

Reprinted, Freeport, N.Y.: Books for Libraries, 1967.

Offers a general introduction to Crashaw's life and poetry (pp. 152–58), calling him "one of the truest lyrists in the English language" and maintaining that "his emotional temperament resounded in sustained song which gives us many of the finest singing lines in literature" (p. 153). Sees Crashaw's secular poetry as inconsequential and acknowledges that occasionally Crashaw fell into the excesses of his age, especially in "The Weeper." Comments generally on Crashaw's uses of imagery, figures of speech, and the music of sounds, as well as the emotional intensity of his sacred verse, maintaining that "he can, at his best, produce a sustained lyric quality that is rare in any poetry" (p. 155).

Concludes that, after Crashaw, English poetry "turned to rolling numbers and merely splendid diction or into the sheer jog trot of Alexander Pope" and that, "for two hundred years, an England that repressed its emotions was not to hear lyrics like these" (p. 158). Briefly compares and contrasts Crashaw with Southwell, Herbert, Shelley, Byron, Poe, Swinburne, and Tom Moore.

◄§ 583. Kelly, Blanche Mary. "The Renaissance: III. More Earth, Less Heaven," in *The Well of English*, 105–15. New York and London: Harper & Brothers.

Stresses the centrality of Catholicism to the greatness of English literature. Claims that Crashaw, by his conversion, returned to the essential source of inspiration. Praises the Teresian poems, calling them "sublime and soaring verses," but adding that "it is in his translations of the *Adoro Te* and the *Dies Irae*, in the *Hymn on the Glorious Assumption of Our Lady*, that he achieves what Donne groped for in vain, not metaphysics but mystical vision" (p. 111). Admits that "the metaphysical way of writing had execrable faults and some of the worst were committed by Crashaw," but concludes that "not even the greatest of his contemporaries succeeded as he did in demonstrating the fellowship of soul and body, which after all is one of the purposes of all art" (p. 111).

◄§ 584. Meozzi, Antero. "Marinismo inglese," in *Il secentismo e le sue manifestazioni europee in rapporto all'Italia*, 111–35. Pisa: Nistri-Lischi Editori.

Suggests that Crashaw's sacred epigrams evidence a direct contact with Marino's poetry. Notes, in particular, a closeness in the imagery of the two poets. Maintains, however, that Crashaw is not a mere imitator of the Italian poet and that they differ greatly in temperament, Crashaw being metaphysical and spiritual and Marino being sensual and superficial. Concludes that Crashaw has "accenti che nessun secentista del commune gregge ha mai pensato" (p. 128). Suggests that in some ways Crashaw's verbal dexterity can be compared to that of Poe, Keats, Victor Hugo, Rossetti, Swinburne, Jean Lorrain, and D'Annunzio.

◄§ 585. Olivero, Federico. *Lirica religiosa inglese*. Turin: S. Lattes & Co. 474p.

Expanded version, Turin: Società Editrice Internazionale, 1941.

Mentions Crashaw throughout. In "Scuola Metafisica" (pp. 231–78) comments on certain metaphysical qualities of Crashaw's thought and style, translates lines from "The Flaming Heart" into Italian prose (p. 236), and notes in particular the influence of emblems in Crashaw's verse. Comments specifically on the spiritual ardor and mystical exaltation of Crashaw's poems: "un ardore assai più intenso è nelle smaglianti pitture del Crashaw, nel suo amore al sacrificio e ad una spiritualità marziale, al combattimento contro le passioni" (p. 238). Contrasts and compares Crashaw briefly with Donne, Herbert, Quarles, Thomas Parnell, Isaac Watts, John Norris, and the Romantics.

◆§ 586. Pickel, Margaret Barnard. "Other Royalist Poets," in *Charles I as Patron of Poetry and Drama*, 69–94. London: Frederick Muller.

Observes that Crashaw "was in steady poetical attendance on the royal family for some years" (p. 81), noting that he wrote complimentary poems on the occasion of the King's coronation as well as several poems to Queen Henrietta Maria, including poems on the births of the Duke of York (1633), Princess Elizabeth (1635), Princess Anne (1637), and Prince Henry (1640). Briefly comments on the support the Queen gave Crashaw when he was introduced to her by Cowley in Paris in 1646.

◆§ 587. Pulsford, Daniel B. "The Passion and the Poets: Devotional Poets of [the] Seventeenth Century." *Sign* 15:505–7.

Offers a general introduction to Herbert, Vaughan, and Crashaw as devotional poets and stresses that, although their religious poems are "quaintly pretty" and "have a fascinating exotic quality" (p. 505), they never achieve the grandeur and genius of Milton's poems. Maintains that all three poets were reacting against Puritanism but suggests that what distinguishes Crashaw's poetry from that of Herbert or Vaughan is its passionate strain of devotion and its mystical ardor. Claims that Crashaw's poetry is often florid, overly sweet, too sensuous, and exotic and that "it must be admitted that Crashaw was not entirely successful in his attempt to anglicize a devotional spirit which needed Spanish or Italian in which fully and properly to express itself" (p. 507). Cites lines from "Song upon the Bleeding Crucifix" to illustrate Crashaw's use of figures of speech that are alien to modern taste. Concludes that "the interest of Crashaw and his fellow-poets consists largely in that they constitute the poetic channel through which Catholicism returned to their native land" and suggests that "the somewhat academic and Tory character of the Oxford Movement carried on the tradition which they helped to create" (p. 507). Notes the influence of Crashaw on Francis Thompson.

◆§ 588. Taketomo, Sōfū. "Crashaw," in *Eibungaku-shi*, 670–1660 [A History of English Literature, 670–1660]. Kobe: Kawase-shoten.

General introduction to Crashaw's life and poetry for the Japanese student. Sees Crashaw as a disciple of Donne and comments on his influence on such later poets as Pope, Coleridge, and Shelley.

◆§ 589. Warren, Austin. "Crashaw's Reputation in the Nineteenth Century." *PMLA* 51:769–85.

Surveys the critical reception of Crashaw's poetry during the nineteenth century. Observes that throughout the period Crashaw's reputation was handicapped by three factors: his use of conceits, his Catholicism, and his conceited treatment of religious themes. Notes that, except for Coleridge and the American Transcendentalists, the metaphysical poets were not greatly admired by the Romantic critics and poets. Describes Coleridge's patronage of Crashaw and observes that Grosart "dramatically reverses the estimate of the preceding century by assigning to Pope mere talent, but to Crashaw, genius" (p. 784). Points out that later nineteenth-century critics discovered in some of the Romantic poets certain "figures and aesthetic attitudes which, by their analogy to Crashaw, assisted in the genuine—as distinct from the purely historical—appreciation of the earlier poet"; thus "Keats' sensuousness, Shelley's mixture of heaven and earth, his fire, his tense music: these recalled Crashaw" (p. 784). Suggests that "in the second half of the century, Swinburne and Francis Thompson performed a similar office" (p. 784). Stresses that, except for Alice Meynell, even nineteenth-century Catholics "were as distant from sympathy with Crashaw's aesthetic as were the Protestants and free-thinkers" (p. 785). Concludes that it is only with the works of Canon Beeching (entry 342), Mario Praz (entry 459), George Williamson (entry 516), and T. S. Eliot (entry 483) "that we reach an attitude unarmed with *a priori* prejudice against the conceit" (p. 785).

✎§ 590. Watkins, W. B. C. "Spenser to the Restoration," in *Johnson and English Poetry Before 1660*, 58–84. (Princeton Studies in English, no. 13.) Princeton: Princeton University Press; London: Humphrey Milford, Oxford University Press.

Mentions that Dr. Johnson, like Pope, was an admirer of Crashaw, "preferring his poetry, in spite of its Catholic inspiration, to that of the Anglican Herbert," and that he "was perfectly aware, too, that Pope at times copied Crashaw" (p. 83). Suggests that it seems curious that Johnson liked the sacred poetry of both Crashaw and Herbert but seemingly did not care for Donne's religious verse. Notes that Johnson often quoted from Crashaw in the *Dictionary*—twenty-three times, for instance, under the letters *M*, *N*, and *O*. See also A. D. Atkinson (entry 732), David Perkins (entry 756), and Samuel Johnson (entry 81).

✎§ 591. White, Helen C. *The Metaphysical Poets: A Study in Religious Experience*. New York: Macmillan. ix, 444p.
Reprinted, New York: Collier Books, 1962, 1966.
Studies the lives and poetry of Donne, Herbert, Crashaw, Vaughan, and Traherne. In the introduction discusses how mysticism and poetry are alike and how they differ and concludes that, although none of the poets discussed is a mystic in the strict sense of the word, all evidence elements of mysticism in their poetry. Chapter 1, "The Intellectual Climate"; chapter 2, "The Religious Climate"; and chapter 3, "Metaphysical Poetry," set up background for the discussion of the individual poets (two chapters to each poet). Chapter 8, "Richard Crashaw: Little Gidding to Rome" (pp. 202–29), presents a sketch

of Crashaw's life and a discussion of his religious sensibilities. Notes that Crashaw's reputation as a wit antedates his reputation as a saint but focuses primarily on his fundamentally Catholic temper and spirit, evident long before his formal conversion to Rome. While recognizing the influence of St. Teresa, the members of the Little Gidding community, his contemporary High Anglican friends and colleagues, and others, points out also that Crashaw's "turning to the great Latin hymns of Thomas Aquinas and Thomas of Celano and Jacopone da Todi is not without its significance as to the development of his mind and feeling" (p. 229). Chapter 9, "Richard Crashaw: 'Poet and Saint'" (pp. 230–58), discusses in some detail the particulars of Crashaw's religious sensibility and attitudes as reflected in his poetry, such as the intensity of his personal, intimate feeling; his delight in color, movement, and brilliance; his ability to sustain flights of ecstasy; his musical virtuosity; his ritualistic uses of images and paradoxes; and his dwelling on the human aspects of Christ's life. Sees Crashaw's poetry as "homogeneous to an extraordinary degree" and maintains that, although in time he abandoned Latin for English, "it is essentially the same man singing on the same themes to the same ends" (p. 231). Finds the same thing true of Crashaw's religious development, noting that "whatever his specific church allegiance, his controlling religious attitudes are the same" (p. 232). Stresses that, for Crashaw, "the central fact in the world's history" was the Incarnation, "not that Christ died for man to satisfy God's justice and redeem his elect, but that God should have come into the world, stooping his glory to the meaness of earth, adding to his ancient cares the littleness of human life" (p. 233). Notes the particularly affective, contemplative, and devotional nature of his poetry, in contrast to the strictly theological, but insists on the intellectual development and control in his often highly embellished poems. Finds Crashaw's rhapsodic temperament highly reflective of the mystical experience but stops short of assenting to the notion that the poet was, in fact, a genuine mystic. Throughout the discussion comments on numerous influences on Crashaw's art and sensibility, including St. Teresa, the Counter Reformation, Herbert, classical Latin poetry, Jesuit poetry, Marino, emblems, and Ignatian meditation, and compares Crashaw to Donne, Herbert, Vaughan, and Traherne, most specifically in the conclusion of the book (pp. 375–411).

≈§ 592. Woesler, Richard. "Über englisches Literaturbarock." *LJGG* 8: 139–50.

Reviews recent studies of English baroque literature. Suggests that the term *baroque* is simply a convenient label to cover a confusion of differing forces, caused by "die Unfähigkeit eine Synthese von Katholizisimus, Rittertum, patristischem Gedankengut, Puritanertum, antiker Mythologie und der sensualistischen Kultur der italiienischen Renaissance" (p. 139). Comments extensively on Paul Meissner's *Die geistesgeschichtlichen Grundlagen des englischen Literaturbarocks* (entry 553) and finds fault with the author's understanding of the baroque aesthetic and his attempt to fit individual works into a preconceived pattern of discordance. Briefly comments on Crashaw, noting that often stanzas could be interchanged without destroying the structure of his poems and pointing out his intention of incarnating the supernatural. Maintains that, although the metaphors of the period appear sensual, they are intended to evoke concepts in the reader.

1937

≈§ 593. Barker, Francis E. "Crashaw and Andrewes." *TLS*, 21 August, p. 608.

Asks if any known copies of the second edition of *XCVI Sermons* by Lancelot Andrewes (1631) contain the engraved portrait of Andrewes by John Payne, with Crashaw's unsigned tribute to the bishop, later included in *The Delights of the Muses* (1646, 1648) under the title "Upon Bishop Andrewes his Picture before his Sermons." Notes that if the poem were published in 1631, as Martin suggests, then it would be the earliest known verse by Crashaw, in either Latin or English, to appear in print, but thinks that Grosart's suggestion that the lines first appeared in the third edition (1635) is more likely. For a reply, see K. N. Colville (entry 596).

≈§ 594. Berchmans, Sister Louise. "Poets and Mystics All." *America* 56 (20 February): 477.

Essentially a review of Helen White's *The Metaphysical Poets* (entry 591). Calls Crashaw "the essential mystic" of the metaphysical poets and sees him in a direct line of descent from Julian of Norwich. Claims that "sublime ecstasy was scored once, at least, in English seventeenth century literature by the Divine Love outpourings of Crashaw."

≈§ 595. Černý, Václav. "Hlavní zjevy barokní poesie náboženské," in *Esej o Básnickém baroku*, 63–81. (A. R. S. Sbirkarozprav Oumĕní, 18.) Prague: Orbis.

Discusses the contribution of mysticism to baroque Spanish literature and comments briefly on the element of mysticism in English baroque poetry, in which domain he includes Milton and the metaphysical poets (Donne, Herbert, Crashaw, and Herrick). Admires Crashaw's use of nature and his portrayal of Mary Magdalene in "The Weeper."

≈§ 596. Colville, K. N. "Crashaw and Andrewes." *TLS*, 28 August, p. 628.

Reply to Francis E. Barker (entry 593). Notes that he has before him a copy of the second edition (1632) of *XCVI Sermons* of Lancelot Andrewes that contains the engraved portrait of the bishop by John Payne and the unsigned verses by Crashaw, later included in *The Delights of the Muses* and entitled "Upon Bishop Andrewes his Picture before his Sermons."

◆§ 597. Johnson, Thomas H. "Edward Taylor: A Puritan 'Sacred Poet.'"
NEQ 10:290–322.

Briefly notes that there are certain similarities between Edward Taylor's religious poetry and Crashaw's sacred verse, such as "a seraphic exaltation and prodigality of fanciful tropes, passionate outburst, the language of amorous poetry adapted to religious expression, gaudy color, cloying sweetness" (p. 319). Notes also that Taylor used figures or tropes in "Meditations" that are identical to those in "Hymn to the Name of Jesus."

◆§ 598. Praz, Mario. "L'Èta di Milton," in *Storia della letteratura inglese*, 143–54. Florence: G. C. Sansoni.
Numerous later editions.

Enlarged 2 volume edition, in which the same Crashaw material appears in the first of the two volumes, *La letteratura inglese: Dal medioevo all'illuminismo* (Florence: Sansoni-Accademia, 1967), 237–52.

Places Crashaw within the tradition of metaphysical poetry and calls him one of Donne's disciples in the sacred tradition. Offers a brief sketch of Crashaw's life and poetry (pp. 147–48), noting the influence of Herbert, Little Gidding, and the Jesuit poets, especially Rémond, Cabilliau, and Malapert. Suggests that Crashaw is a precursor of certain modern poets, especially Shelley and Swinburne. Points out that Southwell anticipated the baroque in English poetry but that Crashaw "rappresenta in letteratura, in minori proporzioni, quello che le apoteosi di un Rubens, i languori di un Murillo, e le estasi di un Greco rappresentano in pittura" (p. 148).

◆§ 599. Schirmer, Walter F. "Donne und die religiöse metaphysische Dichtung," in *Geschichte der englischen und amerikanischen Literatur von den Anfängen bis zur Gegenwart*, 297–308. Halle (Saale): Max Niemeyer Verlag.

Discusses the nature of metaphysical style and sensibility and suggests that they reflect the tension created by the breakdown of the old world view. Presents a general critical evaluation of Crashaw's poetry (pp. 301–2), noting in particular baroque elements in his style and his frequent use of extravagant conceits and erotic imagery. Calls "The Weeper" a rosary of epigrams, lacking precise and logical structure. Suggests that Crashaw's poems are built about sensations, not thought, and that they attempt to present a sense of the highest expression of mysticism. Briefly compares and contrasts Crashaw to Donne, Herbert, Bernini, Marino, Vaughan, and Dryden.

◆§ 600. Winters, Yvor. *Primitivism and Decadence: A Study of American Experimental Poetry*. New York: Arrow Editions. xiii, 146p.

Chapter 5, "The Influence of Meter on Poetic Convention," reprinted in *In Defense of Reason* (Chicago: Swallow Press, 1947; London: Routledge and Kegan Paul, 1960), 103–50.

In Chapter 3, "Poetic Convention" (pp. 64–78), points out that Crashaw, "who carries certain experimental qualities of diction and image found in Donne much farther from the norm than even Donne ventured, is nevertheless traditional in that he utilizes by means of discreet suggestion the more emphatic and experimental metrical forms of the sixteenth century to suggest complexities of feeling not possible in those metrical forms as the poets of the sixteenth century used them" (p. 73). Notes that Crashaw's devotional poems often suggest the songbooks, "as he utilized the common imagery of the Petrarchan love lyric" (p. 73), and suggests that the traditional in Crashaw is "ordinarily thrust aside as merely literary" or "it is completely overlooked because the reader is nonplussed by experimental elements" (p. 75). In Chapter 4, "Primitivism and Decadence" (p. 79–92), notes that "the experimenting of Donne and of Crashaw is subject to the check of a comprehensible philosophy, as the experimenting of Pound and of Crane is not" (p. 91). In Chapter 5, "The Influence of Meter on Poetic Convention" (pp. 93–143), points out that in his devotional poetry Crashaw often uses cadences and images suggestive of earlier love poetry and of drinking songs, noting, for example, that lines 17–18 of "Psalme 23" correspond closely to the last stanza of "Out of the Italian. A Song" and that in his treatment of St. Teresa and of the Virgin Mary he often borrows imagery and wit from Petrarchan love poetry, "as if he were like some celestial tumbler, displaying his finest training and ingenuity for the greater glory, and out of purest love, of God" (p. 124). Maintains that, in fact, Crashaw's poetry shows most obviously the relationship between the Petrarchan conceit and the metaphysical conceit. Comments on the "spiritualization" of meter, images, and diction in "Psalme 23" and in other devotional poems, pointing out that, "by fleeting nuances of language, he suggests an anterior mode of poetic expression and hence of experience, and in a context which is new to it" (p. 125). Claims, therefore, that "it is in ways such as this that Crashaw is traditional; he is experimental in the ways in which he pushes metaphor beyond the bounds of custom and frequently even of reason" (p. 125). Concludes that, although Crashaw is highly experimental, "the large amount of poetry in which the traditional predominates and the experimental is under full control is too seldom appreciated" (p. 125).

1938

⋙ 601. Anon. "Devotional Poetry: Donne to Wesley: The Search for an Unknown Eden." *TLS*, 24 December, pp. 814, 816.

Maintains that "religious verse is seldom the statement of assured belief but more often the passionate protestation of a mind that wishes to believe and believes and doubts again" and that, therefore, "the periods most prolific of devotional masterpieces are those in which a certain body of religious faith is counterbalanced by a definite strain of inquietude" (p. 814). Points out that Crashaw imports to the tradition of English religious poetry "the splendours of the Counter-Reformation and develops his English piety into patterns of baroque magnificence" and observes that "the effect of his verse is both intoxicating and, in the end, a little cloying," maintaining that "erotic and religious symbolism have seldom been more innocently yet wildly confused" (p. 814). Points out Crashaw's "sensuous devotionalism" and concludes that "his religious love-poems are as exquisite as they are disconcerting and lack the slightly saccharine quality of Coventry Patmore" (p. 814). Suggests also that in the poetry of Charles Wesley one finds "something of that eloquence and that troubled fervour which we distinguish in the work of Crashaw and Donne, though the expression of it is less elaborate and less elusive" (p. 816).

⋘ 602. Anon. "T. S. Eliot on 'George Herbert.'" *The Salisbury and Winchester Journal*, 27 May.

A report of a lecture on Herbert and his poetry delivered by Eliot at the Chapter House of Salisbury Cathedral on Wednesday, 25 May 1938, in which, among other things, Eliot compares and contrasts Herbert with other English religious poets, including Crashaw. Discussing the intellectual and yet ardent nature of Herbert's poems, Eliot notes that "in Crashaw, and in some modern poets who resemble Crashaw we find a more passionate, even erotic mood, which . . . is like a diversion of human emotions to divine objects."

⋘ 603. Black, Matthew W., ed. "The Devotional Lyricists," in *Elizabethan and Seventeenth-Century Lyrics*, 479–530. Chicago: J. B. Lippincott Co.

Presents a general introduction to the devotional lyric of the seventeenth century. Sees Crashaw as a disciple of both Donne and Herbert but points out that Crashaw's predisposition to intense and sensuous visualization of religious events and personages makes him "a poet of a very different sort" (p. 482). Maintains that, although Crashaw's poems are "full of extravagances and grave lapses in taste," he is "capable of a sustained rhapsodic flight, of a splendor and warmth of color and light unknown to Herbert" (pp. 482–83). Suggests that Crashaw's conceits are "based upon sensations rather than upon intellectualized abstractions" but notes that "in the closing lines of *The Flaming Heart*, probably his most perfect achievement, he rises above conceit altogether" (p. 483). Claims that Crashaw's poems have scarcely any logical process or design and suggests that they be read as Crashaw wrote them, "in great intoxicating draughts of dizzy emotion" (p. 483). Calls "Wishes. To his (supposed) Mistresse" "a charming and original bit of Platonism" that "deserves its fame" (p. 483). Contrasts Crashaw also with Vaughan and Traherne. Anthologizes selections from five poems (pp. 504–12).

⋘ 604. Brooks, Cleanth, and Robert Penn Warren. *Understanding Poetry: An Anthology for College Students*. New York: Henry Holt & Co. xxiv, 680p.

2d ed., 1950; 3d ed., 1960, includes only "The Teare," 303–5; 4th ed., 1976, does not include Crashaw.

Anthologizes "The Teare" (pp. 447–49) and "Hymn in the Holy Nativity" (pp. 455–58) with questions intended to provoke critical analysis. Asks if the imagery of "The Teare" is "too far-fetched" and if the poem creates "an impression of sentimentality" (p. 449) and suggests that it be compared to Marvell's "The Definition of Love." Notes that "Hymn in the Holy Nativity" is "built on a succession of paradoxes" (p. 458) and asks which of the paradoxes seem appropriate in the light of Vaughan's "The Night."

605. Chandler, Albert R. *Larks, Nightingales and Poets: An Essay and an Anthology.* Columbus, Ohio: Published by the author at University Hall. vii, 190p.

Limited to 200 copies

Discusses the poetical treatment of the songs of the nightingale and the lark from the ancient Greeks to 1934 and anthologizes poems on the subject from twelve languages. Includes "Musicks Duell" (pp. 107–9) and maintains that Crashaw "not only translates Strada's poem but surpasses his *tour de force* by expanding it," noting that "in the middle of the poem about one hundred lines by Crashaw correspond to fourteen by Strada" (p. 178). Gives a table to show the correspondences between the two poems. Lists other English versions of Strada's poem (p. 178). Notes that Marino imitated it also in *L'Adone*, canto VII (1623), and suggests that his version may have been known to some English poets (p. 179).

606. F., R. O. L. "The Editor of Crashaw's 'Steps to the Temple.'" *N&Q* 175:263.

Asks if any new information about Crashaw's life has come to light in recent years and, in particular, if anyone has conjectured concerning the unnamed editor who wrote the "Preface to the Reader" for the 1646 edition. Notes that Martin says he is "unknown." For a reply, see James Seton-Anderson (entry 610).

607. Ford, Ford Madox. *The March of Literature: From Confucius' Day to Our Own.* New York: Dial Press. vii, 878p.

Reprinted, London: George Allen and Unwin, 1939, 1947.

Scattered references to Crashaw. Suggests that English poetry during the early seventeenth century, "in the hands of Donne, Crashaw, Milton, Herbert, and the rest, was beginning to crystallize itself more and more into the aspect of a sweetmeat" (p. 452). Calls Crashaw, Herbert, Donne, Vaughan, Marvell, and Dryden "the most English of all writers" and suggests that "if there is any sustained beauty in the Anglo-Saxon soul it was they who proved its existence" (p. 477). Quotes lines 61–72 of "Letter to the Countess of Denbigh" and calls lines 70–72 "the most exquisite of all passages of English-devotional—but, indeed, of all devotional verse" (p. 479). Contrasts Donne to Crashaw, noting that Donne "had nothing like the metrical skill of a mere Herrick, nor had he the clear, still apprehension of English that were Herbert's and Crashaw's" (p. 483).

◄§ 608. Maycock, A. L. *Nicholas Ferrar of Little Gidding.* London: SPCK. xiii, 322p.

Reprinted, 1963 (paperback), Grand Rapids, Mich.: Eerdmans, 1980.

References throughout to Crashaw and his connection with the members of the Little Gidding community, especially with Mary Collet and Ferrar Collet. Suggests that Crashaw may have met Nicholas Ferrar in London when the poet was only a boy of twelve, since both John and Nicholas Ferrar likely knew William Crashaw. Notes that Crashaw makes several clear references to Little Gidding in his poems and suggests that he may have been introduced to the community by Robert Mapletoft in 1632. Comments on Crashaw's visits and on the appeal that the life at Little Gidding had for the young poet. Maintains that there is good reason to believe that Crashaw composed the epitaph on the tomb of Nicholas Ferrar, Jr.

◄§ 609. Rohr-Sauer, Philipp von. "Poetry of the Baroque Tradition," in *English Metrical Psalms from 1600 to 1660: A Study in the Religious and Aesthetic Tendencies of That Period,* 80–103. Freiburg: Universitäts-druckerei Poppen & Ortmann. (Published dissertation.)

Discusses Crashaw's translations of Psalm 23 and Psalm 137. Finds it curious that Crashaw based his translations upon the Authorized Version, apparently assuming that at the time of their composition Crashaw was already a Catholic. Suggests that Crashaw's rendering of Psalm 137 shows "a less slavish manner of metaphrase than Herbert's, the result being more fantastic poetry, having at times more powerful expression" (p. 91). Points out that Psalm 23, "rendered in octosyllabic couplets of rather melodious verse," was greatly admired by Pope and notes that "it is substantially a free enlargement of the 1611 version, explaining each of the Davidic images in metaphorical turns of expression" (p. 91). Calls Crashaw's style "baroque fancy in its extreme form" (p. 92) and maintains that "to select the most characteristic psalmodist would be to mention Crashaw or Vaughan, for both have written good versions, and both show distinct baroque leanings, even though they did not render so many psalms as Herbert or Carew" (p. 101). Briefly compares and contrasts Crashaw as a metrical psalmodist to Donne, Carew, Fletcher, Sandys, Oldham, Habington, Herbert, and Vaughan.

◄§ 610. Seton-Anderson, James. "The Editor of Crashaw's 'Steps to the Temple.'" *N&Q* 175:305.

A reply to R. O. L. F. (entry 606). Ask if the author of the "Preface to the Reader" for the 1646 edition is not Thomas Car, Crashaw's friend. See also Martin, p. 432, and Austin Warren (entry 619), p. 220.

◄§ 611. Untermeyer, Louis. "The Religious Conceit: Play for God's Sake," in *Play in Poetry*, 27–51. New York: Harcourt, Brace & Co.

Contrasts the seriousness of Herbert's playfulness with Crashaw's efforts: "Crashaw pushed his comparisons further than they could bear to go, and thus made his metaphors not only incongruous, but unpleasantly comic" (p. 38). Claims that Crashaw's conceits "are so ugly as to be unspeakable" and suggests that even the modern reader "inured to the uninhibited candor of the present day might be offended by the symbols of Crashaw's paraphrases of Scripture and his 'translation' of *Dies Irae*" (p. 38). Maintains that in "The Weeper" "the sublime and the ridiculous are inextricably mingled" (p. 38) and that "elsewhere Crashaw's luxuriance runs from the turbulent to the absurd" (p. 39), as, for instance, in "Wishes. To his (supposed) Mistresse." Contrasts Crashaw with Vaughan and with Emily Dickinson and suggests that the latter represents "the continuation, possibly the culmination, of the strain begun by Donne and Herbert: the mingling of rapture and irreverence which makes death a plaything and God a playfellow" (p. 51).

1939

◄§ 612. Carayon, Marcel. "Les trois poèmes de Crashaw sur Sainte Thérèse," in *Hommage à Ernest Martinenche: Études hispaniques et américaines*, 83–92. Paris: Editions d'Artry.

Comments on the profound influence of St. Teresa on the development of Crashaw's thought and religious sensibility as revealed in his poems. Points out that "c'est l'essence spirituelle et passionnée du thérèsianisme, sa grandeur humano-divine, qu'il a voulu chanter et rechanter à divers stades de sa propre vie" (p. 83). Presents translations into French of the three Teresian poems, noting that "le raccourci des mots composés à la saxonne permet en anglais des compressions d'images impossibles dans un idiome néo-latin, et toutes les audaces d'une langue poétique ne passent pas directement dans une autre" (p. 92).

◄§ 613. Honey, William Bowyer, ed. *The Sacred Fire: An Anthology of English Poems from the Fourteenth Century to the Present Day*. London: George Routledge & Sons. xii, 488p.

Includes "Ode on a Prayer-book" (pp. 130–33). Observes in the notes that he deliberately chose this poem "as the most exaggerated and 'excessive' poem in Crashaw's characteristic manner" and claims that "its moral tone is odious, but its poetry is magnificent" (p. 473).

◄§ 614. McPeek, James A. S. *Catullus in Strange and Distant Britain*. (Harvard Studies in Comparative Literature, no. 15.) Cambridge: Harvard University Press; London: Humphrey Milford, Oxford University Press. xvii, 411p.

Discusses the influence of Catullus on English poetry. Maintains that Crashaw's debt to Catullus is slight in comparison to his debt to Horace and Claudian. Notes, however, that Crashaw's "Out of Catullus" is the earliest complete translation of Carmen v into English and adds that, "despite its breathless movement and a few inadequacies in phrasing, it is certainly one of the best" (p. 122). Points out Catullian themes and symbolism in "Epithalamium" and in "The Teare" as well as other minor echoes in Crashaw's poetry.

◄§ 615. Panhuijsen, Jos. "Hymne bij de geboorte van Christus zooals die gezongen werd door de herders van Richard Crashaw." *De Neuwe Gids* (Amsterdam) 54, no. 2:979–83.
Translation into Dutch of the second version of "Hymn in the Holy Nativity," without notes or commentary.

◄§ 616. Praz, Mario. *Studies in Seventeenth-Century Imagery*. 2 vols. (Studies of the Warburg Institute, edited by Fritz Saxl, 3.) London: Warburg Institute, 1939, 1947. 233p.; xi, 209p.
Italian edition, *Studi sul concettismo* (Florence: G. C. Sansoni, 1946), vii, 321p.
2d ed. (considerably enlarged), Rome: Edizione di Storia e Letteratura, 1964 (pt. 1); 1974 (pt. 2).
Vol. 1 (1939) is an English version (expanded with revisions and a new appendix) of *Studi sul concettismo* (Milan: Soc. Ed. La Cultura, 1934). This first Italian edition does not mention Crashaw. The second Italian edition (1946) is an Italian version of the English edition. Comments on Crashaw are contained essentially in Praz's earlier essay (entry 554). In addition, notes that Crashaw "was well versed in Jesuit emblem books" and points out that in *Carmen Deo Nostro* the engraving heading "Letter to the Countess of Denbigh" is a well-known emblem that can be found in *Imago primi saeculi S.J.*, that the engraving heading "Hymn to the Name of Jesus" can be found in Typotius's *Symbola*, and that in "To [Mrs M.R.] Councel Concerning her Choise" Crashaw uses images "that may have been suggested by certain pictures in *Typus Mundi* (emblems 10, 9, 3)" (p. 205). Volume 2 (1947) is a bibliography of emblem books.

◄§ 617. Spencer, Theodore, and Mark Van Doren. *Studies in Metaphysical Poetry: Two Essays and a Bibliography*. New York: Columbia University Press. 88p.
Reprinted, Port Washington, N.Y.: Kennikat Press, 1964.
Part 1 consists of two essays: (1) "Recent Scholarship in Metaphysical Poetry" (pp. 3–18), by Spencer, in which he briefly outlines some of the major developments in metaphysical criticism and scholarship, especially Donne scholarship, which he calls "a kind of microcosm of scholarship relating to

metaphysical poetry in general" (p. 14) and (2) "Seventeenth-Century Poets and Twentieth-Century Critics" (pp. 21–29), by Van Doren, in which he reviews various notions of metaphysical poetry, especially T. S. Eliot's concept of unified sensibility. Maintains that the outstanding feature of metaphysical poetry is its humor: "Humor is the life of their poetry; wit is its language" (p. 28). Part 2 presents an unannotated bibliography of studies in metaphysical poetry from 1912 to 1938 (pp. 33–83) by Spencer, with the assistance of Evelyn Orr. Items are arranged chronologically for each of the poets, with an additional section entitled "General Studies." There are 33 items listed under Crashaw, as compared to 44 for Herbert and 199 for Donne.

◄§ 618. Thompson, Elbert N. S. "The Octosyllabic Couplet." *PQ* 18: 257–68.
Briefly discusses Crashaw's use of the octosyllabic couplet. Notes that some of the poems, such as "Hymn in the Holy Nativity," "are written line by line, with little enjambment either in line or couplet" and yet avoid monotony, whereas "A Hymn to Sainte Teresa" contains both run-on lines and couplets, the result being "a swiftly moving verse written in effective periods that disregard the couplet" (p. 264). Maintains that "A Hymn to Sainte Teresa," therefore, "stands midway between Crashaw's lyrics in regular rhythm and the choral hymns, which rise and fall with changing time in harmony with the musical accompaniment" (p. 264). Notes that in "Hymn to the Name of Jesus" the octosyllabic couplets "are so interspersed with other forms that they seem sporadic" and suggests that the poem is possibly "the finest example of the blending of the couplet with other forms" (p. 267). Maintains that, later in the seventeenth century, "a formal rhetoric came to prevail over the more subtle music of Milton and Crashaw" (p. 267).

◄§ 619. Warren, Austin. *Richard Crashaw: A Study in Baroque Sensibility.* University: Louisiana State University Press; London: Faber & Faber. xv, 260p.
Reprinted, London: Faber and Faber, 1957; Ann Arbor: University of Michigan Press (Ann Arbor Books, AA6), 1957; Ann Arbor: University of Michigan Press, 1967.
Section 6 of Chapter 4, "Symbolism" (176–93) reprinted in *Seventeenth Century English Poetry,* ed. William R. Keast (entry 879), 252–63; rev. ed. (1971), 312–33.
Selections (pp. 133–34, 139–46, 176–93, 238–39) reprinted in *The Metaphysical Poets: Key Essays on Metaphysical Poetry and the Major Metaphysical Poets,* ed. Frank Kermode (entry 980), 257–75.
States in the preface (pp. vii–xii) that "this study chiefly addresses itself to translating the twentieth-century reader of Crashaw into the position of one who, three centuries ago, was informed upon the principal movements in English and Continental religion and art, and conversant with Latin, Italian,

and English poetry" (p. ix). Contents (pp. xiii–xiv) and a list of seven illustrations (p. xv) (not included in reprint). Chapter 1, "The Laudian Movement and the Counter-Reformation" (pp. 3–17), outlines the religious history and spirit of early seventeenth-century England, noting in particular the effects of the Laudian movement, and comments on the religious sensibility that emerged on the Continent during and following the Council of Trent. Claims that "what Catholicly minded Anglicans were most likely to miss, and to seek outside the national church, was the provision for the contemplative life" (p. 11) and the possibilities of a richer devotional life that fostered higher states of mystical prayer, as reflected in the Catholic saints of the period. Chapter 2, "The Man" (pp. 18–62), presents a detailed biography of Crashaw and comments on various influences that shaped his temperament: "Two interests, the arts and religion, dominated his whole life" and, "in both, he found his way, without apparent struggle, toward the goal predestined by his temperament" (p. 61), that is, the Catholic Church. Maintains that, "sensuous rather than intellectual," Crashaw "might have proved voluptuary, libertine or aesthete; and, devoted to the cause of beautifying college chapels and elaborating their ceremonials, he might be set down as a ritualist," but "such he clearly was not" (pp. 61–62). Concludes that "a sensuous nature, coupled with an ardent devotion to unseen realities: the two become approximately fused in the spiritual atmosphere and in the aesthetic of the Counter-Reformation" (p. 62). Chapter 3, "Interlude: Baroque Art and the Emblem" (pp. 63–76), discusses major themes and attitudes found in Tridentine art and discusses the baroque style in art, architecture, and sculpture, a style that is "exuberant, rhetorical, sensual, grandiose" and becomes a "Catholic counterstatement to the reformer's attacks on the wealth of the Church and her use of painting and sculpture" (p. 65). Emphasizes the dominant role played by the Jesuits and Ignatian spirituality in the arts and discusses the history and development of emblem books, especially religious ones, as both a reflection of and a shaping influence on the religious spirit and art of the times. Chapter 4, "The Poetry" (pp. 77–193), presents a critical evaluation of Crashaw's secular and sacred poetry and is divided into six sections. (1) "The Latin Epigrams" (pp. 77–90) points out the influence of Renaissance epigrammatists, especially the Jesuits, on Crashaw's Latin epigrams; contrasts the "metallic and hard" (p. 81) style of the epigrams with Crashaw's later Marinistic poetry; notes his skillful uses of metaphor, paradox, and antithesis; and calls them "the best Latin epigrams written by an Englishman," noting that they can hardly be said to belong to English poetry at all, not only or chiefly because they are written in Latin but also because, "though they restrict themselves in theme to the New Testament and never transcend the theology of High Anglicanism, their method was borrowed from the Jesuits, and their spirit is that of the Counter-Reformation" (p. 89). (2) "The Secular Poems and Translations" (pp. 90–110) compares and contrasts Crashaw's secular poems with those of the Elizabethans and many of his contemporaries, noting that "almost all the verses are either translations or 'occasional' elegies" (p. 91); singles out "Wishes. To his (supposed) Mistresse" as Crashaw's "chief piece in the manner of the Jonsonians," calling it "a delicate and accomplished performance" (p. 97) and finds "Loves Horoscope" somewhat in the style of Donne, but notes that Donne's influence on Crashaw generally is slight; and maintains that most of the secular pieces can be admired as "accomplished studies in rhythm and imagery" (p. 102). Discusses Crashaw's skill as a translator of both Latin and Italian; offers a detailed analysis of "Musicks Duell," praising its music, calling it "the secular triumph of the Crashavian style," and claiming that "it remains, of its kind, the most impressive achievement in English poetry" (p. 110). (3) "The Sacred Muse of Marinism" (pp. 111–32) discusses the pervasive influence of Marino and marinism on Crashaw's poetry and maintains that his "exhibition piece in the manner of Marino" (p. 126) is not his translation, "Sospetto d'Herode," but "The Weeper." Discusses in detail both "The Weeper" and "On the wounds of our crucified Lord" as reflective of the marinistic mode and presents a detailed analysis of "Sospetto d'Herode." Notes that, except in "Charitas Nimia," Herbert's poetry had little influence on Crashaw's and suggests that in temper and style Crashaw is closer to Robert Southwell and Giles Fletcher. (4) "Catholic Themes and Attitudes" (pp. 132–58) surveys the principal themes of Crashaw's mature genius, especially Mary Magdalene, St. Alexis, St. Teresa, nuptial mysticism, the mysticism of the *via negativa*, and martyrdom, and discusses his paraphrases of medieval Latin hymns. Calls "A Hymn to Sainte Teresa" "one of Crashaw's four or five best pieces,"in which the metaphors are structural, not ornamental, and in which he "unites two themes intensely dear to him—martyrdom and mysticism" (p. 146) and discusses in some detail "Hymn in the Glorious Epiphanie" as a moving exploration of the *via negativa*. (5) "Versification: From the Couplet to the Ode" (pp. 159–75) discusses Crashaw's prosody and notes that often he invites us "to concentrate our attention upon some sensuous object like the crucifix, some sensuous symbol like wounds or tears, while the poet, by means of meter, liturgical rhymes, assonance, and alliteration, creates an atmosphere which lulls the critical intellect while the poem insistently repeats its motif" (pp. 174–75). (6) "Symbolism" (pp. 176–93) surveys Crashaw's uses of images, metaphors, and symbols and suggests that, "for Crashaw, the world of the senses was evidently enticing; yet it was a world of appearances only—shifting, restless appearances" and, since he was a believer in the miraculous, "his aesthetic method may be interpreted as a genuine equivalent of his belief, as its translation into a rhetoric of metamorphosis"; for "if in the Gospels, water changes to wine and wine to blood, Crashaw was but imaginatively extending this principle when he turned tears into pearls, pearls into lilies, lilies into pure Innocents" (p. 192). Chapter 5, "The Reputation" (pp. 194–206), comments briefly on Crashaw's critical reception during the eighteenth, nineteenth, and twentieth centuries and summarizes his aesthetic. Notes that the special domain of Crashaw's poetry "is the world of man's inner life at its mystical intensity, the world of devotion expressing itself through the sacraments and cere-monial and liturgy; it is a world which knows vision and rapture, tears and fire; it is a world of the supernatural, wherein the miraculous becomes the prob-able; and this world manifests itself to the senses in a rhetoric brilliant, expres-sive, and appropriate" (p. 206). Detailed notes (pp. 207–40); selected bibli-ography of editions, as well as primary and secondary sources (pp. 241–55); and index (pp. 257–60).

1940

◄§ 620. Anon. "Baroque Sensibility." *TLS*, 10 August, p. 387.

Claims that, unlike the classical and the Gothic, baroque art "wears artifice on its sleeve" and views rococo as "fricasseed baroque." Agrees with Austin Warren (entry 619) that the baroque is a particular kind of sensibility—"not so much a period of art as a 'taste' in art, more or less persistent and often taking the lead in fashion." Maintains that "it is better to remember Jack Sprat and his wife, and, pooling sensibilities in the music of Mozart or the poetry of Crashaw, agree to differ when it comes to painting and architecture."

◄§ 621. Bradner, Leicester. *Musae Anglicanae: A History of Anglo-Latin Po-etry, 1500–1925.* New York: Modern Language Association of America; London: Oxford University Press. xii, 383p.

Calls Crashaw "by far the greatest writer of the conventional sacred epigram in England" (p. 92) and discusses the style of his Latin epigrams, noting the influence of Jesuit Latin poets and Renaissance phrase books on his early Latin poetry. Comments on such features as his uses of the question and the answer, the repetition of key words in a very short space, word play, irony, brevity, conceits, and paradoxes. Claims that "the fundamental paradox that an Almighty God sent his Son to suffer pain and defeat upon earth in order to redeem man is always before him" (p. 92). Stresses the devotional nature of Crashaw's epigrams and notes that "in spite of all his superficial rhetoric, there is a passionate seriousness running through all his religious poems, whether Latin or English" (p. 93). Points out that Crashaw, though living in an age of controversy, did not treat controversial or doctrinal subjects: "Instead of setting himself up as wiser and holier than his brothers in other sects, he casts aside all such comparative considerations in ecstatic wonder at the divine mercy of God and dismay at the hard-heartedness of men who reject such a God" (pp. 93–94). Singles out for comment "Joann. 16:33. Ego vici mundum," "Joann. 2. Aquae in vinum versae," and "Joann. 20. Christus ad Thomam." Surveys briefly Crashaw's Latin poetry in addition to his epigrams, noting that "about half of them are occasional verse of various sorts; most of the rest are on moral themes, or approach the epigram in spirit and style" (p. 94). Dis-cusses Crashaw's use of and experimentation with a variety of meters and praises his technical skill. Notes that he also wrote a number of regular sapphic and alciac odes in which he did not strive for conceit or wit but expressed himself in the language and style of classical Rome, citing the second half of "Hymnus Veneri. dum in illius tutelam transëunt virgines" as an example. Compares and contrasts Crashaw to Herbert, John Owen, John Saltmarsh, James Duport, and Peter Du Moulin. Includes a list of Anglo-Latin poetry (pp. 346–73). See also entry 947.

◆§ 622. Cecil, David, ed. *The Oxford Book of Christian Verse.* Oxford: Clarendon Press. xxxiii, 560p.
  Introduction (pp. xi–xxxiii) comments on the nature and limitations of religious poetry and outlines the history of English religious verse from Richard Rolle to T. S. Eliot. Briefly notes that Browning, Coventry Patmore, Gerard Manley Hopkins, and Christina Rossetti "are the equals if not the superiors of Vaughan and Crashaw" (p. xxvii) and points out that Crashaw is not equal to Donne or Herbert at their best. States that Crashaw's poems, "like Bernini's sculpture, communicate a semi-erotic mysticism, all pierced hearts and tender flames and ecstatic swoonings," and maintains that, "often hysterical and over-luscious, his inspiration can yet take fire and flare up in a throbbing lyrical rush, unequalled by any other English religious poet" (pp. xviii–xix). Anthologizes seven of Crashaw's poems (pp. 190–209), without notes or commentary.

◆§ 623. Crashaw, Richard. *Herderszang.* Vertaling van Gabriël Smit. Schiedam: P. J. Venemans. [8]p.
  Limited to 350 copies.
  Translates into Dutch twelve stanzas of "Hymn in the Holy Nativity," without notes or commentary.

◆§ 624. Daniels, R. Balfour. "Some Remarks on Richard Crashaw," in *Some Seventeenth-Century Worthies in a Twentieth-Century Mirror*, 29–34. Chapel Hill: University of North Carolina Press.
  Reprinted, New York: Russell and Russell, 1971.
  Finds that "of all the devotional poets of his time Crashaw is the most difficult to understand" because "he demands not only a feeling for poetry but also a form of religious experience similar to his own if one would know exactly what he is writing about" (p. 29). Challenges the notion that Crashaw lacked good taste and judgment and suggests that perhaps the modern reader, unfamiliar with seventeenth-century diction and figurative language, may be at fault. Maintains that Crashaw, at least, "was never lacking in delicacy; and delicacy was a virtue often too little esteemed by the Caroline poets" (p. 31). Compares and contrasts Crashaw briefly with Donne and finds parallels between Crashaw's art and sensibility and those of Giovanni Bellini, Giorgione, and Botticelli. Notes that Crashaw portrays "the beauty and the pathos of the life of Christ and His saints through tender and mystical verses that appeal to

the emotions; and in so doing he achieves at times a wistful loveliness" (pp. 32–33). Praises lines from "Hymn in the Holy Nativity" and "The Weeper." Concludes that, although he finds no appeal in perhaps nine-tenths of Crashaw's poems, "no doubt there are many who see poetry and life as Crashaw did and can go with him further along the road" (p. 34).

⋙ 625. Eleanore, Sister M. "My Beloved to Me, and I to Him: The Poetry of Richard Crashaw." *Magnificat* 65:158–64.
  Discusses Crashaw's religious sensibility as it is reflected in his sacred poems, stressing his intimate understanding of the mystical experience. Comments on Crashaw's particularly Catholic sensibility and suggests that his poetry "is always sane and true because he found its source in the Gospels and safeguarded himself by steadfast faith and profound scholarship" (p. 160). Admits, however, that "The Weeper" contains "two of the most absurd lines in English poetry" but attributes them simply to "the vice of juvenile Euphuism so prevalent in Crashaw's day" (p. 161). Concludes that "there is a subtle something" in Crashaw's poems that "makes us know that his lines on ecstatic union with His Beloved are not mere digests of the revelations of the experiences of the saints" (p. 164), but come rather from his personal experience of Christ, on whom "he spent the affectionate interest and loving sympathy most of us spend on our families and friends" (p. 162).

⋙ 626. Fitzgerald, Maurus. "Catholic English Literature in the XVII, XVIII, and XIX Centuries." *Franciscan Educational Conference Report* 22:81–102.
  Calls Crashaw the only "Catholic luminary" (p. 81) in seventeenth-century English poetry and suggests that his poetry has "the impassioned lyricism of Herrick, without the latter's sensuality" (p. 83). Surveys briefly Crashaw's life and poetry (pp. 82–84). Calls "Hymn to the Name of Jesus" a "landmark of religious poetry" and "a prayer that the Fathers of the Church would have been proud to acknowledge as their own" (p. 83). Admits that, although Crashaw was "sincerity personified," even his most brilliant poems are often marred by excesses and extravagances and singles out "The Weeper" and "The Flaming Heart" as examples, calling the latter a "blend of pyrotechnics and seraphic curiosity" (p. 84). Praises Crashaw's "warmth of language, a color and a harmony that is a never-ending pleasure" (p. 84), and concludes that, on the whole, Crashaw's lyrics have "song and passion and imagination combined with a flowing rhythm" (p. 85) and that England was not to have such poetry again until Shelley.

⋙ 627. Heywood, Terence. "Some Notes on English Baroque." *Horizon* 2:267–70.
  Favorable review of Austin Warren (entry 619) that recommends the study "for anyone who aims at a better understanding of one of our most colourful

and European poets" (p. 270). Observes that, since the baroque is "so essentially a Catholic Latin manifestation," its appearance in the "Protestant Teutonic North is curiously instructive" (p. 267). Maintains that, even before Crashaw, the baroque spirit existed in varying degrees in both visual arts and literature in England. Notes that "alongside the poetical edifices of Donne and the other Metaphysicals, which may be said to reflect in varying degrees a sort of Barocco-Palladian compromise, the florid piles of Crashaw sprouted into existence revealing showy façades which, on examination, were found to be non-structural, decorative screens unrelated to the interiors" (p. 269). Agrees with Warren that Crashaw's poetry should be seen apart, but not exclusively so, from the so-called metaphysical tradition and as having more immediate affinities with the work of such poets as Southwell, Giles Fletcher, Benlowes, certain of the emblemists, and some of the less-known Recusant poets. Notes that Warren's study serves to correct the notion that Crashaw was a unique poet of his time in that "his conceits, oxymora and paradoxes are nearly all shown to have been the stock property of the *Seicento* Catholic literature in which he had so thoroughly steeped himself" (p. 269). Cautions, however, that it is very difficult to say just how exclusively Crashaw belonged to the Catholic, Continental, Counter-Reformation tradition. Concludes that, "fortunately, baroque no longer needs an apology; nor, with such delicious Crashavian examples as we have, need we speculate concerning others that might have been produced" (p. 270) if he had lived longer and had moved away from Marinism to the organic conceit used by Donne, as both Austin Warren (entry 619) and George Williamson (entry 516) see in his later work.

◄§ 628. Jonas, Leah. "George Herbert, Richard Crashaw, and Henry Vaughan," in *The Divine Science: The Aesthetic of Some Representative Seventeenth-Century English Poets*, 211–27. (Columbia University Studies in English and Comparative Literature, no. 151.) New York: Columbia University Press.

Contends that Donne provided "the corner stone for the theory of Herbert, Crashaw, and Vaughan, each of whom felt that there was but little virtue in the poetry that was not religious" (p. 211). Notes that, although Crashaw wrote secular poems and translated secular works, these "were apparently interpolations and by their innocuous nature reassert his dominantly religious interests" (p. 213). Finds "Wishes. To his (supposed) Mistresse," "Musicks Duell," and "To the Morning" notable exceptions that do not, however, invalidate the general rule. Comments on the principles informing Crashaw's poetic creed and suggests that, like Herbert, Crashaw "sought an eloquence proper to divine poetry" and believed that "true poetry should result when a soul burning with the love of God tries to manifest its experience in words" (p. 222). Notes the influence of St. Teresa and suggests that Crashaw attempted "to reproduce in English the excellences of foreign religious poetry" (p. 223). Stresses that his great aim was "to apply the full richness of poetic art by expressing the consummate 'sweetness' of divine love" and that he found "no conflict between his love of art and his love of God, nor did he ever question the sincerity of his most florid figures" (p 223). Discusses Herbert's influence on Crashaw and Vaughan, compares and contrasts the three poets, and concludes that their common purpose was "to divert some of the beauty of poetry to the praise of its great Creator," a theory and practice that were ultimately constrictive and limiting: "The divine poet assumes more the function of a priest" (p. 227).

◆§ 629. Kuranga, Makoto. *Chūseki no okeru English Shinpi Bungaku* [English Mystical Literature of the Middle Ages]. Kyōbunkan.
Cited in Yoshihisa Aizawa's "A Bibliography of Writings about Metaphysical Poetry in Japan" (entry 1118). Not located.

◆§ 630. Sharp, Robert Lathrop. *From Donne to Dryden: The Revolt Against Metaphysical Poetry*. Chapel Hill: University of North Carolina Press. xiii, 221p.
Reprinted, Hamden, Conn.: Archon Books, 1965.
Traces the revolution in taste in the seventeenth century from poetry that the author calls extravagant, obscure, and harsh to poetry that exalts the standards and practices of propriety, clarity, and harmony. Examines both literary and nonliterary forces that set up a reaction to metaphysical poetry and notes that "the revolt was not a silent one; it was articulate in criticism as well as in poetry" (p. xii). Suggests that the revolt "reached to the roots of poetry and affected the experience underlying literary creation" and that "by following it, the reader should get a clearer notion of what happened in English poetry between 1600 and 1700" (p. xii). Several references to Crashaw. Claims that, like Herbert and Vaughan, his best poetry is religious; mentions Herbert's influence on Crashaw; and points out that Crashaw, like a number of other metaphysical poets, was a brilliant lyricist, suggesting that "in no period have lyric and song been sweeter" (p. 51).

◆§ 631. Shuster, George N[auman] "Crashaw, Cowley, and the Pindaric Ode," in *The English Ode from Milton to Keats*, 93–122. (Columbia University Studies in English and Comparative Literature, no. 150.) New York: Columbia University Press.
Reprinted, Gloucester, Mass.: Peter Smith, 1964.
Calls both Crashaw and Cowley "medievalists," "classicists," and "harbingers of modernity" who "assured the longevity of the English ode" (p. 93). Suggests that, for Crashaw, music was perhaps the bridge between art and religion. Claims that Crashaw's Greek verse "is probably the best ever written by an English poet of any importance," that his Latin poetry is "highly commendable," and that his versions of the ancient Latin hymns of the Church "are still unsurpassed" (p. 99). Discusses the friendship of Crashaw and Cowley, maintains that it is more likely that Crashaw introduced Cowley to Pindar

than the reverse, and compares and contrasts "Hymn to the Name of Jesus" to Cowley's "The Plagues of Egypt," maintaining that Crashaw's poem is "a singularly musical poem in which all the senses have their roles" (p. 112). Comments on Crashaw's understanding of and feeling for Greek poetry and discusses a number of his patterns and meters to show that "these are in several ways landmarks in the history of the ode" (p. 100). Notes, for example, that "Hymn in the Holy Nativity" is "a forerunner of what would later be termed the 'cantata ode' and may have been based upon either the new 'opera' or the Oratorian 'Cantata Spirituale'" (p. 101), observing, however, that Crashaw was "less dependent upon the Italian models in vogue than is commonly supposed" and that, although he translated Marino and Strada, "they taught him nothing of moment about form" (p. 102). Praises Crashaw's metrical skill and points out two notable feats that he achieved: (1) "skipping unstressed syllables and thus making his verse depend upon the stresses" (p. 103), as in "The Weeper" and (2) his uses of irregular stanzas, as exemplified in the second version of "Ode on a Prayer-book." Suggests that Crashaw "must have possessed an unusually deep insight into what may be termed quantitative possibilities of English speech—that is, the uses of pauses to create effects similar to those produced in classical verse by the substitution, for example, of spondees for dactyls" (p. 104). Calls "A Hymn to Sainte Teresa," "after Milton's Nativity Ode, the most illustrious blending of art and hymnody in seventeenth-century verse" (p. 105) and sees it as "the culmination of one great English poetic adventure" (p. 106). Notes the possible influence of Spenser, Herbert, Thomas Stanley, Jonson, and perhaps even Milton on Crashaw and very briefly compares Crashaw to Shelley and Francis Thompson.

◄§ 632. Smith, Lewis Worthington, J. Hal Connor, and Maxwell D. Edwards, eds. "Richard Crashaw," in *Types and Times in English Literature*. Book 2: *Seventeenth Century*, 154–57. Oklahoma City: Harlow Publishing.

Presents a biographical note on Crashaw and contrasts him with Herbert and Donne, noting that "in its rhetorical aspects and in its devotional ardor Crashaw's poetry is somewhat more glowing than Herbert's" and that "less intellectual and more mystical than Donne or Herbert, he found a livelier pleasure in the employment of language for its own sake" (p. 154). Anthologizes selections from "The Flaming Heart," "Hymn in the Holy Nativity," "A Hymn to Sainte Teresa," and "A Song ('Lord, when the sense of thy sweet grace')" (pp. 154–57), without notes or additional commentary.

1941

◄§ 633. Daniels, Earl. *The Art of Reading Poetry*. New York: Farrar & Rinehart. vii, 519p.
Reprinted, 1942, 1949.

Anthologizes "An Epitaph upon a Young Married Couple" with critical questions and brief comments (pp. 241–42). Notes the "lovely movement" of lines 7–14; points out that Crashaw "is celebrated in English poetry for his use—many would say misuse—of the conceit" (p. 242), cites stanza 6 (from the 1646 version) and stanza 5 (from the 1648 version) of "The Weeper," which he calls "a poem on the tears of the Blessed Virgin"; and notes that "it is hard to distinguish degree of badness in these two specimens" (p. 242).

◄§ 634. Hatzfeld, Helmut. "El predominio del espíritu español en la literatura europea del siglo XVII." *RFH* 3:9–23.

Reviews the critical confusion in literary studies concerning the nature of and the distinctive characteristics of baroque style and sensibility and surveys the extensive influence of the baroque in Spanish, Italian, German, French, and English literature of the sixteenth and seventeenth centuries. Sees the baroque as the last collective European literary movement and stresses the central leadership provided by Spain: "Nosotros creemos que el barroco existe ciertamente como movimento literario europeo, y que es el influjo que el espíritu y estilo españoles ejercieron en todas partes, suplantando el carácter italiano y clásico-antiguo de la literatura europea del siglo XVI" (p. 10). Maintains that from early Roman times to the Renaissance, Spanish literature demonstrated elements that later came to be identified with the baroque and discusses the relationship between English and Spanish baroque poets. Suggests that Southwell's "St. Peter's Complaint" marks the first introduction of Spanish baroque spirituality into English letters and discusses the baroque sensibility and style of several late sixteenth- and seventeenth-century English writers, especially Milton and the metaphysical poets. Maintains that Crashaw studied the works of St. Teresa in depth and that in "The Flaming Heart" he "reproduce el espíritu y la forma de su misticismo" (p. 22).

◄§ 635. L., G. G. "Nympha Pudica Deum Vidit, et Erubuit." *N&Q* 181:246.

Notes that William King (entry 275) attributes to Crashaw both the Latin epigram and the English translation "The conscious water saw its God, and blushed." Also notes a translation that may be either Crashaw's or perhaps Thomas Campbell's (entry 123) that reads "The modest water . . ." and asks which is correct. Points out that the 1941 *Oxford Dictionary of Quotations* attributes the English translation of the epigram to Crashaw as well, but that the English version does not appear in Martin's edition. Asks also for information on the passage from Grotius to which Crashaw is indebted.

◄§ 636. ———. "A Passage from Crashaw." *N&Q* 181:246–47.

Maintains that in lines 17–20 of the 1652 version of "Ode on a Prayer-book" the word *their* should read *your*. Suggests that the error came from a misinterpretation of "yr," taking the "y" for "th" (as in "ye"). Notes that "very likely this correction has been made," but that he has not seen it. (Both Grosart and Martin have *your*, not *their*, based on the 1648 version of the poem.)

◄§ 637. Potter, George Reuben. "A Protest Against the Term *Conceit*," in *Renaissance Studies in Honor of Hardin Craig*, edited by Baldwin Maxwell et al., 282–91. Stanford: Stanford University Press.

Reprinted in *PQ* 20 (1941):474–83.

Surveys the various denotative and connotative meanings of the word *conceit* from the medieval period to modern times and urges that it be discontinued as a critical term. Comments specifically on the confusion that the term has caused when applied to the metaphysical poets. No specific mention of Crashaw.

◄§ 638. Ransom, John Crowe. "Eliot and the Metaphysicals." *Accent* 1: 148–56.

Reprinted, with slight revisions, in *The New Criticism* (Norfolk, Conn.: New Directions, 1941), 175–92.

Attacks Eliot's concept of "unified sensibility" as ineffectively descriptive of what happens in the metaphysical conceit. Uses Donne primarily to illustrate the notion of the metaphysical conceit as a functional metaphor, which "has no explicit tenor or fact-structure but only a 'vehicle' covering it" (p. 154) and which functions as both structure and texture in the poem. No specific mention of Crashaw, but responds to Eliot's essay (entry 417), which makes several mentions of Crashaw.

◄§ 639. Sampson, George. "Cavalier and Puritan," in *The Concise Cambridge History of English Literature*, 344–400. Cambridge: Cambridge University Press.

Reprinted several times.

Offers a biographical sketch and contrasts Crashaw with Herbert: "Herbert suggests the quiet devotion of the Collects in the English Prayer Book; Crashaw suggests the ecstasy of a devotee before the relics of a saint" (p. 347). Notes the pervasive influence of Spanish and Italian models on Crashaw's art and suggests that his translations still "have compelling interest" (p. 348). Calls "Wishes. To his (supposed) Mistresse" Crashaw's most famous secular lyric and suggests it is memorable "because it is altogether his own" (p. 348). Claims however, that Crashaw's place in English literature has been secured by his religious poems. Maintains that Crashaw's poetry is "very uneven and somewhat excessive, but he is never tepid, and his best is superb" (p. 348).

1942

◄§ 640. Bethell, S. L. "The *Adoro Te Devote* of St. Thomas Aquinas and Crashaw's English Version, the *Hymn in Adoration of the Blessed Sac-*

rament, Compared." *Comparative Literature Studies* (Cardiff) 6–7: 38–42.

Compares St. Thomas Aquinas's thirteenth-century eucharistic hymn with Crashaw's baroque paraphrase. Maintains that, "although the latter retained intellectually all the dogmas of the medieval Church, it was affected, despite itself, by the spirit of the Reformation, which laid new emphasis upon the relation of the individual soul with God" (p. 41). Points out resemblances between the two poems, such as their use of traditional Catholic symbolism and of a conceited style, but concludes that there are also profound differences that arise from a difference in intellectual outlook and not simply from differences in the personalities of the two poets. Notes, for instance, that Crashaw's version, which is exactly twice as long as that of Aquinas, subordinates tersely expressed doctrinal exactness to a more intimate, colloquial plea for God's mercy. Points out that Aquinas states his position as one of faith based on reason, whereas Crashaw expresses "not a reasonable faith, but a faith that denies reason for love's sake—not quite in the spirit of *Credo quia impossible est*, but approaching it"—in which "improbability is welcomed as a test of faith in the beloved Lord" (p. 40). Finds also in Crashaw's version much emotionalism, sublimated eroticism, and sensationalism, characteristic elements of Catholic baroque art. Maintains that "there is at times an unhealthiness in Crashaw which we never detect in the more intellectual devotion of St. Thomas" (pp. 40–41). Notes that, in spite of the elaborate "intellectual dexterity" in St. Thomas's hymn, the tone is "dignified, restrained, and impersonal" and is thus "admirably suited for congregational use," whereas Crashaw's approach is so "personal and impassioned" that "one cannot imagine it in congregational use" (p. 41). Suggests that the conceited style and the peculiar wit of metaphysical poetry have their origin in the Latin literature of the early medieval Church. For a correction, see Bethell (entry 641).

◄§ 641. ———. "Corrections to Vols. VI–VIII." *Comparative Literature Studies* (Cardiff) 8:27.

Notes that Dom Gregory Dix in *A Detection of Aumbries* (Dacre Press, 1942) denies that St. Thomas Aquinas is the author of the hymn *Adoro Te Devote* and suggests that the hymn is German in origin. Maintains that, if this is true, it does not materially affect the argument of his earlier essay (entry 640), but, in fact, "makes the original even more broadly representative of the medieval mind": "That the scholastic mode of thought should be found incorporated in a devotional poem of German origin is added evidence of the comparative homogeneity of European culture in the Middle Ages—one of the facts most relevant to my theme."

◄§ 642. Brandenburg, Alice Stayert. "The Dynamic Image in Metaphysical Poetry." *PMLA* 57:1039–45.

Suggests that the underlying quality connecting many of the seemingly unrelated features of metaphysical poetry might be called "the dynamic image."

Distinguishes between two types of images: the static image, which "describes the appearance, taste, smell, feel, or sound of an object—the qualities in short, which medieval philosophers called accidents," and the dynamic image, which "describes the way in which objects act or interact" (p. 1039). Comments primarily on the nature and function of Donne's dynamic images. Notes that Donne's followers continued to use dynamic images but "did not turn so frequently to science for their material or neutralize their images so thoroughly" (p. 1044). Notes that "the grotesqueness of the images used by men like Cleveland arose from their functional character, for the dynamic figure, which is not primarily decorative, loses its point when used as decoration instead of as an integral part of the poem" (p. 1045). No specific mention of Crashaw.

◄§ 643. Fethaland, John. "Crashaw [a Poem]." *TLS*, 21 March, p. 142.
An original poem praising Crashaw's wit, scholarship, poetic ability, and religious vision.

◄§ 644. Frye, Northrop. "Music in Poetry." *UTQ* 11, No. 2:167–79.
Calls Crashaw "the most ambitious musician" among the metaphysical poets and notes that "Musicks Duell" "describes a typically baroque form, the aria with instrumental accompaniment which had been increasingly popular since about 1600" (p. 175). Maintains that "to carry on an elaborate detailed description of the most abstract and wordless of arts for nearly two hundred lines, and make the result successful poetry, is (so far as I know) an unrivalled feat" (p. 175). Points out that Crashaw is "one of the few musical poets whose diction presents a smooth surface" and notes that "his imagery, though often called sensuous, has a musical suggestiveness, depending both on precision of sound and vagueness of sight" (p. 176). Claims that typically Crashaw begins a religious poem by focusing on some kind of icon (a biblical text, an emblem, a religious object or picture) and that "the poem itself is a mental response, controlled by his ear, to the devotional stimulus of that icon" (p. 176). Notes that, therefore, "the sound of his poetry is more *legato* than that of most musical poets" and "has a haunting, evocative quality to it worthy of Coleridge, and generally found in unmusical poets like him" (p. 176). Explains that in most of his best religious poems Crashaw uses "a free fantasia or ode, which he often calls a hymn," and that "the organization of these hymns is purely musical, and for the most part they require a very fluent line which can lengthen or shorten at will, a relentless pushing enjambement, and a fortissimo climax at the end" (p. 176). Briefly compares Crashaw to Cowley and Milton.

◄§ 645. Hutton, Edward. "Some Catholic Poets and Writers in Tudor and Stuart and Hanoverian Times," in *Catholicism and English Literature*, 73–99. London: Frederick Muller.
2d ed., 1948.

Brief survey of Crashaw's life and poetry (pp. 95–98). Calls him "the greatest of the religious poets of the seventeenth century" (p. 95) and calls his poetry "the best, if not the only, example in our language of the enthusiasm of the Catholic reaction, led by St. Teresa and St. Ignatius of Loyola" against "Protestant heresy" (p. 96). Claims that Crashaw's poetry is the most complete example of the baroque in English. Suggests that Crashaw saw Bernini's famous statue of St. Teresa in Rome (though not until after he had written his Teresian poems) and maintains that, even if he did not, his poetry "has everything in common with the almost hysterical emotion and ecstasy, the furious enthusiasm and force of the baroque" (p. 97). Calls "Wishes. To his (supposed) Mistresse" "one of the most exquisite lyrics in the language" (p. 97). Concludes that Crashaw's poems are "the last expression" of English Catholic literature "and have in fact already taken on the foreign air to which English Catholicism had been condemned by its exile" (pp. 97–98).

◄§ 646. Muñoz Rojas, José A. "Los Poemas de Crashaw a Santa Teresa (estudio y version)." *Escorial: Revista de Cultura y Letras* 9, no. 26: 447–68.

Calls Crashaw one of the most attractive of seventeenth-century English poets and insists that an understanding of Spanish influence on English poetry is essential for appreciating his verse. Gives a general biographical sketch, suggesting that it was during his Cambridge years that Crashaw first learned Spanish and took notice of St. Teresa. Discusses the three Teresian poems, emphasizing their visual aspects. Comments on several editions and translations of the life of St. Teresa in circulation during the early seventeenth century and, while acknowledging that there is no evidence about which, if any, of these editions Crashaw actually knew, suggests that the biography served as the inspiration for the Teresian poems. Points out several similarities between the biography and both "The Flaming Heart" and "A Hymn to Sainte Teresa" and asserts that the latter is the best of the Teresian poems. Translates into Spanish: "A Hymn to Sainte Teresa" (pp. 456–62), "An Apologie for the foregoing Hymne" (pp. 462–64), and "The Flaming Heart" (pp. 464–68).

◄§ 647. Witherspoon, Alexander M. "Richard Crashaw," in *The College Survey of English Literature*. Vol. 1: *The Early Period, The Sixteenth Century, The Seventeenth Century, The Eighteenth Century*, edited by B. J. Whiting et al., 612–15. New York, Chicago, Burlingame: Harcourt, Brace & World.

Presents an introduction to Crashaw's life and work and anthologizes "Wishes. To his (supposed) Mistresse" along with selections from "Hymn in the Holy Nativity" and "The Flaming Heart," with brief notes. Suggests that Crashaw, in some ways, is "the least English poet of seventeenth-century England" and contrasts him to Herbert, noting that "there is little of the essential Herbert in his work, and there is nothing in the rapturous devotion and mystical splendor of his poetic cathedral which suggests the chaste simplicity of Herbert's parish church or Herbert's English countryside" (p. 612). Claims that Crashaw's fondness for Marino and the Spanish mystics "led him to introduce elaborate conceits and enthusiasms which at times offend good taste, and at other times startle the reader with their exotic beauty" (p. 612). Concludes that "no poet in the language has more glaring faults than Crashaw, and his love of elaborate conceits and lack of restraint resulted in some of the worst lines in the language"; nonetheless, "he belongs at his best with Shelley" (p. 613).

1943

◄§ 648. Clemens, Cyril. "Richard Crashaw: Catholic Shelley." *Ave Maria* 58 (7 August): 175–78.

A somewhat factually inaccurate biographical sketch of Crashaw along with a brief account of his poems. Suggests that Crashaw had an "ardent nature, sensuous rather than intellectual," which could have led him to become "a voluptuary, libertine, or some kind of ineffectual aesthete" (p. 178), but claims that, in fact, he was a true ascetic. Notes that, "although many of his secular poems attain untroubled rapture, in the religious ones it is often joy consisting of three-fourths pain" (p. 178). Makes no direct comparison between Crashaw and Shelley.

◄§ 649. Davies, Hugh Sykes. "Donne and the Metaphysicals," in *The Poets and Their Critics: Chaucer to Collins*, 63–89. (Pelican Books.) Harmondsworth, Eng.: Penguin Books.

Rev. ed., 1960; reprinted, London: Hutchinson Educational, 1969.

Collection of critical comments on the metaphysical poets, especially Donne, from Chapman to T. S. Eliot. Includes Pope's comment on Crashaw from Spence's *Anecdotes* (entry 131) and Eliot's comment on how Crashaw fits into the direct current of English poetry in "The Metaphysical Poets" (entry 417).

◄§ 650. Sackville-West, V. "Saint Teresa of Avila," in *The Eagle and the Dove: A Study in Contrasts—St. Teresa of Avila, St. Thérèse of Lisieux*, 7–100. London: Michael Joseph.

Suggests that the common notion in England of St. Teresa as "the prototype of the hysterical, emotional woman writhing in a frenzy of morbid devotion at the foot of the Crucifix" (p. 13) is partly due to Crashaw's portrayal of her in his Teresian poems. Regrets that "English readers have seized upon the excitable note [in Crashaw's poems] to the neglect of the other note he was discerning enough to introduce—the reference to her 'large draughts of intellectual day'" (p. 14).

⋙ 651. Vancŭra, Zdeněk. "Počátek a konec baroku" [The Beginning and End of the Baroque Period]. SaS 9:169–81.

Presents a cross-cultural view of the baroque, focusing on literature but also referring to the plastic arts. Singles out Crashaw as the foremost religious poet of the baroque period in England, comments on his religious temperament, and notes the influence of the Italians on his baroque style. Relates Crashaw to the metaphysical school and suggests that historically he is the most important poet in the group.

⋙ 652. Winters, Yvor. "John Crowe Ransom or Thunder Without God," in The Anatomy of Nonsense, 168–228. Norfolk, Conn.: New Directions.

Reprinted in In Defense of Reason (New York: Swallow Press & William Morrow Co., 1947; London: Routledge and Kegan Paul, 1960), 502–55.

Sections 7–9 of the essay, including the discussion of Crashaw, reprinted in Perspectives on Poetry, ed. James L. Calderwood and Harold E. Toliver (New York: Oxford University Press, 1968), 51–68.

Discusses Crashaw's use of tears in "The Weeper" (pp. 209–10) in a defense of his theory of poetry against the criticism of John Crowe Ransom. Calls the fifth stanza "one of the most remarkable triumphs of irrelevance with which I am acquainted" (p. 209). Maintains that, on the whole, the poem is "foolish and displays in an extreme form an error of method" and is "a chaos of irrelevancies not much better organized than a section of Finnegans Wake" (p. 210). Suggests that "The Weeper" is not one poem but rather "an agglomeration of minor poems very loosely related to each other" and concludes that "this is what is called baroque, or decorative, poetry" and that, "although a man of genius may sometimes engage in it with brilliant if fragmentary results, it is fundamentally frivolous" (p. 210).

1944

⋙ 653. Bernard, Sister Miriam. "More than a Woman." CathW 160:52–57.

Comments on Crashaw's admiration of St. Teresa, speculates on his knowledge of her life and works, and evaluates the three Teresian poems. Praises the strength, warmth, and effectiveness of the diction in all three poems, but finds in each "a distinct difference in the feeling" (p. 54). Suggests that the spirit of "A Hymn to Sainte Teresa" is "bright and childishly serious," as befits the subject, although the poem contains some "rough, flat lines" (p. 54), and maintains that "An Apologie for the fore-going Hymne," while more personal, is somewhat marred by the strained metaphor of the vine. Concludes that of the three poems "The Flaming Heart" is the most polished in thought, emotion, imagery, and form and calls it "his greatest poem" (p. 55). Claims that in it "the height of his praise and the swiftness of his lines leave no place for self" (p. 55) and that especially in the concluding lines Crashaw expresses a kind of mysticism not unlike that of St. Teresa.

◄§ 654. Gardner, W[illiam] H[enry]. *Gerard Manley Hopkins (1844–1889): A Study of Poetic Idiosyncrasy in Relation to Poetic Tradition.* London: Martin Secker & Warburg. Vol. 1, 1944. xvi, 304p. Vol. 2, 1949. xiv, 415p.

Vol. 1, 2d rev. ed., 1948; vols. 1 & 2 reissued by Oxford University Press, 1958, 1961, 1966, 1969.

Numerous references to Crashaw and a number of specific comparisons between Hopkins and Crashaw. Suggests that Hopkins's "The Blessed Virgin Compared to the Air We Breathe" (1883) is "nearer to the style and spirit of Crashaw than any other poem by Hopkins" (p. 188).

◄§ 655. Grierson, Herbert J. C., and J. C. Smith. "The Carolines," in *A Critical History of English Poetry,* 158–71. London: Chatto and Windus.

1st American ed., 1946; 2d rev. ed., 1947; reprinted, 1950, 1956, 1962; 1965; New York: Oxford University Press, 1970; [s.l.]: Arden Library, 1980; Atlantic Highlands, N.J.: Humanities Press, 1983.

Suggests that Crashaw's study of Marino merely encouraged his "natural bent to extravagance" but that his interest in the Spanish mystics "fanned his zeal to a flame in which his very extravagances are transfigured till they seem the natural language of adoration" (p. 165). Notes, however, that "when the glow fades they reveal themselves as ludicrous conceits" (p. 165), as evidenced in "The Weeper." Concludes that readers with "colder natures" may find "something febrile in a piety that clothes itself in erotic imagery" but that, nevertheless, nothing in English poetry matches "the rapturous eloquence" of "A Hymn to Sainte Teresa" or the "adoring tenderness" of "Hymn in the Holy Nativity" (p. 165). Claims that "Wishes. To his (supposed) Mistresse" shows that Crashaw "could have held his own with the courtly poets" (p. 165). Briefly contrasts Crashaw to Herbert, Donne, and Vaughan.

◄§ 656. Logan, Sister Eugenia. "An Indebtedness of Coleridge to Crashaw." *MLN* 59:551–53.

Notes Coleridge's admiration of Crashaw and maintains that because of Coleridge's "discerning criticism" Crashaw "regained a place of prominence among the poets after a century or more of neglect" (p. 552). Points out, in particular, the central image of a large black letter in the heavens foreshadowing wrath in Coleridge's "Coeli Enarrant" (lines 5–11) and Crashaw's use of the same figure in "Hymn in the Glorious Epiphanie" (lines 183–89) and suggests the similarity "makes the parallel seem more an echo than a chance resemblance" (p. 553).

◄§ 657. Moloney, Michael Francis. "In the Wake of Donne," in *John Donne: His Flight from Mediaevalism,* 196–213. (Illinois Studies in Language and Literature, vol. 29, no. 2–3.) Urbana: University of Illinois Press.

Reprinted, New York: Russell & Russell, 1965; Folcroft, Pa.: Folcroft Library Editions, 1975; Norwood, Pa.: Norwood Editions, 1975; Philadelphia: R. West, 1977; Norwood, Pa.: Norwood, 1978.

Contrasts the concluding lines of "The Flaming Heart" and Herbert's "Love (I)" to show that Crashaw, unlike Herbert, finds no conflict between human and divine love but rather sees human love "as a stepping stone, a foretaste of the Divine" (p. 208). Suggests that Crashaw's attitude is essentially medieval and "was a way of thinking still understandable in the England of the seventeenth century but in the direct descent from the past it occurs in him for the last time" (p. 208). Suggests also that Crashaw's use of sensuous imagery rests upon "an acceptance of the sacramental idealism of the Middle Ages" and, whether tasteful or not, reflects "a total obliviousness to the divorce of sense and thought which was appearing in much of the poetry of his time" (p. 208). Concludes that, regardless of his debt to Donne and Herbert, Crashaw is "a poet of a different world" and thus agrees with Eliot that "the poetic lineage of Crashaw has not yet been accurately traced" (p. 208). Briefly notes, however, that something of the spirit of Crashaw can be found in the poetry of Francis Thompson and especially Coventry Patmore.

≈§ 658. Sypher, Wylie. "The Metaphysicals and the Baroque." *PR* 11:3–17.

Reprinted in *Partisan Reader*, ed. William Phillips and Philip Rahv (New York: Dial Press, 1946), 567–81.

Argues that our modern admiration of Donne "is in a sense hollow and affected" and that "our depreciation of Milton is wilful" and maintains that, "if we understand the baroque, it is a questionable tactic to elevate Donne at the expense of Milton" (p. 4) since Milton is "the greatest of the baroque poets, the most polyphonic" (p. 17). Surveys baroque "manners" in sculpture, painting, architecture, and poetry. Calls Crashaw's rhetoric "entirely baroque" and contrasts it to the more "romantic" rhetoric of Shelley: "The feeling of both poets is intense; yet in Crashaw the substance can be more readily detached from the eccentric and distorted rhetoric" (p. 12). Notes also that Crashaw's rhetoric, unlike Shelley's, "is more 'external,' possibly because the imagery is *not* a matter of feeling" (p. 12). Suggests that Crashaw's rhetoric has certain affinities with "the rhetoric of the Gesu Church [in Rome], of Correggio in painting away the dome of the cathedral of Parma, or of Bernini in designing the baldachin of St. Peter's" and also has something in common with "the extravagant handling of drapery in counter-reformation statuary" (p. 12). Briefly notes Crashaw's calculated uses of extravagant wit.

≈§ 659. Taketomo, Sōfū. *Eishi-shi* [A History of English Poetry]. Tokyo: Kenkyusha.

Considers Crashaw, along with Herbert and Vaughan, as forming a school of poetry that originated with Donne. Comments particularly on the uses of conceits and quaint imagery in metaphysical poetry and suggests that

Crashaw's Catholic and baroque sensibility sets him apart from Herbert. Discusses briefly "The Weeper" as representative of the strengths and weaknesses of metaphysical poetry.

1945

◆§ 660. Berkeley, Lennox, comp. *Lord, when the sense of Thy sweet grace: Anthem for Mixed Voices and Organ*. Words by Richard Crashaw; music by Lennox Berkeley. (Contemporary Church Music Series.) London: J. & W. Chester/Edition Wilhelm Hansen.

Musical setting of "A Song ('Lord, when the sense of thy sweet grace')."

◆§ 661. Bush, Douglas. *English Literature in the Earlier Seventeenth Century, 1600–1660* (Oxford History of English Literature, edited by F. P. Wilson and Bonamy Dobrée, vol. 5.) Oxford: Clarendon Press. vi, 621p.

Reprinted, 1946, 1948, 1952, 1956; rev. ed., 1962; reprinted with corrections, 1966; first issued as an Oxford University paperback, 1973 (without chronological tables and bibliography).

Section on Crashaw reprinted in *George Herbert and the Seventeenth-Century Religious Poets*, ed. Mario Di Cesare (entry 1133), 270–73.

General critical and historical survey of seventeenth-century poetry and prose (1600–1660). Discusses Crashaw's poetry primarily in Chapter 4, "Jonson, Donne, and Their Successors" (pp. 104–69, especially pp. 139–43). Presents a general survey and critical evaluation of Crashaw's poetry as well as a biographical note. Calls him "the one conspicuous English incarnation of the 'baroque' sensibility" (p. 140) and points out that "for us the simplest definition [of baroque] is 'poetry like Crashaw's'" (p. 141). Notes that Crashaw's "abundant revision" of his poems "always led to further elaboration and rarely to improvement" (p. 141), citing, in the 1962 edition, "Hymn in the Holy Nativity" as an exception. Maintains that Crashaw was "not a theologian or thinker, or a troubled soul like Donne and Herbert, but a secure, single-hearted worshipper whose feeling for the central paradoxes of faith does not lessen his sense of the human values in the story of the Son of Mary" (p. 141). Suggests that, for all his skill as a poet of Greek and Latin verse, Crashaw was "one of the most unclassical, and uncertain, of English poets" (p. 141). Claims that "The Weeper" "offers a severe though not final test for appreciation of Crashaw and baroque religiosity" (p. 141). Maintains that Crashaw "was to go far beyond Marinism in power of vision and symbol, but even in his greater poems he generally hovered between the organic unity of baroque inspiration and a dazzling spray of associated images" and warns that "the reader who lacks a special temperament or a knowledge of the symbolic code may sometimes think of the dreams of a convert who has eaten rich food and slept on his back" (p. 142). Notes that, although Crashaw's images and diction are not vague or even esoteric in some senses, the reader "may not have patience to find the controlling motive" (p. 142). Comments briefly on a number of individual poems, especially "Musicks Duell," "Sospetto d'Herode," and "Hymn to the Name of Jesus" and suggests that the reader probably "comes back most often to the strong and simple 'Hymn' to St. Teresa, and to the sequel, 'The Flaming Heart,' in which cool ingenuity becomes incandescent" (p. 142). Concludes that, at times, Crashaw appears to be "a beautiful angel beating his luminous wings in a richly coloured Catholic heaven" and notes that the ordinary reader "may feel uneasy when the authentic motives of adoration and self-surrender issue in an undisciplined fervour which has never been rational and never ceases to be sensuous and excited" (p. 143). Compares and/or contrasts Crashaw to Southwell, Donne, Herbert, Giles Fletcher, Milton, John Owen, Thomas Campion, Quarles, Joseph Beaumont, Edward Benlowes, Cleveland, Cowley, Davenant, Vaughan, and Dryden. Extensive bibliography (pp. 440–610, with a section on Crashaw, pp. 516–17).

◆§ 662. Daniells, Roy. "Baroque Form in English Literature." *UTQ* 14: 393–408.

Discusses the renewed interest in and appreciation for baroque art and sensibility in the twentieth century; outlines difficulties that critics encounter in applying the term *baroque* to literature, especially English poetry and prose; and argues that, despite these difficulties, *baroque* is a useful critical term in evaluating English seventeenth-century literature. Discusses Donne, Crashaw, and Milton as "the most interesting exponents of baroque form in poetry: Donne on account of his early and deliberate dislocation of conventional shapes, Crashaw because of his direct connections with continental Catholic art, and Milton for the large structures and very deliberate artistry of his major works" (p. 401). Maintains that, of the three, Crashaw's poetry "affords the best, or at least the most obvious, example of baroque technique" and comments on his uses of decoration and elaboration, his "capacity for achieving unity in complication and for subordinating the validity of a single line to the internal cohesion of the total passage," and his ability "to present what would be a baroque subject or design if graphically portrayed" (pp. 402–3). Points out that all baroque poets run the danger of allowing "adroitly handled devices to become an end in themselves, of permitting the delight in overcoming difficulties and achieving effects by superb manipulation to run riot," noting that Crashaw "is always on the edge of this pitfall" and that "all the 'metaphysicals' fall into it sooner or later" (p. 401). Finds that the term *baroque* can be applied meaningfully to many of Crashaw's contemporaries or near contemporaries—Marvell, Carew, Herbert, and Traherne as well as to Donne and Milton.

◆§ 663. Feist, Hans. "Richard Crashaw," in *Ewiges England: Dichtung aus Sieben Jahrhunderten von Chaucer bis Eliot*, 280–91, 578. Zurich: Verlag Amstutz, Herdeg & Co.

Anthologizes (without critical notes or commentary) "An Epitaph upon a Young Married Couple," several stanzas from "Hymn in the Holy Nativity," "On our crucified Lord Naked, and bloody," stanzas from "Song upon the Bleeding Crucifix," and lines from "Hymn in the Assumption"—with facing German translations. Biographical note points out the influence of Southwell, the Spanish and Italian mystics, and Herbert (p. 578).

✒ 664. Gregory, Horace. "The 'Vita Nuova' of Baroque Art in the Recent Poetry of Edith Sitwell: A Note in Appreciation." *Poetry* 66:148–56.
Discusses "baroque elements" in Sitwell's poetry and notes that "in English there has been but one clearly defined Baroque poet, Richard Crashaw, who held during his short life an almost unenglish devotion to the 'Baroque idea' that had come to him through the media of the Roman Church and Spanish and Italian poetry" (p. 152). Quotes lines from "Hymn in the Holy Nativity" and calls them "a true example of Baroque art in English poetry" written by "a fully matured Baroque artist" (p. 152). Suggests that Sitwell's affinity with Crashaw "is one of knowing, consciously or unconsciously, those demands that Baroque art makes upon the poet" (p. 153) but denies any direct borrowings. Maintains rather that "both illustrate a mastery of the Baroque imagination in poetry, which is a control and an art that Francis Thompson, who was all too consciously Crashaw's disciple, did not fully achieve" (p. 154).

✒ 665. Halley, Thomas A. "Father Richard Crashaw: Convert." *Ave Maria* 62 (15 September): 165–67.
Popularized biographical sketch of Crashaw that emphasizes various stages in his conversion to Catholicism. Claims that it is likely Crashaw became a Catholic and was ordained a priest at Oxford, just after returning from his stay in Leyden. Sees striking parallels between Crashaw and Newman.

✒ 666. Hess, M. Whitcomb. "Descartes and Richard Crashaw." *Commonweal* 42:455–57.
Commemorates 1945 as the tercentenary of Crashaw's conversion to Catholicism and contrasts Crashaw's approach to truth with the rationalism of Descartes and his seventeenth-century followers. Notes Crashaw's unworldly mind, his asceticism, his devotion to Christian truth, and his exercise of faith and calls him "the most metaphysical of the metaphysicals" (p. 456). Briefly comments on Crashaw's poems, pointing out his uses of musical metaphors, images of nesting, and Christian symbols. Calls "Nympha pudica Deum vidit, et erubuit" "the most famous line of Latin ever written by an English author" (p. 456). Briefly compares Crashaw to Newman.

✒ 667. Lowell, Robert. "The Verses of Thomas Merton." *Commonweal* 42:240–41.
Suggests the influence of Crashaw on Merton's early poetry and notes that one of Merton's faults "is a contrivance that he may have learned from some

of the less successful poems of Crashaw," for example, "The Weeper" (p. 241). Suggests that Merton's use of conceit in "The Blessed Virgin Mary Compared to a Window" may owe something to both Donne and Crashaw but that their contributions to the poem "detract nothing from its sincerity and freshness" (p. 241). Observes that Merton's "For My Brother Reported Missing in Action, 1943" should be compared to "An Epitaph upon a Young Married Couple" and claims that, in Crashaw's poem, "the metaphors are worked out with logic and care and the meter is firmer" (p. 242).

◆§ 668. Moloney, Michael F. "Richard Crashaw." CathW 162:43–50.
   Presents a biographical sketch of Crashaw and laments that he has been indiscriminately lumped with the other metaphysical poets and is still viewed in the reflected light of Donne and Marino. Finds Crashaw, on the whole, quite unlike Donne. Notes, for example, that the music of Crashaw's lines "most certainly owes nothing to the gnarled and stubborn rhythms of Donne" (p. 44) and maintains, in contrast, that "his versification is the regular and controlled product of the conscious seventeenth century classicist" (p. 45). Suggests that, in versification and form, Crashaw's more likely master is Jonson, not Donne or Spenser. Argues that in thought processes, choice of images, subject matter, and sensibility, "the divergence between Crashaw and Donne remains absolute" (p. 46). Discusses Crashaw's qualities as a poet, such as his distinctive and original craftsmanship in verse; his expertise in Latin verse, especially the epigram; his mastery of pun, paradox, and concentration; and his intellectual and symbolic uses of images. Notes that Crashaw is "the lone voice in English poetry of the baroque aesthetic" (p. 48) and discusses how identification with the baroque has often damaged Crashaw's reputation and made it difficult for English readers to appreciate his art. Calls Crashaw "a true medievalist" (p. 47) and maintains that, although much that is uninspired and tasteless in his poetry comes from his mystical propensity, "only as the heir of the medieval mystics may Crashaw be rightly understood" (p. 50). Warns that, "dislike his verse we may and with good reason, but dismiss it as trivial we cannot with integrity" (p. 48).

◆§ 669. Praz, Mario. Richard Crashaw. Brescia: Morcelliana. 200p.
   Reprinted with appendix (selections from Crashaw's poetry in English), Rome: Mario Bulzoni—Editore Libreria «Richerche», 1964. 231p.
   Abridged English version, "The Flaming Heart: Richard Crashaw and the Baroque," in The Flaming Heart: Essays on Crashaw, Machiavelli, and Other Studies of the Relations between Italian and English Literature from Chaucer to T. S. Eliot, Doubleday Anchor Books (Garden City: Doubleday & Co., 1958), 204–63; reprinted, New York: Norton, 1973.
   Revised edition (with a new preface and bibliography) of the Crashaw section of Secentismo e Marinismo in Inghilterra: John Donne—Richard Crashaw (entry 459).

◄§ 670. Scott, W[alter] S[idney]. "Richard Crashaw," in *The Fantasticks: Donne, Herbert, Crashaw, Vaughan*, 95–130. London: John Westhouse.

Presents a biographical sketch of Crashaw and comments generally on the nature of his poetry (pp. 95–99). Suggests that Crashaw's poetry "clearly shows the dual effect of a strongly inhibited character and a somewhat sensuous religion" and that in him "the natural desires of an ordinary human being, and the mystical understanding of the supernatural were blended together in such a way that the one was hopelessly underdeveloped, while the other was given an uncontrolled freedom" (p. 96). Maintains that Crashaw's use of conceits; the deeply religious, even mystical, nature of his verse; and especially his uses of images of sexual love in treating religious themes show his indebtedness to Donne but notes that, unlike Donne, whose "basic emotion was his need to touch the divine, a need which he expressed, and in his youth attempted to satisfy, through the medium of the love of woman," Crashaw's need "was the satisfaction of his emotional and sensuous nature, a satisfaction whose attainment he attempted to disguise by colouring it with the pale tints of an Italianate and somewhat repellent religiosity" (p. 98). Asks the reader not to be put off by Crashaw's religio-eroticism and sentimentalism but to see the beauty evident in much of his poetry. Includes selections from Crashaw's secular and sacred verse (pp. 101–30), without additional notes or commentary.

◄§ 671. Wilson, F. P. "Poetry," in *Elizabethan and Jacobean*, 53–83. Oxford: Clarendon Press.

Reprinted, 1946, 1959, 1969; Folcroft, Pa.: Folcroft Library Editions, 1969.

Points out some major differences between Elizabethan and Jacobean poetry. Briefly compares and/or contrasts Crashaw with Donne, Herbert, Marvell, Giles Fletcher, and Southwell. Notes that "it is this 'sequaciousness,' this follow-through of logic and passion, which makes it possible to say that George Herbert and Marvell (with all their many differences from Donne and from each other) belong to the same 'school' of poetry as Donne, and that Southwell and Crashaw do not" (p. 58). Points out that Crashaw's hymns, like those of Donne and Herbert, are not suitable for congregational singing. Suggests that in *Christ's Victory and Triumph* (1610) Giles Fletcher, who "with tender and reverential wit lavishes upon his sacred themes the conceits and sensuous imagery and decoration with which secular poets had worshipped Venus" (pp. 71–72), reminds one of Crashaw and notes that, except for "The Weeper," which springs from the same tradition, there is nothing comparable in English poetry to Southwell's "St. Peter's Complaint."

1946

◄§ 672. Anon. "Poet and Saint." *TLS*, 1 June, p. 258.

Commemorates the tercentenary of the publication of the first edition of Crashaw's English poems with a biographical sketch of the poet and a critical survey of his poetry. Notes that the English epigrams in the 1646 edition "show more ingenuity than religious insight" and that "the English cannot preserve the concinnity of the Latin [originals]." Agrees with Praz that "Sospetto d'Herode" is "more typically Baroque in imagination and style than the original" and that "the general effect is apt to appear bizarre." Finds "Musicks Duell" "prettily designed" but too long and praises "Wishes. To his (supposed) Mistresse" as "dainty." Suggests that "The Weeper" shows both Crashaw's strengths and his weaknesses and claims that the stanzas of the poem are "strung together like the beads of a rosary" and that "one order is as good, or as inconsequent, as the other." Singles out "Hymn in the Holy Nativity" as one of Crashaw's most successful pieces. Comments on Crashaw's knowledge of and admiration for St. Teresa and discusses the three Teresian poems, noting that the last twenty-four lines of "The Flaming Heart" "are among the most brilliant that he ever wrote." Maintains that Crashaw "was never happier than in his use of the octo-syllabic line" and notes that "in his hands it moves with a tripping swiftness that is unsurpassed by any English poet." Concludes that "the faults that disfigure much of his work—oversweetness, extravagant fancies, diffuseness—will not in the end tell against the great qualities that he reveals in his best poems." Mentions the influence of Joseph Beaumont, Herbert, Marino, Strada, and Continental models.

◄§ 673. Cazamian, Louis, trans. "Richard Crashaw," in *Anthologie de la póesie anglaise*, 86–87. Paris: Éditions Stock.

Includes lines from the second version of "Letter to the Countess of Denbigh" with a French translation on facing pages. Notes that Crashaw "montre assez souvent, parmi des erreurs de goût et des préciosités incroyables, un essor lyrique, une pureté d'image et de langue, qui placent ses meilleures inspirations au sommet de la poésie religieuse anglaise du XVIIe siècle" (p. 86).

◄§ 674. Coffin, Robert P. Tristram, and Alexander M. Witherspoon, eds. "Richard Crashaw (1612?-1649)," in *Seventeenth-Century Prose and Poetry*, 173–84. New York: Harcourt, Brace and Co.

Two volumes bound as one with separate introductions and pagination; prose section is an expansion of *Seventeenth-Century Prose* (New York: Harcourt, Brace, and Co., 1929).

Reprinted, 1957.

2d ed., with new introduction to Crashaw, ed. Alexander M. Witherspoon and Frank J. Warnke (entry 895); enlarged, 1982.

Presents a general introduction to Crashaw's life, character, and poetry.

Calls him "a Shelley in the church; a poet who makes the idea of loveliness so alive, so breathless, so compelling, and so rich that it casts a spell over the mind" and claims that "his best poems, at their best, become like Shelley's incantations" (p. 173). Notes that, "nervous, restless, avid of sensation, he tries to explain the mystery of life in the richest of rhetoric" and calls him "the most sheerly mystical poet in our tongue" (p. 173). Suggests that *fire* is the only adequate word to describe Crashaw's poetry and claims that he wins his readers "by setting them into such flames as he burns in himself" (p. 174). Comments briefly on Crashaw's art, especially his uses of rich language, elaborate rhetoric, striking and sometimes grotesque figures of speech, repetition, and color. Suggests that Crashaw "has come close to the core of the mystery of being" and characterizes his poetry as "a drowning of one's reasoning and a singing of one's self to sleep by the spell of a fierce, compelling insistence upon man's being a part of the unifying principle of passion which holds suns and stars together in fiery action and adherence" (p. 174). Calls "A Hymn to Sainte Teresa" and "The Flaming Heart" "two of the greatest religious poems in the language" (p. 181). Briefly compares and contrasts Crashaw to Donne, Herbert, and Milton and stresses the influence of the Spanish mystics on Crashaw's life and art. Includes eight selections (pp. 174–84), with brief explanatory notes.

◄§ 675. Daniells, Roy. "English Baroque and Deliberate Obscurity." *JAAC* 5:115–21.
    Attempts to define the baroque as it is applied to English literature. Claims that "baroque may be regarded as the logical continuation and extension of High Renaissance art, with conscious accentuation and 'deformation' of the regular stock of techniques," which "become more dynamic and (in both good and bad senses of the word) theatrical" (p. 117). Points out that "a sense of triumph and splendour, a strenuous effort to unify opposite terms of paradoxes" and "a high regard for technical virtuosity" are some marks of the baroque (p. 117). Suggests that English baroque appears as early as 1590. Specifically comments on the uses of deliberate obscurity as "a cult of significant darkness" (p. 119) in baroque poetry. Notes that seventeenth-century poets, including Crashaw, "take on fresh interest when regarded as Baroque craftsmen" (p. 118). Concludes that the concept of the baroque is useful in the study of English literature in that "it advances fresh relationships, permits new perspectives, leads to a better understanding of the formal intentions of the authors, gives the English-speaking student a link with Continental baroque, forges links between types of sensibility and kinds of style, and generally acts as a catalyst to combinations of critical ideas" and, above all, "adds to our pleasure in the seventeenth-century" (p. 121).

◄§ 676. Doughty, W. L. "Cross and Crucifix: The Sacred Poetry of Richard Crashaw." *LQHR* 171:301–17.

Reprinted (in slightly revised form) in *Studies in Religious Poetry of the Seventeenth Century* (London: Epworth Press, 1946), 34–59; reprinted, Port Washington, N.Y.: Kennikat Press, 1969.

Presents a biographical sketch of the poet, comments on his religious sensibility, and surveys his sacred themes and poetic techniques. Notes that, in spite of defects in his poems, "most intelligent readers hold today that the best of Crashaw's poetry will last as long as the English language endures or men are moved by the beauty of an exquisite line and a graceful fancy" (p. 302). Suggests that modern readers are, in fact, more accepting of Crashaw's lapses in taste because "this is an age that does not expect perfection and which readily forgets the anguish of such infelicities for the joy that some phrase or thought of rapturous beauty has been born into the world" (p. 303). Maintains that, although Crashaw's themes are few, they are "like the four strings of a violin, capable of many melodies" (p. 303). Emphasizes that Crashaw lived "in the presence of the Cross, which, in all his thought, is never far away" (p. 303) and is "the central emblem of his faith" (p. 304). Discusses Crashaw's artistic uses of suffering, tears, and sorrow and comments on his uses of emotionally charged imagery and diction, noting that hallmarks of his style are utter sincerity, quiet intensity, and restrained passion. Praises "Hymn to the Name of Jesus" as among Crashaw's "supreme achievements: a rushing, breathless exuberance of sheer, infectious music: a very cataract of praise; a Niagara of jubilation, that when the surge and cadence of it are over, leaves the dazed, enchanted reader buoyant upon waves that dance and rock and sparkle, memories and motions of the impetuous flood that has borne him in its strong, exhilarating flow" (p. 311). Draws attention to parallels between "Hymn in the Holy Nativity" and Virgil's eclogues. Praises especially the three Teresian poems, noting that "The Flaming Heart" "has the distinction of containing some of Crashaw's most irritating lines and bizarre fancies and also what is generally regarded as his most magnificent flight of unfettered eloquence" (p. 315). Compares and contrasts Crashaw to Dante, Shakespeare, Milton, Isaac Watts, G. B. Shaw, and especially Charles Wesley.

◄§ 677. Hess, M. Whitcomb. "Recalling Crashaw." *America* 74:381–82.

An appreciative tribute to Crashaw commemorating his formal reception into the Catholic Church. Stresses that Crashaw was both a poet and a saint and maintains that, although his command of poetic imagery and mastery of verse techniques are evidence of his ability as a poet, it is primarily his saintliness, his religious and mystical vision of reality, his dedication to his "Christocentric muse" (p. 381), and his ability to transport his reader to a transcendental experience that attract his modern readers. Points out that Crashaw's poetry consists "not in rendering abstract that which is sensible but in rendering sensible that which is abstract" and observes that his poetry is primarily addressed "to those who would live within the spirit" (p. 381). Briefly compares Crashaw to Newman.

◄§ 678. Milch, Werner J. "Metaphysical Poetry and the German 'Barock-lyrik.'" *Comparative Literature Studies* (Cardiff) 23–24:16–22.

Comments on possible areas of comparative studies between the German *barock* poets and the English metaphysicals as well as between the larger aspects of each movement. Sees in the work of the *barock* poets and the metaphysicals "the last great European attempt to bring about a unified world of thought since the rift between contemplative and active life, between unquestioned faith and scientific urge had become the central feature of all philosophy" (p. 20). Suggests that Crashaw should be compared to Johann Scheffler in order to determine the effects of their conversion to Catholicism on their poetry. Maintains that a comparative study of Donne, Crashaw, and Traherne with Andreas Gryphius, Johann Scheffler, and Daniel Czepko would show "striking resemblances in the choice of words and phrases, in metre, in subject matter, and even in titles and headings of single poems" (p. 22). See also entry 687.

◄§ 679. Praz, Mario. "Poesia metafisica inglese del Seicento: Versioni di Donne, Crashaw, Herbert, Vaughan, Herbert of Cherbury, King, Marvell." *Poesia* 3–4:232–312.

Presents a summary of modern critical reaction to metaphysical poetry. In a brief critical evaluation of Crashaw (p. 236) notes especially the influence of the Jesuit Latin epigrammatists and Marino. Contrasts Crashaw to Donne, noting that "poco o nulla troviamo in lui della tormentata introspezione del Donne; vi troviamo invece elevato a temperatura incandescente quel misticismo voluttuoso che spirava dai libri di devozione continentali, sopratutto dai libri d'emblemi gesuiti in cui il linguaggio dell'amor profano era applicato a fini religiosi." Claims that in all of seventeenth-century literature "non v'e forse espressione più alta di quello spiritualizzamento del senso che si configura come miracoloso e vertiginoso ascendere d'immagini travolte e infocate in certi passi degl'inni del Crashaw." Notes that "talvolta il suono in lui sembra avere ragione del senso. . . . ma dal pericolo a cui doveva più tardi soccombere lo Swinburne, il vago e confuso degli effetti, il Crashaw è di solito preservato grazie all'abito analitico del concettismo, che infustisce anche le immagini più stravaganti, e mette a fuoco le emozioni più sottili ed eteree: a questo modo il sentimento è tradotto in pensiero senza per questo cessare d'essere sentimento, e la poesia del Crashaw, pur così diversa da quella del Donne, può dirsi metafisica anch'essa" (p. 236). Translates into Italian "Wishes. To his (supposed) Mistresse," "Letter to the Countess of Denbigh," and the closing of "The Flaming Heart" (pp. 272–82).

◄§ 680. ———. *Studi sul concettismo*. (Biblioteca Sansoni Critica, 9.) 2d ed. Florence: G. C. Sansoni. vii, 321p.

Specific comments on Crashaw do not appear in the first Italian edition of *Studi sul concettismo* (Milan: Soc. Ed. La Cultura, 1934) but do appear in

Studies in Seventeenth-Century Imagery, vol. 1 (entry 616), an English version (with revisions and a new appendix) of the first Italian edition. The second Italian edition is essentially an Italian version of the English revised edition. Comments on Crashaw found in both the English version and the second Italian edition first appeared in an essay in *English Studies* (entry 554).

✒ 681. Watkin, E[dward] I. "British Baroque." *CQR* 142:48−60.

Defines baroque art as "the employment of classical forms and themes by the Gothic spirit" (p. 48) and claims that "Baroque was born of the inspiration which had earlier given birth to Gothic, namely Christian faith" (p. 49). Sees Counter-Reformation art as a reaction not only to Protestantism but also to "the nascent secularism and irreligious humanism of the Renaissance" and thus "diametrically opposed to the classical temper of the latter" (p. 50). Surveys examples of British baroque art, primarily in architecture. Comments briefly on the chapel of Peterhouse, noting that it brings "memories of our most Baroque poet, Crashaw" (p. 55). Suggests that the real triumph of the baroque in England took place in poetry, singling out Crashaw as more baroque than Marino. Notes that, unlike Donne, Crashaw "never halts the reader with a difficult passage to construe or chills him with an unfeeling subtlety" and suggests that even "his most preposterous conceits are ornaments dropped by love before his Lord's feet or in more secular poems aglow with a lofty enthusiasm" (p. 60). Compares Crashaw briefly with Herbert and Vaughan and concludes that to know the English baroque poets "is to have entered the heart of British Baroque" (p. 60).

✒ 682. Wellek, René. "The Concept of Baroque in Literary Scholarship." *JAAC* 5:77−109.

Reprinted in *Concepts in Criticism* (New Haven: Yale University Press, 1963), 69−127.

Surveys historically and critically the various uses of the term *baroque*, primarily as it is applied by scholars and critics to describe the poetry and prose of several countries. Mentions Crashaw several times and calls him a mystical poet. Points out that, although *baroque* is used to describe both literary style and/or emotional attitudes and ideological categories, its application is most successful "with poets like Crashaw where the integration of belief and expression is complete" (p. 95). Concludes that whatever defects the term may have it is "a term which prepares for synthesis, draws our minds away from the mere accumulation of observations and facts, and paves the way for a future history of literature as a fine art" (p. 97). Bibliography of writings on the baroque, arranged chronologically from 1888 (Wölfflin) to 1947 (pp. 97−103); notes (pp. 103−9).

✒ 683. Zanco, Aurelio. "L'Età di Milton," in *Storia della letterature inglese*. Vol. 1: *Dalle origini alla restaurazione*, 650-1660, 520−55. Turin: Chiantore.

2d ed., Turin: Loescher Editore, 1964.

Presents a brief sketch of Crashaw's life and works (pp. 532–33). Notes Spanish and Italian influences, especially those of Marino and St. Teresa. Maintains that Crashaw "fu un virtuoso dell'immagine, un ricercatore di concetti peregrini e di modi di dire inconsueti, ma in lui, più che nel Herbert, di cui, del resto, subì l'influsso, predomina una ricchezza di linguaggio che ne fa veramente un «verborum artifex», sovente paragonabile, per libertà e sottigliezza, allo stesso immaginifico ed esaltato Shelley, di cui lo si considerò un remoto precursore" (p. 533). Notes that in *Carmen Deo Nostro* "il sentimento religioso si raffina e con esso la potenza dell'espressione, non scevra, tuttavia, da difetti analoghi a quelli che abbiamo riscontrati nel Herbert e nel Donne, specialmente per quanto riguarda la ricercatezza grottesca delle immagini e la mania dei paragoni strani, barocchi e ridondanti" (p. 533). Points out that in "The Flaming Heart" "il tumulto delle immagini d'amore e di entusiasmo acquista intensità di delirio, in una progressione addirittura sinfonica" (p. 533).

1947

◄§ 684. Allison, A. F. "Some Influences in Crashaw's Poem 'On a Prayer Booke Sent to Mrs. M. R.'" *RES* 23:34–42.

Considers "Ode on a Prayer-book" as Crashaw's "most successful description of the mystical progress of the soul" (p. 34) and discusses several works that may have influenced the poem, especially St. Teresa's *Vida* and her account of the mystical life in *The Interior Castle*. Notes that lines 1–58, which describe the stage of purgation, not only reflect the main features of St. Teresa's account of mystical experience but also show the influence of the language of early seventeenth-century English poetry, especially that of Herbert. Points out, however, that lines 58–74, which describe the stage of illumination, show little influence of Herbert but rather contain language and symbols borrowed directly from St. Teresa. Notes that the language of Western mysticism, including that of St. Teresa, was itself often borrowed from the secular tradition and was a spiritualization and artistic refinement of the language of romantic passion. Claims that when he came to express the last stage of mystical union, Crashaw found even the language of St. Teresa, borrowed from the *Song of Songs*, "too restrained" to provide him "with the material for a magnificent peroration" (p. 40) and thus he sought his imagery and language in the baroque fusion of Christian and pagan classical poetry. Points out that "nowhere is the fusion more remarkable than in Crashaw, in whose verse may be seen a two-fold extension of human experience, the development of the mystical life on the one hand, and, on the other, an increasing preoccupation with the sensuous" (pp. 40–41). Notes that especially in lines 81–117 of the poem, his description of the spiritual nuptials, Crashaw introduces into the floral setting of the *Song of Songs* images taken from Carew's most licentious poem, "The Rapture." Concludes that "as an expression of mystical experience it is more complete than any of the later poems which were influenced by St. Teresa; and, in its attempt to find a metaphor for conceptions before which even she was silent, it explored the sensuous possibilities of language more thoroughly than much of the love-poetry of the Renaissance" (p. 42).

◄§ 685. Finzi, Gerald. *Lo, The Full, Final Sacrifice: Festival Anthem for Chorus and Organ (or Orchestra)*. With words by Richard Crashaw. New York: Boosey & Hawkes. 31p.
A musical setting for a combination of lines from Crashaw's versions of St. Thomas Aquinas's "Adoro Te" and "Lauda Sion Salvatorem." Dedicated to Rev. Walter Hussey and the organist and choir of the Church of St. Matthew (Northampton) on 21 September 1946, the fifty-third anniversary of the consecration of the church.

◄§ 686. Hayward, John, comp. *English Poetry: A Catalogue of First and Early Editions of the Works of the English Poets from Chaucer to the Present Day Exhibited by the National Book League at 7 Albemarle Street, London.* Cambridge: Published for the National Book League by the Cambridge University Press. x, 140p.
Illustrated ed. (with 7 additional pages), 1950.
Calls the exhibit "the most comprehensive and valuable loan collection of first and early editions of English poetry ever shown in public" (p. v). Item 82 (p. 43) is a copy of the first edition of *Steps to the Temple. Sacred Poems. With other Delights of the Muses* (1646), bound in early nineteenth-century polished calf with sprinkled edges and lacking the original blank leaf A1 before the title; C5-C8 (pp. 33–40); G11, the second of two leaves of "The Table"; and G12, the final blank. Lent by Roger Senhouse. Item 83 (p. 43) is a copy of the second edition of *Steps to the Temple,* bound in contemporary sheep, "a perfect, untouched copy with a fine impression of the engraved title preceding the letterpress title." Notes that "at the foot of the latter the (?) original owner has written in a delicate hand: 'Ex libris Fran: Fitt'" and that "in this second edition twenty-four pieces were added to Part I, and nineteen to Part II." Lent by Richard Jennings.

◄§ 687. Milch, Werner. "Deutsche Barocklyrik und 'Metaphysical Poetry.'" *Trivium* 5:65–73.
Comments on the contemporaneity of the metaphysical poets and certain seventeenth-century German baroque poets and suggests areas of comparative studies between individual poets in each country as well as between larger aspects of the two periods. Comments on various religious, political, and philosophical conditions in both Germany and England that favored the development of baroque poetry. Suggests that Crashaw should be compared to Johann Scheffler, especially with regard to the effects of their conversion to Catholicism on their poetry. See also entry 678.

◄§ 688. Minkov, Marko Konstantinov. *Baroque Literature in England*. (Annuaire de l'Université de Sofia. Faculté Historico-Philologique, 43.) Sofia: Impr. de l'Université. 71p.

Focuses on Fletcher as the first English baroque dramatist and attempts to show how the term *baroque* is useful and fully justifiable when discussing literature. Defines the characteristics of the baroque in the light of and with the limitations of Wölfflin's principles for the baroque in art. Finds that the way of looking at things in the seventeenth century was connected with definite social, political and religious forms. Distinguishes among three types of baroque art that arose from three cultural strains: the religious culture of the Catholic Church, the courtly culture of the aristocracy, and bourgeois culture. Claims that English literature is complicated by the contrast not only between the Renaissance and baroque but also between the aristocratic and the bourgeois. In a broad comparison of sixteenth- and seventeenth-century English literature, states that in the Catholic Crashaw, "in whom Donne's influence was reinforced by that of the Italian Marino, we have English literature at its most Baroque, even in the strictest sense of the word" (p. 24). Argues that, because England has all three strains of the baroque, one could use its literature to define baroque more adequately than Wölfflin's categories do. Discusses broadly lyric poetry of the sixteenth and seventeenth centuries, as well as epic poetry, character books, prose style, and drama, and maintains that the ultimate difference between Renaissance and baroque is the former's delight in the world around it and the latter's more self-centered, introspective nature. Sees further distinctions in the objectivity of the Renaissance in contrast to the subjectivity of the baroque, and sees Renaissance literature as multiple, episodic, and digressive, whereas the baroque expresses a unity of all reality. Finds a static quality in the Renaissance and a dynamic one in baroque (evidenced, for example, by the conceit).

◄§ 689. Tuve, Rosemond. *Elizabethan and Metaphysical Imagery: Renaissance Poetic and Twentieth-Century Critics*. Chicago: University of Chicago Press. xiv, 442p.

Reprinted, 1961, 1968.

Extracts appear in *Discussions of John Donne*, ed. Frank Kermode (Boston: D. C. Heath, 1962), 106–17.

Reconsiders Elizabethan and metaphysical modes of expression in terms of contemporary habits of thought, principally in terms of Renaissance theories of rhetoric and logic. Inquires into the nature and function of imagery and offers a corrective evaluation of twentieth-century critical approaches to Renaissance poetry. Views many of the so-called unorthodox and new qualities of metaphysical poetry as much less novel than many modern critics suggest and regards these features as part of a large and consistent tradition. Briefly mentions Crashaw throughout, primarily as a vehicle for explaining general critical points about rhetoric, logic, imagery, poetical convention, and so on.

See especially pp. 131n, 217–18, 220, 224n, 303, 307, 327n, and notes K and R in the appendix. Notes, for example, that "images like Crashaw's have a deceptively sensuous character which promotes misreading if the intellectual process of abstracting is relaxed" (p. 131n) and suggests that "a young undergraduate with no knowledge of liturgy or Catholic thought, reading Crashaw, one with no knowledge of classical myth, reading Spenser, finds exactly similar blocks to comprehension of images that he and other persons find in reading such a volume as Yeats's *Winding Stair* (1933)" (p. 220). Points out that the old pattern of cataloging the beauties of the mistress left its mark on the formal structure of "Wishes. To his (supposed) Mistresse" (p. 307).

1948

⋘ 690. Allison, A. F. "Crashaw and St. François de Sales." *RES* 24: 295–302.

Discusses the influence of *Le Traité de l'Amour de Dieu* of St. François de Sales on Crashaw's later poetry. Claims that, although the poet never explicitly refers to the works of the saint, he undoubtedly knew them and points out that Thomas Car (Miles Pickney) made the first English translation of *Le Traité* in 1630. Suggests that "The Authors Motto" was inspired by the concluding chapter of *Le Traité*; notes that in "An Apologie for the fore-going Hymne" there is a direct borrowing from a letter of St. François de Sales to André Fremyot, Archbishop of Bourges (dated 5 October 1605); and cites several metaphors in "An Apologie for the fore-going Hymne," "The Flaming Heart," and "Sancta Maria Dolorum" that indicate that Crashaw's "mind was imbued with the language of *Le Traité de l'Amour de Dieu*" (p. 302).

⋘ 691. Bethell, S. L. "Two Streams from Helicon," in *Essays on Literary Criticism and the English Tradition*, 53–87. London: Dennis Dobson, 1948.

Expanded version of a series of four essays first appearing in *New English Weekly*, 7, 28 February, 21 March, and 4 April 1946 (pp. 162–64, 193–94, 223–24, 243–44).

Contrasts two principal traditions in English poetry, one represented by Shakespeare and Donne and the other by Spenser, Milton, and Tennyson. Contrasts the uses of language, rhythms, imagery, and subject matter in each tradition and challenges F. R. Leavis and the *Scrutiny* critics for their assumptions about the superiority of the first group. Notes that there is no trace of folk tradition in the poetry of Crashaw, Donne, Vaughan, and Marvell and very little in Herbert. Briefly contrasts Crashaw's sexual analogies with those of Donne to show that the later can "explore such ideas without running into those nauseating half-sublimations from which Crashaw, for instance, at times suffers" (p. 69).

⊷ 692. Britting, Georg, ed. "Richard Crashaw," in *Lyrik des Abendlands*, 250–51, 623. Gemainsam mit Hans Hennecke, Curt Hohoff und Karl Vossler, ausgewählt von Georg Britting. Munich: Carl Hanser.
Reprinted several times.
Biographical sketch of Crashaw (p. 623) and translations into German by Curt Hohoff of "On our crucified Lord Naked, and bloody" and lines from "On Hope" (pp. 250–51).

⊷ 693. Brooke, Tucker. "Seventeenth-Century Poetry: II. The Moral Tradition," in A *Literary History of England*, edited by Albert C. Baugh, 637–50. New York and London: Appleton-Century-Crofts.
2d ed., 1967.
General introduction to Crashaw's poetry (pp. 646–48). Notes that "The Weeper," "The Teare," "Sancta Maria Dolorum," and other stanzaic poems "are as full of conceited language as of pious fervor" (p. 646), singles out "Hymn to the Name of Jesus" as "an unusually fine example of the pseudo-Pindaric ode" (p. 647), and calls "Hymn in the Holy Nativity" "quaint and lovely, a remarkable blend of childlike piety and the pastoral convention (p. 646). Suggests that Crashaw's best religious poems are the Teresian hymns and singles out "Musicks Duell" and "Wishes. To his (supposed) Mistresse" as outstanding examples of his secular verse. Concludes that Crashaw, "though in some of his poems diffuse and over-ridden with conceits, was as pure a poet as his age can show" and suggests that, "less ingenious than Cowley, he had a richer and deeper nature and by honest faith traversed the whole range of Christian belief" (p. 648).

⊷ 694. Cammell, Charles Richard. "Sonnet: On the Divine Poets, Herbert and Crashaw." *New English Review Magazine* 1 (November):187.
Original sonnet praising the religious poems of Crashaw and Herbert.

⊷ 695. Clarke, George Herbert. "Christ and the English Poets." *QQ* 55: 292–307.
Surveys the portrayal of Christ by English poets from Cynewulf to John Masefield. Briefly observes that Crashaw's religious poetry is "intensely mystical and reflects an unusually sensitive imagination" (p. 297). Cites as particularly good examples of Crashaw's deep feeling for Christ "Hymn in the Holy Nativity," "The Weeper," and "The Flaming Heart," calling the last "deeply Christian" (p. 297).

⊷ 696. Connolly, Francis X., ed. "Richard Crashaw," in *Literature: The Channel of Culture*, 594–96. New York: Harcourt, Brace and Co.
Anthologizes "A Song ('Lord, when the sense of thy sweet grace')," "The Flaming Heart," "Charitas Nimia," "An Epitaph upon a Young Married

Couple," and lines from "Song upon the Bleeding Crucifix," without notes or commentary. Points out in a headnote that, "an uneven writer, occasionally descending from the pitch of great poetry to bathos, Crashaw at his best reached heights rarely attained by any other English lyricist" (p. 594). Suggests that *Steps to the Temple* is "in the manner of George Herbert" and that Marino "was partly responsible for a peculiarly Latin flamboyance" (p. 594).

◄§ 697. Curtin, C. J. "Crashaw: A Great Religious Poet." *IER* series 5, 70:816–31.

Notes that modern interest in metaphysical poetry as well as the decline of anti-Catholic bias in literary circles has created a new audience for Crashaw's poems. Calls Crashaw "a great lyric poet and within the narrow sphere of the religious lyric one of the greatest" (p. 816). Surveys several secular poems and suggests that they show Crashaw "in the process of apprenticeship, experimenting with styles and modes till he developed a style which was peculiarly his own and which shone forth in all its splendour when Crashaw turned to religious poetry" (p. 819). Praises "Wishes. To his (supposed) Mistresse" for its "effortless grace, the exact correspondence of sound with sense, and the exquisite daintiness of the 'conceits'" (p. 817); finds "Loves Horoscope" a "rather unusual poem" that is "worked out with a power akin to Donne" (p. 819); and dismisses "Musicks Duell" as lacking in "genuine passion and feeling, that warmth and tenderness which is present in some of his less elaborate verse" (p. 819). Suggests that Crashaw's best religious poetry "has a combination of the soaring ardour of Shelley together with the sensuousness of Keats and the tenderness of Blake" (p. 820). Discusses the influence of Counter-Reformation devotional life and Continental models on Crashaw's religious verse and maintains that Crashaw is the "most brilliant exponent" (p. 821) in English of the baroque. Points out that the central theme of Crashaw's religious poetry is the humanity of Christ, comments on his admiration of St. Teresa, and compares his poetry to traditional Catholic religious poetry to show that "the underlying spirit is the same in each" (p. 825). Notes Crashaw's influence on Francis Thompson and compares the nativity poems of Crashaw and Milton. Praises the religious intimacy of Crashaw's poems, notes that, unlike Donne and Herbert, he is "almost completely objective" (p. 830) and Christocentric, and points out the "extraordinary buoyancy and optimism" (p. 831) of his religious vision.

◄§ 698. Freeman, Rosemary. *English Emblem Books.* London: Chatto and Windus. xiv, 256p.

Reprinted, 1966; New York: Octagon Books, 1978.

Presents a broad study of the history and development of emblem books in the sixteenth and seventeenth centuries, especially in England, and discusses the influence of the emblem tradition on English poets. Observes that, because of his particular religious sensibility, Crashaw was greatly attracted by the themes of the Jesuit emblem books and notes that his imagery is often emblematic. Points out that, although English Protestants used plates from the Continental emblem books in their own emblem books, their poetry remained thoroughly Protestant. Cites lines from "Hymn to the Name of Jesus" and suggests that they "are in closer accord with the sensuous qualities of the plates of the Jesuit emblem books than is any of the poetry of Quarles or Harvey" (p. 139). Points out Crashaw's use of the popular emblem of the pelican feeding its young in "Vexilla Regis" and in "Adoro Te." Notes that there are several emblematic plates in *Carmen Deo Nostro*, some of which were probably designed by Crashaw himself.

≈§ 699. Fuson, Benjamin Willis. *Browning and His English Predecessors in the Dramatic Monolog*. (State University of Iowa Humanistic Studies, edited by Franklin H. Potter, vol. 8) Iowa City: State University of Iowa. 96p.

Points out that Crashaw wrote two objective monologues, "Alexias" and "Our Lord in his Circumcision to his Father." Suggests that his most notable technical feature is his use of the "hovering" device, wherein "the poet 'projects' himself as literal witness of some imaginary or historical event as if it is occurring" (p. 59, n. 131), finding in "Song upon the Bleeding Crucifix" and "Hymn in the Assumption" especially remarkable examples.

≈§ 700. Husain, Itrat. *The Mystical Element in the Metaphysical Poets of the Seventeenth Century*. With a foreword by Evelyn Underhill. Edinburgh and London: Oliver and Boyd. 351p.

Reprinted, New York: Biblo and Tannen, 1966.

Contains an introduction on the general characteristics of mysticism, followed by individual studies of Donne, Herbert, Crashaw, Henry and Thomas Vaughan, and Traherne. Attempts "to establish the amount of personal spiritual experience which lies behind the work of these poets" (p. 5) and "to estimate the *content* of the religious thought of these poets in order to determine the nature and significance of the mystical element in their poetry" (p. 13). Chapter 4, "The Mystical Element in the Religious Poetry of Richard Crashaw" (pp. 159–92), stresses the influence of the Laudian movement and of Counter-Reformation Catholicism on both his poetic art and his faith. Suggests that Crashaw may have first become acquainted with Catholic devotional literature in his father's library and comments on the influence exercised on him by his association with Nicholas Ferrar and Little Gidding and by his reading of the mystical works of St. Teresa. Maintains that Crashaw's formal conversion to Catholicism was simply "the confirmation of a spiritual state which had already existed" and that "this state was mainly emotional, an artistic abandonment to the ecstasy of divine love expressed through sensuous symbolism" (p. 163). Argues that, although Crashaw's poetry describes and expresses mystical experience and often delineates the mystical experiences of the saints, it contains no accounts of personal mystical encounters: "Crashaw is a devotee rather than a mystic" (p. 165). Discusses the major themes of Crashaw's religious poetry: the life of Christ (especially aspects of the Passion), the Virgin Mary, and the saints and martyrs (especially St. Teresa and Mary Magdalene) and notes that none of his poems reveals "the inner struggle for self-purification and the complexity of the aspirations of the soul in its attempt to apprehend God" (p. 167) that one finds in Donne and Herbert. Points out that Crashaw's poetry primarily expresses the joy of discovery common to the convert but that it contains "no subtle and argumentative evolution of feeling or its fusion with intellect" but is rather "controlled more by emotion than intellect" (p. 168). Notes in Crashaw's poetry baroque luxuriance; intense feeling; familiarity with the divine; a tone of reverence, wonder, and joy; and a way of seeing and feeling divine truths that is particularly Catholic. Throughout compares Crashaw to Donne, Herbert, Vaughan, and Traherne and to the great Christian mystics, especially St. Augustine, St. Bernard, St. Teresa, and St. John of the Cross, as well as to Vondel, Robert Southwell, and Francis Thompson. Concludes that Crashaw is a "great devotional poet," that he has "given supreme expression to the moods of religious ecstasy"; that he "knows how to express in exquisite imagery, and soft musical cadences, the ardour, the rapture and exaltation of Divine Love"; and that, although no mystic himself, his poetry "has a ring of deep, sincere and authentic understanding of the almost inaccessible heights of mystical life" (p. 192). In an appendix (pp. 301 – 3) lists Crashaw's religious poems by theme. Bibliography (pp. 305–45).

◄§ 701. Miles, Josephine. *The Primary Language of Poetry in the 1640's.* (University of California Publications in English, vol. 19, no. 1.) Berkeley and Los Angeles: University of California Press; London: Cambridge Press. 160p.

Incorporated into *The Continuity of Poetic Language: Studies in English Poetry from the 1540's to the 1940's* (Berkeley and Los Angeles: University of California Press; London: Cambridge University Press, 1951).

Distinguishes the major poetic vocabulary of the 1640s from the language that preceded and followed it. Notes that Crashaw, unlike Vaughan, was "a poet of fuller measure in accent and vocabulary, was more apt to include than ignore, though he too lacked interest in Donne's concepts of abstract value," but observes that he used "with major stress most of the major words of the decade, especially the visual and structural *fair, eye, heaven, make,* and *see,* along with Donne's and Vaughan's *death, tear,* and *world,* the metaphysical negatives, a vast store of precious adjectives like *bright, dark, full, high, new, old, poor, rich, true,* most of the terms stressed by anyone else in the decade, along with his own *black* and *proud*" (p. 73). Maintains, however, that, "where Vaughan differs in nouns, in the direct subjects and means of his attention, Crashaw differs in adjectives, in the world of sense which he elaborates" (p. 73). Suggests that "Crashaw sensed, Donne judged, and Vaughan felt, and all, as they recognized their mortality, wept" (p. 73). Points out how Crashaw typically "extends the poetic line into a fairly steady pentameter, coupleted or alternated, even in his mixed lyrical forms lengthening the line away from its intermittent two-accent articulations" (p. 76) but maintains that, when he alters this standard, he "does so, as we have seen in both vocabulary and measure, by extension, by certain filling out of extremes, not changing but increasing" (p. 77). Thus "the primary structure of address is still evident, but it is filled out by many exclamations, questions, imperatives" and "the line is lengthened and increased with adjectives, nouns, verbs, abundant all three" but still "the eye's fair sight and tear are the fully repeated theme" (p. 77). Finds that because of his amplificatory stresses, Crashaw writes "apart from his fellow poets of the metaphysical divine, and closer to the cosmical divine of More, Quarles, Milton" (p. 77). Concludes that, unlike Donne, Herbert, or Vaughan, Crashaw wishes "to make poetry soar on wings very broad and well feathered" (p. 77) and that his taste is "for the elaborate rather than the homely, the cosmical rather than the social, the angel rather than the gnat" (p. 78). Suggests that it is not "darkness" and "light," as Wallerstein suggests, nor "sweet" and "delicious," as Warren asserts, but rather "weeping" that is Crashaw's "most central and abundant" figure (p. 147).

◄§ 702. Mims, Edwin. "Richard Crashaw: Sensuous Priest," in *The Christ of the Poets*, 84–92. New York and Nashville: Abingdon-Cokesbury Press, 1948.
Reprinted, New York: Greenwood, 1969.
Presents a biographical sketch of the poet and suggests that he would not have left the Anglican community but for the religious dissension and disruptions of his time. Calls Crashaw "the one poet in England who expressed in characteristic verse the spirit and the martyrdom of the Counter Reformation" and points out that his poetry is characterized by "a voluptuousness of language, a richness and sometimes folly of conceits, [and] an atmosphere of incense, which represent the influence of the Spanish mystics" (p. 88). Maintains that of all the seventeenth-century religious poets Crashaw "visualizes best the human life of Jesus, throwing about it all the sensuous beauty that is characteristic of the Catholic approach," and suggests that his poems often "reproduce the tone and atmosphere of medieval hymns and ballads" (p. 92). Points out Crashaw's intense, personal, and intimate feeling for Christ in such poems as "A Hymn to Sainte Teresa," "The Flaming Heart," "Hymn to the Name of Jesus," "Hymn in the Holy Nativity," "Charitas Nimia," and "A Song ('Lord, when the sense of they sweet grace')." Briefly compares and/or contrasts Crashaw with Donne, Herbert, and Southwell.

◄§ 703. Neill, Kerby. "Structure and Symbol in Crashaw's 'Hymn in the Nativity.'" *PMLA* 63:101–13.
Argues that in his revisions of "Hymn in the Holy Nativity" Crashaw evi-

dences "a growing sense of form" and that the final version (1652) "has a conceptual unity that raises it to a level of poetry considerably above that of the
1646 version" (p. 101). Through a stanza-by-stanza comparison of the earlier
and later versions demonstrates that this greater conceptual unity is achieved
"by substituting structural symbols for mere sense images, by emending a few
lines, by dropping one stanza, and by adding two very important new stanzas
that make the structural pattern of the poem much clearer" (p. 101). Argues
that the major theme of the poem is "the contrast between the natural and the
supernatural" and that primarily it "deals with the reconciliation of the material and the spiritual, lost since Adam's sin, and mysteriously solved by the
Incarnation through a human Vessel" (p. 102). Maintains that, although most
of the basic ideas contained in the later version are present in the 1646 version, "they become clear to the reader only when the structural pattern is
tightened, and the recurrent image of the light and fire of love is introduced in
the second line to fuse the whole" (p. 102). Suggests that, in a sense, the two
versions can be seen as two different poems: the earlier praises the Virgin
Mary and her Son, while the later praises the Christ Child "and *through Him*
His mother" (p. 113). Concludes that "what gives the poem its new unity is
the unity of its underlying theological concept, and the changes in imagery
that introduced new figures and placed the old ones in new contexts tended to
bring all these figures into closer structural harmony with the whole" (p. 113).

◄§ 704. O'Connor, William Van. "The Influence of the Metaphysicals on
    Modern Poetry." *CE* 9:180–87.
    Appears in revised form in *Sense and Sensibility in Modern Poetry* (Chi-
cago: University of Chicago Press, 1948), 81–92.
    Surveys the importance and the extent of the modern revival of interest in
seventeenth-century metaphysical poetry, especially the poetry of Donne, and
comments on the influence of this renewed interest on the poetry of certain
modern poets, especially T. S. Eliot, Wallace Stevens, Conrad Aiken, Edith
Sitwell, the Fugitive Poets, Robert Lowell, and Elinor Wylie. No specific
mention of Crashaw.

◄§ 705. Williams, George W. "Crashaw's 'Letter to the Countess of Den-
    bigh.'" *Expl* 6: item 48.
    Reprinted in *The Explicator Cyclopedia* (Chicago: Quadrangle Books,
1968), 2:94–95.
    Notes a "most exquisite" pun on Christ as the Lamb of God, filled with
divine fire or love, in lines 67 of the 1653 edition of "Letter to the Countess of
Denbigh." Points out that the pun recalls the *Song of Solomon* 2:8, which was
conventionally allegorized as Christ's marriage to the Church.

◄§ 706. ————. "Textual Revision in Crashaw's 'Upon the Bleeding Cru-
    cifix.'" *SB* 1(1948–1949): 191–93.

Compares the two versions of "Song upon the Bleeding Crucifix" to show that Crashaw, like Herbert, consciously tried "to make the form of the poem reproduce the movement of the thought" (p. 191). Notes that the progressive change of title shifts the emphasis "from the wounds through the body to the crucifix" and that the later version (1648/52) "has been made consciously cruciform" (p. 192). Points out that, although no major change occurs in the thought, "the deceptively simple transposition in lines two and three of the first stanza and the consequential rearrangement of the order of the following four stanzas evidence a certain intention to provide the 1648 version with an articulated structure in keeping with the new name for the poem" (p. 192). Suggests, furthermore, that the words *head, feet, hands, side* "parallel the movement of the hand in making the sign of the cross" (p. 192). Concludes that "it is evident that this is no casual rearrangement, but that Crashaw is consciously revising to create a cruciform poem which outlines a small crucifix in the lines and proceeds to enlarge the picture in the body of the poem" (p. 193).

1949

◄§ 707. Anon. "A Poet of Delights." *TLS*, 19 August, p. 536.
Presents a biographical sketch of Crashaw and surveys his poetry in commemoration of the tercentenary of his death. Calls him "the English poet of the Counter-Reformation" and his poetry "perhaps the least native, the most un-English, of any that we possess." Maintains that Crashaw's conversion to Catholicism was aesthetic, not theological: "In a world disordered by dispute and speculation he sought again for order." Finds that "acceptance, not doubt; joy, not perplexity; worship, not disputation—these things are the keynotes of his poetry" and points out that, although Crashaw wrote excellent poetry, he seldom wrote excellent poems. Characterizes the poetry as baroque, "delighting in incident rather than in ideas, preferring to portray in the life of Christ those occasions which give scope to sensational treatment, and especially the life of Mary Magdalene, universally the favourite of the Counter-Reformation." Contrasts Crashaw's religious temperament and sensibility to those of Milton and notes resultant differences in their nativity odes. Agrees essentially with Pope's criticism of Crashaw's poetry and suggests that because Crashaw was "first and foremost a mystic, not an artist, his poetry can drop suddenly from heights of passionate intensity to almost bottomless bathos." Maintains that, since the defects in Crashaw's poems most often come from his unbridled religious enthusiasm, his most finished poems are the secular pieces, singling out for praise "Wishes. To his (supposed) Mistresse," in which, "not troubled by the uncontrolled intensity of his feeling, he can display his eclectic delight in visual beauty, his gentle, ironic humour, and what Pope called his 'neat cast of verses.'" Briefly compares Crashaw to Donne, Herbert, Vaughan, and Sir Thomas Browne.

᪥ 708. Boase, Alan M. "Poètes anglais et français de l'époque baroque."
    RSH 55–56:155–84.

Suggests that there was a poetry comparable to English metaphysical poetry
in France during the late sixteenth and early seventeenth centuries. Outlines
some of the major characteristics of the metaphysical poets, using Donne as
the touchstone. Suggests that le Père de Saint Louis (Jean-Louis Barthelemy),
whom Gautier called "le Titan du Baroque" (p. 181), most closely represents
in French poetry what Crashaw represents in English poetry. Notes that both
poets were highly baroque and were influenced by Marino and his followers.
Maintains that Crashaw, however, is much less facile than his French counterpart and was saved from the worst excesses of baroque taste by his solid classical education, by his knowledge of the *Greek Anthology* and emblem books,
and by the influence of Donne and other metaphysical poets. Notes Crashaw's
love for the irregular strophe and suggests that his careful manipulation of
verse forms also kept him from the uncontrolled excesses so easily demonstrated in the poetry of le Père de Saint Louis. Notes Crashaw's influence on
Cowley.

᪥ 709. Crashaw, Richard. *The Verse in English of Richard Crashaw . . . To-*
    gether with a critical chronology selected from the writings of various
    commentators, from 1652 to the present day. (Evergreen Books, no. 2)
    New York: Grove Press. 255p.

A biographical sketch of Crashaw with selected criticism on the poet (pp.
9–21) by Thomas Car (1652), Cowley (1656), Pope (1710), Hazlitt (1819),
Swinburne (1852 [1862] and 1883), Coventry Patmore (1881), Edmund
Gosse (1883), Francis Thompson (1897), William Empson (1930), Yvor
Winters (1937), and Wylie Sypher (1944). Offers a brief history of the publication of Crashaw's poems (pp. 22–23) and indicates that the present edition
of the English poems is based upon the 1646 edition of *Steps to the Temple*
and *The Delights of the Muses*, the 1652 edition of *Carmen Deo Nostro*, the
1653 text of "Letter to the Countess of Denbigh," and poems in manuscripts
"which can be attributed to him on good 'external' as well as 'internal' evidence" (p. 22). English poems (pp. 25–227), with modernized spelling and
minor changes in the original punctuation. Reproduces photographs of original title pages and of two emblems in *Carmen Deo Nostro* thought to be by
Crashaw and includes a table of contents for each of the three volumes included. Very brief notes (pp. 247–49) and an index of first lines (pp. 251–55).

᪥ 710. Gros, Léon-Gabriel. "Métaphysiques anglais, du raisonnement en
    poésie." *Cahiers du Sud* 293:3–30.

Critical preface to a group of translations into French of poems by Donne,
Jonson, Quarles, Habington, Herbert, Carew, Lovelace, Marvell, Vaughan,
and Traherne. Evaluates metaphysical poetry primarily in terms of Eliot's
criticism. Excludes Crashaw from the selections but notes, in speaking of the

metaphysical poets, that "même ceux d' entre eux qui versèrent dans le formalisme précieux, notamment Crashaw si difficilement défendable, parlent toujours à voix d'homme" (p. 9).

◆§ 711. Hutton, Edward. "Richard Crashaw: A Tercentenary." *The Tablet* (London) 194 (10 September): 167.

Commemorates the tercentenary of Crashaw's death with a biographical sketch and an appreciative evaluation of his poetry. Calls Crashaw "the only 'baroque' poet, the only poet of the Catholic Reaction of the seventeenth century in English literature," and praises his poetry as "the only expression in English poetry of the exuberance and passionate fervour of the Counter-Reformation," noting that Crashaw's enthusiasm is "wedded to a marvellous verbal technique, a 'dazzling intricacy and affluence in refinements' quite without parallel in our poetry." Calls "Wishes. To his (supposed) Mistresse" "an exquisite lyric" but maintains that "as lovely and far more extravagant are his sacred poems to St. Mary Magdalen and St. Teresa," citing the concluding lines of "The Flaming Heart." Wonders if Crashaw ever saw Bernini's famous statue of St. Teresa in Rome.

◆§ 712. Knox, R[onald] A[rbuthnot]. "Richard Crashaw (Died 1649)." *Clergy Review* n.s. 32:373–88.

Reprinted in *Literary Distractions* (New York: Sheed & Ward, 1958), 59–77.

Contrasts Crashaw as a religious poet to Donne, Herbert, and Herrick and finds his poetry fully integrated and superior to that of the other three: "Crashaw's poetry was all religion, and Crashaw's religion was all poetry" (p. 373). Notes that Crashaw wrote comparatively little secular verse and that even in these poems he avoids the stock-in-trade of his contemporaries: "There is nothing about love-affairs, nothing about quarrels, nothing about pets, nothing about May-day revelry or haymaking or getting drunk" (p. 374). Discusses the importance of the Latin classics on Crashaw's art, especially Martial and Ovid, and points out that his epigrams, Latin and English, remind the reader of the paradoxes and puns St. Augustine employed in his commentaries on Scripture. Argues that, fine as many of them are, the epigrams are essentially the work of "an agile scholar who could Latinize for you gracefully" (p. 380) but do not suggest that Crashaw would become a great poet. Stresses that Crashaw was foremost an ascetic and a mystic, "a holy man who wrote verses" (p. 384), not simply a poet who wrote on pious and religious themes and certainly not one who wrote poetry for poetry's sake. Rather he wrote epitaphs when his friends died, he celebrated events at court when they occurred, and "on much rarer, all too rare occasions, he got up from his knees and sang to God" (p. 381). Suggests that "Hymn in the Glorious Epiphanie" most clearly reveals Crashaw's mysticism. Notes that, as one who sought mystical union in prayer, Crashaw most likely tried to eliminate all images from his prayer but, having done so, they rushed back into his consciousness after prayer and that his poems are the result: "I see Crashaw, then, coming back from his prayer to his poetry with a great wealth of images running through his brain—all the more tumultuously, perhaps, for their recent cold-shouldering. He plays around his theme untiringly, seeing it from a hundred angles, and each view must go down on paper. He is writing for St. Mary Magdalen, for St. Teresa, not for a set of critics who will read it over his shoulder and say, 'This is good . . . that is bad'" (pp. 386–87).

◄§ 713. Meath, Gerard. "The Tumbling Images of Richard Crashaw." *The Listener* 42:366–67.

Presents a biographical sketch of the poet; praises his translations from Greek and Latin, calling "Nympha pudica Deum vidit, et erubuit" "one of the most memorable lines penned outside classical Rome" (p. 366); and stresses his commitment to preserving in English poetry traditional Christianity against the growing threats of secularized humanism and Puritan excess. Admits that, like other metaphysical poets, Crashaw's defects as a poet "were largely the defects of his good qualities" and notes that "his love of the quaint and intricate conceit, his diffuseness, and his unbridled enthusiasm often produced grotesqueries" and that sometimes "he had not the complete control of image and phrase that only the finest artists possess" and thus "his images tumble over one another, and sometimes they trip up both reader and poet" (p. 366). Maintains, however, that "when he does light on the right phrase Crashaw is magnificent, and in economy and in precision can even surpass Donne" (p. 367). Suggests that the fundamental inspiration behind Crashaw's poetry, both religious and secular, "is the love of God in all its forms, and particularly as it is symbolised in blood, tears and water" and that "traditional theology of the incarnation and the sacraments shapes and deepens his imagery" (p. 367). Comments briefly on Crashaw's sacramental theology and maintains that, even when his skill as an artist fails, the defects are due "not to the dullness of his vision, but to the subtlety of the pattern and the vigour of his own enthusiasm which threatened to stretch and disfigure it" (p. 367).

◄§ 714. Moloney, Michael F. "Richard Crashaw: 1649–1949." *CathW* 169:336–40.

Points out that the tercentenary of the death of Crashaw "offers no evidence of a radical awakening to his poetic merits among his co-religionists" and that "even to many Catholic readers this most Catholic of poets is little more than a name in literary history" (p. 336). Maintains, however, that "to any genuine renewal of Catholic poetry in English Crashaw will have much to contribute by way of example and inspiration" (p. 336). Praises Crashaw's craftsmanship as a poet. Suggests that "no poet of the century shows more clearly how impossible it is to separate absolutely the classical and the 'metaphysical' influences which in fusion gave the seventeenth-century lyric its characteristic flavor" and notes that "the concentrated metaphor with its sometimes unreasonable intellectual demands upon the reader Crashaw did utilize as had Donne" but his versification "is classical in the Jonsonian sense" (p. 337). Presents a biographical sketch and suggests that, "in a smaller way, he was a seventeenth-century Augustine who, as his world crashed about his ears, lived and wrote with his eyes on eternity" (p. 337). Discusses Crashaw's religious sensibility as it was reflected in both his life and his art. Singles out his concept of self-realization through Christian self-abasement and notes that he had the capacity to keep his poetry free from external distractions, pointing out that, in spite of a life of trials and disappointments, Crashaw allowed no notes of bitterness or despair to enter his poems. Concludes that, although Crashaw is not one of the major English poets, his poetry "genuinely expresses valid human experience in masterful form" and that "even the profane world will not willingly let it die" (p. 340).

➳ 715. Murdock, Kenneth B. *Literature and Theology in Colonial New England*. Cambridge: Harvard University Press. xi, 235p.

Reprinted, New York and Evanston: Harper & Row (Harper Torchbook), 1963; Westport, Conn.: Greenwood Press, 1970.

Discusses the attitude of New England Puritans toward literature, pointing out that one central issue for the Puritan artist was "to decide just what sensuous material was proper in religious art and how it could be fittingly presented" and noting that on that issue "the Catholic and Puritan positions were far apart" (p. 10). Cites four stanzas from "On the wounds of our crucified Lord" and the concluding lines of "The Flaming Heart" as representative of Catholic practice (pp. 11–13). Notes that "it would be useless to hunt for a Puritan poet who could write, as the Catholic Crashaw did, of the wounds on Christ's feet as mouths with full-bloomed lips, to be kissed with rapture," for he "would say that such imagery would so stir the sensual in man as to blind him to anything spiritual in the poem" (p. 38). Points out that even today Crashaw "may often be too luscious, too perfumed, too sensually—or even sexually—evocative for Anglo-Saxon tastes, at least where religion is concerned, but it is worth remembering that his best poems, and the best of other Catholic writers, have power to stir the reader to an actual and intense physical experience of the emotion which the author feels in the presence of the divine" (p. 13).

➳ 716. Praz, Mario. "Drummond and Crashaw." *TLS*, 21 October, p. 681.

Notes that both Crashaw's "Out of the Italian ('Would any one the true cause find')" and Drummond's "Naked Love" are imitations of a sestet by Valerio Marcellini that was set to music by Luca Marenzio in *Il quarto libro de'madrigali a cinque voci* (Venice: Giacomo Vincenti, 1584), no. 18. Points out that the imitation is "another witness of the widespread popularity of Italian madrigals in England."

◆§ 717. Turnell, Martin. "Richard Crashaw After Three Hundred Years."
    Nineteenth Century and After 146:100–114.

Contrasts the themes and spirit of medieval and Renaissance art with those of baroque art in order to show that Crashaw was thoroughly representative of his time and stresses that in order to understand Crashaw's artistry one must have an understanding of the baroque spirit. Discusses major features of Crashaw's poetry, particularly its erotic, artificial, and deliberately stylized imagery; its exaggeration and flamboyancy; its uses of synaesthesia; and its lack of precise, logical structure. Notes, for example, that Crashaw's poetry is "extremely rich in visual, concrete, physical images" and that "not merely one but all five senses are solicited on every page, almost in every line" (p. 102). Points out that, whereas Donne and Herbert wrote religious poems firmly rooted in human emotion, Crashaw attempted to present the more extraordinary and transcendental aspects of mystical ecstasy. Suggests also that, unlike the images of Donne and Herbert, used as vehicles to convey experience, in Crashaw's poems "the image itself becomes an object of contemplation" that "precedes the emotion and is used to generate it" (p. 106). Shows that, unlike the logical, almost mathematical precision in the poems of Donne and Herbert, Crashaw's poems have a looser and more associational development, noting that typically "one image suggests another image, and the process continues until the poet has exhausted all the possibilities of the original association" (p. 106). Maintains that, although Crashaw's baroque images are "ingenious and entertaining" and his poems contain genuine religious fervor, his uses of "free association and the lack of intellectual control" are weaknesses and that "it involves a more and more determined appeal to the senses in the attempt—the impossible attempt—to reach *through the senses* something which lies outside the field of sense-perception" (p. 107). Sees his use of erotic imagery as a weakness in Crashaw's art. Discusses "Ode on a Prayer-book" as representative of Crashaw's poetry and presents a brief analysis of "Hymn in the Glorious Epiphanie" to show that, unlike "The Weeper" and "A Hymn to Sainte Teresa," the Epiphany hymn is "much less lush" and "reveals to the full the poet's metaphysical wit and his remarkable gift of phrase" (p. 110). Calls Crashaw "the most striking expression in English of the spirit of the Counter-Reformation" but suggests that the sectarian spirit of his poetry "marks a break with English tradition and the loss of valuable qualities which we rightly regard as distinctively English" (p. 114).

◆§ 718. Willey, Basil. *Richard Crashaw (1612/13—1649)*. Cambridge: University Press. 25p.
    Reprinted, Norwood, Pa.: Norwood Editions, 1978.

A memorial lecture delivered at Peterhouse, Cambridge, on 11 July 1949. Presents a biographical sketch of Crashaw and comments on some of his major themes and poetic techniques. Claims that in spirit Crashaw "belonged essentially to the Counter-Reformation" and that Rome was his "true spiritual destination" (p. 15) and suggests that, until recently, Crashaw had little appeal for English readers who were often offended by his lush imagery, uses of conceits and paradoxes, and his ecstatic and exotic spirituality: "The fact is that the Counter-Reformation baroque, of which his poetry is the distillation, represents a mode of feeling and expression as far removed as possible from the native sentiment and tradition, or at any rate from the standards, whether religious or aesthetic, which on the whole dominated the eighteenth and nineteenth centuries" (pp. 16–17). Points out that Crashaw "fixes his attention continually upon the physical manifestation of Christianity" (p. 17) and that even his heaven is "too warm, roseate and honeyed for most English tastes" (p. 18). Observes that even the modern revival of interest in Donne has done little for Crashaw, "for he lacks in general that toughness and sinew, that blend of logic and passion, and that tumult of spirit which our generation has found congenial in Donne" (p. 25). Comments primarily on the religious sensibility in such poems as "Ode on a Prayer-book," "On the wounds of our crucified Lord," "The Weeper," "To the Name of Jesus," and "Hymn in the Glorious Epiphanie," noting that the latter shows "a degree of intellectual concentration rare in Crashaw" (pp. 22–23). Finds Crashaw to be most fully himself in the conclusion of "The Flaming Heart," "where fire and sweetness and ecstatic love are fused together in the pure passion of prayer, and where, transcending all sensuous fancies, he soars on eagle-wings straight toward the sun" (p. 25). Suggests that resemblances between Crashaw and either Shelley or Keats are mostly superficial, noting that most of Crashaw's nature images are nonnaturalistic emblems and his joys are mystical. Compares and/or contrasts Crashaw to Shakespeare, Donne, Herbert, Sir Thomas Browne, Pope, Isaac Watts, and Charles Wesley.

1950

✥ 719. Arms, George, and Joseph M. Kuntz. *Poetry Explication: A Checklist of Interpretations since 1925 of British and American Poems Past and Present.* New York: Swallow Press and William Morrow & Co. 187p.

2d ed. by Joseph Kuntz (Denver: Swallow Press, 1962); 3d ed. by Joseph Kuntz and Nancy C. Martinez (Boston: G. K. Hall & Co., 1980).

Lists explications for nine of Crashaw's poems drawn from five sources (pp. 50–51). Second edition gives explications for sixteen poems from thirteen sources (pp. 63–66), and third edition lists explications for twenty-one poems from twenty-five sources.

✥ 720. Bullett, Gerald. "Some Seventeenth-Century Poets," in *The English Mystics,* 94–112. London: Michael Joseph.

Reprinted, Folcroft, Pa.: Folcroft Library Editions, 1979.

Briefly contrasts Crashaw and Herbert as religious poets: "where, even in his most rapturous moment, Herbert is quiet and gentle, Crashaw writes at white heat, yet too often softens and oversweetens his effects by a surfeit of amorous fancies and metaphors" (p. 103). Notes that at his best, such as in the concluding invocation of "The Flaming Heart," Crashaw can be magnificent.

⊷§ 721. Cammell, Charles Richard. "The Divine Poet: Richard Crashaw." *National and English Review* 135:230–35.

An appreciative introduction to Crashaw's life and poetry for the general reader. Contrasts Crashaw briefly to Donne, Cowley, and especially Herbert; notes the debt of Pope and Milton to Crashaw's poems; and points out the influence of Marino. Suggests that in his use of sound and color and in his rapturous spirituality Crashaw surpasses the other metaphysical poets. Maintains that "The Weeper" is "a masterpiece wherein poetry and music have united to create a rapture around the tears of the Magdalene" (p. 234) and singles out "Wishes. To his (supposed) Mistresse" and "Musicks Duell" as the most notable of the secular verses. Concludes that Crashaw was "without question one of the most inspired and loveliest lyrists in our literature" (p. 235).

⊷§ 722. Daiches, David, and William Charvat, eds. "The Seventeenth Century," in *Poems in English, 1530–1940*, 53–121, 661. Edited with critical and historical notes and essays. New York: Ronald Press.

Introductory survey of seventeenth-century poetry (pp. 53–58). Contrasts Crashaw with Donne, Herbert, Vaughan, and Traherne, and anthologizes "A Song ('Lord, when the sense of thy sweet grace')" (pp. 76–77). Calls it an "intense little poem" that "derives much of its effect from the adaptation of the imagery of secular love poetry to describe a religious experience" and comments briefly on its stanzaic form and metrical features, noting that its metrical variations "produce a fine flexibility that enables the verse to follow the curve of the emotion to its climax" (p. 661).

⊷§ 723. Keast, William R. "Johnson's Criticism of the Metaphysical Poets." *ELH* 17:59–70.

Reprinted in *Essential Articles for the Study of John Donne's Poetry*, ed. John R. Roberts (Hamden, Conn.: Archon Books, 1975), 11–19.

Reevaluates Johnson's criticism of the metaphysical poets in an attempt to determine "how far our disappointment with Johnson's treatment of the metaphysical poets reflects genuine deficiencies in Johnson and how far it reflects merely our own present conviction that Donne is a greater poet than, say Gray or even Milton" (pp. 59–60) and how much of our disagreement with Johnson simply reflects "our preferences for a critical theory that specializes in detailed accounts of metaphorical structure to one that emphasizes the general conditions of literary pleasure" (p. 60). Argues that, given Johnson's assumptions and premises about the nature and function of poetry, his censure of metaphysical poetry is understandable and just. Points out that Johnson developed no comprehensive literary theory but applied his taste and judgment to individual writers. Suggests that Johnson's comments on the metaphysicals can be more readily put into a proper perspective if one reads his *Life of Cowley* "in relation to the *Rambler*, the *Preface to Shakespeare*, and the other *Lives*" (p. 61). No specific mention of Crashaw.

◄§ 724. Mahood, M[olly] M[aureen]. *Poetry and Humanism*. New Haven: Yale University Press. 335p.
Reprinted, Port Washington, N.Y.: Kennikat Press, 1967; New York: W. W. Norton, 1970.

Comments on baroque style and notes that "the gilded conceits and sensuous transports of Roman and Neapolitan Baroque are found only in Crashaw and in a small group of lesser poets" but that even "the more insular writers, such as Herbert, Vaughan and Traherne, share with Continental artists the fundamental qualities of the style" (p. 134). Points out that the term *baroque* can embrace a wide range of works from many different cultures and religious sects, including such diverse works as Crashaw's "The Flaming Heart," the lyrics of Gryphius and certain other German contemporaries, the sermons of Donne and Bossuet, the heroic plays of Vondel and Corneille, and Milton's *Samson Agonistes* and his heroic poems. Suggests that "Musicks Duell" is the best-known example in English of attempting to give the effect of music in poetry and points out that its "complex sensuousness" (p. 138) is typical of the art that the Society of Jesus practiced and supported. Maintains that, unlike Donne, Crashaw's baroque temper is "of a purely southern kind" and that "he is an exile in his own land" (p. 168). Briefly contrasts "Hymn in the Holy Nativity" to Milton's Nativity Ode but suggests that both poems reflect baroque humanism. Suggests that Vaughan's *Silex Scintillans* contains echoes of Crashaw and Jesuit devotional writers.

◄§ 725. Maxwell, J. C. "*Steps to the Temple*: 1646 and 1648." *PQ* 29: 216–20.

Takes issue with Martin's brief account of the relationship between the 1646 and 1648 editions of *Steps to the Temple* on three grounds: (1) it is not just "for several consecutive pages" of unrevised poems that the 1648 version follows the 1646 exactly, but for a much greater bulk of them; (2) the differences between unrevised 1648 poems and 1646 poems cannot be explained merely in terms of compositors with different habits, for the texts are identical while misprints and differing punctuation are common; and (3) among poems revised in 1648, at least one was set up from a corrected copy of 1646 and not from manuscript. Notes that "The Teare" of 1648 is the first unrevised poem with widely variant texts but points out that the differences are all literal, not verbal. Notes also that the epigrams down to, but not including, "Sospetto d'Herode" also have numerous literal, but not verbal, differences and suggests that no single direction can be traced. Hypothesizes that these poems were set up from a new manuscript in 1648, while those from "Sospetto d'Herode" on were set up from the 1646 version. Consequently feels that the 1648 text should have a higher estimate than Martin gives it. Points out that unrevised poems set from 1646 contain far fewer misprints than Martin suggests and that far more misprints exist in those set up from the manuscript. Maintains that there is no consistent tendency toward less expressiveness or greater modernity, as Martin suggests. Points out that "In praise of Lessius" was set up from the corrected 1646 edition, not from manuscript. Admits that the importance of these facts for textual criticism of Crashaw is not great.

◄§ 726. Nicolson, Marjorie Hope. *The Breaking of the Circle: Studies in the Effect of the "New Science" upon Seventeenth Century Poetry*. Evanston: Northwestern University Press. xxii, 193p.
    Rev. ed., New York: Columbia University Press, 1960, 1962, 1965.
    Points out that, with the encroachment of a mechanistic view of the world, the cosmological metaphors (especially the circle) that grew out of an earlier world view ceased to have the force of actuality and became mere similies. Uses Crashaw's poetry to illustrate the world view commonly held before the introduction of the New Science. Comments briefly on his uses of tears, of the circle as a symbol for spring and happiness, and of the microcosm-macrocosm, and briefly notes his concept of time as finite.

◄§ 727. Ōsawa, Mamoru. "'Wishes to his (supposed) Mistress,' Translation and Comment." *EigoS* 96, no. 5:204–8.
    Translates into Japanese "Wishes. To his (supposed) Mistresse" and briefly comments on the poem. Notes that when he was first introduced to Crashaw twenty-five years before, he found his poetry warmer and more congenial than Herbert's.

◄§ 728. Towers, Gladys V. "A Note on Richard Crashaw." *Ave Maria* 71: 75–78.
    Presents a brief introduction to Crashaw's life and poetry intended primarily for the Catholic reader and calls him "one of the major Catholic poets of all time, however inferior his genius is to Francis Thompson, one of the greatest of them all" (p. 75). Notes that Crashaw will be remembered best as the poet of St. Teresa and suggests that modern Catholic poets "will do well to study Crashaw for his rare ability to express timeless truths timelessly" (p. 78).

◄§ 729. Wallerstein, Ruth. *Studies in Seventeenth-Century Poetic*. Madison: University of Wisconsin Press. x, 421p.
    Reprinted, 1961, 1965.
    Mentions Crashaw throughout but has no extended discussion of his poetry. Comments briefly on Crashaw's use of witty emblems and his uses of the senses in portraying religious ecstasy. Suggests that Crashaw's "single-lined paradoxes and ejaculations are one perfect type of the strong line" (p. 74) and

maintains that in English poetry he is the only poet who "carries one to an understanding" of Dionysius the Areopagite (p. 193). Briefly compares the poetic diction of Crashaw and Joseph Beaumont and comments on Marvell's possible indebtedness to Crashaw.

◄§ 730. Wedgwood, C[icely] V[eronica]. "John Donne and Caroline Poetry," in *Seventeenth-Century English Literature*, 66–89. (Home University Library of Modern Knowledge, 218.) London, New York, Toronto: Geoffrey Cumberlege and Oxford University Press.
   Reprinted, 1961, 1970, 1977, 1978.
   Claims that, after Donne, Crashaw is "the greatest of the metaphysical poets" (p. 72) and "one of the greatest of our sacred poets" (p. 73). Suggests that his poetry clearly reflects the faults and merits of metaphysical poetry as a whole. Notes that Crashaw's comparison in "The Weeper" of Mary Magdalene's eyes to "Two walking baths; two weeping motions; / Portable, and compendious oceans" is "nothing less than a catastrophe in the work of a man whose heights are among the highest in the language" (pp. 72–73). Suggests, however, that one finds lines in "Musicks Duell" in which "the forced juxtapositions and bold metaphors are perfectly mingled with a just observation and controlled by an exquisitely sensitive ear" (p. 73) and praises "A Hymn to Sainte Teresa" and "The Flaming Heart" for combining "ecstatic adoration suitable to the great Saint with a wonderful tenderness" (p. 74). Maintains that Crashaw's most serious faults are an "uncritical seriousness" and a rather morbid preoccupation with the physical symptoms of death: "It is strange that a poet who at this best has the incandescent depth of sunset or dawn is, at his worst, rather foetid" (p. 74). Suggests that Herbert "can never stir the emotions as Crashaw or Donne can stir them" (p. 83).

1951

◄§ 731. Aliandro, Higino. *John Donne no movimento literário metafísico*. (Universidad de São Paolo. Faculdade de Filosofia, Ciências e Letras. Boletim 127. Lingua e Literatura Inglêsa, no. 1.) São Paolo: Universidad de São Paolo. 121p.
   Considers Crashaw a disciple of Donne but notes that, in many respects, he modeled his poetry more after the Elizabethans than after Donne. Presents a biographical sketch and comments generally on aspects of his poetry and on his religious temperament (pp. 75–76). Notes the influence of St. Teresa on Crashaw's religious development and that of Italian and Spanish models on his art. Points out that Crashaw's nature was essentially emotional and sensual and that he used sexual images to express the spiritual longing of the soul for God. Contrasts Crashaw to Donne and suggests that, whereas Donne's poetry reflects a virile spirit, Crashaw's reflects a kind of feminine love characterized by tenderness, gentleness, and sweet melody.

◆§ 732. Atkinson, A. D. "Donne's Quotations in Johnson's Dictionary." N&Q 196:387–88.

Notes 384 quotations ascribed to Donne in Johnson's *Dictionary* and points out that the quotation under *cragged*, ascribed to Crashaw, is actually from Donne. See also Samuel Johnson (entry 81), David Perkins (entry 756), and W. B. C. Watkins (entry 590).

◆§ 733. Bateson, F. W. "Contributions to a Dictionary of Critical Terms. II. Dissociation of Sensibility." *EIC* 1:302–12.

Reprinted in *Essays in Critical Dissent* (Totowa, N.J.: Rowman and Little-field, 1972), 142–52; and in *Essential Articles for the Study of John Donne's Poetry*, ed. John R. Roberts (Hamden, Conn.: Archon Books, 1975), 58–65.

Traces the development of Eliot's notion of "dissociation of sensibility" to the critical writings of Rémy de Gourmont, particularly his *Problème du style* (1902), which provided Eliot with "a *framework* to which his own critical ideas and intuitions—even when incomparably profounder and more original than Gourmont's—were able to attach themselves" (p. 308). Suggests that Eliot transferred "to the nation Gourmont's analysis of the mental processes of the individual" and points out that "the unified sensibility that Gourmont found in LaForgue Mr. Eliot finds in the England of the early seventeenth century" (p. 307). Notes certain inconsistencies in Eliot's use of the term *dissociation of sensibility* and traces the evolution of Eliot's thoughts on the concept. Concludes that "its use today as a loose, honorific synonym for 'taste' or 'personality' can only be deprecated" (p. 312). For a reply, see Eric Thompson (entry 748). For Bateson's reply to Thompson, see entry 740. No specific mention of Crashaw.

◆§ 734. Bethell, S. L. *The Cultural Revolution of the Seventeenth Century*. London: Dennis Dobson. New York: Roy. 161p.

Reprinted, London: Dennis Dobson, 1963.

Divided into two parts: (1) a detailed discussion of the concept of dissociation of sensibility as it is reflected in seventeenth-century literary theory and practice and especially as it related to certain theological questions of the period (pp. 11–120) and (2) a study of Henry Vaughan (pp. 121–61). Notes that Crashaw was not anti-rational and that his theology was essentially orthodox and included a high estimation of natural reason. Comments briefly on Crashaw's imagery, his "employment of a rich but generalised vocabulary of sensation (sight, sound, scent, taste, touch: jewels, music, perfumes, sugar, down) coupled with the traditional imagery of sexual love, in order to express the ardour of mystical devotion" (p. 93). Compares and contrasts Crashaw briefly with Donne, Herbert, and Vaughan.

◆§ 735. Buffum, Imbrie. *Agrippa d'Aubigné's Les Tragiques: A Study of the Baroque Style in Poetry*. New Haven: Yale University Press; Presses Universitaires de France. 151p.

Reprinted, New York: AMS Press, 1978.

Calls Crashaw "that poet most generally conceded by critics to be baroque" (p. 9) and points out that "he excels in expressing by means of concrete and sensuous imagery states of agitated and ecstatic mysticism" (p. 132). Notes that the subject matter of many of Crashaw's poems is influenced by the Counter-Reformation and the baroque and claims that he regarded poetry primarily as a means to win converts to religious faith and to glorify the Catholic religion and that he would have repudiated the notion of art for art's sake. Discusses briefly the uses of erotic imagery in "Ode on a Prayer-book" and in "The Flaming Heart" and notes that baroque sensibility found nothing shocking in describing divine love in human terms. Compares Crashaw's translation of Psalm 23 with the King James version in order to show its baroque features, such as elaboration; its uses of exclamatory sentences, sensuous metaphors, elaborate imagery and rhetoric, puns and conceits, personification, and argumentative metaphors; its pastoral atmosphere; its uses of synaesthesia; and its baroque theatricality. Points out parallels between Crashaw and D'Aubigné, not only in *Les Tragiques* but very specifically in the latter's rendering of Psalm 58 in *Les Chambre dorée* to show how both poets were baroque. Points out parallels between Crashaw's poetry and the works of the great baroque painters and sculptors, especially Murillo, Bernini, El Greco, Rubens, Poussin, Claude Lorrain, and Pozzo.

◄§ 736. Jacquot, Jean. "«Le duel musical» de Richard Crashaw et sa source italienne." *RLC* 25:232–41.

Notes that Strada's neo-Latin verses on the contest between the nightingale and the lutenist published in *Prolusiones academiae* . . . (1617) exercised a strong influence on his English contemporaries: "c'est que leur culture et leur sensibilité musicales les disposait tout particulièrement à les apprécier" and suggests that of all the English adaptations of Strada's poem Crashaw's is "la plus intéressante" (p. 232). Discusses the sources of Strada's poem, traces the long poetic tradition of its theme, and surveys a number of Renaissance poets who employed it. Compares and contrasts Strada's poem with Crashaw's version, noting that Crashaw employed more alliteration, created new images, achieved greater lyrical improvisation, produced more masterfully the qualities of sound, and generally tried to surpass his model. Notes that Crashaw's poem has a voluptuous intensity that ends in ecstasy and suggests that Strada's stanzas seem to have a classical sobriety in contrast to Crashaw's more baroque approach. Sees in "Musicks Duell" a foreshadowing of many of the baroque characteristics that Crashaw developed more fully in his later religious poems and comments on the importance of music throughout his poetry.

◄§ 737. Praz, Mario. "The Critical Importance of the Revived Interest in Seventeenth-Century Poetry," in *English Studies Today*, edited by C. L. Wren and G. Bullough, 158–66. London: Oxford University Press.

Reprinted in *Essential Articles for the Study of John Donne's Poetry*, ed. John R. Roberts (Hamden, Conn.: Archon Books, 1975), 3–10. Maintains that the revival of interest in the metaphysical poets, especially Donne, in the twentieth century "has not only resulted in a change of perspective in literary criticism, but has also furthered the reaction against the critical standards and poetic theory of romanticism" (p. 166). Argues that the revaluation of the metaphysical poets "has been more than a literary fashion, has resulted not only in the adoption of certain images, in the cult of certain conceits and imaginative processes; it has rather amounted to the awareness of a similar disposition of spirit, of the same perplexity in facing life, of the same ironical reaction" (p. 163). Outlines Eliot's key role in this process. No specific mention of Crashaw.

⋙ 738. Smith, Harold Wendall. "'The Dissociation of Sensibility.'" *Scrutiny* 18:175–88.

Reexamines Eliot's theory and suggests that the split between thought and feeling has social and religious roots. Argues that Eliot's evaluation of Donne and the metaphysicals was an effort to canonize his own tastes and reflects the tensions of his own sensibility. Suggests that, by the time of the metaphysicals, "the two realms of abstract and sensible had already been divided" and notes that "it was in the distance which separated them that the 'metaphysicals' worked between them." Concludes that "Eliot's very term 'unification' implies both elements must have been clearly distinguishable and in need of being utterly fused into one" (p. 178). Brief references to Crashaw.

⋙ 739. White, Helen C., Ruth C. Wallerstein, and Ricardo Quintana, eds. "Richard Crashaw," in *Seventeenth-Century Verse and Prose.* Vol. 1: *1600–1660,* 369–92. New York: Macmillan.

2d ed., 1971, entry 1047.

General introduction to Crashaw's life and poetry, followed by a highly selected bibliography (pp. 369–70). Points out that Crashaw's religious poetry "does not reflect the intellectual problems of the religious life nor even the conflicts of doubt and faith, nor the tension of the rival claims of the world and the spirit" but rather "seeks to focus the senses, the imagination, and the reflective powers on a religious emotion awakened by the enraptured consideration of great religious themes and by the resources of art" (p. 369). Notes that "his themes and his treatment of them, his endeavor by sensuous sublimation to break open the finite and ascend to the world of the intelligences make him in English the great representative of *baroque* art in one of the important uses of that term" (p. 370). Briefly discusses the influence of the Bible, the classics, emblem books, Marino, Spenser, and Continental devotion on Crashaw's themes and techniques. Suggests that "the finest element of his sensibility is the music which gives unity and expressiveness to even his most conceited images" (p. 370). Anthologizes fifteen poems (or selections therefrom) with brief explanatory notes (pp. 371–92).

1952

◆§ 740. Bateson, F. W. "The Critical Forum: 'Dissociation of Sensibility.'"
EIC 2:213–14.

Replies to Eric Thompson (entry 748), who challenges Bateson's attack on the notion of "dissociation of sensibility" (entry 733). Insists that "however much we dress it up, the Dissociation of Sensibility cannot be made respectable" and suggests that "it's a lovely mouthful, full of sound and fury, but unfortunately it doesn't signify anything" (p. 214). No specific mention of Crashaw.

◆§ 741. Bush, Douglas. "The Renaissance," in *English Poetry: The Main Currents from Chaucer to the Present*, 21–79. New York: Oxford University Press.

Reprinted, with minor corrections, London: Methuen (Home Study Books, vol. 18), 1961; New York: Oxford University Press (A Galaxy book GB93), 1963; London: Methuen (University Paperbacks, 138), 1965; New York: Oxford University Press, 1966; London: Methuen, 1971.

Suggests that, "if we base our definition of metaphysical poetry on Donne and Herbert, or on them and Marvell, it hardly touches Richard Crashaw" and maintains that, although one can find Italianate and Spanish excesses in some Elizabethans, in Giles Fletcher, and in the early Donne, Crashaw "represents a later wave of more extravagant conceitism, and in his original as well as his translated work we may be more conscious of the un-English than of the English elements in his sensibility and poetic manner" (p. 63). Contrasts Crashaw and Herbert and calls Crashaw baroque. Notes that, although Crashaw "can be plain and direct" and can "display a genuine if sophisticated tenderness," on the whole "his name suggests flights of flamboyant adoration" (p. 63). Comments briefly on Crashaw's uses of imagery (especially erotic imagery), of paradox, and of baroque form. Suggests that "The Weeper" lacks logical organization and that there is no apparent reason it "should not be half as long, or ten times as long, as it is" (p. 64).

◆§ 742. Cazamian, Louis. *The Development of English Humor*. Pts. 1 and 2. Durham: Duke University Press. viii, 421p.

Reprinted, New York: AMS Press, 1965.

Studies the development of English humor from Old English through the Renaissance. Maintains that Crashaw, as well as such religious poets as Herbert, Vaughan, Lord Herbert of Cherbury, and Traherne, are humorless as poets: "The devout seriousness of their purpose precludes the possibility of a half-conscious element of intentional grotesqueness in their manner" (p. 356, n. 1). Suggests that "their conceits do not lend themselves to any suspicion of double meaning" (p. 388).

◆§ 743. Jenkins, Harold. *Edward Benlowes (1602–1676): Biography of a*

Minor Poet. London: University of London, Athlone Press; Cambridge: Harvard University Press; Leiden: E. J. Brill. x, 371p.

Suggests that Benlowes may have read Crashaw's poetry but it is not possible to be certain. Stresses that, in temperament, the two poets were very similar and notes the influence of Catholicism and the emblem tradition on both. Claims that, like Crashaw, Benlowes had "an inability to describe passion without some physical insignia" (p. 196) but maintains "delight in triumph through surrender is particularly characteristic of Crashaw and occasions some of his most passionate verses" whereas "it is less common in Benlowes, and less ecstatic when it comes" (p. 188n.). Notes similarities between Crashaw's diction and imagery and those of Benlowes.

✍ 744. Kunitz, Stanley J., and Howard Haycraft, eds. "Crashaw, Richard," in *British Authors Before 1800: A Biographical Dictionary*, 127–29. (The Authors Series.) New York: H. W. Wilson Co.

General introduction to Crashaw's life and poetry. Suggests that, although Crashaw is mainly known as a religious poet, his secular verses are "charming and graceful" (p. 128) and often avoid the faults of his devotional poetry. Maintains that "at his best he is almost Shelleyan, if a devout Shelley can be imagined," but that he is "one of the most unequal and uneven poets who ever wrote," noting that "passages of sheer felicity and fiery loveliness are interspersed with clumsy, awkward images and pure bathos" and that he is capable of "ethereal beauty married to gross banality" (p. 128). Lists Crashaw's major faults as "those of excess, of crowding imagination, of complete lack of self-evaluation or self-criticism" as well as a "meretriciousness of style if not of feeling" (p. 128). Highly selected bibliography.

✍ 745. Martin, L. C. "An Unedited Crashaw Manuscript." *TLS*, 18 April, p. 272.

Describes a recently discovered manuscript (six leaves, in two hands) of Crashaw's "A Hymn to Sainte Teresa" and "An Apologie for the fore-going Hymne" attached to a copy of *Las Obras de la S. Madre Teresa de Iesus . . . Primera Parte que contiene su Vida* (Antwerp, 1630), now in the Pierpont Morgan Library. Notes that the manuscript preserves several unique readings but points out that in several places where the manuscript differs from the printed versions, its readings "seem inferior and probably reveal an earlier stage of composition." Lists variants between the manuscript and the printed versions of the two poems. Notes also that the manuscript contains nine additional lines to the title of "A Hymn to Sainte Teresa," which have apparently never been printed before, and suggests that these lines are very likely by Crashaw. Speculates that perhaps one hand is that of Crashaw. Reproduces the first page of the manuscript.

✍ 746. Mazzeo, Joseph Anthony. "A Critique of Some Modern Theories of Metaphysical Poetry." *MP* 50:88–96.

Reprinted in *Seventeenth-Century English Poetry: Modern Essays in Criticism*, ed. William Keast (entry 879), 63–74, rev. ed. (1971), 77–88; in *Discussions of John Donne*, ed. Frank Kermode (Boston: D. C. Heath & Co., 1962), 118–25; in *John Donne's Poetry: Authoritative Texts, Criticisms*, ed. A. L. Clements (New York: W. W. Norton & Co., 1966), 134–43; and in *The Metaphysical Poets: Key Essays on Metaphysical Poetry and the Major Metaphysical Poets*, ed. Frank Kermode (entry 980), 158–71.

Comments on several modern theories about the nature of metaphysical poetry, such as the idea that metaphysical poetry is a decadent, exaggerated use of the Petrarchan and troubadour traditions; is best accounted for by the influence of Ramist logic; is closely allied to the baroque; or is closely related to the emblem tradition. Approaches the problem from the perspective of sixteenth- and seventeenth-century theorists, especially Giordano Bruno, Baltasar Gracián, and Emmanuele Tesauro, and finds all modern theories wanting and, at times, inconsistent. Argues that "the principle of universal analogy as a poetic, or the poetic of correspondences, offers . . . a theory of metaphysical poetry which is simpler, in great harmony with the evidence, and freer from internal contradictions than the major modern theories that have yet been formulated" (p. 89). Points out that, according to the contemporary critics, "the conceit itself is the expression of a correspondence which actually obtains between objects and that, since the universe is a network of universal correspondences or analogies which unite all the apparently heterogeneous elements of experience, the most heterogeneous metaphors are justifiable" and "thus, the theorists of the conceit justify the predilection of the 'school of wit' for recondite and apparently strained analogies by maintaining that even the more violent couplings of dissimilars were simply expressions of the underlying unity of all things" (pp. 88–89). Mentions Crashaw briefly in several instances and comments on Praz's study (entry 459).

◆§ 747. Raiziss, Sona. *The Metaphysical Passion: Seven Modern American Poets and the Seventeenth-Century Tradition.* Philadelphia: University of Pennsylvania Press. xv, 327p.
Reprinted, 1969; Westport, Conn.: Greenwood Press, 1970.
Discusses the influence of the metaphysical poets on the work of certain modern poets, especially Eliot, John Crowe Ransom, Allen Tate, Robert Penn Warren, Hart Crane, Elinor Wylie, and Archibald MacLeish. Suggests that "if, from many of Donne's poems, we remove a seventeenth-century construction here and there or revert an inversion, we discover the experience and the language of contemporary writing" (p. xiii). Part 1 (pp. 3–56) examines the temper of metaphysical poetry, its subject matter, method, modes, and wit. Part 2 (pp. 59–164) discusses the sources of the metaphysical impulse, those tensions and conflicts that are parallel between the seventeenth century and the twentieth century. Part 3 (pp. 167–241) discusses seven modern poets in the light of the preceding comments. Refers throughout to Crashaw, primarily to illustrate some of his major themes, his uses of the con-

ceit, and his wit. Calls Crashaw a Catholic mystic and comments on the influence of Spanish and Italian poetry on his work, noting that "his transcription of spiritual ecstasy into erotic symbols had conscious and involuntary kinship with the Italian literature of that time" (p. 77). Notes also that Crashaw can exhibit startling instances of bad taste. Briefly compares and contrasts Crashaw to Shakespeare, Donne, Herbert, Vaughan, G. M. Hopkins, Emily Dickinson, Eliot, John Crowe Ransom, Hart Crane, Samuel B. Greenberg, and the Symbolists.

◄§ 748. Thompson, Eric. "The Critical Forum: 'Dissociation of Sensibility.'"
      EIC 2:207–13.
   Challenges F. W. Bateson (entry 733). Suggests that Eliot's study of F. H. Bradley is central to understanding his concept of "dissociation of sensibility." For a reply, see Bateson (entry 740).

1953

◄§ 749. Bethell, S. L. "Gracián, Tesauro, and the Nature of Metaphysical
      Wit." Northern Miscellany of Literary Criticism 1:19–40.
   Reprinted in Discussions of John Donne, ed. Frank Kermode (Boston: D. C. Heath & Co., 1962), 136–49; and in The Metaphysical Poets: A Selection of Critical Essays, ed. Gerald Hammond (entry 1085), 129–56.
   Agrees with Rosemond Tuve's position in Elizabethan and Metaphysical Imagery (entry 689) but attempts "to supplement and somewhat rectify her account of metaphysical poetry by means similar to her own, that is by going to contemporary theorists" (p. 20). Presents an account of metaphysical wit and of the nature of the conceit based primarily on a reading of Gracián's Agudeza y Arte de Ingenio (1642) and Tesauro's Il Cannocchiale Aristotelico (1654). Suggests that both Gracián and Tesauro "are engaged with the general nature and specific modes of the conceit rather than the wider functions of literary criticism, so what they have to say applies almost as much to English as to Spanish or Italian poetry" (p. 22). Maintains that "there is, of course, no suggestion that they are 'sources' of anything or 'influences' upon anybody" but, "coming as they do after Europe had been soaked for a half a century in metaphysical wit, we might expect them to articulate the methods by which poets and other writers had been perhaps only half-consciously working" (p. 22). No specific references to Crashaw.

◄§ 750. Cutts, John P. "A Bodleian Song-Book: Don. C. 57." M&L 34:
      192–211.
   Describes and comments on the contents of a pre-1650 manuscript of seventeenth-century songs in the Bodleian Library (Don. C. 57). Notes that Crashaw's "A Song ('Lord, when the sense of thy sweet grace')" appears in the manuscript and that, except for lines 13 and 14, it is substantially the same as

in Martin's edition. Suggests that these two lines in the manuscript are from an earlier version of the song.

◄§ 751. Duncan, Joseph E. "The Revival of Metaphysical Poetry, 1872–1912." *PMLA* 68:658–71.
Reprinted in *Discussions of John Donne*, ed. Frank Kermode (Boston: D. C. Heath & Co., 1962), 126–35.
In revised form appears as chap. 4 of *The Revival of Metaphysical Poetry: The History of a Style, 1800 to the Present* (entry 831), 113–29.
Suggests that Grierson's edition of Donne (1912) "marked the end of the first stage of the metaphysical revival" (p. 658) and that Eliot's essays "were not so much a new note as a sensitive formulation of ideas that had become familiar by 1912" (p. 658). Traces the ever-growing acceptance of metaphysical poetry from 1872 (Grosart's edition of Donne) to 1912. Primarily concerned with the nineteenth-century fascination with Donne the man and with surveying the background of Eliot's criticism of the metaphysicals, but also illustrates the changing attitude toward all the metaphysical poets. Mentions Crashaw in several places.

◄§ 752. Malloch, A. E. "The Unified Sensibility and Metaphysical Poetry." *CE* 15:95–101.
Attempts to limit more precisely the terms *unified sensibility* ("an epitome of all that is most cryptic and pretentious in modern criticism" [p. 95]) and *metaphysical poetry* and to indicate the relationship between the two. Concludes that "the relation of the unified sensibility to metaphysical poetry is the relation of poetic process to poetic technique" and notes that "certain techniques can validly be said to distinguish Donne, Herbert, Crashaw, and Marvell as a school (and there are significant differences within that school)" whereas "the unification or dissociation of sensibility, on the other hand, is a judgment on a poet's mode of creation, whatever the nature of his techniques" (pp. 100–101).

◄§ 753. Mazzeo, Joseph Anthony. "Metaphysical Poetry and the Poetic of Correspondence." *JHI* 14:221–34.
Discusses the revival of interest in the nature and function of metaphor among certain European critics and rhetoricians in the seventeenth century, especially Baltasar Gracián, Emmanuele Tesauro, Cardinal Sforza-Pallavicino, Pierfrancesco Minozzi, and Matteo Pellegrini, and suggests that these theorists "envisaged the poet's universe as a complex system of universal analogical relationships which the poets expressed and revealed" (p. 234). Points out that such a universe "contained relationships which no longer exist for us" since "they have been eliminated from our perception by Baconianism and Cartesianism" (p. 234). Concludes, therefore, that "what may seem to us strange and far-fetched similitudes were often truths, even commonplaces, in

their world of insight" (p. 234). Makes no specific references to Crashaw but quotes from Austin Warren's study (entry 619) to support his position.

◄§ 754. Mourgues, Odette de. *Metaphysical Baroque & Précieux Poetry.* Oxford: Clarendon Press. vii, 184p.
Reprinted, Folcroft, Pa.: Folcroft Library Editions, 1970, 1973; Norwood, Pa.: Norwood Editions, 1976, 1977; Philadelphia: R. West, 1978; [s.l.]: Arden Library, 1980.
Distinguishes the term *baroque* from *metaphysical* and *précieux* and compares French "baroque" poets with certain late sixteenth- and early seventeenth-century English poets, including Crashaw. Suggests that baroque poetry relies "on unbridled fancy to bridge the gap between the pagan and spiritual world" and maintains that "it is the disorders of this imagination enlisted in the service of God which will account for the main features of baroque mystical poetry" (p. 78). Considers Crashaw as representative of the Counter-Reformation baroque but stresses that all baroque poets are not Catholics. Outlines some of the major features of Crashaw's poetry, especially his uses of music; rhetoric; ritualistic, decorative, and sensuous images and metaphors; and devotional and objective symbols and emblems. Notes that in Crashaw's poetry one often finds "a strange mixture of crude pathos and sensuous pleasure" (p. 80) and attributes his "distorted vision" to his use of "the possibilities offered by Catholic hagiography and the ritual of the Church" (p. 82). Briefly compares Crashaw to La Ceppède, Durant, le Père de Saint-Louis, Saint-Amant, Théophile, Tristan, and d'Aubigné. Notes similarities between Crashaw and Southwell, Giles Fletcher, and John Davies.

◄§ 755. Oates, J. C. T. "Cambridge Books of Congratulatory Verse 1603–1640 and Their Binders." *TCBS* 1, pt. 10:395–421.
Describes and discusses thirteen books of congratulatory verse issued by Cambridge University on royal occasions before 1641, one of which, *Rex redux, Sive Musa Cantabrigiensis . . .* , 1633, contains a poem by Crashaw (entry 5). Notes that Charles I was crowned at Edinburgh on 18 June 1633 and that the book was published by 28 July of the same year. Reproduces photographs of two bindings of the book and discusses other bindings.

◄§ 756. Perkins, David. "Johnson on Wit and Metaphysical Poetry." *ELH* 20:200–217.
Reevaluates Dr. Johnson's attitude toward metaphysical poetry, especially his "*favorable* approach to qualities—such as 'wit' and 'novelty' in the uses of imagery and language—that are now commonly associated with the 'metaphysical style'" (p. 201). Points out the value that Johnson placed on "intellectual activity in the language of poetry" (p. 202) and on wit. Redefines Johnson's concept of wit. Points out that Johnson quotes Crashaw 103 times in the *Dictionary*, as compared with 408 citations from Donne, 290 from Cow-

ley, 125 from Cleveland, 78 from Herbert, 32 from Carew, and none from Vaughan. Maintains that, although Johnson's admiration for the metaphysical poets was not without certain reservations, it was "strong enough, however, to make him the first critic to analyze and define them—in a sense, even to resurrect and justify them critically" (p. 217). See also A. D. Atkinson (entry 732), Samuel Johnson (entry 81), and W. B. C. Watkins (entry 590).

◄§ 757. Peter, John. "Crashaw and 'The Weeper.'" *Scrutiny* 19:258–73.
    Pages 272–73 reprinted in *The Critical Temper: A Survey of Modern Criticism on English and American Literature from the Beginnings to the Twentieth Century*. Vol. 1: *From Old English to Shakespeare*, gen. ed. Martin Tucker (New York: Frederick Ungar, 1969), 299–300.
    Reacts to those critics who focus on Crashaw's use of startling imagery and thereby neglect "the more significant questions that his poems suggest" (p. 258). Examines in detail "The Weeper" as typical of Crashaw's work. Denies that Crashaw's extravagant imagery results from "a deficiency of judgment or taste" (p. 260) and explains how it is in the poetry by design. Argues that Continental influences alone do not adequately explain what Crashaw does and discusses several poems by Donne to demonstrate how extravagant imagery can be both flippant and serious at the same time. Emphasizes that the images of "The Weeper" are not realized concretely nor fused together but rather are employed to achieve a "jubilant, impulsive, rapturously incoherent" tone (p. 264). Sees a problem in the nature of the emotions that Crashaw attempts to express, which, however, cannot be attributed to his conversion to Catholicism, for the poem must have been written by 1635. Argues that the poet does not control the imagery but allows it to control him, noting that Crashaw often has "a too complete preoccupation with the mere sound of words at the expense of their meaning" (p. 268). Charges also that the vehicle and tenor of the poem are not closely related and thus attention is not directed to the theme but to the ingenious imagery of the poem. Maintains that "what should concern us . . . is the evident disproportion between the weight of his imagery and the slightness of the theme upon which it is made to depend—a slightness which is the poet's own responsibility and in no sense inherent in the subjects which he chose" (p. 272). Notes that both Donne and Herbert avoid such misjudgments and concludes that "it is not only artistry that makes them superior to him, but integrity as well" (p. 273).

◄§ 758. Ross, Malcolm M. "A Note on the Metaphysicals." *HudR* 6:106–13.
    Discusses the decline of Christian poetic sensibility in the seventeenth century. Argues that the change can best be seen in "those Christian symbols which at one and the same time are rooted in dogma and which convey—or seek to convey—the immediate sense of existence" (p. 107). Comments on the breakdown of the Christian symbol from analogy to mere metaphor as a result of the reform of Christian dogma. Suggests that it is in Anglican poetry,

especially Herbert's, "hovering precariously as it must between Catholic and Protestant symbol, that one is able to see most clearly a far-reaching crisis in the Christian aesthetic" (p. 107). Mentions Crashaw only briefly, suggesting that "the years from Donne to Dryden—the years of the Fletchers, Herbert, Milton, Crashaw—could these be indeed the last years of the Christendom of the arts?" (p. 107). For a more thorough discussion, see Ross's *Poetry and Dogma*, entry 766.

◆§ 759. Turnell, Martin. "Baroque Art and Poetry." *Commonweal* 56: 146–49.

Examines Crashaw's poetry in the light of the baroque period and the spirit of the Counter-Reformation. Sees baroque art as an attempt to convert, assimilate, and transform the vitality released by the Renaissance to the service of the Church. Notes that, like baroque sculpture, Crashaw's poetry is "extremely rich in visual, concrete, physical images" and that "not merely one, but all five of the sense are solicited on every page" (p. 147). Suggests that the baroque artists' realistic representations of mystical ecstasy or death were attempts "to get as close as possible to the content of experience" and that this tendency "seems to explain the peculiar position of the image in Crashaw's poetry" (p. 147). Notes that in Crashaw's poetry "we have the impression that attention has shifted away from the experience to the image, that *the image itself becomes an object of contemplation*" and that "the image precedes the emotion and is used to generate it" (p. 147), which is quite unlike what one finds in Donne, Herbert, and Marvell. Suggests that Crashaw's images are "ingenious and entertaining" and that there is "a genuine fervor in his poetry which is often impressive" but maintains that "it is difficult to avoid the conclusion that free association and the lack of intellectual control which it implies is something of a weakness in a poet" (p. 148). Discusses Crashaw's use of erotic images and finds it a weakness in his poetry. See also Martin Turnell (entry 869).

◆§ 760. Unger, Leonard, and William Van O'Connor. "Richard Crashaw (1613?–1649)," in *Poems for Study: A Critical and Historical Introduction*, 166–83. [New York]: Rinehart & Co.

Reprinted, 1956.

Presents a brief introduction to Crashaw's life and poetry; explicates "A Hymn to Sainte Teresa"; and anthologizes "The Weeper," "Charitas Nimia," and lines from "The Flaming Heart" with study questions. Maintains that Crashaw's themes and techniques can only be understood in the light of Counter-Reformation spirituality and the spirit of the baroque. Comments briefly on Crashaw's use of highly elaborate rhetoric, highly imaginative metaphors, and sensuous and sometimes gaudy diction to present his religious attitudes and suggests how these means are appropriate to his specific end. Outlines the structure of "A Hymn to Sainte Teresa" and discusses the nature and function of oxymora, puns, paradoxes, antitheses, startling metaphors, and conceits in the poem.

❧ 761. Watkin, E[dward] I. "William Crashaw's Influence on His Son." *DubR* 223:1–25.

Reprinted in *Poets and Mystics* (New York and London: Sheed and Ward, 1953), 164–87; reprinted, Freeport, N.Y.: Books for Libraries Press, 1968.

Discusses William Crashaw's influence on his son. Disagrees with those who believe that Richard was reacting against his father's religion when he chose to embrace Catholicism and maintains that the poet derived from his father "a positive Anglican Christianity which, when he became a Catholic, he would not deny but complete" (p. 2). Argues that, although William made virulent attacks on Papists and Jesuits and saw the Pope as the Anti-Christ, he was not a Puritan, Dissenter, or Independent but rather was a devout and zealous Anglican and royalist. Comments on William's great love of the Anglican Prayer Book, his respect for episcopal hierarchy, his appreciation of ancient religious tradition, and his agreement with the basic doctrines of the Church of England. Stresses that anti-Catholic sentiment was prevalent in seventeenth-century Anglicanism, even in Laudianism, and that the kind of Anglo-Catholicism that developed in the nineteenth century was not prevalent. Points out that at times William Crashaw evidences a conflict in his attitude "between his virulent hatred of the Catholic Church and a devotion, not so remote from his son's" (p. 14). Notes that William translated Catholic hymns and devotions for the edification of Protestants and suggests that Richard was first exposed to Catholic theology and devotion in his father's library, where the elder Crashaw had numerous Catholic books used primarily for his own polemical purposes. Rejects the notion that Richard's connection with Little Gidding contributed to his conversion to Catholicism, suggesting that its strong commitment to the Church of England held him back at a time when he was already showing signs of moving toward Rome. Concludes that William Crashaw had a strong and positive influence on his son's religious attitudes, his love of prayer, and his poetry. Notes parallels between Crashaw's poetry and the passionate mystical writings of Francis Rous, a Puritan zealot, to show that mystical devotion of an "erotic and Baroque colour was in the spiritual atmosphere of the time" (p. 23).

1954

❧ 762. Bottrall, Margaret. *George Herbert.* London: John Murray. 153p.

Reprinted, Folcroft, Pa.: Folcroft Library Editions, 1971; Norwood, Pa.: Norwood Editions, 1975; Philadelphia: R. West, 1977.

Briefly contrasts Crashaw to Herbert, especially "the sane temper of Herbert's religious lyrics" to the "fevered devotional verse" of Crashaw (p. 142). Notes that Crashaw "was always liable to lapses in taste, especially when the

distinction between sacred and profane love is involved" (p. 143). Comments
briefly on the possibility of Herbert's influence on Crashaw, noting that, although Crashaw paid homage to Herbert, "his poems owe nothing discernible
to Herbert's example" (p. 144).

◄§ 763. McCann, Eleanor. "Donne and Saint Teresa on the Ecstasy." *HLQ*
    17:125–32.
    Compares Donne and St. Teresa and draws special attention to similarities
between Donne's "The Extasie" and the middle portion of Teresa's *Vida*, noting that, "although far apart in history, politics, and religion, Donne and
Teresa have left records of their ecstatic experience which illuminate not only
the life of love but each other as well" (p. 132). Briefly contrasts Crashaw's
response to the Spanish saint to that of Donne and points out that, "although
Crashaw was warmed by the erotic element in Teresa's *Vida*, he tended to
etherealize both her and her heavenly discourse," whereas Donne "knew how
to bring the subject down to earth" (p. 131). Suggests that the same reason
that Donne suppressed any mention of his indebtedness to the saint accounts
for Crashaw's "An Apologie for the fore-going Hymne."

◄§ 764. Martz, Louis L. *The Poetry of Meditation: A Study in English Reli-
    gious Literature of the Seventeenth Century.* (Yale Studies in English,
    vol. 125.) New Haven: Yale University Press; London: Oxford University
    Press. xiv, 375p.
    Rev. ed., 1962; reprinted, 1969, 1978.
    Pages 135–44 reprinted in *The Modern Critical Spectrum*, ed. Gerald Jay
Goldberg and Nancy Marner Goldberg (Englewood Cliffs, N.J.: Prentice-
Hall, 1962), 244–50.
    Pages 211–48 (with revisions from the 2d ed.) reprinted in *Seventeenth
Century English Poetry: Modern Essays in Criticism*, ed. William Keast (entry
879), 144–74, rev. ed. (1971), 118–51.
    Pages 220–23 and 228–48 reprinted in *John Donne: A Collection of Criti-
cal Essays*, ed. Helen Gardner (Englewood Cliffs, N.J.: Prentice-Hall, 1962),
152–70.
    The primary purpose of this study is "to modify the view of literary history
which sees a 'Donne tradition' in English religious poetry. It suggests instead a
'meditative tradition' which found its first notable example not in Donne but
in Robert Southwell" (p. 3). Argues that the metaphysical poets, though obviously widely different, are "drawn together by resemblances that result, basically, from the common practice of certain methods of religious meditation"
(p. 2). Mentions Crashaw throughout. Briefly contrasts the "baroque extravagance" of Crashaw with the "delicate restraint" of Herbert (p. 4) and notes
how Crashaw's poetry has marked affinities to that of Southwell but differs
greatly from that of Donne. Shows that Crashaw not only reflects the influ-

ence of Continental methods of meditation but also evidences the influence of Continental poetry that was itself shaped, in part, by these devotional techniques. Notes the element of mystical contemplation in Crashaw's poetry; comments briefly on his rendering of the Psalms into English; and maintains that his poetry reflects a meditative style, that is, "'current language heightened,' molded, to express the unique being of an individual who has learned, by intense mental discipline, to live his life in the presence of divinity" (p. 324). Presents a brief analysis of "Hymn in the Holy Nativity" (pp. 165–67) and contrasts it to Milton's Nativity Ode to show the differences between the spirituality of the Counter-Reformation and that of English Puritanism: Crashaw "produces a ritual love-song; Milton, a hymn in praise of the Power and Glory" (p. 167). Comments on "Sancta Maria Dolorum" (pp. 115–17) to show how it reflects the influence of meditational techniques and how it differs from Jacopone da Todi's original. Comments on "The Weeper" (pp. 201–3) as representative of the popular literature of tears. Discusses in some detail "Hymn to the Name of Jesus" (pp. 61–64) to demonstrate how it conforms to the usual tripartite structure of discursive meditation. Calls the hymn "a masterwork in the poetry of meditation, and one of the very last in its kind" (p. 64) and especially notes how the hymn, for all its flamboyant rhetoric, is controlled by "wit in the sense of intellectual ingenuity, producing a hundred surprises of word and phrase; wit in the sense of humor, which plays delicately throughout the earlier part of the poem, in Herbert's way; and above all, wit in the sense of intellectual power, planning and executing a careful movement of the whole through prologue, *mise en scène*, developing action, climax, and epilogue" (p. 62). In "Appendix 1: Mauburnus, Hall, and Crashaw: The 'Scale of Meditation'" (pp. 331–52), compares "Hymn to the Name of Jesus" to the *Rosetum* (Zwolle, 1494) of Joannes Mauburnus (Jean Mombaer) and to *The Arte of Divine Meditation* (London, 1606) of Joseph Hall and concludes that "in this poem the art of meditation has provided the fundamental unity of structure necessary to control the daring adventures of the baroque imagination" and that the hymn "stands with Donne's *Second Anniversary* as one of the greatest achievements in the poetry of meditation" (p. 352). Briefly compares and/or contrasts Crashaw to Southwell, Donne, Herbert, Milton, Vaughan, Traherne, and Marvell.

◄§ 765. Mishra, Jayakanta. "The Metaphysical Style in Seventeenth-Century English Literature." *University of Allahabad Studies (English Section)* 30:47–77.

Presents a general account of critical response to metaphysical poetry, comments on the use and misuse of the term *metaphysical* as applied to some seventeenth-century poetry, and surveys certain basic elements of metaphysical style. Claims that the distinctive features of metaphysical poetry are its intellectuality, its psychological realism, its uses of the dramatic, and its creation of a new diction and rhythm. Only briefly mentions Crashaw, noting that his piety and mysticism "are expressed in an erotic imagery which would not be possible in any other style" (p. 75).

✎§ 766. Ross, Malcolm Mackenzie. *Poetry and Dogma: The Transfiguration of Eucharistic Symbols in Seventeenth Century English Poetry*. New Brunswick: Rutgers University Press. xii, 256p.

Reprinted, New York: Octagon Books, 1969.

Studies "some of the consequences for religious poetry in England of the Protestant revision of Eucharistic dogma" and maintains that "the dogmatic symbolism of the traditional Eucharistic rite had nourished the analogical mode of poetic symbol, indeed had effected imaginatively a poetic knowledge of the participation (each in the other) of the natural, the historical, and the divine orders" (p. vii). Argues that Crashaw "serves to illustrate the numbing and narrowing effect of the revolution in dogma on even the Catholic sensibility" (p. ix) during the seventeenth century. Suggests that, "by contrast with the corporate tone of Puritans on the march," Crashaw's poetry seems "utterly individualistic and subjective" and that the contrast provides "insight into the bewildering, restless firmament of the Christian symbol in seventeenth century poetry" (pp. 53–54). Notes that there was nothing Tridentine in the spirituality of Little Gidding that would have moved Crashaw toward Catholicism and points out that Crashaw's Catholicism and Milton's Protestantism should be regarded "not as belonging to utterly separate poetic firmaments but as expressing, with a final clarity, the opposite horns of the Anglican dilemma, indeed of the Christian dilemma, in an age of disintegration" (p. 67). Maintains that, for Crashaw, "the certitudes of faith, while real and intense, are limited not only by a Tridentine conservatism of the intellect, but also by something more crucial to the poetic activity, by a loss of the certitude 'that the impact of his freedom on his destiny gives his life a movement which is *oriented . . .* and which has to do, in one way or another, with the whole fabric of being'" (p. 234). Calls Crashaw's poetry "a-historical" and suggests that in it "interiority of religious experiences leaves no room at all for the *corporate human act*" and that "the movement of his life is inevitably oriented inward, away from the unruly order of event, and even, in the proper analogical sense, away from the fragmented order of things" (p. 234). Argues, therefore, that Crashaw's poetry "stands at the last extreme of the aesthetic predicament of Catholicism in seventeenth century Protestant England" (p. 234). Maintains that "continental Catholicism, with its bitter-sweet raptures and blinding surfaces lifted Crashaw not only out of place but out of time" (p. 241). Suggests that only in the symbolization of human love can Crashaw create analogically and notes that his nature images are "always metaphorical rather than analogical" (p. 242). Suggests that, although Crashaw used the great wealth of image and symbol contained in the liturgy, he turned liturgy, for the most part, into private devotion. Compares and/or contrasts Crashaw to Southwell, Herbert, Vaughan, Joseph Beaumont, Milton, and Christopher Lever.

✎ 767. Sayama, Eitarō [Sakae Iwasaki]. "Richard Crashaw," in *Keijijōshi no Dentō* [The Tradition of Metaphysical Poetry], 78–87. Tokyo: Kenkyūsha. 2d ed., 1965.

General critical evaluation of Crashaw's poetry. Maintains that, although Crashaw's poetry reflects the influence of Donne and Herbert, his voluptuous mysticism is uniquely his own. Comments on certain baroque features of Crashaw's art, especially his use of sensuous and erotic images and conceits. Discusses in particular "Letter to the Countess of Denbigh," "On Hope," "A Hymn to Sainte Teresa," and "The Flaming Heart." Maintains that Crashaw was the first poet in the seventeenth century to develop a Romantic style.

✎ 768. Summers, Joseph H. *George Herbert: His Religion and Art*. Cambridge: Harvard University Press; London: Chatto & Windus. 246p.

Reprinted, Cambridge: Harvard University Press, 1968; Binghamton, N.Y.: Center for Medieval and Early Renaissance Studies, 1981.

Compares Crashaw briefly to Herbert. Notes, for instance, that "Herbert's imagery characteristically concerns the creator and the architect, rather than the 'nests' and 'tears' of Crashaw" (p. 89) and points out that Herbert could not divorce celebration from examination and that even his pattern poems contain messages that are "precise and clear even if complex and subtle," whereas "a differing conception of the religious hieroglyph led Crashaw to ecstatic adoration and worship" (p. 145). Suggests that the pattern poems of Joseph Beaumont and Edward Benlowes are closer to Crashaw's than to Herbert's.

✎ 769. Wallis, P. J. "William Crashaw—Puritan Divine, Poet and Bibliophile." *N&Q* n.s. 1:101–2.

Seeks additional information about William Crashaw. Suggests that the best account of the poet's father is in vol. 2 of Grosart's edition but that Grosart probably knew more about the Crashaws than he printed in the edition.

1955

✎ 770. Adams, Robert Martin. "Taste and Bad Taste in Metaphysical Poetry: Richard Crashaw and Dylan Thomas." *HudR* 8:61–77.

Reprinted, in revised form, in *Strains of Discord* (entry 813), 128–45; and in *Seventeenth Century English Poetry: Modern Essays in Criticism*, ed. William R. Keast (entry 879), 264–79.

Discusses what it is in Crashaw's poetry that leads many critics, both past and present, to label his poems as lacking in good taste and questions what sound critical basis there can be for saying, for example, that even such a notorious metaphor as "Portable, and compendious oceans" in "The Weeper" is in bad taste, since it produces the strong effect that Crashaw presumably intended. Suggests that the judgment resides not so much in Crashaw's metaphors, images, and conceits per se as in the effect produced and that they are called "bad" because the critics disapprove of the kind of feeling such figurative language produces in the reader. Notes that Crashaw's favorite theme is "the unity of opposites, of pain with pleasure, life with death, fruition with denial, assertion with surrender" and that such unity "always involves a degree of incongruity, often of incongruity unresolved, a sense of strain and grotesquerie" and suggests that "it is precisely because he succeeds so well in unifying into one assertion, over the most intense opposition, his 'highest' thoughts and 'lowest' feelings, his most physical sensations and his most spiritual aspirations, that contemporary taste is sometimes revolted and sometimes amused by Crashaw" (pp. 65–66). Cites aspects of Crashaw's "bad taste" that disturb critics, such as "his deliberate injection of a homely word or circumstance amid lofty spiritual reflections" (p. 66) and his uses of physical orifices in his poems. Suggests, however, that, in spite of the "absurdity" of some of the images and metaphors, "a Christian poet, at least, can scarcely be blamed for assuming, and asking his readers to assume for the moment, a definition of reality which includes more than the humanly demonstrable" (p. 70). Disagrees with Ruth C. Wallerstein's argument (entry 575) that Crashaw's later poetry show signs of his moving away from the grotesque and maintains that Crashaw's taste "simply included an area of 'very bad taste' within a larger area of 'inoffensive taste,' and rose occasionally to something we can call 'impeccable taste,' always provided our standards of taste are purely conventional" (p. 70). Briefly compares and contrasts Crashaw to Dylan Thomas.

≈§ 771. Bairstow, Edward C. "Come, lovely Name," in *Five Poems of the Spirit, for Baritone Solo, Chorus, and Orchestra*, 1–9. London: Novello.
Musical setting of twenty lines of "Hymn to the Name of Jesus" for baritone solo and optional chorus of women's voices.

≈§ 772. Blunden, Edmund. "Some Seventeenth-Century Latin Poems by English Writers." *UTQ* 25:10–22.
Translates into English lines 121–37 of "Bulla" (pp. 15–16). Calls the poem "a deliberate *tour de force*" but notes that "yet one would say that a glory descended on the writer as soon as he began his frolic" (p. 15). Quotes Archbishop Trench's praise of the poem in *Sacred Latin Poetry* (entry 209). Points out that about a third of Crashaw's poems are classical and are "quintessentially important" (p. 15). Also includes translations from Donne, Herbert, and Milton.

≈§ 773. Brinkley, Roberta Florence, ed. *Coleridge on the Seventeenth Century*, edited by Roberta Florence Brinkley with an introductory essay by

Louis I. Bredvold. Durham, N.C.: Duke University Press. xxxviii, 704p.
Reprinted, New York: Greenwood Press, 1968.
Selections reprinted in *The Metaphysical Poets: A Selection of Critical Essays*, ed. Gerald Hammond (entry 1085), 59–60.
Collection of Coleridge's comments on the seventeenth century arranged under seven headings: (1) the seventeenth century in general, (2) the philosophers, (3) the divines, (4) science, (5) literary prose, (6) poetry, and (7) the drama. See especially "Richard Crashaw" (pp. 612–14). (See entries 116, 150, 151.)

◄§ 774. Bush, Douglas. "Seventeenth-Century Poets and the Twentieth Century." *Annual Bulletin of the Modern Humanities Research Association* no. 27:16–28.
Comments on the revival of interest in the metaphysical poets, especially Donne, from the nineteenth century through the twentieth. Gives reasons for the extraordinary attention given the metaphysical poets by both scholars and practicing poets, especially during the 1920s and 1930s, and for the decline of interest since that period. Also considers the effects of the metaphysical revival on the fate of Milton in the twentieth century and concludes that Milton, "far from having been dislodged from his throne, appears to sit more securely than ever on a throne that has partly new and even more solid foundations" (p. 26). Suggests that while "amateur criticism restored Donne and banished Milton, scholarly criticism kept Donne and restored Milton" (pp. 26–27). Briefly mentions Crashaw.

◄§ 775. Esch, Arno. *Englische religiöse Lyrik des 17. Jahrhunderts: Studien zu Donne, Herbert, Crashaw, Vaughan.* (Buchreihe der Anglia Zeitschrift für englische Philologie, 5.) Tübingen: Max Niemeyer Verlag. xi, 225p.
Studies the problems of seventeenth-century religious poetry by analyzing and comparing the works of individual poets. Chapter 4 (pp. 97–141) presents a biographical sketch of Crashaw, describing his life as a yearning for motherly love that was finally fully satisfied by his embracing of Holy Mother the Church, and comments on themes and techniques of some of his major poems. Notes that Crashaw's poetry is centered about the mystery of divine love, a love that finally eliminates the differences between heaven and earth. Argues that Crashaw's poetry shows much less homogeneity than is often assumed and maintains that it develops through three stages: (1) the youthful period, characterized by the use of wit and epigrammatic structure; (2) a second stage, characterized by the influence of the mysticism of St. Teresa and during which he developed the free hymn style and replaced mere wit by divine love; and (3) a final stage in which he moved on to a poetry of Logos, characterized by a deepening intellectual awareness and by a more ordered,

logical structure while, at the same time, retaining deep emotional intensity. Discusses in some detail "Song upon the Bleeding Crucifix," "The Weeper," "Hymn in the Holy Nativity," "Ode on a Prayer-book," "Hymn in the Assumption," "A Hymn to Sainte Teresa," and "Letter to the Countess of Denbigh" in order to show Crashaw's spiritual and aesthetic development, paying close attention to those changes made between early and later versions of the same poem. Briefly contrasts Crashaw to Herbert and Donne. Chapter 5 (pp. 142–59) discusses Crashaw's versions of medieval Latin hymns and suggests that they are neither translations nor paraphrases in the strict sense but rather are free variations upon the themes of the originals. Maintains that those that differ most from the originals are, in fact, the most successful. Discusses in detail "Adoro Te," noting that Crashaw transforms the rigid Thomistic structure "in eine bewegte und gespannte Strukur . . . , die dem emotionalen Erleben reichere Entfaltungsmöglichkeit bot" (p. 151) and breaks up the clear divisions of the original, with their rigid intellectual progressions, replacing them with a rhapsodic structure. Discusses in less detail the other versions of medieval hymns. Concludes that Crashaw "versetzt sich nicht in den Geist seiner Vorlagen, er spannt die alten Kirchenhymnen in sein Erleben ein" (p. 159).

⋙ 776. Groom, Bernard. "The Spenserian Tradition and Its Rivals to 1660," in *The Diction of Poetry from Spenser to Bridges*, 48–73. Toronto: University of Toronto Press; London: Geoffrey Cumberlege, Oxford University Press.

Reprinted, Toronto: University of Toronto Press, 1960, 1966.

Sees Crashaw as part of the new poetic culture that arose as a rival of Spenserianism and comments generally on his uses of imagery and diction. Notes that his imagery and diction "remind one vividly of the florid art fostered by the counter-Reformation"; that, although at times he rises to "a burning eloquence," his poems are "marked by extravagance," citing "On our crucified Lord Naked, and bloody" as an example; and that, although he "delights in a soft and sensuous imagery," there is also "a virile vein in Crashaw, expressing itself in many turns of phrase and reminding one of the healthier side of his opulent imagination" (p. 69). Suggests that in *Carmen Deo Nostro* Crashaw "adapted his earlier style to the spirit of his adopted religion" (p. 68). Cites "Musicks Duell" as an example of Crashaw's mastery of a rich poetic vocabulary and of his resourcefulness in language. Briefly compares and/or contrasts him to Herbert, Vaughan, Quarles, and Francis Thompson.

⋙ 777. Manning, Stephen. "The Meaning of 'The Weeper.'" *ELH* 22: 34–47.

Discusses the influence that the spiritual tradition available to Crashaw, in emblem books, Jesuit spirituality, Carmelite mysticism, contemporary devotional lyrics, and the patristic and medieval heritage, had on his imagery.

Maintains that the imagery of "The Weeper" reflects its theme, which is "spiritual perfection, the progress toward the mystical union of Christ and the soul" (p. 37). Points out, in particular, images that suggest spiritual marriage, coming from both secular and sacred love poetry; images that suggest the superiority of the Magdalene's tears to nature because they are spiritual; images that emphasize copious tears as a sign of repentance; and images that suggest the timelessness of the saint's tears. Discusses in some detail the general movement of the poem. Suggests that in stanzas one to five Crashaw generalizes upon the Magdalene's spiritual state and shows how, having repented of her sins, she begins the way to perfection. Maintains that in stanzas six to eighteen the poet traces the steps of her arrival at this spiritual state and in stanza nineteen, the very center of the poem, he extols her both as a penitent and as a follower of Christ. Sees this central stanza as a summing up of the preceding stanzas and as a preparation for stanzas twenty to twenty-seven. Concludes that, "finally, having addressed the eyes up to this point, Crashaw turns to the tears, and they, in answer, confirm that Magdalene has renounced all earthly things for Christ" (pp. 46–47).

◆§ 778. Miles, Josephine. "Eras of English Poetry." *PMLA* 70:853–75.
Reprinted in *Eras & Modes in English Poetry* (Berkeley and Los Angeles: University of California Press, 1957), 1–19.
Questions the practice of dividing English poetry arbitrarily into historical periods and defines three recurrent modes in poetry based upon various kinds of sentence structure and word usage favored by English poets: the clausal (or active predicative), the phrasal (or sublime), and the balanced (or classical). Considers the clausal mode as the most English and traces it to Chaucer. In a chart, lists Crashaw as belonging to the balanced mode, which "is not merely a scale of degrees between extremes, but a mode of statement characterized by a balance between clausal and phrasal elements" (p. 854). Suggests that an analysis of ten of Crashaw's lines shows that there are roughly as many adjectives as verbs. Sees Donne's and Herbert's poetry as predominantly clausal.

◆§ 779. Rickey, Mary Ellen. "Crashaw and Vaughan." *N&Q* n.s. 2:232–33.
Suggests that Vaughan was familiar with Crashaw's poems and that he probably read them, at least in part, because of their mutual respect for Herbert. Discusses a number of Crashavian phrases and figures in *Silex Scintillans*.

◆§ 780. Sypher, Wylie. *Four Stages of Renaissance Style: Transformations in Art and Literature, 1400–1700.* (Anchor Books Original, A44.) Garden City: Doubleday & Co. 312p.
Reprinted, Gloucester, Mass.: Peter Smith, 1978.
Studies the development of various Renaissance styles from 1400 to 1700, stressing relationships between literature and the fine arts. Sees most of the metaphysical poets as "mannerists" but calls Crashaw "the most characteristic

poet of baroque piety" (p. 189). Discusses those elements of Crashaw's style that can be regarded as baroque, such as his uses of sensuous and literal images, his buoyant ardor and triumphalism, and his uses of witty language. Maintains that Crashaw's verse reflects the revolution against mannerist distrust of the flesh and notes that he "gives to the conceit, and to wit, a sensuousness more ornate and voluptuous than appears in the other English devotional poets" (p. 189). Suggests that "Sancta Maria Dolorum" reminds one of Murillo and that "Ode on a Prayer-book" reminds one of Sassoferrato or Carlo Dolci. Briefly contrasts Crashaw with Donne, Herbert, and Milton.

≈§ 781. Warnke, Frank J. "Marino and the English Metaphysicals." *SRen* 2:160−75.

Argues that "it is difficult to accept the hypothesis of a general European baroque style, a style which embraces both Marino and the English metaphysicals," and shows how Marino's poetry differs from that of the metaphysicals "in its use of mythological reference and pastoral machinery, in its auditory smoothness, in its sensuous imagery, and in its diffuse metaphorical patterns" as well as "in its continued use of the characteristic Renaissance forms of epic, sonnet, and madrigal" (p. 174). Suggests that the true English equivalents of Marino are Giles and Phineas Fletcher, not Crashaw, as has often been argued. Discusses "Sospetto d'Herode" to demonstrate that in letter and spirit Crashaw's poem diverges significantly from Marino's original. Notes, for example, that Crashaw excludes the machinery of the classical myth from the argument to the canto; that he places greater emphasis on paradox, especially Christian paradox; and that he employs more conceptual metaphors. Maintains, therefore, that "despite a certain temperamental kinship to Marino which manifests itself in a love of diffuse and startling metaphor, Crashaw, in 'Sospetto d'Herode' as in his independent works, differs from the Italian poet in both style and vision" and notes that Crashaw "fashioned from material of the utmost diversity a poetry of spiritual unity" and that he "aims always at the mystical rather than the marvelous" (pp. 173−74).

≈§ 782. Watson, George. "Hobbes and the Metaphysical Conceit." *JHI* 16:558−62.

Argues that the metaphysical conceit was killed by a change in literary theory and illustrates this change by referring to the critical writings of Hobbes. Suggests that, in time, the conceit lost its intellectual force and was dismissed as mere sound. No extended discussion of Crashaw. For a reply, see T. M. Gang (entry 792).

1956

≈§ 783. Birrell, T. A. "Sarbiewski, Watts and the Later Metaphysical Tradition." *ES* 37:125−32.

Discusses the reception of the neo-Latin poems of Casimire Sarbiewski in England and comments on his extraordinary influence on certain later metaphysical and eighteenth-century poets, especially Isaac Watts. Notes that both Sarbiewski and Crashaw were first published in England in 1646. Points out that the use of erotic and sensuous imagery is often seen by later critics as somehow un-English, notes that "there are things in Watts every bit as startling as any to be found in Crashaw," and that "a 17th century metaphysical poet would hardly have understood what was meant by un-Englishness, or, as a poet, would he have understood much of a division between Anglican, Romanist or Non-Conformist poetry" (p. 132).

◅§ 784. Collmer, Robert G. "Crashaw's 'Death More Misticall and High.'" *JEGP* 55:373–80.

Discusses meanings the word *death* held in the Renaissance and concludes that, by the phrase "death more misticall and high" in "A Hymn to Sainte Teresa," Crashaw is referring to the mystical experience of the union of the soul with God, not to physical death. Traces the uses of the figure in Catholic mystical writings from Saint Bernard of Clairvaux (1091–1153) to Madame de Guyon (1648–1717) to show how it was used consistently by Catholic mystics to describe the goal of mystical union. Points out that the figure of mystical death can be found in several of Crashaw's other poems, in particular "Ode on a Prayer-book" and "The Flaming Heart." Rejects the notion that in Crashaw's poetry death may refer to sexual orgasm, argues that such a reading "violates the peculiarity of Crashaw's language" (p. 379), and supports this position by stressing that Crashaw did not borrow his language from Donne or from native English poetry but from the writings of Catholic mystics.

◅§ 785. Compton-Rickett, Arthur. "Jacobean Poetry," in A *History of English Literature from Earliest Times to 1916*, 181–90. London: Thomas Nelson and Sons.

Reprinted, 1958, 1964.

Presents a biographical note on Crashaw and comments briefly on his poetry. Notes that Crashaw "has less intellectual breadth than Carew, less imaginative by-play than Herrick, but his work, though extremely uneven, rises at times to heights of rare excellence" (p. 184). Suggests that Crashaw's best poem is "The Flaming Heart" and notes that "some of his lighter things have a pleasant grace about them" (p. 185), quoting stanzas from "Wishes. To his (supposed) Mistresse" by way of example. Compares and contrasts Crashaw briefly with Herrick, Carew, and Vaughan.

◅§ 786. Cox, R. G. "A Survey of Literature from Donne to Marvell," in *From Donne to Marvell*, edited by Boris Ford, 43–85. (The Pelican Guide to English Literature, vol. 3.) Harmondsworth, Eng.; Baltimore: Penguin Books.

Several reprints (see entry 790).

Broad survey of poetry and prose from Donne to Marvell. Discusses Crashaw in a subsection titled "The Metaphysical Manner and Religious Poetry" (pp. 54–59). Notes that Crashaw's "combining a fondness for paradox with sensuous warmth in the manner of the Italian poets of the Counter-Reformation, especially Marino and the Jesuit writers of Latin epigrams," often leads him to use the conceit "as isolated ornament rather than as an integral part of a poem's total meaning" (p. 57). Suggests that Crashaw "carries to extremes the traditional use of erotic metaphor to convey the ecstasies of adoration" and that "his uncontrolled lyric fervour sometimes collapses into an exclamatory verbal haze" (p. 58). Notes that, on the whole, Crashaw's poetry "moves away from the tradition of Donne and Herbert" but that in certain poems, such as his reply to Cowley on hope and his "Letter to the Countess of Denbigh," Crashaw's "approximation to Metaphysical wit adds strength and substance to his ecstatic lyricism" (p. 58). Briefly compares Crashaw to Southwell, Giles Fletcher, and Quarles and contrasts him with Donne, Herbert, Milton, and Vaughan.

787. Denonain, Jean-Jacques. *Thèmes et formes de la poésie "métaphysique": Étude d'un aspect de la littérature anglaise au dix-septième siècle.* (Publications de la faculté des lettres d'Alger, 28.) Paris: Presses Universitaires de France. 548p.

In the introduction (pp. 5–18), states his intention to define as precisely as possible the nature of metaphysical poetry and challenges several of the better-known definitions. Divided into five major parts: (1) a tentative definition of metaphysical poetry (pp. 21–95); (2) an analysis of major themes in metaphysical poetry (pp. 99–326); (3) a discussion of the psychological processes by which the themes of the poetry are developed and expanded (pp. 329–64); (4) a study of poetic forms employed by the metaphysical poets (pp. 367–449); and (5) a conclusion that seeks to discern the unifying characteristics of metaphysical poetry (pp. 453–80). Although mentioned throughout, Crashaw is specifically discussed in three sections: (1) "Les thèmes religieux chez Richard Crashaw" (pp. 221–34), which comments on his life and religious sensibility; outlines his major religious themes, especially the sufferings of Christ, divine love, the Virgin Mary, St. Mary Magdalene, and St. Teresa; and discusses major characteristics of his poetic style, such as ornamentation, verbal ingenuity, and intense passion; (2) "Images, métaphore et conceit chez Crashaw" (pp. 394–96), which contrasts Crashaw's use of figurative language with Donne's practice; and (3) "La technique poetique chez Crashaw" (pp. 437–40), which discusses Crashaw's versification, primarily contrasting him to Donne and Herbert. Maintains that Crashaw is not particularly original in versification and points out that Crashaw, "poète a l'imagination visuelle intense, et a l'intellect acéré, ne semble pas avoir d'oreille" (p. 440). Calls Crashaw's poetry "une effervescence sentimentale uncontrólée" (p. 361) and suggests that he "s'abandonnes à l'ivresse des mots" (p. 369). Notes that the term *felt thought* was first employed by Grosart in his edition of Crashaw. Among the several appendixes, presents a chronological table of Crashaw's life and works (p. 487). Selected bibliography.

◄§ 788. Enright, D. J. "George Herbert and the Devotional Poets," in *From Donne to Marvell*, edited by Boris Ford, 142–59. (The Pelican Guide to English Literature, vol. 3.) Harmondsworth, Eng.; Baltimore: Penguin Books.

Several reprints (see entry 790).

Calls Crashaw "pre-eminently the English poet of the Counter-Reformation" (p. 156) and surveys his life and poetry. Asserts Crashaw's art can be related to Catholic ritual and to the masque, for, in spite of all its flamboyance, it is "a formal, public act of worship which tastes simultaneously of the cathedral, the stage, and the study" (p. 159). Suggests that the epigrammatic aspect of Crashaw's poetry most nearly resembles that of the other metaphysicals but considers the Catholic poet outside the English tradition and more like Marino and the Italians. Maintains that, in spite of some flaws, Crashaw's poems can have intellectual force, neatness, and immediacy. Points out that the most notorious feature of his verse is the use of the sensuous, in particular the use of metaphors of human love as vehicles for expressing spiritual love. Suggests that the ornate, baroque conceit "is the very basis of Crashaw's poetry," noting that often "it is lovingly handled, but sometimes too lovingly fondled" (pp. 157–58). Cites "A Hymn to Sainte Teresa" as Crashaw's finest English poem, calling it "dramatic," "unusually masculine for Crashaw," and tender but "weakened by a cloud of abstractions" (p. 158). Briefly compares and contrasts Crashaw to Herbert, Vaughan, and Francis Thompson.

◄§ 789. Farnham, Anthony E. "Saint Teresa and the Coy Mistress." *Boston University Studies in English* no. 2:226–39.

Contrasts, through a detailed reading of both poems, Marvell's "To His Coy Mistress" and Crashaw's "A Hymn to Saint Teresa" and comments on their differences in theme, uses of rhythm and meter, imagery, rhetoric, and tone. Suggests that, although both employ the octosyllabic couplet, their poetic methods are quite different: "In contrast to the succinct brevity and swift pace with which Marvell conveys a controlled passion, Crashaw with equal control uses a stately rhythm and expansive richness to express ecstatic ardor" (p. 232). Notes that one of the major differences between the two poems "can be regarded as one of philosophical spirit and background, involving the conceptual distinction of classical and Christian" (p. 226). Points out that, unlike Marvell, Crashaw's poem reaffirms the Christian notion of "the annihilation of joy by time" and asserts that "there is *no* joy in created time" and that "worldly happiness is the expectation of joy in eternity" (p. 231). Suggests that the theme of Crashaw's hymn is "the love between God and man, with emphasis on the passion of man's attempt to receive that love in full measure" (p. 231). Sees the poem as a reflection of the mystical spirit of St. Teresa, noting that she belonged to that group of mystics who "approach God through an attempted union in the mind of all sense perceptions" (p. 231) and who describe their spiritual experiences in terms of human love and marriage. Maintains that the rich sensuousness of Crashaw's poetry "is raised to the level of ritual, where it becomes symbolic and transcends its own sensuousness" (p. 232).

꼭 790. Ford, Boris, ed. *From Donne to Marvell*. (The Pelican Guide to English Literature, vol. 3.) Harmondsworth, Eng.; Baltimore: Penguin Books.

Reprinted, 1960; new and revised ed., London: Cassel, 1962; revised ed., Harmondsworth, Eng.; New York: Penguin, 1968; revised and expanded ed., Harmondsworth, Eng.; New York: Penguin, 1982 (The New Pelican Guide to English Literature, vol. 3).

Crashaw is mentioned in several places in this collection of original essays on various seventeenth-century topics. Essays in which Crashaw is given special consideration have been entered separately in this bibliography (entries 786, 788, 796). Biographical note and selected bibliography (p. 255).

꼭 791. Frankenberg, Lloyd. *Invitation to Poetry: A Round of Poems from John Skelton to Dylan Thomas Arranged with Comments*. Garden City, N.Y.: Doubleday & Co. 414p.

Reprinted, New York: Greenwood Press, 1968.

Presents brief critical comments on "On our crucified Lord Naked, and bloody" and suggests that the phrase "Opening the purple wardrobe of thy side" reminds one of the early paintings of Salvador Dali. Claims that Crashaw's poems "create their own strange world of devotion" and that, in spite of elaborate uses of metaphor and conceit, "everything in them is in scale with it" (p. 236). Points out that Crashaw attempts "to give permanence to what is most transitory" (p. 236).

꼭 792. Gang, T. M. "Hobbes and the Metaphysical Conceit: A Reply." *JHI* 17:418–21

In part, a reply to George Watson (entry 782), challenging Watson's view of Hobbes's critical theory. In the second part of the essay discusses the metaphysical conceit, maintaining that it was possible for metaphysical poets "to use the language and assumptions of metaphysics because they believed these to have validity" but that later on, in the 1650s and 1660s, "both the verbiage and the general method had become, or were fast becoming, meaningless" (p. 419). Suggests that what makes a conceit "metaphysical" is "not the wildness of the comparison, but the fact that the comparison is between a concrete thing and an abstraction, and that the double meanings are produced by tak-

ing the concrete part of the comparison 'seriously,' that is, writing literally
about the vehicle of the metaphor" (p. 421). No specific mention of Crashaw.

◆§ 793. Ishii, Shōnosuke, Anthony Thwaite, and Ann Thwaite. "From *The
     Flaming Heart* by Richard Crashaw: Jūana-seik Eishi gohyō." *EigoS*
     102, no. 12:21–24.
A critical dialogue among Ishii and Anthony and Ann Thwaite on the last
thirty lines of "The Flaming Heart." Discusses the selection as representative
of the merits and weaknesses of Crashaw's religious poetry and comments on
individual lines, words, and images. Thwaite suggests that Crashaw is inferior
to the other major metaphysical poets: "I think I can honestly say I've never
heard a good word spoken of Crashaw" (p. 22). Notes the influence of Marino
and the Continental poets and concludes that, "with Crashaw, one often has
the feeling that either he is unconscious of his peculiarity, or else is exaggeratedly cultivating it," a fault that gives him "a line with Swinburne, Shelley
and Francis Thompson—very different poets, but their lack of taste is often
remarkably similar" (p. 24). Ishii's comments, on the whole, are much more
positive. He praises the closely knit structure and effective thematic focus in
"The Flaming Heart" and stresses the influence of the Catholic faith and its
liturgy on Crashaw's art.

◆§ 794. Lamson, Roy, and Hallett Smith, eds. "Richard Crashaw, 1612–
     1649," in *Renaissance England: Poetry and Prose from the Reformation
     to the Restoration*, 962–85. New York: W. W. Norton & Co.
Expanded version, *The Golden Hind: An Anthology of Elizabethan Prose
and Poetry* (New York: W. W. Norton & Co., 1942), does not include Crashaw.
    Presents a brief introduction to Crashaw's life and poetry, with a selected
bibliography (pp. 962–63), and anthologizes, with brief notes, eight poems
(pp. 964–85). Claims that Crashaw is "the best representative in English of
the baroque style in literary art" (p. 962) and that his poetry can be compared
to Bernini's sculpture of St. Teresa. Maintains that "the characteristics of
baroque art—a swelling, flamboyant movement which presses against the
boundaries of the space, and, if we consider baroque to be the art of the
Counter Reformation, a transfer of the stimuli of earthly passions to sacred
subjects so that 'the five senses are made portals to heaven'—these are the
salient traits of Crashaw's verse" (p. 962).

◆§ 795. Melchiori, Giorgio. "Fry: The Popular Theatre," in *The Tightrope
     Walkers: Studies of Mannerism in Modern English Literature*, 150–74.
     London: Routledge & Kegan Paul; New York: Humanities Press; New
     York: Macmillan.
Reprinted, Westport, Conn.: Greenwood Press, 1974.
    Suggests similarities of movement between a passage from Christopher Fry's
Venus Observed and "Musicks Duell" but notes that in Crashaw's poem "we

can detect a greater balance, a sense of symmetry and conclusion" that "is indeed the distinction between late Mannerism and full Baroque" (p. 165).

*◄§ 796. Mourgues, Odette de. "The European Background to Baroque Sensibility," in *From Donne to Marvell*, edited by Boris Ford, 89–97. (The Pelican Guide to English Literature, vol. 3.) Harmondsworth, Eng.; Baltimore: Penguin Books.
Several reprints (see entry 790).
Surveys European baroque sensibility and its influence in England. Calls the baroque "a crisis of sensibility" (p. 97) and sees it as the "artistic outcome" of the "destruction of the balance between feeling and intellect," the "distortion of reality through the cravings of unruly emotions and the desperate vagaries of imagination," and a "conflict between the spirit and the senses" (p. 90). Notes the influence of the Counter-Reformation on Crashaw's art and sensibility, especially that of the Jesuits and of devout humanism, and suggests that the excessive appeal to the senses of this period "leads to a distorted view of life in which religious themes, such as the repentant Magdalene, the ecstatic Teresa, the Sacred Heart, the crucified Saviour, the Holy Innocents, are translated into undulating marble raptures in sculpture or pictorial symbolic metaphors in poetry" (pp. 90–91). Suggests that Crashaw, along with Théophile, St. Amant, Góngora, and Marino, "replaced the living universe by a world of correspondences" and that in their poetry "a network of recurrent motifs is consistently being interposed between reality and ourselves," which is "made even more artificial by a riot of colours and a profusion of jewels" (p. 94).

◄§ 797. Powers, Perry J. "Lope de Vega and *Las Lágrimas de la Madalena*." *CL* 8:273–90.
Discussed the tradition of poetry on Mary Magdalene and the larger tradition of the literature of tears and suggests how Lope de Vega's long narrative poem on the saint, *Las Lágrimas de la Madalena*, both employs the conventions of the tradition and transcends them. Briefly notes Crashaw's participation in the tradition of poetry on the saint's tears and suggests that, although Lope's poem is quite different from "The Weeper," there are resemblances, primarily "in the conversion of a sensual image, the tear, into a series of images that depend less upon a visual perception of the object than upon purely intellectual associations: seed-tear, the drink of Cherubs, pearls, dewdrops, silver, all tending to make the tear a tear-not-tear (like Lope's *cabellos* that are not *cabellos* in any literal sense), an object freed from material limitation, a thing of great tenderness, yet quite dissociated from human grief" (p. 287). Notes that Crashaw's metaphor in "The Weeper" of tears that flow upward can be traced back at least as far as Peter Chrysologus's *De Conversione Magdalenae* (fifth century).

❧ 798. Rao, A. V. "The Religious and Meditative Poetry of England." *Prabuddha Bharata; or Awakened India* (Calcutta) 61:139–42.

Briefly comments on some of the major devotional and mystical poets of England from the thirteenth century to T. S. Eliot. Assures Indian readers that "a rich vein of religious, devotional, and meditative poetry runs through the literature of England, though at first sight it would seem incredible, because the English people have been looked on as fighters, colonizers, empire-builders, sturdy John Bulls, a 'nation of shopkeepers', and what not—anything but mystics and devotional poets" (p. 139). Briefly mentions Crashaw and suggests that he and Traherne "reveal intense feeling, a quality almost or apparently absent in Marvell and Cowley, whose intelligence and wit so often triumphed over emotion" (p. 141).

❧ 799. Rickey, Mary Ellen. "Chapman and Crashaw." *N&Q* n.s. 3:472–73.

Suggests that Crashaw "was struck both by certain recurrent motifs of Chapman's imagery—particularly in *The Shadow of Night*—as well as by certain turns of phrase which Chapman employed here and in subsequent work" (p. 472) and examines several passages from Chapman, especially his treatment of the Phoenix legend, that suggest Crashaw's indebtedness. Concludes that these resemblances show that "the young Crashaw inaugurated in his verse a system of imagery which, while common enough in his time, is closely enough paralleled in Chapman to lead one to speculate on Chapman's verse as a probable source" and that, "when Crashaw later shifted to exclusively devotional verse, he retained the phoenix myth as a poetic staple, reinforcing his interpretation of human love as a type of the soul's union with God" (p. 473).

❧ 800. Schücking, Levin L., ed. *Englische Gedichte aus sieben Jahrhunderten. Englische-Deutsch.* (Sammlung Dieterich, Band 109.) Leipzig: Dieterich'schen Verlagsbuchhandlung; Bremen: Schünemann. 390p.

Includes translations into German with English on facing pages of "An Epitaph upon a Young Married Couple" (pp. 100–101), translated by L. L. Schücking, and two stanzas from "Song upon the Bleeding Crucifix" (pp. 102–3), translated by Richard Flatter. Brief biographical-critical note (p. 356).

❧ 801. Smith, A. J. "An Examination of Some Claims for Ramism." *RES* n.s. 7:348–59.

Reprinted in *Essential Articles for the Study of John Donne's Poetry*, ed. John R. Roberts (Hamden, Conn.: Archon Books, 1975), 178–88.

Challenges Rosemond Tuve's claim in *Elizabethan and Metaphysical Imagery* (entry 689) that Ramism "provides a satisfactory explanation not only of certain major elements in so called 'Metaphysical' poetry, but even of the very thought processes of the greatest 'Metaphysical' poet, Donne" (p. 348). Discusses the nature of Ramism, in particular its relation to verse. Concludes that "too much has been made of the attempt at reform in teaching method called Ramism, in itself and as an influence" (p. 359) and that "for the true explanation of 'Metaphysical' qualities and techniques one need seek no farther than the great sixteenth-century tradition of which Ramism was but a backwater—that of wit as it was developed in conventional rhetoric" (p. 359). No specific discussion of Crashaw. For a reply, see George Watson (entry 824).

◆§ 802. Wallis, P. J. "The Library of William Crashawe." *TCBS* 2, pt. 3:213–28.
Presents a biographical sketch of William Crashaw, father of the poet, and a survey of his printed works. Discusses William Crashaw's extensive personal library and comments on his books and manuscripts, many of which were given to St. John's College, Cambridge, through a gift of the Earl of Southampton. Notes that, "although not so well known now as his son Richard, William's contemporary influence was probably greater" (p. 228).

◆§ 803. Wellek, René. "The Criticism of T. S. Eliot." *SR* 64:398–443.
Reviews T. S. Eliot's basic comments on metaphysical poetry and poets (pp. 437–40). Points out that, although his criticism has proved to be an important impetus to the so-called metaphysical revival, his ideas are, for the most part, neither original nor consistent, but that he is the first critic to link the metaphysical poets so definitely with the French Symbolists. Briefly comments on Eliot's appreciation of Crashaw: "He calls him a 'finished master,' compared to whom Keats and Shelley were 'apprentices with immense possibilities before them'" (p. 439). Observes that Eliot "finds a kind of intellectual pleasure even in the entirely preposterous images of Crashaw" and that he "endorses Mario Praz who puts Crashaw 'above Marino, Góngora, and everybody else as the representative of the baroque spirit in literature'" (p. 439). Notes that the notion of "dissociation of sensibility" or "felt thought" goes back at least to Grosart's edition of Crashaw and thus is not a new way of describing metaphysical poetry.

◆§ 804. Williams, George W. "Richard Crashaw and the Little Gidding Bookbinders." *N&Q* 3:9–10.
Suggests that Crashaw's specific references to the technical aspects of bookmaking and bookbinding reflect his acquaintance with the work of the community of Little Gidding. Points out seven such images in his verse and notes that, though few in number, they show that Crashaw had a more intimate knowledge of bookbinding than did most contemporary poets.

1957

◆§ 805. Anon. "The Puzzle of Richard Crashaw." *TLS*, 3 May, p. 274.
Essentially a review of Martin's second edition (1957). Argues that, al-

though Crashaw is an important poet, "it is not easy to say what precisely it is in his verse that constitutes his claim to our attention" and faults Martin for not making a more convincing case for the poetry. Finds Crashaw inferior to Donne, Herbert, Vaughan, and Milton and points out a number of his poetic flaws. Attributes Crashaw's positive achievement to his enthusiasm and bursts of energy. Suggests that his only complete successes are those poems, such as "Wishes. To his (supposed) Mistresse," in which Crashaw writes "in a convention of manageable proportions" and concludes that in the sacred poems, "those that promise most and achieve, on the whole, least, the convention was too flexible to support him" and thus "he was driven back too much on his own, not quite adequate, resources."

◄§ 806. Berkeley, Lennox, composer. *Look Up, Sweet Babe: Anthem for Treble Solo, Mixed Choir and Organ.* Words by Richard Crashaw; music by Lennox Berkeley. London: J. & W. Chester/Edition Wilhelm Hansen London. 8p.
Musical setting of lines 10–14 and 22–25 of "Hymn in the Glorious Epiphanie."

◄§ 807. Gardner, Helen, ed. *The Metaphysical Poets.* Selected and edited by Helen Gardner. (The Penguin Poets, D38.) Harmondsworth, Eng.; Baltimore: Penguin Books. 328p.
Reprinted, 1959, 1961, 1963, 1964; rev. ed., 1966; 2d ed., London: Oxford University Press, 1967; reprinted, 1967; 3d ed., Baltimore: Penguin Books, 1972, 1975, 1978.
Pages xix–xxiv reprinted in *Seventeenth Century English Poetry: Modern Essays in Criticism,* ed. William Keast (entry 879), 50–62, rev. ed. (1971), 32–44.
An anthology of metaphysical poetry in which Crashaw is represented by nine poems. Includes a biographical note and selected bibliography (p. 308). In the introduction outlines and comments on characteristics of metaphysical poetry as a whole (pp. 15–29). Mentions the dramatic element in metaphysical poetry, the "particular situations out of which prayer or meditation arises," pointing out that, although "the sense of the poet's own situation" (p. 27) is less important in Crashaw's verse than in the poetry of other metaphysicals, his poetry is essentially dramatic rather than narrative. In a note on the text, points out that, for the most part, she reproduced the poems from the 1648 edition, not the 1652, and wonders if some negative judgments on Crashaw have arisen because of "the exotic printing of *Carmen Deo Nostro,* whose heavy punctuation, weird spellings, and absurd over-capitalization impede recognition of his melodic power" (p. 31).

◄§ 808. Kermode, Frank. "Dissociation of Sensibility." *KR* 19:169–94.
Reprinted in *Essential Articles for the Study of John Donne's Poetry,* ed. John R. Roberts (Hamden, Conn.: Archon Books, 1975), 66–82.

Challenges T. S. Eliot's theory of "dissociation of sensibility" and points out that the tension between reason and theological truth was not solely confined to, nor begun in, seventeenth-century England. Maintains that, as far as poetry is concerned, especially metaphysical poetry, the theory is simply an "attempt on the part of the Symbolists to find an historical justification for their poetics" (p. 194). Discusses how the term and concept are closely related to the twentieth-century revival of metaphysical poetry. No specific discussion of Crashaw. The same material is examined in a revised form in entry 809.

◄§ 809. ———. "'Dissociation of Sensibility': Modern Symbolist Readings of Literary History," in *Romantic Image*, 138–61. London: Routledge and Kegan Paul; New York, Macmillan.
Reprinted many times.
Relevant parts of this chapter that deal with metaphysical poets and the seventeenth century are explored in much expanded form in his "Dissociation of Sensibility" (entry 808).

◄§ 810. Oxford University, Bodleian Library. *English Literature in the Seventeenth Century: Guide to an Exhibition held in 1957*. Oxford: Bodleian Library. 167p.
Guide to an exhibition of seventeenth-century books and manuscripts in the Bodleian (including three that were borrowed) that were "read then or now for their literary merit" (p. 5). Includes a 1646 copy of *Steps to the Temple. Sacred Poems, With other Delights of the Muses* (number 43) and a manuscript made by Archbishop Sancroft of poems, English and Latin, by Crashaw and others (number 44). In the note on the first item points out that, although Crashaw had become a Catholic by 1646, the title of his volume clearly echoes Herbert's *The Temple* and *A Priest to the Temple* and notes the signatures of two earlier owners on the title page—"Jo. Wogan" and "T. Sanderson." In the note on the second title points out that both Grosart and Martin used the manuscript in the preparation of their editions of Crashaw's poems.

◄§ 811. Pettoello, Laura. "A Current Misconception Concerning the Influence of Marino's Poetry on Crashaw's." *MLR* 52:321–28.
Refutes those critics who attribute Crashaw's bad taste and verbal extravagance to the influence of Marino and argues that Crashaw's occasional incongruities in style are due mainly "to his being a transitional poet who has many traditions of poetical style to assimilate and fails to do so" (p. 321). Points out differences between Italian and English as poetic media and suggests that the complexity of English "helps to explain why Crashaw was far more likely to pick up 'a fanciful extravagance of diction' at home than in Italy" (p. 323). Stresses that, although Marino's style is extravagant by the

standards of Italian poetry, which relies much less on metaphor and conceit than does English poetry, it is not particularly extravagant by English standards of the period. Points out that Crashaw more likely got his taste for elaborate diction and word play from his English contemporaries such as Cowley, Benlowes, and Cleveland, in whose poems "Metaphysical wit frequently runs to seed" (p. 327). Shows that Crashaw's "Sospetto d'Herode" is much richer than Marino's original and points out that when Crashaw borrows a conceit or metaphor from Marino he invariably makes it more opulent and extended.

৺§ 812. Stamm, Rudolf. "Prosa und Dichtung im 17. Jahrhundert," in *Englische Literatur*, 141–98. (Wissenschaftliche Forschungsberichte geisteswissenschaftliche Reihe, herausgegeben von Professor Dr. Karl Hönn, Band 2.) Bern: A. Francke AG Verlag.
Briefly surveys and evaluates modern critical studies of Crashaw (pp. 167–68), especially the work of A. F. Allison (entries 684, 690), Kerby Neill (entry 703), Mario Praz (entry 459), Ruth Wallerstein (entry 575), Austin Warren (entry 619), and Basil Willey (entry 718). Notes that, because of the excellence of modern editions, Crashaw's poetry is readily available to modern critics.

1958

৺§ 813. Adams, Robert M. *Strains of Discord: Studies in Literary Openness.* Ithaca, N.Y.: Cornell University Press. xi, 220p.
Reprinted, Freeport, N.Y.: Books for Libraries Press, 1971.
Includes a revised version of "Taste and Bad Taste in Metaphysical Poetry: Richard Crashaw and Dylan Thomas" (entry 770) entitled "Crashaw and Dylan Thomas: Devotional Athletes" (pp. 128–45). In the concluding chapter, "Some Aesthetic Adjustments" (pp. 201–15), suggests that Crashaw's poetry creates "a kind of baroque structure the energy and audacity of which remove it entirely from the criterion of good and bad taste" (p. 204) and observes that "The Weeper" is simply "a string of stanzas on a theme" without beginning or end and thus "the pearls could be strung in another order, and in greater or lesser number, without the slightest harm to the poem" (p. 208).

৺§ 814. Burgess, Anthony [John Burgess Wilson]. "The Age of Milton: End of a Period," in *English Literature: A Survey for Students*, 131–53. London: Longmans, Green and Co.
Reprinted, 1964, 1965, 1966; new edition, 1974; reprinted, 1976.
Calls Crashaw "one of the most un-English of English poets" and notes that "his richness and extravagance are too much for some tastes" (p. 141). Admits, however, that "the skill of his work cannot be denied, even when his metaphysical fancies appall the reader" (p. 141). Sees "The Weeper" as representative of "the metaphysical mind at its most grotesque" (p. 141) and sug-

gests that the images are baroque, adding that "the baroque is really a kind of elaboration approaching—and sometimes reaching—the absurd" (p. 142). Quotes a stanza from "Hymn in the Holy Nativity," however, to show that Crashaw is capable of "dignified simplicity" (p. 142).

◄§ 815. Bush, Douglas. "Tradition and Experience," in *Literature and Belief*, edited with a foreword by M. H. Abrams, 31–52. (English Institute Essays, 1957.) New York: Columbia University Press.

Reprinted in *Engaged and Disengaged* (Cambridge: Harvard University Press, 1966), 143–63.

Discusses non-Christian responses to, and experience of, poetry that is firmly rooted in Christian belief. Observes that Crashaw's poetry, unlike much of the poetry of Donne, Herbert, Vaughan, and Marvell, has little appeal for modern readers. Points out that in his classes at Harvard, students of diverse or no belief respond to such poems as Herbert's "Love (III)" but that, as far as he recalls, none respond to "The Weeper" or to "the more flamboyant odes" of Crashaw (p. 40).

◄§ 816. Coleman, Elliott, "'Not what you make of it, but what it makes of you.'" *Poetry* 91:273–76.

Essentially a review of Austin Warren's *New England Saints* (Ann Arbor: University of Michigan Press, 1956) and the 1957 paperback reprint of his *Richard Crashaw: A Study in Baroque Sensibility* (entry 619). Suggests that reading the two works together "is a poetic experience of unusual pleasure and a critical experience of unusual value" (p. 273–74). Comments briefly on Crashaw's poetry, calling it "a glowing product of the Golden Age of Anglicanism" and suggesting that, by the time of his death, Crashaw's poetry "had become his complete prayer" (p. 275) and that "each of the religious compositions of Crashaw is one of those to-be-continued moments of the complete prayer that was his life and being" (p. 276). Maintains that Crashaw's verse is "a poetry of belief and self-abnegating love" and that "this was the faith of the New England Saints, whether they called themselves Christian or not" (p. 276).

◄§ 817. Hagstrum, Jean H. *The Sister Arts: The Tradition of Literary Pictorialism and English Poets from Dryden to Gray.* Chicago: University of Chicago Press. xxii, 336p.

Reprinted, 1974.

Discusses "The Flaming Heart" to illustrate how Crashaw belongs to the iconic and pictorialist tradition of poetry. Maintains that, "in spite of some tasteless and ridiculous ingenuity, the poem in its revised form is one of the most intense iconic poems in the language and also an impressive embodiment in verse of the qualities that prevailed in baroque art after the Council of Trent" (p. 120). Comments, in particular, on Crashaw's use of the convention of having the poet directly address the painter, a convention ultimately derived from Anacreon, and suggests that "nowhere else is the painter so vigorously expostulated with as in Crashaw's poem" (p. 119). Briefly mentions Pope's comments on Crashaw.

◄§ 818. Madsen, William G. "A Reading of 'Musicks Duell,'" in *Studies in Honor of John Wilcox*, edited by A. Dayle Wallace and Woodburn O. Ross, 39–50. Detroit: Wayne State University Press.

Reprinted, Freeport, N.Y.: Books for Libraries Press, 1972.

Argues that "Musicks Duell" is "built up on a basic intellectual contrast between the music of man and the music of the nightingale that is not found in either Strada's poem or in any of the other translations and paraphrases of it, and that this basic contrast is supported by the imagery" (p. 39). Surveys the tradition of the singing-duell as well as other translations and adaptations of Strada's poem and points out that "only in Crashaw does the musical duel appear to have religious significance" (p. 42). Examines in detail the imagery of Crashaw's poem to show that, although he uses relatively few technical terms from music, he picks those terms with great care and purpose in order to suggest that "the bird's music, however various and complicated, is purely melodic or horizontal, while the music of the lute is both melodic and harmonious or vertical" (p. 42). Maintains that the poem is anagogical, not allegorical, and that it "invites us to lift our minds from the narrative to a contemplation of the eternal verity of which it is a concrete embodiment: earthly realities, while not losing their rich particularity, become symbols—or types, to continue the biblical terminology—of spiritual realities" (pp. 45–46). Maintains, therefore, that melody and harmony in the poem are types or symbols of time and eternity and that the imagery suggests "a complex interaction between nature and grace rather than the irreconcilable conflict that the bare narrative might suggest" (p. 49).

◄§ 819. Peterkiewicz, Jerzy, ed. and trans. "Richard Crashaw," in *Antologia liryki angielskiej (1300–1950)*, 74–75. London: Veritas Foundation Press.

Includes "On the wounds of our crucified Lord" (p. 74) and a Polish translation (p. 75), without notes or commentary.

◄§ 820. Praz, Mario. "The Flaming Heart: Richard Crashaw and the Baroque," in *The Flaming Heart: Essays on Crashaw, Machiavelli, and Other Studies in the Relations between Italian and English Literature from Chaucer to T. S. Eliot*, 204–63. (Doubleday Anchor Books.) Garden City: Doubleday & Co.

Reprinted, New York: Norton, 1973.

Abridged English version of the Crashaw section of *Secentismo e Marinismo in Inghilterra: John Donne—Richard Crashaw* (entry 459), which was later published separately, with revisions, as *Richard Crashaw* (entry 669); reprinted with appendix (selections from Crashaw's poetry), Rome: Mario Bulzoni-Editore Libreria «Richerche», 1964. Excludes the biographical sketch that appeared in the original essay.

❧ 821. Saveson, J. E. "Richard Crashaw." *TLS*, 28 February, p. 115.

Based on information contained in two letters of Dr. John Worthington, dated 1667 (entry 38), speculates that after Crashaw left Cambridge at the end of January 1642/43 and before he reached Leyden, he visited an unidentified friend in Lincolnshire to whom he delivered an autograph of his poems. Maintains that, slight as the information is, it is a more tangible possibility than Martin's suggestion that, after leaving Cambridge, Crashaw spent time at Little Gidding. See also Edwin Greenlaw (entry 486).

❧ 822. Shinoda, Hajime. "Shudai to Hensō: Hitotsuno Shi-taiken" [Themes and Variations: A Poetic Experience]. *Eibungaku-Kenkyū* 35, no. 1:107–19.

Compares the interpretations of "The Weeper" by Austin Warren (entry 619), Mario Praz (entry 459), and William Empson (entry 566) and concludes that Empson's reading of the poem is closest to his own experience of it. Sees "The Weeper" as a collection of thirty-one variations on the two-line epigraph ("Loe where a WOUNDED HEART with Bleeding EYES conspire. / Is she a FLAMING fountain, or a Weeping fire?") but suggests that the theme is too weak to hold the stanzas together, calling the poem a variation without a definite theme. Points out, however, that the poem excites a strong emotional response by its abundance of startlingly brilliant images but suggests that some of the images are clumsily handled.

❧ 823. Warnke, Frank J. "Jan Luyken: A Dutch Metaphysical Poet." *CL* 10:45–54.

Argues that metaphysical poetry "constitutes a distinct style, unlike the continental baroque, and that this style is not limited to English poetry" (p. 46). Asserts that the religious poetry of Dutchman Jan Luyken (1649–1712) demonstrates the presence of something analogous to English metaphysical verse in Continental literature. Maintains that the Dutch poet is more closely related to Vaughan or Traherne and thus belongs "to that last phase of metaphysical poetry, in which the traditional view of the world expresses itself through a meditative attention to the observed nature, an attention which in many ways anticipates that of those Romantics who a century and a half later were also to look for the Creator in the creation" (pp. 53–54). Notes Crashaw's use of conceptual imagery and the "sensuous, ritualistic" (p. 45) nature of his poetry. Briefly compares Luyken and Crashaw, noting in particular their similar uses of emblems as illustrations rather than for purposes of static allegory.

◄§ 824. Watson, George. "Ramus, Miss Tuve, and the New Petromachia."
MP 55:259–62.
Challenges A. J. Smith's attack (entry 801) on Rosemond Tuve's claims for
Ramism in *Elizabethan and Metaphysical Imagery* (entry 689). Agrees with
Smith that Tuve's argument is "too ambitious and will not stand" (p. 260) but
concludes that Ramism, "so far as the English were concerned, was a quick
handbook for logic with Cambridge and Puritan associations" and that "it is
still not clear that there is any need to seek a connection between Ramism and
English poetry" (p. 262). Suggests that, "if one must be sought at all, the neo-
Ramists might surely have found a happier hunting-ground than the poems of
men as un-Puritanical and unsimple as the English metaphysicals" (p. 262).
No specific discussion of Crashaw.

◄§ 825. Wilson, Edward M. "Spanish and English Poetry of the Seventeenth
Century." *Journal of Ecclesiastical History* 9:38–53.
Reprinted in *Spanish and English Literature of the 16th and 17th Centuries: Studies in Discretion, Illusion, and Mutability* (Cambridge, New York:
Cambridge University Press, 1980).
Declares his intent to show that "there was unity as well as diversity in two
contemporary religious literatures and to hint at the sources of that unity"
(p. 38). Suggests that "in each country there was a common way to express
religious truths in vivid everyday terms" and that this "was partly due to the fact
that both countries had a medieval heritage in common, but still more to the
fact that a devotional literature spread from Spain through Roman Catholic
Europe into England, in spite of fundamental differences of religious belief
and practice" (p. 53). Discusses the art of sacred parody and the uses of divine
analogy (or continued metaphor) in English and Spanish devotional poetry
and comments on the influence of discursive meditation on both. Mentions
Crashaw only briefly and claims that he, like Herbert and Donne, "almost
certainly knew and read Spanish" (p. 47). Calls Crashaw's poems "extravagant" but observes that even his poetry lacks "the extreme character that so
many of the Spanish poems display" (p. 46).

1959

◄§ 826. Anon. "Anglicanism and the Poets." *TLS*, 20 March, Religious
Books Section, pp. i–ii.
Comments on the great diversity of Anglican poets and suggests that many
of them, though not always agreeing on points of doctrine, seem to share "an
understanding of the peculiarly indefinable Anglican temperament" (p. 153).
Claims that the local nature of the Anglican Church accounts for a great deal
of this diversity: "This ability of their age can occasionally make clear distinctions difficult, and the absence of an inflexibly orthodox line has led many

critics into what in one sense are almost bizarre comparisons between, for example, Wordsworth and Vaughan, for intellectually these poets differ greatly" (p. 153). Points out that, although born a Catholic, Donne was "most conscious of the true nature of the church of his adoption" and suggests that "a comparison of his poetry with that of Crashaw soon reveals a considerable difference between the local and the Italianate tradition" (p. i).

◄§ 827. Attal, Jean-Pierre. "Qu'est-ce que la poésie 'métaphysique'?" *Critique* (Paris) 15:682–707.
Review of six critical studies: (1) Jean-Jacques Denonain's *Thèmes et formes de la poésie «métaphysique»* (entry 787); (2) Odette de Mourgues's *Metaphysical Baroque & Précieux Poetry* (entry 754); (3) Alan Boase's *Sponde* (Geneva: Pierre Cailler, 1949); (4) Boase's "Poètes anglais et français de l'époque baroque" (entry 708); (5) Joan Bennett's *Four Metaphysical Poets* (entry 552); and (6) T. S. Eliot's "The Metaphysical Poets" (entry 417). Maintains that metaphysical poetry is indeed *metaphysical* in that it deals with first principles and first causes, that it is above all concerned with truth rather than beauty, and that it scorns the heritage of the classics and traditional poetic phraseology: "Ils se sont tournés verse le quotidien et le familier pour atteindre la «réel»" (p. 706). Briefly comments on Crashaw as a baroque poet and questions his inclusion among the metaphysical poets.

◄§ 828. Bald, R. C., ed. "Richard Crashaw (1612–1649)," in *Seventeenth-Century English Poetry*, 315–32. (The Harper English Literature Series.) New York: Harper Brothers.
Biographical sketch with a bibliographical note on seventeenth-century editions and modern studies. Anthologizes fourteen Crashaw poems or selections from poems, with brief explanatory notes.

◄§ 829. Boyd, George W. "What Is 'Metaphysical' Poetry?" *MissQ* 12:13–21.
Traces the meaning of the term *metaphysical poetry* from Dryden to the present, "taking account of its sometimes gradual, sometimes drastic shifting and giving especial attention to the wide-ranging discussion of the subject in the criticism of the past decade" (p. 13). Maintains that the "classic definition and delineation of metaphysical poetry laid down by Messrs. Grierson, Eliot, and Williamson . . . has not been superseded in modern criticism, indeed, . . . it has hardly been basically modified" (p. 21). Sees the work of Joseph Mazzeo and Louis Martz as possible new directions, however. No specific discussion of Crashaw.

◄§ 830. Danchin, Pierre. *Francis Thompson: La vie et l'oeuvre d'un poète.* Paris: A.-G. Nizet. 554p.
Discusses throughout Thompson's debt to Crashaw (see especially pp. 434–37, 473–78). Finds numerous parallels between the religious sensibility

and the poetry of the two poets, noting many analogies in imagination, vocabulary, and style. Calls Thompson a disciple of Crashaw but "un disciple à qui le maître a permis de se trouver lui-même" (p. 478). Comments on Thompson's critical writings on Crashaw and points out that contemporary critics often compared Thompson to Crashaw. Suggests that Thompson may have been led to Crashaw by reading Coleridge's criticism.

◄§ 831. Duncan, Joseph E. *The Revival of Metaphysical Poetry: The History of a Style, 1800 to the Present.* Minneapolis: University of Minnesota Press. 227p.

Reprinted, New York: Octagon Books, 1969.

Pages 118–26 reprinted as "The Background of Eliot's [Donne] Criticism," in *The Metaphysical Poets: Key Essays on Metaphysical Poetry and the Major Metaphysical Poets*, ed. Frank Kermode (entry 980), 136–45.

Presents a general overview of the critical reputation of metaphysical poetry from the seventeenth century to the present. Emphasizes "the line of successive interpretations rather than individual evaluations, and treats poetic style as a vital force guiding creative efforts in a later period" (p. 5). Attempts "to show in what ways the metaphysical style, as it was interpreted and varied through successive periods, was both like and unlike the metaphysical style of the seventeenth century" (p. 4). Divided into ten chapters: (1) "The Early Conceptions of Metaphysical Poetry" (pp. 6–28); (2) "Seeds of Revival" (pp. 29–49); (3) "John Donne and Robert Browning" (pp. 50–68); (4) "The Beginnings of the Revival in America" (pp. 69–88); (5) "The Catholic Revival and the Metaphysicals" (pp. 89–112); (6) "The Metaphysical Revival: 1872–1912" (pp. 113–29); (7) "Yeats, Donne and the Metaphysicals" (pp. 130–42); (8) "Eliot and the Twentieth-Century Revival" (pp. 143–64); (9) "Metaphysicals and Critics since 1912" (pp. 165–81); and (10) "Metaphysical Fluorescence" (pp. 182–202). Chapter 3 first appeared as "The Intellectual Kinship of John Donne and Robert Browning in *SP* 50 (1953): 81–100, here slightly revised; chapter 6 first appeared as "The Revival of Metaphysical Poetry, 1872–1912" (entry 751), here slightly revised. Many references throughout to Crashaw. Comments on Crashaw's influence on later poets, especially Gerard Manley Hopkins and Francis Thompson, and surveys his critical reception. Points out that Crashaw stands apart from the other metaphysicals since his style "is intertwined with a Continental Catholic baroque style" and "his poetic structures are frequently loose, almost epigrammatic, while his conceits tend to depend on an all-suffusing sensuous and emotive appeal rather than on aptness and precision" (p. 8).

◄§ 832. Gamberini, Spartaco. *Poeti metafisici e cavalieri in Inghilterra.* (Biblioteca dell' «Archivium Romanicum»: Serie 1: Storia-letteratura-paleografia, vol. 60.) Florence: Leo S. Olschki. 269p.

Discriminates between such critical terms as *wit, conceit, metaphysical po-*

etry, euphuism, baroque, and *mannerism.* Compares and contrasts Donne, Jonson, and Chapman as leaders of different poetic schools. Presents a general survey of Crashaw's poetry, both secular and religious, for an Italian audience (pp. 92–109). Comments primarily on Crashaw's religious sensibilities as reflected in the thematic and stylistic concerns of his poetry. Points out that Crashaw, less insular than the other metaphysical poets, has much in common with Continental baroque poets: "Nella sua personalità confluiscono insieme la tradizione inglese e quella dei grandi mistici cattolici, ma l'esame stilistico della sua poesia conferma che il barocco metafisico inglese è sostanzialmente creazione autonoma della grande stagione barocca europea" (p. 92). Stresses, in particular, Crashaw's ability to use the language of sensual, human love to express sacred love: "È questo forse l'aspetto più spettacolare della poesia crashawiana, e il cui valore viene spesso esaltato dalla critica" (p. 108). Concludes that the religious theme of Crashaw's poetry "è si sorreto da un sentimento di estrema sincerità, le capacità espressive hanno bensì una illimite possibilità d'invenzione," but perhaps Crashaw "non riesce mai a superare totalmente la convenzione poetica, sì che un sospetto di secentismo aleggia sin nei più sinceri brani di poesia, donde il continuo richiamo del critico al concetto, alla rettorica, al grottesco, alla esagerazione, al tema d'obbligo, al linguaggio sensuoso, all' espressione miracolosa, e insomma a tutte quelle caratterizzazioni che impediscono a questa poesia quell'attributo che, nonostante le poetiche d'ogni tempo, è il coronamento dello sforza della grande poesia, l'attributo della bellezza assoluta" (p. 109).

◄§ 833. Hocke, Gustave René. *Manierismus in der Literatur: Sprach-Alchimie und esoterische Kombinationskunst.* (Rowohlts deutsche Enzyklopädie, gen. ed. Ernesto Grassi.) Reinbek bei Hamburg: Rowohlt Taschenbuch Verlag. 341p.
Reprinted, 1967, 1969.
Translated by Raffaele Zanasi into Italian: *Il manerismo nella letteratura,* La cultura, storia, critica, testi, vol. 103 (Milan: Casa Editrice Il Saggiatore, 1965); reprinted, Milan: Garzanti, 1975.
Briefly discusses Crashaw as a Mannerist and Marinist. Suggests that Crashaw is more exuberant and more mystical than Donne and calls "A Hymn to Sainte Teresa" one of the greatest English poems of the baroque period, comparable to the works of Lubrano, Góngora, and Marino. Briefly discusses the musical qualities of Crashaw's poetry and comments on his uses of images of sound. Translates into German two stanzas of "The Weeper" (pp. 288–89).

◄§ 834. Kranz, Gisbert. "Crashaw," in *Christliche Literatur der Neuzeit,* 66–68. (Der Christ in der Welt. Eine Enzyklopädie. XIV Reihe. Die Christliche Literatur, 3 Band.) Aschaffenburg: Paul Pattloch Verlag.
Rev. ed., *Europas Christliche Literatur,* 1500–1960 (Aschaffenburg: Paul

Pattloch Verlag, 1961), 113–15; reprinted as *Europas Christliche Literatur von 1500 bis heute* (Munich: Ferdinand Schöningh, 1968). Translated by J. R. Foster as *Three Centuries of Christian Literature* (London: Burns and Oates, 1961) and as *Modern Christian Literature* (New York: Hawthorn Books, 1961), 71–73.

Comments on the relation of the worldly and the spiritual in Crashaw's poetry and discusses his uses of imagery, paradox, oxymoron, and antithesis. Suggests that the prominent feature of Crashaw's verse is "seine Innigkeit und Wärme" (p. 67). Acknowledges that much of Crashaw's poetry is alien to modern taste but maintains that his enthusiasm and fervor are genuine. Points out that much of Crashaw's religious poetry attempts to reconcile heaven and earth but notes that he wrote several poems about nature that are filled with genuine emotion and reflect a baroque joy in the beauty of this world. Stresses the influence of St. Teresa: "So erweckte die Spanierin Theresia den Engländern einen geistlichen Lyriker, der mit dem Höhenflug seines Geistes, mit seiner unerhörten Einbildungskraft, seiner ekstatischen Glut und seiner bewegten Farbigkeit der grösse seiner Zeit wurde" (pp. 66–67).

✒ 835. Kusunose, Toshihiko. "Richard Crashaw's Poetry and Steps to Loreto." Kansei-gakuin University, *Ronkō* no. 6: 153–74.

Revised version included in *Shi to Shin* [Poetry and Faith] (entry 1038).

Presents a general survey of Crashaw's life and poetry, stressing the fundamentally Catholic nature of his religious sensibility and art. Discusses the major themes of Crashaw's poetry and comments on the general characteristics of his art, especially its emotionalism and optimism and its uses of sensuous images and metaphors. Maintains that, contrary to what many critics suggest, Crashaw's life and his poetry reveal much personal inner affliction and agony. Briefly contrasts Crashaw to Southwell, Donne, Herbert, Vaughan, and the classical Latin poets.

✒ 836. Untermeyer, Louis. "After the Renaissance," in *Lives of the Poets: The Story of One Thousand Years of English and American Poetry,* 137–69. New York: Simon and Schuster; London: W. H. Allen.

Reprinted in paperback, New York: Simon and Schuster, 1963.

Biographical sketch of Crashaw followed by a general evaluation of his poetry (pp. 142–44). Contrasts Crashaw with Herbert: "Where Herbert is restrained, Crashaw reflects Italian and Spanish intemperance; where Herbert is a strict observer of ceremony, never confusing ritual and religion, Crashaw wallows in the debris as well as the excessive decoration of theatrical properties" (p. 143). Calls Crashaw's work "rococo" and observes that his poetry "is so ornate, so overembellished, that it is sometimes hard to see the poetry because of the words" (p. 143). Maintains that Crashaw's imagery is "alternately gorgeous and grotesque" and suggests that some of his religious poems "are so inflated that what begins to be grandiose becomes ludicrous" (p. 143). Maintains that the most successful are the Teresian poems, in which "the abstractions and cloudy metaphors are blown away in a sweep of pure exaltation" (p. 144).

1960

✒ 837. Bennett, Joan. *Four Metaphysical Poets: Donne, Herbert, Vaughan, Crashaw. With an Anthology of Their Poetry Especially Selected for the Vintage Edition.* New York: Vintage Books (Random House). 233, viip. Reprinted, 1965.

A reprint of the corrected second edition (1957) of *Four Metaphysical Poets: Donne, Herbert, Vaughan, Crashaw* (first published in 1934; entry 552), with selections from their poetry. Includes four poems by Crashaw (pp. 217–33) without notes or additional commentary: "Wishes. To his (supposed) Mistresse," "On Mr. G. Herberts booke, The Temple," "A Hymn to Sainte Teresa," and "The Flaming Heart."

✒ 838. Claydon, Sister Margaret. *Richard Crashaw's Paraphrases of the Vexilla Regis, Stabat Mater, Adoro Te, Lauda Sion, Dies Irae, O Gloriosa Domina.* Washington, D.C.: The Catholic University of America Press. 167p.

Published Ph.D. dissertation. Analyzes in detail Crashaw's paraphrases of six medieval Latin hymns to show that, far from being mere translations, they are completely new poems with "entirely new emphases" (p. vii). Chapter 1 (pp. 1–10) presents a brief history of the nature and development of the six Latin hymns and maintains that, whereas they exhibit wide differences in tone and structure, Crashaw's paraphrases possess "basic likenesses" and are clearly "poems typical of a particular style and era" (p. 10). Calls Crashaw a *sine qua non* example of baroque style and sensibility and maintains that his uses of conceits, metaphors, and hyperboles produce a "poetry which appeals to the senses, the imagination, the emotions" (p. 10). In chapters 2–7 discusses the history and stylistic characteristics of each of the Latin hymns and shows how Crashaw's renditions differ greatly from the originals: "Sancta Maria Dolorum" (pp. 11–30), "Adoro Te" (pp. 31–51), "Laudia Sion Salvatorem" (pp. 52–77), "Dies Irae" (pp. 78–99), "O Gloriosa Domina" (pp. 100–110), and "Vexilla Regis" (pp. 111–31). Chapter 8 (pp. 132–37) summarizes the conclusions of the preceding analyses. Notes that Crashaw's paraphrases reflect Counter-Reformation spirituality and modes of meditation; are characterized by extensive use of personification, the imperative mood, exclamatory utterances, the active rather than passive voice, the present and future tenses rather than the past; and especially rely upon an abundance of adjectives to attain their emotive and affective meanings. Defends Crashaw against the charge that his conceits are too ingenious, too daring, and often forced, by pointing out that he simply follows the traditional imagery of the

Church and uses conceits in order to attempt "to utter the ineffable" and "to convey supernatural truths by natural means" (p. 136). Stresses that, whereas the Latin hymns are "predominantly static, expository, cognitive, [and] objective," the center of-interest of which is the exposition of doctrine, Crashaw's renditions tend to be "dynamic, dramatic, affective, [and] subjective" and that, although paradox, oxymoron, and hyperbole "are not found in the medieval poems to any extent," in Crashaw's paraphrases they are "part of the whole texture of the poems" (p. 135). Appendix 1 (pp. 138–39) contains two charts comparing the Latin hymns with Crashaw's versions: (1) Means used to achieve dynamic, dramatic emphasis (imperative mood, personification, present or future tense, past tense, active voice, passive voice) and (2) means used to achieve the emotive and affective emphasis (adjectival occurrences, exclamatory utterances, and change in address). Appendix 2 (pp. 140–58) gives the Latin versions of the six hymns and Crashaw's paraphrases. Selected bibliography (pp. 159–62) and index (pp. 163–67).

≈§ 839. Daiches, David. "Poetry after Spenser: The Jonsonian and the Metaphysical Traditions," in A *Critical History of English Literature*, 1: 346–89. New York: Ronald Press Co.

2d ed., London: Secker & Warburg, 1969; reprinted, New York: Ronald Press, 1970.

General survey and evaluation of Crashaw's poetry (pp. 371–73). Maintains that Crashaw has "none of Herbert's quietly controlled cunning in developing a Christian theme at the same time personally and publicly" and that "his pressing of all the senses into the service of the expression of religious passion, his use of erotic and other images of physical appetite in a deliberately paradoxical religious sense, his relish of extravagant paradox involving the secular and the divine, tears and ecstasy, the sensuous and the spiritual, show not so much the union of passion and thought which is characteristic of Donne as the deliberate search for startling and paradoxical expression which will shock and excite the reader" (pp. 371–72). Observes that Crashaw, "with a lushness of religious experience which is typical of one aspect of the Counter Reformation throughout Europe, explores with an almost feverish enthusiasm every way of presenting the spiritual world in sensuous terms" (p. 372). Suggests that "A Hymn to Sainte Teresa" reveals Crashaw "at his most concentrated and intense" and maintains that the strength and power of the poem "are beyond anything else in his poetry" (p. 373). Relates Crashaw to the Continental baroque movement and concludes that "whether one considers the whole movement a disease or a laudable extension of the scope of figurative language depends perhaps on individual taste and sensibility" (p. 373). Briefly compares and/or contrasts Crashaw to Southwell, Donne, and Herbert.

≈§ 840. Ellrodt, Robert. L'*Inspiration personnelle et l'esprit du temps chez les poètes métaphysiques anglais*. Paris: José Corti. 2 parts in 3 vols.

Part 1 (vols. 1–2), 2d ed. (with new bibliography), 1973. General introduction (pp. 14–77) reviews various definitions of metaphysical poetry using certain historical, stylistic, and psychological grounds and dismisses each as inadequate. Presents a tentative definition of metaphysical poetry and concludes that, since the metaphysical conceit comes from "la perplexité de l'esprit en présence des contradictions inhérentes à l'existence," Herbert, Donne, and Marvell "sont les vrais «poètes métaphysiques»", car leur poésie reproduit la démarche même et l'inquiétude du métaphysicien" (p. 30). Part 1, "Les Structures fondamentales de l'inspiration personnelle," is divided into two volumes. Volume 1, "John Donne et les poètes de la tradition chrétienne" is subdivided into two books: "John Donne" (pp. 80–264) and "Les Poètes de la tradition chrétienne" (pp. 265–452). In the second book, one chapter is devoted to Crashaw (pp. 375–449) and has four major sections, in addition to a biographical sketch (pp. 375–76): (1) "Le Mode de sensibilité fondamental" (pp. 377–98), (2) "L'Univers de Crashaw" (pp. 399–415), (3) "Le paradoxe et les mystères chrétiens" (pp. 416–28), and (4) "Les divers modes d'expression et la sincérité artistique" (pp. 429–49). Calls Crashaw "le plus grand poète lyrique du XVIIe siècle" but notes that "son lyrisme tend à l'impersonnalité" (p. 377). Focuses on Crashaw's religious lyricism and on his desire to lose himself in the beloved: "la conscience de Crashaw . . . n'aspire qu'à se projeter hors d'elle même" (p. 378). Points out a development in Crashaw's poetry toward an increasing purity of sentiment and sublimation of sexuality, noting that the later poems are more joyous and triumphant than the earlier ones. Discusses in some detail Crashaw's religious sensibility but concludes that he was probably not a mystic. Comments on Crashaw's uses of images, especially images of liquidity; his lack of irony and humor; his sense of wonder; his sincerity; and his uses of symbols, paradoxes, and conceits. Analyzes also Crashaw's perceptions of space and time and maintains that his art is musical in that it presents "des mouvements de l'âme que toute perception éxcite en nous" (p. 415) in the same way music does. Suggests that Crashaw's problem was his visual imagination and that his conceits are "ces fautes de goût" (p. 433). Maintains that the evolution seen in Crashaw's images reflects his movement from "la sensualité mystique" to "une spiritualité authentique" (p. 437). Concludes that, although Crashaw is predominantly a Christian poet, his egotism prevented his Christianity from being totally Christocentric. Volume 2 of part 1 is divided into two books: "Poètes de transition" (pp. 9–170) and "Poètes mystiques" (pp. 171–399). Throughout compares and contrasts Crashaw to Donne, Herbert, Lord Herbert of Cherbury, Cowley, Vaughan, Marvell, and Traherne. Three tables summarize the major characteristics of the metaphysical poets (pp. 411–12, 416, 422). In part 2 (pp. 9–400) discusses the social, psychological, and literary origins of metaphysical poetry at the turn of the sixteenth century with only brief references to Crashaw.

୶ 841. Fukuchi, Shirō. "Crashaw: Loretto e no Michi" [Crashaw: A Way to Loreto]. *Mie-University Bulletin* 3, no. 1.
Discusses Crashaw's religious sensibility and traces his spiritual development from Anglicanism to Catholicism.

୶ 842. Hoiby, Lee. A *Hymn of the Nativity, for Soprano and Bass Soli, Mixed Chorus and Orchestra, with Text after Richard Crashaw*. New York: G. Ricordi & Co. 91p.
Musical setting for lines selected from the 1646 and 1648 versions of "Hymn in the Holy Nativity" and from the 1648 version of "Hymn in the Glorious Epiphanie."

୶ 843. Judson, Jerome. "On Decoding Homer." *Antioch Review* 20: 479–93.
Discusses the problem of determining tone in a literary work. Suggests that in "Song upon the Bleeding Crucifix" Crashaw intentionally employs humor "to intensify and sharpen tragic feeling" and that "the pathetic inadequacy of words, concepts, imagination, to deal with the tragedy of Christ's bleeding is deliberately part of the poem's effect" and suggests that the poet seems to be saying, "Laugh, if you dare—but this is the blood of God I am talking about—a transcendent paradox in itself. Would naturalism, would taste be sufficient to convey its magnitude?" (p. 486).

୶ 844. Maddison, Carol. "The English Ode," in *Apollo and the Nine: A History of the Ode*, 286–401. Baltimore: Johns Hopkins University Press; London: Routledge and Kegan Paul.
Discusses Crashaw as an Anglo-Latin poet and especially as the first important writer of the English ode (pp. 336–61). Observes that "the bulk of Crashaw's work, and the most important part, is his odes" (pp. 360–61). Critically surveys Crashaw's secular and religious odes and comments on his experimentation with various forms, especially the irregular ode. Points out that Crashaw's odes move from "epigram odes" to "epigram-built emblem book odes" to the irregular ode and suggests that his odes are influenced by Neo-Latin mixed odes and dithyrambs, by vernacular mixed odes, and by Italian madrigals and the Neo-Latin triadic Pindaric. Discusses in some detail "The Weeper," "Hymn in the Glorious Epiphanie," and "The Flaming Heart" and comments in less detail on a number of other poems. Calls the later religious odes "symphonies of adoration" (p. 360). Points out that, because Crashaw was often so very exotic and was also a Catholic, he had little influence in establishing the vogue of ode writing that developed in the mid-seventeenth century. Compares Crashaw to Cowley as an ode writer and discusses Cowley's elegy on the death of Crashaw.

◄§ 845. Miles, Josephine. *Renaissance, Eighteenth-Century, and Modern Language in English Poetry: A Tabular View.* Berkeley and Los Angeles: University of California Press. iii, 73p.

Reprinted, Folcroft, Pa.: Folcroft Library Editions, 1970, 1975; Norwood, Pa.: Norwood Editions, 1976, 1978; Philadelphia: R. West, 1977.

Presents information gathered from two hundred poets, from Chaucer to the present, "in such a way as to suggest the basic patterns of relation between poet and poet in the use of language, and at the same time to provide the most straightforward chronological arrangement of materials for those who may have other questions to ask, about single poets, single eras, single types, or single terms" (p. 1). Tabulates Crashaw's use of language, examining the number of nouns, adjectives, and verbs in the first 1,080 lines from Waller's edition (1904). Also lists the most frequently used adjectives, nouns, and verbs in Crashaw's verse.

◄§ 846. Sayama, Eitarō [Sakae Iwasaki]. *Igirisu Bungaku-shi Taikei* [A Historical Survey of English Literature: 17th Century]. Book 4. Tokyo: Tokyo University Press.

Considers Crashaw a baroque poet, influenced by the religious sensibility and aesthetics of the Counter-Reformation, and questions his being grouped with Donne and Herbert as a metaphysical poet (pp. 85–89). Comments especially on Crashaw's uses of sensual imagery, symbolic metaphors, and paradox and observes that his emotional flights, lyrical rhapsody, and mystical exaltation will appear alien to most Japanese readers.

◄§ 847. Schlauch, Margaret. "Angielscy poeci metafizyczni 17 wieku" [English Metaphysical Poets in the Seventeenth Century]. *PHum* 4 & 5:47–74.

Discusses the nature of baroque poetry and suggests that its main features are intensity, ecstasy, animation, and a particular sensibility, all of which can best be summarized by the word *exaltation*. Briefly discusses Crashaw as a baroque poet, suggesting that certain of his themes can be profitably compared to baroque painting and sculpture; his Teresian poems, for example, can be compared to Bernini's statue of the saint in Rome. Points out Crashaw's use of paradox and antithesis in "Hymn in the Holy Nativity."

◄§ 848. Wallis, P. J. "William Crashawe, The Sheffield Puritan." *Transactions of the Hunter Archaeological Society* 8 (1960–1963): 37–49, 111–21, 169–93, 245–62.

Reprinted, with addenda and index, as a monograph, 1963. 77p.

Presents a biographical study of William Crashaw, the father of the poet, and surveys his printed sermons and polemical writings. Reproduces his 1621 will (pp. 41–49), much of which is given to denouncing Roman Catholicism and to professing his Christian faith. Gives a genealogical chart of the

Crashaw family (p. 40) and comments briefly on the date of Richard Crashaw's birth (p. 179). Presents a bibliography of the works of William Crashaw (pp. 247–62).

◄§ 849. White, Helen C. *Poetry and Prayer*. (Wimmer Lecture VIII.) Latrobe, Pa.: Archabbey Press. viii, 59p.

Suggests that if asked to contribute to an anthology of "religious horrors" she would be tempted to include Crashaw's description of the weeping eyes of St. Mary Magdalene in "The Weeper" ("Two walking baths; two weeping motions; / Portable, and compendious oceans") but if asked to contribute to an anthology of "the sublimest verse in English literature" she would include the conclusion of "The Flaming Heart" (p. 58). Observes that "ecstasy is a brittle business in poetry as in life" and that "we are wise today to be chary of it when it can produce such atrocities as the description of the Magdalene's eyes, but it would be a pity if we laughed another Crashaw—if there could be another Crashaw—out of his progress from Mary Magdalene to Santa Teresa, and a tragedy if our more rationally disciplined imaginations lost their capacity to rise to the height of that praise of Santa Teresa" (p. 51).

1961

◄§ 850. Alvarez, A[lfred]. *The School of Donne*. London: Chatto & Windus.

Reprinted, New York: Pantheon Books, 1962; New American Library, 1967; London: Chatto & Windus, 1970.

Announces his intent "to show how Donne affected the language and form of poetry in a way that is still peculiarly meaningful to us, and is rapidly becoming yet more meaningful" and "to define a kind of intelligence which, though it was first expressed at the end of the sixteenth century, is still vital and urgent" (p. 12). Argues for the notion of a "School of Donne," united not so much by various poetic methods and techniques as by the intellectual attitude and tone that formed it: the desire to portray dramatically in poetry the complexities of thought and feeling. In Chapter 4, "Metaphysical Rhetoric: Richard Crashaw" (pp. 91–103), argues that Crashaw belongs to the "School of Donne" "only because it is difficult to see where else in the English Tradition he belongs" and that, although he occasionally echoes both Herbert and Donne, the resemblances "are rarely important and have nothing to do with his unique quality" (p. 91). Admits that Crashaw's poetry is uneven but points out that "there are moments when he sounds like one of the greatest poets in the language" (p. 92). Maintains that essentially Crashaw "was a Continental poet writing in English" and "was the forbear not of Hopkins but of Poe" (pp. 92–93). Discusses Crashaw's uses of rhetoric, symbols, images, conceits, and paradoxes and finds in his poetry a clash "between an ornamental logical ingenuity and an overall impressionism" as well as between "precise effects and what seem to be imprecise feelings" (pp. 96–97). Calls Crashaw's use of imagery "centrifugal" and contrasts it with Shakespeare's "centripetal" use: "The more Shakespeare adds image to image, the more sharply he defines the feelings which give rise to them; the more complex he is, the more accurate," whereas Crashaw's images "recede from focus" and "imaginative rightness gives way to a perverse logic of ornamentation" (p. 94). Maintains that Crashaw "expressed himself so completely through his technical devices that extreme passion automatically meant extreme artifice" and the result was "some of the most artificial verse in the language" (p. 101). Calls Crashaw a "ritualistic poet" (p. 98) and comments on the public nature of his verse, contrasting it to the private nature of the works of Donne, Herbert, and Vaughan. Discusses specifically "The Teare," "On the wounds of our crucified Lord," "The Weeper," and "Letter to the Countess of Denbigh," calling the last his "most perfect and most mature" poem and claiming that it is, "in its flexible, subtle and wide-ranging intelligence, nearest to the style of Donne" (p. 103). Discusses the relationship between metaphysical and baroque styles. Compares and/or contrasts Crashaw with Shakespeare, Donne, Herbert, Vaughan, Southwell, Giles Fletcher, Quarles, Marvell, and Marino.

◆§ 851. Bamonte, Gerardo. "La poesia barocca in Inghilterra," in *Poeti dell'età barocca*, with a preface by Giancinto Spagnoletti, 523–637, 656–57. (Collezione Fenice, diretta da Attilio Bertolucci, 49.) Parma: Ugo Guanda.

Reprinted in 2 vols., Milan: Garzanti, 1973, 2:189–303, 312–13.

A general discussion of English baroque poetry (pp. 523–35), followed by selections from the poets, with Italian translations on facing pages (pp. 536–637). Includes Crashaw's "Wishes. To his (supposed) Mistresse," "The Weeper," two stanzas from "Song upon the Bleeding Crucifix," and the conclusion of "The Flaming Heart" (pp. 576–95). Calls Crashaw "il poeta metafisico che meglio rientra nella cornice barocca" (p. 531) and comments on the baroque features of his style. Includes a biographical note (p. 656).

◆§ 852. Banzer, Judith. "'Compound Manner': Emily Dickinson and the Metaphysical Poets." *AL* 32:417–33.

Argues that Dickinson, like the metaphysical poets, "practiced the metaphysical awareness of the unity of experience" and that "the discipline that wrought many of her poems was the metaphysical one of a 'Compound Vision,' by which the eternal is argued from the transient, the foreign explained by the familiar, and fact illuminated by mystery" (p. 417). Comments on Dickinson's familiarity with the metaphysical poets and notes that "her pencil-markings of several poems argue close attention to their vision and technique" (p. 418). Suggests an influence of Crashaw on Dickinson and points out that during her most creative years she had access to a number of works containing poems by Crashaw. Notes, for example, that in Edward Dickinson's copy of Robert Chambers's *Cyclopedia of English Literature* (entry 165) "the Vaughan

section, like that of Crashaw, is well-thumbed and creased from right to left"
(p. 431).

❧ 853. Collmer, Robert G. "The Meditation on Death and Its Appearance
in Metaphysical Poetry." *Neophil* 45:323–33.

Discusses the *meditatio mortis* tradition and comments on some of its appearances in the poetry of Crashaw, Donne, Herbert, and Vaughan. Suggests
that Crashaw, as well as other poets influenced by the Catholic mystical tradition, "provides the choicest examples of devotional exaltation induced by
meditation on death" and points out that in his poems "we find many passages
referring to the possibility of entering upon some aspects of death before
dying" (p. 328). Maintains that because of his mystical tendencies Crashaw
"never concerns himself with the mundanities of physical dying" but rather
"his interest is in the present possibility of union with God" (p. 331). Compares and contrasts Crashaw with Donne, Herbert, and Vaughan.

❧ 854. Dalglish, Jack. *Eight Metaphysical Poets*. Edited with an introduction and notes by Jack Dalglish. New York: Macmillan; London:
Heinemann. viii, 184p.

Reprinted, 1963, 1965, 1970.

General introduction to the nature and style of metaphysical poetry (pp.
1–10). Considers the intellectual and introspective nature of much of metaphysical poetry, its fusion of thought and feeling, its uses of imagery and conceits, its verse movement and dramatic qualities, and so on. Anthologizes
poems by Donne, Herbert, Carew, Crashaw, Vaughan, King, Marvell, and
Cowley. Includes "Loves Horoscope," "Adoro Te," and "A Hymn to Sainte
Teresa" (pp. 61–70) with commentary and notes on individual poems (pp.
155–58). In the notes for Crashaw presents a biographical sketch and a brief
essay on general features of his poetry, such as ornamental conceits, passionate lyrical intensity and eloquence, sensuous and erotic imagery, and musical
facility. Maintains that Crashaw is quite unlike Donne and Herbert and is a
very uneven poet, "lacking in discipline and critical sensibility," and that at
times his conceits "are impossibly extravagant" and his "sensuous sweetness
becomes cloying" (p. 157).

❧ 855. Fukuchi, Shirō. "Crashaw: Teresa Sanka" [Crashaw: Saint Teresa].
Mie-University Bulletin 4, no. 1:33–45.

Translates into Japanese "A Hymn to Sainte Teresa." Comments on the per-
vading influence of the saint on Crashaw's life and art and discusses his religious sensibility. Briefly discusses Francis Thompson's criticism of Crashaw.

❧ 856. Goldfarb, Russell M. "Crashaw's 'Suppose He Had Been Tabled at
Thy Teates.'" *Expl* 19: item 35.

Reprinted in *The Explicator Cyclopedia* (Chicago: Quadrangle Books, 1968), 2:95.

Points out that "Luke 11: Blessed be the paps which Thou hast sucked" is addressed to "the certain woman" who speaks to Christ as recorded in Luke 11:27, not to the Virgin Mary, as William Empson suggests (entry 509). Maintains that the poem is resolved in a simple paradox: "The woman, no matter how hungry, would not feel what Jesus ate at her breast, and after Jesus himself becomes Man's source of nourishment because of his bloody death, the woman, Mary, and all mothers must get nourishment from Jesus," while "he, in turn, will not hunger after what they take from Him." Calls Empson's interpretation "a strange Freudian dance, more grotesque than the music Crashaw piped."

◆§ 857. Hollander, John. *The Untuning of the Sky: Ideas of Music in English Poetry*, 1500–1700. Princeton: Princeton University Press. xii, 467p. Reprinted, 1970.

Discusses certain beliefs about the nature and function of music during the Renaissance and about how English poetry of the sixteenth and seventeenth centuries expressed and employed these beliefs. Describes "the successive stages in the de-mythologizing of poetry's view of music" (p. 19) and suggests that "from the canonical Medieval Christian view that all actual human music bears a definite relation to the eternal, abstract (and inaudible) 'music' of universal order, to the completely de-Christianized, use of such notions in late seventeenth-century poetry as decorative metaphor and mere turns of wit, a gradual process of disconnection between abstract musical mythology and concrete practical considerations of actual vocal and instrumental music occurs" (p. 19). One section of Chapter 4, "What Passions Cannot Music Raise and Quell?" (pp. 220–38), discusses the wide range of musical images, figures, and terminology as well as the more generalized musical effects in "Musicks Duell." Suggests that, "if ever an elaborate, even overexpressive representation of the musical theory of the passions seems to stand out above all others," then "it is surely in the work of the avowedly Baroque poet, Richard Crashaw" (p. 223). Calls "Musicks Duell" Crashaw's most successful secular poem and an outstanding example of baroque style and suggests that "it remains a model of a kind of propriety seldom attained by the practice of so extravagant a style" (p. 223). Discusses seventeenth-century fondness for poems about the nightingale, compares and contrasts Crashaw's version with Strada's original, and comments extensively on the artistry of "Musicks Duell," pointing out, for example, that the poem "fairly overflows with technical musical language, ranging from items of general musical usage to terms which remain today in the arcana of the lutenist's specialized vocabulary" (p. 228) and contains many "actual references to the practice of lute playing" and even the "visual phenomena of written notation" (p. 229). Concludes that "it was Crashaw's accomplishment not only to record increasingly a current view of music as passion, but to imitate its production and effects, transforming material facts of music-making and human feeling in another domain, none the more ethereal for being more general" (pp. 237–38).

◀§ 858. Izzo, Carlo. *Storia della letteratura inglese.* Vol. 1: *Dalle origini alla restaurazione.* (Storia delle letterature di tutto il mondo, directed by Antonio Viscardi.) Milan: Nuova Accademia Editrice. 622p.

General introduction to Crashaw's life and poetry (pp. 480–83). Comments on the baroque features of Crashaw's art, especially his use of images of human love and passion to convey his love for God and the saints. Suggest that the conclusion of "The Flaming Heart" gives one "un'idea dello slancio lirico di cui egli è capace quando il fuoco della fede e della concitazione poetica brucia e annulla nel suo calore quanto di goffo, e persino di grottesco, presenta lo sfrenato barocchismo cui ricorrono le sue ineguali capacità creative nelle depressioni più artificiosamente letterarie del suo poetare" (p. 481). Cites "Wishes. To his (supposed) Mistresse" as Crashaw's best secular poem, calling it "deliziosa" and "particolarmente felice anche nel metro" (p. 482).

◀§ 859. Leishman, J. B. "Some Themes and Variations in the Poetry of Andrew Marvell." *PBA* 47:223–41.

Briefly points out that Marvell's descriptions and images often have "both the colour and the crystalline purity of Crashaw's, but, although he is free from Crashaw's not infrequent mawkishness and sentimentality, he also lacks both Crashaw's child-like tenderness and his rapture" (p. 224). Maintains that Marvell's early poems indicate that he was more likely a disciple of Crashaw and the Neo-Latin epigrammatists whom Crashaw imitated than of Donne. Claims that Marvell's "Eyes and Tears" was suggested by "The Weeper" and finds certain allusions in the poem that seem to be borrowed directly from Crashaw's poem.

◀§ 860. McCann, Eleanor. "Oxymora in Spanish Mystics and English Metaphysical Writers." *CL* 13:16–25.

Discusses the use of oxymora by such English metaphysical poets as Crashaw, Southwell, Donne, Vaughan, and Joseph Beaumont and suggests that they were influenced directly or indirectly by the great Spanish mystics. Points out that the oxymoron "was the most natural way of expressing a core idea of Spanish mysticism: that the great unifying force of God's love blots out apparent contrarieties in the mind of the truly devout" (p. 16) and observes that certain of the traditional oxymora "were directly transplanted, others hybridized after arriving by ingenious methods of seed dispersal into the English soul-garden" (p. 25). Points out specific oxymora and paradoxes that Crashaw borrowed from the mystical writings of St. Teresa, St. John of the Cross, and Diego de Estella, such as "dying life," "sweet wounds of love," "blind sight," and the "wholesome, healing shaft or dart of love," as well as paradoxes of light-dark, the ladder, and the blending of fire and water.

◄§ 861. Nelson, Lowry, Jr. *Baroque Lyric Poetry*. New Haven and London: Yale University Press. viii, 244p.
Reprinted, 1963; New York: Octagon Books, 1979.
Pages 6–15 reprinted in *The Metaphysical Poets: Key Essays on Metaphysical Poetry and the Major Metaphysical Poets*, ed. Frank Kermode (entry 980), 88–96.
Through a close examination of some of the major poems of the period discusses the features of the European literary baroque and sees it as the prevailing literary style in England and on the Continent from the late 1500s to the late 1600s. Dissociates the baroque from the Counter-Reformation and from the other arts and concentrates primarily on the structure of poems rather than on imagery. Discusses in some detail new and complex manipulations of time in the poems and comments extensively on their varied uses of dramatic elements. Maintains that "those who speak of the Baroque style in poetry as decadence or disease are guilty of a number of misconceptions" and "usually they make Baroque too narrow and find it only in the most extravagant works of poets like Marino, Crashaw, and Góngora" and usually define it "only in terms of the conceits or other rhetorical devices" (p. 161). Mentions Crashaw in several instances. Discusses in particular his uses of time, especially in "Musicks Duell," a poem that "departs from the usual narrative technique and works out a structure in terms of a progression of tenses" (p. 55). Shows how the poem has "an unexpected structuring in the progression from past to historical present to actual present" (p. 55). Briefly compares Crashaw and Góngora in their use of tenses.

◄§ 862. Pagnini, Marcello, ed. *Lirici carolini e repubblicani* (Collana di letterature moderne, 15.) Naples: Edizione scientifiche italiane. xii, 420p.
Anthology of seventeenth-century English lyrical poetry for the Italian reader. Contains a general introduction as well as critical comments on each of the poets included (pp. 3–40). Textual note (pp. 41–42) and a selected bibliography of critical works on the period and on individual poets (pp. 43–51). Includes a biographical sketch of Crashaw and a list of editions of his works, followed by heavily annotated texts of five poems—"Wishes. To his (supposed) Mistresse," "The Weeper," "An Epitaph upon a Young Married Couple," "A Hymn to Sainte Teresa" and a selection from "The Flaming Heart" (pp. 161–92). Texts in English; introduction and notes in Italian.

◄§ 863. Poulet, Georges. "L'époque baroque," in *Les métamorphoses du cercle*, 22–48. Paris: Librairie Plon.
Reprinted, Paris: Flammarion, 1979.

Translated into English by Carley Dawson and Elliott Coleman in collaboration with the author (Baltimore: Johns Hopkins University Press, 1967), 15–31.

Calls Crashaw "le plus dramatique de tous les poètes baroques" (p. 28) and briefly discusses his uses of the circle in "An Elegy upon the Death of Mr. Stanninow" and the bubble in "Bulla," in which "un gonflement sphérique illusoire se dissipe, et tout retourne au rien" (p. 30). Comments on how Crashaw's use of such figures reflects the philosophical preoccupations of baroque art and sensibility.

⋙ 864. Reeves, James. "The Seventeenth Century: Donne and the Metaphysicals," in *A Short History of English Poetry, 1340–1940*, 75–88. London: Heinemann.

Reprinted, New York: E. P. Dutton, 1962, 1964.

Brief introduction to Crashaw's life and poetry. Claims that his best devotional poems are unsurpassed and suggests that "nowhere perhaps outside the plays of Marlowe is to be found the note of sustained and rapturous ecstasy we hear in the address to Saint Teresa in *The Flaming Heart*" (p. 82). Comments briefly on Crashaw's reputation and notes that his poems can be understood only in the context of baroque flamboyancy. Points out that even in "The Weeper" there are beautiful lines and that if some of the images and metaphors appear un-English, that does not make them unpoetic.

⋙ 865. Rickey, Mary Ellen. *Rhyme and Meaning in Richard Crashaw*. Lexington: University of Kentucky Press. 98 [1]p.

Reprinted, New York: Haskell House, 1973.

Discusses Crashaw's highly conscious use of rhyme and stanza patterns to shape and structure his poems. In the introduction (pp. 1–4) argues that Crashaw "not only liked rhyme patterning in general, but he enjoyed repeating certain specific rhyme words" and maintains that the rhymes recur in his poems "because of connotations which they acquired for Crashaw and because he could insert substantial volumes of meaning and emotion into a passage of verse by using some of these charged rhyme words" (p. 3). In Chapter 1, "Crashaw's Rhyme Vocabulary" (pp. 5–24), lists and comments on Crashaw's favorite rhyme words and argues that certain word combinations and rhymes became for him personal symbols. In Chapter 2, "Crashaw's Early Use of Rhyme: Epigrams and Secular Poems" (pp. 25–36), examines the poet's youthful, imitative verse to show that his uses of repetition in these poems, "regardless of how clever or effective, do not attempt the more elaborate patterns which are the hallmark of his later verse" and thus "form no significant designs" (p. 36). In Chapter 3, "The Verse of *Steps to the Temple* and *Carmen Deo Nostro*" (pp. 37–61), discusses Crashaw's mature religious poems, especially "Charitas Nimia," "Ode on a Prayer-book," "Hymn to the Name of Jesus," and "A Hymn to Sainte Teresa," to show that his uses of rhyme "are unobtrusive but firm emphases of the structures of the poems and hence of their logical force, but their very nature gives the verse an appearance of flexibility and spontaneity which at once intensifies the emotional climax that each poem reaches, and yet belies the labor of the poet in the expression of his emotion" (p. 61). In Chapter 4, "Crashaw's Rhyme Revisions" (pp. 62–76), surveys rhyme revisions in Crashaw's poems that appear in more than one version, such as "Song upon the Bleeding Crucifix," "The Weeper," and "Letter to the Countess of Denbigh," to show that "he discards some kinds of imperfect rhymes, conceals some end rhymes, eliminates the lines of demarcation between irregular stanzas, and retains some rhyme words even while fundamentally changing the import of the lines in which they occur" (p. 76). In Chapter 5, "Some Backgrounds of Crashaw's Technique" (pp. 77–91), comments briefly on the poet's indebtedness to the Italian poets (especially Marino, Tasso, and Guarini), to such devotional exercises as Lancelot Andrewes's *Private Devotions,* and to his poetic predecessors (especially Herbert, Joseph Beaumont, and Carew). Suggests that "the remarkable thing about Crashaw's borrowings is that their sum total makes his verse unlike that of any of his poetic models," for "he assimilated, not merely copied, the techniques which he found" (p. 91). In the conclusion (pp. 92–93) briefly reviews the preceding chapters and stresses that Crashaw's poems clearly show his "particularly keen concentration on matters of form, structure, and management of sound" and that "his handling of rhymes, both in their selection and arrangement, demonstrates care and skill" (p. 92). Notes (pp. 95–98) followed by an index of Crashaw's poems discussed in the text.

◆§ 866. Sanesi, Roberto, ed. *Poeti metafisici inglesi del Seicento.* (Collezione Fenice, gen. ed. Attilio Bertolucci, no. 45.) Parma: Guanda. 2d ed. (revised and augmented), 1976.

General introduction to the poetry of the period (pp. vii–xvi), with selections from Donne, Lord Herbert of Cherbury, Aurelian Townshend, Henry King, Quarles, Herbert, Carew, Davenant, Crashaw, Cleveland, Marvell, Vaughan, and Traherne. English and Italian on facing pages. Includes "Psalme 137," "Epitaph upon a Young Married Couple," "Wishes. To his (supposed) Mistresse," "Upon two greene Apricockes," "Letter to the Countess of Denbigh," "A Hymn to Sainte Teresa," and the conclusion to "The Flaming Heart" (pp. 146–83). In the notes (pp. 264–68), gives a biographical sketch, a brief bibliography, and notes on individual poems. Second edition adds "On the wounds of our crucified Lord" and "On our crucified Lord Naked, and bloody."

◆§ 867. Souris, André, comp. and arr. *Poèmes de Donne, Herbert et Crashaw mis en musique par leurs contemporains G. Coperario, A. Ferrabosco, J. Wilson, W. Corkine, J. Hilton.* Transcriptions et réalisation par André Souris après des recherches effectuées sur les sources par John Cutts.

Introduction par Jean Jacquot. Paris: Editions du centre national de la recherche scientifique. xix, 26, 10p.

Comments briefly in the introduction on Crashaw's life and poetry, notes the influence of Marino and Strada, and discusses "Musicks Duell" and the two seventeenth-century musical settings contained in this collection. Presents John Wilson's musical setting for "Out of the Italian ('Love now no fire hath left him')" (Bodleian Library Ms. Mus. b 1 ff. 138v–139) and an anonymous contemporary musical setting of "A Song ('Lord, when the sense of thy sweet grace')" (Bodleian Library Ms. Don. c. 57, f. 68).

◄§ 868. Sudo, Nobuo. "Eikoku Shukijo shi-bun-sho" [Extracts from Various Works of Religious Literature], in *Eikoku no Shukyo-bungaku* [Religious Literature in England], 232–306. Tokyo: Shinozaki Shorin.

Cited in A *Bibliography of English Renaissance Studies in Japan*, compiled by Kazuyoshi Enozawa and Miyo Takano (Tokyo: Renaissance Institute, 1979). Not located.

◄§ 869. Turnell, Martin. "The Changing Pattern: Contrasts in Modern and Medieval Poetry," in *Modern Literature and Christian Faith*, 1–21. London: Darton, Longman & Todd.

Discusses the relation between literature and religious faith in six poets from Chaucer to Eliot. Briefly discusses Crashaw's work as a reflection of Counter-Reformation and baroque sensibility. Maintains that baroque art attempts to convert, assimilate, and transform the vitality of the Renaissance into the service of the Church. Suggests that baroque artists' realistic representations of mystical ecstasy and death were attempts "to get as close as possible to the content of experience" but that "in the end this involved a more and more determined appeal to the senses in the attempt—the impossible attempt—to reach through the senses something which lay outside the field of sense-perception" (p. 15). Notes that, like baroque sculpture, Crashaw's poetry "is extremely rich in visual, concrete, physical images" and that "not merely one, but all five of the senses are solicited on every page, almost on every line" (p. 14). See also entry 759.

◄§ 870. Warnke, Frank J. *European Metaphysical Poetry.* (The Elizabethan Club Series, 2.) New Haven and London: Yale University Press. xi, 317p.

Reprinted, 1974.

Pages 5–21 reprinted in *The Metaphysical Poets: Key Essays on Metaphysical Poetry and the Major Metaphysical Poets*, ed. Frank Kermode (entry 980), 97–112.

Anthology of French, German, Dutch, Spanish, and Italian metaphysical poetry. In the introduction (pp. 1–86) distinguishes between baroque and metaphysical style and suggests that the latter is one of several related styles that can be seen within the generic category of the baroque. Maintains that the European metaphysical poets show "the extent to which not only the Baroque style but also its Metaphysical variation ought to be regarded as international phenomena, further manifestations of the real unity of our culture" (p. 4). Defines the baroque as "the dominant European literary style from the late 1500's to the late 1600's, characterized by a general extravagance of language, a tendency to exceed the limits of its medium, and a concern (thematic, but consistently mirrored in technique) with the relations of appearance and reality" and maintains that "the Baroque vision, conditioned by the Reformation and Counter-Reformation quickening of the religious impulse, by the disturbing teachings of the new science, and by a consequent intensification of the conflict between humanism and religion, has as its core a systematic doubt in the validity of appearance, a doubt which expresses itself as an obsessive concern for appearance" (pp. 1–2). Maintains that, although most readers associate metaphysical poetry primarily with Donne, his poetry must not be used exclusively in determining the nature of all metaphysical poetry: "certain of his crucial themes, techniques, and emphases will occur in all Metaphysical poetry, but others will not" (p. 5). Argues that metaphysical poetry "has, when tried on the ear, a 'metaphysical' sound; that is to say, it sounds significantly like the poetry of John Donne," but "each Metaphysical poem has also the unique sound of the individual poet" (p. 5). Discusses some of the characteristic elements of Donne's style and throughout compares and contrasts Crashaw with Donne, Herbert, Vaughan, and Marvell. Argues that all the metaphysical poets "display differing aims and differing sensibilities" but "are united by a set of shared stylistic traits—ingenious metaphor, consistent intellectuality, radically all-inclusive diction, and colloquial tone—and, ultimately, by a shared habit of vision—the tendency to view their experience in the light of total reality, with a consequent concern for metaphysical problems and contradictions" (p. 21). Calls Crashaw "one of the closest English relatives of the Continental High Baroque religious poets" yet maintains that, "if we compare him to the recognized masters of that manner—to Marino, Vondel, even to Giles Fletcher—we find him clearly Metaphysical" (p. 15). Comments on specific features of Crashaw's poetry: its use of sensuous and ornamental detail, its use of sexual imagery in a religious context, its colloquial and even conversational diction, its intellectuality and impersonality, and so on. Compares and contrasts Crashaw with European poets such as Jean de Sponde, Andreas Gryphius, Joost van den Vondel, Johann Scheffler, Jan Luyken, Friedrich von Spee, Heiman Dullaert, Jean de La Ceppède, Théophile de Viau, David Schirmer, Jean-Baptiste Chassignet, Jacobus Revius, and Paul Fleming.

◄§ 871. Willy, Margaret. "Richard Crashaw," in *Three Metaphysical Poets* (Writers and Their Work, no. 134), 7–19, 43–44. London: Longmans, Green and Co.

Reprinted in the American series, British Writers and Their Work, no. 4 (Lincoln: University of Nebraska Press, 1964), 87–103, along with Frank Kermode's *John Donne* (London, New York: Published for the British Council and the National Book League by Longmans, Green, 1957) and T. S. Eliot's *George Herbert* (London, New York: Published for the British Council and the National Book League by Longmans, Green, 1962), with an updated bibliography; reprinted in *British Writers*. Vol. 2: *Thomas Middleton to George Farquhar*, ed. Ian Scott-Kilvert (New York: Charles Scribner's Sons, 1979), 179–84, with an updated bibliography.

Presents a general introduction to Crashaw's life and poetry. Comments on influences on his art, especially the Latin and Greek epigrammatists, the emblem books, Spenser, Marino and the Italian poets, and St. Teresa, and discusses major aspects of his poetry, particularly his use of sensuous and erotic images, his vivid depiction of physical agony in a religious context, and the pictorial and musical qualities of his verse. Points out that "the nest, both as refuge sheltered by parental protection and the nourishing source of all love, is one of the most frequently recurring symbols in Crashaw's work" (p. 13) and notes that "the wounds of martyrdom symbolized for Crashaw the most complete and eloquent physical expression of spiritual love" (p. 14). Comments on Crashaw's use of tear images and notes how he uses images of physical love "to communicate his perceptions of its spiritual and divine counterpart" (p. 12). Calls "A Hymn to Sainte Teresa" one of his "finest and most fully realized poems" and points out that the conclusion of "The Flaming Heart" "rises to a height of lyrical rapture unsurpassed anywhere in Crashaw's works" (p. 15). Suggests that sometimes Crashaw's poetry is extravagant and excessive and plunges into a kind of bathos but notes that "the strong sensuous vein lends his work a special purity, warmth and sweetness; a limpid flow of cadence whose music appeals to the ear as powerfully as its impressions of scent, light and colour entrance the other senses" (p. 17). Concludes that at his best Crashaw "has the vernal freshness, delicacy, and radiance of Botticelli" (p. 19). Selected bibliography (pp. 43–44).

1962

◄§ 872. Abrams, M. H., ed. "Richard Crashaw," in *The Norton Anthology of English Literature*, 1:842–49, 1743. New York: W. W. Norton and Co. 2d ed., 1968; 3d ed., 1974; 4th ed., 1979.

Biographical and critical introduction (pp. 842–43), followed by selections from Crashaw's poetry, including "Hymn in the Holy Nativity," a selection from "The Flaming Heart," "On the wounds of Our Crucified Lord," and six epigrams, with notes. Calls Crashaw "a figure almost unique in English literary history" and points out that "his verse has undergone wildly fluctuating judgments, alternately ridiculed and admired—and usually in extremes—ever since it appeared" (p. 842). Suggests that because of his imitation of Italian models, especially Marino, Crashaw's poems are "deliberately artificial and deliberately lacking formal structure" and maintains that he typically strings his "extravagant metaphors loosely together" and combines them "with almost grotesque effects" (pp. 842–43). Points out that Crashaw's best poems, such as "Hymn in the Holy Nativity" and "The Flaming Heart," culminate "in a swirling, grandiose phantasmagoria of sensual and spiritual ecstasy" and concludes that his verse reminds the reader of the great baroque churches of Rome, "where ornate theatricalities work on every hand to dissolve everyday solidities into a vision of florid, artificial grandeur" (p. 843). Bibliographical note (p. 1743). Third edition has expanded introduction, deletes "Hymn in the Holy Nativity," and adds "Letter to the Countess of Denbigh."

≈§ 873. Artz, Frederick B. "The Baroque, 1600–1750," in *From the Renaissance to Romanticism: Trends in Style in Art, Literature, and Music, 1300–1830*, 158–218. Chicago: University of Chicago Press. Reprinted, 1965, 1975.

Discusses the nature of baroque style in art, literature, and music. Suggests that, in England, Crashaw "represents the essence of the Catholic Baroque spirit" and that "nowhere else in the Baroque period is poetry so close to works like the 'St. Teresa' of Bernini" (p. 196). Maintains that Crashaw is "the most daring of the metaphysical poets in his imagery" and that his long religious lyrics, though uneven, "rise at times to an electric fervor and an ecstatic grandeur" (p. 196). Suggests that Milton, however, is the greatest genius of the baroque in England.

≈§ 874. Bawcutt, N. W. "A Seventeenth-Century Allusion to Crashaw." *N&Q* n.s. 9:215–16.

Points out that in a collection of poems by a group of seventeenth-century Catholics first published by Arthur Clifford in 1813 as *Tixall Poetry* (entry 121) appears a poem entitled "Letters to Mr. Normington" by Edward Thimelby (died circa 1690) that contains two allusions to Crashaw. See also Thimelby (entry 30).

≈§ 875. Berry, Francis. *Poetry and the Physical Voice*. London: Routledge and Kegan Paul; New York: Oxford University Press. x, 205p.

Discusses the importance of vocal sounds in poetry. Contrasts Crashaw's line "Love, thou art Absolute Lord" from "A Hymn to Sainte Teresa" with Marvell's "Had we but world enough, and time" from "To His Coy Mistress" to show that, although metrically identical, Crashaw's line has "an ecclesiastical solemnity" (p. 9, n.) because of his use of long syllables and lower pitch, whereas Marvell's use of short syllables and higher pitch creates the effect of speed. Notes that Crashaw's poem is "public and ceremonial," that it "assumes a vast and splendid congregation," and thus it "should be said more gravely and sonorously than Marvell's" (p. 10). Notes also Crashaw's interest in the use of echo devices in his poetry.

◆§ 876. Finney, Gretchen Ludke. *Musical Backgrounds for English Literature: 1580–1650.* New Brunswick, N.J.: Rutgers University Press. xiii, 292p.

Reprinted, Westport, Conn.: Greenwood Press, 1976.

Discusses musical theory that served as a background to English literature from 1580 to 1650. Points out that "speculative music dealt with the nature of sound, with the position and function of music in the entire system of human knowledge, and with music's usefulness to man" and that "it included, finally, metaphysical speculations on the harmony of the universe, for it was widely taught in the Renaissance that the whole cosmos operates according to musical law" (p. ix). Comments on the development of the poetic image of the world as an instrument, on poets' emphasis on the usefulness of music, and on the relationship between love and music, since both are forms of harmony. Briefly mentions Crashaw's uses of music and musical images, noting, for example, that in "Hymn to the Name of Jesus" he describes the spheres in terms of the "chest" of viols and "sets" of instruments (p. 241, n. 36).

◆§ 877. Hopkins, Kenneth. *English Poetry: A Short History.* Philadelphia and New York: J. B. Lippincott Co. 568p.

Reprinted, Carbondale: Southern Illinois University Press, 1969.

Maintains that, although Crashaw's "stock stands higher than ever before." and although his poems contain "occasional flashes," the bulk of his verse is "a wilderness of unprofitable reading" (p. 116). Suggests that one finds in Crashaw "a feverish and rather unwholesome element underlying many of his ecstasies" and that "he is too preoccupied with blood and tears" (p. 116). Briefly contrasts Crashaw to Herbert and Vaughan.

◆§ 878. Ishii, Shōnosuke. *Eibei Bungakushi Kōza* [History of English and American Literature]. *Book IV* (17th Century). Tokyo: Kenkyusha.

Brief introduction to Crashaw's life and poetry (pp. 42–43). Gives examples from "A Hymn to Sainte Teresa" and "The Weeper" to illustrate Crashaw's use of sensuous imagery, elaborate conceits, wit, and paradox. Suggests that, because of the influence of Marino, Crashaw's poems have a Continental rather than English flavor.

◆§ 879. Keast, William R., ed. *Seventeenth Century English Poetry: Modern Essays in Criticism.* (A Galaxy Book, 89.) London, Oxford, New York: Oxford University Press. 434p.

Rev. ed., 1971.

Collection of previously published items. Includes five general essays on metaphysical poetry: (1) H. J. C. Grierson, "Metaphysical Poetry," from *Metaphysical Lyrics & Poems of the Seventeenth Century* (entry 420), pp. xiii–xxxviii; (2) T. S. Eliot, "The Metaphysical Poets" (entry 417); (3) F. R. Leavis, "The Line of Wit," from *Revaluation: Tradition & Development in English Poetry* (London: Chatto & Windus, 1936, 1949; New York: W. W. Norton

Co., 1947), pp. 10–36; (4) Helen Gardner, "The Metaphysical Poets," from *The Metaphysical Poets* (entry 807), pp. xix–xxxiv; and (5) Joseph Anthony Mazzeo, "A Critique of Some Modern Theories of Metaphysical Poetry" (entry 746). Includes two items specifically on Crashaw: (1) Austin Warren, "Symbolism in Crashaw," from *Richard Crashaw: A Study in Baroque Sensibility*" (entry 619), pp. 176–93; and (2) Robert Martin Adams, "Taste and Bad Taste in Metaphysical Poetry: Richard Crashaw and Dylan Thomas" (entry 770). The revised edition adds Earl Miner's "Wit: Definition and Dialectic," from *The Metaphysical Mode from Donne to Cowley* (entry 984), pp. 118–58, but does not include Adams's or Leavis's essays.

◄§ 880. Praz, Mario. "Il barocco in Inghilterra," in *Manierismo, barocco, rococò: Concetti e termini*, 129–46. (Accademia Nazionale dei Lincei, no. 52: Problemi attuali di scienza e di cultura.) Rome: Accademia Nazionale dei Lincei.
Reprinted in *I Volti del tempo* (Naples: Edizioni Scientifiche Italiane, 1966), 1–26.
Abridged English version, "Baroque in England" (entry 905).
Maintains that in art and architecture the baroque was essentially alien to English sensibility and taste and that, although examples of English baroque art can be found, the baroque period in England was "un episodio, una breve, e in un certo senso splendida aberrazione nella storia dell'arte inglese" (p. 135). Points out, however, that Milton, Beaumont and Fletcher, Dryden, and especially Crashaw were influenced by baroque models. Calls Crashaw the "più inequivocabilmente barocco dei poeti inglesi" (p. 142) and maintains that, because of the strong Continental influence on his poetry, he is closer to the baroque than to the tradition of metaphysical poetry. Maintains that Crashaw's mature religious poetry reflects "l'espressione più alta di quella spiritualizzazione del senso a cui tende la migliore arte barocca" (p. 142). Suggests that Crashaw's religious lyrics can be seen as literary counterparts to the art of Rubens, Murillo, and El Greco. Discusses also the revival of interest in metaphysical poetry in the twentieth century, commenting in some detail on T. S. Eliot.

◄§ 881. Sito, Jerzy S. "Angielska poezja metafizyczna 17 wieku" [English Metaphysical Poetry in the Seventeenth Century]. *Więź* [Connection], 3:50–53.
Briefly comments on the nature of metaphysical poetry and translates into Polish "On our crucified Lord Naked, and bloody."

1963

◄§ 882. Cohen, J. M. *The Baroque Lyric*. London: Hutchinson University Library. 207p.

Calls Crashaw "the most Italianate of English Metaphysicals" (p. 105) and briefly compares and contrasts him with Marino, Claudio Monteverdi, and Girolamo Fontanella. Discusses briefly "Musicks Duell" and suggests that Crashaw's nightingale, "even more certainly than Marino's, is really a female soprano in feathery disguise" (p. 105). Observes that both Crashaw and Marino saw nature "through the lenses of literary convention, which cast a green shade that is not exactly the natural green" (p. 106). Comments also briefly on "The Weeper," pointing out that in it Crashaw "is concerned not with the Magdalene's character or story, nor with her conversion from sinner to saint, but solely with the flowing of her eyes, upon which he builds a succession of conceits" (p. 154).

⊷ 883. C[ohen], J. M. "Crashaw, Richard," in *The Concise Encyclopedia of English and American Poets and Poetry*, edited by Stephen Spender and Donald Hall, 102–3. London: Hutchinson; New York: Hawthorn Books. 2d rev. ed., London: Hutchinson, 1970.

A brief account of Crashaw's life and a critical evaluation of his poetry. Stresses the unevenness of his poetry: "At times as magnificent in style as any poet of the century, he fell easily into absurd bathos or empty rhetoric" (p. 102). Claims that Crashaw is most eloquent "when addressing his ideal of saintly womanhood, Mary Magdalen or Santa Teresa," yet "there is no conception of female character in any of his poems, which are built from loosely associated successions of conceits, each stanza a separate unit" (p. 102). Praises "Sospetto d'Herode" as superior to Marino's original. Points out that in several poems Crashaw "by dint of fervour transcends the limits of the conceited style to achieve greatness" but that most of his poems are "undistinguished" (p. 103).

⊷ 884. ———. "Foreign Influences on English Poetry," in *The Concise Encyclopedia of English and American Poets and Poetry*, edited by Stephen Spender and Donald Hall, 130–39. London: Hutchinson; New York: Hawthorn Books. 2d rev. ed., London: Hutchinson, 1970.

Discusses briefly Crashaw's Italianate manner. Notes that "Sospetto d'Herode" is more elaborate than Marino's original. Calls "The Weeper" "an extreme example of the Baroque style in English" and suggests that the poem can be seen as "the ancestor of Shelley's *To a Skylark* and of poems by Patmore and Francis Thompson" (p. 135).

⊷ 885. Crashaw, Richard. *Caritas Nimia* by Richard Crashaw (1612–1649). Worcester, Eng.: Stanbrook Abbey Press. 4p.

Reprints "Charitas Nimia" without notes or commentary. Handset in Spectrum and printed on Millbourn Lexpar.

⊷§ 886. Day, Martin S. "Richard Crashaw," in *History of English Literature: A College Course Guide.* Vol. 1: *To 1660,* 407–8. Garden City: Doubleday & Co.

A brief introduction to Crashaw's life and poetry, calling him "the chief English poet representing the Catholic Counter Reformation" (p. 408) and pointing out that, unlike the other metaphysical poets, he is baroque, not manneristic. Maintains that Crashaw "extravagantly explores every device presenting the spirit in sensuous terms" and that "daring paradox, startling confrontation of tears and ecstasy, characterize his dazzlingly intense religious verse" (p. 408). Briefly comments on "The Weeper," "The Flaming Heart," "A Hymn to the Name of Jesus," and "Hymn in the Holy Nativity."

⊷§ 887. Kuna, F. M. "T. S. Eliot's Dissociation of Sensibility and the Critics of Metaphysical Poetry." *EIC* 13:241–52.

Maintains that the dissociation of sensibility is "a poetic theory, and nothing more, which cannot be applied to any poetry written before the eighteenth century without distorting all historical truth, and which must not be separated from its original context" (p. 243). Argues that the concept is primarily the result of Eliot's theorizing about the nature of his own early poetry. No specific mention of Crashaw.

⊷§ 888. Leach, Elsie. "Some Commercial Terms in Seventeenth-Century Poetry." *N&Q* n.s. 10:414.

Points out that Crashaw's use of the business term *draw a dividend* in "Sancta Maria Dolorum" (stanza 9) antedates the first recorded instance in the *OED.*

⊷§ 889. Martz, Louis L., ed. *The Meditative Poem: An Anthology of Seventeenth-Century Verse.* With an introduction and notes. (Anchor Seventeenth-Century Series, AC6.) Garden City: Doubleday & Co. xxxii, 566p.

Reprinted in hardback (Stuart Editions), New York: New York University Press, 1963.

Rev. ed., *The Anchor Anthology of Seventeenth Century Verse,* vol. 1 (Garden City: Doubleday & Co., 1969); reprinted as *English Seventeenth Century Verse,* vol. 1 (1973).

Introduction is partially reprinted in *The Poem of the Mind: Essays on Poetry, English and American* (entry 938), 33–53.

In the introduction (pp. xvii–xxxii), distinguishes between metaphysical and meditative poetry and outlines the essential features of the meditative mode, suggesting that "the central meditative action consists of an interior drama, in which a man projects a self upon a mental stage, and there comes to understand that self in the light of a divine presence" (p. xxxi). Discusses briefly the influence of the meditative mode on Crashaw and points out that he could, "at his best, tame and control his extravaganzas by the firm structure of a meditation" (p. xxiii), noting, for example, the traditional tripartite structure of "Hymn to the Name of Jesus." Suggests that Crashaw, "though resembling Herbert and Jonson in places, finds his central poetical allegiance in the Continental Baroque" and maintains that "the kinship that he truly holds with Donne and Herbert does not lie within poetical traditions, strictly so-called," but in his "own underlying mastery of the art of meditation, by which he often gives the firm and subtle structure of his 'wit of Love' to violent sensory effects that may on the surface seem to escape all reasonable control" (p. xxx). Includes eleven of Crashaw's poems (pp. 271–318), with notes and commentary and a biographical sketch (pp. 540–45).

◄§ 890. Mirollo, James V. "The Marinesque Current in England," in *The Poet of the Marvelous: Giambattista Marino*, 243–64. New York and London: Columbia University Press.

Discusses Crashaw's indebtedness to Marino (see especially pp. 248–51). Maintains that "it was the Catholic poet rather than the modern disciple of Ovid whom Crashaw admired" (p. 250) and concludes, therefore, that since he "was concerned with a minor part of Marino's output, with those elements of his style which are the least original with him," Marino's influence on Crashaw "was important but not crucial" (p. 251). Warns that, since both poets drew on the same Latin and Italian models, caution must be exercised in suggesting that Crashaw borrowed a particular theme or image from Marino. Points out, however, adaptations and translations from *La Mira* in both the epigrams and *The Delights of the Muses* and notes similarities between Marino's imagery and the images in "The Weeper." Calls "Sospetto d'Herode" "undoubtedly one of the best translations ever made from Italian" but points out that the poem is "a curious example of a fairly restrained Marino being heightened in sensuous imagery and emotional intensity" (p. 249).

◄§ 891. Sito, Jerzy S. "Richard Crashaw," in *Śmierć i miłość. Mała antologia poezji według tekstów angielskich mistrzów, przyjaciół, rywali wrogów i násladowców Johna Donne'a* [Love and Death. A Small Anthology of Poetry Based on the Works of the English Forerunners, Friends, Rivals, Enemies and Followers of John Donne], 77–87. [Warsaw]: Czytelnik.

Translates into Polish "On our crucified Lord Naked, and bloody," lines from "The Flaming Heart," "On the wounds of our crucified Lord," "Matthew 27. And he answered them nothing," selected stanzas from "Wishes. To his (supposed) Mistresse," "An Epitaph upon a Young Married Couple," two quatrains from "Song upon the Bleeding Crucifix," and lines from "On Hope," without notes or commentary.

◄§ 892. Sparrow, John. "Hymns and Poetry." *TLS*, 11 January, p. 32.

Points out that several poems by Crashaw, Donne, Herbert, and other religious poets of the period were adapted for congregational singing and included in the *Collection of Hymns* (1754), edited by John Gambold (entry 80) for the "Brethren's Church" of the Moravians. For a listing and fuller discussion, see John Sparrow (entry 910).

◄§ 893. Swanston, Hamish. "The Second Temple." *DUJ* 55:14–22.

Reexamines the affinity between Crashaw and Herbert and argues that their similarities are more than superficial. Comments on technical features that both poets exhibit such as use of language, means of manipulating the metaphor, and recurring verbal patterns and points out similar constructive elements, especially their uses of the conceit. Notes also the similarity in their general attitudes toward sensible and suprasensible objects and suggests that Crashaw's "general attitude towards the world and all that is in it resembles, at certain points, that of Herbert" and that "in some respects what the Schoolmen would have called their general metaphysics corresponds closely" (p. 21). Tends to agree with those seventeenth- and eighteenth-century critics who recognized many affinities between the two poets and suggests that modern critics who exaggerate their differences miss the mark.

◄§ 894. Williams, George Walton. *Image and Symbol in the Sacred Poetry of Richard Crashaw*. Columbia: University of South Carolina Press. ix, 151p.

Declares that his intent is to discover the meaning of the religious symbols in Crashaw's sacred poetry and how they interrelate with the poems. Chapter 1, "The Poet-Saint and the Baroque" (pp. 1–11), presents a summary of the major influences on Crashaw's art—the Bible, Catullus, Martial, Donne, Herbert, Southwell, Giles Fletcher, Marino, St. Teresa, and Dionysius the Areopagite. Maintains that "their greatest contribution to his development as a poet lay in their transmitting to him the commonplace symbols of the Christian church" and suggests that, as a result, "Crashaw's symbology was composed of commonplaces" (p. 7). Sees Crashaw as baroque, and sees the main characteristics of baroque as redundancy, movement, fluidity, power, and excess. Chapter 2, "Quality" (pp. 12–32), discusses the symbolic concept of quality, which is basic to Crashaw's artistry, and divides it into three aspects: (1) the abundance of God (as in overflowing rivers or the feeding of the multitudes), (2) *maxime in minimis* (as in drops of water, wine, or blood and in crumbs), and (3) man's insignificance (suggested in images of dust, worms, and flies). Chapter 3, "White and Red" (pp. 33–56), discusses how Crashaw used white to symbolize purity and red to symbolize the sacrifice of Christ or the shame of sinful man. Points out that these colors are worked out in images of flowers, gems, and other contrasts. Chapter 4, "Light and Dark" (pp. 57–83), explains how Crashaw used the Bible as the source of his color contrasts and points out that, for him, divine light represented goodness while darkness represented evil. Discusses "Hymn in the Glorious Epiphanie" as an extended example of the uses of light and dark to suggest the goodness of the Divine and the darkness of the world. Chapter 5, "Liquidity" (pp. 84–104), comments on Crashaw's use of flowing images and shows how the concepts of quality and color are related to them. Points out, for example, that the basic white liquid in his poetry is water, the properties of which are thirst, cleansing, and cooling, and maintains that, for Crashaw, water as tears is even more important because tears represent the confession of the sinner's guilt. Notes that the basic red liquids in his poems are blood (the blood of the Redemptive Christ) and wine (the state of divine intoxication). Shows how white and red liquids are often contrasted, as, for instance, in "The Weeper," and discusses the poem at some length. Chapter 6, "Other Symbols and Images" (pp. 105–35), discusses Crashaw's use of animal symbolism; images of fire and the instruments of love, the crucifixion and instruments of hate, containers, protection and nourishment, hardness and softness; commercial images; and Crashaw's cosmology. Selected bibliography (pp. 137–45); index of images and symbols (pp. 146–47); and index of first lines and titles, with cross references (pp. 147–51).

⋙ 895. Witherspoon, Alexander M., and Frank J. Warnke, eds. *Seventeenth-Century Prose and Poetry.* 2d ed. New York and Burlingame: Harcourt, Brace & World. xxvi, 1094p.

First ed., entry 674; reprinted, 1957; 2d enlarged ed., 1982.

Includes a general introduction to seventeenth-century English poetry with a selected bibliography (pp. 707–18), in which Crashaw is called a poet of "frenzied extremes" (p. 713) and "the least typical, the most Italianate, of the Metaphysical poets" (p. 714). Maintains that a case can be made for excluding Crashaw from the metaphysical mode: "his poetry, it is true, operates through conceit, paradox, and oxymoron, and it is notable for its witty ingenuity, but it consistently shows an associational rather than a logical type of structure, it is exclamatory rather than dramatic in method, and it employs a type of opulent sense-imagery totally alien to most Metaphysical poetry" (pp. 713–14). Suggests that in these respects Crashaw is more like Giles Fletcher and Joseph Beaumont than like Donne, Herbert, Vaughan, and Marvell. Notes the influence of the Continental baroque poets, especially Marino. Maintains, however, that his best poems "display, besides their High Baroque features, a psychological perceptiveness and theological subtlety which suggest Herbert far more potently than they do Fletcher or Marino" (p. 714) and therefore concludes that Crashaw should still be considered a metaphysical poet. Presents a general introduction to Crashaw's life and poetry and a selected bibliography (pp. 916–17) and anthologizes nine poems or selections from poems, with explanatory notes (pp. 917–30). Stresses that Crashaw's art is "an inimitable and unforgettable fusion of the traditions of Metaphysical devotional verse with the wider traditions of European Baroque art" (p. 917).

1964

➤§ 896. Berry, Lloyd E., comp. *A Bibliography of Studies in Metaphysical Poetry, 1939–1960.* Madison: University of Wisconsin Press. xi, 99p.

A continuation of Theodore Spencer and Mark Van Doren's *Studies in Metaphysical Poetry: Two Essays and a Bibliography* (entry 617). Lists 1,147 critical studies on metaphysical poetry from 1939 to 1960. Notes that "entries were compiled after a search of more than 1000 journals, about 480 of which are not listed in the PMLA bibliography" (jacket). No annotations. Includes 49 items specifically on Crashaw.

➤§ 897. Ellrodt, Robert. "Scientific Curiosity and Metaphysical Poetry." *MP* 61:180–97.

Accounts for the prevailing scientific curiosity in much metaphysical poetry and for the differences in the use of science among the various poets. Suggests that the problem of disagreement between faith and reason never troubled Crashaw and that, "incurious of science" and of the major intellectual problems of his age, he borrowed his images and metaphors "from ritual and the mystical tradition" (p. 194). Points out that Herbert is "like Donne and unlike Crashaw in stressing paradox rather than mystery or miracle" (p. 196).

➤§ 898. Ferry, Anne D., ed. *17th Century English Minor Poets.* (The Laurel Poetry Series, gen. ed., Richard Wilbur.) New York: Dell Publishing. 192p.

Includes a general introduction to the "minor" poets of the seventeenth century: Henry King, Carew, Suckling, Lovelace, Cowley, Crashaw, Vaughan, Traherne, Waller, John Wilmot, Earl of Rochester (pp. 9–18); a biographical note on Crashaw (pp. 21–22); a selection of eleven of Crashaw's poems (pp. 88–106); and notes on individual poems (pp. 189–90).

➤§ 899. Gilman, Harvey. "Crashaw's Reflexive Recoil." *SCN* 22, no. 1:2–4.

Defines "the reflexive recoil" as a device in which "an object is first personified and then is made to perform its customary function upon itself" and notes that its use results in "a kind of Baroque transformation of startling and arresting power" (p. 2). Points out that Crashaw most often uses the device "for intensification, amplification, and to bring about the climax of a poem" (p. 2) and gives numerous examples of its use in his secular and sacred poems. Observes that "what distinguishes the device in the verse of Crashaw from that to be found in the poetry of his contemporaries is the frequency and variety with which he employs it" (p. 3). Claims that "the reflexive recoil" represents Crashaw's "own image for the logical extreme boundary of Baroque transformation" and that it occurs most often whenever he "stretches his imagination to its limit in an attempt to describe, in concrete terms, the incredible paradoxes of Christian dogma" (p. 4).

❧ 900. Hauser, Arnold. "Die Hauptvertretre des Manierismus in der Literatur des Abendlandes," in *Der Manierismus: Die Krise der Renaissance und der Ursprung der modernen Kunst*, 299–352. Munich: Verlag C. H. Beck.
Translated into English (with the assistance of Eric Mosbacher) as *Mannerism: The Crisis of the Renaissance and the Origin of Modern Art* (London: Routledge & Kegan Paul; New York: Knopf, 1965).
Briefly considers Crashaw as one of the last mannerist poets in England and warns that the term *metaphysical* can be applied to Donne, Herbert, Crashaw, and Marvell only with great reservations.

❧ 901. Kenner, Hugh, ed. "Richard Crashaw (1613–1649)," in *Seventeenth Century Poetry: The Schools of Donne and Jonson*, 229–54. New York: Holt, Rinehart and Winston.
Presents a brief introduction to Crashaw's life and poetry (pp. 229–30) and anthologizes ten of his poems, without commentary (pp. 230–54). Suggests that "each poem of Crashaw's is a great *performance*" and points out his "unflagging fecundity of elaboration" (p. 229). Notes the influence of the baroque on Crashaw's sensibility and art and calls him the "least native of English devotional poets" (p. 230).

❧ 902. Melchiori, Giorgio. *Poeti metafisici inglesi del Seicento.* (Scala Reale: Antholgie Letterarie, no. 4.) Milan: Casa Editrice Dr. Francesco Vallardi. 673p.
Anthology of seventeenth-century English poetry for the Italian reader. The introduction (pp. 1–45) is divided into seven sections: (1) "Eufuismo," (2) "Wit eufuistico e wit metafisico," (3) "Universo medievale e nuova filosofia," (4) "Il linguaggio del Manierismo," (5) "L'evoluzione barocca," (6) "Dalla meditazione alle visione," (7) "La poesia metafisica oggi." Selected general bibliography (pp. 53–58). Includes a brief introduction to Crashaw's life and poetry and a selected bibliography of works on Crashaw (pp. 339–41). Maintains that Crashaw "si afferma un nuovo stile poetico, che solo per estensione del termine può esser considerato metafisico" (p. 340) and suggests that he represents "l'aspetto romantico, entusiastico ed estroso del Barocco inglese, come Milton ne rappresenterà l'aspetto classico, disciplinato e dotto" (p. 341). Contrasts Crashaw with Donne and Herbert and points out his link with the Continental baroque, Marino, the Jesuit emblemists, and such English predecessors as Joshua Sylvester, Giles Fletcher, and Southwell. Claims that "la poesia è per lui musica, pittura e architettura" and that "all'estasi intellettuale e carnale si sostituisce l'estasi auditiva, visuale, e l'estasi data

dalle esalazione dei profumi" (p. 340). Translates into Italian twenty-five of Crashaw's English poems (pp. 343–401), with notes (pp. 651–53) and twenty of his Latin poems (pp. 597–619), with notes (p. 662).

◄§ 903. Miller, Clarence H. "The Order of Stanzas in Cowley and Crashaw's 'On Hope.'" *SP* 61:64–73.

Suggests that the intended order of the alternating stanzas of "On Hope" may have been disturbed through a scribal or printer's error when the 1646 edition was prepared and argues that "Cowley's arguments follow a logical plan, which Crashaw's stanzas, if re-arranged, answer point by point" (p. 66). Claims that in such a reordering Crashaw's metaphors become sacred symbols that match exactly Cowley's stanzas and that Crashaw, in answering him, "transforms Cowley's human hope into the traditional theological virtue of hope" (p. 70). Maintains that in the reordered arrangement "the debate moves on the orders of nature and grace like parallel lines which always correspond but meet only at infinity" and "is like a disputation between Aristotle and St. Augustine or between Averrhoes and St. Bonaventure" and that, "in the spirit of the baroque, it seeks not so much to harmonize as to exploit the tensions between the secular and the sacred, between the human and the divine" (p. 70). For a reply, see George Walton Williams (entry 999).

◄§ 904. Patrides, C. A. *The Phoenix and the Ladder: The Rise and Decline of the Christian View of History.* (University of California Publications, English Studies, 29.) Berkeley and Los Angeles: University of California Press. 101p.

Expanded and much revised as *The Grand Design of God: The Literary Form of the Christian View of History* (London: Routledge & Kegan Paul; Toronto and Buffalo: University of Toronto Press, 1972).

Briefly contrasts "Hymn in the Holy Nativity" and Milton's Nativity Ode, pointing out that "no two poets of the seventeenth century are more diametrically opposed than Crashaw and Milton, whether we consider their temperaments, their loyalties, or their approach to poetry" (p. 60). Suggests that, "while Crashaw focused his attention on the manger and dwelt on the relation of God directly perpendicular to man, Milton's concurrent interest was in the horizontal significance of 'the rude manger,' the way it affected the relations not between God and man but between God and men considered in their totality" (p. 60). Points out that, while Milton affirms the universal scope of Christ's birth, Crashaw focuses on "one specific moment in history that witnessed the union of God and man" (p. 60).

◄§ 905. Praz, Mario. "Baroque in England." *MP* 6:169–79.

An abridged English version of "Il Barocco in Inghilterra" (entry 880).

◆§ 906. Preston, Thomas R. "*Christabel* and the Mystical Tradition," in *Essays and Studies in Language and Literature* (Duquesne Studies, Philosophical Studies, 5), edited by Herbert H. Petit, 138–57. Pittsburgh: Duquesne University Press.

Discusses Coleridge's admiration for Crashaw's poetry, especially the Teresian hymns, and comments on the influence of "A Hymn to Sainte Teresa" on *Christabel*. Discusses the mystical language and themes in Crashaw's poem, especially his uses of sexual and military imagery.

◆§ 907. Pritchard, Allan. "Puritan Charges Against Crashaw and Beaumont." *TLS*, 2 July, p. 578.

Points out a Puritan view of Crashaw and Beaumont, as well as others associated with them in Cambridge, that appears among the miscellaneous papers in the Harley MS 7019 (no. 11, fols. 52–93), now in the British Library. Notes that, although the manuscript is undated and its author or authors unidentified, it was probably written in the early months of 1641, two years before Crashaw departed from Cambridge, and is undoubtedly the work of Puritan investigators. Points out that the investigators were especially severe in their attacks on Laudian practices permitted at Peterhouse and presents a number of specific charges against Crashaw, such as, that he reportedly urged admiration of a picture of the Virgin Mary, perhaps celebrated what could be termed private liturgies at Little St. Mary's, used forbidden church plate, washed his hands before the Communion service and consumed crumbs and remaining wine following it, and insisted on designating the sanctuary of the church as a place of particular holiness.

◆§ 908. Richmond, H. M. *The School of Love: The Evolution of the Stuart Love Lyric.* Princeton: Princeton University Press. 337p.

Briefly mentions "Wishes. To his (supposed) Mistresse" and calls the poem "diffuse and disordered" (p. 35). Compares Crashaw to Martial, noting that the love expressed in several of Martial's epigrams, though more sophisticated than that of the Greek epigrammatists, is paradoxically more likely to be unrealized because "the more elaborate the anticipations the more certain is the falsification of at least some of them by an actual relationship" (p. 26). Notes that "this defect is shared by the yet more charming but no less ominously elaborate fancies in Crashaw's 'Wishes. To his Supposed Mistresse' and in the twentieth century by the unabashed sentimentality of 'The girl that I Marry' in that interestingly feminist American musical *Annie Get Your Gun*" (p. 26). Suggests that "all these lyrics illustrate the feeble self-delusions of the daydream, doomed almost necessarily to frustration by actual experience" (p. 26). Observes that although there is "a steady progression, like Plato's ladder, from the crudely physical desires of many pagan classical poets to the more romantic ideas of the post-Renaissance era, such wishful or wistful thinking lacks decisive patterns of thought, expression, and action" (p. 27). Briefly compares and contrasts Crashaw also with Donne, Jonson, and Thomas Hardy.

◄§ 909. Rowland, Daniel B. "John Donne: Mannerist Style in the Meditative Genre," in *Mannerism—Style and Mood: An Anatomy of Four Works in Three Art Forms*, 49–72. New Haven and London: Yale University Press.

Distinguishes mannerism from Renaissance and baroque modes of expression and discusses Crashaw as representative of the baroque. Compares and contrasts "Hymn in the Assumption," Donne's *The First Anniversary*, and Spenser's *Astrophel*, detailing the prosody, syntax, structure, rhetorical features, imagery, and general sensibility of each poem. Discusses in particular Crashaw's use of musical devices, sound patterns, sensuous imagery, conceits, and loose structure and points out that, "in sensibility as in verse music, he lies far closer to Spenser than he does to Donne" (pp. 62–63).

◄§ 910. Sparrow, John. "George Herbert and John Donne among the Moravians." *BNYPL* 68:625–53.

Reprinted in *Hymns Unbidden: Donne, Herbert, Blake, Emily Dickinson and the Hymnographers* by Martha Winburn Englander and John Sparrow (New York: Public Library, 1966), 1–28.

Points out that no edition of Crashaw's poems appeared after 1670 until the selection of his poetry published in 1785 by Peregrine Phillips (entry 93) and that, although he was included in collections by Robert Anderson (entry 102) and Alexander Chalmers (entry 119), "no serious attention was paid to his poetry until the 1850's" (p. 625), during which time appeared the editions by George Gilfillan (entry 186) and William B. Turnbull (entry 191). Points out, however, that ten adaptations of Crashaw's poems were included in the Moravian hymnbook *A Collection of Hymns* (1754), edited by John Gambold (entry 80). Notes that the adapter "allows himself to select and abridge, but he does not alter the text much more than is necessary in order to make it fit existing tunes" (p. 643).

◄§ 911. Sugimoto, Ryūtarō. "Crashaw no Shi—Donne, Herbert to no Renkansei" [Crashaw's Poetry—The Relationship of Donne and Herbert]. *Jimbun Kenkyū* 15, no. 3:23–34.

Discusses the major characteristics of Crashaw's poetry, contrasting him to Donne, Herbert, and, to a lesser extent, Marvell. Suggests that, because of his uses of highly decorative and sensuous images, Crashaw should not be classified as metaphysical but as baroque. Comments on the influence of Spanish and Italian models, especially St. Teresa, Marino, and the Jesuit Latin poets. Finds Crashaw's poetry often flawed by his use of sensuous and inconsistent conceits and images. Comments on "The Weeper," "Hymn to the Name of

Jesus," and "Hymn for New Year's Day" and finds the last most aesthetically satisfying. Suggests that the religious poems reflect a kind of sublimated sexuality that can be detected in the use of highly sensuous and erotic imagery.

❧ 912. Yoklavich, John. "A Manuscript of Crashaw's Poems from Loseley." *ELN* 2:92–97.
Describes a collection of eighteen secular poems by Crashaw (all known to modern editors) found among the Loseley manuscripts in the Folger Library (L. b. 708). Dates the manuscript before 1635 and points out that the Crashaw poems derive from no known manuscript or printed version. Argues that the manuscript provides "one more piece of evidence that Crashaw's early poems enjoyed a wide circulation before the publication of *Steps to the Temple* in 1646" and points out that it is "especially interesting since it comes from Loseley House and Anne Donne's family, the Mores" (p. 97).

❧ 913. ———. "Not by Crashaw, but Cornwallis." *MLR* 59:517–18.
Argues that three elegies and an epitaph from Bodleian MS Tanner 465— "On the death of Wm Henshaw, student in Emān. Coll.," "An Elegy vpon the death of Mr Wm Carre, student in Emān: Colledge," and "An Elegy upon the death of Mʳ Christopher Rouse Esquire" with its attached epitaph—that L. C. Martin included in his second edition of Crashaw's poems (pp. 401, 402, 404) on internal evidence and with many qualifications were written by Philip Cornwallis, a kinsman of Rouse. Supports his argument by evidence in two of the Loseley manuscripts (L. b. 675 and L. b. 674) in the Folger Library.

1965

❧ 914. Beaty, Jerome, and William H. Matchett. *Poetry: From Statement to Meaning.* New York: Oxford University Press. 353p.
General introduction to the study of poetry. Briefly comments on the imagery of "The Weeper" by noting that "it is quite possible for an image to be too vivid and thus to interfere with, or even destroy, what would seem to have been the intended effect of the poem" (p. 179). Suggests that "sometimes this may be due to the poet's having been at least momentarily inept (as when Crashaw writes of the cherub who sips from the waters of Mary Magdalene's tears, and adds the repellent idea that his song 'Tastes of this breakfast all day long'), but sometimes it is apparently due to the poet's having been carried away by an image admittedly impressive or beautiful, which unfortunately overpowers the context in which it appears" (p. 179).

❧ 915. Bouyer, Louis. "Le protestantisme après les réformateurs et les débuts de l'anglicanisme," in *La spiritualité orthodoxe et la spiritualité protestante et anglicane,* 137–225. (Histoire de la spiritualité chré-

tienne, vol. 3, ed. Louis Bouyer, Jean LeClercq, François Vanden-
broucke, and Louis Cognet.) Paris: Aubier.
Translated into English by Barbara Wall (London: Burns & Oates; New
York: Desclée Co., 1969); reprinted, New York: The Seabury Press, 1982.
Briefly discusses Crashaw as a semi-mystical poet,"très sincère, à sa man-
ière un peu hystérique" (p. 181). Suggests that in Crashaw's poetry all the tendencies of the school of Donne run to seed: "Le concettisme en est fondu dans
les liquéfactions et les incandescences les plus baroques de toute la littérature
anglaise" (p. 181). Suggests that the Teresian poems present a kind of "sensualité moite" and contain embarrassing erotic images that "laisse vite un ar-
rière-goût de fadeur" (p. 181). Maintains that "cette impudeur est bien celle
de l'innocence, mais d'une innocence qui a passé la maturité sans l'atteindre"
and "ce punch faussement sensuel ne brule que sur un océan de sucreries"
(p. 181). Concludes that "les psychanalystes qui croient déceler derrière la
débauche d'image pseudo-nuptiales de Crashaw la suele nostalgie du sein ma-
ternel ne sont sans doute pas loin du compte" (p. 181).

◀§ 916. Collmer, Robert G. "The Function of Death in Certain Metaphysical
    Poems." McNR 16:25–32.
    Reprinted in BSE 6 (1966): 147–54.
    Discusses the treatment of death in the poetry of Crashaw, Donne, Herbert,
and Vaughan. Suggests that Crashaw's language about death differs greatly
from that of the other metaphysical poets and can be properly understood only
in the light of Counter-Reformation mysticism. Observes that Crashaw says
nothing about his own literal death and seems unconcerned about the question of the resurrection of the body. Points out that, although he views death
as a destructive force in some of his funeral elegies, those poems that seem to
reflect his own personal experiences view death as a positive, uniting force
that frees the soul to enjoy the Beatific Vision. Cites examples from "A Hymn
to Sainte Teresa" as reflecting Crashaw's use of the mystic's language about
death. Compares and contrasts Crashaw to Donne, Herbert, and Vaughan
and maintains that, in their belief that death is fundamentally positive,
Crashaw and Herbert are similar.

◀§ 917. Dewey, Thomas B. "Some 'Careless' Seventeenth-Century Rhymes."
    BNYPL 69:143–52.
    Challenges critics who allege that Cleveland's poetry is marred by care-
less rhymes. Compares rhymes in 1,800 lines each of Cleveland, Cowley,
Crashaw, Vaughan, and Waller to show that "none of them was careless, that
they were using rhymes that fitted the spoken language of their time; or that, if
occasionally they strained for a rhyme, they held to tradition" (p. 147).

◀§ 918. Eliot, T. S. "To Criticize the Critic," in To Criticize the Critic and
    Other Writings, 11–26. New York: Farrar, Straus & Giroux.

Comments on his role in the modern revival of interest in metaphysical poetry: "I think that if I wrote well about the metaphysical poets, it was because they were poets who had inspired me. And if I can be said to have had an influence whatever in promoting a wider interest in them, it was simply because no previous poet who had praised these poets had been so deeply influenced by them as I had been" (p. 22). He adds: "As the taste for my own poetry spread, so did the taste for the poets to whom I owed the greatest debt and about whom I had written. Their poetry, and mine, were congenial to that age. I sometimes wonder whether that age is not coming to an end" (p. 22). Points out that for pure delight and pleasure he turns now more and more to the poems of Herbert, rather than to those of Donne. No specific comments on Crashaw.

◆§ 919. Gorlier, Claudio. "La poeta e la nuova alchimia." *Paragone* 16, no. 182:55–78; no. 184:43–80.
Suggests that Crashaw's highly baroque poetry represents a decline in wit. Comments on the pyrotechnics of Crashaw's rhetoric, his uses of emblems, and his employment of verbal decoration and sensuous images. Discusses, in particular, the marinistic features of Crashaw's poetry, pointing out how he converts the technique of the Italian poet for his own purposes. Calls "The Flaming Heart" Crashaw's most representative poem and briefly contrasts him with Milton, Donne, Herbert, Vaughan, and Marvell, especially regarding their uses of wit.

◆§ 920. Grennen, Joseph E. "Richard Crashaw," in *The Poetry of John Donne and the Metaphysical Poets*. 69–71. (Monarch Notes and Study Guides.) New York: Monarch Press.
Includes a sketch of Crashaw's life followed by brief paraphrases of "The Flaming Heart" and "A Hymn to Sainte Teresa."

◆§ 921. Hibbard, Howard. *Bernini*. (Pelican Books, A701.) Harmondsworth, Eng.; Baltimore: Penguin Books. 255p.
Reprinted, 1966, 1968, 1971, 1974, 1976.
Briefly points out that, although "A Hymn to Sainte Teresa" "seems at times to be inspired by a representation of the scene of Teresa's vision," Crashaw saw Bernini's statue of the saint in Santa Maria della Vittoria in Rome "only after he wrote the poem" (p. 241). Maintains that the conclusion of "The Flaming Heart" "describes the state Bernini desired to create in the mind of the beholder better than any other English poem" (p. 241). Suggests, therefore, that, "if Anglo-Saxons are, as has often been maintained, more susceptible to literary than visual imagery, it may be useful to approach [Bernini's] *Ecstasy of St. Teresa* through Crashaw, remembering that his poetry and Bernini's are not the same except in ultimate goal" (p. 241).

◆§ 922. Hunter, Jim. *The Metaphysical Poets*. (Literature in Perspective.) London: Evans Brothers. 160p. Reprinted, 1968, 1972.

A general introduction to metaphysical poetry for the "ordinary man who reads for pleasure" (p. 5). Contains nine brief chapters: (1) "Backgrounds," (2) "Characteristics of Metaphysical Poetry," (3) "Verse," (4) "Diction," (5) "Imagery," (6) "John Donne," (7) "George Herbert," (8) "Vaughan, Marvell, Crashaw, and Others," and (9) "Critical Estimate Over the Years." Mentions Crashaw throughout and in Chapter 8 presents a brief biographical account of him and a general survey of his poetry (pp. 141–46). Maintains that Crashaw's poetry is "extremely artificial" and can "lack an onward force, as it lingers over its devices" and claims that, because of its Italianate and baroque elements, "many readers find themselves out of sympathy with it" (p. 142). Comments on major features of Crashaw's poetry, especially its uses of elaboration, ornamentation, ritualistic and musical forms, and erotic, sensuous imagery. Praises the tenderness and easy grace of many of Crashaw's poems. Finds "The Weeper" impressive and remarkable but limited and too impersonal; praises "A Hymn to Sainte Teresa" as Crashaw's finest poem because in it "the poet is not decorating but saying" (p. 145) and because he expresses strong emotion; suggests that "Letter to the Countess of Denbigh" has a similar "urge to communicate"; and praises it and "Charitas Nimia" as containing lines that come as near as Crashaw ever did "to personal, direct involvement in his poetry" (p. 146). Briefly compares and contrasts Crashaw to Vaughan and Marvell.

◆§ 923. Inglis, Fred, ed. *English Poetry, 1500–1660*. London: Methuen & Co. xix, 242p.

Anthologizes "Matthew. 27. And he answered them nothing," "On our crucified Lord Naked, and bloody," "Letter to the Countess of Denbigh," and "The Weeper" (pp. 171–80) with brief notes (p. 221) and a biographical sketch (p. 224).

◆§ 924. Jauernick, Stephanie. "Crashaw's Hymne auf Santa Teresa." *NS* 14:449–61.

Presents a detailed explication of "A Hymn to Sainte Teresa" and discusses Crashaw's admiration of the saint and knowledge of her works. Comments on the versions of the poem and calls the 1652 version one of Crashaw's most beautiful works, comparable in some respects to Bernini's famous statue of the saint in Rome. Discusses the structure of the poem and divides it into four closely related parts: lines 1–15, 16–65, 66–105, and 106–183. Suggests that the poem is informed not only by the biography of St. Teresa and by her mystical writings but also by Crashaw's own personal experiences. Points out various ways in which Crashaw weds his poetic techniques to the subject matter of the poem. Concludes that the poem exactly parallels some of St.

Teresa's writings and shows that Crashaw was himself mystically inclined and was able to unveil that which is beyond the senses and to transform the sensual into the spiritual.

◄§ 925. Jennings, Elizabeth. "The Seventeenth Century," in *Christianity and Poetry*, 48–63. (Faith and Fact Books, 122.) London: Burns & Oates.

General survey of religious poetry in England during the seventeenth century. Suggests that Crashaw "is not one of the most accessible or most popular of the metaphysical poets" because "his imagery is often too far-fetched and his manner of approach too indirect for him to appeal to the kind of reader who admires Vaughan, Herbert or Traherne" (pp. 59–60). Points out that "he draws much on the New Testament," which "tends to give his verse an air of unreality and remoteness to the feelings which he is trying to express" (p. 60). Claims that, although there is passion in Crashaw's poetry, "it often seems diluted simply because the poet is either too shy or else to awed to present it nakedly" (p. 60). Calls "A Hymn to Sainte Teresa" Crashaw's most celebrated poem and notes that it contains genuine religious feeling in spite of its artificial baroque style. Praises the lucidity and simplicity of "A Song ('Lord, when the sense of thy sweet grace')."

◄§ 926. Pinkham, Daniel. *Three Lenten Poems of Richard Crashaw*. Boston: Ione Press, distributed by E. C. Schirmer Music Co. 15p.

Musical settings of "On the still surviving markes of our Saviours wounds," "On our crucified Lord Naked, and bloody," and the antiphon from compline of "Office of the Holy Crosse" by Daniel Pinkham, for mixed voices, string quartet (contrabass ad libitum), or string orchestra and handbells (or celesta or harp) or with keyboard accompaniment (handbells ad libitum).

◄§ 927. Rogers, David M. "*Carmen Deo Nostro*," in *Masterpieces of Catholic Literature in Summary Form*, edited by Frank N. Magill, with associate editors A. Robert Camponigri and Thomas P. Neill, 600–605. New York: Harper & Row.

A brief introduction to Crashaw's life, poetry, and religious sensibility. Argues that the poems in *Carmen Deo Nostro* result from the poet's "complete dedication of himself to God throughout a life of intellectual and spiritual achievement" (p. 601). Suggests that Crashaw's poetry is characterized by "the use of antithesis and paradox within a verbal structure whose chief end is exaltation and ecstasy, not insight" and by "that efflorescence of spiritual and imaginative energy we now call the Counter-Reformation" (p. 602). Points out that typically Crashaw "asks us to contemplate an object such as the crucifix, or an event such as the Epiphany, realized, of course, in all the concrete details of the wise men and their gifts, while the poet uses meter, assonance, and alliteration to create an atmosphere in which the analytical intellect is put to sleep and the soul may glimpse, at last, the glories of Paradise beyond the wall of contraries" (p. 603). Suggests that Crashaw's most inspired poetry is the conclusion of "The Flaming Heart" but points out his ability to express whimsical humor in "In praise of Lessius" and his sheer delight in verbal manipulation in "Letter to the Countess of Denbigh." Claims that Crashaw's artistic evolution "was marked by a movement from formalism to improvisation" (p. 604). Briefly traces Crashaw's critical reputation and concludes that he "has received more attention in the past thirty years than he did in the preceding three hundred" and that "he is now regarded as one of the finest devotional poets in the language" (p. 605). Briefly compares and contrasts Crashaw with Herbert and Vaughan.

❧ 928. Steese, Peter. "Herbert and Crashaw: Two Paraphrases of the Twenty-Third Psalm." *Journal of Bible and Religion* 33:137–41.

Compares Crashaw's and Herbert's paraphrases of Psalm 23 and contrasts their achievements with the rendition by Sternhold and Hopkins (1562). Points out that, although Crashaw elaborates on the original, he retains its basic spirit and structure. Comments on stylistic features of Crashaw's poem, such as its elaboration of basic biblical images, its prevailing mood of enthusiasm, its intensely personal tone, and its uses of alliteration, repetition, and sensuous images. Concludes that both Crashaw's and Herbert's paraphrases, though quite different, "represent a level of achievement seldom equalled in the history of the genre" (p. 141).

❧ 929. Taira, Zensuke. "Barokushi to Keijijōshi" [Baroque and Metaphysical Poetry], in *Keijijōshi no Shomondai* [Some Problems of Metaphysical Poetry], edited by Isamu Muraoka, 91–102. Tokyo: Nan'un-do.

Argues that baroque art should not be seen solely as deriving from and related to the Counter-Reformation and the Jesuits. Points out that many baroque poets were Protestants and that many secular as well as sacred poems were written in the baroque style. Comments on Odette de Mourges's definitions of baroque and metaphysical styles in *Metaphysical Baroque & Précieux Poetry* (entry 754) and notes that, according to her restrictive classifications, only Crashaw among the metaphysical poets was distinctively baroque. Finds more satisfactory Frank Warnke's explanation in *European Metaphysical Poetry* (entry 870) and summarizes his points in some detail.

❧ 930. Woodhouse, A. S. P. "The Seventeenth Century: Donne and His Successors," in *The Poet and His Faith: Religion and Poetry in England from Spenser to Eliot and Auden*, 42–89. Chicago and London: University of Chicago Press.

Comments on the general conditions of English religion and poetry in the seventeenth century that made the period such an important one for religious verse. Presents a biographical sketch of Crashaw and comments on his religious sensibility as reflected in his poetry. Suggests that Crashaw's religious ardor is "expressed in poems fraught with sensuous and erotic imagery and marked by a constant play of wit" (pp. 74–75) and that these elements can be seen at their best in "Hymn in the Holy Nativity" and the Teresian poems and at their worst in "The Weeper." Comments on "Adoro Te" to show that Crashaw can at times strike "a simpler and less florid note" (p. 76). Contrasts "Hymn in the Holy Nativity" to Milton's Nativity Ode and briefly compares and contrasts Crashaw with Donne, Herbert, and Vaughan.

1966

◄§ 931. Collmer, Robert G. "The Function of Death in Certain Metaphysical Poems." *BSE* 6:147–54.
First appeared in *McNR* (entry 916).

◄§ 932. Eliot, T. S. "A Tribute to Mario Praz," in *Friendship's Garland: Essays Presented to Mario Praz on His Seventieth Birthday*, edited by Vittorio Gabrieli, 1:[3]. (Storia e Letteratura: Raccolta di Studi e Testi, 106.) Rome: Edizioni di Storia e Letteratura.
Points out that he first became aware of the work of Praz when the *TLS* sent him a copy of *Secentismo e Marinismo in Inghilterra* (1925) to review: "I immediately recognized these essays—and especially his masterly study of Crashaw—as among the best that I had ever read in that field." Calls the book "essential reading for any student of the English 'metaphysical poets.'"

◄§ 933. Fitts, Dudley. "Crashaw: 'The Teare,'" in *Master Poems of the English Language*, edited by Oscar Williams, 196–200. New York: Trident Press.
Presents an analysis of "The Teare" and discusses Crashaw's uses of ingenious conceits, elaborate images, and hyperbolic metaphors in the poem. Suggests that it is "less extravagant, less mannered, than 'The Weeper'" and "carries greater conviction, that is on the whole a more reasonable expression of religious experience" (p. 198). Maintains that Crashaw is "above all an ecstatic" and that "his mind works by a logic that achieves its solutions and discoveries by forcing metaphors, tropes in general, to the very limits of sense, beyond which lies madness" (p. 198). Points out that "The Teare" "is flawed perhaps, though it does not, as 'The Weeper' does, become silly" and that "the flaws, if they are flaws, are the inevitable blemishes of the baroque in any form of art: a sinning by excess, a temporary plunging beyond control" (p. 200).

◄§ 934. Geha, Richard, Jr. "Richard Crashaw: (1613?-1650?) The Ego's Soft Fall." *AI* 23:158–68.
A psychoanalytical interpretation of Crashaw's life and poetry. Suggests that

the two major motivations underlying the poet's religious sensibility and in particular his conversion to Catholicism were a negative reaction to his father and an attempt to rediscover the love of his lost mother. Claims, for example, that Crashaw's "deepest psychic needs drew him toward the calm atmosphere of a monastic life" (p. 160), which he partially enjoyed at Little Gidding, and suggests that Mary Collet represented to him his first mother and that, like her, she was unreachable, whereas in St. Teresa, Crashaw found the "mystical mother" figure he always desired. Characterizes Crashaw as "a man who walked around the mind and attempted to return to the lost mother, to narcissism, to unity via the bleeding heart and the gushing tears" (p. 163). Suggests that the poet's preference for hyperbole and lushness, "his persistent association of pain with pleasure, his tireless dwelling on fluidic imagery, his fascination with death, all mark him as a forerunner of the Decadent Movement of the nineteenth century" (p. 162). Presents a psychoanalytical analysis of "A Hymn to Sainte Teresa" and "The Flaming Heart" and sees them as poems that most reveal "the major motivations and distinctions of Crashaw's life and art" (p. 163). Calls "A Hymn to Sainte Teresa" a "song of the masochistic Christ-son resolving his oedipal difficulty through the romance of religion" (p. 165) and finds in "The Flaming Heart" that Crashaw "becomes the mother, finally recovering that eternity that was lost; the mother who abandoned him as an infant to the father" (p. 168).

⋖§ 935. Kusunose, Toshihiko. "Richard Crashaw no Sei to Shi—Ritualism no Katei" [Richard Crashaw's Life and Poetry—The Process of Ritualism]. *Ronko* (Kanseigakuin Daigaku) no. 13 : 101–18.

Revised version included in *Shi to Shin—Donne o meguru shijintachi* (entry 1038).

Presents a general critical evaluation of Crashaw's sensibility and art. Comments on major features of his poetry, especially his uses of sensuous images, his rich sense of color, his uses of paradox, and his blending of the emotional with the intellectual. Stresses the ritualistic nature of Crashaw's poetry.

⋖§ 936. Leishman, J. B. *The Art of Marvell's Poetry.* London: Hutchinson & Co. 328p.

Mentions Crashaw throughout. Argues that Marvell's poetry "has far deeper affinities with Crashaw's than with Donne's" (p. 36) and that his indebtedness to Crashaw "seems, on the whole, to have been greater than to any other single poet" (p. 49). Points out Marvell's specific borrowings from Crashaw and notes numerous echoes. Maintains that "some of Marvell's descriptions and images have both the colour and the crystalline purity of Crashaw's" but that, "although he lacks Crashaw's not infrequent mawkishness and sentimentality, he also lacks both his childlike tenderness and his rapture" (p. 11). Calls Crashaw the most brilliant epigrammatist of the period and comments in some detail on "Joann. 2. Aquae in vinum versae," "To Pontius washing his blood-stained hands," and "Joann. 5. Ad Bethesdae piscinam positus."

◄§ 937. Loiseau, J. "The Baroque Element in English and French Poetry of the Late Sixteenth and Early Seventeenth Century," in *English Studies Today*, 4th series, edited by Iliva Cellini and Giorgio Melchiori, 187– 209. Rome: Edizioni di storia e letteratura.

Maintains that "the only English poet of the age who fulfills all the qualifications required of an orthodox Baroque poet is Richard Crashaw" and suggests that he is "the best exponent of what is considered by some critics as the very soul of the Baroque, 'the spiritualization of sense'" (p. 205). Asserts that, influenced by Italian poets and Spanish mysticism, Crashaw is "an authentic member of the Counter-Reformation" and that, as such, "he stands isolated among his brother poets" (p. 206). Briefly compares Crashaw to Jean de La Ceppède and François de Malherbe.

◄§ 938. Martz, Louis L. "Meditative Action and 'The Metaphysical Style,'" in *The Poem of the Mind: Essays on Poetry, English and American*, 33–53. New York: Oxford University Press; London: Hutchinson.

First appeared, in a shorter version, in the introduction to *The Meditative Poem: An Anthology of Seventeenth-Century Verse* (entry 889).

Includes material from an essay on Donne in *Master Poems of the English Language*, ed. Oscar Williams (New York: Trident Press, 1966).

2d ed., 1968; reprinted in paperback, 1969.

Discusses the nature of meditative action in seventeenth-century English poetry and attempts to distinguish between meditative action and metaphysical style. Maintains that Crashaw, "though resembling Herbert and Jonson in places, finds his central poetic allegiance in the Continental baroque" and that "the kinship that he truly holds with Donne and Herbert does not lie within poetical traditions, strictly so called" but "in Crashaw's own underlying mastery of the art of meditation, by which he gives the firm and subtle structure of his 'wit of Love' to violent sensory effects that may on the surface seem to escape all reasonable control" (p. 52). Points out the meditative structure of "Hymn to the Name of Jesus" and notes that the Teresian poems employ a Jonsonian use of the tetrameter couplet.

◄§ 939. Miles, Josephine, and Hanan C. Selvin. "A Factor Analysis of the Vocabulary of Poetry in the Seventeenth Century," in *The Computer and Literary Style: Introductory Essay and Studies*, edited by Jacob Leed, 116–27. (Kent Studies in English, no. 2.) Kent, Ohio: Kent State University Press.

Reprinted in *The Metaphysical Poets: A Selection of Critical Essays*, ed. Gerald Hammond (entry 1085), 182–96.

A "factor analysis of the sixty nouns, adjectives, and verbs used at least ten times in a consecutive thousand lines by each of at least three of thirty poets in the seventeenth century" revealing "a number of factors useful for characterizing certain groups of poets and poetic habits" (p. 116). Includes *Steps to the Temple* in this study. Argues that certain emphases become more obvious through such a study than they do in literary histories, such as "the primacy of the Donne tradition; the ethical allegiance of Herbert to Jonson; the early innovative forces of Sandys and Quarles toward the Biblical aesthetic; and the isolation of Vaughan from his religious confrères, in contrast to the surprising general continuity in Prior and Pomfret" (p. 125). Finds Crashaw's word choice most strongly correlated with that of Milton and points out that they share the use of such words as *high, new, old, sweet, god, heaven, night, come, gone, hear,* and *make.*

◄§ 940. Osborn, James M., ed. *Joseph Spence. Observations, Anecdotes, and Characters of Books and Men. Collected from Conversation.* Vol. 1. Oxford: Clarendon Press. civ, 476p.

Spence was first published in 1820 (entry 131). Additional comments on Crashaw included in this edition. Indicates that Pope's ranking of Crashaw as higher than Herbert but lower than Sir John Beaumont and Donne exemplifies his neoclassical attitude toward metaphysical poetry and observes that Dr. Johnson excluded both Crashaw and Herbert from the *Lives of the Poets* (pp. 187–88). Reports that after May 1732 Holdsworth reputedly said that he could never find Crashaw's epitaph at Loreto: "I hunted the church all over and read all the epitaphs, and enquired of an English Jesuit whom I saw there, but could find nor hear of no such thing" (p. 316). Notes that Spence's travel papers identify the Jesuit as Father Atkinson (1688–1763) (p. 316).

◄§ 941. Raspa, Anthony. "Crashaw and the Jesuit Poetic." *UTQ* 36:37–54.

Agrees with Louis Martz (entry 764) that Crashaw's sacred poems, as well as some of Donne's and Southwell's religious poems, were greatly influenced by Jesuit poetry and poetical theory. Argues, however, that this influence "is not confined to the structure of individual poems" (p. 37), but is more pervasive and came into English poetry through Jesuit poetic theory. Finds in *Carmen Deo Nostro* the three major characteristics of Jesuit poetry and theory: a particular psychology, an epigrammatic style, and a clear distinction between sacred and profane genres. Discusses the nature of Jesuit psychology in relation to Crashaw's poetry and notes that he translated and borrowed directly from several Jesuit poems and would have been familiar with the work of certain Jesuit theorists. Discusses the three stages of the typical Ignatian meditation (use of memory, understanding, and will) and compares and contrasts them with "the way in which a reader achieved an apprehension" (p. 43) or experienced a religious truth in poems written under Jesuit influences. Concludes that "a poem could be considered a meditation comparable to a spiritual exercise" and that a poem could provide the experience of a meditation "in a fashion resembling that of the *Exercises*" (p. 52).

◄§ 942. Sito, Jerzy S. "Richard Crashaw: Maria Magdalena albo płaczka." *Więz* 9:40–49.

A Polish translation of "The Weeper" (pp. 40–48) followed by a brief introduction to Crashaw's life and poetry entitled "Mistyk płomienia" [The Mystic of the Flame] (pp. 48–49). Speaks of the special appropriateness of calling Crashaw a "mystic of the flame," not only because of his use of *flame* as a key word in his poems, but also because he burned with the fire of God's love in his personal life. Suggests that twentieth-century, post-Freudian readers often cannot fully appreciate Crashaw because they have not experienced such divine fire and innocence in their own lives.

◄§ 943. Stanwood, P. G. "Crawshaw [*sic*] at Rome." *N&Q* n.s. 13:256–57.

Points out the frequent appearance of Crashaw's name in the *Pilgrim-Book* (a visitors' register) of the English College in Rome and comments briefly on his connection with the college and its English residents and visitors. Suggests that Crashaw likely met Edward Thimelby there. Observes that the names of all four of the Fellows ejected from Peterhouse who converted to Catholicism—Crashaw, Francis Blakiston (nephew of John Cosin), Christopher Bankes, and Richard Nicols—appear in the book. Notes also that John Cosin's only son was a student at the college from 1652 and, as a Jesuit priest, returned to England in 1659. See also Henry Foley (entry 251) and Kenneth Larsen (entry 1039).

◄§ 944. Stewart, Stanley. *The Enclosed Garden: The Tradition and the Image in Seventeenth-Century Poetry*. Madison, Milwaukee, London: University of Wisconsin Press. xiv, 226p.

Briefly suggests that Crashaw's use of passionate language in "Ode on a Prayer-book" links him to the tradition of the Song of Songs. Suggests that the "proper context" for "Vexilla Regis" is found in the legends of the cross and the tree (p. 79). Calls attention to Crashaw's use of "the paradox of Christ's simultaneous role as both sun and shade" in "Hymn in the Glorious Epiphanie" (p. 90) and notes the traditional portrayal of the Virgin Mary as the prototype of the bride in "Hymn in the Assumption" (pp. 31; 194–95n.).

1967

◄§ 945. Anderson, James Bruce. "Richard Crashaw, St. Teresa, and St. John of the Cross." *Discourse* 10:421–28.

Challenges the notion that Crashaw's "baroque" style was greatly influenced by St. Teresa and St. John of the Cross. Compares typical poems by the two Spanish mystics with Crashaw's poems, especially "The Weeper," to show that Crashaw "did not become a formal disciple of the mystics, and never knew their writings in a way that would supply him with a writing style" (p. 427). Maintains that, although Crashaw's admiration for St. Teresa was great and probably life-long, "the main stream of his river of images flows from a source other than Spain" (p. 427). Regards "A Hymn to Sainte Teresa" and "The Flaming Heart" simply as products of a young student's enthusiasm for a saint who aroused the imagination of nearly all Europe and suggests that they do not show that Crashaw was particularly advanced in or existentially knowledgeable about the mystical experience: "I do not think he was farther along the mystical road than George Herbert; he was less far than John Donne" (p. 426).

&ᔣ 946. Binkerd, Gordon. *The Recommendation. Poem by Richard Crashaw.* London, Paris, Bonn, Sydney, Toronto, Johannesburg: Boosey & Hawkes. 19p.

Musical setting of "The Recommendation" from "Office of the Holy Crosse."

&ᔣ 947. Bradner, Leicester. "*Musae Anglicanae*: A Supplemental List." *Library* 5th series, 22:93–103.

Adds more than a hundred items to his list of Anglo-Latin poems in *Musae Anglicanae: A History of Anglo-Latin Poetry, 1500–1925* (entry 621) and makes minor corrections and revisions in some items previously included. Under 1634 suggests that the "second edition in 1670" should be deleted from his entry on *Epigrammatum sacrorum liber* and adds a new entry under 1670 pointing out that *Poemata et epigrammata* contains the 1634 epigrams with additional poems and was reissued with a newly dated title page in 1674.

&ᔣ 948. Chambers, Leland. "In Defense of 'The Weeper.'" *PLL* 3:111–21.

Presents a detailed critical analysis of "The Weeper" and argues that, although it has often been considered "an exhibition piece, an easily ridiculed example of the uncontrolled ingenuity identified with Baroque bad taste," the poem "displays neither bad taste nor lack of poetic discipline" but is "carefully ordered, flamboyant but not unrestrained in its imagery, and if ingeniously devised, deeply religious in its tone" (p. 111). Maintains that the poem is often misunderstood by critics and readers who fail to recognize its emblematic character and that the poem is not a hymn to Mary Magdalene but a hymn that glorifies the bleeding heart of God. Suggests that, "once the object of the poem's extravagant hyperboles and metaphors is established, what appears as ludicrous when considered solely in relationship to the Magdalen assumes the aspect of high devotional art" (p. 111). Discusses how the weeping eyes of the saint are emblematically related to the bleeding heart of God and argues that thus the saint unconventionally symbolizes God's love for man and is not the conventional symbol of man's love for God. Points out also that the traditional association of the Magdalene "with the language and imagery of secular love poetry makes it possible for Crashaw to address her in terms which convention and good taste would not otherwise have permitted him to address to God" (p. 112). Compares the 1646 and 1648 versions of the poem to show that the later "is not a mere expansion and revision of an already solidified poetic concept" but rather "represents a new, radical, and complex attitude towards its symbols and its subject" (p. 121).

◆§ 949. Davis, Bernard, and Elizabeth Davis, eds. *Poets of the Early Seventeenth Century.* (Routledge English Texts, ed. T. S. Dorsch.) London: Routledge & Kegan Paul. x, 246p.

Presents a general introduction to early seventeenth-century English poetry (pp. 1–6); anthologizes five poems or lines from poems by Crashaw (pp. 121–31); and gives a biographical sketch of the poet and a brief introduction to his poems (pp. 223–24), followed by notes to the poems (pp. 224–25). Suggests that Crashaw has more in common with Cowley than with Donne but "derives most from the works of Spanish and Italian poets and mystics of the Counter-Reformation, whose influence is widely perceptible in his choice of sacred themes, the impassioned fervour of his devotional apostrophes, and the 'fine excess' of his 'baroque' imagery and style" (p. 224). Points out that in some of his spiritual ecstasies "his reach is apt to exceed his grasp" and his poetry collapses into bathos, but that, at his best, in "A Hymn to Sainte Teresa," for instance, he "attains a high level of lyrical power" (p. 224). Suggests that in such poems as "Wishes. To his (supposed) Mistresse" and "Letter to the Countess of Denbigh" Crashaw "shows his command of familiar, natural style and compact expression, adapted alike to the play of wit and fancy and to the serious exercise of persuasive argument" (p. 224).

◆§ 950. Harrison, Robert. "Erotic Imagery in Crashaw's 'Musicks Duell.'" *SCN* 25:47–49.

Argues that critics too often regard Crashaw only as a religious poet and "have chosen either to dismiss his profane poems with faint praise or to explicate them wholly from the standpoint of the religious poems," thereby denying him "the privilege of wearing two hats" (p. 47). Through an analysis of "Musicks Duell" challenges the assumption that Crashaw "was interested in sexual imagery only as a vehicle, a 'language of accommodation' designed to express an ecstatic religious experience" and insists that the poem clearly demonstrates that he "had more than a metaphysical interest in sex" (p. 47). Compares Crashaw's version with Strada's original to show that the English poet greatly expanded upon the Latin poem and that in his expansions he often counterpointed a persistent erotic subcurrent to the poem's musical terminology. Maintains, therefore, that, as the poem develops, "it seems clear that not only is a musical duel taking place, but that the counterpoint of an unmistakeably erotic experience, deriving its movement from the rhythm of the music, is fitted into every line" and that at points in the poem Crashaw's imagery becomes "so infused with sensuality that the universe of music has all but disappeared" (p. 48).

◀§ 951. Milward, Peter. *Christian Themes in English Literature*. Tokyo: Kenkyuska. xvi, 269p.
Reprinted, Folcroft, Pa.: Folcroft Press, 1970, 1971.
Mentions Crashaw throughout. Points out lines 205–12 of "Hymn in the Glorious Epiphanie" as representative of the mystical *via negativa* and notes that Crashaw is more Continental than English in his use of this idea. Maintains that Crashaw derives his inspiration from the various mysteries of the life of Christ and that, although he dwells equally on the joyful and sorrowful mysteries, "it is perhaps in the former that his inspiration is strongest" (p. 151), citing in particular "Hymn in the Holy Nativity." Finds "tasteless exaggeration" in Crashaw's poems on Christ's passion, for example, "Song upon the Bleeding Crucifix." Comments on Crashaw's devotion to the Virgin Mary and contrasts his intense fervor in "O Gloriosa Domina" to Donne's coolness in *The Second Anniversary*. Briefly compares and contrasts Crashaw also with Francis Thompson and Gerard Manley Hopkins.

◀§ 952. Nuttall, A[nthony] D[avid]. "The Use of the Imagination in the Sixteenth and Seventeenth Centuries," in *Two Concepts of Allegory: A Study of* The Tempest *and the Logic of Allegorical Expression*, 73–107. London: Routledge and Kegan Paul; New York: Barnes and Noble.
Briefly discusses Crashaw's use of sensuous and often extravagant imagery. Suggests that "one function of bizarre imagery, like Crashaw's, is, as it were, to stretch the imagination until it surprises itself" (p. 83). Comments briefly on Crashaw's tendency to link the immense with the small and points out that the effect often is "to precipitate the reader into a state of wonder" (p. 84). Suggests that "the actualizing imagination," which makes the reading of Crashaw's poems "so strangely shocking may, on occasion, be the proper faculty to use" (p. 84), citing the image of the pelican shooting forth blood on a sinful world in "Adoro Te." Calls the description of the Magdalene's eyes as "Two walking baths; two weeping motions; / Portable, and compendious Oceans" the "most indigestible lines in the whole of Crashaw" (p. 85) and suggests that the shock contained in the lines survives any attempt to educate our modern sensibility.

◀§ 953. Reilly, R. J. "God, Man, and Literature." *Thought* 42:561–83.
Suggests that, "since the writer's felt apprehension of his relationship to God shapes his literary imagination, it might well be used as a principle of classification of literature" (p. 561). Outlines five basic categories: (1) "the 'rapt' writers, those who have a sense, or awareness, of their intimate union with God" (p. 568); (2) "the 'excited' writers, those who also apprehend that

the relationship between God and man is an intimate one, but whose apprehension is more intellectual than that of the writers in Group I" (p. 568); (3) "the 'normal' writers or 'humanistic' writers, those who accept the close relationship posited for them by their religions or philosophies but for whom the relationship is not existentially central" (p. 568); (4) "the writers in whose work there is less than normal recognition of the relationship, whether or not their religion or philosophy posits such a relationship" (p. 568); and (5) "the 'fervid deniers' of the relationship" (p. 568). Places Crashaw in the second category.

954. Roscelli, William John. "The Metaphysical Milton (1625–1631)." *TSLL* 8:463–84.

Comments on the possibility of the influence of the metaphysical poets on Milton and concludes that "(1) in at least six English poems which he composed between 1625 and 1631 and which have survived, Milton did employ images which can be considered metaphysical; (2) the use of metaphysical images, in general, is restricted to poems whose ostensible subject is death; (3) some of these metaphysical images find parallels in the poems of George Herbert, but the echoes are not so strong as to suggest direct influence; (4) the internal evidence provided by the English poems substantially confirms Raleigh's judgment that Milton was 'untouched' by Donne" (p. 484). Suggests no direct influence of Crashaw on Milton's early poems. Notes, however, that Crashaw's witty images are much more extravagant than Milton's and briefly contrasts Milton's use of conceit in "The Passion" (stanza 7) with Crashaw's use in "Upon the Death of a Gentleman [Mr. Chambers]" (lines 27–30), pointing out that Crashaw "particularizes his conceit precisely, thereby suggesting genuine feeling, albeit a feeling tinged with sentimentality," whereas Milton, "by not dramatizing his emotion with the same precision, was foredoomed to failure" (p. 475).

955. Shinoda, Kazushi. "Kantan nite-Gendai yoroppa Gungakuron." *Kenkyu Hokokushu* (Shokei Jogakuin Tanki Daigaku), no. 14.

Cited in Yoshihisa Aizawa's "A Bibliography of Writings about Metaphysical Poetry in Japan" (entry 1118). Not located.

956. Shudō, Tomoko. "St. Mary Magdalene o Megutte—Herbert to Crashaw" [About St. Mary Magdalene—Herbert and Crashaw]. *Shō-Kei Joshi Tanki Daigaku. Kenkyū Hōkokushū* [Reports of Shō-Kei Junior College for Women], no. 114.

Contrasts the quiet simplicity of Herbert's "Marie Magdalene" to the exuberant, ecstatic treatment of the saint by Crashaw in "The Weeper." Points out that Crashaw's poem clearly shows the influence of the baroque as well as that of the literature of tears. Suggests that "The Weeper" reflects Crashaw's highly emotional, Catholic fervor and maintains that he uses sensuous and even erotic imagery and symbols only in order to portray the ecstasy that results from total abandonment to the love of God. Claims that beneath the elaborate images of the poem lies a much deeper, hidden meaning that may escape the facile reader who is dazzled by the superficial aspects of the poem. Suggests that in his later poems Crashaw strikes a note of exultation that results from his contentment and joy in Catholicism.

≈§ 957. Stanford, D[erek]. "Crashaw, Richard," in *The New Catholic Encyclopedia*, 4:414–15. New York: McGraw Hill.
    Reprinted, Palatine, Ill.: J. Heraty, 1981.
    Presents a biographical account of Crashaw; briefly mentions the influences on his thought, art, and sensibility, such as Marino, the Jesuit epigrammatists, and St. Teresa; and briefly summarizes critical opinion on his poetry. Suggests that Crashaw's best-known poem is "A Hymn to Sainte Teresa." Points out that "a handful of Crashaw's poems have been universally appreciated" but that "critical opinion is divided as to the bulk of his work" (p. 415), even among his supporters. Briefly contrasts Crashaw to Herbert and points out his influence on Francis Thompson.

≈§ 958. Starkman, Miriam K., ed. *Seventeenth-Century English Poetry*, vol. 1. (Borzoi Anthology of 17th-Century English Literature, vol. 1.) New York: Alfred A. Knopf. xiii, 294, viip.
    Includes a general critical introduction to metaphysical poetry (pp. 3–24). Maintains that, although Crashaw "stands in the tradition of seventeenth-century devotional poetry, he is in a sense, atypical: extreme, sensuous, and decorative rather than logical and organic; synaesthetic, a little a-rational, unbalanced in his poetic usage, Baroque" (p. 20). Comments on major themes and techniques of Crashaw's sacred poetry. Points out that in his poetry Crashaw treats "the mystical theme" (p. 21) rather than mysticism itself and suggests that it is in the Teresian poems that he "approaches mysticism most explicitly, and there more speculatively than otherwise" (p. 22). Claims that Crashaw's originality as a devotional poet can be seen most clearly in his liturgical hymns and suggests that the main subject of his hymns is religious ardor. Comments briefly on the musical, ritualistic, and symbolic qualities of the hymns, citing "Hymn in the Glorious Epiphanie" as "the most intellectually substantial" (p. 22). Presents a brief biographical account of Crashaw (pp. 225–26) and anthologizes eighteen poems (pp. 226–88), with explanatory notes. Selected bibliography (pp. 289–94).

≈§ 959. Warnke, F[rank] J. "Baroque Poetry and the Experience of Contradiction." *CollG* 1:38–48.
    Appears, in revised form, as Chapter 3 of *Versions of Baroque: European Literature in the Seventeenth Century* (entry 1067), 52–65.
    Discusses the theme of contradiction as it is related to both metaphysical

and high baroque poetry. Suggests that both manners, while distinctive in some ways, are rooted in the same habit of mind and the same conception of art. Points out that baroque works of art typically search for "the reality behind the apparent fact of contradiction" and thus become objects "to be experienced rather than a text to be paraphrased or a message to be decoded" (p. 47). Observes that Crashaw "is notoriously the most Italianate of English seventeenth-century poets" (p. 38). Maintains that, "like his Continental coevals, he creates a phantasmagoric effect through an imagery which, though appealing vividly to the senses, is so disposed as to present a series of powerful contradictions of normal sensuous experience" and that "the typical structure of Crashaw's lyrics, associational rather than logical, works with his sensuous conceits to create a frankly imaginative world which insists on its difference from ordinary life even as it utilizes the sense data of that life" (p. 38). Discusses "A Hymn to Sainte Teresa" and points out that in the poem "the contraries of pain and rapture, flesh and spirit, multiplicity and unity, are fused into a single experience of the imagination through the agency of a sensibility which utilizes the sense data of worldly experience but rearranges those data in such a way as to transcend them, creating thus a world in which ordinary contradictions have lost their capacity for enforcing choice" (p. 47).

◄§ 960. Whitlock, Baird W. "From the Counter-Renaissance to the Baroque." *BuR* 15:46–60.

Discusses certain differences between sixteenth- and seventeenth-century art forms, between the Counter Renaissance (circa 1520–1620) and the baroque (circa 1620–1720). Maintains that in English poetry Donne and Herbert "represent the shift that took place in formal experimentation between the two periods" but suggests that "Donne's metrical and rhyme innovations very seldom add to the unification or meaning of the whole poem, whereas Herbert's variations almost without exception do" (p. 48). Points out that in baroque art "decoration maintains the appearance of structure" and that "vocal decorations are included by the composer to heighten the ongoing structure of the piece and become part of the meaning of the song, just as the apparently overdone piling of conceits in Crashaw is an inherent part of the emotional meaning of the poems" (p. 58).

◄§ 961. Williamson, George. "Richard Crashaw," in *Six Metaphysical Poets: A Reader's Guide*, 119–44. New York: Farrar, Straus and Giroux. Reprinted, London: Thames and Hudson, 1968.

Presents a general introduction to Crashaw's life and poetry. Suggests that Crashaw tends to offend modern taste by "his excesses in the expression of devotional love" and by "his feeling for the beauty of holiness" (p. 119) and maintains that "none of the Metaphysical Poets understood the rhetoric of contrariety better than Crashaw" (p. 133). Contains brief analyses of "Upon the ensuing Treatises [of Mr. Shelford]," "The Weeper," "Wishes. To his (supposed) Mistresse," "Loves Horoscope," "Upon the Death of a Gentleman [Mr. Chambers]," "An Elegy upon the death of Mr. Stanninow," "Upon two green Apricocks," "On Hope," "Hymn in the Holy Nativity," "Hymn in the Glorious Epiphanie," "Hymn to the Name of Jesus," "A Hymn to Sainte Teresa," "Ode on a Prayer-book," "On Mr. G. Herberts booke, The Temple," and "Letter to the Countess of Denbigh."

◅§ 962. Winters, Yvor. "Aspects of the Short Poem in the English Renaissance," in *Forms of Discovery: Critical and Historical Essays on the Forms of the Short Poem in English*, 1–120. Chicago: Alan Swallow.
   Comments on the difficulty of expressing mystical experience through sexual analogy and maintains that "the poet who insists on dealing with the experience and who becomes involved emotionally in the sexual analogy runs the risk of corrupting his devotional poetry generally with sexual imagery" (p. 92). Focuses on the weaknesses in Crashaw's poetry that result from his use of sexual analogy and imagery. Argues that "A Hymn to Sainte Teresa," for example, is "greatly over-estimated," calls it "a fairy-tale of childish pietism," finds it "not credible" and "far from interesting," and suggests that a comparison of it to Jonson's "To Heaven" or Herbert's "Church Monuments" will show "the extraordinary nature of the decay of poetic intelligence within a very few years" (p. 93). Maintains that "Hymn in the Holy Nativity" is a better poem but shows similar weaknesses and "tends to disintegrate, the more carefully one inspects it" (p. 94). Finds "Psalme 23" "more nearly successful" but with certain weaknesses as well. Singles out "The Weeper" and "Wishes. To his (supposed) Mistresse" as Crashaw's worst pieces, exemplifying "the faults of the Metaphysical poets at their extreme" (p. 96). Concludes that "there are many brilliant passages scattered through Crashaw's work" (p. 95), citing stanza 23 from "Sospetto d'Herode" as an example, but maintains that his most successful poems, "are minor in intention and fact" (p. 96). Suggests that the best poems in Crashaw's canon are "The Recommendation" at the conclusion of "Office of the Holy Crosse" and "Marke 4. Why are yee afraid, O yee of little faith?"

1968

◅§ 963. Bertonasco, Marc F. "Crashaw and the Emblem." *ES* 49:530–34.
   Supports the position of Ruth Wallerstein, Helen White, and Austin Warren that Crashaw's imagery is "purely symbolical" and that "ignoring its emblematic nature has led to numerous misinterpretations" (p. 530). Argues that Crashaw's images are "almost always emblematic" and traces certain of his key images "(especially those criticized by unfriendly critics) to specific sources in emblem books circulating throughout England in the second and third decade of the seventeenth century" (p. 530). Discusses Crashaw's use of such images as the nest, breast, wounds of love, water and flames, as well as his use of

wing and animal symbolism, and shows that their sources can often be found in popular emblem books. Suggests that the "most disturbing" image to modern critics is that of breast sucking, as found in "Luke 11. Blessed be the paps which Thou hast sucked," but argues that "the graphic representation of breast sucking is not uncommon in seventeenth-century emblem books" (p. 533). Maintains that "a few hours spent with Quarles will do much to dispel the notion that Crashaw was exotic, continental, foreign-hearted" (p. 533) but insists that "it was the emblematic mode of expression, even more than individual emblem plates, that affected his poetic utterance" (p. 534).

◆§ 964. ————. "A New Look at Crashaw's 'The Weeper.'" *TSLL* 10: 177–88.
Revised version included in *Crashaw and the Baroque* (entry 1026), 94–117.
Argues that "The Weeper" is "modeled on the method of formal meditation developed and popularized by St. Francis de Sales" (p. 177) and that, when read as a Salesian meditation, it "takes on a firm, actually predictable structure, and even the grotesqueries of the poem, to a great degree, emerge as aesthetically justifiable" (p. 178). Distinguishes between the Ignatian and the Salesian methods of meditation. Maintains that the principal subject of the poem is supernatural repentance. Presents a prose paraphrase of the poem in order to show its formal structure: "The beauty of the Magdalene's contrition (and that of any sincere Christian) is more beautiful, more precious, than anything in nature, for it secures salvation (I–XIII)"; but "most Christians, like the Magdalen, can enjoy the security of God's love only after a period of intense grief (XIV–XVII), and although their repentance may be in some measure free, the ultimate cause is the grace of Christ (XVIII), to whom conversion gives such great glory (XIX–XXII)" (p. 183). Comments on how the meditative purposes of the poem influenced Crashaw's choice of highly emblematic imagery and argues that Crashaw's imagery "is hardly ever truly redundant or even *merely* iterative for purposes of dramatic emphasis," as many critics have suggested, but that his employment "of the same *basic* concept in a series of increasingly lush images usually represents a steady, subtle, but quite significant development of thought" (p. 183). Suggests that his comments on "The Weeper" can be profitably applied to other Crashaw poems, especially those in *Carmen Deo Nostro*.

◆§ 965. Fischer, Hermann. "Richard Crashaw," in *Die englische Lyrik: Von der Renaissance bis zur Gegenwart*, edited by Karl Heinz Göller, 1: 175–93, 411–15. Düsseldorf: August Bagel Verlag.
Translates into German "Easter day" and "Hymn in the Assumption," explicates each poem, and compares and contrasts their effectiveness in unifying disparate baroque elements. Describes "Easter day" as simultaneously ecstatic and highly mannered and suggests that the poem is, in a sense, a third version

of Crashaw's paradoxical treatment of the theme of Christ's resurrection, the
two earlier attempts being his epigrams "In resurrectionem Domini" and
"Upon our Saviours Tombe wherein never man was laid." Discusses the biblical sources and allusions in "Easter day" and notes that, although the intricate
theological reasoning in the poem and its elaborate rhetorical and stylistic features have little immediate appeal for modern readers, it shows Crashaw's attempt to unify disparate elements. Suggests that "Hymn in the Assumption,"
on the other hand, carries the "Einheitsprinzip" (p. 186) of baroque painting
into poetry and finds it a highly unified poem that successfully combines such
disparate elements as sensuality and spirituality, and highly mannered details
and organic unity. Calls the hymn a great liturgical work and notes that it is
"stilstark in ihrer konstrucktiven Synthese von sakralem und profanem Be-
reich; faszinierend in ihrem an Geist, Gefühl und Sinne gerichteten Appell;
foomischer in ihrer Strukturfähigkeit und in ihrer Verwirklichung des harmo-
nischen 'Gesamtkunstwerks'" (p. 192). Detailed notes on both poems (pp.
411–15).

⋙ 966. Gorlier, Claudio. "Maturazione del <<wit>> barocco: Richard
    Crashaw," in *La poesia metafisica inglese*, 107–23. (Biblioteca di studi
    inglesi e americani, 1.) Milan: La Goliardica.
    A biographical sketch of Crashaw and a general critical discussion of his
poetry, stressing the poet's spiritual evolution and the baroque features of his
style—its sensuousness, ingenuity, and uses of harmony and music; its pictorial effects; and its use of sacred parody. Calls Crashaw "il D'Annunzio della
poesia metafisica inglese" (p. 107). Discusses the major themes of Crashaw's
poetry and points out influences on his sensibility and art, especially Marino
and his followers, Guarini, the Counter-Reformation, and the Latin emblemists, but stresses how Crashaw brings baroque wit to a kind of maturity.
Suggests that Crashaw sees poetry as an instrument of salvation and comments on the sacramentality of his view of poetic language. Discusses in some
detail the theme and poetic technique of "Wishes. To his (supposed) Mistresse," "On the wounds of our crucified Lord," and "The Flaming Heart."
Briefly contrasts Crashaw to Donne and Herbert.

⋙ 967. Honig, Edwin, and Oscar Williams, eds. *The Major Metaphysical
    Poets of the Seventeenth Century: John Donne, George Herbert, Richard
    Crashaw, and Andrew Marvell.* New York: Washington Square Press.
    902p.
    In a detailed critical introduction to metaphysical poetry (pp. 1–33), Honig
comments on major features of Crashaw's art and sensibility, such as his use
of emblems, elaborate rhetoric and decoration, and verbal ingenuity, and
compares and contrasts him with Donne, Herbert, and Marvell. "Richard
Crashaw" (pp. 505–705) presents a biographical account of the poet and anthologizes the English poems, without notes or commentary. Includes a se-

lected bibliography prepared by Milton Miller and Beverly Goldberg (pp. 867–77).

◆§ 968. Howard, Thomas T. "Herbert and Crashaw: Notes on Meditative Focus." *GorR* 11:79–98.

Maintains that, although Crashaw and Herbert were products of a similar religious tradition and shared a devotion to the liturgy, the sacraments, and spiritual meditation, there is a fundamental difference between them: "Whereas Herbert's vision of religion and the world was a truly sacramental one, albeit tempered with an Anglican reticence about becoming too baroque, Crashaw felt at home in the excruciatingly physical forms of Counter-Reformation meditation, an idea which is borne out in his shift to Rome as well as in his poetic focus" (p. 84). Suggests that Herbert's "devotional and meditative posture takes on the form of scrutiny, analysis, self-calumny, dialogue with God, reflection on the implications of grace, and so forth, with the full consciousness of liturgical and traditional forms and the significance of ecclesiastical ornament, the figural, and sacramental understanding of the creation as 'God-bearing images'"; whereas Crashaw "is disposed to adoration, and baroque elaboration of objects of veneration as though by the artistic expansion of the objects the soul will be that much the more impressed and aware of its overwhelming debt of gratitude" (p. 84). Comments on a number of Crashaw's poems, especially "The Teare," "The Weeper," "Hymn to the Name of Jesus," "Hymn in the Holy Nativity," "Sancta Maria Dolorum," "O Gloriosa Domina," "Hymn in the Assumption," "Adoro Te," "Lauda Sion," and several of the divine epigrams, to illustrate Crashaw's religious convictions and sensibilities.

◆§ 969. Kelliher, W. Hilton. "Crashaw's Contemporary Reputation." *N&Q* n.s. 15:375.

Notes the mention of Crashaw in an unsigned, twenty-one stanza, irregular Pindaric ode on the Charterhouse that appeared in the prefatory matter of Samuel Herne's *Domus Carthusiana: or an Account of the Noble Foundation of the Charter-House* . . . (entry 46). Notes that the mention does not appear in Martin. Suggests that the writer of the ode is Herne (or Hearne) himself and reproduces the fifteenth stanza in which Crashaw is discussed.

◆§ 970. Shudō, Tomoko. "Divine Love e no Michi: Richard Crashaw: St. Teresa Poems no hitotsu no Kaishaku." *Shokei Jogakuin Tanki Daigaku. Kenkyu Hokoku* no. 15 (October):91–100.

Discusses the three Teresian poems to show how Crashaw's deepening attraction to Teresa reflects his spiritual development from pious Anglicanism to mystical Catholicism. Suggests that in "A Hymn to Sainte Teresa" Crashaw merely describes the saint's life and mystical experiences, which serve as a model for him; that in "An Apologie for the fore-going Hymn" he apologizes to his countrymen for praising a Spaniard and confesses his love for Christ, gained through the example and writings of St. Teresa; and that in "The Flaming Heart" Crashaw expresses complete self-surrender and spiritual unity with the great saint, as poetic and spiritual ecstasy become one.

◄§ 971. Turnell, Martin. "The Mystic and the Critic." *TLS*, 29 February, pp. 201–2.

Comments on the confusion created by critics who indiscriminately use the word *mysticism* (as well as such closely associated words as *ecstasy, vision, contemplation,* and *hallucination*) and maintains that "genuine mystical writing is a record of a personal or, more accurately, an autobiographical religious experience, that is different in kind from all other forms of religious writing and from the imaginative work of the creative writer" (p. 201). Suggests that in lines 65–74 of "Ode on a Prayer-book" Crashaw may not be reflecting his own mystical experience but may simply be imaginatively interpreting what he had read in the Second Epistle to the Corinthians or in St. Teresa.

◄§ 972. Whitlock, Baird W. "The Baroque Characteristics of the Poetry of George Herbert." *Cithara* 7, no. 2:30–40.

Argues that Herbert, not Crashaw, is the most typical English baroque poet and maintains that "to study the characteristics of the Baroque without seeing George Herbert as a central figure in the movement is to miss most what is central to the concept" (p. 39). Cites twelve generally accepted major characteristics of baroque art and illustrates each with specific examples from Herbert's poems. No extended discussion of Crashaw.

1969

◄§ 973. Binkerd, Gordon W. *Memorial.* (Text by Richard Crashaw.) [New York]: Boosey & Hawkes. 20p.

Musical setting of "A Song ('Lord, when the sense of thy sweet grace')" for soprano, alto, tenor, and bass.

◄§ 974. Crum, Margaret, ed. *First-Line Index of English Poetry 1500–1800 in Manuscripts of the Bodleian Library Oxford.* 2 vols. New York: Index Committee of the Modern Language Association; Oxford: Clarendon Press. 1–630; 631-1257p.

Includes five indexes: (1) Bodleian manuscripts listed by shelfmarks; (2) authors; (3) names mentioned; (4) authors of works translated, paraphrased, or imitated; and (5) references to composers of settings and tunes named or quoted. Includes 113 entries for Crashaw.

◄§ 975. Davie, Donald. "Christopher Smart: Some Neglected Poems." *ECS* 3:242–64.

Briefly compares Christopher Smart's *Hymns and Spiritual Songs* (1765) to *Steps to the Temple* to suggest that, in some respects, Smart was a baroque poet. Points out, for example, that two characteristics of Crashaw's poetry are "a disparity between the complexity of the surface and the simplicity beneath" and that it does not reflect "a divided or tormented, self-doubting or self-questioning attitude in the writer" (p. 250). Suggests that in these respects Smart is like Crashaw.

◄§ 976. The Editors. "A Correction and an Apology." *SCN* 27:57.

Expresses regret for the publication of "Richard Crashaw and Thomas Traherne: A Bibliography, 1938–1966" by Edward E. Samaha, Jr. (entry 993). Acknowledges that the intended update "wrongly stated that Lloyd E. Berry excluded both poets from his *Bibliography of Studies in Metaphysical Poetry*" (entry 896) and that Samaha's list "imperfectly duplicates part of what he covered soundly" and includes "titles which do not deserve listing inasmuch as they contain little or nothing on the two authors."

◄§ 977. Hardy, Stan. "Source Wanted." *N&Q* n.s. 16:194.

Asks for the source of a stanza beginning "That he whom the Sun serves should faintly peepe through clouds of Infant flesh." Notes that his impression is that it "appeared as an entry in a Literary Competition, probably in the 1915–1918 period" but suggests that it "may be authentic seventeenth-century verse." For a reply, see Anthony Shipps (entry 996).

◄§ 978. Iwabuchi, Satoru. "Richard Crashaw no Shūkyō-shi ni okeru Shim-pishisō" [Mysticism in Richard Crashaw's Divine Poems]. *Fukushima Kōtō-senmon Gakkō Bulletin* 5, no. 1:96–101.

Discusses the influence of medieval thought on Crashaw and comments on the mystical elements of his poetry. Points out that Crashaw's mysticism, which is termed "Platonic," has the tone of the *via negativa* recommended by the Pseudo-Dionysius, that is, a searching for the invisible God by denying visible creation and by entering into mystical darkness in order to find the eternal brightness of God, an attitude that pervades all of Crashaw's religious verse. Suggests that "Hymn in the Glorious Epiphanie" best expresses Crashaw's mysticism and notes the influence of the *Spiritual Exercises* of St. Ignatius Loyola.

◄§ 979. Kawata, Akira. "Richard Crashaw to Banshō no Kusari" [Richard Crashaw and the Chain of Being]. *Ichinoseki Technical College Bulletin* no. 3:89–99.

Discusses how the concept of the Great Chain of Being is reflected in Crashaw's poetry, especially his religious verse. Suggests that the poet's use of rich, abundant, and colorful imagery may have been influenced by the theory of emanation proposed by the Pseudo-Dionysius. Observes that in his poetry

Crashaw depicts a God who descends to penetrate the world with his grace rather than a transcendent God.

◆§ 980. Kermode, Frank, ed. *The Metaphysical Poets: Key Essays on Metaphysical Poetry and the Major Metaphysical Poets.* Edited with introduction and commentary by Frank Kermode. (Fawcett Premier Literature and Ideas Series, ed. Irving Howe.) New York: Fawcett Publications. 351p.

Presents a general introduction to metaphysical poetry and comments on critical trends (pp. 11–32). Briefly discusses the relationship between metaphysical and baroque poetry and notes that, although Continental critics are not reluctant to call Milton a baroque poet, "nobody ever seriously called him metaphysical," whereas Crashaw, "described as a metaphysical, is called baroque because of his frenetic Counter-Reformation piety and his link with Bernini and St. Teresa" (p. 16). Suggests that Crashaw represents a fusion between metaphysical and baroque. Points out that his poetry "is devoted to spiritual ecstasy of a kind that—like the face of Bernini's Teresa seen from certain angles—seems to have a strong sexual model; and in some famous passages, such as the great crescendo of the last section of 'The Flaming Heart' there is surely a building up of an explosive, as it were orgasmic, force" (p. 26). Suggests that of all the English poets Crashaw most resembles Marino, "although he had more élan—not more virtuosity, but more impetus, witness the secular, Italianate, and beautiful 'Musicks Duell'" (p. 26). Maintains that, although Crashaw's conceits are often considered tasteless, they are "no more so than many other aids to pious meditation, of a less exciting kind" (p. 26). Notes that poems like "The Weeper" "can sometimes remind one of those shops, full of cheaply made junk, that one sees outside great cathedrals" but claims that "it is Crashaw's merit to have made poetry from this fact—to have made English poems out of this foreign and suspect ecstasy" (p. 27). Concludes that Crashaw is "the metaphysical poet we might, most of us, most happily surrender to baroque" but points out that "he enriches, as well as confuses, the history of metaphysical poetry" (p. 27). Contains twenty-six previously published essays and/or selections from book-length studies arranged under five headings: (1) The English Background, (2) Baroque, (3) Metaphysical Poetic, (4) the Major English Metaphysical Poets, and (5) Epilogue. The following items are especially relevant to Crashaw: (1) Lowry Nelson, Jr., "The Baroque Style" (pp. 88–96), from *Baroque Lyric Poetry* (entry 861), pp. 6–15; (2) Frank J. Warnke, "Baroque and Metaphysical" (pp. 97–112), from *European Metaphysical Poetry* (entry 870), pp. 5–21; (3) T. S. Eliot, "The Metaphysical Poets" (pp. 126–35), first published in 1921, from *Selected Essays* (entry 417); (4) Joseph E. Duncan, "The Background of Eliot's [Donne] Criticism" (pp. 136–45), from *The Revival of Metaphysical Poetry* (entry 831), pp. 118–26; (5) Joseph A. Mazzeo, "A Critique of Modern Theories of Metaphysical Poetry" (pp. 158–71), from *MP* (entry 746), (6) selection from

"The Preface to the Reader" from *Steps to the Temple* (pp. 255–56); and (7) Austin Warren, "Crashaw's Themes and Images" (pp. 257–75), from *Richard Crashaw: A Study in Baroque Sensibility* (entry 619), pp. 133–34, 139–46, 176–93, 238–39.

◄§ 981. Krzeckowski, Henryk, Jerzy S. Sito, and Juliusz Żuławski, eds. "Richard Crashaw (1613?-1649)," in *Poeci języka angielskiego* [Poets of the English Language], 1:653–72, 864–65. (Biblioteka poezji i prozy.) Warsaw: Panstwowy Instytut Wydawniczy.

Reprinted, 1971, 1974.
A general introduction to Crashaw's life and poetry (p. 653), a very selected bibliography (p. 653), and eleven poems or selections from poems, translated into Polish by Jerzy S. Sito and Aleksander Mierzejewski (pp. 654–72), with brief notes (pp. 864–65). Calls Crashaw one of the outstanding metaphysical poets and an author of deep and beautiful religious lyrics.

◄§ 982. Martz, Louis L. *The Wit of Love: Donne, Carew, Crashaw, Marvell.* (University of Notre Dame Ward-Phillips Lectures in English, vol. 3.) Notre Dame and London: University of Notre Dame Press. xv, 216p.

Series of four lectures (revised and expanded) first given at the University of Notre Dame in March 1968. Chapter 3, "Richard Crashaw: *Love's Architecture*" (pp. 113–47), defines the baroque through the visual arts, especially Bernini's Baldacchino in St. Peter's, Gaulli's ceiling of Il Gesù in Rome, the altarpiece of the Lady Chapel at the University of Notre Dame, and the font-cover ascribed to Grinling Gibbons in the church of All Hallows Barking in London, seeing these artifacts as examples of the "Renaissance ideal of harmony" holding in place "the violent aspirations of the Baroque spirit" (p. 116). Discusses Bernini's statue of St. Teresa in the Cornaro Chapel in Rome, stating that knowledge of its baroque techniques is especially helpful in an understanding of Crashaw's poetry. Discusses "The Flaming Heart" in the light of the painting of St. Teresa by Crashaw's contemporary, Gerhard Seghers, which was displayed in the Church of the Discalced Carmelites in Antwerp, where the poet could have seen it in the 1640s. Points out that a copy of the painting, attributed to Velásquez, exists in the English Convent at Bruges and suggests that more copies existed, thus explaining why Crashaw perhaps thought of it as representing the way "she is usually expressed"—pale-faced, rather than inflamed, as she ought to be. Also points out that Crashaw's description of the seraph in "The Flaming Heart" fits the figure in the painting. Distinguishes between metaphysical and baroque conceit, claiming that the first is based upon the philosophical doctrine of correspondences, whereas the second is a paradox or symbol viewed from various angles, "reviewing and revising and restating and expanding the issue until some truth of emotion gradually grows out from all the glittering elaboration" (pp. 127–28). Comments on the 1652 additions to "The Flaming Heart," seeing them as indicative of a movement from the concrete to the abstract and maintaining that "the Baroque tries, by multiplication of sensory impressions, to exhaust the sensory and to suggest the presence of the spiritual" (p. 131). Regards "A Hymn to Sainte Teresa" as more successful because it is more controlled. Calls it a perfect poem, rare in Crashaw, "partly because of the very nature of the Baroque, which depends upon the daring cast of imagination for its most powerful effects, and also perhaps because Crashaw himself is living in a world of imagination that does not have its roots in England" (p. 135). Maintains that Crashaw had no English models of a baroque poet, except Southwell. Points out that from Herbert, Crashaw learned the "use of simple language and homely images in devotion" (p. 136) and discusses "On Mr. G. Herberts booke, The Temple," which raises the central problem of Crashaw's use of sensuous imagery to speak of his love of God or saints. Discusses "Ode on a Prayer-book" as an example of Crashaw's use of imagery commonly found in popular Cavalier love songs, such as Carew's "A Rapture," for religious subjects. Asserts that the argument of the poem fails because it suggests a rivalry for God's love as if there were not enough to go round. Briefly comments on the weaknesses of "The Weeper" and the strengths of "Hymn in the Glorious Epiphanie." Suggests that "Hymn in the Holy Nativity" is "one of Crashaw's nearly perfect pieces" (p. 142) and discusses it as a lover's dawn-song and also as an example of the baroque method of repetition to achieve a unity of impression. In Chapter 4, "Andrew Marvell: *The Mind's Happiness*" (pp. 151–90), compares the careers of Crashaw and Marvell and briefly contrasts their poetry, illustrating the differences by commenting on "The Teare" and Marvell's "Eyes and Tears."

◀§ 983. Mazzaro, Jerome. "Robert Lowell and the Kavanaugh Collapse." *UWR* 5 : 1–24.
   Briefly suggests similarities between images in Robert Lowell's "The Mills of the Kavanaughs" and "An Epitaph upon a Young Married Couple" and points out that Lowell cites Crashaw's poem in his "The Verse of Thomas Merton" (entry 667).

◀§ 984. Miner, Earl. *The Metaphysical Mode from Donne to Cowley*. Princeton: Princeton University Press. xix, 291p.
   Pages 99–117 reprinted in *The Metaphysical Poets: A Selection of Critical Essays*, ed. Gerald Hammond (entry 1085), 197–214.
   Pages 118–58 reprinted in *Seventeenth Century English Poetry: Modern Essays in Criticism*, ed. William R. Keast (entry 879), 45–76, rev. ed. (1971), 45–76.
   States that the purpose of this study is "to discriminate poetic features that are particularly important to the metaphysical style and differences possible within the style; in other words, what is lasting and what changes, what is general to the style and what is peculiar to individual writers" (p. xi). Argues

(1) that Metaphysical poetry is "private in mode, that it treats time and place in ways describable in terms of the 'dramatic,' the 'narrative,' the transcendent, the 'meditative,' and the 'argumentative'—and that these terms provide in their sequence something of a history of the development of Metaphysical poetry" (p. xi); (2) that "the wit of Metaphysical poetry can be characterized as definition, that is, as those logical or rhetorical processes bringing together or separating (whether in metaphor or idea) matters of similar or opposed classes; and as that dialectic, or those processes, that extend such matters by their relation in logical and rhetorical procedures" (pp. xi–xii); and (3) that "the thematic range of Metaphysical poetry can best be represented in terms of satiric denial and lyric affirmation" (p. xii). Chapter 1, "The Private Mode" (pp. 3–47), argues that the private mode is "the chief 'radical' of Metaphysical poetry, . . . differentiating it from the social and public modes of other poetry written in modern English before the late eighteenth century and the Romantic poets" (p. x). Chapter 2, "Forms of Perception: Time and Place" (pp. 48–117), explores various "forms, modes and structures of Metaphysical poems in terms of their versions of time and place" (p. x). Chapter 3, "Wit: Definition and Dialectic" (pp. 118–58), defines the "major features of Metaphysical wit in terms reflecting the poets' use of an older logic and rhetoric" (p. xi). Chapter 4, "Themes: Satire and Song" (pp. 159–213), comments on "the thematic range of Metaphysical poetry in terms of complementary elements," in terms of song and satire, "the former a tendency to affirmation, the latter a tendency to denial, both being capable of expression in lyricism or in satire, or in mixtures" (p. xi). Chapter 5, "Three Poems" (pp. 214–71), examines in detail Donne's "The Perfume," Herbert's "The Flower," and Marvell's "Nymph complaining for the death of her Faun." Mentions Crashaw throughout and compares and contrasts him with Donne, Herbert, Vaughan, Marvell, Traherne, and Cowley. Comments on Crashaw's use of the private and meditative modes, his employment of ingenious wit in his religious poems, his "identification of religious ardor with sexual ecstasy" (p. 141), and his uses of sacred parody. Maintains that Crashaw is primarily a poet of affirmation, not one of satiric denial. Calls him "the least satiric of the major Metaphysical poets" and points out that, "so given is he to praise and affirmation that the satirical element, the personal antagonism, the tension of opposed elements— the things that give Donne's poetry much of its drive—are either absent or transformed in his best-known poetry" (p. 186), such as "A Hymn to Sainte Teresa." Suggests that "the only tension is normally that between erotic imagery and religious ecstasy, but since such imagery is common enough in mystical poetry and because Crashaw uses it for traditional sacred parody, his usual treatment does not warrant the name of satire, even in an extended sense" (p. 187). Points out, however, that in some of his lesser-known poems, such as "To Pontius washing his blood-stained hands" and especially "Sospetto d'Herode," some elements of satiric antagonism can be found but that even in his adaptation of Marino's poem "his theme is affirmation, and even Herod

slaughtering the Innocents seems scarcely to pose a threat" (p. 188). Maintains that Crashaw sometimes "invents a style (which is usually not very successful) that can be termed neither dramatic nor narrative, because it has no situation or specifiable actors to give its intensity a dramatic effect, nor yet any discernible sequence to give its details narrative succession" (p. 98), citing "Hymn to the Name of Jesus" as an example. Briefly comments on "Hymn in the Holy Nativity" as a metaphysical pastoral and calls "The Weeper" a "ludicrous poem" and a "ransacking of the resources of definition" (pp. 126–27).

◄§ 985. Murrin, Michael. "The Auditor's Response," in *The Veil of Allegory: Some Notes Toward A Theory of Allegorical Rhetoric in the English Renaissance*, 98–134. Chicago and London: University of Chicago Press.
Discusses how Crashaw achieves a "medley of historical periods" (p. 111) in "Hymn in the Glorious Epiphanie" and praises the poem for its skillful blending of literal history, theological vision, and philosophical mysticism. Points out that in the poem Crashaw includes three historical events—the visitation of the Magi, the death of Christ, and the triumph of Christianity over pagan heliolatry—and suggests that he may have included yet a fourth and contemporary event—the proclamation of Tommaso Campanella that Louis XIV "would unite all peoples in a new city of the sun and be himself the new Sun King" (p. 112). Maintains that "the constant, brilliant paradoxes of the poem rest upon a simple opposition, which, once grasped, clarifies practically all the difficult passages"—"day represents theological and moral darkness; and darkness, light" (p. 130). Calls the hymn "unique among Crashaw's works" (p. 130).

◄§ 986. Okuda, Hiroko. "Mizu no Henshin" [A Transformation of Water]. *Idee* no. 2:1–12.
Argues that the imagery of "The Weeper" is highly emblematic and that the whole poem contains the three basic elements of an emblem: the *pictura* (portrait of the saint), the *inscriptio* (initial epigraph), and the *subscripto* (thirty-one stanzas). Notes also the pervasive influence of the Ignatian application of the five senses on the imagery of the poem. Maintains that, although the poem lacks a strictly logical unity, each of the stanzas comments on the initial epigraph and together they form a thematic unity.

◄§ 987. Ōsawa, Minoru, ed. "Richard Crashaw," in *Sekai Meishi Kanshō Jiten* [A Dictionary of World-Famous People], 87–88. Tokyo: Tokyōdo.
A brief introduction to Crashaw's life and poetry. Praises "The Flaming Heart" as Crashaw's finest work. Points out the influence of Marino and Góngora and comments briefly on the exaggerated effects of the baroque on Crashaw's style.

◄§ 988. Perella, Nicholas James. "Medieval Mystics," in *The Kiss Sacred and Profane: An Interpretative History of Kiss Symbolism and Related*

Religio-Erotic Themes, 51–83. Berkeley and Los Angeles: University of California Press.

Points out that in "A Hymn to Sainte Teresa" Crashaw envisions the death of the saint as a kiss "by which God ravished her soul unto himself" (p. 70) and suggests that he may have derived the image not only from the medieval Catholic mystical tradition but also from the kiss symbolism found in medieval Jewish writings.

◆§ 989. Perosa, Sergio. "L'Età di Milton," in *Storia della letteratura inglese*, 1:108–34. (Letteratura universale, vol. 21, ed. Luigi Santucci.) Milan: Fratelli Fabbri Editori.

A brief introduction to Crashaw's life and poetry (pp. 121–22), suggesting that the literary influences on Crashaw's poetry, especially that of the Jesuit Latin poets and Marino, "possono farci capire il tono generale della poesia di Crashaw, piena di concetti, di immagini sbilanciate ed ardite, di variazioni che si ripetono all'infinito come in una sinfonia il cui tema viene riproposto in modo sempre identico e diverso, di pensieri che si sperdono in musica e di musica che vorrebbe sostituirsi ai pensieri" (p. 122). Claims that the richness of Crashaw's poetry reminds one of Rubens and that his languidness recalls Murillo. Points out that in color and sound Crashaw's poetry belongs to the baroque. Singles out "Musicks Duell" and "The Flaming Heart" as "le due espressioni più significative di questa estasi religiosa che ha tutti i languouri, i suoni e i colori di una esperienza carnale" (p. 122).

◆§ 990. Rothschild, Philippe de. "Richard Crashaw, 1612(?)-1649," in *Poèmes élisabéthains*, 302–15, 394–95. Préface de André Pieyre de Mandiargues. Introduction de Stephen Spender. Notices biographiques de Christopher Ricks. Paris: Seghers.

A brief introduction to Crashaw's life and poetry (pp. 302–5) followed by selections from "Wishes. To his (supposed) Mistresse," "Epithalamium," "New Years Day," "On our crucified Lord Naked, and bloody," "Hymn to the Name of Jesus," and "The Flaming Heart," with French translations on facing pages (pp. 306–15). Notes and variants on the text (in English and French) (pp. 306–15). Calls Crashaw "un poète religieux de l'exaltation et du désepoir" (p. 305) and comments briefly on his baroque sensibility and mystical attitudes, noting that "le paysage de Crashaw n'a rien d'anglais dans ses splendeurs et misères" (p. 304). Briefly compares and contrasts Crashaw to Milton, Herbert, Vaughan, and Traherne.

◆§ 991. Roy, V[irendra] K[umar], and R. C. Kapoor. "Metaphysical Poetry," in *John Donne and Metaphysical Poetry*, 18–44. Delhi: Doabo House.

General introduction to the major characteristics of metaphysical poetry with brief critical comments on Donne, Herbert, Carew, Crashaw, Vaughan, Marvell, Cowley, and Herrick. Suggests that Crashaw "does not possess the intellectualism of Donne or the control and artistic finish of Herbert's poetry" and that, on the whole, he "does not have any sense of discipline and critical sensibility" (p. 42). Maintains that in Crashaw's religious poetry "there is passion and lyrical intensity, but no analysis of feelings and emotions or of moods and attitudes" and that his secular poems "do not have any real amorous experience as background" (p. 42). Suggests that Crashaw's conceits are purely ornamental and "do not form an integral part of the poems" (p. 42).

◆§ 992. Ruthven, K. K. *The Conceit.* (The Critical Idiom, ed. John D. Jump, vol. 4.) London: Methuen & Co. 70p.

Discusses the word *conceit,* the theoretical bases of conceits, some common types of conceits, and the decline of conceits. Briefly comments on Crashaw's use of conceits drawn from Scripture, especially in the sacred epigrams. Notes that Crashaw tends "to condense and sharpen the contrasts or parallels in order to heighten the wit, the inference being that certain subtleties of the Holy Ghost's were lost on Matthew and Luke but not on Crashaw, whose pointed epigrams restore to the divine *concetti* something of their original crispness" (p. 47). Calls some of Crashaw's conceits "divine Clevelandisms" (p. 47).

◆§ 993. Samaha, Edward E., Jr., comp. "Richard Crashaw and Thomas Traherne: A Bibliography, 1938–1966." *SCN* 27:42–46.

Intended as an updating for 1938–1966 of the Crashaw and Traherne sections of Theodore Spencer and Mark Van Doren's *Studies in Metaphysical Poetry: Two Essays and a Bibliography* (entry 617). Incorrectly states that Lloyd E. Berry excluded both poets from his *A Bibliography of Studies in Metaphysical Poetry, 1939–1960* (entry 896). Crashaw items are divided into four sections: (1) editions and anthologies, (2) milieu and general studies, (3) analyses of individual poems, and (4) miscellaneous. Lists (without annotations) ninety-eight items for Crashaw, fifty-six of which are not listed in Berry but only nine of which appear before Berry's cutoff date of 1960. See also "A Correction and An Apology" (entry 976).

◆§ 994. Schaar, Claes. "The 'Sospetto d'Herode' and 'Paradise Lost.'" *ES* 50:511–16.

Briefly surveys critical opinion on the influence of "Sospetto d'Herode" on *Paradise Lost.* Maintains that Milton knew both Marino's original and Crashaw's version and comments specifically on verbal parallels among Marino's poem, Crashaw's translation, and Milton's epic to show how these echoes "affect our appreciation of various details in *Paradise Lost*" (p. 512).

◆§ 995. Shawcross, John T., and David Ronald Emma, eds. *Seventeenth-Century English Poetry.* (Lippincott College English Series.) Philadelphia and New York: J. B. Lippincott Co. xvii, 636p.

Includes a general introduction to seventeenth-century poetry (pp. 1–11) and a general selected bibliography (pp. 13–14). Presents a brief introduction to Crashaw's life and poetry, with a selected bibliography (pp. 319–21), and reproduces twenty-three poems with explanatory notes (pp. 321–49). Suggests that, although compelling in its intensity, Crashaw's religious poetry may seem quite extravagant to the non-Catholic or even to the sophisticated Catholic reader. Points out that "the effects are sometimes grotesque" and maintains that it can be best understood as "poetry of inspiration which cannot be contained by ordinary bounds of form or taste" (p. 320).

◄§ 996. Shipps, Anthony W. "Sources Wanted." *N&Q* n.s. 16:303.
Reply to Stan Hardy (entry 977). Identifies the quoted lines as stanza 23 of "Sospetto d'Herode."

◄§ 997. Shudō, Tomoko. "Crashaw no Zeppitsu—'A letter to the Countess of Denbigh' ni tsuite" [A Letter from Mr. Crashaw to the Countess of Denbigh as His Swan Song]. *Shokei Jogakuin Tanki Daigaku Kenkyū Hōkoku* [Research Report of the Shokei Women's Junior College] no. 16 (December): 79–88.
Presents a detailed comparison of the earlier and later versions of "Letter to the Countess of Denbigh" to show how the later version is superior, especially in its second part. Points out that the poem does not discuss the differences between Catholicism and Anglicanism but only urges the Countess to stop hesitating and to receive God's love. Suggests that the main theme of the poem is also the major informing influence in Crashaw's life. Traces Crashaw's life after his conversion to Catholicism and comments on his letter written from Leyden. In an appendix prints both versions of the poem.

◄§ 998. Strier, Richard. "Crashaw's Other Voice." *SEL* 9:135–51.
Reprinted in *George Herbert and the Seventeenth-Century Religious Poets*, ed. Mario Di Cesare (entry 1133), 284–95.
Maintains that Crashaw's characteristic voice in poetry is "exultant and assured," a voice that is "wholly free from anxiety or painful self-consciousness," and suggests that his conversion to Catholicism "set Crashaw free of the preoccupation with painful diagnosis of emotions and states of mind which Protestant eschatology stimulated" (p. 135). Argues, however, that in certain poems in *Carmen Deo Nostro* there is "the kind of tension, concern, and doubt associated with introspection and the kind of language associated with this tension" (p. 135). Points out that these poems are written to other people, dealing with their concerns, not his own: "For himself, Crashaw could be sure, for others he could not" (p. 136). Illustrates this "other voice" by a detailed analysis of "Letter to the Countess of Denbigh" and briefly contrasts it with "Hymn to the Name of Jesus," a poem written in Crashaw's more characteristic voice. Points out that the verse letter to the Countess is "austerely controlled," "reverberates with the pressure of passion on argument," echoes "pro-

found human concern," and is motivated by "the compassion of a deeply religious man" (p. 136). Claims that, when not writing on heavenly things, Crashaw's poetic language and voice "take on something of the sinewy, nervous quality of metaphysical poetry" (p. 151). Briefly compares Crashaw to Keats.

◄§ 999. Williams, George Walton. "The Order of Stanzas in Cowley and Crashaw's 'On Hope.'" *SB* 22:207–10.
     In part, a reply to Clarence H. Miller (entry 903). Presents what he considers to be the most satisfactory ordering of Crashaw's and Cowley's stanzas in "On Hope." Using the numbers that refer to the order of the poem in all seventeenth-century texts, suggests that the stanzas should be arranged 1, 2, 3, 4, 6, 5, 8, 7, 9. Points out that apparently Crashaw wrote an extra ten lines (one extra stanza), "where tradition dictated he should have provided only forty," in order to match Cowley's poem stanza-by-stanza and that "how best to fit in the usual Crashavian excess is the editor's problem" (p. 210).

1970

◄§ 1000. Bradbury, Malcolm, and David Palmer, eds. *Metaphysical Poetry.* (Stratford-Upon-Avon Studies, 11.) London: Edward Arnold; New York: St. Martin's Press. 280p.
     Reprinted, 1971.
     Collection of ten essays that reflects "the shifts of emphasis that have taken place since the revival of modern interest in 'metaphysical poetry'" and shows that "there is an evident desire to see these poets in new contexts, and to relate them to a more varied and extensive awareness of the different kinds of poetic activity that belong to this period" (pp. 6–7). Essays in which Crashaw is discussed have been entered separately in this bibliography (entries 1011, 1020, 1024).

◄§ 1001. Cirillo, A. R. "Crashaw's 'Epiphany Hymn': The Dawn of Christian Time." *SP* 67:67–88.
     Maintains that Crashaw's best religious poetry "contains a richness of detail and evocation, a pattern of careful, orderly development that is not only especially significant, but also perfectly welded to the form and temper of its expression" (p. 67) and that it has "a profundity not usually associated with his art" (p. 68). Discusses "Hymn in the Glorious Epiphanie" as the climax of a highly structured and unified sequence of poems in *Carmen Deo Nostro*, beginning with "Hymn to the Name of Jesus" and followed by "Hymn in the Holy Nativity" and "New Year's Day." Maintains that the sequence reflects the liturgical cycle of Christmas as contained in the *Roman Breviary*. Discusses the theme of harmony, the cyclic structure, the uses of a threefold concept of

advent, as described by St. Bernard, and the importance of light symbolism in the sequence and shows how "Hymn in the Glorious Epiphanie," "working on simultaneous orders of meaning, prunes the more sensuous elements of the earlier poems and joins the themes of light, advent, and harmony inherent in a Christian hymn into the conclusion of one cycle of liturgical and Christian time, the cycle of the Incarnation—or of the first advent and its accompanying moral advent into the soul of man" (p. 73). Presents a detailed analysis of "Hymn in the Glorious Epiphanie" to demonstrate that the poem "develops its own cycle of movement from darkness in light through light in darkness, while it continues the cycle of Incarnation instituted in 'Hymn to the Name'" and thus is "the liturgical climax of the incarnation cycle—the celebration of the inner manifestation of the second advent" (p. 88).

◄§ 1002. Crashaw, Richard. *The Complete Poetry of Richard Crashaw*. Edited with an Introduction, Notes, and Variants by George Walton Williams. (The Anchor Seventeenth-Century Series, ACo–12.) Garden City, N.Y.: Doubleday & Co. xxvi, 707p.

Reprinted, New York: New York University Press (Stuart Editions), 1972; New York: Norton, 1974.

Abandons the traditional ordering by volumes and divides the poems into "Sacred Poems" and "Secular Poems," providing the Latin, Greek, and Italian originals that Crashaw translated, as well as English prose translations of Crashaw's Latin poems (prepared by Phyllis S. Bowman). Poems that appear in only one version are printed on *seriatim* pages, and translated poems and poems that appear in two versions are printed on facing pages in parallel texts. Poems are introduced by general and critical headnotes, and glosses and commentary appear in footnotes. Acknowledgments (p. vii), table of contents (pp. ix–xiv), general introduction to Crashaw's life and poetry (pp. xv–xxii), chronology of Crashaw's life and works (p. xxiii), and note on the arrangement of the edition (pp. xxv–xxvi), followed by eight divisions: (1) sacred poems in one English version (pp. 3–74), (2) sacred poems in two English versions (pp. 75–153), (3) sacred poems translated into English from Latin and Italian (pp. 155–253), (4) sacred poems in Latin and Greek (pp. 255–447), (5) secular poems in one English version (pp. 451–98), (6) secular poems in two English versions (pp. 499–513), (7) secular poems translated into English from Greek, Latin, and Italian (pp. 515–49), and (8) secular poems in Latin (pp. 551– 621). Contains also an appendix of dedications and other preliminary matter in Crashaw's collections of poems, with English translations of the Latin (pp. 625–34); supplementary poems (pp. 655–58); notes, including a first-line index of the epigrams in *Epigrammatum Sacrorum Liber* and those in Bodleian MS Tanner 465; a list of events, miracles, and parables in the sacred epigrams; a scriptural index to the sacred epigrams; a table of contents to the 1646, 1648, and 1652 volumes (pp. 659–94); and an index of first lines and titles (pp. 695–707).

❧ 1003. ————. *Steps to the Temple (1646). Together with Selected Poems in Manuscript.* Menston, Eng.: Scolar Press. 138, [30]p.

Facsimile reprint (original size) of the Bodleian Library copy of the 1646 edition of *Steps to the Temple. Sacred Poems, With other Delights of the Muses* (Douce. C. 96) along with selected pages from the Tanner manuscript (MS Tanner 465). In a prefatory note, presents a brief sketch of Crashaw's life and printed works. Notes that "in addition to the printed works sixteen manuscripts survive containing poems by Crashaw" and that "the most important is the Bodleian Library's MS Tanner 465 which is the only source for several poems not found in print" (preface).

❧ 1004. Editors. "Crashaw in the Eighteenth Century." *N&Q* n.s. 17:470.

Reply to Brijraj Singh (entry 1021). Points out that the two eighteenth-century mentions of Crashaw's works cited by Singh were briefly mentioned by Arthur H. Nethercot in "The Reputation of the 'Metaphysical Poets' During the Age of Pope" (entry 458).

❧ 1005. Ellrodt, Robert. "George Herbert and the Religious Lyric," in *English Poetry and Prose, 1540–1674,* edited by Christopher Ricks, 173–205. (History of Literature in the English Language, vol. 2.) London: Barrie & Jenkins.

Paperback ed., Sphere Books, 1970.

Discusses the nature of Crashaw's religious verse, contrasting his themes and style with those of Donne, Herbert, Vaughan, and Traherne. Maintains that "a strong flavour of individuality is the distinguishing mark and excellence of the religious lyric in seventeenth-century England, as compared with earlier devotional verse or with the Baroque lyric of the Continent" (p. 173). Discusses the theological and philosophical thought that shaped Crashaw's vision and briefly comments on the influence of Herbert, Ignatian and Salesian devotion, Jesuit epigrammatists, Marino, and the Spanish mystics. Points out that Crashaw, like Herbert, "wrote in the liturgical tradition of the Church" and "lived in a sacramental world," whereas Vaughan and Traherne "chose to raise a freer world of spiritual meditation, Hermetic or Platonic, in Nature" (p. 173). Suggests that Crashaw's "ecstatic piety aims at self-annihilation" (p. 185) and that his "faith and imagination are centrifugal" (p. 186). Discusses aspects of Crashaw's sacred verse, such as its lyrical intensity, emotional yet impersonal tone, use of sensuous and even erotic images, employment of the rhetoric of contraries, lack of rational structure, uses of music, and use of symbols that have emotional value. Suggests that Crashaw's poetry reflects a spiritual evolution that can be seen in his later poems, especially the Teresian hymns. Claims that Crashaw "might have been a greater poet if his imaginative association had been dictated only by his deeper feelings and the major symbols" but "he often succumbed to an intellectual irritability which, in the literary atmosphere of the age, bubbled up in superfluous conceits."

◄§ 1006. Esch, Arno. "Die 'metaphysische' Lyrik," in *Epochen der englischen Lyrik*, edited by Karl Heinz Göller, 100–128. Düsseldorf: August Bagel Verlag.

A general introduction to metaphysical poetry (pp. 100–104) followed by discussions of individual poets, including Crashaw (pp. 117–20). Attributes the 1920s rebirth of interest in metaphysical poets to the similarities that the poets of the time perceived between their situation and that of Donne and his disciples. Maintains that metaphysical poetry evidences a continuity with Renaissance poetry, not a sudden rupture. Calls Crashaw's poetry "philosophisch-theologische Vertiefung" (p. 10) and points out that the poet repeatedly attempts to convey the mystical experience of apprehending the mystery of divine love. Notes that his poetry is greatly influenced by three major traditions: epigrammatic poetry, the emblem, and Marinism. Discusses briefly "The Weeper," "Ode on a Prayer-book," the Teresian poems, and "Letter to the Countess of Denbigh." Observes that Crashaw's poetry is more difficult to relate to than that of the other metaphysical poets and thus has been less important in the current rediscovery of the metaphysicals.

◄§ 1007. Farmer, Norman K., Jr. "A Theory of Genre for Seventeenth-Century Poetry." *Genre* 3:293–317.

Argues that "a critical method that acknowledges the objective features of poetry, a method able to define genre in terms of the rhetorical motives that distinguish some poems from others" (p. 294) is more valuable in arriving at precise aesthetic distinctions than are such unsatisfactory terms as *metaphysical* and *cavalier* and that "individual genius may often be best discovered through a comparative study of genres and the conventions which shape them" (p. 295). Presents a taxonomy of such Renaissance genres as the verse letter, funeral elegy, epithalamion, epigram, philosophical poem, satire, ode, Ovidian elegy, allegorical poem, and sacred lyric to show that such an approach "offers an explanation for the richness of seventeenth-century poetry by showing how the lyric stood in relation to other more public genres commonly practiced at the time and how poets were able to develop the 'I' of the lyric poem with greater facility than their predecessors by virtue of cutting across generic lines and developing rhetorics of various other modes as well" (p. 312). Only passing references to Crashaw.

◄§ 1008. Hanak, Miroslav John. "The Emergence of Baroque Mentality and Its Cultural Impact on Western Europe after 1550." *JAAC* 28:315–26.

Considers the emergence of baroque mentality after 1550 in Italy, Spain, France, Germany, and England. Argues that baroque art and literature are "a reflection of a new and distinct world view which continues to employ Renaissance forms but loads them with an entirely different world concept" (p. 315) and suggests that the baroque is "a spiritualization of the Renaissance lust for life" (p. 316) and "has its *raison d'être* in the never-ending struggle between flesh and spirit, and between reason and the emotions" (p. 317). Surveys the political and historical events of 1550–1600 to show "how this spiritualized elation replaced Renaissance *élan vital*" (p. 318). Surveys also modern scholarship on the baroque and discusses some of the major features of baroque art. Briefly comments on the baroque in English literature and claims that "it is not Crashaw's (1613–1649) Catholicism, Latinity, sojourn in Spain, or translations from Marino that make him a baroque poet, but rather his innermost attunement to the times 'out of joint'" (p. 323).

⋙ 1009. Ishii, Shōnosuke. *An Anthology of World Famous Poems* [Sekai Meishishu], vol. 9; English Poetry, 1. Heibon-sha.
Translates into Japanese "Loves Horoscope" (p. 118) and "Letter to the Countess of Denbigh" (p. 122).

⋙ 1010. Jacobus, Lee A. "Richard Crashaw as Mannerist." *BuR* 18, no. 3:79–88.
Observes that Crashaw "had more than one style at his disposal" (p. 88) and argues that, although he is often considered "the English baroque poet *par excellence*," certain of his poems "are not so much baroque as they are mannerist in style" (p. 79). Contrasts the baroque and mannerist modes and claims that the latter emphasizes "tension, shock value, distortion, and psychological pressures of an unusual nature" (p. 80). Discusses these qualities of mannerist style in "The Weeper," "On our crucified Lord Naked, and bloody," "Hymn in the Holy Nativity," and "Luke 11. Blessed be the paps which Thou hast sucked." Maintains that such plain-speaking poems as "Adoro Te" and "Sancta Maria Dolorum" "show only that Crashaw must have been aware of pushing himself and us to the limits in his extreme moments, those moments which, because of their studiousness, their sense of dislocation, intensity of pitch, and frequent absurdity" (p. 88) can be termed mannerist.

⋙ 1011. Martz, Louis L. "The Action of the Self: Devotional Poetry in the Seventeenth Century," in *Metaphysical Poetry*, edited by Malcolm Bradbury and David Palmer, 100–121. (Stratford-Upon-Avon Studies, 11.) London: Edward Arnold; New York: St. Martin's Press.
Claims that seventeenth-century devotion involved "an active, creative state of mind, a 'poetical' condition . . . in which the mind works at high intensity" and that thus the devotional poetry of the period "should not . . . be taken to indicate verse of rather limited range, 'merely pious' pieces without much poetic energy" (p. 103). Points out that Crashaw's poetry "remains an anomaly in English literature, an example of a continental importation which never struck a firm hold upon the English scene" and examines "Hymn in the Assumption" as one example of his departing "from the central modes of English poetry, adapting the phraseology of Herbert, the couplet-rhetoric of Ben Jonson, the techniques of the Elizabethan love-song, and bringing all

these modes into an idiom that was essentially foreign to the English tradition" (p. 117). Suggests that the poem "represents Crashaw's art of baroque celebration at its best, with its subtly shifting voices, varied repetitions, multiple perspectives, and modulating verse forms, all its variety held together under the artful control of the human speaker, whose simple language opens and concludes his hymn" (p. 121).

᪥ 1012. Miller, Paul W. "The Decline of the English Epithalamion." *TSLL* 12:405–16.

Traces the epithalamic tradition in England from Spenser to Crashaw and contends that the decline of the tradition "reflects the decline of the marriage myth that originally inspired the genre" (p. 405), the myth that "wedlock, when properly entered upon and celebrated, is a potent force, to unify and bless the bridal pair and to avert evil from them" (pp. 406–7). Comments on possible historical and religious reasons for the decline of the myth and argues that "as the myth of marriage loses its vigor the epithalamia increasingly find their inspiration not in the myth itself, but in the distortion or perversion of this myth for rhetorical or poetic effect" (p. 406). Briefly discusses Crashaw's "Epithalamium" and suggests that, although a beautiful poem, it represents the nadir of the genre. Argues that Crashaw deliberately misapplies many of the traditional elements of the genre "so as to shift attention from the marriage myth to his wit" (p. 414). Maintains that, "in his immensely complex and arabesque of a poem, Crashaw destroys almost at one blow the high seriousness and dignity of the epithalamic tradition so evident in Spenser's wedding poem" (p. 414).

᪥ 1013. Molho, Blanca and Maurice, eds. *Poetas ingleses, metafísicos del siglo XVII.* (Preparación de textos originales, María Gomis.) Barcelona: Barral Editores. 181p.

General introduction to metaphysical poetry and poets for the Spanish reader with selections from the poetry of Donne, John Fletcher, William Drummond, William Browne, Herbert, James Shirley, Waller, William Cartwright, Crashaw, Lovelace, Marvell, and Vaughan. In the introduction, "Prologo: John Donne y la poesia metafísica" (pp. 11–36), calls Crashaw's poetry "una curiosa mezela de «wit» inglés ye de poesia meridional voluptuosamente barroca" (p. 33) and comments on his Catholic sensibility, in particular his devotion to the Virgin Mary and St. Teresa. Sees Crashaw "partido entre ese mundo intelectual, del que quiere librarse, y un mundo de la forma que le atrae apasionadamente" (p. 34). Anthologizes, without notes or commentary, "An Epitaph upon a Young Married Couple," "Hymn in the Holy Nativity," two stanzas from "On the wounds of our crucified Lord," the conclusion of "The Flaming Heart," and "A Song ('Lord, when the sense of thy sweet grace')" (pp. 137–55), with English and Spanish on facing pages.

◆§ 1014. Ostriker, Alicia. "The Lyric," in *English Poetry and Prose, 1540–1674*, edited by Christopher Ricks, 119–36. (History of Literature in the English Language, vol. 2.) London: Barrie & Jenkins.

Reprinted in paperback, Sphere Books, 1970.

Outlines the rise and decline of the lyric during the Renaissance and seventeenth century and comments on the interplay between the traditions of communal song and individual speech in the lyric. Points out that in the early seventeenth century "the balance between communal song and individual speech shifted" and, "instead of quasi-anonymous singers sharing conventional ideas and techniques," such poets as Crashaw, Donne, Herbert, Herrick, and Suckling wrote "ostensibly not as personae but as persons" (p. 121). Suggests that Crashaw, "in the violence and extravagance, and commonly the eroticism, of his religious rhapsodies is more like Donne than any other English poet" (p. 131). Maintains, however, that Crashaw's conceits "do not depend on intellect but on enthusiasm" and that his art was "more influenced by the European Counter-Reformation than by any English movement," thus earning him the title of "England's sole 'baroque' poet" (p. 131).

◆§ 1015. Paley, Morton D. "The Dream of Reason," in *Energy and the Imagination: A Study of the Development of Blake's Thought*, 80–121. Oxford: Clarendon Press.

Points out Blake's parody of the opening lines of "A Hymn to Sainte Teresa" ("Love, thou art Absolute sole lord / Of Life and Death") in *The Four Zoas*, Night the Fifth, line 42 ("King of Love thou art the King of rage & death") (p. 104).

◆§ 1016. Peterkiewicz, Jerzy. "The Failure of Mystical Verse," in *The Other Side of Silence: The Poet at the Limits of Language*, 109–19. London, New York, Toronto: Oxford University Press.

Discusses the difficulties that poets encounter in attempting to present mystical experience in poetry. Maintains that "A Hymn to Sainte Teresa" "as a whole fails to convince one of its mystical subject, partly because it is mounted in the panegyrical manner of the age, and partly because its figures of speech seem to intensify the freakish aspect of holiness" (p. 110). Points out, however, that Crashaw does succeed "in creating the mood of rapture in the St. Teresa poem by his display of rhetoric" and notes that, although he "certainly indulges in metaphysical freaks," nonetheless "he has no desire to explain them away in a steady argument" (p. 111), as Vaughan does in "The World." Briefly compares and contrasts Crashaw to St. John of the Cross, Vaughan, Traherne, and Marvell.

◆§ 1017. Petersson, Robert T. *The Art of Ecstasy: Teresa, Bernini, and Crashaw*. London: Routledge & Kegan Paul. xv, 160p.

First American ed., New York: Atheneum, 1970, 1974. xvi, 183p.

Compares the autobiography of St. Teresa with Bernini's Cornaro Chapel in Rome and Crashaw's "A Hymn to Sainte Teresa." Part 1, "The New Carmelite" (pp. 1–42), discusses Teresa's life in terms of her historical context, her accomplishments as a reformer, and her mystical experiences. Part 2, "Bernini's Teresan Cosmos" (pp. 43–81), explains the "illusionistic" manner of Bernini's treatment of the saint's ecstasy, the setting of the statues within the larger Cornaro Chapel, and the symbolism and artistry of his statues of Teresa and the Seraph. Part 3, "Text of Crashaw's Poem" (pp. 83–90), reproduces the poem. Part 4, "Crashaw's Ascent Beyond Time" (pp. 91–134), contrasts the successful, extroverted life of Bernini with the exiled, introverted life of Crashaw and comments on the artistry of the hymn. Discusses the musical quality of Crashaw's poetry as more central than its visual quality and sees "the abstraction, energy, and harmony of music" (p. 97) as related to his mysticism. Comments on the poet's use of synesthesia to express his notion of the unity of all aspects of man and of time. Defines the baroque and the metaphysical and places Crashaw in the context of both. Views Crashaw as a poet of sensations rather than as a sensuous poet, pointing out that his purpose is to express the inexpressible. Calling "A Hymn to Sainte Teresa" Crashaw's "most accomplished, most fully developed work" (p. 105), discusses how his life led to its writing, and relates the poem to Teresa's *Vida*, seeing the poem's first two movements as closely based on her autobiography but suggesting that the third movement comes essentially from Crashaw's imagination. Points out likenesses between Bernini's statue and Crashaw's poem and presents a detailed critical analysis of the hymn, emphasizing that its theme is love, which descends into Teresa and gives her existence and the poem energy. Shows how the techniques of speaker, sound, rhythm, and movement contribute to the presentation of the experience of ecstasy. Part 5, "Epilogue" (pp. 135–41), relates the works of Teresa, Bernini, and Crashaw to the metaphor of fire. Notes (pp. 142–56) and index (pp. 157–60).

◄§ 1018. Praz, Mario. "The Curve and the Shell," in *Mnemosyne: The Parallel Between Literature and the Visual Arts*, 109–51. The A. W. Mellon Lectures in Fine Arts, no. 16, 1967. (Bollingen Series 35.) Princeton and London: Princeton University Press.
Reprinted, with minor corrections, 1974.
First Princeton paperback edition, 1974.
Briefly compares Crashaw to various baroque artists, especially Rubens, Borromini, Bernini, and Lanfranco. Maintains that "there is nothing either in Marino or in the Jesuit poets whose Latin verse Crashaw studied and imitated to suggest that marvelous energy of soaring imagination which associates the English poet with the masterpieces of the visual arts" (pp. 137, 142). Praises the ecstatic quality, opulence, and uses of rhetoric in such poems as "To the Morning. Satisfaction for sleepe," "Hymn to the Name of Jesus," and "A Hymn to Sainte Teresa." Suggests that when we read the Teresian hymn,

the baroque effigies of saints and martyrs found in Italian and Spanish churches and art galleries "become suddenly clear, as if we had been given a commentary on them and were reading them in the light of those few lines of a great 'minor' English poet, which transcend them and seem to contain *in nuce* the quintessence of the whole seventeenth century" (p. 143).

◆§ 1019. Reinsdorf, Walter. "Edward Taylor's Baroque Expression." *Greyfriar: Siena Studies in Literature* 11:31–36.
Discusses Edward Taylor's use of baroque metaphors and images to express spiritual states and relationships and suggests that his baroque techniques are similar to those employed by Crashaw. Points out that both poets used emblems and that thus their metaphors "are sometimes external and sensuous" (p. 33). Briefly contrasts Crashaw's emotionally charged metaphors with Donne's more intellectual ones.

◆§ 1020. Saunders, J. W. "The Social Situation of Seventeenth-Century Poetry," in *Metaphysical Poetry*, edited by Malcolm Bradbury and David Palmer, 236–59. (Stratford-Upon-Avon Studies, 11.) London: Edward Arnold; New York: St. Martin's Press.
Argues against the simplistic notion that the seventeenth century is only "a transition period of total conflict sandwiched between two opposed ages of relative clarity and stability, so that its social phenomena may be rationalized as developments en route between the starting-point and an end venue of a completely different kind" (p. 237) and explores some of the "particular deficiencies in the Tudor fabric which required change and which indeed began to change with the poets of 1600 to 1660" (p. 241). Suggests that the main development in the social context of poetry was "the emergence of an educated and intellectual printed-book public" (p. 257), resulting in "poetry as a national and learned art, which increasingly takes itself seriously and draws away from its roots in popular entertainment" (p. 258). Argues that, although this intellectualization produced many good effects (not the least of which was the poetry of Milton and Pope), "it lost the saving grace of the courtly age, the unity of the audiences, and through that unity, the universality of poetry" (pp. 258–59). Mentions Crashaw only briefly, noting his connection with the court in exile of Queen Henrietta Maria and pointing out that, like many other poets of the age, Crashaw's major poems did not appear in print until within a few years of his death.

◆§ 1021. Singh, Brijraj. "Crashaw in the Eighteenth Century." *N&Q* n.s. 17:251–52.
Notes two mentions of Crashaw's work between 1727 and 1756 (1) a summary in the June 1732 issue of *The Gentleman's Magazine* (pp. 786–87) of an anonymous article entitled "A Critique on English Poets" that appeared in *Applebee's Journal* on 3 June 1732 (see entry 73) in which *Steps to the Temple*

is mentioned but not Crashaw by name, and (2) a summary of an article in the same issue of *The Gentleman's Magazine* (p. 802) by an A. B. (entry 74), who notes that Crashaw is the author of *Steps to the Temple* and gives a biographical sketch of the poet, based presumably on Wood's account in *Athenae Oxonienses* (entry 56). Points out certain inaccuracies in the sketch and notes that "Pope, then, was not the only one who read Crashaw in the first half of the eighteenth century" (p. 252). Suggests that if the author of "A Critique on English Poets" was familiar with Crashaw's works, "there is some evidence that some people at his own university remembered both the man and his poems" (p. 252). Observes that, although Pope regarded Crashaw as primarily a wit, A. B. recognized him as a religious poet. For a reply see entry 1004.

◄§ 1022. Söderholm, Torbjörn. *The End-Rhymes of Marvell, Cowley, Crashaw, Lovelace and Vaughan: A Study of Their Reflection of the Pronunciation of Stressed Vowels and Diphthongs in the Mid-Seventeenth Century.* (Acta Academiae Aboensis, Ser. A: Humaniora, vol. 39, no. 2.) Abo: Abo Adademi. 167p.

A synchronic, descriptive, analytical study of the end rhymes of Crashaw, Marvell, Cowley, Lovelace, and Vaughan to determine English pronunciation of stressed vowels and diphthongs in the mid-seventeenth century. Introduction; three chapters: (1) "Aim, Method, and Scope of the Investigation" (pp. 13–17), (2) "Analyses of the Rhymes" (pp. 19–82), (3) "Concluding Remarks & Summary of Findings" (pp. 83–88); bibliography (pp. 89–92); two appendixes: (1) "List of Rhymes on which the Investigation is Based" (pp. 95–138) and (2) "Complete List of Marvell's End-Rhymes" (pp. 139–67). Examines 5,870 rhymes by Crashaw and points out, for example, that he rhymes such words as *heaven, seven, driven, given,* and *even* and that he frequently uses aI/ɔI/ rhymes. Finds thirty-four examples of "inaccurate" rhymes and four cases of "impossible" rhymes in Crashaw's poetry.

◄§ 1023. Summers, Joseph H. *The Heirs of Donne and Jonson.* London: Chatto and Windus; New York and London: Oxford University Press. 198p.

Argues that "most of the interesting poets of the period were in some sense heirs of both Donne and Jonson and that they wrote successfully a large number of different kinds of poetry" and maintains that "granted the general condition of the language, the literary and intellectual currents, the 'spirit of the age,' and other large and vaguely apprehended abstractions, for the seventeenth century as for other periods, one can discover almost as many aesthetics as there are interesting poets" (p. 7). Rejects the notion of "schools" and finds the term *metaphysical poetry* unsatisfactory. Proposes that Crashaw, Herbert, Herrick, Suckling, Carew, Henry King, Vaughan, and Marvell may best be seen as heirs of Donne and Jonson, "not with the implication that later poets had any familial or natural right or that either Donne or Jonson intended that they should inherit, but in simple recognition that they came to occupy a good deal of the literary estate of their two great predecesors" (p. 15). In Chapter 4, "A Foreign and a Provincial Gentleman: Richard Crashaw and Henry Vaughan" (pp. 102–29), comments on the merits and weaknesses of Crashaw's secular and sacred poetry, calling him an unusual poet and "the chief English poet of the Counter Reformation" (p. 105). Suggests that his poems "do not usually invite us primarily to rational understanding or even the appreciation of a performance, but to rapt participation in ecstatic joys and sufferings or delight in decorative and sensuous ornament" (p. 105). Argues that extreme reactions, both positive and negative, in Crashavian criticism "tend to obscure not only some of the radical problems but also some of the unusual possibilities in Crashaw's poetry" (p. 106) and makes a case for Crashaw's particular kind of "poetry of excess" (p. 111), admitting, however, that he "cannot read Crashaw every day" (p. 113). Discusses major features of Crashaw's art, especially his tendency to use copious variations on a theme, his sensitivity to the emotional effects of sounds, and his uses of synaesthesia and sexual language to describe exalted spiritual states. Suggests that, among the secular poems, "Upon two greene Apricockes" demonstrates Crashaw's "mastery of the sort of ingenious, witty, tightly-organized seventeenth-century poem so admired in the first half of the twentieth century" (p. 107) and praises aspects of "On Hope," "Upon Venus putting on Mars his Armes," "Out of Virgil: In the praise of the Spring," "Wishes. To his (supposed) Mistresse," and "Musicks Duell." Suggests that Crashaw's most successful religious poems are the Teresian hymns and "Hymn in the Holy Nativity" and comments on their merits. Maintains that in the concluding lines of "The Flaming Heart" Crashaw "most successfully transformed the hyperboles and ardours of ordinary lovers' language into a triumphantly new language for a new and supreme love" (p. 114). Notes Crashaw's indebtedness to Spenser and/or the Spenserians; the Jesuit Latin poets, especially Rémond, Cabilliau, and Hugo; Marino; and the classical poets. Briefly compares Crashaw with Donne, Herbert, Cowley, Vaughan, and Blake. In Chapter 5, "The Alchemical Ventriloquist: Andrew Marvell" (pp. 130–55), briefly discusses the possibility of Marvell's indebtedness to Crashaw, especially in his "Eyes and Tears."

◄§ 1024. Warnke, Frank J. "Metaphysical Poetry and the European Context," in *Metaphysical Poetry*, edited by Malcolm Bradbury and David Palmer, 261–76. (Stratford-Upon-Avon Studies, 11.) London: Edward Arnold; New York: St. Martin's Press.

Argues that metaphysical poetry is simply one of several versions of baroque literature and points out similarities between the English metaphysical poets and Continental poets (Jean de La Ceppède, Francisco de Quevedo, Lope de Vega, Constantijn Huygens, Tommaso Campanella, Paul Fleming, Jean Bertaut, Peter Motin, Théophile de Viau, Hofmann von Hofmannswaldau, and Marc-Antoine de Saint Amant, among others) in order to demonstrate that "metaphysical poetry is an international European phenomenon" (p. 276). Maintains that "to assume that the native English style is metaphysical and that the continental style contemporaneous with it is high baroque is misleading—almost as misleading as to consider the metaphysical a Protestant style balanced against the high baroque as a Catholic style" (p. 265). Points out that Crashaw, like most of the other metaphysical poets, wrote in more than one style. Calls "The Weeper," for instance, "a horrid example of high baroque style carried to an extreme" but suggests that "A Hymn to Sainte Teresa" is "a notable triumph of the same style," while such poems as "Charitas Nimia" and "Letter to the Countess of Denbigh" "are in the controlled, colloquial, intellectual manner of the metaphysicals" (p. 265). Points out how Crashaw's world view and religious sensibility, as well as his uses of formal meditation, sacred parody, elaborate forms of wit, and emotionally charged symbols, link him with certain Continental poets. Maintains that, at times, Crashaw's poetry is high baroque and, like Marino's, is theatrical "in its showy impact, in its representation of reality as a shifting phantasmagoria of unstable stage sets" (p. 275). Maintains that in Crashaw, as in Góngora, Marino, and Gryphius, "we find an imagery of fantasy and distortion, the deployment of which suggests as assumption that the world of sensuous experience, essentially unreal, may be toyed with at the artist's discretion: that world may be formed and reformed into verbal artifacts which, previously non-existent, possess as much validity as what we think we perceive in what we think is nature" (p. 275).

◄§ 1025. Williams, A. M. Introduction to *Conversations at Little Gidding. 'On the Retirement of Charles V.' 'On the Austere Life': Dialogues with Members of the Ferrar Family*, xi–lxxxvi. Edited with Introduction and notes by A. M. Williams. London: Cambridge University Press.

An account of the Ferrar family, the life and discipline observed at Little Gidding, and the historical and religious events that shaped the spiritual temper of the community. Briefly comments on Crashaw's association with the High Anglican community. Notes that Crashaw may have been introduced to the works of Lessius by the Ferrars and suggests that, although "Description of a Religious House and the Condition of Life" is, in part, a translation based on John Barclay's *Argenis*, Crashaw's poem described "a religious foundation not unlike that of Little Gidding" (p. lxiv).

1971

◄§ 1026. Bertonasco, Marc F. *Crashaw and the Baroque*. University: University of Alabama Press. vii, 158p.

Chapter 3 is a revised version of "A New Look at Crashaw's 'The Weeper'" (entry 964).

Contains an appreciative preface by Linda Van Norden (pp. v–vii) that outlines the aim and approach of the book. In the introduction states that the purpose of the study is "to readjust the popular image of Crashaw, to suggest several lines of approach to his religious lyrics, and to demonstrate that this major poet exercises a far firmer control over his materials than critics have generally recognized" (p. 4). Chapter 1, "Crashaw and the Emblem" (pp. 6–42), discusses the poet's uses of emblems and emblematic imagery to figure forth complex Christian concepts and argues that readers who remain immersed in the sensuous details of Crashaw's images or visualize them too vividly misunderstand the intellectual and conceptual nature of his art. Delineates Crashaw's juxtaposition of the sacred and profane, his intellectual integrity, his elaborate ornamentation, the possible sources for his emblems, and the dominant images and symbols in his poetry. In Chapter 2, "The Influence of St. Francis de Sales" (pp. 43–93), suggests that Crashaw's tendency to image religious thought and feeling derives in part from the increased interest during the period in meditative practices. Discusses the symbolic imagery as a "point of similarity between seventeenth-century Puritanism and continental Catholicism" (p. 52) and points out that Crashaw was indebted not only to Continental writers but also to popular English culture, such as English emblem writers. Argues, however, that the writer with the most influence on Crashaw was St. Francis de Sales, whose spiritual writings were quite popular in England. Notes direct borrowings from the saint but claims that the Salesian spirit in general is what marks Crashaw's poetry. Describes this spirit as "an unquestioning faith in God's overwhelming love for His creation" (p. 50) and shows how this spirit is most evident in Crashaw's poetry. Shows also that neither St. Francis nor Crashaw dealt much with self, sin, hell, or death. Maintains that Crashaw's imagery was also greatly influenced by the saint, quoting passages that show his fondness for images of honey and bees and gems. Outlines the steps of a Salesian meditation, stressing how it differs from the Ignatian model, and discusses how Crashaw's poetry approximates it. Chapter 3, "A New Look at 'The Weeper'" (pp. 94–117), argues that the poem is a formal Salesian meditation and that the images are not redundant but are repeated with significance. Discusses the explications of the poem by Stephen Manning (entry 777) and John Peter (entry 757) and then analyzes "The Weeper" to show that each embellishment of image is grounded in precise thought. In the conclusion (pp. 118–21) reemphasizes the importance of the emblem and the spirituality of St. Francis de Sales on Crashaw's poetry and how both inform "The Weeper." Appendix I, "Crashaw Scholarship in the Twentieth Century: Survey and Assessment" (pp. 123–43), presents a brief, selective survey and evaluation of Crashavian criticism from Tutin (1905) to the 1970s, maintaining that, on the whole, "the body of criticism on Crashaw's poetry forms the least satisfactory part of seventeenth-century literary scholarship" (p. 143). Points out that "one can arrange almost all critics in two camps: those who are cognizant of the purely symbolic and emblematic nature of Crashaw's imagery and who are familiar with the history of Christian thought and devotion; and those who are unable or unwilling to assume the necessary historical orientation" (p. 143). Appendix II, "The Imagery in Certain Representative Lyrics" (pp. 144–50), examines characteristic images in "Sancta Maria Dolorum," "On the wounds of our crucified Lord," and "Ode on a Prayer-book." Selected bibliography (pp. 151–56) and index (pp. 157–58).

◈ 1027. Blake, Kathleen. "Edward Taylor's Protestant Poetics: Nontransubstantiating Metaphor." *AL* 43:1–24.
Discusses Taylor's poetry as an example of Protestant poetics, especially his uses of metaphor as a bridge between the spiritual and the physical. Maintains that, for Taylor, the Lord's Supper, like nature and Scripture, functions metaphorically and that he repudiates the Catholic notion of transubstantiation in both his theology and his poetics. Contrasts Taylor's view with Crashaw's celebration of the doctrine and points out that Crashaw's view of the relationship of sensation to the apprehension of reality is thoroughly Catholic and is reflected in his uses of images, metaphors, and conceits. Observes that, although Crashaw's imagery is sensuous, he views sense objects as mere appearance and illusion and attempts to transcend them, a viewpoint rejected by Protestants. Compares and contrasts Taylor's use of conceits with Crashaw's. Claims that Crashaw "is probably the most genuinely mystical of the seventeenth-century English/American Metaphysicals" (p. 21) and therefore his poetry is less introspective and less personal than Taylor's.

◈ 1028. Crane, D. E. L. "Crashaw," in *The Penguin Companion to English Literature*, edited by David Daiches, 126–27. Harmondsworth, Eng.: Penguin Books; New York: McGraw-Hill Co.
Encyclopedic account of Crashaw's life and poetry, with a highly selected bibliography. Suggests that Crashaw "is best known, perhaps notorious, as the major exponent of the baroque style in English poetry" and points out that "the baroque, as it appears in Crashaw, is difficult to define but easy to illustrate, most obvious in its more tasteless manifestations" (p. 126). Discusses in particular Crashaw's use of sensuous, extravagant conceits. Singles out "A Hymn to Sainte Teresa" and "The Flaming Heart" as Crashaw's best poems.

◈ 1029. Day, W. G. "The Athenian Society: Poets' Reputations 1692–1710." *N&Q* n.s. 18:329.
Comments on a section on poetry in "An Essay upon all sorts of learning" in *The Young-Students-Library, containing Extracts and Abridgments of the Most Valuable Books . . .* written by the Athenian Society and published by John Dunton in 1692, after which appear two columns of recommended authors, one entitled "Latins" and the other "English" (entry 55). Notes that Crashaw is one of nineteen of the recommended English poets. Points out

that, when the essay was reprinted in A *Supplement to the Athenian Oracle* (1710), the English reading list was altered to include Prior, Addison, Milton, and Waller but that Drayton and Donne were excluded.

❧ 1030. Edwards, Paul, and MacDonald Emslie. "'Thoughts so all unlike each other': The Paradoxical in Christabel." *ES* 52:236–46.

Discusses the inconsistency in the hypothetical conclusions to Coleridge's unfinished *Christabel* by James Gillman and Derwent Coleridge. Suggests that certain cruxes in the poem can be explained by comparing it to "A Hymn to Sainte Teresa," to which Coleridge acknowledges his indebtedness. Calls attention to Crashaw's "customary . . . dealing with religious matters in sexual terms" (p. 243) and suggests that Coleridge's poem is one of sexual initiation. Points out that both St. Teresa and Christabel "must go beyond the protection of father and mother . . . and encounter sufferings . . . brought by 'Blest Seraphims'" (p. 244).

❧ 1031. Fischer, Hermann, ed. *Englische Barockgedichte: Englisch und Deutsch*. Stuttgart: Philipp Reclam Jun. 440p.

General introduction to English baroque poetry (pp. 51–81); includes "The Flaming Heart," "Hymn in the Assumption," "Death's Lecture," "To Pontius washing his blood-stained hands," and "Easter day" with German translations (pp. 243–49); a biographical note on Crashaw (pp. 397–98); and notes on the individual poems (pp. 398–99). Selected bibliography (pp. 417–28).

❧ 1032. Gardner, Helen. "Seventeenth-century Religious Poetry," in *Religion and Literature*, 171–94. New York: Oxford University Press.

Reprinted, 1983.

Surveys English religious poetry of the earlier seventeenth century and attempts to account for the fact that this period, perhaps more than any other, was propitious for religious verse. Suggests that three things make seventeenth-century religious poetry appealing to modern readers: (1) the "poems are made poems, not effusions of feeling" (p. 192); (2) the poetry is highly intellectual, "though full of feeling, emotion, strength of devotion and personal faith" and "is laced by, and built upon, a scheme of thought, and a universe of discourse that is not the poet's own invention, but has the toughness of systems that have been debated and argued over for centuries" (p. 193); and (3) the poetry reflects "the unembarrassed boldness and naturalness with which these poets approach their subject, and the freedom with which they bring the experiences of daily life, their experience of art, their native powers of mind, their skill in argument and their wit, to play over religious doctrine, religious experience and religious imperatives" (p. 193). Suggests that the most important bond among the religious poets of the time was the common religious tradition that they shared, such as the practice of discursive meditation, as well as "their readiness to assimilate Continental influences" (p. 175).

Points out that, although Crashaw converted to Catholicism, his language, like that of his Protestant contemporaries, was greatly influenced by the English Bible and the Book of Common Prayer. Briefly compares and contrasts "Hymn in the Holy Nativity" with Milton's Nativity Ode. Calls Crashaw's poem "an elaborate cantata" and maintains that "the tradition of classical pastoral, developments in sacred music, and the effort of theologians to make precise meaning of the Incarnation lie behind Crashaw's poem" (p. 181).

⮑ 1033. George, A[rapara] G[hevarghese]. "Metaphysical Poetry," in *Studies in Poetry*, 37–59. New Delhi and London: Heinemann.
A general introduction to metaphysical poetry for students and the general reader, focusing on Donne. Calls Crashaw "pre-eminently the English poet of the counter-Reformation" and suggests that, in spite of his "exquisite fancy, the great melody of his verse, and that power over the reader which springs from deep sensuousness, he suffers from long intervals of dullness and tortured conceits, characteristic of Metaphysical Poetry at its worst" (p. 42). Singles out "Wishes. To his (supposed) Mistresse" as Crashaw's best and most famous secular poem.

⮑ 1034. Graham, Paul T. "The Mystical and Musical Realism of Richard Crashaw." *ESRS* 20, no. 1:5–49.
Maintains that "Crashaw's use of the emblematic form and the musical idiom allows him to succeed formalistically and allegorically" (p. 5) and that both link his poetry to *The Spiritual Exercises* of St. Ignatius Loyola and the Counter-Reformation. Presents a close reading of "Hymn to the Name of Jesus" to show that "its structure, style, and theme have aspects in common with both the emblem and *The Spiritual Exercises* because of their emphasis upon Transubstantiation" (p. 7). Discusses "To our Lord, upon the Water made Wine," "The Teare," and "Upon Lazarus his Teares" as variations upon an emblem common to all three and upon images of liquidity, to speak of transubstantiation. Discusses Crashaw's interest in Jesuit emblem books and epigrams. Suggests that his use of end rhymes relates him to the emblem tradition and comments on "The Flaming Heart" to show how its end-rhyme scheme has emblematic overtones. Noting that Crashaw's poems concern incarnation, salvation, and love, discusses "Marc. 10. The blind cured by the word of our Saviour," "Upon the Sepulchre of our Lord," and "Easter day." Compares also "Charitas Nimia" and "Upon the ensuing Treatises [of Mr. Shelford]," declaring that the latter is an inversion of the theme of "Love loved." Discusses St. Ignatius Loyola's "Third Method of Prayer" that links devotion with music and comments on Crashaw's adoption of this link. Maintains that "Crashaw's use of music is his way of 'composing place' and his particular way of applying the senses" (p. 33). Compares "Out of the Italian. A Song" with the work of Palestrina "because it is a paraphrase and resembles the descant on a plainsong that was the core of 79 of Palestrina's 102 Masses"

(p. 35). Concludes with a discussion of "Musicks Duell" to show how its musical idiom creates a "composition of place." Selected bibliography (pp. 48–49).

◄§ 1035. Helsztyński, Stanisław. "Crashaw, Richard," in *Mały sLownik pisarzy angielskich i amerykańskich* [A Concise Dictionary of English and American Writers], edited by Stanisław Helsztyński, 122. Warsaw: Wiedza Powszechna.
Biographical sketch of Crashaw and listing of his works. Emphasizes the mystical tendencies and the baroque qualities of his poetry.

◄§ 1036. Hernádi, Miklós. "Metaphysical Bards and Modern Reviewers." *Angol es americai filogiai tanulmanyak* [Studies in English and American Philology] 1:227–41.
Discusses the role "new criticism" played in the modern revival of interest in metaphysical poetry and suggests that the metaphysical poets provided a "convenient hunting-ground for 'new critics' who insist that the various ingredients of wit, so inherent in seventeenth-century English poetry, should be regarded as governing properties of all poetry" (p. 231). Notes that several of the most influential of the "new critics" (Pound, Eliot, Ransom, Tate, Richards, Blackmur, and others) were also practicing poets and sees a strong tie between their evaluative criticism and the directions of much modern poetry. Argues that the most unfortunate aspect of the "new criticism" has been its "extension of a Metaphysical doctrine of poetry over other kinds of poetry," an extension that "leads to the exclusion of all poetries that do not 'toe the line' of that doctrine" (p. 236), such as the poetry of Milton and the Romantics. Mentions Crashaw only briefly.

◄§ 1037. Hughes, Richard E. "Metaphysical Poets as Event." *HSL* 3: 191–96.
Argues for the development of a "mythico-religio-poetics" so that the twentieth-century reader might better understand and appreciate metaphysical poetry: "Writing in a time of anxiety amenable to myth; nurtured by a faith supportive of a sacramental response to reality; accepting the world as a panorama of symbol-saturated events rather than neuter objects: the poets of the earlier seventeenth century were involved in poem, myth and religious insight all at once" (p. 196). No specific mention of Crashaw.

◄§ 1038. Kusunose, Toshihiko. "Richard Crashaw—Bi to Junkyo" [Richard Crashaw—Beauty and Martyrdom], in *Shi to Shin—Donne o meguru Shijintachi* [Poetry and Faith—Donne and His Circle], 106–34. Kyoto: Keibunsha.
Revised version of "Richard Crashaw's Poetry and Steps to Loreto" (entry 835) and "Richard Crashaw no Sei to Shi—Ritualism no Katei" (entry 935). General introduction to Crashaw's life, religious sensibility, and poetry, de-

scribing him as fundamentally mystical and ritualistic. Comments in particular on his uses of sensuous imagery, especially his keen sense of color; his uses of elaborate conceits and wit; and his sensationalism, pointing out that these are all characteristics of the baroque style. Suggests that there is often a tension between the emotional and the intellectual and between the sensational and objective in Crashaw's poetry that is reflected in his uses of the paradox. Comments on the major themes of Crashaw's poetry and suggests that he was always attempting to find a balance between the world of sin and heavenly grace and that he searches for the eternal in the reality of this world.

১৩ 1039. Larsen, Kenneth J. "Some Light on Richard Crashaw's Final Years in Rome." *MLR* 66:492–96.

Points out that the *Pilgrim-Book* and the *Account Book* in the archives of the Venerable English College (Rome) supply important information on Crashaw's life and movements in the city from 1646 to 1649. Notes that Crashaw's name first appears in the *Pilgrim-Book*, a list of guests and visitors compiled by the Rectors from 1580 to 1656, as an entry on 28 November 1646, and that the last entry is dated 4 April 1649. Indicates that Crashaw opened an account at the college on 7 January 1647, with a final entry, which balances his account after his death, appearing in September 1649. Points out that three entries in the *Account Book* are in Crashaw's own hand. Discusses each entry that relates to Crashaw in the two books and shows how together they give clues about the poet's final years. Also comments on the English College as the center of English life in Rome during the period and mentions several of Crashaw's Cambridge acquaintances who were associated with the college during his time there. Points out Cardinal Palotto's connection with the college, suggests that Crashaw was never ordained a Roman Catholic priest, points out that his position at Loreto as a "beneficiatus" would not have required him to be in major orders, although it is likely he received tonsure and minor orders in order to sing in the choir. Further contends that "the frequent assumption that he had been obliged to read the Roman breviary as a Roman priest may be disregarded" (p. 496). See also Henry Foley (entry 251) and P. G. Stanwood (entry 943).

১৩ 1040. Orgel, Stephen. "Affecting the Metaphysics," in *Twentieth-Century Literature in Retrospect*, edited by Reuben A. Brower, 225–45. (Harvard English Studies, 2.) Cambridge: Harvard University Press.

Points out that the label *metaphysical* is largely a creation of critics, not of the poets themselves, and that "from the time 'metaphysical' was first formulated as a critical term its definition has remained relatively constant, but the list of poets whom critics regarded as metaphysical has varied wildly from generation to generation" (p. 226). Points out that Dr. Johnson does not mention Crashaw in his list of metaphysical poets and that sometimes Crashaw is classified by modern critics as baroque rather than metaphysical. Presents a brief history of the term and considers how a seventeenth-century reader would have regarded seventeenth-century poetry. Reasons that "no theory of metaphysical poetry has proved adequate" because "'metaphysical' really refers not to poetry, but to our sensibilities in response to it" (p. 245). Discusses Renaissance concepts of poetic images, especially emblems, stressing that even in emblem books the verbal element is basic: "Renaissance poets tended to think of images as tropes or rhetorical figures, that is, verbal structures" (p. 238). Suggests that Crashaw and Herbert are the most emblematic of the poets we call metaphysical and that even for them the "strictly pictorial aspects of emblematic poetry held little interest" (p. 233). Notes the influence of "concettismo" and "marinismo" on Crashaw. Concludes that "what we find as critics in works of art is largely determined by what we are looking for, and it is one of the functions of criticism to make us look again and again at works of art in ways that are valid but untried" (p. 245).

◄§ 1041. Parfitt, G. A. E. "Renaissance Wombs, Renaissance Tombs." *RMS* 15:23–33.

Discusses the use of the common "womb-tomb" *topos* in Renaissance poetry and attempts "to show something of the range of occasions and themes which the pairing is called upon to serve" and also tries "to see whether different poets' use of a common topos is a useful index to their abilities as poets" (p. 23). Briefly comments on Crashaw's use of the *topos* in "Upon our Saviours Tombe wherein never man was laid" and maintains that, although the figure could have provided Crashaw with a number of rich associations, "he concentrates wittily upon a limited application of the *topos*" and thus "one is left with the impression that Crashaw is being extravagantly witty without backing extravagance with perception and imagination" (p. 30). Claims that Crashaw's sacred epigrams "are usually simultaneously witty and witless" (p. 29). Briefly suggests that Crashaw's habit of pairing "breast" and "nest" is psychologically revealing and notes that, unlike Lovelace, Crashaw possessed an imagination that "is likely on one occasion to be perversely eccentric and on another to work fruitfully through wit upon the great Christian mysteries" (p. 33).

◄§ 1042. Sandbank, S[himon]. "On the Structure of Some Seventeenth-Century Metaphors." *ES* 52:323–30.

Discusses ways to approach seventeenth-century images and metaphors and challenges "the neutralization-of-the-vehicle doctrine" or the "never-try-to-visualize-it rule" (p. 325) supported by certain modern critics. Concentrates on images found in character books and shows that often "the vehicle is not the faceless carrier of a logical truth" (p. 328) but must be visualized. Opens up questions about the "metaphysicalness" of metaphysical poetry. Argues that, whereas the Spenserian poet tends to relate sense impressions harmoniously to one another, the metaphysical poet typically sees "logical resemblances while being aware of sensory disparities" (p. 330). Mentions Crashaw only in passing.

꣠ 1043. Schaar, Claes. *Marino and Crashaw*: Sospetto d'Herode: A Commentary. (Lund Studies in English, 39.) Lund, Sweden: C. W. K. Gleerup. 300p.

In the introduction (pp. 9–29) defends both Marino's original poem and Crashaw's version and argues that Marino's poem has not received the appreciation it deserves because critics have lacked the classical, biblical, and Renaissance backgrounds required to understand it. Maintains that Marino's poem is not inferior to Crashaw's rendering but has a unified structure, consistency of tone, and allusive richness. Discusses Crashaw's version in the context of seventeenth-century theories of translation and points out that, although the two poets "represent entirely different types of 17th-century poetry," Crashaw's poem "marks an important stage in the development of his poetical method" (p. 13). Comments on the classical, medieval, and Renaissance treatment of the Infernal Council motif, surveys the criticism on the two poems, and points out stylistic differences. Rejects *baroque* as a useful critical term. Presents on facing pages noncritical texts of Marino's "Sospetto d'Herode" and Crashaw's translation (pp. 32–77), followed by a detailed exegesis of both poems (pp. 81–288), in which they are compared and contrasted and in which numerous analogues to Crashaw's diction are noted. Selected bibliography (pp. 289–94); two selected indexes: (1) names (pp. 295–96) and (2) topics and words (pp. 297–99); and a list of abbreviations (p. 300).

꣠ 1044. Sugimoto, Ryūtarō. *Keijijōshi no Sugata to Nagare* [Metaphysical Poetry—Its Forms and Development]. Tokyo: Shinozaki Shorin. 232, 13p.

General critical introduction to metaphysical poetry. Chapter 1, "An Introduction to Metaphysical Poetry," describes its historical background and uses of wit and the conceit; Chapter 2, "John Donne"; Chapter 3, "The Poems of Crashaw," discusses Crashaw's relation to Donne and Herbert; Chapter 4, "Metaphysical Poetry and Marvell"; Chapter 5, "Milton and Metaphysical Poetry"; Chapter 6, "Coleridge's Criticism of Metaphysical Poetry"; Chapter 7, "T. S. Eliot and Metaphysical Poets"; and Chapter 8, "Donne in the Twentieth Century," a review of scholarship and criticism. Suggests that, although influenced by Donne, Crashaw's so-called Donnean qualities enter his verse through the poetry of Herbert and others rather than directly. Points out Crashaw's use of elaborate conceits and his blending of sensuous and spiritual images. Maintains that Crashaw, unlike Donne, does not fuse thought and feeling but achieves his effects through elaborate, loosely jointed figurative language.

◄§ 1045. Thomson, Virgil, composer. *The Nativity as Sung by the Shepherds: For Four-Part Chorus of Mixed Voices with Piano Accompaniment.* New York and London: G. Schirmer. 24p.

A musical setting for "Hymn in the Holy Nativity," composed to celebrate the seventy-fifth anniversary of the University of Chicago and first performed in the Rockefeller Chapel on 7 May 1967.

◄§ 1046. Tytell, John. "Sexual Imagery in the Secular and Sacred Poems of Richard Crashaw." *L&P* 21:21–27.

Maintains that in certain poems, especially those addressed to women, Crashaw employs sexual allusions and images that "do not directly support the religious subjects of those poems" and that "several passages are so manifestly erotic as to seduce the reader from the immediate argument to a distracting sexual metaphor that has little apparent function when the context of the poem is considered" (p. 21). Points out, however, that in his secular poems, such as "Loves Horoscope" and "Wishes. To his (supposed) Mistresse," Crashaw tends to understate sexuality and to handle it very modestly and calmly and that even in "The Epithalamium" he "deals with human love in conventional terms which are not especially sexual" (p. 23). Argues that when Crashaw introduces highly erotic allusions and images in "Musicks Duell" as well as in his religious poems, he creates a confusing ambiguity that does not add levels of richness and multiplicity of meanings to the poem, an ambiguity created by "a use of a series of images which evoke an action not directly expected or conceivable, given the ideological or thematic context of the poem" (p. 23). Discusses examples of such ambiguity in "The Weeper," "Ode on a Prayer-book," "A Hymn to Sainte Teresa," "Letter to the Countess of Denbigh," and "The Flaming Heart." Points out that Crashaw "seems on the whole, unaware of the larger implications of the sexual terms integral to his celebration of a union with God" (p. 27).

◄§ 1047. White, Helen C., Ruth C. Wallerstein, Ricardo Quintana, and A. B. Chambers, eds. "Richard Crashaw," in *Seventeenth-Century Verse and Prose.* Vol. 1: 1600–1660, 391–417. 2d ed. New York: Macmillan; London: Collier-Macmillan.

Revision of the 1951 edition (entry 739), with a new introduction to Crashaw and new notes, selections, and bibliography. Presents a general introduction to Crashaw's life and poetry (pp. 391–92) and anthologizes nineteen poems (or selections therefrom), including two different versions of "Wishes. To his (supposed) Mistresse," to illustrate Crashaw's poetical development (pp. 392–417). Points out that no matter how much he revised his poems, certain qualities remain: "forceful and occasionally forced paradox; violent contrast; reliance on sensual detail, particularly of color and touch, to indicate moral condition and religious theme; deliberate distortion of regular structures to produce the asymmetric effect of baroque art; and unity of thought more dependent on imagery than on logic" (p. 391). Notes that Crashaw "often approached his subjects from an epigrammatist's point of view" and that even his longer poems "are constructed from small units—couplets, triplets, stanzas—which, if printed separately, might be mistaken for complete, though highly compressed, poems" (p. 391). Suggests that the revisions made between 1646 and 1648 show "so remarkably quick a development of Crashaw's poetic powers that one is tempted to speculate what the verse would have become had Crashaw been spared even another five years" (p. 391). Comments on the themes and techniques of Crashaw's devotional poetry.

◆§ 1048. Wilcher, Robert. "Notes on Recurrent Images in Seventeenth-Century Poetry." *N&Q* n.s. 18:288–90.

Points out the popularity of the periphrasis "feathered rain" for snow among several mid-seventeenth-century poets and notes Crashaw's use of it in line 1 of "An Elegy upon the death of Mr. Stanninow." Suggests that, whatever its origin, the figure "seems to have been disseminated through its use in William Strode's lyric 'On a Gentlewoman walking in the Snowe'" (p. 288), which was first printed in W. Porter's *Madrigals and Airs* (1632) and later as "On Chloris walking in the Snow" in *Wits Recreations* (1640).

◆§ 1049. Willy, Margaret, ed. *The Metaphysical Poets*. (The English Library, ed. James Sutherland.) London: Edward Arnold; Columbia: University of South Carolina Press. x, 149p.

Includes three poems by Crashaw—"Upon the Death of a Gentleman [Mr. Chambers]" (pp. 59–60), "Letter to the Countess of Denbigh" (pp. 131–34), and "Easter day" (pp. 134–35)—with brief critical introductions and explanatory notes. Selected bibliography.

1972

◆§ 1050. Beaty, Frederick L. "With Verse Like Crashaw." *N&Q* n.s. 19: 290–92.

Suggests that negative references to Crashaw in the May 1817 issue of *Blackwood's Edinburgh Magazine* (entry 122) may be the source for Byron's derogatory comment on Crashaw in *Don Juan* (entry 132). Points out that, except for "Sospetto d'Herode," Byron probably knew little about Crashaw's poetry and notes that Crashaw "was apparently little read in Byron's day" and "was remembered chiefly because his translation of Marino seemed to have influenced Milton's *Paradise Lost*" (p. 291). Points out also that Byron was familiar with Thomas Campbell's *Specimens of the British Poets* (entry 123), which contains equally pejorative remarks about Crashaw, but suggests that, since there is no evidence that Byron received his copy in Rome before May

1820, after he had composed his line, the comments in Campbell may have only confirmed his earlier view.

◄§ 1051. Beer, Patricia. *An Introduction to the Metaphysical Poets.* London and Basingstoke: Macmillan; Totowa, N.J.: Rowman & Littlefield. 115p.

Reprinted, Atlantic Highlands: Humanities Press, 1982.

General introduction to metaphysical poetry and poets designed for students in their first year of reading for an English honors degree. Although Crashaw is listed and/or mentioned in several places as a metaphysical poet, no extensive treatment of his poetry is given. Comments briefly on "A Hymn to Sainte Teresa," calling it one of Crashaw's "most characteristic and most impressive poems" and pointing out that it is "full of emotional warmth" and sensuousness that seem "particularly suitable for his Catholic themes" (p. 31).

◄§ 1052. Campbell, Jane. *The Retrospective Review (1820–1828) and the Revival of Seventeenth-Century Poetry.* (Waterloo Lutheran University Monograph Series.) Waterloo, Ont.: Waterloo Lutheran University. 76p.

Outlines the history of the *Retrospective Review* and comments on its literary background and the important role it played in the reevaluation of seventeenth-century poetry and poets during the Romantic period. Specifically outlines and comments on the treatment of Crashaw (entry 130). Observes that the review "was content to share the prevalent view" of Crashaw, "while broadening the readers' knowledge of the poet by reprinting excerpts from his work," noting that, on the whole, early nineteenth-century critics, "when reading Crashaw at all, tended to place him above Herbert and also to exempt him from some of the censure which was allotted to the other metaphysicals" and pointing out that, "for the average nineteenth-century reader of the poet, however, Crashaw was not nearly as congenial a religious poet as Wither, Habington, or even Herbert, and the *Retrospective* belongs with the majority" (p. 39). Suggests that the most perceptive comment on Crashaw appears in an article on Beaumont's *Psyche* (11[1825]: 288–307), "in which the author compares Beaumont's way of treating the theme of evil to Crashaw's and comments on the poets' idea of 'a mystical union between moral and physical good'" (p. 39).

◄§ 1053. Carrive, Lucien. "Les principales variétés," in *La Poésie religieuse anglaise entre 1625 et 1640: Contribution à l'étude de la sensibilité religieuse à l'âge d'or de l'anglicanisme*, 1:53–259. Caen: Assoc. des Publs. de la Faculté des Lettres et Science Humaines de l'Université de Caen.

Comments on such matters as biblical imagery, paraphrases of the psalms, emblems, prayer, spiritual exercises, and mysticism and discusses English religious poetry from 1625 to 1640 in the light of these topics. Briefly discusses

"Psalme 23" and "Psalme 137" and suggests that they are "plutôt des commentaires ou des méditations que des traductions" (p. 131). Notes that Crashaw "est trop totalemente en dehors de la tradition de poésie religieuse qui nous occupe et ces psaumes répondent à de tout autres préoccupations" (p. 132). Comments briefly on Crashaw's use of emblematic images and suggests that, at times, whole passages in his poems seem very much like emblems. Disagrees generally with Louis Martz concerning the dominance of discursive meditative modes in the period but suggests that Crashaw, a Counter-Reformation Catholic, may be an exception.

◄§ 1054. Crashaw, Richard. *Richard Crashaw*. Selected with an introduction by Michael Cayley. (Fyfield Books.) Oxford: Carcanet Press. 90p.
    Brief introduction to Crashaw's life and poetry (pp. 1–9); selections from forty poems, both sacred and secular (pp. 11–89); and a note on the text followed by a highly selected bibliography (p. 90). Notes that the texts are, on the whole, from *Carmen Deo Nostro* (1652) and *The Delights of the Muses* (1648), although "earlier versions, where relevant, have always been consulted, and in one or two cases substantially different readings have been incorporated," and notes that both spelling and punctuation have been modernized "to facilitate comprehension of Crashaw's frequently difficult syntax" (p. 90). Suggests that "the valid distinction in Crashaw's work lies not in chronology but between sacred and secular, and here the distinction is more one of subject-matter than of style" (p. 5). Sees many similarities, therefore, in the sacred and secular poems, noting that "The Weeper" and "Wishes. To his (supposed) Mistresse" both consist of a sequence of largely self-contained witty stanzas, a succession of brilliants connected by a fragile string of logical progression" (p. 6). Stresses the lack of logic in Crashaw's longer poems; his sensuousness and sensationalism; his uses of the pastoral; his employment of paradox, wit, and elaborate conceits; and his use of strongly sexual imagery. Comments in some detail on "Hymn in the Holy Nativity," noting that it is "not as artificial as it at first appears"; in fact, it is "on the whole fairly simple" while the tone "is one of slightly humorous warmth" (p. 7). Suggests that "much of Crashaw's best work" is in the Teresian poems (p. 8). Concludes that Crashaw is "a poet of feelings rather than the intellect" and is "the only truly Baroque poet of importance in English" (p. 9). Briefly compares and contrasts Crashaw to Southwell, Herbert, Donne, Milton, Keats, and Bernini.

◄§ 1055. Ditsky, John. "Symbol-Patterns in Crashaw's *Carmen Deo Nostro*." *North Dakota Quarterly* 40, no. 3:31–36.
    Calls Crashaw "a skilled poet of the traditional Christian symbols" and maintains that a distinctive feature of *Carmen Deo Nostro* is "the occurrence of patterns or groupings of a number of symbols which frequently recur, singly or in overlapping sets, throughout the entire set of poems" (p. 31). Suggests that these "families of symbols" (p. 31) can be grouped, more or less, into five

major categories: (1) lamb symbols, including the concept of sacrifice; (2) fire-dawn-day-light-spring-heat and cold symbolism; (3) king-lover-soldier-battle-wound symbolism; (4) bodily symbols (life and death-blood-tears-etc.); and (5) miscellaneous symbols of minor or rarer usage. In order to show that these symbols "occur in definite developmental patterns" (p. 36), points out their appearance in "Letter to the Countess of Denbigh," "Hymn to the Name of Jesus," "Hymn in the Holy Nativity," "New Year's Day," "Hymn in the Glorious Epiphanie," "Office of the Holy Crosse," "Vexilla Regis," "Charitas Nimia," "Sancta Maria Dolorum," "Song upon the Bleeding Crucifix," "Adoro Te," "Dies Irae Dies Illa," "O Gloriosa Domina," "Hymn in the Assumption," "The Weeper," the Teresian hymns, "Alexias," "Description of a Religious House and Condition of Life," and "On Hope."

৯§ 1056. Dobrez, Livio. "The Crashaw-Teresa Relationship." *SoRA*, 5: 21–37.

Argues that the most distinctive characteristic of Crashaw's poetry is a sense of surrender, a prodigal, witty, rhetorical abandon, seen most vividly in his poems about women, and relates this tendency to St. Teresa's concept of rapture in her *Life* and *Interior Castle*. Points out that for both "the important thing is the 'wounding' or 'killing' of the egocentric impulse" (p. 25). Finds images of wounds, especially of the pierced heart, in Crashaw's poems written before his acquaintance with Teresa's life and writings and suggests that the concept of surrender is more confirmed than influenced by her. Maintains that for both the concept of surrender is "from death to a life which is the life of the Other, transformation by love" (p. 27), reflecting a "cycle of regeneration" (p. 29). Discusses "The Weeper," "A Hymn to Sainte Teresa," and "Letter to the Countess of Denbigh" as examples of this pattern. Finds less successful those poems that portray surrender only, but not regeneration, especially "Hymn to the Name of Jesus." Labels this trait "infantilism" and points out instances of it in "The Weeper," "Sancta Maria Dolorum," and "Luke 11. Blessed be the paps which Thou hast sucked." Argues that this "infantilism" has nothing in common with Teresa's writings and suggests that Crashaw's interest in the saint taught him how to control his abandon and excess. Examines also the erotic imagery in Crashaw's poetry and suggests that it has its roots not only in literary and religious tradition but also in an unfulfilled sexual motive. Sees the image of the pierced heart as "undeniably a picture of neurosis" (p. 36) for Crashaw and as the reflection of a "circumscribed personality, forced to play a passive role to itself" for both Crashaw and Teresa, yet suggests that this symbol of self-conflict "provides its own solution, either partial or complete" (p. 37) in the mystical death and creative union. Concludes that at its best Crashaw's style of surrender is "an integrated style, a controlled abandon—abandon controlled not from the outside but from *within*, that is, not by a restraint alien to Crashaw but by the inner logic of surrender" (p. 37).

◄§ 1057. Ellrodt, Robert. "De Platon à Traherne: L'intuition de l'instant chez les poétes métaphysiques anglais du dix-septième siècle," in *Mouvements premiers: Études critiques offertes à Georges Poulet*, 9–25. Paris: Librairie José Corti.

Relates the views of the metaphysical poets toward the "instant" or "moment" to those of Plato, Plotinus, Aristotle, and Kierkegaard and suggests that an evolution of human spirit toward interiority and subjectivity can be observed. Maintains that Crashaw's poetry ignores the present moment: "Tout en elle est flux ou mouvement musical, élan vers un apogée qui est une expiration ou un engloutissement" (p. 20). Asks, however, if we cannot consider as "une série d'instants extatiques" (p. 20) the successive "deaths" of amorous fainting in Crashaw's poetry, profane in the young spouse, mystic in the saint. Suggests that "A Hymn to Sainte Teresa" is characterized by a repetition of dissonant chords, directed, as in music, toward a final resolution. Briefly compares Crashaw to Ernest Hemingway in his attachment to the moment of experience.

◄§ 1058. Gillie, Christopher. *Longman Companion to English Literature.* London: Longman Group. 885p.

Reprinted, New York: Longmans, 1974; 2d ed., London, 1977, 1978; new ed. 1980.

Mentions Crashaw under different headings. Under "Crashaw" (p. 470), gives a biographical sketch and a brief introduction to Crashaw's poetry. "Metaphysical Poets" (pp. 643–44) outlines the history of the term *metaphysical poets* and major features of the metaphysical style. Suggests that Crashaw belongs to the metaphysical school "but in a special sense"; notes the influence of Marino, calling Crashaw "the most sensuous of the English poets of this tendency"; points out the impersonal quality of his verse; and suggests that Herbert was Crashaw's "first master" (p. 470). Singles out "A Hymn to Sainte Teresa" as Crashaw's masterpiece and suggests that "The Weeper" "shows his extravagances most obtrusively" (p. 470).

◄§ 1059. Kelliher, Hilton. "Crashaw at Cambridge and Rome." N&Q n.s. 19:18–19.

Adds additional information about Crashaw's acquaintances at Cambridge and in Rome contained in the 1813 *Tixall Poetry* (entry 121). Notes that twice in his verse-letters Edward Thimelby refers to "our Crashaw" and suggests that these references indicate that both Thimelby and the recipient of his letters, Thomas Normanton, knew Crashaw personally. Points out that Normanton was at the English College during Crashaw's stay in Rome and that he traveled with Thomas (or Thomas's brother, William) Keightly and Thomas Playters, all of whom Crashaw may have known at Cambridge. Further suggests that Crashaw met Thimelby in Rome and that two poems in the Tixall collection,

"On the Translation of the House of Loretto" and "A Sigh to St. Monica's Teares," though not by Crashaw, may have been inspired by his example.

◄§ 1060. Leach, Elsie. "T. S. Eliot and the School of Donne." *Costerus* 3:163–80.

Summarizes the shifts in Eliot's critical position toward the metaphysical poets and argues that "the changing emphases of Eliot's criticism parallel developments in his own verse" (p. 163). Surveys Eliot's criticism of Crashaw and claims that his views were significantly shaped by Praz. Points out that in the 1920s Eliot "wrote more about Crashaw than any other seventeenth-century poet" (p. 166) and regarded him as "the greatest Baroque poet of any nationality" (p. 167). Observes that during this period Eliot began to write his own explicitly Christian poems and that perhaps he was attracted to Crashaw because he saw him as "the best poet on the 'extreme Right' of Christianity in seventeenth-century England" (p. 166). Discusses Eliot's comparisons of Crashaw to Dante and to Herbert. Shows that after 1931 Eliot evidenced an increasing interest in Herbert as his interest in Donne, Crashaw, and Marvell diminished.

◄§ 1061. Montgomery, Lyna Lee. "The Phoenix: Its Use as a Literary Device in English from the Seventeenth Century to the Twentieth Century." *DHLR* 5:268–323.

Comments on selected uses of the phoenix legend in English literature from the seventeenth to the twentieth century and concludes that, "from its full splendor and vitality as a literary device in the seventeenth century the phoenix sank into the nest of eighteenth and nineteenth century literature, relatively dead, to rise once more in contemporary literature, renewed and vigorous, as a rich and almost endlessly versatile symbol" (p. 321). Discusses Crashaw's use of the phoenix legend in "Hymn in the Holy Nativity" pointing out how it informs many of the images in the poem and how it provides Crashaw with an appropriately paradoxical symbol to discuss the paradoxes of the Incarnation. Points out briefly Crashaw's use of the phoenix legend and symbol in "Office of the Holy Crosse," "Easter day," "Phaenicis Genethliacon & Epicedion," and "On a foule Morning, being then to take a journey."

◄§ 1062. Nakamura, Mineko. "A Ring Without a Stone: A Study of Baroque Quality in *The First Anniversary* (2)." *Insight* (Notre Dame Joshi Daigaku, Kyoto), no. 4 (May):59–75.

Disagrees with Odette de Mourgues's definition of baroque in *Metaphysical Baroque & Précieux Poetry* (entry 754) and offers a broader definition of the term. Discusses Donne's *The First Anniversary* as a baroque poem and contrasts it with "The Weeper." Suggests that Crashaw's poem "wallows in the pleasure of sweet sorrow," whereas Donne's poem "is steeped in the terror and deploration of losing something dear and indispensable to him" (p. 60).

Maintains that "The Weeper" is characterized by a "reckless flow of clustered images" and suggests that, unlike Donne's poem, it is "illogical in the sequence of the stanzas and has a loose sense of form" (pp. 69–70).

◄§ 1063. Parks, Edna D. *Early English Hymns: An Index*. Metuchen, N.J.: Scarecrow Press. viii, 9–168p.

Presents an index of early English hymns, in part to challenge the assumption that English hymn writing dates from Isaac Watts (1674–1748). Includes much religious poetry of the seventeenth century since "much which was suitable was soon adapted and joined with a tune" (p. iv), even though it was not originally designed for congregational singing. Includes some poems that were never set to music, if they conform to the definition of the hymn. Arranges the hymns in alphabetical order by first line and also presents (1) the meter, (2) the number of lines or stanzas in the earliest publication of the poem, (3) the name of the author, (4) date of publication and page or line numbers where the hymn can be found, and, when possible, (5) information about the tune and composer. Lists thirteen items for Crashaw, all but three of which first appeared as hymns in *A Collection of Hymns of the Children of God in All Ages* (entry 80). Bibliography (pp. 143–54), author index (pp. 155–62), composer index (pp. 163–65), and tune index (pp. 166–68).

◄§ 1064. Schlüter, Kurt. "Die Lyrik der englischen Renaissance," in *Renaissance und Barock*, vol. 10, edited by August Buck et al., 216–56. (Neues Handbuch der Literaturwissenchaft, vols. 9 & 10, ed. Klaus von See.) Frankfurt am Main: Akademische Verlagsgesellschaft Athenaion.

Reprinted in *Englische Dichtung des 16. und 17. Jahrhunderts*, by Horst Oppel und Kurt Schlüter, Athenaion Essays, 3; Studienausgaben zum "Neues Handbuch der Literaturwissenschaft," ed. Klaus von See (Frankfurt am Main: Akademische Verlagsgesellschaft, 1973), 54–94.

General historical and critical survey of English lyric poetry of the Renaissance—from Wyatt to Milton. Briefly evaluates Crashaw's poetry (pp. 246–47) and describes it as uncommonly baroque for England. Notes that Crashaw was influenced more than other poets of his time by Marino, the Jesuits, and the Counter-Reformation and, therefore, seems "zu schwül, zu süss und zu rosig" (p. 247) for most English tastes. Suggests that Crashaw "schwelgt in innigem Liebesverlangen und steigert sich in rauschhafte Ekstasen" (p. 247). Briefly comments on "The Weeper," "Song upon the Bleeding Crucifix," and "Ode on a Prayer-book."

◄§ 1065. Steele, Thomas J. "The Tactile Sensorium of Richard Crashaw." *SCN* 30:9–10.

Maintains that, when dealing with Crashaw's poetry, it is useful to broaden the usual definition of synesthesia and see it not as a compact figure of speech but as "the stimulation of two or more senses within an image-group which may occupy several lines" (p. 9) and points out that "the reader finds Crashaw so consistently relating the other four senses to the tactile that in nearly every image-group in his mature poetry some type of tactility emerges" (pp. 9–10). Maintains that "Crashaw's synesthesias run from the very simple joining of images from two senses to extended combinations of several," all centered about the tactile, and that his tactility "tends to dominate space and time and even infinity and eternity" (p. 10). Concludes that synesthesia was Crashaw's way "to drive the reader past sensory disparateness to an understanding of ideal relations" and that, "by engaging and outraging the senses by the powerful catachresis of synesthesia, Crashaw forces the reader to unify the image-object on the level of reason or faith" (p. 10).

◆§ 1066. Szenczi, Miklós, Tibor Szobotka, and Anna Katona. "A korai Stuar-tok és a polgári forradalom Kora (1603–1660)" in *Az Angol irodalom története* [The History of English Literature], 126–216. Budapest: Gondolat.

Presents a biographical sketch of Crashaw and contrasts him with Herbert. Agrees with Douglas Bush that Crashaw is the only outstanding example of baroque religious sensibility in English literature. Comments briefly on the influence of Marino, the Spanish mystics, and the Jesuit poets on Crashaw's style, especially in his choice of images.

◆§ 1067. Warnke, Frank J. *Versions of Baroque: European Literature in the Seventeenth Century.* New Haven and London: Yale University Press. ix, 229p.

Chapter 3, in different form, first appeared in *CollG* (entry 959).

Most of Chapter 4 first appeared as "The World as Theatre: Baroque Varia-tions on a Traditional Topos," in *Festschrift für Edgar Mertner,* ed. Bernard Fabian and Ulrich Suerbaum (Munich: Wilhelm Fink Verlag, 1968), 185–200.

A portion of Chapter 5 was first published as "Das Spielelement in der Liebeslyrik des Barock," in *Arcadia* 4 (1969):225–37.

Uses the term *baroque* "to denote not a precisely definable style but a period complex made up of a whole cluster of more or less related styles—a complex which, in its earlier phases (approximately 1580–1610), contains significant survivals of the preceding complex, or period style (i.e. the Renaissance), and, in its later phases (approximately 1650–90), anticipations of the subsequent complex (i.e. Neoclassicism)" (pp. 1–2). Maintains that a "literary period cannot be conceived of as a time span populated by authors expressing them-selves in virtually identical styles, style itself being too individual a phenome-non to allow for such a conception," and suggests that "a literary period is rather a time span in which underlying shared spiritual preoccupations find expression in a variety of stylistic and thematic emphases (p. 9). Isolates a number of these emphases, preoccupations, and topoi of baroque literature in nine chapters: (1) "Terms and Concepts," (2) "Appearance and Reality," (3) "The Experience of Contradiction," (4) "The World as Theatre," (5) "Art as Play," (6) "Metaphysical and Meditative Devotion," (7) "The Baroque Epic," (8) "The Sacrificial .Hero," and (9) "The End of the World." Considers Crashaw a primary example of the "ornate, exclamatory, emotional, and extravagant" (p. 12) baroque style, designated the "high baroque" and typified by such Continental poets as Gryphius, Marino, Góngora, d'Aubigné, and Vondel, and points out high baroque characteristics of his poetry throughout. In Chapter 2 (pp. 21–51) argues that "the contradictory vision and the attempt to capture absolute reality constitute the unifying elements of Baroque poetry" (p. 23) and contrasts Spenser's "Hymn to Heavenly Beautie," lines from Donne's *The second Anniversary*, and Crashaw's "Hymn in the Assumption" to show major divisions of baroque style. Suggests that Crashaw's poem "combines the sensuousness of the Renaissance and the intellectual extravagance of the Baroque in a fusion which typifies one whole international tendency in seventeenth-century poetry" (p. 30) and maintains that Crashaw uses sensuous imagery in the poem "not in a manner that significantly imitates or represents the world of ordinary experience but in a manner that constructs phantasmagoric heaven out of chunks of sensuous experience regarded simply as raw material for an artifact" (pp. 31–32). Maintains that "in his dramatic concentration on an individual protagonist, as in his rejection of the phenomenal, Crashaw is a Baroque poet of the truest sort" (p. 32). Compares Crashaw to Giles Fletcher. In Chapter 3 (pp. 52–65) maintains that Crashaw is "notoriously the most Italianate of English seventeenth-century poets" and that, "like his Continental coevals, he creates a phantasmagoric effect through an imagery which, though appealing vividly to the senses, is so disposed as to present a series of powerful contradictions of normal sensuous experience" (p. 54). Contrasts Crashaw with Donne, Herbert, and Marvell. Briefly discusses "A Hymn to Sainte Teresa" to show that "the contraries of pain and rapture, flesh and spirit, multiplicity and unity, are fused into a single experience of the imagination through the agency of a sensibility which utilizes the sense data of worldly experience but rearranges those data in such a way as to transcend them, creating a world in which the ordinary contradictions have lost their capacity for enforcing choice" (p. 63).

1973

◄§ 1068. Adams, Robert M. *Proteus, His Lies, His Truth: Discussions of Literary Translations*. New York: W. W. Norton & Co. xii, 192p.

Comments briefly on Crashaw's translations of his own Latin epigrams into English. Points out that it is "not altogether a foregone conclusion that every one of the epigrams was written first in Latin, then translated into English," for "some of them may have undergone the contrary process" (p. 133). Maintains that Crashaw "did not exercise any difficult options in one tongue that he avoided in the other" and suggests that, "because he was deft in both, the results are often equivalent or nearly so" (p. 133). Briefly contrasts Crashaw to Marvell in this respect. Suggests ways in which Crashaw's "Sospetto d'Herode" is superior to Marino's original yet maintains that Crashaw's poem remains faithful in many respects to the original. Points out, for example, that Crashaw "is particularly good at warming and animating images of Marino which in the original seem cold and nerveless because they don't have strong verbs or because the adjectives used have a distancing, a commentator's effect"; that he has "extraordinary assurance in manipulating rhythmic syncopation" (p. 166); and that his stanzas are "much fuller and more crowded than those of Marino" (p. 167). Concludes that, "trained on bilingual epigrams, Crashaw was an expert at getting *multum in parvo*" (p. 168).

⋙ 1069. Allison, A. F. *Four Metaphysical Poets: George Herbert, Richard Crashaw, Henry Vaughan, Andrew Marvell: A Bibliographical Catalogue of the Early Editions of Their Poetry and Prose (To the end of the the 17th Century)*. (Pall Mall Bibliographies, no. 3) Folkestone & London: Dawsons of Pall Mall. 134p.

Brief account of Crashaw's life and chronological listing of the publication of his poetry to the end of the seventeenth century (pp. 27–28). Bibliographical description of each separate edition (pp. 28–32); facsimiles of each title page, keyed to the entries (pp. 86–96), and index of printers and publishers, also keyed to the entries (pp. 133–34)

⋙ 1070. Hollander, John, and Frank Kermode, eds. "Richard Crashaw," in *The Oxford Anthology of English Literature*. Vol. 1: *The Middle Ages through the Eighteenth Century*, 1178–89. New York: Oxford University Press.

Reissued as *The Literature of Renaissance England*, The Oxford Anthology of English Literature, vol. 2 (New York: Oxford University Press, 1973), 678–89.

Brief introduction to Crashaw's life and poetry. Agrees with Douglas Bush that Crashaw is the very incarnation of baroque sensibility and points out that "his religious verse is far more excitedly sensual than a good deal of Caroline erotic poetry" and that "his use of the paradox of self-contradiction and of excruciatingly insistent conceits was energized by a belief that only by the intensification of the concrete realms—of body, picture, or thing—could the abstract ones of soul and significance be released" (p. 1178). Observes that some of Crashaw's more intense secular verse, such as "Musicks Duell," "shares with his devotional verse a delight in expressive energy itself, banishing good taste and rhetorical control as a Cavalier love lyrist would banish prudence, a delight that found no strength save at the brink of rage, no fullness save in overflow" (p. 1179). Suggests that "The Weeper" is only a "string of glittering epigrams" that "lacks total coherence" (p. 1183) and that the Teresian hymns are characterized by "a controlled linguistic frenzy" (p. 1187). Anthologizes "Musicks Duell," "The Weeper," "On our crucified Lord Naked, and bloody," "Upon our Saviors Tombe wherein never man was laid," "Upon the Infant Martyrs," and lines from "The Flaming Heart," with notes.

◄§ 1071. Lewalski, Barbara K., and Andrew J. Sabol, eds. *Major Poets of the Earlier Seventeenth Century: Donne, Herbert, Vaughan, Crashaw, Jonson, Herrick, Marvell*. Indianapolis and New York: Odyssey Press, a Division of Bobbs-Merrill Co. xxxv, 1330p.

Includes a general introduction to earlier seventeenth-century lyric poetry (pp. xix–xxxi); a selected bibliography of studies of seventeenth-century poetry and its backgrounds (pp. xxxiii–xxxv); an introduction to Crashaw's life and poetry (pp. 611–21); a selected bibliography of editions and studies on Crashaw's life and poetry (p. 622); extensive selections from Crashaw's secular and sacred poetry (including the whole of *Carmen Deo Nostro*) with explanatory notes (pp. 623–739); an introduction to musical settings of seventeenth-century lyrics (pp. 1209–12), including a musical setting of "A Song ('Lord when the sense of thy sweet grace')" (pp. 1222–34); textual notes on Crashaw's poems included in the anthology (pp. 1288–92); and an index of titles and first lines (pp. 1301–30). In the general introduction Lewalski outlines major critical trends in the study of early seventeenth-century poetry; notes the modern tendency to break down the rigid dichotomy between metaphysical and neo-classical poetry as well as to relate English poetry to Continental poetry of the period; comments on the trend to divert "attention away from broad generalizations about common features of style toward the unique poetic experience which each of these poets can offer" (p. xxvii); and discusses the relationship between the lyric and music. In the introduction to Crashaw briefly outlines his life and comments on major characteristics of his poetry and some influences on his sensibility and art—emblems, Counter-Reformation spirituality, Latin epigrammatists, Marino, Southwell, and Giles Fletcher. Maintains that Crashaw is "the only important English poet who can be called 'baroque' with complete accuracy" (p. 612). Suggests that, although Crashaw's sensibility often repels modern readers, he has many merits as a poet, noting that "he alone among the English religious poets attempted the poetic rendering of religious ecstasy and rapture" (p. 615) and suggests that his "apparent formlessness, metrical irregularity, and plethora of seemingly confused images are explicable in terms of this intention, for it is by collapsing the logical categories of thought and producing a synesthetic blending of sensations, a phantasmagoria, a constant metamorphosis of one thing into another, that Crashaw suggests transcendence" (pp. 615–16). Maintains that Crashaw's Latin epigrams are among the best ever written by an Englishman and calls "Wishes. To his (supposed) Mistresse" "an elegant exception, a triumph in the

Jonsonian manner of simplicity and restraint" (p. 616). Comments on "Musicks Duell" as Crashaw's masterpiece of secular verse but maintains that his most distinctive poems are his original religious hymns and odes.

♦§ 1072. Mares, F. H. "Translating Catullus: A Grammato-Critical Examination of 'Vivamus, mea Lesbia' and some English Versions." *SoRA* 6:223–37.

Points out that Catullus's work, now very much in vogue, was also translated in the earlier seventeenth and in the late nineteenth centuries, but that each period reads Catullus "in the light of its own preoccupations" and "brings out something slightly different in its translations" (p. 223). Focuses on "Vivamus, mea Lesbia" (*Carmina* V). Briefly questions Crashaw's translation of line 1 in "Out of Catullus" and suggests that his translation of line 18 "anticipates the self-conscious pose of the Restoration rake" (p. 229). Concludes that, on the whole, earlier seventeenth-century translations "use a syntax which provides a more cheerful, more volitionist and more simply sensual reading of the poem," while nineteenth-century translation "puts passion into fancy-dress with a syntax (and lexis) littered with archaisms" (p. 231)

♦§ 1073. Quennell, Peter, and Hamish Johnson. "The Seventeenth Century," in *A History of English Literature*, 93–201. London: Weidenfeld and Nicolson; Springfield, Mass.: G. C. Merriman Co.
(Hamish Johnson does not appear on the title page of the American edition.) Reprinted, London: Ferndale Editions, 1981.

Brief introduction to Crashaw's life and poetry (pp. 133–34), relating him to the Counter-Reformation and to baroque art. Maintains that, although capable of "fiery eloquence," Crashaw "was seldom capable of long-sustained flights" and points out that critics who dislike metaphysical poetry "have often picked on his more unbalanced fancies—for example, on his ludicrous picture of the weeping Magdalen" (p. 133). Singles out "A Hymn to Sainte Teresa" as typical of Crashaw's baroque art, quotes lines from the hymn, and suggests that Dr. Johnson's phrase about "the most heterogeneous images" being "yoked by violence together" is an appropriate description of the poem (p. 134).

♦§ 1074. Ramsaran, John A. "Divine Infatuation: Crashaw and Mīram Baī; Herbert and Mīram Baī," in *English and Hindi Religious Poetry: An Analogical Study*, 89–108. (Studies in the History of Religions, 23.) Leiden: E. J. Brill.

Compares and contrasts Crashaw's life, religious sensibility, and poetry with those of Mīrām Baī, a late fifteenth- and early sixteenth-century Indian poetess. Suggests that Mīrām Baī "is in her religious ecstasies like an Indian St. Teresa" and "in her poems like Crashaw a poet of divine love" (p. 94). Maintains that "nowhere in English poetry is the lover-beloved mood, akin to the mādhurya-bhāva of bhakti, so clearly expressed as in Crashaw" (p. 90) and observes that Crashaw's liturgical poems suggest similarities between him and "the Hindi Aṣṭachāpa poets who dedicated their poetic gifts to the service of Kṛṣṇa in the Vaiṣṇava temple at Govardhana in Vraja" (p. 91). Observes that both the Indian poetess and Crashaw use rich symbolism, sensuous images, and high emotional intensity to depict spiritual states and that both often strike a note of joyous surrender to God. Concludes, however, that Mīrām Bāī resembles George Herbert more than Crashaw, "whose emotional range is more limited" (p. 101).

•ᢒ 1075. Rogers, Robert. "A Gathering of Roses: An Essay on the Limits of Context." *HSL* 5:61–76.
Surveys the metaphorical uses of the rose and comments briefly on Crashaw's use of it in "The Weeper" and his depiction of Christ as a rose in "New Year's Day."

•ᢒ 1076. Sundararajan, P. K. "Richard Crashaw." *BB* 30:69–75.
Lists (1) 18 editions of Crashaw's poems and 5 anthologies that "are remarkable for some reason, such as an introduction or extensive notes" (p. 69); (2) 31 books either exclusively on Crashaw or that contain extensive discussions of him; (3) 103 critical articles specifically on Crashaw; and (4) 6 bibliographical sources. Excludes pre-1900 critical studies, except for those that are part of editions or anthologies. Annotates briefly each item, except for early editions.

•ᢒ 1077. Wagner, Jürgen. "'Amor' in den geistlichen Gedichten Richard Crashaws," in *No More Lewd Layes: Eine Untersuchung zum Verhältnis zwischen weltlicher und geistlicher Dichtung im 16. und 17. Jahrhundert in England*, 235–90. Bonn: Rheinischen Friedrich-Wilhelms-Universität.
Studies Crashaw's transformation of the pagan figure of "Amor" into Christ and the figure of Venus into the Virgin Mary in his religious poems and observes that his attempts to overcome the pagan associations and mythological sources are not always successful. Examines the uses of red and white as conventional colors in the description of female beauty and notes that for Crashaw these colors connote sin and repentance. Maintains that Crashaw often goes beyond mere conceit and creates highly elaborate symbols but that he never abandons conceit altogether, since he recognizes the effectiveness of surprise that could be achieved by its use. Suggests that Crashaw thought that images of secular love in spiritual poetry had been fully sanctioned by St. Teresa's sensual descriptions of her most ecstatic moments. Compares the earlier and later versions of *Steps to the Temple* to show that the arrow-shooting figure of Amor is used more extensively in the later. Explores also the motifs of the arrow and the nest in Crashaw's poetry.

1974

❧§ 1078. Adkins, Joan F., and J. H. Adamson. "Via Negativa: Spanish Mystics and English Poets." *Literary Criterion* 11, no. 2:43–57.

Discusses the influence of the *via negativa* of sixteenth-century Spanish mystics on English poets of the seventeenth century and maintains that, "whatever their methods of expression," both "are drawn together by a common thread: they believe that God in His absolute reality is dark to man's intellect" (p. 43). Discusses briefly the theme and the light-dark imagery of "Hymn in the Glorious Epiphanie" to show that it "clearly reflects the Spanish mystical vision of the *via negativa*" (p. 56). Concludes that, "although it is not always possible to demonstrate that the English writers borrowed directly from the Spanish mystics," it is clear that "the heightened mystical activity in sixteenth-century Spain created a religious current which informed the intellectual, spiritual, and artistic milieu of seventeenth-century England" (p. 57).

❧§ 1079. Broadbent, John, ed. *Signet Classic Poets of the 17th Century,* Vol. 1. (The Signet Classic Poetry Series, gen. ed. John Hollander.) New York and Scarborough, Ontario: New American Library; London: New English Library. xviii, 377p.

In the introduction briefly compares and contrasts Crashaw and Herrick, noting that, like Herrick, Crashaw "is a poet of more private and peculiar talent" and suggests that "he accepts the improbable, he crystallises the most far-out metaphor of religio-erotic mysticism into an actual trinket" (p. 8). Brief introduction to Crashaw's poetry (pp. 249–51) and ten poems (pp. 251–74), with brief explanatory notes. Suggests that three things are extraordinary about Crashaw: (1) "he hyper-realises the metaphorical, or the personification" (p. 249), (2) he is sexually fixated and obsessed, almost to the point of perversity, and (3) he reflects an "emphatic individuation of tone" in which "he mixes musical pomp with colloquial carelessness, and refuses to obey metre," which is "partly an effect of his opportunistic sensationalism; and of the obsessional sexualising" (p. 250). Concludes that Crashaw is "a test of what is vulgar, especially of what is kitsch, in poetry" (p. 250).

❧§ 1080. Campbell, Gordon. "Words and Things: The Language of Metaphysical Poetry." *Lang&L* (Copenhagen) 2, no. 3:3–15.

Translated into Spanish as "Palabras y objetos: El lenguaje de la poesia metafísica," by Virginia Zúñiga. Tristán and Roger Wright, *Kañina* 3, no. 2(1979): 63–72.

Challenges critics, such as Rosemond Tuve, who attempt "to experiment with the analytical tools of the Renaissance in an attempt to recreate the sixteenth- and seventeenth-century readers' understanding of poetry" and argues that "these methods of analysis, although historically justified, are ultimately destructive, and that an appreciation of Renaissance poetry, particularly metaphysical poetry, is predicated on a knowledge of the poets' ideas about the nature of poetry rather than an ability to implement the philosophers' ideas on how a poem should be analysed" (p. 3). Challenges also the notion that Ramism accounts for metaphysical poetry and summarizes the Renaissance debate about the primacy of words or things. Concludes that metaphysical poetry is "primarily a poetry of words rather than things" and "we should be content to admire it at that level" (p. 11). Points out that it was common among the religious poets to reject ideas in favor of a language of devotion and cites Crashaw briefly as an example, noting, in particular, that in "The Teare" words take primacy over ideas.

◄§ 1081. Chinol, Elio. "The Metaphysical Poets," in *English Literature: A Historical Survey*. Vol. 1: *To the Romantic Revival*, 315–22. Naples: Liguori.
Briefly mentions Crashaw as an admirer of Herbert and suggests that he "blends metaphysical conceits and paradoxes with a vein of voluptuous mysticism typical of Italian and Spanish baroque art" (p. 315).

◄§ 1082. Dörrie, Heinrich. *Pygmalion: Ein Impuls Ovids und seine Wirkungen bis in die Gegenwart*. (Geisteswissenschaften, Vorträge-Rheinisch-Westfälische Akademie der Wissenschaften; G 195.) Opladen: Westdeutscher Verlag. 102p, 16 plates.
Discusses the Pygmalion theme in poetry and prose. Reproduces Crashaw's "In Pigmaliona" (p. 88) and notes that Crashaw "hat die Form eines Figuren-Gedichtes gewahlt; die Verse, symmetrische unter einander gesetzt, sollen die Gestalt der 'Pygmaliona' erkennen lassen" (p. 88).

◄§ 1083. Fisher, R. M. "The Predicament of William Crashawe, Preacher at the Temple, 1605–1613." *Journal of Ecclesiastical History* 25: 267–76.
Based on new biographical evidence, discusses the many difficulties encountered by the poet's father, William Crashaw, during the period of his tenure at the Temple from 1605 to 1613. See also entries 1084 and 1105.

◄§ 1084. Fisher, R. M. "William Crashawe and the Middle Temple Globes 1605–15." *Geographical Journal* 140: 105–12.
Suggests that the Molyneux globes, dated 1592 and 1603, at the Middle Temple, often assumed to have been donated by Robert Ashley, were, in fact, the gift of William Crashaw, the poet's father, who from 1605 to 1613 was preacher to the Temple. See also entries 1083 and 1105.

◄§ 1085. Hammond, Gerald, ed. *The Metaphysical Poets: A Selection of Critical Essays*. (Casebook Series, gen. ed. A. E. Dyson.) London and Basingstoke: Macmillan. 254p.
Collection of previously published essays. General editor's preface (p. 9); general introduction outlining the reputation of metaphysical poetry and metaphysical poets from the seventeenth century to the present, with brief com-

ments on Crashaw (pp. 11–32); twenty-four essays or parts of essays (pp. 34–241); selected bibliography (pp. 243–45); notes on contributors to part 3 (pp. 247–48); and index (pp. 249–54). Part 1: "Seventeenth- and Eighteenth-Century Criticism" (pp. 34–54) contains selections from Thomas Sprat, Edward Phillips, William Winstanley, Giles Jacob, the anonymous editor of *Select Hymns Taken out of Mr Herbert's Temple* (1697), Joseph Addison, John Oldmixon, the anonymous author of *A Dialogue on Taste* (1762), and Samuel Johnson. Part 2, "Nineteenth- and Early Twentieth-Century Criticism" (pp. 59–88), contains selections from Coleridge, Hazlitt, De Quincey, Emerson, George Macdonald, Alexander Grosart, Arthur Symons, and T. S. Eliot. Part 3, "Recent Studies" (pp. 89–241), contains selections from Rosemond Tuve, "The Criterion of Decorum," from *Elizabethan and Metaphysical Imagery* (1947); Leo Spitzer, "'The Extasie,'" from *A Method of Interpreting Literature* (1949); S. L. Bethell, "The Nature of Metaphysical Wit," from *Northern Miscellany of Literary Criticism* (1953); Joseph H. Summers, "George Herbert: The Conception of Form," from *George Herbert: His Religion and Art* (1954); Josephine Miles and Hanan C. Selvin, "A Factor Analysis of the Vocabulary of Poetry in the Seventeenth Century," from *The Computer and Literary Style* (1966); Earl Miner, "The Metaphysical Mode: Alteration of Time," from *The Metaphysical Mode from Donne to Cowley* (1969); and Rosalie L. Colie, "Andrew Marvell: Style and Stylistics," from *'My Echoing Song'—Andrew Marvell's Poetry of Criticism* (1970). Observes in the introduction that Peregrine Phillips's edition of Crashaw (1785) "aroused widespread hostility because of his accusations of plagiarism against a number of English poets, including Gray, Pope, and Milton" (p. 19), and points out that, in spite of his inclusion in most modern anthologies of metaphysical poetry and despite the excellent critical work of such scholars as Ruth Wallerstein and Austin Warren, Crashaw "is still thought of as essentially foreign" (p. 28).

⊷§ 1086. Ishii, Shōnosuke. "Richard Crashaw no 'The Weeper'" [Richard Crashaw's "The Weeper"]. *Sella* (Shirayuri Women's College) no. 3:1–5.

Translates into Japanese stanzas from "The Weeper" and briefly discusses its imagery and structural coherence. Suggests, that, although the imagery may at first appear repetitious, it is subtle, rich, and interconnected, forming various layers of figures and color that all contribute to the basic image of liquidity. Claims that all the images reinforce the basic notion of the saint's contrition for sin and her love of God. Argues that stanzas 1–5 center about the Magdalene's repentance that enables her tears to flow up to heaven, that stanzas 6–15 contain comparisons of her tears to various precious things, that stanzas 16–18 give explanations of the divine fire and love in her soul and how these were stirred up in her by Christ, that stanzas 19–22 comment on the saint's devotion to Christ, that stanzas 23–27 comment on the sweetness of her love as represented in descriptions of her weeping and tears, and that the poem ends with a colloquy between the poet and the tears, by which we learn that the saint has renounced all worldly things for Christ. Stresses that such images as the tears take on changing and deeper meanings as the poem progresses.

◄§ 1087. Kawata, Akira. "Richard Crashaw no Christo kotan-sanka—John Milton no bai to kikaku-site" [On Richard Crashaw's Hymn on the Nativity with reference to John Milton's Nativity Ode]. *Bulletin of the Faculty of Education* (Fukushima University), 26, no. 2.

Contrasts "Hymn in the Holy Nativity" with Milton's Nativity Ode to show the distinctive characteristics of Crashaw's religious verse, pointing out his uses of rhythms and images and his attitudes toward the Virgin Mary and the Mystery of the Incarnation. Maintains that, whereas Milton's poem is grand and majestic, full of rhetoric and classical allusions, Crashaw's hymn is an ardent religious love lyric, full of sensuous and rich colors, that emphasizes the love of God revealed in the birth of Christ.

◄§ 1088. Larsen, Kenneth J. "Richard Crashaw's *Epigrammata Sacra*," in *The Latin Poetry of English Poets*, edited by J. W. Binns, 93–120. London and Boston: Routledge & Kegan Paul.

Detailed historical and critical survey of Crashaw's Latin epigrams. Maintains that the individual epigrams can be dated precisely as beginning on 24 August 1631 and concluding on 17 May 1635, based on the liturgical cycle of the English Church for those years. Suggests that the dating of the epigrams allows one to see Crashaw's religious development toward a High Church position and points out that by mid-1634 the epigrams, as well as Crashaw's prefatory poem to Robert Shelford's *Five Pious and Learned Discourses* (entry 9) clearly indicate he had by then gone over completely to the Laudian camp. Points out that, in Laudian terms, love, not faith, was the essential virtue for salvation and that Crashaw's early epigrams "concern themselves primarily with eliciting from the Gospel incidents a strengthening of faith" whereas "those of the later years concentrate on the motive of love" (p. 98). Shows that, whether dealing with saints, miracles, the Virgin Mary, the passion of Christ, or the Eucharist, Crashaw progressively moves toward an emphasis on love. Comments on the influence of William Crashaw, John Tourney, Benjamin Laney, and Laudian sympathizers on Crashaw's religious attitudes and maintains that, although he was influenced stylistically by Continental models, the spirit and theology of his epigrams reflect his growing allegiance to Laudian theology and practice. Maintains that "the critical reaction, which has misconstrued his Latin epigrams as continental, has similarly clouded and misjudged his later English poetry" (p. 119).

◄§ 1089. Leicester, Richard. "Modest or Conscious." *TLS*, 12 July, p. 749.

Asks whether "Crashaw's own translation" of line 4 of "Joann. 2. Aquae in vinum versae" should read "the modest water" as quoted by Sir William

Temple in his *Readings of St. John's Gospel* (London: Macmillan, 1959), p. 37, or "the conscious water" as indicated in the *Oxford Dictionary of Quotations* (London: Oxford University Press, 1941).

◄§ 1090. Levitt, Paul M. "Crashaw's 'The Weeper,'" 113–14." *Expl* 32: item 56.

Explains the lines "Two walking baths; two weeping motions; / Portable, and compendious oceans" in the light of metaphysical wit and seventeenth-century word usage to show that in the poem Crashaw "has the eyes and tears of the Magdalen stand for the baptism waters, a tearful universe (rain), and the sorrow of the world, to be endured for the death of Christ."

◄§ 1091. McCanles, Michael. "The Rhetoric of the Sublime in Crashaw's Poetry," in *The Rhetoric of Renaissance Poetry from Wyatt to Milton*, edited by Thomas O. Sloan and Raymond B. Waddington, 189–211. Berkeley, Los Angeles, London: University of California Press.

Maintains that Crashaw attempts to arouse in the reader the emotion of the sublime "through hyperbole and paradox in which image and statement mediate a trans-human reality primarily by manifesting their own inadequacy for doing so" (p. 194) and suggests that both Kant's account of the sublime and contemporary rhetorical theory illuminate "certain aspects of conceiving the inconceivable in Crashaw's poetry" (p. 193). Discusses as examples of this technique "Hymn in the Holy Nativity," "New Year's Day," and especially "Hymn in the Glorious Epiphanie," all poems that employ "the image of the sun to praise Christ, primarily through amplifying its inadequacy for doing so" and in which the poet "places natural images and their divine referents together as if they were comparable and one could move univocally from one to the other" until "this compatibility is pushed to such hyperbolic extremes as to call it into question" (p. 195). Maintains that the ultimate goal of Crashaw's religious poetry is "the communication of 'something like' the blanking out of both sensation and thought at the moment of mystical union with God" and points out that "the critic's difficulty in talking about this aspect of Crashaw's poetry parallels the poet's difficulty in speaking about the divine: both must continually signal the need for discounting affirmations and affirming discountings" (p. 202). Discusses Crashaw's use of sexual symbols, images, and allusions in "Ode on a Prayer-book," "To [Mrs. M. R.] Councel Concerning her Choise," "A Hymn to Sainte Teresa," and "The Flaming Heart" to show that by "counterpointing" eros and agape Crashaw's final intention is not to reduce eros to agape but "to sunder agape and eros completely and totally" (p. 203). Suggests that all four poems "operate on the assumption that the aesthetic experience of a 'sublime' transcendence of conceptualization is analogous to a trans-human religious or mystical experience" (p. 210). Concludes that Crashaw's poetry "requires the reader to become a rhetorical critic, and to incorporate his recognition of the 'exaggerations' and 'inadequacies' of *hyperbole* into his understanding of the poetry itself" and that the poetry "expresses the possibilities and limits of its own rhetoric by mediating realities that are non-rhetorical—the limits of human concepts and names as they confront divine mysteries" so that "these realities are not only mediated by the rhetoric" but "likewise comment in turn on the rhetoric itself" (pp. 210–211).

◄§ 1092. Magill, Frank N., ed. "Richard Crashaw," in *Cyclopedia of World Authors* (revised edition), 1:442–43. Englewood Cliffs, N.J.: Salem Press.

Reprinted in *English Literature: Middle Ages to 1800* (entry 1178).

General introduction to Crashaw's life and poetry, noting that he is "among the best of England's Roman Catholic poets" (p. 422). Suggests that his poetry "reveals a joy in art and beauty that helps explain his preference for the ceremonies of the Roman Catholic Church" (p. 442). Notes that Crashaw "remains a well-established minor poet, one of the few English writers with the 'baroque sensibility,' the love for rich colors, sensuous imagery, and intense emotion that inspired the sculptors, painters, and poets of seventeenth century France and Italy" (p. 443). Selected bibliography (p. 443).

◄§ 1093. Miller, Carroll. "'Down the Arches of the Years': Richard Crashaw and Francis Thompson." *Journal of the Francis Thompson Society* 4–5:4–11.

Discusses the pervasive influence of Crashaw on Francis Thompson and comments on Thompson's criticism of Crashaw to show that it "demonstrates conclusively that its author was thoroughly acquainted with his subject" and "also provides a useful source for identifying materials which he borrowed from his forerunner" (p. 4). Points out close parallels and echoes of Crashaw in specific poems by Thompson. Calls "St. Monica" Thompson's "most sustained imitation of Crashaw" and suggests that it "duplicates both the imagery and structure of 'On the Bleeding Wounds of Our Crucified Lord'" (p. 5). Points out that Thompson's criticism devotes as much attention to Crashaw's secular verse as to his religious poetry, confirming "that the Victorian poet was more interested in his forerunner's technical skill than in his use of religious materials" (p. 6). Singles out "The Poppy" to illustrate Thompson's adaptation of Crashaw's imagery to a secular context. Claims that "The Hound of Heaven," though quite different from any of Crashaw's poems, uses a kind of impressionistic imagery reminiscent of the seventeenth-century poet.

◄§ 1094. Parfitt, G. A. E., ed. *Silver Poets of the Seventeenth Century.* Edited, with an introduction by G. A. E. Parfitt. London: J. M. Dent; Totowa, N.Y.: Rowman and Littlefield. xxi, 266p.

Presents a general introduction to Crashaw's poetry and points out that his secular verse "is important because it shows an ability to write with orthodox

control and accuracy, sufficiently to make it clear that he was not technically incompetent, although his religious verse often seems to say that he
was" (p. xi). Maintains that often Crashaw "seems to lack self-control, self-
criticism, and intelligence" (p. xi), but that certain poems in *Carmen Deo
Nostro* "show him moving away from his earlier witty style towards a manner
which is altogether more valuable" (p. xii). Singles out "Hymn to the Name of
Jesus" as the best example of Crashaw's mature style. Maintains that "the best-
known Crashaw poems are the wrong ones to concentrate on," for "as a poet
of wit Crashaw is usually disastrous" (p. xiii), and recommends, in addition to
"Hymn to the Name of Jesus," "Letter to the Countess of Denbigh" and
"Hymn in the Glorious Epiphanie." Concludes that "at his best and most important Crashaw creates an artefact which *is* his experience of God and which
is unlike Donne's self-analysis, Herbert's concern with God-in-life and
Vaughan's flashes of insight" (p. xiii). Anthologizes thirty-five Crashaw poems
(pp. 139–90) with brief explanatory notes (pp. 257–59). Highly selected bibliography (p. xxi).

⋙ 1095. Pearcy, Roy J. "Blake's 'Tyger' and Richard Crashaw's Paraphrase of
   Thomas of Celano's 'Dies Irae.'" *BlakeN* 7, no. 4:80–81.
   Suggests that Blake's "The Tyger" was influenced by Crashaw's "Dies Irae
Dies Illa." Points out that both poems are concerned with the theme of divine
wrath and the punishment of sin and that both employ similar metrical patterns, rhetorical features, poetic rhythms, figures of speech, and diction to
create religious awe. Maintains that "the most significant effect of seeing in
'The Tyger' reminiscences of the 'Hymn' is to focus attention on Blake's poem
as an apocalypse, to fasten certain of its activities in time, and to make it a
manifestation of divine wrath *in actu* rather than *in posse*" (p. 81).

⋙ 1096. Roston, Murray. "Mannerist Perspective," in *The Soul of Wit: A
   Study of John Donne*, 21–70. Oxford: Clarendon Press.
   Surveys and defends mannerist art, distinguishing it from both Renaissance
and baroque art. Maintains that "the common denominator of religious mannerism is the dematerialization of the physical universe and the tormented
striving towards a more satisfying spiritual reality beyond the empirically veri-
fiable world" (p. 69) and finds parallels in perspective and technique between
Donne's poetry and the art of such mannerists as El Greco and Tintoretto.
Contrasts Crashaw and Donne and suggests that Crashaw "seems even in his
most admired poems to be oblivious of the distasteful implications of his imagery whilst Donne, in his most audaciously provocative moods, remains in
firm artistic control, foreseeing the apparent absurdity or discrepancy and preparing to trap his reader by twisting it suddenly to his own advantage" (p. 56).
Maintains that, on the whole, Crashaw is ineffective in his attempts to translate religious experience into satisfying poetry and suggests that he lacks genuine wit and often lapses into a kind of "voluptuous self-indulgence" (p. 58).

Links Crashaw with Murillo, calling them both baroque, but pointing out that "there is no trace in their work of that weighty, dogmatic assertion which serves as the main baroque thrust" and suggests that their works seem like "the effulgent, heavenly opulence painted on the ceiling of a baroque cathedral but without the massivity of the dark structure below that creates the powerful aesthetic tensions of the true baroque" (p. 58).

◄§ 1097. Segel, Harold B. *The Baroque Poem: A Comparative Survey*. New York: E. P. Dutton & Co. xx, 328p.
Reprinted, New York: Irvington Publishers, 1983.
Presents "a comprehensive survey of the Baroque: the state of scholarship in the field, problems in the definition and use of Baroque as a term and concept, the relationship of mannerism to Baroque, the political, religious, scientific, and philosophical background of the age, the possible impact of nonliterary events on the evolution of Baroque taste, art, and outlook, the various types of Baroque poetry and aspects of Baroque poetic style" and illustrates "points made in the first, or survey, part of the book by giving a broad selection of representative poems, mostly lyrics, in the original languages and accompanying English translations" (pp. xix–xx). Contains 150 poems from the following literatures: English, American, Dutch, German, French, Italian, Spanish, Mexican, Portuguese, Polish, Modern Latin, Czech, Croatian, and Russian. Mentions Crashaw throughout and calls him "an outstanding Baroque poet" (p. 71). Points out that Crashaw is still labeled a metaphysical poet by most specialists in English poetry of the seventeenth century but maintains that the term is too restrictive and less apt than baroque in describing Crashaw's art. Briefly notes the influence of post-Tridentine Catholicism, Marino, and especially St. Teresa on Crashaw's poetry and points out his highly elaborate uses of rhetoric and sensuous imagery. Includes in the introduction lines and/or brief comments on "Hymn in the Holy Nativity," "The Weeper," "Wishes. To his (supposed) Mistresse," "Sospetto d'Herode," and "A Hymn to Sainte Teresa" but includes none of Crashaw's poems in the anthology. Selected bibliography (pp. 140–43).

◄§ 1098. Thwaite, Anthony. "Henry Vaughan (1621–1695), Richard Crashaw (?1612–1649), Thomas Traherne (1638–1674)," in *The English Poets from Chaucer to Edward Thomas*, by Peter Porter and Anthony Thwaite, 118–29. London: Secker & Warburg.
Reproduces the conclusion of "The Flaming Heart" as an example of Crashaw's "magnificent rhetoric" (p. 125). Calls Crashaw "England's only baroque poet" and suggests that at his best Crashaw "has a superbly rich commanding tone" but that "often there's something too hectically ingenious about his exaltations and adorations" (pp. 124–25).

1975

⌘ 1099. Baker, Herschel, ed. "Richard Crashaw," in *The Later Renaissance in England: Nondramatic Verse and Prose, 1600–1660,* 299–315. Boston: Houghton Mifflin Co.

Biographical sketch of Crashaw and a general introduction to his poetry (pp. 299–301), followed by a selected bibliography (p. 301) and selections from *Steps to the Temple* and *Carmen Deo Nostro* (pp. 301–16), with notes.

⌘ 1100. Barbato, Louis R. "Marino, Crashaw, and *Sospetto d'Herode.*" *PQ* 54:522–27.

Disagrees with recent critics who question the influence of Marino on Crashaw and, by extension, the influence of *marinismo* on English metaphysical poetry. Demonstrates that, if one compares Marino's *La Strage degl'Innocenti* (Naples, 1632) with Crashaw's version, it becomes apparent that Crashaw borrowed not only his subject matter from the Italian original but also "an integrated set of classical and Christian allusions, a pattern of paradoxical expansion, and the inspiration for metaphorical development" (p. 523). Maintains that Crashaw follows Marino "to the extent of retaining most of the mythological references wherever they occur" (p. 523) and that, "far from distinguishing between the worlds of classical myth and Christian reality, Crashaw follows Marino in effectively engaging the former to illuminate the latter" (p. 524). Points out also that Crashaw uses several techniques in his poem, such as balanced construction and alliteration, that are usually associated with *marinismo*.

⌘ 1101. Chambers, A. B. "Christmas: The Liturgy of the Church and English Verse of the Renaissance," in *Literary Monographs,* vol. 6, edited by Eric Rothstein and Joseph Anthony Wittreich, Jr., 109–53. Madison and London: University of Wisconsin Press.

Discusses the history, theology, and symbolism of the liturgy of the Christmas cycle, comments on how seventeenth-century divines interpreted these materials, and shows how an understanding of the Christmas liturgy is useful in interpreting late sixteenth- and early seventeenth-century poems on the birth of Christ. Notes that Crashaw wrote two epigrams on the Slaughter of the Holy Innocents and freely translated Marino's *Sospetto d'Herode* and briefly comments on "Hymn in the Glorious Epiphanie," noting that it deals with two traditional motifs—"the wisdom and insight of the Magi, even though they were guided by a miraculous star, in discerning the badges of royalty within circumstances of poverty" and "the conversion of the Magi and the symbolic, if not literal, end of pagan religions" (p. 124). Points out that in the 1646 edition of *Steps to the Temple,* "Hymn in the Holy Nativity" and "New Year's Day" are separated and the Epiphany hymn, which was written after 1646, does not appear, but that the revised order of the 1648 edition suggests that Crashaw "had come to see the religious and aesthetic advantages gained by joining the three poems together" and "may have been influenced by the rite or by Herbert or by both" (p. 131). Briefly compares and contrasts Crashaw to Donne, Herbert, Vaughan, Jonson, and Milton.

✎§ 1102. Cragg, Gerald R. "The English Catholics and the Problem of Authority," in *Freedom and Authority: A Study of English Thought in the Early Seventeenth Century*, 193–218. Philadelphia: Westminster Press.
Surveys the situation of English Catholics during the first half of the seventeenth century, when "Catholic fortunes reached their lowest ebb" (p. 193), commenting on the problems of authority both within the Catholic community and between it and the state. Points out, however, that in spite of all the bitter controversies, the English mystical tradition persisted and that "a select company of Catholics discovered the full intensity of religious experience" and "by its means they found that the authority of faith was most persuasively mediated" (p. 193). Discusses Crashaw briefly as a representative of baroque, Continental art and sensibility and suggests that "what separates Crashaw from his fellow countrymen is the extravagance with which he multiplies his metaphors, the unpruned luxuriance of his imaginative exploration of religious emotion" (p. 217). Maintains that Crashaw served only to confirm Protestant suspicions that "much of the piety and devotion of English Catholicism was permeated by a foreign atmosphere" but notes that his poetry "also struck with unique intensity the authoritative note that belongs to a certain type of religious experience" (p. 217).

✎§ 1103. Davies, Horton. "Spirituality: Preparation for Public Worship," in *Worship and Theology in England*. Vol. 2: *From Andrewes to Baxter and Fox, 1603–1690*, 68–132. Princeton: Princeton University Press.
Discusses Roman Catholic spirituality and devotional life in seventeenth-century England and comments briefly on Crashaw as the only Catholic among the metaphysical poets. Suggests that Crashaw's spirituality, as reflected in his poetry, "is Baroque in the brilliance of its tortured sensibility, its vivid portrayal of the religious emotions of awe, ecstasy, and piety" but that "it easily degenerates into sentimentality or mere theatrical posturing" (p. 87). Briefly contrasts "Hymn in the Holy Nativity" to Milton's Nativity Ode to show the differences in religious sensibility between the two poets.

✎§ 1104. Ferrari, Ferrucio. *La poesia religiosa inglese del Seicento*. (Biblioteca di cultura contemporanea, 115.) Messina and Florence: Casa editrice G. D'Anna. 202p.
Two major parts: (1) "Un secolo di poesia religiosa" (pp. 9–125), which consists of a series of essays on English religious poetry of the seventeenth century, and (2) "Robert Herrick, poeta religioso" (pp. 127–79). Mentions Crashaw throughout the first part and briefly contrasts him with Herrick in the

second. Compares "Hymn in the Holy Nativity" with Milton's Nativity Ode and briefly discusses the influence of Little Gidding, the *Spiritual Exercises* of St. Ignatius Loyola, the literature of tears, and emblem books on Crashaw's devotional verse. In "Il culto mariologico in Inghilterra dopo la Riforma. Richard Crashaw, poeta mistico" (pp. 99–110) surveys the renewed interest in the Virgin Mary after the Reformation, noting that of all the English poets Crashaw celebrated her most fully and passionately. Suggests that Crashaw is "senza dubbio l'espressione mistica più genuina della poesia inglese" (p. 104). Presents a biographical sketch of the poet and offers a general critical evaluation of his poetry, stressing the baroque features of his art and contrasting his religious temperament with that of Donne and Herbert. Maintains that "le immagini ridondanti, i termini a volte esagerati, gli abbandoni, i rapimenti, le sue estasi voluttuose di poeta innamorato, non sono artifici, ma l'effusione di una natura sensuale d l'espressione genuina della sua fede, che è latina e meridionale, nei momenti di più intensa religiosità e commozione" (p. 107). Comments briefly on "A Hymn to Sainte Teresa" as an example of Crashaw's mystical poetry.

◄§ 1105. Fisher, R. M. "William Crashawe's Library at the Temple." *The Library* 30:116–24.
    Reproduces an undated letter (probably mid-1613) in which William Crashaw, the poet's father, offered for sale to the Temple his extensive library of two hundred manuscripts and four thousand books as well as a pair of globes. Notes that the books offered were primarily on Scripture, the councils, Fathers of the Church, Protestants, Catholics, law, cosmography, and history—books directly related to his personal activities as scholar, preacher, and polemicist as well as to his keen interest in cosmology and geography. Points out that the offer was rejected and discusses the later disposition of the impressive collection. See also entries 1083 and 1084.

◄§ 1106. Galdon, Joseph A. *Typology and Seventeenth-Century Literature.* (De proprietatibus litterarum. Series maior, 28.) The Hague and Paris: Mouton. 164p.
    Explains biblical typology to those not trained in theology and comments on the pervasiveness of typological images and themes in seventeenth-century literature. Comments briefly on Crashaw's use of typology in "Hymn in the Assumption," noting that in the poem the Virgin Mary is equated with the beloved of the Canticle of Solomon. Points out also the extensive use of the lamb to symbolize Christ in Crashaw's poetry and his use of temple typology.

◄§ 1107. Gibaldi, Joseph. "Petrarch and Baroque Magdalene Tradition." *HUSL* 3:1–19.

Maintains that Petrarch's poem on the Magdalene "served as the fountainhead for a major literary tradition that began about two hundred years after the composition of the lyric and was to last for over a century" (p. 18) and points out how many elements in Petrarch's poem were imitated and developed in baroque poems on the subject. Observes, however, that, although Petrarch barely mentions the tears of the saint, baroque poets often focus on them. Calls "The Weeper" "a dazzling display of lachrymose images" and points out that metaphoric ingenuity often brings such poets as Crashaw "to the brink of the incredulous, if not the ridiculous" (p. 12). Maintains that baroque poets, such as Crashaw, Marino, Desportes, Vondel, and others, were not innovators but "planted themselves firmly within the Petrarchan tradition" and "attempted to out-Petrarch their master by restating familiar themes and repeating poetic techniques in a more exuberant, more dynamic, and more sensuous manner that continually sought the unexpected, the farfetched, and the marvellous" (p. 14). Suggests that the Petrarchan Magdalene "offered the baroque poet the opportunity to harmonize the esthetic of Renaissance poetry with the demands of his own age" and that "it is this synthesis which is probably the very essence of the sacred Baroque" (p. 19).

◄§ 1108. Hill, J. P., and E. Caracciolo-Trejo, eds. *Baroque Poetry*. Selected and translated, with an introduction by J. P. Hill and E. Caracciolo-Trejo. London: J. M. Dent & Sons; Totowa, N.J.: Rowman and Littlefield. xx, 276p.

In the introduction defines *baroque* as a literary term and explains the rationale and organization of this anthology of English, French, Spanish, Italian, and German baroque poems of the sixteenth and seventeenth centuries. Suggests that, although individual poets and national literatures differ, baroque poetry is characterized by its uses of the conceit; the manipulation of syntax that creates ambiguity or drama; excess, exaggeration, and a relatively uncontrolled energy; individualism; and certain similar themes. Divides the anthology into five sections, each introduced by a brief critical essay: (1) "Vision of Nature," (2) "Artifice," (3) "Love," (4) "On Life, Time and Death," which includes "Death's Lecture," and (5) "The Love of God," which includes "The Flaming Heart," "Adoro Te," "A Hymn to Sainte Teresa," "The Weeper," and "Song upon the Bleeding Crucifix." Gives literal translations of poems in foreign languages with text of the original. Selected bibliography (p. xviii).

◄§ 1109. Ishii, Shōnosuke. "Keijijōshijin to Shūkyō—yonin no Keishijōshijen—Donne, Herbert, Crashaw, Vaughan" [Metaphysical Poetry and Religion—Four Metaphysical Poets—Donne, Herbert, Crashaw, Vaughan], in *Eikoku Renaissance to Shūkyō* [Renaissance and Religion in England], edited by Shōnosuke Ishii and Peter Milward, 113–58. Tokyo: Aratake Shuppan.

Discusses the religious sensibility and theological view of Crashaw as reflected in his poetry (pp. 131–39) and presents a biographical sketch.

❧ 1110. Laurens, Pierre. "Un grand poème latin baroque: *La Bulle* de Richard Crashaw." *Vita Latina*, no. 57 (March): 22–33.

Reproduces "Bulla" and gives a prose translation of it in French. Discusses the poem as a baroque poem on the vanity of human existence, analyzing its images and stylistic devices, and pointing out numerous deliberate ambiguities. Shows that the poem owes much to late, or Silver Age, Latin poets, especially Claudian, and to biblical tradition, especially the Book of Wisdom. Also compares the poem to poems on the Virgin Mary written by John de Howden.

❧ 1111. Laurens, Pierre, in collaboration with Claudie Balavoine, eds. and trans. "Richard Crashaw," in *Musae Reduces: Anthologie de la poésie latin dans l'Europe de la Renaissance*, 2:493–513. Leiden: E. J. Brill.

Includes a biographical sketch of Crashaw (p. 493); an introduction to his Latin poetry, especially the sacred epigrams (pp. 493–94); a selected bibliography of studies on his Latin poems (p. 495); and prose translations of fifty-eight Latin epigrams, "In Pigmaliona," and "Bulla" (pp. 496–513), with Latin and French on facing pages. Calls the sacred epigrams the first collection of its kind in England and the masterpiece of the genre. Points out stylistic features of Crashaw's epigrams, notes influences on his style, and suggests that it is "cet accord profond entre le sujet et le style qui fait des *Epigrammes sacrées* une réussite incontestable, où se réconcilient la doctrine et le sentiment, l'esprit et la poésie" (p. 494).

❧ 1112. LeClerq, R. V. "Crashaw's *Epithalamium*: Pattern and Vision," in *Literary Monographs*, vol. 6, edited by Eric Rothstein and Joseph Anthony Wittreich, Jr., 71–108. Madison and London: University of Wisconsin Press.

Argues that "Epithalamium" both meets and exceeds the expectations of the genre. Maintains that the first four stanzas present the typical epithalamic movement from the moment preceding consummation to its completion: "The themes, images, and structural devices of the initial stanzas (the battle theme; the phoenix; the grave-cradle; the 'funeral-pyle: marriage-bed'; and numerological symbols, *two, three, five,* and *twelve*) suggest that the act will find its natural conclusion in progeny" (p. 73). Argues that the images of stanza five interject a mystical dimension suggesting that consummation is a metaphor for the mystic's union with God. Maintains that Crashaw's metaphor of marriage as divine union is more than simply a metaphor and that it reflects seventeenth-century Catholic belief that marriage is a sacrament that is not merely a sign of Christ's presence but the actuality of it. Discusses St. Robert Bellarmine's views on the sacramental nature of marriage and contrasts them with those held by Protestant divines who argued against the Catholic position. Details the argument that the poem exceeds conventional epithalamic conventions by analyzing its images and the significance of the numbers 2, 3, 5, 8, and 12 in the poem. Suggests that these considerations add the ideas of time, eternity, Christ, charity, and external resurrection to the conventional epithalamium. Analyzes, for example, the numerological significance of the seventh stanza, which concludes the first half of the poem, pointing out that 7 is made up of 3, representing the Trinity, and 4, representing the material world, and suggests that the sum represents "the penetration of matter with spirit" (p. 89). Discusses Crashaw's use of the persona as both *praeceptor amoris* and *paranymph*, whose function is to advise the couple on spiritual union. Concludes that, in exceeding the convention, Crashaw "simply tried to load the genre with more meaning—drawn from incompatible quarters—than it could easily handle" yet maintains that he is a master of a "kind of renaissance art, wherein things inconceivable are made perceivable through metaphoric structure" (p. 108).

✎§ 1113. Milward, Peter. "Anglican and Catholic in the Religious Poetry of the XVIIth Century." *ELLS* (Tokyo) 11:1–12.
Suggests that had the Civil War and the resultant triumph of Puritanism not occurred, the Anglican Church might have been reunited with the Catholic Church by the end of the seventeenth century. Sees the poetry of Herbert and Crashaw as representative of two successive and continuous stages in the development of Anglicanism, noting that many of Crashaw's most baroque poems were written while he was still an Anglican. Recognizes Herbert's negative attitudes about the Papacy and the fundamentally Protestant temper of much of his theology but maintains that in his poems he "expresses an ideal of the Church and Christian worship which is fundamentally at one with Catholic tradition" (p. 6). Discusses Crashaw's Anglo-Catholicism and the reasons for his conversion to Rome. Suggests that the merits and defects in the poetry of both Herbert and Crashaw "correspond in varying degrees to the merits and defects in the Anglican and Catholic communions of their period" (p. 10). Sees Herbert as more parochial and more English than Crashaw, who was more open to the Continental, baroque expression of Christianity: Crashaw "is Catholic not only in name, but also in the breadth of his vision; while his combination of sensuous imagery with metaphysical, even mystical insight accords well with the ideal of the Incarnation" (p. 11).

✎§ 1114. Nakao, Setsuko. *A Study of Richard Crashaw*. (Renaissance Monographs, 2.) Tokyo: The Renaissance Institute, Sophia University. iii, 124p.
Discusses the poetic and spiritual development of Crashaw to "give us at least a suggestion of a solution to the paradox of existence" (p. 6). "Point of Departure" (pp. 1–7), announces the intention of investigating how Crashaw's

life and poetry affect each other, especially by examining the characteristics of his three major published volumes, and points out that Crashaw's poetic exuberance, the high emotional pitch of his poems, and his religious enthusiasm stand "squarely against the sober, succinct taste of traditional Japanese sensibility" (p. 4–5). Three main sections, each of which contains several chapters. "Part I. First Steps: *Epigrammata Sacra*" (pp. 7–29) discusses the background of Crashaw's early life; comments on the distinguishing features of his epigrams, especially their themes and spiritual temper; and suggests that *Epigrammatum Sacrorum Liber* reflects elements associated with the purgative stage of the mystical life. "Part II. *Steps to the Temple*" (pp. 31–56), surveys Crashaw's life at Peterhouse, Leyden, and Paris; discusses the influence of St. Teresa; and suggests that the poems in *Steps to the Temple* reflect his spiritual progress and demonstrate his understanding of and appreciation for the illuminative stage in mystical advancement. "Part III. In the Temple: *Carmen Deo Nostro*" (pp. 57–86) surveys Crashaw's life from 1646; discusses the style and spiritual themes of the poems in *Carmen Deo Nostro*, especially "Charitas Nimia," "Hymn to the Name of Jesus," "Sancta Maria Dolorum," and "Hymn in the Glorious Epiphanie," suggesting that in the latter Crashaw succeeded "in conveying his knowledge and understanding of the essence of Christian contemplation" (pp. 76–77). While never claiming that Crashaw himself actually reached the pinnacle of mystical ascent, the unitive stage, in the conclusion (pp. 87–94) states that his poetry "confidently announces that there is a transcendental world beyond the visible, where man's existential thirst will finally be slaked" and that, "by means of his sincere appeal, in ardour and radiance, he suggests a solution to the conundrum of existence, inspiring us to seek the world beyond the senses, taste the supernatural and love that allembracing Reality" (p. 94). Notes (pp. 95–97); bibliography (pp. 98–101); and appendix, "Crashaw in Japan" (pp. 103–24), which surveys Japanese scholarship on Crashaw and includes a bibliography of translations and biographical and critical studies in Japanese.

◄§ 1115. Pop-Cornis, Marcel. "Early Seventeenth Century Poetry and the Traditions of Modern English Verse," in *Modern English Poetry: A Critical and Historical Reader*. Vol. 1: *From John Donne to Alexandre* [*sic*] *Pope* (1590–1730), 1–54. Timisoara, Rumania: Timisoara University Press.

Suggests that any survey of modern English poetry must begin with a study of seventeenth-century poetry and comments briefly on a metaphysical tradition from Donne to T. S. Eliot and Edith Sitwell. Surveys the political, intellectual, and religious history of the seventeenth century and comments on how the temper of the times is reflected in the poetry. Outlines major features of metaphysical poetry and briefly surveys the history of the term, especially commenting on Dr. Johnson's criticism of metaphysical poetry. In "Richard Crashaw (1613?–1649)" (pp. 32–35) discusses some of the major characteristics of Crashaw's poetry, such as his use of erotic metaphors, sensuous imagery, musical cadences, and epigrammatic rhetoric, and points out various influences on his art and sensibility, such as Marino, Spenser, and emblem books. Reproduces "The Teare" with study questions as well as the last sixteen lines of "The Flaming Heart" with study questions and a brief commentary. Calls "The Flaming Heart" Crashaw's "most lyrical production, rising to unsurpassed heights and poetic rapture" (p. 35). Selected bibliography (pp. 51–54).

◄§ 1116. Ruoff, James E. "Crashaw, Richard," in *Crowell's Handbook of Elizabethan & Stuart Literature*, 87–89. New York: Thomas Y. Crowell Co.
Published in England as *Macmillan's Handbook of Elizabethan & Stuart Literature* (London: Macmillan, 1975).
Biographical sketch of Crashaw with commentary on major features of his poetry. Suggests that, although Herbert and Donne were his "leading masters," Crashaw's "febrile and humid metaphors, florid superlatives, and ecstatic freedom from intellectual discipline owe far less to the English metaphysical poets than to the lavish sensuousness of . . . Marino" (pp. 87–88), the Continental emblem writers, and the Jesuits. Observes that, "to the ornate and hyperbolic diction of Marino, Crashaw brings a terse, epigrammatic syntax learned from the Latin poets, and combines with these a metaphysical stress on paradoxes" and notes that, unlike Donne and Herbert, the paradoxes in Crashaw's poetry "are hung on poems like tinsel on Christmas trees" (p. 88). Calls "The Weeper" a "rosary poem," its conceits "notorious," and its lines "spongy" (p. 88). Suggests that "his verbal intoxication and the single-minded ecstasy of his metaphors" place Crashaw outside the mainstream of English poetry and "make his lines read as if they were being strained through the foreign sensibilities of Marino, the continental emblemists, St. Ignatius Loyola, and the Spanish mystics," the result being "an impression of cloying overripeness" (p. 88). Stresses the baroque nature of Crashaw's art and sensibility and suggests that his efforts at verbalizing mystical experience as well as his "failure to realize the limits of language" (p. 88) set him apart from the other metaphysical poets and alienate him from English readers. Highly selected list of modern editions, critical studies, and bibliographical checklists of Crashaw's poetry.

◄§ 1117. Trautmann, Joanne, and Carol Pollard, eds. *Literature and Medicine: Topics, Titles, and Notes.* Hershey, Pa.: Department of Humanities, Hershey Medical Center. x, 209p.
Rev. ed., Pittsburgh: University of Pittsburgh Press, 1982.
Annotated bibliography of literary works that refer to medical topics, with a topical index. Lists four items by Crashaw (p. 16)—poems that treat sexuality, old age, and suffering. Suggests that "Epithalamium" contains "a curiosity—

mourning the death of a maidenhead" and that in the poem Crashaw "transforms the wedding into a funeral, with such relish that the concluding blessings upon the couple ring false" (p. 16). Calls "The Flaming Heart" the "most extreme expression of the Renaissance and Baroque fusion of religion and sexuality" and suggests that Crashaw's praise of St. Teresa "is almost indistinguishable from praise of a sexually-fulfilled woman" (p. 16). Claims that Crashaw's praise of temperance in "In praise of Lessius" is extravagant and that his portrayal of Christ's sufferings in "On the wounds of our crucified Lord" is "very immediate and grotesquely violent" (p. 16).

1976

◆§ 1118. Aizawa, Yoshihisa. "Nihon ni okeru Keijijoshi Kenkyu Sho-shi" [A Bibliography of Writings about Metaphysical Poetry in Japan], in *Keijijōshi Kenkyū* [Metaphysical Poetry Studies], 1–32. Tokyo: Japan Society of 17th-Century English Literature.

Lists books, articles, and reviews by Japanese critics on the metaphysical poets from 1927 to 1975. Includes seventeen studies specifically on Crashaw, revealing that, although Japanese scholars and critics have written less on Crashaw than on Donne, Herbert, and Marvell, they have shown more interest in him than in Vaughan or Traherne.

◆§ 1119. Arakawa, Mitsuo. "Richard Crashaw," in *Shimpishisō to Keijijoshi-jintachi [Mystical Thought and Metaphysical Poets]*, 122–49. Tokyo: Shohakusha.

Discusses Crashaw's mystical thought and his attitude toward God through an analysis of a number of his religious poems, especially "The Weeper," "A Hymn to Sainte Teresa," "Hymn in the Holy Nativity," "Hymn in the Glorious Epiphanie," "On the wounds of our crucified Lord," and "Ode on a Prayerbook." Stresses that Crashaw's mystical attitude is fundamentally Christocentric with an emphasis on Christ's sufferings. Points out that Crashaw's style is sensuous, ornamental, and Continental and that he characteristically employs sublimated erotic imagery to describe the mystical path to God.

◆§ 1120. Berry, Boyd M. *Process of Speech: Puritan Religious Writing and Paradise Lost*. Baltimore and London: Johns Hopkins University Press. xi, 305p.

Compares "Hymn in the Holy Nativity" briefly to Herbert's "Easter Wings" (p. 33) and contrasts it with Milton's Nativity Ode (pp. 113–22). Maintains that what distinguishes Milton's poem from Crashaw's "is the process of thought and speech by which they move their focus and our attention from time to eternity," noting that Crashaw "begins in time and opens out to eternity," while Milton "swirls divinely above time and then finally descends into it" (p. 114). Contrasts the structure, language, use of paradox, and tone of the two poems and argues that Milton's vision in his poem "is not composed of discrete units as was Crashaw's but is unified or interwoven" (p. 119). Comments on changes Crashaw made in the later version of his poem and suggests that, although several are improvements, the inserted two stanzas in the later version somewhat disrupt the movement of the poem. In a parenthetical comment, calls Crashaw's poetry "a sport in the literary history of his nation" (p. 113).

◄§ 1121. Edwards, A. S. G. "Libertine Literature in Restoration England: Princeton MS AM 14401." *BC* 25:354–68.

Points out that "Loves Horoscope" appears in a late seventeenth-century commonplace book by an unknown compiler (Princeton MS AM 14401), not noted by Martin. Describes the diverse contents of the manuscript, noting that, in addition to Crashaw's poem, it contains "libertine" works; prose orations; political and satirical poems by Marvell, Oldham, and Rochester; and love poems by Etheredge and Sedley.

◄§ 1122. Elder, David. "L'image de l'épine dans la poésie métaphysique anglais: Exergue et analyse," in *Études anglo-americaines*, 21–35. (Annales de la faculté des lettres et sciences humaines de Nice, 27.) Paris: Minard.

Discusses the wide-ranging use of the figure of the thorn in poetry, notes its appearances in metaphysical poetry, but warns that it is not found with obsessional frequency in metaphysical poems. Points out that for the English metaphysicals the thorn most often has biblical associations: "La couronne des martyrs et les épines du péché sont les plus caractéristiques de ses multiples emplois" (p. 23). Briefly comments on Crashaw's use of the thorn in "Sospetto d'Herode," "On the still surviving markes of our Saviours wounds," and "On the wounds of our crucified Lord." Notes Crashaw's "obsession" with images of liquidity.

◄§ 1123. Kelliher, Hilton. "Crashaw as University Preacher." *N&Q* n.s. 23:231–32.

Points out that a transcript of a Cambridge combination paper for 1642/43 (BM Add. MS 5821, f. 1b) by the antiquarian William Cole "preserves the merest detail relating to Crashaw's preaching duties in the University" (p. 231). Notes that Crashaw's name appears in a list of those scheduled to preach at Great St. Mary's on Sunday afternoons and feast days—for the afternoon of 13 November 1642, the Twenty-third Sunday after Trinity. Suggests that if Warren is correct in assuming that Crashaw left Cambridge in January 1643, the sermon was his last. Points out also that, according to the rules that established the sermons, Crashaw would have become eligible to preach no earlier than July 1641 and would have thus been eligible to preach no more than a total of four sermons during his Cambridge years.

⊷§ 1124. Mayer, Lloyd G. "An Unnoticed Life of Richard Crashaw." *N&Q* n.s. 23:230–31.

Points out a biographical account of Crashaw in *The Lives of the Poets of Great Britain and Ireland, to the Time of Dean Swift . . . by Mr. Cibber,* published by R. Griffiths in 1753 (entry 79). Suggests that, although it provides no new information on Crashaw's life and is derived essentially from Anthony Wood's account in *Athenae Oxonienses* (entry 56), the sketch is worthy of attention "because of its author's censure of Crashaw's defection from the Anglican Church and his presumed disloyalty to the Royalist cause" (p. 230). Suggests that the author is Robert Sheils, the Scottish Jacobite and Tory, and that the attack on Crashaw was politically motivated.

⊷§ 1125. Milward, Peter. "Keijijogaku to Meiso" [Metaphysical Studies and Meditation], in *Keijijōshi to Meisōshi* [Metaphysical Poetry and Meditative Poetry], edited by Peter Milward and Shōnosuke Ishii, 3–38. Tokyo: Aratake.

Translated into Japanese by Yamamoto Hiroshi. Discusses the influence of the tradition of discursive meditation on seventeenth-century English poetry, including Crashaw's religious verse.

⊷§ 1126. Nakao, Setsuko. "Crashaw no Shukyoshi ni okeru Catholicism" [Catholicism in Crashaw's Religious Poetry], in *Keijijōshi to Meisōshi* [Metaphysical Poetry and Meditative Poetry], edited by Peter Milward and Shōnosuke Ishii, 125–58. Tokyo: Aratake.

Traces the religious development of Crashaw reflected in his poetry and suggests that the three major volumes of his poetry *(Epigrammatum Sacrorum Liber, Steps to the Temple,* and *Carmen Deo Nostro)* evidence elements that roughly correspond to the three stages in the mystical life (via purgativa, via illuminativa, and via unitiva). Maintains that the poems in *Carmen Deo Nostro* demonstrate that Crashaw finally reached the highest state in the mystical life. Comments in some detail on the Catholic nature of his later poems. See also entry 1114.

⊷§ 1127. Schwenger, Peter. "Crashaw's Perspectivist Metaphor." *CL* 28: 65–74.

Comments on Emmanuele Tesauro's discussion in *Il Cannocchiale Aristotelico* (Turin, 1654) of the uses of metaphor to create deliberate literary illusionism and a sense of the marvelous and argues that, although the treatise did not directly influence Crashaw's "The Weeper," it does reveal a contemporary aesthetic theory that sheds light on Crashaw's practice. Points out that in "The Weeper" the tears of the saint, "as metaphorized by Crashaw, are multiplied into images of pearls, dew, wine, oceans, and so forth, which are the measure of each other's illusionism at the same time that they provide a sense of marvel" (p. 70) and suggests that, although the metaphors themselves are not dazzling, "it is the multiplicity and movement of metaphors, the reiterated sense of transition, which creates a sense of the marvelous" (p. 71). Maintains that the use of shifting metaphors and conceits is consistent throughout the poem, creating a unifying force, and suggests that the pleasure that the reader obtains from watching these shifts "is precisely the pleasure which Tesauro argues is innately present in the transition from illusion to disillusion" (p. 71). Points out that, although point of view on the tears of the Magdalene "may be said to shift continually in one sense, in the emotional sense it remains constant" and "the variety of viewpoints extends the emotion rather than undercutting it" (p. 74).

1977

◄§ 1128. Byard, Margaret M. "Poetic Response to the Copernican Revolution." *Scientific American* 236, no. 6:120–29.
Discusses the impact of the Copernican revolution on seventeenth-century poets, including Crashaw. Suggests that, in his religious poetry Crashaw is "as much at home in an outer world of stars and planets as Herbert is" and that he "conveys a sense of space" and "imagines even as to the feel of the clouds and the sounds that he hears: music is omnipresent" (p. 125). Briefly notes the use of star images and other cosmological referents in "The Weeper."

◄§ 1129. Fabry, Frank J. "Crashaw's 'On the Wounds of our Crucified Lord.'" *CP* 10, no. 1:51–58.
Presents a detailed reading of "On the wounds of our crucified Lord" and suggests that the poem is "the purest example of Crashaw's metaphysical style, a poem which brings Crashaw as close as he ever got to his contemporary English poetic mentor, George Herbert" (p. 51). Maintains that "the poem's structure is consistent throughout; that, though ultimately the poem's meaning is anagogical, the play of paradox, pun, and allusion is the way to its mystery and the basis of its appeal; that a comparison of Crashaw's early Latin epigram on the same subject ['In vulnera Dei pendentis'] illuminates the English version; and that understanding the poem as an instrument of [Ignatian] meditation accounts for its curious but purposeful disjunction in perspective (from wounds to Magdalene) and tone (from reflection to direct address)" (p. 52). Suggests that the ultimate anagogical meaning of the poem is that "at her death Christ will be Magdalene's Heavenly Bridegroom" but that, "meanwhile even in death he is her spiritual suitor" (p. 54). Concludes that "this dense poem shows us a Crashaw unlike the celebrative poet of the Theresa pieces, where lyrical exuberance sweeps us along; or unlike the eccentric poet of certain epigrams and some stanzas in 'The Weeper,' where extravagant and bizarre conceits evoke the patronizing smile, despite our awareness of their post-Reformation context," for "here, where metaphor is carefully controlled, tone deftly handled, and meaning obliquely revealed, is evidence of a true metaphysical poet functioning in the service of his faith" (p. 57).

◄§ 1130. Kawata, Akira. "R. Crashaw to A. Marvell—Namida o megutta" [Richard Crashaw and Andrew Marvell on Tears]. *Bulletin of the Faculty of Education* (Fukushima University), no. 29, 2:75–83.

Discusses Crashaw and Marvell in the light of the tradition of the literature of tears. Contrasts "The Weeper" and Marvell's "Eyes and Tears" to show the major characteristics of each poet. Points out that, whereas Marvell's poem is highly intellectual and logical, tightly structured, and employs images closely connected to the subject, Crashaw's poem is typically sensuous and descriptive, uses very colorful and even sensual images, and is so loosely constructed that it seems to be almost a collection of self-sufficient beautiful images.

◄§ 1131. Parrish, Paul A. "Crashaw's Two Weepers." *CP* 10, no. 2:47–59.

Challenges earlier criticism of "The Weeper" and maintains that a comparison of the 1646 and 1652 versions of the poem shows "the basis for the final version and Crashaw's thematic and structural intentions" (p. 48), that the poem is not fragmented and lacking in stanzaic development and coherence, and that the revision indicates Crashaw was aware of certain weaknesses in the earlier version and consciously improved the poem. Points out that Crashaw's changes are of five kinds: (1) minor changes in punctuation or type, (2) slight improvements in choices of individual words and phrases, (3) important deletions of stanzas, (4) significant scattered additions, and (5) several major central additions. Focuses on the last three to show that in the later version "the stanzas are effectively presented, that they give a new and valuable emphasis to the devotional basis of the poem, and that they provide the element which Praz found missing in the original, 'a central point round which the poem . . . gravitate[s] in a harmonious coordination of its parts'" (p. 55). Points out that the earlier version focuses "almost entirely on sorrow and sadness, even to the extent of a prominent allegorical presentation of those emotions," whereas the later version "includes that side of the penitential act but reminds us, too, of the love and the lamb which are equally necessary" so that ultimately "thematically the poem is more attractive and more balanced, and structurally, more coherent and unified" (p. 58).

1978

◄§ 1132. Benito Cardenal, Luis Carlos. *El manierismo inglés. John Donne.* (Colección monográfica, 62.) Granada: Universidad de Granada. 327p.

Discusses Crashaw as an extreme example of the Catholic baroque and contrasts his uses of the conceit and the grotesque with Donne's uses (pp. 204–12). Claims that Crashaw imitates Marino servilely, is more Continental than English, and "lleva a la exasperación del mal gusto, de lo realmente grotesco, la manía de los 'concetti' continentales" (p. 204). Characterizes Crashaw's poetry as lacking intellectual control, elaborating profusely sensorial effects, and piling up uncontrolled images: "Todo es desmayo y éxtasis, jadeos y suspiros, sangre de heridas y leche de pechos; todo ello apilado sin solución de continuidad, sin descanso para el lector, sin la progresión dialética characterística de Donne" (p. 205). Maintains that, rather than spiritualizing the senses, Crashaw sensualizes almost unbearably interior and spiritual experience. Points out that, whereas Donne's conceits are personal, original, and functional, Crashaw's are overly decorative and often become grotesque. Suggests that, although Donne occasionally uses details or presents feelings that may be called grotesque, Crashaw habitually indulges in bad taste.

⋙ 1133. Di Cesare, Mario A. ed. *George Herbert and the Seventeenth-Century Religious Poets: Authoritative Texts/Criticism.* (A Norton Critical Edition.) New York: W. W. Norton & Co. xiv, 401p.
Anthology of poems by Herbert, Crashaw, Marvell, Vaughan, and Traherne. Calls Herbert and Marvell "major poets" and Crashaw, Vaughan, and Traherne "poets of real distinction" (p. xiii). "Richard Crashaw" (pp. 71–91) includes a biographical sketch and sixteen secular and sacred poems (in part or in whole) with explanatory notes. Bibliographical introduction to Crashaw's poems and textual notes (pp. 211–13). Includes an original essay by Anthony Low (entry 1140) and four previously published essays and/or sections from books that deal specifically with Crashaw: (1) Douglas Bush, "Crashaw: Single-hearted Worshipper," from *English Literature in the Earlier Seventeenth Century,* 2d ed. (entry 661), pp. 147–50; (2) Helen C. White, "Richard Crashaw: Intellectual Poet," from *The Metaphysical Poets* (entry 591), pp. 228–30; (3) Austin Warren, "Crashaw's Symbolism," from *Richard Crashaw: A Study in Baroque Sensibility* (entry 619), pp. 177–93; and (4) Richard Strier, "Crashaw's Other Voice" (slightly abridged, with minor changes by the author) from *SEL* (entry 998). Partially annotated bibliography (pp. 387–401).

⋙ 1134. Evans, Gillian. *The Age of the Metaphysicals.* (Authors in Their Age, gen. eds., Anthony Adams and Esmore Jones.) Glasgow and London: Blackie & Sons. 140p.
Introduces metaphysical poets and their era to students. Defines the nature of metaphysical poetry; outlines the religious, educational, and political backgrounds that the poets shared; presents brief biographical comments on the major poets; comments on the society in which the poets lived; sketches the world view of the early seventeenth century and changing social structures; discusses the major genre that engaged the interest of the metaphysical poets and their shared view of the nature and function of poetry; comments on the major subject matter of the poems and how the poets shared certain habits of thought; and outlines the history and development of criticism of metaphysical poetry, suggesting that "twentieth-century readers, perhaps for the first time since the age of the metaphysical poets themselves, are in a position to appreciate their work on two levels at least: that of the pleasure of problem-

solving, and that of the more familiar pleasure of poetry, the sharing of some-
one else's experience, the recognition of common sensations and shared responses to the happenings of life" (p. 131). Mentions Crashaw throughout
and points out that he is the most baroque of the metaphysical poets "because
of the sometimes cloying richness of his poetry" but notes that "other metaphysical poets on occasion let their love of elaborate images run away with
them" (p. 16). Selected bibliography (pp. 132–35).

◄§ 1135. Greenblatt, Daniel L. "The Effect of Genre on Metrical Style."
    Lang&S 11:18–29.
Uses statistical profiles based on the Halle-Keyser theory of iambic pentameter "to demonstrate that the genre of a poem has an appreciable effect on
its metrical style, at least for several important seventeenth-century poets, and
that the effect of certain genres on metrical style is to some extent predictable"
(p. 18). Presents statistical profiles of selected poems by Crashaw, Donne,
Jonson, Herbert, Carew, and Marvell and shows that, "for all the poets tested
except Marvell, the data suggest strongly that genre can exert a powerful influence on the metrical stylistic feature of complexity" and that, "in many cases
not only do these poets adapt their styles to different genres, they deal with
their common genres in approximately the same way" (p. 23). Notes that
Crashaw's "genre mean for epigrams is, like Jonson's, considerably above his
overall mean, and his mean in the genre of funeral elegy is, like both Jonson's
and Donne's, substantially below his overall mean" (p. 24).

◄§ 1136. Ishii, Shōnosuke. "A Plea for Crashaw's 'The Weeper': A Reconsid-
    eration of Its Emblematic Qualities." *Studies in English Language and
    Literature* (Sofia University) 3, no. 2:41–62.
Revised version appears in Robert M. Cooper, ed., *Essays on Richard
Crashaw* (entry 1153), 196–204.
Presents a brief survey of critical interest in Crashaw by Japanese scholars,
noting that, although Crashaw was referred to as early as 1891 by Tamotsu
Shibue in his *Eibungaku-shi* [A History of English Literature], it was not until
the mid-fifties that Crashaw "began to be taken up and dealt with as a unique
figure among the metaphysical poets" (p. 42). Points out that the first book-
length study of Crashaw written in English by a Japanese was Setsuko Nakao's
A Study of Richard Crashaw in 1975 (entry 1114). Notes that the poems most
frequently discussed by Japanese critics are "Wishes. To his (supposed) Mistresse," "Hymn in the Holy Nativity," "The Flaming Heart," and "The
Weeper." Comments on Japanese studies of "The Weeper" and offers an interpretation of the poem, focusing on its emblematic and pictorial qualities.
Maintains that the poem can be read "as a series of emblems in which the
poetry is speaking pictures,—that is, though there is no actual illustration, the
verse of every stanza helps the reader to have in his mind a picture vividly
painted" (p. 50). Suggests that the poem resembles the ancient Japanese pic-

ture scroll (*Emakinono*). Reproduces "The Weeper" in English as an appendix (pp. 54–62), without notes or additional commentary.

◆§ 1137. Labriola, Albert C. "Herbert, Crashaw, and the *Schola Cordis* Tradition." *GHJ* 2, no. 1:13–23.

Discusses the influence of the *schola cordis* tradition on the poetry of Herbert and Crashaw and suggests that their reliance on the tradition indicates that there are often more resemblances than differences between Catholic and Protestant devotional poetry of the seventeenth century. Comments specifically on how both poets use the tradition to create images that have "complex and profound meanings and insights far exceeding those of cardiomorphic icons" found in emblem books and maintains that "these meanings and insights are directly related to the perceptions of the speaker, the diversity of his attitudes, and the range of his tone" (p. 15). Points out five major characteristics of *schola cordis* poetry: (1) the quotation or paraphrasing of scriptural passages that refer to the human heart, (2) a reflection of a typological perspective into biblical history, (3) an emphasis on Christ's Paschal mystery, (4) allusion to the sacramental celebration of the Paschal mystery, and (5) an acknowledgment of the importance of liturgical and communal worship. Illustrates the influence primarily by a detailed reading of Herbert's "The Bunch of Grapes," but points out the appearance of the tradition in a number of Crashaw's poems, especially "Vexilla Regis," noting that "as many as thirty of his poems depict the heart as the *locus* of man's relations with the Lord" (p. 21). Maintains that *schola cordis* poetry "collapses time and internalizes landscape, so that Christ's cross and Adam's tree, respective images of fertility and desolation, are indeed planted in the same place, none other than every Christian's heart" (p. 22) and that "what the speaker sees and says, but also feels, is a spiritual drama initiated long ago in biblical history, undergone by Christ, and presently re-enacted in the liturgy and sacraments" (p. 23). Notes also that in "I am the Doore" and "Joh. 10. Ego sum ostium" Crashaw uses the common image of the heart kept under lock and key, an image found in Petrarch's *Canzoniere* and in numerous English sonnets written under his influence. See also entry 1164.

◆§ 1138. Leighton, Kenneth. *Lord, When the Sense of Thy Sweet Grace*. For Mixed Voices, S. A. T. B. and Soprano Solo, a capella. Words by Richard Crashaw. Music by Kenneth Leighton. Chapel Hill, N.C.: Hinshaw Music. 12p.

Musical setting of "A Song ('Lord, when the sense of thy sweet grace')."

◆§ 1139. Low, Anthony. *Love's Architecture: Devotional Modes in Seventeenth-Century English Poetry*. New York: New York University Press. xix, 307p.

Chapter 5, "Richard Crashaw: Sensible Affection" (pp. 116–59), surveys the aesthetic and devotional underpinnings of Crashaw's religious poetry and suggests that his work can only be partially understood in terms of mannerist and baroque aesthetics and various seventeenth-century schools of devotion. Discusses the influence of Laudian liturgy, vocal prayer, and song on Crashaw's verse and comments in this context on "Dies Irae Dies Illa," "Office of the Holy Crosse," "Hymn in the Glorious Epiphanie," and "Hymn to the Name of Jesus." Points out that only a few of Crashaw's poems reflect Ignatian meditation, such as some of the epigrams, "On the wounds of our crucified Lord," "Our Lord in his Circumcision to his Father," and "On our crucified Lord Naked, and bloody." Discusses the nature of sensible devotion and points out that although many of Crashaw's poems evidence much intellectual activity, careful structure, and order, "the affections seem to overflow spontaneously, to require no promptings from reason or discursive imagination" (p. 131). Discusses "The Weeper" as an extreme example of sensible devotion and argues that the poem "moves by the logic of affection and the dream-logic of association rather than intellectual analysis" (p. 138). Comments also on the three Teresian poems as examples of sensible devotion and stresses that Crashaw's use of sensual and even sexual imagery to depict spiritual states and experiences of the soul reflects his attempt "to baptize the passions and desires of natural man by redirecting them" (p. 146). Maintains that, while there is no proof that Crashaw was himself a mystic, such works as "Ode on a Prayerbook" and the Teresian hymns make it clear that he knew a great deal about mystical experience. Suggests that, "what is evident, is that, however far he progressed toward the mystical state he so keenly desired, sensible affection was the means he took toward his goal" (p. 156). Comments on the charge of bad taste leveled against Crashaw and suggests that modern readers tend to reject his aesthetics and devotional mode because "we have not acclimated ourselves to Crashaw as to his fellows" and thus "for the moment his poetry is less accessible" (p. 158). Compares and contrasts throughout the entire study Crashaw's poetic techniques and devotional modes with those of Donne, Herbert, Vaughan, Herrick, Marvell, and Traherne.

◄§ 1140. ———. "Metaphysical and Devotional Poets," in *George Herbert and the Seventeenth-Century Religious Poets: Authoritative Texts/Criticism*, edited by Mario Di Cesare, 221–32. (A Norton Critical Edition.) New York: W. W. Norton & Co.

Discusses the major characteristics of metaphysical poetry, such as masculine expression, naturalness and familiarity of tone, the combination of intellect and feeling, orderly or logical development, sense of drama or process, an interest in the inner movements of thought and feeling, its private versus public mode, and uses of the conceit. Discusses also various kinds of devotional practices in the seventeenth century, such as vocal devotion, discursive meditation, and contemplation, and comments on how these devotional modes shaped and informed the religious poetry of the age. Compares and contrasts Crashaw to Herbert, Vaughan, Marvell, and Traherne. Considers Crashaw and Marvell to be more formal than the others and points out that Crashaw's poems "typically turn on an inner logic of feelings" (p. 224). Observes that Crashaw's images, even those most criticized in "The Weeper," are not tasteless or grotesque if viewed within the context of the whole poem but accord perfectly with the affective development of his poem. Maintains that typically Crashaw subordinates thought to feeling and comments on how his religious sensibility is reflected in his poems, especially his ability "to soar out of an intense evocation of the senses and feelings into a kind of mystical ecstasy" (p. 229), citing the conclusion of "The Flaming Heart" as a well-known example.

◄§ 1141. Mabbott, Thomas O. "Observations on Poets and Poetry." *BI* no. 29:14–35.

Presents excerpts from the notes and letters of Thomas O. Mabbott to Maureen Cobb, later Mrs. Mabbott, mostly written during 1923 and 1924, that contain his observations on poets and on poetry, selected by Mrs. Mabbott. Comments briefly on Francis Thompson's criticism of Crashaw. Observes that Thompson "is most gifted in appreciation of the rare qualities of the highest lyricism, and of ecstatic religious feeling" and that, "when he finds these two qualities combined in a poet, as they are in the matchless Richard Crashaw, he shines and understands what so many modern critics overlook—the really outstanding position of Crashaw among the metaphysical poets, rightly ranking him above Donne for lyric quality, and as an ancestor, in a way, of Shelley" (p. 26).

◄§ 1142. Marcus, Leah Sinanoglou. "The Poet as Child: Herbert, Herrick, and Crashaw," in *Childhood and Cultural Despair: A Theme and Variations in Seventeenth-Century Literature*, 94–152. Pittsburgh: University of Pittsburgh Press.

Sees in a progression from Herbert to Herrick to Crashaw a "narrower definition of the *persona* of child, a progressively more radical retreat from the possibility of acting and achieving" (p. 96), and views this retreat as a response to the political and religious turmoil of seventeenth-century England, as well as an inclination of the poets' personal temperament. Maintains that, if Crashaw could have maintained his life of retirement at Peterhouse, he would likely have remained a High Anglican, but that the circumstances of his life led him "into the phantasmagoric world of baroque Catholic spirituality and the poetic role of infant" (p. 139). Argues that his religious verse is an attempt to escape from the world, pointing out that "most of his lyrics are completely cut from history" (p. 140), and maintains that his poetry suggests a desire to return not so much to childhood as to a form of protected infantilism. Stresses the note of self-abnegation and self-annihilation in Crashaw's poetry that goes far beyond the ideal of childlike humility before God. Suggests that Crashaw's role as an infant is developed primarily through his use of images of nourishment, protection, and enclosure and concludes that his view of Christianity "is a giant projection of the forms and processes of motherhood—the overflowing breast, the warmth of a mother's arms, the protection of the womb, and the joyous liberation of birth" (p. 150).

✠ 1143. Rogers, Robert. *Metaphor: A Psychoanalytic View.* Berkeley, Los Angeles, London: University of California Press. x, 148p.

Suggests that the description of the Magdalene's tears in "The Weeper" as "the suffring rose that's vext . . . Sweating in a too warm bed" (Stanza 27, 1648) has overtones of anality and that the description of Christ as a rose in "New Year's Day" is couched in "the language of erotic passion" and is "a kind of speaking in tongues" (p. 124). Briefly suggests the erotic possibilities of fire and flame metaphors in the Teresian poems, "Ode on a Prayer-book," "Song ('Lord, when the sense of thy sweet grace')," and "Epithalamium."

✠ 1144. Strier, Richard. "Changing the Object: Herbert and Excess." *GHJ* 2, no. 1:24–37.

Contrasts Herbert's and Crashaw's uses of sensual, especially sexual, indulgence in positive religious contexts and argues that Herbert "does not participate at all in Counter-Reformation cultivation of ecstasy, in the campaign to 'change the object, not the passion'" (p. 28). Points out that Herbert's poems, unlike Crashaw's, tend to end in praise, not ecstasy, and they do not court pain for the purpose of self-immolation but rather plead for an end of pain or ask God to allow him to endure and derive some spiritual good from the undesired experience.

✠ 1145. Wong, Tak-Wai. *Baroque Studies in English, 1963–1974: A Survey & Bibliography.* Richmond, Va., and Carnegie, Victoria, Australia: New Academic Press. 137p.

Presents a detailed survey of scholarship and criticism on baroque literature (pp. 15–67) and comments specifically on studies on Crashaw (pp. 38–39). Points out that "of all the seventeenth-century English writers, Crashaw is probably the poet most widely accepted as Baroque" (p. 38). Appendix 5 (p. 107) is a chart from Gordon Bennett's Ph.D. dissertation, "The Form and Sensibility of Edith Sitwell's Devotional Poems: A Study of Baroque Tradition" (Kansas, 1969) that distinguishes two baroque styles, one represented by Crashaw's "Hymn to the Name of Jesus" and the other by Donne's *The Second Anniversary.* Annotated bibliography of baroque literature studies, 1932–1976 (pp. 113–37).

✠ 1146. Young, Robert V., Jr. "Truth with Precision: Crashaw's Revisions of *A Letter.*" *Faith and Reason* (The Journal of Christendom College), 4, no. 3:3–17.

Compares the 1652 version of "Letter to the Countess of Denbigh" with the revision to show that "the way in which he alters his expostulation in the second version reveals that Crashaw possessed a clear understanding of the theological issues that divided Protestant Reformers from the Catholic Church" and to demonstrate that "the purpose of the second version was to render a clearer metaphorical definition of the Catholic faith proferred the Countess" (p. 4). Outlines the major differences between Catholic and Protestant theologians of the time concerning free will; maintains that the official theology of Anglicanism was essentially Calvinist; and points out that of all the devotional metaphysical poets "only Crashaw made a clean break with the predestinarian implications of Reformation theology, because only Crashaw became a Catholic" (p. 6). Illustrates this point by contrasting Crashaw's views in "Letter to the Countess of Denbigh" with those of Donne in "Batter my heart." Comments specifically on Crashaw's reordering of lines, making verbal alterations and rearranging punctuation in the first twenty-six lines of the revision so that a more emphatic and confident tone emerges, and points out how in the remainder of the poem he makes significant changes in imagery and address so that the theme and imagery of the poem are brought into greater harmony. Maintains that, "by changing the emphasis in the figurative depiction of the relation between God and man, Crashaw implicitly defines the difference between Protestant and Catholic interpretations of grace and justification, locating the center of the conflict in the question of man's free will" (p. 6). Argues that, although Crashaw did not change his belief about free will, the revised poem "is better organized, and hence the argument is clearer" and, "more important, its metaphorical strategy corresponds more closely to the Catholic understanding of conversion, which is, finally, the theme of the poem" (p. 13). Concludes that "this tighter coherence of figure and idea makes the revision more vivid and compelling, and more mature— in every way a better poem" and that the revision reflects "not the work of naive emotion, but of skilled intelligence, which Crashaw possessed in a degree for which he is too rarely given full credit" (p. 13).

1979

1147. Asals, Heather A. R. "Crashaw's Participles and the 'Chiaroscuro' of Ontological Language," in *Essays on Richard Crashaw*, edited by Robert M. Cooper, 35–49. (Salzburg Studies in English Literature, Elizabethan & Renaissance Studies, ed. James Hogg, no. 83.) Salzburg: Institut für Anglistik und Amerikanistik, Universität Salzburg.

Finds a logical, philosophical, and theological significance in Crashaw's use of present active participles and maintains that the nature of his art can be better understood in terms of scholastic philosophy and theology than in terms of art history. Points out that scholastic theologians such as Francis Suarez maintained that *being* is a verbal adjective, not simply an abstract noun, that implies the continuous working of God in the created universe. Suggests that Crashaw derived his "theology of participles" from the works of Suarez. Notes that in the "Preface to the Reader" of the 1646 and 1648 editions Suarez is alluded to and invoked as "the present expert on 'the language of the Angels'" (p. 35). Argues that Crashaw's use of such participles as *weeping, flaming, bleeding,* and *saving* when seen in the context of Suarez's works is neither extravagant nor pointlessly redundant but figures forth precisely his theological views. Discusses Crashaw's uses of metonymy and active participles in "The Flaming Heart" to show how his poetic techniques reproduce and support his essentially Catholic vision of spiritual reality. Contrasts Crashaw's depiction of God's relationship with His creatures in "A Hymn to Sainte Teresa" with that in "The Flaming Heart" and concludes that in the first, God is presented as "a transcendent and Protestant God" but in the second he becomes "a Catholic and presential God, obscuring and enveloping beings into his universal Being: presently and actively but also perfectly and passively" (p. 46).

❧ 1148. Barker, Arthur E. *The Seventeenth Century: Bacon Through Marvell.* (Goldentree Bibliographies in Language and Literature, ed. O. B. Hardison, Jr.) Arlington Heights, Ill.: AHM Publishing Co. xi, 132p.

Unannotated, selected bibliography of studies on seventeenth-century English poetry and prose to 1975 (excluding Milton, Dryden, the drama, and dissertations). In addition to entries for thirty-nine authors, includes aids to research, major anthologies, general studies of literary history and criticism, and studies in backgrounds. Lists, in addition to Martin's and Williams's editions, forty items for Crashaw (pp. 40–42), all of which appear in this bibliography.

❧ 1149. Benet, Diana. "The Redemption of the Sun: Crashaw's Christmastide Poems," in *Essays on Richard Crashaw,* edited by Robert M. Cooper, 129–44. (Salzburg Studies in English Literature, Elizabethan & Renaissance Studies, ed. James Hogg, no. 83.) Salzburg: Institut für Anglistik und Amerikanistik, Universität Salzburg.

Argues that "Hymn in the Holy Nativity," "New Year's Day," and "Hymn in the Glorious Epiphanie" form a logical sequence firmly controlled by the progressive subordination of the *sun,* a symbol of the natural order that exists to assist men in finding spiritual reality and truth, to the newly born *Son* of God. Maintains that Crashaw's intention in the three poems "is to celebrate the Incarnation by dramatizing successive responses to the Christ child that yield an analysis of the significance of the Advent" and that, "through dramatic speakers, he traces the gradual assimilation of the spiritually-informed perspective made possible by the Incarnation" (p. 129). Contends that in "Hymn in the Holy Nativity" the rustic shepherds, while fully aware of the superiority of the Son to the natural sun and perceiving that the birth of Christ heralds a victory over the material world, sing a love-song to God for his great gift but remain unaware of the full spiritual significance of the Incarnation. Argues that the speaker in "New Year's Day" not only deals confidently with the opposition of Son and sun but also expands the notion to include the opposition of sin and redemption, thereby widening the significance of the event, while in "Hymn in the Glorious Epiphanie" the three pagan kings "comprehend the conflict of the natural and supernatural light personally, in terms of error and liberation from the deception of sin" (p. 136) and then project their vision into the future.

◄§ 1150. Bertonasco, Marc F. "A Jungian Reading of Crashaw's 'The Flaming Heart,'" in *Essays on Richard Crashaw*, edited by Robert M. Cooper, 224–64. (Salzburg Studies in English Literature, Elizabethan & Renaissance Studies, ed. James Hogg, no. 83.) Salzburg: Institut für Anglistik und Amerikanistik, Universität Salzburg.
Argues the need for a Jungian reading of "The Flaming Heart," reviews basic Jungian concepts, and examines the images, symbols, and paradoxes of the poem to demonstrate that "it is to self-actualization that Teresa is summoned in her celebrated dream" (p. 230), in which the seraph is the saint's animus and messenger of the self, urging her to embark on a perilous inner journey. Suggests that the seraph's dart is symbolic of the masculine principle but also represents androgyny and mystical union. Maintains, therefore, that the spearing of Teresa's heart by the seraph, both in her autobiography and in the poem, "represents the destruction of the many impediments to individuation (mystical union with Christ); it is a painful sacrifice, a martyrdom, to dismantle and re-structure the ego and to shift control away from the conscious will to the Self" (p. 233). Argues that the predominant symbol of fire in the poem "represents a spiritual energy that creates, transmutes, sublimates, and purifies through suffering" and "designates also the intellectual and spiritual elements of the animus which the saint eventually assimilates as well as her ardent love of God (Self), her spiritual illumination, privileged insights, and extraordinary ability to inspire and guide souls along the paths she herself has traveled" (p. 236). Maintains that the symbol of the flaming heart symbolizes everything that Crashaw wants to say about Teresa, encompassing all the other symbols, and becomes a symbol of androgyny, "a full development and harmonious integration of both masculine and feminine potentials, of animus and anima, of yang and yin" (p. 239). Finds that in the poem, as in her life, Teresa fulfills the role of the shamaness or female magician, "the penultimate stage in the process of individuation" (p. 247), as well as the "totally venerable and beneficent phallic mother" (p. 252). Structurally regards the poem as essentially a Salesian meditation upon a picture.

◄§ 1151. Bottrall, Margaret. "Crashaw," in *Great Writers of the English Language: Poets*, edited by James Vinson and D. L. Kirkpatrick, 245–47. New York: St. Martin's Press.
Biographical note on Crashaw, a list of his publications, a selected bibli-

ography of critical studies, and a general evaluation of his poetry. Claims that Crashaw is "the odd man out among 17th-century English devotional poets" and that "it is difficult for a 20th-century reader to do justice to his poetry without a well-developed historical imagination" (p. 246). Discusses the baroque features of Crashaw's themes and style and maintains that, although sometimes excessive and rather morbidly preoccupied with sexual equivalents to spiritual experience, Crashaw is a poet "of great enterprise and accomplishment, whose strength of feeling is allied with considerable intellectual force" (p. 246). Compares and contrasts Crashaw to Herbert and suggests that, "in tenderness of tone and sometimes in purity of diction, Crashaw does resemble his predecessor," but his verse lacks Herbert's self-analysis, and "the texture of his verse is less sinewy, his wit less compact" (p. 246). Briefly compares Crashaw to Cowley and Milton. Maintains that, seen in the context of Caroline culture, Crashaw's poetry seems less exotic and notes that the poems in *Carmen Deo Nostro* "are on the whole rather more subdued in tone, more disciplined in feeling, than the earlier pieces" (p. 247).

✒ 1152. Cirillo, Albert R. "Recent Studies in Crashaw." *ELR* 9, no. 1: 183–93.

Evaluative bibliographical survey of Crashaw in four sections: (1) biographies and general studies; (2) selected topics (baroque, meditative techniques, mysticism, sources, rhetoric, numerological and calendrical symbolism); (3) studies of individual poems ("Hymn to the Name of Jesus," "Hymn in the Holy Nativity," "Hymn in the Glorious Epiphanie," "The Weeper," "Ode on a Prayer-book," "Musicks Duell"); and (4) canon and texts, followed by a selective listing of items according to the above categories. Points out that "there tends to be a trend in recent studies to get beyond facile and clichéd preconceptions of Crashaw as 'baroque' in order to deal directly with the poetry in a critical and analytical manner" and suggests that "what is needed, perhaps, is a study along the lines of Rosemond Tuve's *A Reading of George Herbert* (1952), one that will fully reveal both Crashaw's virtues and his failings as a poet and thinker without resorting to vague labels, no matter how convenient" (p. 188).

✒ 1153. Cooper, Robert M., ed. *Essays on Richard Crashaw*. (Salzburg Studies in English Literature, Elizabethan & Renaissance Studies, ed. James Hogg, no. 83.) Salzburg: Institut für Anglistik und Amerikanistik, Universität Salzburg. i, 264p.

The editor points out that, "in the last two decades, critics increasingly have come to realize that Crashaw's work is 'foreign' or 'grotesque' only insofar as it represents the most notable achievement in English of traditions that disappeared in the later seventeenth century, traditions which were normal and accepted parts of a High Church intellectual and devotional climate found in England during the poet's lifetime" and maintains that "the problem for crit-

ics today is no longer one of defending Crashaw" but "one of reappraisal—
of new approaches both to the unique effects that he produced and to the
traditions in which he worked" (p. i). Contains twelve essays on Crashaw's
poetry, each of which has been separately entered in this bibliography: (1) Albert C. Labriola, "Richard Crashaw's *Schola Cordis* Poetry" (pp. 1–13),
(2) Hilton Kelliher, "The Latin Poems Added to *Steps to the Temple* in 1648"
(pp. 14–34), (3) Heather A. R. Asals, "Crashaw's Participles and the 'Chiaroscuro' of Ontological Language" (pp. 35–49), (4) Paul A. Parrish, "Crashaw's
Funeral Elegies" (pp. 50–77), (5) Coburn Freer, "Mirth in Funeral: Crashaw
and the Pleasures of Grief" (pp. 78–101), (6) Eugene R. Cunnar, "Crashaw's Hymn 'To the Name Above Every Name': Background and Meaning"
(pp. 102–28), (7) Diana Benet, "The Redemption of the Sun: Crashaw's
Christmastide Poems" (pp. 129–44), (8) Louise Schleiner, "Song Mode in
Crashaw" (pp. 145–68), (9) Joseph P. Hilyard, "The Negative Wayfarers
of Richard Crashaw's 'A Hymn in the Glorious Epiphanie'" (pp. 169–95),
(10) Shōnosuke Ishii, "A Plea for 'The Weeper': A Reconsideration of Its
Emblematic Qualities" (pp. 196–204), a revised version of his 1978 essay (entry 1136), (11) Lee A. Jacobus, "The Musical Duel in 'Musicks Duell'"
(pp. 205–23), and (12) Marc F. Bertonasco, "A Jungian Reading of Crashaw's
'The Flaming Heart'" (pp. 224–64).

◆§ 1154. Cunnar, Eugene R. "Crashaw's Hymn 'To the Name Above Every
Name': Background and Meaning," in *Essays on Richard Crashaw*,
edited by Robert M. Cooper, 102–28. (Salzburg Studies in English Lit-
erature, Elizabethan & Renaissance Studies, ed. James Hogg, no. 83.)
Salzburg: Institut für Anglistik und Amerikanistik, Universität Salzburg.
Argues that the seeming lack of artistic control in "Hymn to the Name of
Jesus" disappears when one views it in the light of the hymn tradition, the
Laudian-Puritan controversy over bowing at the name of Jesus, and the her-
meneutic problem of expressing the ineffable. Maintains that the hymn was
written to support the Laudian position on the importance of ritual and liturgical worship, specifically the appropriateness of bowing at the name of Jesus,
and that Crashaw "turned to the hymn as a genre with strong ritual associations and composed his own hymn to the Name in such a fashion that it
would argue that the Word is ritual action creating an atmosphere conducive
to the adoration of God" (p. 108), while, at the same time, fully aware that
God is ultimately ineffable. Points out that "in order to name without naming
and to move his poem from the verbal and toward action, Crashaw develops a
strategy of praise derived from two mutually supportive traditions, namely that
of the liturgical feast for the Name of Jesus and the mystical tradition of the
hermeneutics of the divine names as advocated by Pseudo-Dionysius the
Areopagite" (p. 109). Maintains that "the use of excess and expansion as
rhetorical and poetic means of praise serves Crashaw's purpose in moving the
soul to union with God through adoration" and that this excess "suggests

spontaneity, itself characteristic of a living hymn in adoration" (p. 114). Analyzes the poem to show that Crashaw is a poet "who marched to a more profound beat of unity than most New Critics grant him" and that, "in facing the knotty problem of praising that which cannot adequately be praised, Crashaw succeeds in moving his poem from verbal artifact to liturgical action whose reality is always present" and "in doing so he provided an answer to those Puritans who argued against the ritual bowing at the mention of the name of Jesus by transforming himself through his art into a living hymn" (p. 120).

◄§ 1155. Daly, Peter M. *Literature in the Light of the Emblem: Structural Parallels between the Emblem and Literature in the Sixteenth and Seventeenth Centuries.* Toronto, Buffalo, London: University of Toronto Press. xiv, 245p.

An introduction to the study of emblematic structure in English and German literature of the sixteenth and seventeenth centuries. Chapter 1, "The Emblem" (pp. 3–53), discusses the origins and nature of emblem books, comments on forerunners of the emblem, and surveys recent critical developments in emblem theory, especially endorsing the work of Albrecht Schöne in *Emblematik und Drama im Zeitalter des Barock* (Stuttgart, 1964, 2d ed., 1968). Chapter 2, "The Word-Emblem" (pp. 54–102), discusses the various forms and functions of emblematic imagery in English and German literature. Chapter 3, "Emblematic Poetry" (pp. 103–33), Chapter 4, "Emblematic Drama" (pp. 134–67), and Chapter 5, "Emblematic Prose Narrative" (pp. 168–84), comment on the structural affinities between the emblem and poetry, drama, and prose fiction. Brief conclusion (pp. 185–88), notes (pp. 189–223), and selected bibliography (pp. 224–33), followed by an index of names (pp. 235–39) and an index of emblem motifs (pp. 241–45). Mentions Crashaw's use of emblematic imagery and structures throughout, primarily endorsing the work of Marc Bertonasco (entry 1026) as well as studies by T. O. Beachcroft (entry 518), and Ruth Wallerstein (entry 575).

◄§ 1156. Erlebach, Peter. "Das Epigramm des 17. Jahrhunderts," in *Formgeschichte des englischen Epigramms von der Renaissance bis zur Romantik*, 121–84. (Anglistiche Forshungen, 131.) Heidelberg: Carl Winter Verlag.

Maintains that Crashaw was an innovator in introducing spiritual and mystical subject matter into the epigram in England, first in Latin (1634) and then in English (1646). Discusses the structure of Crashaw's religious epigrams, pointing out his uses of biblical paraphrase and paradox to intensify his meaning and commenting on his exploitation of the possibilities of the genre. Analyzes a number of individual poems to show Crashaw's artistic command of the form. Discusses seven epigrams written in couplets and suggests that Crashaw's use of paradox and the unexpected is the key to understanding them, noting how often a play on words carries the meaning. Discusses the four-line epigrams, pointing out that more space allows the poet to introduce paraphrases of Scripture. Comments on the various rhetorical and verbal strategies he employs to achieve a powerful expression of Christian meaning. Observes that often the key to these poems is a conceit or a metaphor and notes that frequently Crashaw saves the revelation of the full meaning of an epigram to the last half-line or even the last word in order to intensify everything that has preceded. Discusses also Crashaw's experimentation with other forms of the epigram and with different meters and comments on his uses of sound and rhetorical devices to achieve his artistic ends.

◄§ 1157. Freer, Coburn. "Mirth in Funeral: Crashaw and the Pleasures of Grief," in *Essays on Richard Crashaw*, edited by Robert M. Cooper, 78–101. (Salzburg Studies in English Literature, Elizabethan & Renaissance Studies, ed. James Hogg, no. 83.) Salzburg: Institut für Anglistik und Amerikanistik, Universität Salzburg.

Discusses the treatment of grief in Crashaw's poetry. Notes that his laments over biblical figures and various saints have more intensity than his personal elegies. Comments on a number of the elegies on individuals, especially "Death's Lecture," to show how Crashaw assumes an air of detachment and presents the act of grief in recurring reflexive metaphors and patterns in which the subject of the poem turns inward and this internal motion "is paralleled by a similar emotion in the bystander or griever" (p. 80). Maintains that, unlike Donne, Crashaw as a poet "is not particularly self-divided" and that, "confident in divine Grace, he is not drawn to a Protestant struggle for self-validation or authenticity" (p. 84). Suggests that Crashaw sees grief as leading to joy and views even death, real or mystical, as a pleasurable self-fulfilling experience in which the self is freed and ultimately led to God. Contrasts this kind of fulfilling introspection with unfulfilling self-scrutiny by contrasting St. Teresa in "A Hymn to Sainte Teresa" with Satan in "Sospetto d'Herode" and comments on the expression of the theme in the poems added to the 1648 edition, especially "Hymn to the Name of Jesus" and "Hymn in the Glorious Epiphanie," calling the latter as "precise a study of fulfilled self-reflection as the *Sospetto* is from the side of frustrated self-knowledge or despair" (p. 89). Examines the prevalent self-reflexive patterns in "Dies Irae Dies Illa," "Letter to the Countess of Denbigh," and "The Flaming Heart" and suggests that the last "documents the movements of a loving self, its life and its death, as fully as anything Crashaw wrote" (p. 94). Suggests that Crashaw's treatment of the self and the theme of grief is so powerful in his later poems because in his early poetry he had "imagined so thoroughly what it means *not* to be free of the self but to become an end in itself" (p. 96). Concludes that, for Crashaw, "grief is the true alms-gift which collapses all the customary distinctions between the selves of sufferer, writer, and reader, in the sweetness of freedom and love" and that his rhetorical pattern "is ultimately a spiritual pattern, which challenges our usual separation of cause and effect and finds the re-accommodation of that challenge a source of pleasure" (p. 97).

◄§ 1158. Goddard, Geoffrey. "From Temple to Holy House: The Story of a 17th Century Convert." *The Ransomer* 27, no. 3:7–14.
Biographical sketch of Crashaw for the readers of this popular Catholic journal, which focuses primarily on his religious development and the influences that led him to the Catholic Church.

◄§ 1159. Grant, Patrick. "Richard Crashaw and the Capucins: Images and the Force of Belief," in *Images and Ideas in Literature of the English Renaissance*, 89–128. Amherst: University of Massachusetts Press.
Maintains that the key problem in reading Crashaw is to determine whether his images refer to the physical or spiritual world. Tries to reconcile the view that Crashaw's poems "attempt to give us a sense of the distortion of the physical world seen without God" with the notion that he "uses physical things emblematically, as signs to be referred in the conventional Augustinian manner to a higher spiritual reality" (p. 94). Maintains that the spirituality of the Capuchins offers a solution to these two seemingly divergent viewpoints. Points out that seventeenth-century Capuchin devotion stressed turning toward good by means of a revulsion from the horrors of a physical world without God. Discusses Capuchin history, the life of Benet of Canfield, his work, *The Rule of Perfection*, and his emphasis on abandoning one's self in doing God's will and seeing the physical world's capacity to reflect spiritual truths. Also discusses his images of fluidity, his fondness for the word *sweet*, and his insistence on meditating on Christ's suffering. Concludes that Benet's spiritual emphasis "is on transcendence, on the selfless abandonment and absorption of individual will into the will of God" (p. 110). Discusses also Benet's disciples, Zacharie of Lisieux and Remi de Beauvais, and their relationship to Crashaw. Points out that Zacharie also believed that sensual passion can be transferred to spiritual ends and that the senses should be shocked by the physical so that one will recoil from it to appreciate the spiritual. Notes that Remi de Beauvais's 746-page poem, *La Magdaleine*, highlights the saint's suffering and ecstatic joy and uses images of fluidity. Maintains that Crashaw inherited a native English and Augustinian spiritual tradition but that he could also have come under the influence of the Capuchins. In Crashaw, "the kissing of wounds, the tears, the mixture of pain and erotic pleasure, the centrality of the cross, the absence of self-scrutiny or autocentricism, the fervent abandonment of the Magdalene, the technique of recoil, and the fluid transformations as literal is transmuted to symbolic sense, have all the hallmarks of Capucin influence" (p. 119). Discusses in more detail Crashaw's mystical theocentrism, his language of transcendence, and his emphasis on "the ambivalence of the human being challenged by God's love in a world given over to distractions

and falsity" (p. 122). Discusses "Luke 11. Blessed are the paps which Thou hast sucked" and "The Weeper" as examples of recoil from the physical to the spiritual level of meaning.

◄§ 1160. Healy, Tom F. "Crashaw's 'Wishes.'" *N&Q* n.s. 26:427–28.

Points out that later editions (five by 1667) of *Wits Recreations* (entry 13), first published in 1640, contain an altered and expanded version of "Wishes. To his (supposed) Mistresse." Notes that the 1645 contains significant alterations and that the 1650 and later editions contain four stanzas that were added after the larger and completed version of the poem was published in the 1646 and 1648 editions of *The Delights of the Muses*. Speculates that the editors may have taken the stanzas from a manuscript that contained an expanded but not yet completed form of the poem but maintains that the appearance of the altered and expanded version in *Wits Recreations* "sheds new light on the growth and reception of the poem" (p. 428). Points out also that MS 68 (James, no. 1.3.16) in Emmanuel College Library (Cambridge) contains a version of "Musicks Duell" in a seventeenth-century hand that has interesting variants.

◄§ 1161. Hilyard, Joseph P. "The Negative Wayfarers of Richard Crashaw's 'A Hymn in the Glorious Epiphanie,'" in *Essays on Richard Crashaw*, edited by Robert M. Cooper, 169–95. (Salzburg Studies in English Literature, Elizabethan & Renaissance Studies, ed. James Hogg, no. 83.) Salzburg: Institut für Anglistik und Amerikanistik, Universität Salzburg.

Argues that "Hymn in the Glorious Epiphanie" is constructed about the central compound paradox "that the brightness of the worldly life is really a darkness and that the apparent darkness of the Deity is really a brightness that can be experienced by the soul only through the obscure groping of the negative way" (p. 169). Suggests that the poem can be seen as "a 'descant upon the devout plainsong' of two passages from Dionysius the Areopagite" (p. 169) in which the mystical philosopher comments on the dazzling darkness of God. Points out, however, that, unlike the Areopagite, Crashaw's Magi are more complex in that they are attracted to the natural world as well as repulsed by it and that "this counterpull of opposed desires may account for the poem's power to move us much more than do the Dionysian passages which seem to have fathered it" (p. 170). Maintains that Crashaw achieves this simultaneous tone of repulsion and attraction by use of oxymoron, by syntactical manipulation of words to convey a sense of paradox, and by sensuous images to embody abstract concepts. Shows how the evolving image of the sun reinforces the central notion of *via negativa*. Comments on the importance of the intermingling of aspects of the birth of Christ with those of his passion and death, which shows that, "as man must travel the negative way to God, so God in the Incarnation becomes a self-darkening negative wayfarer to reach man" (p. 179). Suggests that in the poem the Magi are simultaneously hunters of

God and the hunted by God and that the poem expresses, playfully yet seriously, the complexity of man's relationship with God. Concludes that the complex tone of the poem is basically "that of a would-be mystic, one who speaks constantly in the future tense about his hoped-for union with the Divine Darkness" (p. 192).

⋙ 1162. Jacobus, Lee A. "The Musical Duel in 'Musicks Duell,'" in Essays on Richard Crashaw, edited by Robert M. Cooper, 205–23. (Salzburg Studies in English Literature, Elizabethan & Renaissance Studies, ed. James Hogg, no. 83.) Salzburg: Institut für Anglistik und Amerikanistik, Universität Salzburg.

Approaches the poem from a music historian's point of view. Gives a brief explanation of the Artusi-Monteverdi controversy, a debate that "centered on the degree to which the music was a servant of the words, or the words the servant of the music" (p. 207). Finds "Musicks Duell" a "recension of the Artusi-Monteverdi controversy, with the newer, monodic harmony of the affections eventually forcing the freer, but less resourceful melody into submission" and thus presenting "a triumph over church music and the polyphonic stile antico, but a triumph itself expressed with a mannerist yearning after the old style" (p. 208). Maintains, therefore, that "the innocence of the nightingale suggests a nostalgic affection for what must give way to the new ambitions of the new music" (p. 208). Points out the emblematic nature of "Musicks Duell" and its uses of the affections and suggests similarities between Crashaw's techniques and those of Monteverdi. Discusses Crashaw's use of repetition in the poem (especially the word sweet) and sees it as a verbal counterpart to the repetition of a single chord or tone in music. Concludes that the poem can be read "as an emblem of a genuine musical duel" (p. 219).

⋙ 1163. Kelliher, Hilton. "The Latin Poems Added to Steps to the Temple in 1648," in Essays on Richard Crashaw, edited by Robert M. Cooper, 14–34. (Salzburg Studies in English Literature, Elizabethan & Renaissance Studies, ed. James Hogg, no. 83.) Salzburg: Institut für Anglistik und Amerikanistik, Universität Salzburg.

Discusses the occasions that gave rise to two of Crashaw's Latin poems added to the 1648 edition of Steps to the Temple and suggests that the poems "tell us something about the purposes to which Crashaw was happy to lend his fertile poetic talents during the middle years of his career at Cambridge, and about the nature of his involvement in the religious life of the University" (p. 14). Maintains that "Fides quae sola justificat, non est sine Spe & Dilectione" is an example of academic poetry known as carmina Comitalia (or Tripos verse) and was written in support of John Nowell, who, in 1635, debated the question of justification from the Laudian viewpoint at the Great Commencement in Great St. Mary's Church (Cambridge). Suggests that the poem reflects that Crashaw's High Church views were confirmed while he was yet a student at Pembroke. Maintains that "Votiva Domus Petrensis Pro Domo Dei" closely reflects details of the work undertaken to beautify the college chapel at Peterhouse and argues that the 1648 text probably derives from a 1637 transcript of the poem that was circulated among the wealthier alumni to solicit funds for the college, whereas the 1670 text may derive from Crashaw's own autograph draft. In an appendix reproduces (with English translation) Eleazar Duncon's *carmina Comitalia* of 1633.

◆§ 1164. Labriola, Albert C. "Richard Crashaw's *Schola Cordis* Poetry," in *Essays on Richard Crashaw*, edited by Robert M. Cooper, 1–13. (Salzburg Studies in English Literature, Elizabethan & Renaissance Studies, ed. James Hogg, no. 83.) Salzburg: Institut für Anglistik und Amerikanistik, Universität Salzburg.

Redefines the *schola cordis* tradition, not limiting it to the visual context of cardiomorphic iconography, and maintains that Crashaw's poetry, "when interpreted in relation to this broadened context, is much richer and more variegated than we have supposed" (p. 2). Points out five major features of the *schola cordis* tradition: (1) the use of biblical passages that comment on or depict the human heart, (2) typological perspective in the use of these passages, (3) emphasis on the redemptive mystery of Christ's death and resurrection and the Paschal *triduum* that commemorates these events, (4) allusion to the sacramental celebration of these mysteries, and (5) stress on the importance of liturgical and communal worship. Suggests that all these features are united by "an emphasis on the perception and means by which salvation can be achieved: imitating and participating in Christ's Paschal triumph" (p. 2). Presents an analysis of "Vexilla Regis" and surveys "Sancta Maria Dolorum," "Charitas Nimia," "Hymn in the Glorious Epiphanie," "Office of the Holy Crosse," "Hymn to the Name of Jesus," and "A Hymn to Sainte Teresa" to show how the *schola cordis* tradition informs the paradoxical thought, emotional intensity, hyperbolic language, rhetorical strategy, and passionate exhortation of Crashaw's poetry and provides a means for understanding its richness, profundity, and complexity. See also entry 1137.

◆§ 1165. Lewalski, Barbara Kiefer. *Protestant Poetics and the Seventeenth-Century Religious Lyric*. Princeton: Princeton University Press. xiv, 536p.

Presents a revisionist theory of current views on the English religious lyric of the seventeenth century and argues that Protestant emphasis on the centrality of the Bible and Protestant appreciation and understanding of scriptural language, biblical genres (especially the Psalms and the Canticles), biblical rhetoric, and typology fostered a theory of aesthetics that defines both the poetics of the religious lyric and its spiritual contents. Stresses that the major religious lyricists of the period—Donne, Herbert, Vaughan, Traherne, and Edward Taylor—are much more indebted to contemporary English Protestant meditation, emblematics, and sermon theory than to medieval Catholic and Continental sources. Mentions Crashaw throughout and maintains that he, unlike the Protestant poets, "writes out of a very different aesthetics emanating from Trent and the continental Counter Reformation, which stresses sensory stimulation and church ritual (rather than scripture) as means to devotion and to mystical transcendence" (p. 12). Contrasts, in particular, Crashaw's use of emblems in *Carmen Deo Nostro* with contemporary Protestant practice and argues that Crashaw "clearly calls upon different emblematic resources and exploits them in characteristically different ways" (p. 197). Maintains that, on the whole, Crashaw's use of Christian iconography "is altogether more direct and pervasive" (p. 196) and that, "whereas Crashaw renders an atmosphere by evoking fleeting images from baroque sacred art and Jesuit emblem books, the Protestant poets often interpret biblical and sacred metaphors in images which are, like the Protestant discrete emblems, strongly visual, logically precise, and elaborately detailed" (p. 197). Suggests that more study needs to be done on the relation between Protestant and Tridentine aesthetics, pointing out that comparing and contrasting the Protestant aesthetic with Crashaw's use of emblems and his epigrams on biblical texts might be illuminating.

◄§ 1166. Magill, Frank N., ed. "Richard Crashaw (1612–1649)," in *Magill's Bibliography of Literary Criticism*, 1:461–64. Englewood Cliffs, N.J.: Salem Press.

Reprinted in *English Literature: Middle Ages to 1800* (entry 1178).

Unannotated, highly selective checklist of critical studies on Crashaw's poetry in general and on "Luke 11. Blessed be the paps which Thou hast sucked," "A Hymn to Sainte Teresa," and "The Weeper," in particular.

◄§ 1167. Parrish, Paul A. "Crashaw's Funeral Elegies," in *Essays on Richard Crashaw*, edited by Robert M. Cooper, 50–77. (Salzburg Studies in English Literature, Elizabethan & Renaissance Studies, ed. James Hogg, no. 83.) Salzburg: Institut für Anglistik und Amerikanistik, Universität Salzburg.

Maintains that Crashaw has often been misjudged or improperly evaluated because critics have neglected most of his early secular and occasional poetry and have concentrated on his more baroque sacred poems. Analyzes all eighteen of Crashaw's early elegies—over one-fifth of his secular canon—written between 1631 and 1635 to show that they not only reflect his poetic inclinations and development during his formative years at Cambridge but also make it clear that he was not only a baroque artist but also a "restrained and even classical artist who could praise and lament and console with decorum and moderation" (p. 52). Maintains that the funeral elegies show that Crashaw experimented with several modes—the classical and Renaissance, the metaphysical, and the baroque—and that he could write effectively in each. Summarizes the essential features of the Renaissance elegiac tradition and maintains that Crashaw's best elegiac poems show a "remarkable confluence of tradition, convention, occasion, subject, and poet working harmoniously and efficaciously on a receptive audience" (p. 56). Finds most interesting, both because of number and because of their innovations and variety, the elegies on the death of William Herrys but singles out "Death's Lecture" as Crashaw's best early elegy and as "one of the most metaphysical poems in Crashaw's canon," claiming that it is, "in tone, language, and aim, unique among his elegiac verse" (p. 70). Concludes that, "more often restrained than luxurious, controlled than excessive, the elegies teach us that if Crashaw was most notably a Baroque poet, he could be a Renaissance and Metaphysical one as well" (p. 73).

◄§ 1168. Rollins, Roger B. "Metaphysical Poets, Milton and the," in *A Milton Encyclopedia*, gen. ed. William B. Hunter, Jr., 5:110–14. Lewisburg: Bucknell University Press; London: Associated University Presses.

Surveys similarities and differences between Milton's poetry and that of the metaphysical poets and suggests that, although "there is no evidence that Milton ever read so much as a single verse by John Donne, the preeminent metaphysical poet of the seventeenth century, nor has investigation yielded one unmistakable echo of any of the other metaphysicals in all of Milton's poetry" (p. 110), Milton "*was* a 'metaphysical'—at least in the very broadest sense of that elusive term" (p. 114). Suggests that Milton comes closest to Crashaw's style in "Upon the Circumcision."

◄§ 1169. Schleiner, Louise. "Song Mode in Crashaw," in *Essays on Richard Crashaw*, edited by Robert M. Cooper, 145–68. (Salzburg Studies in English Literature, Elizabethan & Renaissance Studies, ed. James Hogg. no. 83.) Salzburg: Institut für Anglistik und Amerikanistik, Universität Salzburg.

Discusses the influence of contemporary songs, especially madrigals and lute songs, on Crashaw's prosody and rhetoric. Points out how a number of features of Crashaw's poetry, from the early verse translations to the mature odes, such as his use of feminine rhyme, specific metrical forms, and figures of rhetoric, especially anaphora, anadiplosis, ploce, antimetabole, and alliteration, were inspired and shaped by contemporary song modes. Presents a detailed analysis of "Hymn to the Name of Jesus" to illustrate how "speech mode is in Crashaw regularly interspersed with passages displaying features of song mode (smooth, flowing meter, sometimes isometric verse, sometimes variable lines creating patterned rhythms leading to a pause or conclusion, rhyme syncopation, feminine rhymes, and tripping anapestic or dactyllic substitutions, and the favorite rhetorical devices of song poets)" (p. 155). Comments briefly on "Out of the Italian. A Song," "Out of the Italian ('Love now no fire hath left him')," and "A Song ('Lord, when the sense of thy sweet grace')," calling the last "probably Crashaw's purest example of song mode" (p. 153). Also discusses several seventeenth-century and modern musical settings of Crashaw's poems by such composers as John Wilson and Edward Bairstow and points out that often the composers carefully imitated the musical effects they found in the poems. Concludes that, although many poets of the period were influenced by the song mode, Crashaw is perhaps unique "in the frequency with which he created song-related effects for appropriate moments within the capacious scope of his mature poems, and in his ability to integrate these moments of song into his vivid pictorial images" (p. 164).

◄§ 1170. Stanwood, Paul G. "Time and Liturgy in Donne, Crashaw, and T. S. Eliot." *Mosaic* 12, no. 2:91–105.
   Broadly defines liturgy as a religious ceremony that "memorializes or consecrates a past action in order to give to it a present and continuing significance" and argues that, in literature, liturgy functions metaphorically to convey movements of time in space and depends "upon rhetorical and verbal invention, designed to make us feel both still and active, contracted and expansive, filled with the past and alive to the present" (p. 91). Maintains that the form, structure, and rhetoric of much of the best poetry of the metaphysicals, cavaliers, and Milton "presupposes ritual, ceremony, and liturgical action" and that, although not always devotional, the poetry "is always marked by high and often exuberant ceremony which tries to defeat time" (p. 92). Focuses on Donne, Crashaw, and Eliot, including the latter because his poetry helps to understand the earlier poets and "his work clarifies and summarizes their themes and meaning" (p. 92). Maintains that, although Donne and Crashaw differ greatly, "consecration, ceremony, unity of experience, and publicly formalized yet personal feeling—all features of the liturgical mode— belong as much to Crashaw as to Donne" (p. 98). Challenges the notion that Crashaw's art is un-English and suggests that his "ceremonial, adorational mode of expression, his passion, and his alleged Catholic flamboyance are familiar in other and non-Roman writers contemporary with him, as well as in Donne and in earlier English poets such as Sidney and Spenser" (pp. 98–99). Discusses the liturgical mode of Crashaw's poetry, commenting specifically on "Hymn in the Holy Nativity," "The Weeper," and "The Flaming Heart."

◄§ 1171. Trotter, David. "Cowley and Crashaw," in *The Poetry of Abraham Cowley*, 56–82. Totowa, N.J.: Rowman and Littlefield.
   Discusses the friendship of Crashaw and Cowley both in Cambridge and later in Paris and contrasts their personal lives and poetical theories. Comments on the theological and political ambience of Peterhouse during Crashaw's residency and calls attention to the importance of his friendship with Joseph Beaumont. Suggests that Crashaw's devotional poetics were influenced by Gregory of Nazianzanus, pointing out that both the Church Father

and Crashaw emphasize "the loss of self in rapture rather that the controlling function of mind, the value of 'locutionary' form rather than of 'propositional content'" (p. 70). Contrasts Crashaw's and Cowley's stanzas in "On Hope" and discusses Cowley's elegy on Crashaw. Suggests that Cowley influenced Crashaw's revision of "Letter to the Countess of Denbigh."

◄§ 1172. Yoshida, Sachiko. "The Influence of the Father upon the Son— William Crashaw and Richard Crashaw." *Kenkyu Nempo* (Annual Researches of the Faculty of Letters of Nara Women's University) 3(March): 45–67.

Maintains that, although Crashaw's later religious poems clearly reflect the influence of the Counter Reformation, his earlier poems reveal "a strong echo of his father's works" (p. 45). Acknowledges that the extent of William Crashaw's influence on his son's poetry cannot be exactly determined but suggests that some of the poet's images, choice of subject matter, and passionate language and rhetoric may have been shaped by paternal example. Suggests, for example, that William Crashaw's use of such words as *sighes* and *tears* and his mingling of sorrow and joy in his obituary on his second wife influenced his son's choice of theme and language in "The Weeper" and "The Teare." Discusses Crashaw's use of images of tears, blood, milk, and water in his early poetry. Points out that William's translation in *The Jesuites Gospel* of a long poem on the Virgin Mary by the Flemish Jesuit Bonarscius, though undertaken to prove that the poem was theologically unsound and reflective of corrupt Catholic devotion, contains images that Richard may have found appealing and imaginatively exciting. Suggests further that the fiery enthusiasm and passionate vocabulary in some of William's polemical writings may have shaped his son's poetry.

◄§ 1173. Young, R[obert] V., Jr. "Jonson, Crashaw, and the Development of the English Epigram." *Genre* 12:137–52.

Points out that "the adaptation of the classical epigram to the purposes of Renaissance poetry posed problems not only of language, but also of what might be called atmosphere or moral orientation" and shows how Jonson and Crashaw "solved these problems, though in different ways, and made the epigram a successful literary form in seventeenth-century England" (p. 138). Maintains that Crashaw's primary aim in his epigrams was to stun the reader "into an awareness of the supernatural power latent in every earthly experience" and that, unlike Jonson, he employed "the point, concision, the witty turn of the epigram not to close a subject, but to open it up" and hence sought "not 'maximal closure,' but *maximal disclosure*—another term for revelation" (p. 145). Maintains that in *Epigrammatum Sacrorum Liber* Crashaw takes as his "point of departure the delight in the marvelous which occasionally surfaces in Martial" and that he "strains the epigrammatic form to its limits, finding in verbal compression a figure for speechless wonder, in the sudden turn of a conceit or play on words a momentary disclosure of the miracle of the Incarnation" (p. 146). Comments on the artistic success of such Latin epigrams as "Joann. 2. Aquae in vinum versae" and "In spinas demtas à Christi capite cruentatas"; discusses the greater difficulties Crashaw encountered in his English epigrams, such as "Upon the Thornes taken downe from our Lords head bloody" and "On our crucified Lord Naked, and bloody"; and points to "In amorem divinum" as an example of Crashaw's attempt to transcend the form and limits of the epigram. Discusses Crashaw's use of the epigrammatic form in longer poems, less successfully in "The Weeper," which "succeeds only in stringing epigrams together" (p. 150); more successfully in the later odes and hymns, in particular "Hymn to the Name of Jesus." Concludes that Crashaw's epigram of disclosure, "instead of limiting and defining its subject, holds it up to the light and finds an unsuspected iridescence" (p. 152).

1980

1174. Crane, David. "Catholicism and Rhetoric in Southwell, Crashaw, Dryden, and Pope." *Recusant History* 15:239–58.

Calls attention to the fact that English Catholicism changed greatly during the 150 years between Southwell and Pope and finds evidence of those changes in the poetry of Southwell, Crashaw, Dryden, and Pope. Contrasts Crashaw's religious poetry with Southwell's, maintaining that Crashaw "is more at home with the rather overheated fancies of the contemporary Continental Catholic fashion in devotional poetry and imagery" and that, even though most of his poetry was written while he was still an Anglican, "his sensibilities and pieties were often those of the Counter-Reformation" (p. 246). Finds two main points of contrast: (1) Crashaw "has not to the extent of Southwell a medieval sense that God's world is already in its deepest reality *shapely* and capable of rhetorical rendering" and thus he uses wit "to produce displays of skill in holding together the poet's new-made worlds" (p. 247) and (2) "the bonds used to bind together these new-made worlds" are more permanent for Crashaw than they were for earlier writers like Southwell. Observes that typically Crashaw "strives for intensity by attracting the spiritual reality so closely into union with its physical analogue" (p. 247) that the difference between the physical and the metaphorical disappears. Argues that Crashaw's poetry "asserts to an extent that Southwell's never does . . . the primacy of the poet" and suggests that the "element of grotesquery" (p. 248) is more intense in Crashaw than in Southwell.

1175. Dobrez, Livio. "Mannerism and Baroque in English Literature." *Miscellanea Musicologica* 11:84–96.

Argues that the term *mannerism* is fully applicable to much later sixteenth- and early seventeenth-century English literature and that its use by critics would have the advantage of linking certain developments in literature with the wider world of the arts—music, painting, sculpture, and architecture. Analyzes Donne's "The Sunne Rising," passages from Shakespeare's *Othello*, and Crashaw's "Letter to the Countess of Denbigh" and "A Hymn to Sainte Teresa" to show that English literature was "progressively transformed in the course of two centuries, and that this transformation may be characterized as, in its first phase, a movement towards the dynamic, the complex and the uncertain, and, in the second, towards a grander, more affirmative vision" (p. 96), in other words, a movement from mannerism to baroque. Briefly contrasts Donne the mannerist with Crashaw the baroque poet and compares Crashaw's poetry to the work of several baroque masters—Andrea Pozzo, Murillo, Rubens, and especially Bernini. Maintains that Crashaw is not the only baroque English poet, pointing out that baroque elements can also be found in other of the metaphysicals as well as in Milton.

⋙ 1176. Elsky, Martin. "History, Liturgy, and Point of View in Protestant Meditative Poetry." *SP* 77:67–83.

Studies the connections between liturgical presentation of time and Protestant meditative poetry and argues that the traditional Catholic view of the importance of memory in making present the major events of sacred history, both in the Mass and in private devotion, is given a much different emphasis by Protestant theology, which insists that the "real presence" is an internal experience. Maintains that, although Catholic and Protestant meditative poetry often bear striking resemblances, the fundamental difference between the two is that "the center of reformed meditative verse is not just Christ, but Christ as experienced by the meditator" (p. 72). Points out that, "for reformed poets, applying Christ to the self often involves a union of subject and object, or the making present of Christ the object in the heart and soul of the meditating subject in a way that clearly reflects the internalized sacrifice of the Protestant Lord's Supper" (p. 73). Suggests that "the difference is that between a tropological relationship to Christ (an imitation of Christ) and a typological relationship to Christ, in which events in his life are reenacted in the meditator" (p. 79) and thus in the Protestant tradition, salvation history is closely connected with spiritual autobiography. Observes that, unlike Herbert, Crashaw does not evidence an internalized point of view when he meditates on a sacred event but keeps himself and the object of meditation distinct.

⋙ 1177. Hageman, Elizabeth H. "Calendrical Symbolism and the Unity of Crashaw's *Carmen Deo Nostro*." *SP* 77:161–79.

Argues that the poems in *Carmen Deo Nostro* are ordered in accordance with the calendar of the ecclesiastical year of the Roman Catholic Church and that "the calendrical symbolism that guides the selection and arrangement of Crashaw's poems points to what the Roman Catholic Crashaw regards as the true relationship between time and eternity and teaches us to feel the exhilaration so often associated with the baroque" (p. 162). Maintains that following the first poem in the collection, "Hymn to the Name of Jesus," which serves as a joyful invocation and precursor of the whole, the remaining thirty-two poems fit into two main groups: (1) poems patterned on the temporal cycle of Christmas and Easter followed by (2) poems that celebrate the response of the Virgin Mary, the saints, and other holy people to the redemptive actions of Christ depicted in the Incarnation, which, though they do not follow strictly the sanctoral calendar, "deal with experiences in which time is related to eternity" (p. 174). Comments on stylistic features and theological underpinnings of individual poems, stressing that Crashaw attempts to appeal primarily to his reader's emotions, not their intellects, and that, on the whole, the poems in *Carmen Deo Nostro* are about "'letting go,'" about entering into fervent devotion, the kind of devotion in which the self is annihilated and accepts its nothingness in order that it might gain great and indescribable joy" (p. 175). Points out that several of the poems as well as the collection as a whole are informed by numerological principles. Notes, for example, that, in selecting thirty-three poems for inclusion, Crashaw probably followed the tradition that Christ lived on earth for thirty-three years.

◆§ 1178. Magill, Frank N., ed. "Richard Crashaw," in *English Literature: Middle Ages to 1800*, 291–301. (Derived from Library Editions Published by Salem Press.) Pasadena, Calif.: Salem Softbacks.

Reprints "Richard Crashaw" (*Cyclopedia of World Authors* [entry 1092]) and "Richard Crashaw (1612–1649)" (*Magill's Bibliography of Literary Criticism* [entry 1166]). Includes a new "Essay-Review" of Crashaw's poetry (pp. 293–98). Comments briefly on the baroque elements of Crashaw's style and notes that his poems are often "diffuse, impassioned reflections on the life of Christ and the symbols of the Christian Church" (p. 293). Suggests that Crashaw's poems are characterized by rhapsodic tone and high emotional pitch; uses of hyperbole, personification, and direct address; the employment of erotic language in spiritual contexts; and the use of strange, paradoxical images and comparisons. Calls "The Weeper" "one of his most famous and most extravagant poems" and suggests that the flow of images in it "betrayed him into verses which move across the line separating the sublime from the ludicrous" (p. 294). Praises "Sospetto d'Herode," noting that it reveals "an unexpected control of language and dialogue that some of his more extravagant lyrics would not suggest" (p. 296), and calls "Musicks Duell" "one of his best works," a poem "remarkable for the skill with which the poet has manipulated his rhythm and diction to create the most musical effect possible" (p. 297). Suggests that Crashaw's use of short stanza forms and clarity of diction makes "Wishes. To his (supposed) Mistresse" one of his most appealing poems. Maintains that the poems in *Carmen Deo Nostro* are, on the whole, less strained, less characterized by bizarre images, and much more controlled than much of the early work. Concludes that, in spite of their faults, Crashaw's poems are admired by many readers for their technical skill and "for the ecstatic quality of the author's imagination" (p. 298).

◆§ 1179. Parrish, Paul A. *Richard Crashaw*. (Twayne's English Author Series, no. 229, ed. Arthur Kinney.) Boston: Twayne Publishers, A Division of G. K. Hall & Co. 189p.

Portions of Chapter 4 first appeared as "Crashaw's Two Weepers" in *CP* (entry 1131).

Comments in Chapter 3 first appeared in "Crashaw's Funeral Elegies" in *Essays on Richard Crashaw* (entry 1167).

General, comprehensive introduction to Crashaw's life and poetry that attempts to encourage "a recognition of greater variety in Crashaw's poetic achievement" and to discourage "a temptation to reduce his art—as any critical label will result in reduction—to the 'Baroque'" (p. [9]). Chronology of Crashaw's life and works (p. [13]). Chapter 1, "Backgrounds: The Life and the Art" (pp. 15–46), discusses the historical and religious setting of the first half of the seventeenth century, Crashaw's academic life at the Charterhouse and Pembroke College, his years at Peterhouse, his connection with Little Gidding, his conversion to Catholicism, and his last years in Paris and Italy. Discusses also the artistic background of Crashaw's poetry—Renaissance classicism, the metaphysical tradition, the baroque aesthetic—and concludes that "we see in Crashaw a unique fusion of various theological, aesthetic, and personal forces that result in a truly eclectic art" (p. 33). Chapter 2, "Apprenticeship: The Epigrams and Early Translations" (pp. 47–69), shows that Crashaw began writing epigrams as schoolboy exercises, discusses the epigrammatic tradition, and examines *Epigrammatum Sacrorum Liber* for its arrangement, subject matter, uses of persona, and its techniques of repetition, pun, and paradox. Discusses also the early shorter translations and "Sospetto d'Herode" and suggests that in the latter "we see a desire to embellish, to arouse, or more simply, to delight, through language and imagery that, while not shunning the intellect, has a more overtly sensuous appeal" (p. 69). Chapter 3, "*Delights of the Muses*: The Secular and Occasional Poems" (pp. 70–91), comments on the variety of subject matter, meter, and form of Crashaw's secular poetry and claims that it shows that the poet "was capable of classical elegance, Metaphysical abruptness, and Baroque luxuriousness" (p. 73). Discusses the royalty poems; the elegies (the largest group among the secular poems); three love poems—"Wishes. To his (supposed) Mistresse," "Loves Horoscope," and "Epithalamium"—"Musicks Duell"; and several other pieces, concluding that the secular verse "reveals a Crashaw who is more subdued, more controlled in his poetic idiom" (p. 91). Chapter 4, "*Steps to the Temple*: The Sacred Poems" (pp. 92–117), surveys the contents and prefaces of the 1646 and 1648 editions and examines the extent of the influence of Herbert, suggesting that, except in "Charitas Nimia" and "Office of the Holy Crosse," it is slight. Analyzes the yoking of the sacred and profane in

Crashaw's poetry, commenting on "On Hope," "Ode on a Prayer-book," "To
[Mrs. M. R.] Councel Concerning her Choise," and "Letter to the Countess
of Denbigh." Discusses in some detail "The Weeper" in an attempt to answer
negative criticism of the poem and to show that the revisions of the second
version make the poem "more attractive and balanced, and structurally more
coherent and unified" (p. 117). Chapter 5, "The Major Hymns" (pp. 118–
43), discusses five original hymns ("Hymn to the Name of Jesus," "Hymn in
the Holy Nativity," "New Year's Day," "Hymn in the Glorious Epiphanie,"
and "Hymn in the Assumption") and six paraphrases ("Vexilla Regis," "Sancta
Maria Dolorum," "Adoro Te," "Lauda Sion Salvatorem," "Dies Irae Dies
Illa," and "O Gloriosa Domina") and maintains that, although there is great
variety among them, they all have "a more passionate eloquence, a figured
and repetitive style, and a Baroque sensibility that carries a reader by rhetorical waves toward the object of praise and contemplation" (pp. 119–
20). Chapter 6, "The Teresa Poems" (pp. 144–64), discusses the life of
St. Teresa and Crashaw's three poems on her that manifest the meaning of
that life. Concludes that these poems are "his ultimate achievement in Baroque art and the most consequential examples of his allegiance to the *via
affirmativa,* the way to God through expression and feeling" (pp. 149–50).
"Epilogue" (pp. 165–68) reaffirms that Crashaw's greatest achievement "is
not to be found simply in the Baroque quality of his work but in the often
unique fusion of diverse influences and traditions that his poetry reveals"
(p. 167). Notes (pp. 169–81), selected bibliography (pp. 182–85), and index
(pp. 186–89).

1180. Yoshida, Sachiko. "R. Crashaw to Ai no Inyu: Eikoku Shinpi Shiso
to no Kakawari ni oite" [Metaphor of Love in Richard Crashaw's Poetry
in Relation to English Mysticism], in *Suga Yasuo, Ogoshi Kazugo:
Ryokyoju Taikan Kinen Ronbunshu* [Festschrift in Honor of Professor
Suga and Professor Ogoshi], 264–79. Kyoto: Apollonsha.
Suggests that the change in Crashaw's attitude toward love from his earlier
to his later poetry is a key concept in understanding the developments of his
religious sensibility and art. Points out that, although the word *love* appears
often in his earlier poetry, it is not vitally connected with the idea of love,
while in the later poetry love takes on profound mystical connotations and is
employed with various metaphorical meanings. Maintains that these metaphors of love are based on the writings of the medieval English mystics.

1181. Young, Robert V., Jr. "Crashaw, St. John of the Cross, and the Dark
Night of the Soul," in *A Fair Day in the Affections: Literary Essays in
Honor of Robert B. White, Jr.*, edited by Jack M. Durant and M. Thomas
Hester, 101–10. Raleigh, N.C.: Winston Press.
Compares "Hymn in the Glorious Epiphanie" to the mystical writings of
St. John of the Cross and argues that the Spanish saint's concept of the "dark

night of the soul" or the *via negativa* informs and unifies the apparent diffuseness and divergent elements in the hymn. Points out numerous parallels in language, structure, images, and symbolism between the poetry and mystical commentaries of St. John of the Cross and Crashaw's hymn to show that the poem "is a skillful representation of mystical experience" (p. 108) and that "one of Crashaw's major contributions to devotional literature is his unique meditation on the relation between mystical experience and the Church's liturgical celebration of Gospel events" (p. 101).

Index of Authors, Editors, Translators, and Composers

Abrams, M. H., 872
Adams, Robert Martin, 770, 813, 879, 1068
Adamson, J. H., 1078
Addis, John, Jun., 212
Adkins, Joan F., 1078
Aikin, John, 114
Aizawa, Yoshihisa, 1118
Albert, Edward, 434
Albertson, Charles Carroll, 526
Alcott, Amos Bronson, 223
Alexander, William, 317
Alford, Henry, 146
Aliandro, Higino, 731
Allibone, Samuel Austin, 189
Allison, A. F., 684, 690, 1069
Alsop, Thomas, 150
Alvarez, Alfred, 850
Anderson, G. F. Reynolds, 298
Anderson, James Bruce, 945
Anderson, Robert, 102
Anketell, John, 238
Arakawa, Mitsuo, 1119
Arms, George, 719
Arnold, Thomas, 204
Artz, Frederick B., 873
Asals, Heather A. R., 1147, 1153
Aston, Walter Hutchinson, 120
Atkinson, A. D., 732
Attal, Jean-Pierre, 827
Austin, John, 26, 39

Bailey-Kempling, W., 356
Bairstow, Edward C., 771
Baker, Herschel, 1099
Balavoine, Claudie, 1111
Bald, R. C., 527, 828
Bamonte, Gerardo, 851
Banzer, Judith, 852
Barbato, Louis R., 1100
Bargrave, John, 37
Barker, Arthur E., 1148
Barker, Francis E., 435, 593
Barksdale, Clement, 23, 48
Barrett, Alfred, 579
Bates, William, 213

Bateson, F. W., 733, 740
Bawcutt, N. W., 874
Bax, Arnold Edward Trevor, 436
Beachcroft, T. O., 517, 518, 551
Beaty, Frederick L., 1050
Beaty, Jerome, 914
Beaumont, Joseph, 19
Bede, Cuthbert, 181
Beeching, H. C., 299, 335, 342
Beer, Patricia, 1051
Beeton, Samuel Orchart, 235
Belasyse, Henry, 32
Bell, Robert, 159
Bellew, John Chippendale Montesquieu, 214
Benet, Diana, 1149, 1153
Benito Cardenal, Luis Carlos, 1132
Bennett, Gordon, 1145
Bennett, Joan, 552, 837
Bensly, Edward, 328, 357
Bentley, Richard, 177
Berchmans, Sister Louise, 594
Berkeley, Lennox, 660, 806
Bernard, Sister Miriam, 653
Bernardin, Brother, 495
Berry, Boyd M., 1120
Berry, Francis, 875
Berry, Lloyd E., 896
Bertonasco, Marc F., 963, 964, 1026, 1150, 1153
Bethell, S. L., 640, 641, 691, 734, 749
Binkerd, Gordon, 946, 973
Birrell, T. A., 783
Black, Matthew W., 603
Blake, Kathleen, 1027
Blakeney, Edward Henry, 504
Bliss, Geoffrey, 358
Blunden, Edmund, 772
Boase, Alan M., 708
Bottrall, Margaret, 762, 1151
Bouyer, Louis, 915
Bowes, Robert, 294
Bowman, Phyllis S., 1002
Boyd, George W., 829
Bradbury, Malcolm, 1000
Bradner, Leicester, 621, 947

Brandenburg, Alice Stayert, 642
Brégy, Katherine, 341
Brinkley, Roberta Florence, 580, 773
Brittin, Norman A., 581
Britting, Georg, 692
Broadbent, John, 1079
Brooke, Stopford Augustus, 245, 301
Brooke, Tucker, 693
Brooks, Cleanth, 561, 562, 563, 604
Brown, Gulielmi [William] Haig, 231
Browning, Elizabeth Barrett, 164
Browning, Robert, 168
Buckley, W. E., 280
Buffum, Imbrie, 735
Bullen, Arthur Henry, 267
Bullett, Gerald, 720
Burgess, Anthony [John Burgess Wilson], 814
Bury, Samuel, 61
Bush, Douglas, 661, 741, 774, 815, 1133
Butterworth, S., 359
Byard, Margaret M., 1128
Byron, George Gordon (Lord), 132

Cammell, Charles Richard, 694, 721
Campbell, Gordon, 1080
Campbell, Jane, 1052
Campbell, Thomas, 118, 123, 126
Candy, Hugh C. H., 404
Car, Thomas [Miles Pinkney], 27
Caracciolo-Trejo, E., 1108
Carayon, Marcel, 612
Carier, Benjamin, 21
Carrive, Lucien, 1053
Carter, Edmund, 78
Carter, Jane Frances Mary, 291
Carver, George, 460
Cattermole, Richard, 149, 161
Cayley, Michael, 1054
Cazamian, Louis, 449, 673, 742
Cecil, David, 622
Černý, Václav, 595
Chalmers, Alexander, 119
Chalmers, Robert, 448
Chambers, A. B., 1047, 1101
Chambers, Leland, 948
Chambers, Robert, 165
Chandler, Albert R., 605
Charvat, William, 722
Chinol, Elio, 1081
Choate, Isaac Bassett, 292
Cibber, Theophilus, 79
Cirillo, Albert R., 1001, 1152

Clark, Evert Mordecai, 496
Clarke, Charles Cowden, 186
Clarke, George Herbert, 695
Claydon, Sister Margaret, 838
Clemens, Cyril, 648
Cleveland, Charles Dexter, 172
Clifford, Arthur, 121
Clifford, Cornelius, 360
Clutton-Brock, Arthur, 329, 349
Coburn, Kathleen, 115
Coffin, Robert P. Tristram, 674
Cohen, J. M., 882, 883, 884
Colby, Elbridge, 582
Coleman, Elliott, 816
Coleridge, Samuel Taylor, 115, 116, 124, 150, 151
Coleridge, Sara, 173
Coles, Abraham, 199
Collier, Jeremy, 60
Collier, William Francis, 202
Collmer, Robert G., 784, 853, 916, 931
Colville, K. N., 596
Compton-Rickett, Arthur, 785
Confrey, Burton, 426, 469, 481
Connolly, Francis X., 696
Connor, J. Hal, 632
Cook, Albert S., 363
Cooper, Robert M., 1153
Cornwall, Barry. See Procter, Bryan Waller
Corser, Thomas, 302
Cosin, John, 51
Courthope, W. J., 330
Courtney, W. P., 366
Cowley, Abraham, 31
Cox, R. G., 786
Cragg, Gerald R., 1102
Craik, George L., 169
Crane, D. E. L., 1028
Crane, David, 1174
Crisp, Frederick Arthur, 384
Crosse, Gordon, 437
Crouch, Charles H., 320
Crum, Margaret, 974
Cunnar, Eugene R., 1153, 1154
Cunningham, George Godfrey, 152
Curtin, C. J., 697
Cutts, John P., 750

Daiches, David, 722, 839
Dalglish, Jack, 854
Daly, James J., 528
Daly, M., 506
Daly, Peter M., 1155

Dana, Charles Anderson, 192
Danchin, Pierre, 830
Daniell, F. H. Blackburne, 276
Daniells, Roy, 662, 675
Daniels, Earl, 633
Daniels, R. Balfour, 624
Darton, F. J. Harvey, 478
Davie, Donald, 975
Davies, Horton, 1103
Davies, Hugh Sykes, 649
Davis, Bernard, 949
Davis, Elizabeth, 949
Day, Martin S., 886
Day, W. G., 1029
Dearmer, Percy, 482
Denbigh, Countess of [Cecilia Mary Clifford Feilding], 395
Denonain, Jean-Jacques, 787
de Vere, Aubrey, 193
Dewey, Thomas B., 917
Dibdin, Thomas Frognall, 135
Di Cesare, Mario A., 1133
Digby, Kenelm, 18
Ditsky, John, 1055
Dobrez, Livio, 1056, 1175
Dodd, Charles [Hugh Tootell], 75
Dodd, Henry Philip, 232
Dörrie, Heinrich, 1082
Doughty, W. L., 676
Dowden, Edward, 321
Drake, Nathan, 108
Draper, John W., 497
Duckett, Eleanor Shipley, 453
Duncan, Joseph E., 751, 831, 980
Dunton, John, 55, 57, 58

Edwards, A. S. G., 1121
Edwards, Maxwell D., 632
Edwards, Paul, 1030
Egan, Maurice Francis, 250
Elder, David, 1122
Eleanore, Sister M., 461, 625
Eliot, T. S., 417, 418, 454, 462, 463, 468, 471, 483, 507, 508, 529, 565, 879, 918, 932, 980
Ellis, George, 111
Ellrodt, Robert, 840, 897, 1005, 1057
Elsky, Martin, 1176
Elton, Oliver, 530
Emerson, Ralph Waldo, 156, 241
Emma, David Ronald, 995
Emperor, John Bernard, 484
Empson, William, 509, 566
Emslie, MacDonald, 1030

Enright, D. J., 788
Erlebach, Peter, 1156
Esch, Arno, 775, 1006
Evans, Gillian, 1134

Fabry, Frank J., 1129
Falls, Cyril Bentham, 438
Farmer, Norman K., Jr., 1007
Farnham, Anthony E., 789
Fausset, Hugh I'Anson, 439
Fehr, Bernhard, 485
Feist, Hans, 663
Ferrari, Ferrucio, 1104
Ferry, Anne Davidson, 898
Fethaland, John, 643
Findlater, Andrew, 205
Finlayson, John, 242
Finney, Gretchen Ludke, 876
Finzi, Gerald, 685
Fischer, Hermann, 965, 1031
Fisher, R. M., 1083, 1084, 1105
Fitts, Dudley, 933
Fitzgerald, Maurus, 626
Fitzmaurice-Kelly, James, 368
Flatter, Richard, 800
Fleming, William Kaye, 383
Foley, Henry, 251
Ford, Boris, 790
Ford, Ford Madox, 607
Foy, Thomas, 541
Frankenberg, Lloyd, 791
Freeman, Rosemary, 698
Freer, Coburn, 1153, 1157
Friederich, Werner P., 531
Frye, Northrop, 644
Fukuchi, Shirō, 841, 855
Fuson, Benjamin Willis, 699

Galdon, Joseph A., 1106
Gamberini, Spartaco, 832
Gambold, John, 80
Gang, T. M., 792
Gardner, Helen, 807, 879, 1032
Gardner, William Henry, 654
Garrod, H. W., 498
Geha, Richard, Jr., 934
George, Arapara Ghevarghese, 1033
Gerould, Gordon Hall, 401
Gibaldi, Joseph, 1107
Gibbons, Alfred W., 288
Gilfillan, George, 178, 186
Gillie, Christopher, 1058
Gillman, Frederick John, 472
Gillow, Joseph, 300

Gilman, Harvey, 899
Goddard, Geoffrey, 1158
Goldberg, Beverly, 967
Goldfarb, Russell M., 856
Gomis, María, 1013
Goodwin, Gordon, 342
Gorlier, Claudio, 919, 966
Gorton, John, 139
Gosse, Edmund, 257, 273, 306, 331, 419
Graham, Paul T., 1034
Granger, James, 84
Grant, Patrick, 1159
Gray, Thomas, 86
Green, M., 103
Greenblatt, Daniel L., 1135
Greene, Graham, 542
Greenlaw, Edwin, 486
Greg, Walter Wilson, 532
Gregory, Horace, 664
Grennen, Joseph E., 920
Grierson, Herbert J. C., 350, 420, 499, 655, 879
Griswold, Rufus Wilmot, 175
Groom, Bernard, 776
Gros, Léon-Gabriel, 710
Grosart, Alexander B., 224, 225, 226, 227, 228, 233, 237, 239, 274

Hageman, Elizabeth H., 1177
Hagstrum, Jean H., 817
Hall, Samuel Carter, 153
Hall, William C., 344
Hallam, Henry, 160
Halley, Thomas A., 665
Hamilton, George Rostrevor, 464
Hammond, Gerald, 1085
Hanak, Miroslav John, 1008
Hardy, Stan, 977
Harrison, John Smith, 332
Harrison, Robert, 950
Harvey, Paul, 533
Hatzfeld, Helmut, 634
Hauser, Arnold, 900
Haycraft, Howard, 744
Hayley, William, 99
Haynes, Henrietta, 377
Hayward, John, 686
Hazlitt, William, 125, 127, 128
Headley, Henry, 96, 97
Healy, Tom F., 1160
Hearne, Thomas, 69, 70
Hebel, John William, 500
Heide, Anna von der, 396

Helsztyński, Stanisław, 1035
Henrietta Maria (Queen), 17
Hernádi, Miklós, 1036
Herne, Samuel, 46
Hess, M. Whitcomb, 666, 677
Heynsius (Heinsius), Daniel, 15
Heywood, Terence, 627
Hibbard, Howard, 921
Hill, J. P., 1108
Hilyard, Joseph P., 1153, 1161
Hocke, Gustave René, 833
Hodgkin, John, 405
Hodgson, Geraldine Emma, 427
Hohoff, Curt, 692
Hoiby, Lee, 842
Holdsworth (Oldsworth), Richard, 11
Holland, John, 166
Hollander, John, 857, 1070
Holliday, Carl, 372
Honey, William Bowyer, 613
Honig, Edwin, 967
Hopkins, Kenneth, 877
Howard, Thomas T., 968
Hudson, Hoyt H., 500
Hughes, Richard E., 1037
Hughes, T. Cann, 265
Hunt, Leigh, 129, 145, 170
Hunter, Jim, 922
Husain, Itrat, 700
Hutchinson, Francis E., 373, 406, 407, 487
Hutton, Edward, 323, 345, 645, 711
Huxley, Aldous, 534

Inge, William Ralph, 397
Inglis, Fred, 923
Isaacson, Henry, 4
Ishii, Shōnosuke, 793, 878, 1009, 1086, 1109, 1136, 1153
Iwabuchi, Satoru, 978
Izzo, Carlo, 858

Jacob, Giles, 66
Jacobus, Lee A., 1010, 1153, 1162
Jacquot, Jean, 736, 867
Jauernick, Stephanie, 924
Jenkins, Harold, 743
Jennings, Elizabeth, 925
Johnson, Hamish, 1073
Johnson, Samuel, 77, 81, 87, 88
Johnson, Thomas H., 597
Johnstone, John, 140, 144
Jonas, Leah, 628
Jones, Richard Foster, 510

Judson, Alexander Corbin, 473
Judson, Jerome, 843
Julian, John, 289
Jusserand, J. J., 337

Kane, Elisha K., 488
Kapoor, R. C., 991
Katona, Anna, 1066
Kawata, Akira, 979, 1087, 1130
Keast, William R., 723, 879
Keble, John, 137
Kelliher, W. Hilton, 969, 1059, 1123, 1153, 1163
Kelly, Blanche Mary, 583
Kemp, Violet I., 489
Kenner, Hugh, 901
Kermode, Frank, 808, 809, 980, 1070
Kindt, Hermann, 216, 217
King, William Francis Henry, 275
Knowles, R. B., 243
Knox, Ronald A., 712
Kobinata, Teijiro, 440
Kranz, Gisbert, 834
Krzeckowski, Henryk, 981
Kuna, F. M., 887
Kunitz, Stanley J., 744
Kuntz, Joseph M., 719
Kuranga, Makoto, 629
Kurth, Paula, 535
Kusunose, Toshihiko, 835, 935, 1038

Labriola, Albert C., 1137, 1153, 1164
Lamb, Charles, 117
Lamson, Roy, 794
Lang, Andrew, 378
Larsen, Kenneth J., 1039, 1088
Lauder, William, 76
Laurens, Pierre, 1110, 1111
Lea, Kathleen M., 455
Leach, Elsie, 888, 1060
Leavis, F. R., 879
LeClerq, R. V., 1112
Lee, A. H. E, 490
Lee, Kathleen, 511
Lee, Sidney L., 281
Legouis, Émile, 449
Leicester, Richard, 1089
Leigh, John, 24
Leighton, Kenneth, 1138
Leishman, J. B., 859, 936
Leslie, John Randolph Shane, 456
Levitt, Paul M., 1090
Lewalski, Barbara Kiefer, 1071, 1165
Linton, W. J., 258

Lloyd, David, 40
Logan, Sister Eugenia, 656
Loiseau, Jean, 519, 937
London, William, 33
Longfellow, Henry Wadsworth, 157, 210
Loudon, K. M., 428
Low, Anthony, 1133, 1139, 1140
Lowell, James Russell, 167, 208
Lowell, Robert, 667
Lowes, John Livingston, 412
Lyte, H. C. Maxwell, 276

Mabbott, Thomas O., 1141
Mabie, Hamilton Wright, 365
Macaulay, Rose, 520, 536
McBryde, John McLaren, Jr., 315
McCanles, Michael, 1091
McCann, Eleanor, 763, 860
McCarthy, D. F., 194, 195
Macdonald, George, 218
McPeek, James A. S., 614
Maddison, Carol, 844
Madsen, William G., 818
Magill, Frank N., 1092, 1166, 1178
Mahood, M. M., 724
Malloch, A. E., 752
Manning, Stephen, 777
Marcus, Leah Sinanoglou, 1142
Mares, F. H., 1072
Margoliouth, H. M., 413
Marsh, Bower, 384
Marshall, Ed, 246
Martin, L. C., 398, 402, 441, 442, 443, 470, 745
Martinez, Nancy C., 719
Martz, Louis L., 764, 889, 938, 982, 1011
Massey, Gerald, 219
Massingham, Harold J., 414, 429
Masson, David, 200
Masterman, John Howard Bertram, 307
Matchett, William H., 914
Matsuura, Kaichi, 537
Maty, Henry, 94
Maxwell, J. C., 725
Maycock, A. L., 608
Mayer, Lloyd G., 1124
Mayor, John Eyton Bickersteth, 185, 187
Mazzaro, Jerome, 983
Mazzeo, Joseph Anthony, 746, 753, 879, 980
Meath, Gerard, 713
Mégroz, Rodolphe Louis, 474
Meissner, Paul, 553

Melchiori, Giorgio, 795, 902
Mennes, John, 13, 22
Meozzi, Antero, 584
Meynell, Alice, 308, 309, 310
Mierzejewski, Aleksander, 981
Milch, Werner J., 678, 687
Miles, Josephine, 701, 778, 845, 939
Miller, Carroll, 1093
Miller, Clarence H., 903
Miller, Milton, 967
Miller, Paul W., 1012
Milward, Peter, 951, 1113, 1125
Mims, Edwin, 702
Miner, Earl, 879, 984
Minkov, Marko Konstantinov, 688
Mirollo, James V., 890
Mishra, Jayakanta, 765
Mitford, John, 141
Molho, Blanca, 1013
Molho, Maurice, 1013
Moloney, Michael Francis, 657, 668, 714
Monaghan, John, 444
Montgomery, James, 142
Montgomery, Lyna Lee, 1061
Moore, Thomas, 143
Morley, Henry, 240
Moulton, Charles Wells, 324
Mourgues, Odette de, 754, 796
Mullinger, James Bass, 374
Muñoz Rojas, José A., 646
Murdock, Kenneth B., 715
Murrin, Michael, 985
Musser, Benjamin Francis, 567

Nakamura, Mineko, 1062
Nakao, Setsuko, 1114, 1126
Neill, Kerby, 703
Nelson, Lowry, Jr., 861, 980
Nethercot, Arthur H., 430, 450, 457, 458, 512, 521
Newbolt, Henry, 431, 465
Newdigate, Bernard H., 568
Nichols, John, 89
Nicholson, Brinsley, 230
Nicoll, W. Robertson, 351
Nicolson, Marjorie Hope, 726
Nolan, Joseph A., 254
Nott, Charles Cooper, 211
Nuttall, Anthony David, 952

Oates, J. C. T., 755
O'Brien, Edward J., 369
O'Connor, William Van, 704, 760

Ōjima, Shōtarō, 513
Okuda, Hiroko, 986
Oldys, Alexander, 59
Olivero, Federico, 409, 585
O'Neill, George, 391, 466
Orgel, Stephen, 1040
Orr, Evelyn, 617
Ōsawa, Mamoru, 727
Ōsawa, Minoru, 987
Osborn, James M., 940
Osgood, Charles Grosvenor, 569
Osmond, Percy Herbert, 385, 415
Ostriker, Alicia, 1014

Pagnini, Marcello, 862
Paley, Morton D., 1015
Palgrave, Francis Turner, 203, 283
Palmer, David, 1000
Panhuijsen, Jos., 615
Parfitt, G. A. E., 1041, 1094
Parks, Edna D., 1063
Parrish, Paul A., 1131, 1153, 1167, 1179
Patmore, Coventry, 255, 295
Patrides, C. A., 904
Patterson, Richard Ferrar, 543
Pearcy, Roy J., 1095
Peckard, Peter, 101
Perella, Nicholas James, 988
Perkins, David, 756
Perosa, Sergio, 989
Peter, John, 757
Peterkiewicz, Jerzy, 819, 1016
Petersson, Robert T., 1017
Pettoello, Laura, 811
Phare, Elsie Elizabeth, 538, 544
Phillips, Edward, 45
Phillips, Peregrine, 93
Pickel, Margaret Barnard, 586
Pinkham, Daniel, 926
Pollard, Carol, 1117
Pop-Cornis, Marcel, 1115
Pope, Alexander, 62, 63, 65, 71
Porter, Alan, 467
Potter, George Reuben, 637
Poulet, Georges, 863
Powers, Perry J., 797
Praz, Mario, 459, 475, 522, 554, 570, 598, 616, 669, 679, 680, 716, 737, 820, 880, 905, 1018
Preston, Thomas R., 906
Pritchard, Allan, 907
Procter, Bryan Waller, 138
Prynne, William, 29
Pulling, Alexander, 476

Pulsford, Daniel B., 587

Quennell, Peter, 545, 1073
Quiller-Couch, Arthur, 410, 501
Quinn, John Francis, 432
Quintana, Ricardo, 739, 1047

Raiziss, Sona, 747
Ramsaran, John A., 1074
Ramsay, Mary Paton, 403
Ransom, John Crowe, 638
Rao, A. V., 798
Raspa, Anthony, 941
Read, Herbert, 491
Reed, Edward Bliss, 379
Reed, John Curtis, 502
Reeves, James, 864
Reeves, Jeremiah Bascom, 451
Reilly, R. J., 953
Reinsdorf, Walter, 1019
Renton, William, 293
Reynolds, John, 67
Rhys, Ernest, 386
Ricci, Seymour de, 571
Richmond, H. M., 908
Rickey, Mary Ellen, 779, 799, 865
Ricks, Christopher, 990
Roberts, Michael [William Edward Roberts], 555
Roberts, Sydney C., 445
Robinson, Eloise, 392
Rogers, David M., 927
Rogers, Robert, 1075, 1143
Rohr-Sauer, Philipp von, 609
Rollins, Roger B., 1168
Roscelli, William John, 954
Ross, Malcolm M., 758, 766
Roston, Murray, 1096
Rothschild, Philippe de, 990
Rowe, Elizabeth Singer, 68
Rowland, Daniel B., 909
Rowley, James, 234
Roy, Virendra Kumar, 991
Ruffhead, Owen, 85
Ruoff, James E., 1116
Ruthven, K. K., 992

Sabol, Andrew J., 1071
Sackville-West, V., 650
Saintsbury, George, 277, 314, 361, 421, 422
Saito, Takeshi, 477
Samaha, Edward E., Jr., 993
Sampson, George, 639

Sandbank, Shimon, 1042
Sanesi, Roberto, 866
Sanford, Ezekiel, 126
Saunders, J. W., 1020
Saveson, J. E., 821
Sawyer, Charles J., 478
Sayama, Eitarō, 767, 846
Schaar, Claes, 994, 1043
Schaff, Philip, 220, 256
Schelling, Felix E., 316, 387, 479
Schirmer, Walter Franz, 452, 523, 599
Schlauch, Margaret, 847
Schleiner, Louise, 1153, 1169
Schlüter, Kurt, 1064
Schücking, Levin L., 800
Schwenger, Peter, 1127
Scott, Cyril Meir, 446
Scott, Mary Augusta, 303
Scott, R. F., 325
Scott, Walter Sidney, 670
Scrymgeour, Daniel, 179
Sears, Clara Endicott, 399
Seccombe, Thomas, 351
Segel, Harold B., 1097
Selden, John, 54
Selvage, Watson Bartemus, 338
Selvin, Hanan C., 939
Seth-Smith, Elsie Kathleen, 393
Seton-Anderson, James, 610
Shafer, Robert, 411
Sharland, E. Cruwys, 380
Sharp, Robert Lathrop, 572, 630
Shaw, Martin, 482
Shawcross, John T., 995
Shelford, Robert, 9
Shepherd, R. A. Eric, 389
Shiels, Robert, 79
Shinoda, Hajime, 822
Shinoda, Kazushi, 955
Shipley, Orby, 259
Shipman, Thomas, 50
Shipps, Anthony W., 996
Shorthouse, Joseph Henry, 252, 260
Shudō, Tomoko, 956, 970, 997
Shuster, George Nauman, 631
Simcox, G. A., 253
Singh, Brijraj, 1021
Sito, Jerzy S., 881, 891, 942, 981
Skipton, H. P. K., 354, 423
Smit, Gabriël, 623
Smith, A. J., 801
Smith, Chard Powers, 573
Smith, Hallett, 794
Smith, Harold Wendall, 738

Smith, J. C., 655
Smith, James, 546
Smith, Lewis Worthington, 632
Smith, T. C., 196
Smith, W. Bradford, 556
Söderholm, Torbjörn, 1022
Souris, André, 867
Southern, Henry, 130
Southey, Robert, 109
Southwell, Robert, 35
Sparrow, John, 892, 910
Spence, Joseph, 131
Spencer, Theodore, 617
Spender, Constance, 416
Spurgeon, Caroline F. E., 388
Stamm, Rudolf, 812
Stanford, Derek, 957
Stanwood, Paul G., 943, 1170
Starkman, Miriam, 958
Stebbing, William, 355
Steele, Thomas J., 1065
Steese, Peter, 928
Stevens, William Bagshaw, 95
Stewart, Stanley, 944
Strier, Richard, 998, 1133, 1144
Stubbe (Stubbs, Stubbes), Henry, 25
Sudo, Nobuo, 868
Sugimoto, Ryūtarō, 911, 1044
Summers, Joseph H., 768, 1023
Sundararajan, P. K., 1076
Swann, John H., 346
Swanston, Hamish, 893
Swinburne, Algernon Charles, 206, 244,
    261, 271
Sypher, Wylie, 658, 780
Szenczi, Miklós, 1066
Szobotka, Tibor, 1066

Taggard, Genevieve, 503
Taira, Zensuke, 929
Taketomo, Sōfū, 588, 659
Taylor, Una, 304
Testor, Ita, 322
Thimelby, Edward, 30
Tholen, Wilhelm, 492
Thomas, Philip Edward, 370
Thompson, A. Hamilton, 433
Thompson, Elbert N. S., 424, 618
Thompson, Eric, 748
Thompson, Francis, 284, 290, 311, 312,
    326, 339, 347, 362
Thompson, J. E., 269
Thompson, W. Meredith, 574
Thomson, Virgil, 1045

Thwaite, Ann, 793
Thwaite, Anthony, 793, 1098
Todd, Henry John, 112
Torry, Alfred Freer, 282
Towers, Gladys V., 728
Townsend, Anselm, 514
Traill, Henry Duff, 296
Trautmann, Joanne, 1117
Trench, Richard Chenevix, 176, 209
Trotter, David, 1171
Turmann, Margaritha, 557
Turnbull, William B., 191, 197
Turnell, Martin, 717, 759, 869, 971
Tutin, J. R., 272, 285, 305, 318, 319,
    327, 342
Tuve, Rosemond, 689
Tynan, Katharine, 297
Tytell, John, 1046

Ueda, Bin, 515
Unger, Leonard, 760
Untermeyer, Louis, 611, 836

Vancŭra, Zdeněk, 651
Van Doren, Mark, 617
Van Norden, Linda, 1026

Wagner, Jürgen, 1077
Walker, John, 64
Walker, Thomas Alfred, 352, 381
Waller, A. R., 336
Wallerstein, Ruth C., 575, 729, 739,
    1047
Wallis, P. J., 769, 802, 848
Walpole, Horace, 100
Walsh, Michael, 558
Walsh, Thomas, 480, 493
Walton, Izaak, 44
Ward, C. A., 262, 263, 270
Warnke, Frank J., 781, 823, 870, 895,
    959, 980, 1024, 1067
Warren, Austin, 494, 524, 539, 540,
    547, 548, 559, 560, 576, 577, 589,
    619, 879, 980, 1133
Warren, Charles Frere Stopford, 313
Warren, Robert Penn, 604
Warton, Joseph, 82, 107
Waterton, Edmund, 264
Watkin, E. I., 549, 681, 761
Watkins, John, 110
Watkins, W. B. C., 590
Watson, George, 782, 824
Watt, Robert, 136
Waugh, Arthur, 400

Wedgwood, C. V., 730
Wellek, René, 682, 803
Wesley, Samuel, 52
White, Helen C., 525, 591, 739, 849, 1047, 1133
Whitlock, Baird W., 960, 972
Whitlock, John, 34
Whittier, John Greenleaf, 247
Wilcher, Robert, 1048
Wild, Friedrich, 578
Willey, Basil, 718
Williams, A. M., 1025
Williams, George Walton, 705, 706, 804, 894, 999, 1002
Williams, I. A., 447
Williams, Oscar, 967
Williams, Ralph Vaughan, 482
Williamson, George, 516, 961
Willis, Thomas, 49
Willmott, Robert Aris, 148, 207
Willy, Margaret, 871, 1049
Wilson, Edward M., 825

Wilson, F. P., 671
Winstanley, William, 36, 53
Winters, Yvor, 600, 652, 962
Witherspoon, Alexander M., 647, 674, 895
Woesler, Richard, 592
Wong, Tak-Wai, 1145
Wood, Anthony à, 56
Woodberry, George Edward, 425
Woodhouse, A. S. P., 930
Wordsworth, Christopher, 248
Worthington, John, 38, 41
Wright, Edward, 340

Yeats, William Butler, 394
Yoklavich, John, 912, 913
Yoshida, Sachiko, 1172, 1180
Young, Robert V., Jr., 1146, 1173, 1181

Zanco, Aurelio, 683
Zouch, Thomas, 105
Żulawski, Juliusz, 981

Subject Index

(The following is an index of subjects mentioned in the annotations in this bibliography. The reader is advised to check all general studies related to a specific topic.)

Abdy, Alice, 441
Account Book (English College, Rome), 1039
Addison, Joseph, 262, 309, 1029
Aiken, Conrad, 704
Alexis, Saint, 619
Allison, A. F., 812
Almack, Edward, 423
Ambrose, Saint, 180
American Transcendentalists, 589
Amoris Divini et Humani Antipathia, 554
Anacreon, 817
Anderson, Robert, 115, 116
Andrewes, Lancelot, 2, 36, 593, 596, 865
Angelico, Fra Giovanni da Fiesole, 409
Anglican Church (Anglicans and Anglicanism), 46, 47, 51, 56, 79, 186, 242, 349, 385, 415, 426, 435, 500, 520, 531, 538, 548, 549, 559, 619, 758, 761, 766, 783, 816, 826, 841, 968, 970, 997, 1025, 1088, 1113, 1124, 1142, 1153, 1174
Aquinas, Saint Thomas, 427, 514, 591, 640, 641
Aristotle (Aristotelianism), 463, 1057
Arminianism, 307, 539
Arnold, Matthew, 495
Artusi, Giovanni Maria, 1162
Ashe, Thomas, 254
Ashley, Robert, 1084
Aston, Herbert, 30
Atkinson, Father, 940
Attwater, Aubrey L., 559
Augustine, Saint (Augustinianism), 700, 712, 714, 1159
Ausonius, 52

Bacon, Francis (Baconianism), 32, 753
Bairstow, Edward, 1169
Bankes, Christopher, 943
Barclay, John, 1025
Bargrave, John, 112, 158, 450
Barksdale, Clement, 450
Baron, Samuel, 540
Baroque, 523, 531, 551, 578, 592, 609, 619, 620, 627, 634, 651, 658, 661, 662, 664, 675, 681, 682, 687, 688, 708, 711, 717, 724, 735, 759, 767, 780, 794, 796, 846, 847, 851, 861, 863, 869, 873, 880, 882, 894, 909, 929, 937, 959, 960, 966, 972, 982, 1008, 1017, 1018, 1019, 1026, 1062, 1067, 1070, 1097, 1107, 1108, 1110, 1145, 1175
Barthelemy, Jean-Louis (le Père de Saint Louis), 708, 754
Baudelaire, Charles Pierre, 565
Baxter, Richard, 472
Beachcroft, T. O., 1155
Beaufort, Lady Margaret, 282, 547
Beaumont, Charles, 539
Beaumont, Francis, 32, 117, 880
Beaumont, John, 131, 940
Beaumont, Joseph, 333, 392, 415, 539, 661, 672, 729, 766, 768, 860, 865, 895, 907, 1171
Becher, Howard, 64
Beeching, H. C., 589
Bellarmine, Saint Robert, 1112
Bellini, Giovanni, 624
Benlowes, Edward, 627, 661, 743, 768, 811
Bennett, Joan, 570, 827
Bernard of Clairvaux, Saint, 700, 784, 1001
Bernini, Gian Lorenzo, 523, 549, 570, 599, 622, 645, 658, 711, 735, 794, 847, 873, 921, 924, 980, 982, 1017, 1018, 1054, 1175
Berry, Lloyd E., 976
Bertaut, Jean, 1024
Bertonasco, Marc F., 1155
Bible (New Testament, Old Testament), 6, 109, 163, 448, 461, 469, 481, 530, 559, 609, 619, 625, 644, 684, 705, 735, 739, 894, 925, 939, 944, 965, 971, 992, 1032, 1043, 1053, 1088, 1106, 1110, 1156, 1157, 1164, 1165, 1181
Bibliographical information: Crashaw autographs, 532; primary, 227, 237, 294, 302, 343, 346, 404, 443, 470, 593, 596, 686, 755, 810, 1069; manuscripts, 274, 278, 280, 441, 470, 571,

745, 750, 912, 974, 1121; secondary, 346, 617, 619, 661, 719, 894, 896, 993, 1002, 1076, 1114, 1118, 1148, 1152, 1166; textual problems and revisions, 194, 195, 196, 197, 198, 280, 398, 636, 706, 725, 745, 1160
Biographical accounts and information (excluding biographical sketches), 14, 17, 18, 21, 29, 35, 37, 40, 45, 46, 53, 56, 60, 64, 66, 74, 75, 78, 79, 83, 89, 97, 99, 101, 102, 103, 106, 222, 228, 237, 246, 251, 263, 276, 282, 288, 302, 322, 336, 342, 346, 352, 354, 366, 374, 380, 384, 426, 469, 470, 475, 476, 524, 532, 540, 547, 559, 576, 619, 665, 821, 848, 907, 934, 940, 943, 1039, 1059, 1123, 1124, 1163, 1179
Blackmore, Richard, 151
Blackmur, R. P., 1036
Blake, William, 277, 465, 697, 1015, 1023, 1095
Blakiston, Francis, 943
Boase, Alan, 827
Bonarscius (Carolus Scribanius), 1172
Book of Common Prayer, 639, 761, 1032
Borromini, Francesco, 1018
Botticelli, Sandro, 326, 369, 624
Bouchier, Elizabeth, 243
Bousset, Jacques Bénigne, 724
Bradley, F. H., 748
Bramston, Sir John, the Younger, 441
Brome, Alexander, 484
Brooke, Robert, 6, 40, 374
Brooke, Stopford, 327
Browne, Sir Thomas, 469, 707, 718
Browne, William, 342, 1013
Browning, Elizabeth Barrett, 168, 327, 358
Browning, Robert, 239, 279, 311, 416, 622
Bruno, Giordano, 746
Burns, Robert, 327, 372
Butler, Samuel, 208
Byron, George Gordon, Lord, 317, 327, 582, 1050

Cabilliau, Baudouin, 459, 598, 1023
Calvinists (Calvinism), 497, 1146. *See also* Protestants; Puritans
Cambridge Platonists, 469, 551
Campanella, Tommaso, 985, 1024
Campbell, J. Dykes, 359
Campbell, Nancy, 558

Campbell, Thomas, 126, 133, 135, 164, 635, 1050
Campion, Thomas, 661
Canfield, Benedict (Benet of Canfield), 1159
Capuchins, 1159
Car, Thomas (Miles Pinkney), 27, 99, 153, 227, 237, 610, 690, 709
Carew, Thomas, 82, 277, 301, 361, 450, 457, 527, 609, 662, 684, 710, 756, 785, 854, 865, 866, 898, 982, 991, 1023, 1135
Carmelites, 777
Cartwright, William, 501, 1013
Catholic Church (Roman Catholics, Roman Catholicism), 21, 26, 29, 40, 47, 51, 64, 78, 79, 83, 106, 109, 115, 125, 128, 149, 152, 158, 163, 179, 186, 200, 206, 237, 245, 249, 250, 257, 259, 291, 292, 299, 300, 302, 329, 331, 338, 341, 349, 354, 366, 377, 385, 389, 391, 395, 415, 435, 444, 448, 456, 459, 460, 466, 467, 474, 479, 480, 481, 485, 491, 493, 495, 499, 511, 520, 524, 525, 536, 538, 541, 542, 543, 548, 549, 558, 567, 579, 580, 582, 583, 589, 591, 619, 625, 626, 627, 640, 645, 659, 661, 664, 665, 666, 677, 678, 687, 688, 697, 700, 702, 707, 711, 714, 715, 728, 735, 743, 747, 754, 758, 761, 766, 783, 784, 788, 793, 825, 826, 831, 832, 835, 841, 848, 873, 934, 943, 956, 970, 995, 997, 998, 1008, 1013, 1024, 1026, 1027, 1032, 1053, 1092, 1097, 1102, 1103, 1112, 1113, 1126, 1137, 1142, 1146, 1147, 1158, 1165, 1170, 1172, 1176, 1177, 1179
Catullus, 453, 484, 614, 894, 1072
Cavalier poets, 240, 378, 982. *See also individual poets*
Chalmers, Alexander, 54
Chapman, George, 418, 508, 799
Charles I, 282, 352, 547, 586, 755
Chassignet, Jean-Baptiste, 870
Chesterton, G. K., 558
Chrysologus, Saint Peter, 797
Clark, J. H., 254
Classicism (Classical poets, allusions and influence), 281, 328, 347, 449, 497, 523, 575, 591, 621, 631, 668, 681, 684, 712, 739, 772, 835, 871, 908, 1023, 1043, 1100, 1110, 1167, 1179.

See also individual classical poets
Claudian, 614, 1110
Cleveland, John, 32, 86, 204, 450, 457, 642, 661, 756, 811, 866, 917, 992
Codrington, Robert, 226
Cole, William, 1123
Coleridge, E. H., 356, 359
Coleridge, Samuel Taylor, 149, 161, 165, 168, 171, 172, 173, 242, 254, 277, 279, 281, 284, 305, 307, 311, 326, 327, 330, 342, 347, 351, 356, 358, 359, 368, 369, 372, 379, 388, 400, 409, 415, 424, 438, 474, 493, 561, 563, 580, 588, 589, 656, 773, 830, 906, 1030, 1044
Coleridge, Sara, 372
Collet, Ferrar, 291, 380, 381, 540, 608
Collet, John, 14, 380
Collet, Mary, 14, 252, 354, 380, 549, 608, 934
Collins, William Wilkie, 362
Constable, Cuthbert, 69
Constable, Henry, 229
Cornaro, Luigi, 405, 406, 407
Corneille, Pierre, 565, 724
Cornwallis, Philip, 913
Correggio, Antonio Allegri da, 658
Cosin, John, 385, 524, 538
Counter-Reformation (Tridentine), 459, 499, 507, 508, 545, 549, 570, 578, 591, 601, 619, 627, 658, 681, 697, 700, 702, 707, 711, 717, 718, 735, 754, 759, 760, 764, 766, 776, 786, 788, 794, 796, 817, 838, 839, 846, 861, 869, 870, 886, 916, 927, 929, 937, 966, 968, 980, 1014, 1023, 1033, 1034, 1053, 1064, 1071, 1073, 1097, 1129, 1144, 1165, 1172, 1174
Cowley, Abraham, 57, 67, 73, 75, 86, 87, 89, 97, 99, 100, 102, 113, 114, 130, 131, 138, 148, 150, 151, 156, 159, 171, 186, 189, 191, 204, 237, 241, 295, 302, 305, 308, 315, 327, 333, 342, 344, 349, 358, 360, 361, 411, 416, 417, 433, 450, 457, 458, 463, 474, 493, 516, 519, 521, 527, 545, 581, 586, 631, 644, 661, 693, 708, 709, 721, 756, 786, 798, 811, 840, 844, 854, 898, 903, 917, 949, 984, 991, 999, 1022, 1151, 1171
Crabbe, George, 438
Craik, George L., 327
Crane, Hart, 563, 600, 747
Crashaw, Elizabeth (poet's stepmother), 222, 228
Crashaw, John, 322
Crashaw, Richard
—Adaptations, imitations, and borrowings, 34, 39, 61, 68, 71, 72, 80, 219, 264, 447
—Collected editions, 6, 16, 20, 27, 42, 43, 48, 93, 102, 119, 186, 191, 237, 272, 274, 305, 318, 319, 323, 336, 342, 389, 470, 541, 709, 1002, 1003, 1054
—Editions of single poems published in the twentieth century, 353, 364, 367, 371, 375, 376, 382, 390, 564, 885
—Greek translations of epigrams and translations of Greek verse, 25, 42, 1002
—Original poems on Crashaw, 317, 528, 643, 694
—Paintings by Crashaw at Cambridge, 282, 547
—Poems attributed to Crashaw, 67, 69, 70, 84, 97, 99, 101, 104, 105, 119, 185, 213, 230, 275, 423, 447, 568, 608, 635, 913
—Poems that mention Crashaw, 19, 23, 24, 30, 31, 46, 57, 59, 132, 146, 969
—Poems published individually in the seventeenth century, 1, 2, 3, 4, 5, 7, 8, 9, 10, 12, 13, 15, 25, 28, 36, 44, 49
—Romances, novels, in which Crashaw appears as a character, 252, 393, 536
—Translations of Latin Poems, 42, 48, 180, 232, 237, 262, 319, 333, 772, 1002, 1068, 1089
—Translations into foreign languages, 408, 459, 585, 612, 615, 623, 646, 663, 673, 679, 692, 727, 800, 819, 833, 851, 855, 866, 881, 891, 902, 942, 965, 981, 990, 1009, 1013, 1086, 1110, 1111
Crashaw, Richard (poet's godfather), 320, 322
Crashaw, Richard (son of John Crashaw), 322
Crashaw, William, 54, 222, 228, 237, 263, 282, 325, 354, 374, 405, 406, 476, 525, 532, 547, 575, 608, 700, 761, 769, 802, 848, 934, 1083, 1088, 1105, 1172
Crew, Sir Randolph, 263
Cromwell, Henry, 62, 63
Cust, Henry J. C., 465
Czepko, Daniel, 678

Dali, Salvador, 791
D'Annunzio, Gabriele, 584, 966
Dante, Alighieri, 173, 242, 394, 463, 471, 483, 491, 565, 676, 1060
D'Aubigné, Agrippa, 735, 754, 1067
Davenant, Sir William, 661, 866
Davies, Sir John, 125, 754
Denbigh, Countess of (Cecilia Mary Clifford Feilding), 27, 243, 377, 395, 538
Denonain, Jean-Jacques, 827
Descartes, René (Cartesianism), 666, 753
Desportes, Philip, 1107
Devotional tradition and theory, 525, 739, 764, 825, 958, 1011, 1103, 1139, 1140, 1159, 1177. See also Liturgy; Meditation
Dickinson, Edward, 852
Dickinson, Emily, 503, 556, 611, 747, 852
Diego de Estella, 860
Dionysius the Aeropagite, 548, 729, 894, 978, 979, 1154, 1161
Dissociation of sensibility (unified sensibility), 417, 463, 617, 638, 733, 734, 738, 740, 748, 752, 803, 808, 809, 887
Dix, Gregory, 641
Dolce, Lodovico, 304
Dolci, Carlo, 520, 780
Donne, Anne, 912
Donne, John, 32, 86, 131, 138, 160, 169, 171, 186, 204, 208, 239, 293, 299, 302, 316, 326, 334, 341, 349, 360, 362, 378, 383, 387, 403, 416, 417, 419, 420, 421, 438, 450, 454, 457, 459, 463, 464, 469, 472, 474, 477, 491, 497, 503, 507, 508, 516, 518, 519, 523, 527, 529, 541, 546, 550, 551, 552, 556, 561, 562, 572, 575, 581, 583, 585, 588, 590, 591, 595, 598, 599, 600, 603, 607, 611, 617, 619, 622, 624, 627, 628, 632, 638, 642, 649, 655, 657, 658, 659, 661, 662, 667, 668, 670, 671, 674, 678, 679, 681, 683, 688, 691, 697, 700, 701, 702, 704, 707, 708, 710, 712, 713, 714, 717, 718, 721, 722, 723, 724, 730, 731, 734, 737, 738, 741, 747, 751, 752, 756, 757, 759, 763, 764, 767, 772, 774, 775, 778, 780, 784, 786, 787, 790, 801, 805, 815, 825, 826, 833, 835, 839, 840,

846, 850, 853, 854, 859, 860, 866, 867, 870, 889, 892, 894, 895, 897, 900, 902, 908, 909, 911, 915, 916, 918, 919, 922, 930, 938, 939, 940, 941, 945, 949, 951, 954, 960, 966, 967, 984, 991, 1005, 1006, 1013, 1014, 1019, 1023, 1029, 1033, 1044, 1054, 1060, 1062, 1067, 1094, 1096, 1101, 1104, 1115, 1116, 1118, 1132, 1135, 1139, 1141, 1145, 1146, 1157, 1165, 1168, 1170, 1175
Dorrington, Theophilus, 39
Dowden, Edward, 351
Drayton, Michael, 1029
Drummond, William, 211, 716, 1013
Dryden, John, 128, 182, 204, 205, 221, 254, 264, 275, 326, 417, 421, 430, 450, 455, 497, 599, 607, 661, 880, 1174
Du Bartas, Guillaume de Salluste, 512
Duggan, Eileen, 558
Dullaert, Heiman, 870
Du Moulin, Peter, 621
Duncon, Eleazar, 1163
Dunton, John, 1029
Duport, James, 621
Durant, Marc, 754

El Greco, 459, 522, 598, 735, 880, 1096
Eliot, T. S., 494, 563, 570, 589, 617, 638, 657, 704, 710, 733, 737, 738, 747, 748, 751, 803, 808, 827, 829, 880, 887, 1036, 1044, 1060, 1170
Elizabethan poets and poetry, 309, 455, 479, 508, 572, 619, 731, 741, 1011. See also individual Elizabethan poets
Ellis, George, 119, 133, 189
Emakinono (Japanese picture scroll), 1136
Emblems (emblem books and emblematic), 357, 475, 517, 518, 549, 551, 554, 575, 585, 591, 616, 619, 627, 644, 679, 698, 708, 718, 729, 739, 743, 754, 777, 823, 871, 919, 948, 963, 967, 986, 1006, 1019, 1026, 1034, 1040, 1053, 1071, 1104, 1115, 1136, 1137, 1155, 1159, 1162, 1164, 1165
Emerson, Ralph Waldo, 581
Empson, William, 709, 822, 856
English College (Rome), 251, 252, 943, 1039, 1059
Engravings in Carmen Deo Nostro, 27,

104, 191, 196, 237, 302, 336, 487, 518, 554, 616, 698, 709
Erasmus, Desiderius, 499
Etheredge, Sir George, 1121
Eucharist, 420, 640, 766, 1027, 1034, 1088, 1176
Euphuism, 240, 625, 832, 902

Faber, Frederick William, 520
Fairfax, Edward, 97
Fathers of the Church (Patristics), 475, 777. *See also individual Church Fathers*
Felltham, Owen, 208
Fénelon, François de Salignac de la Mothe, 140
Ferrar, John, 14, 380, 608
Ferrar, Nicholas, 14, 101, 291, 323, 354, 405, 406, 407, 472, 575, 608, 700
Farrar, Nicholas, Jr., 101
Fleming, Paul, 870, 1024
Fletcher, Giles, 171, 299, 342, 425, 609, 619, 627, 661, 671, 741, 754, 781, 786, 850, 870, 894, 895, 902, 1067, 1071
Fletcher, John, 32, 117, 688, 880, 1013
Fletcher, Phineas, 171, 224, 342, 425, 781
Fontanella, Girolamo, 882
Ford, John, 117, 127, 129, 148, 167, 168, 212, 244, 260, 272, 293, 303, 342, 438, 551, 564
Framyot, Archbishop André, 690
Francis de Sales, Saint, 690, 964, 1026
Francis of Assisi, Saint, 389
Frank, Mark, 185
Fruitlands (Harvard, Massachusetts), 399
Fry, Christopher, 795
Fugitive Poets, 704
Fuller, Margaret, 223
Fuller, Thomas, 208

Gaddi, Taddeo, 409
Garth, Samuel, 128
Gascoigne, George, 208
Gaulli, Giovanni Battista, 982
Gibbons, Grinling, 982
Gilfillan, George, 327, 495
Giorgione (Giorgio Barbarelli), 624
Góngora y Argote, Luis de (Gongorism), 257, 306, 307, 459, 483, 485, 488, 512, 553, 796, 803, 833, 861, 987, 1024, 1067
Gosse, Edmund, 255, 260, 261, 342,

372, 709
Gottschalk, Laura Riding, 494
Gourmont, Rémy de, 733
Gracián, Baltasar, 746, 749, 753
Gray, David, 272
Gray, Thomas, 93, 302, 723, 1085
Greek Anthology, The, 708
Greenburg, Samuel B., 747
Greene, Robert, 555
Gregory of Nazianzanus, Saint, 19, 1171
Grierson, Herbert J. C., 475, 751, 829
Grosart, Alexander B., 54, 236, 342, 344, 474, 593, 769, 787, 803, 810
Grotius, Hugo, 635
Gryphius, Andreas, 678, 724, 870, 1024, 1067
Guarini, Giovanni Battista, 865, 966
Guyon, Jeanne Marie Bouvier de la Motke, 784
Gwinn, Owen, 325

Habington, William, 250, 469, 497, 609, 710, 1052
Hagreen, Philip, 564
Hall, Joseph, 764
Hallam, Henry, 156
Hardy, Thomas, 558, 563, 908
Harvey, Christopher, 67, 84, 97, 99, 105, 119, 388, 698
Hawkins, Henry, 554
Haydn, Franz Joseph, 262
Hayley, William, 54, 100, 103, 119, 189
Hazlitt, William, 168, 171, 372, 709
Headley, Henry, 108, 119, 120, 172, 189
Heber, Reginald, 264
Hemingway, Ernest, 1057
Henrietta Maria (Queen), 249, 377, 521, 586, 1020
Herbert, George, 16, 19, 23, 36, 40, 44, 58, 59, 67, 82, 97, 99, 102, 111, 119, 131, 137, 146, 151, 154, 155, 163, 171, 193, 200, 205, 207, 240, 241, 242, 253, 281, 284, 291, 299, 300, 309, 321, 326, 330, 334, 337, 339, 345, 349, 350, 360, 372, 373, 378, 387, 388, 405, 406, 407, 409, 416, 417, 419, 420, 428, 433, 439, 449, 450, 455, 463, 465, 469, 472, 477, 478, 479, 485, 490, 491, 497, 499, 500, 507, 510, 514, 515, 516, 518, 522, 523, 527, 529, 531, 535, 541, 542, 543, 551, 552, 562, 565, 573, 579, 580, 581, 582, 585, 587, 590, 591, 595, 598, 599, 602, 603, 607,

609, 611, 617, 619, 621, 622, 628,
630, 631, 632, 639, 647, 655, 657,
659, 661, 662, 663, 671, 672, 674,
681, 683, 684, 691, 694, 696, 697,
700, 701, 702, 706, 707, 710, 712,
717, 718, 720, 721, 722, 724, 727,
730, 734, 741, 742, 747, 752, 756,
757, 758, 759, 762, 764, 766, 767,
768, 772, 775, 776, 778, 779, 780,
786, 787, 788, 805, 810, 815, 825,
835, 836, 839, 840, 846, 850, 853,
854, 865, 866, 867, 870, 877, 889,
892, 893, 894, 895, 897, 900, 902,
911, 916, 918, 919, 922, 925, 927,
930, 938, 939, 940, 945, 954, 956,
957, 960, 966, 967, 968, 972, 982,
984, 990, 991, 1005, 1011, 1013,
1014, 1023, 1044, 1052, 1054, 1058,
1060, 1066, 1067, 1074, 1081, 1094,
1101, 1104, 1113, 1116, 1118, 1120,
1128, 1129, 1133, 1135, 1139, 1140,
1142, 1144, 1151, 1165, 1176, 1179
Herbert of Cherbury, Edward, Baron,
417, 529, 742, 840, 866
Herne (Hearne), Samuel, 969
Herrick, Robert, 169, 277, 361, 479,
541, 595, 607, 626, 712, 785, 991,
1014, 1023, 1079, 1104, 1139, 1142
Herringman, Henry, 41
Hickes, George, 39
Hill, Aaron, 180, 232, 254, 262, 264,
333
Hindi Aṣṭachāpa Poets, 1074
Hobbes, Thomas, 782, 792
Hofmannswaldau, Hermann von, 1024
Holdsworth, Edward, 940
Homer, 19, 452
Hopkins, Gerard Manley, 517, 544, 565,
579, 622, 654, 747, 831, 951
Hopkins, John, 928
Hopton, Lady Susanna, 39
Horace, 19, 452, 614
Hosain, A. S., 506
Hoskyns-Abrahall, John, 259
Howden (Hovedon), John of, 1110
Hugo, Hermann, 554, 1023
Hugo, Victor, 584
Hunt, Leigh, 168, 171, 190
Hussey, Walter, 685
Hutchinson, F. E., 504
Hutton, Edward, 328
Huygens, Constantijn, 1024

Imagist poets, 461

Imago primi saeculi S. J., 616
Incarnation and Incarnationalism, 403,
416, 420, 591, 703, 713, 1001, 1032,
1034, 1061, 1087, 1113, 1149, 1161,
1173, 1177
Ingelo, Nathaniel, 38, 41
Innocent X, Pope, 17, 18, 29, 35, 366,
377

Jacopone da Todi, 472, 591, 764
James, Henry, 542
Jennings, Richard, 686
Jermyn, Lord Henry, 395
Jesuits (Society of Jesus), 330, 454, 459,
463, 475, 508, 516, 522, 554, 570,
575, 578, 591, 598, 616, 619, 621,
679, 698, 724, 761, 777, 786, 796,
902, 911, 929, 941, 943, 957, 989,
1005, 1018, 1023, 1034, 1064, 1066,
1116, 1165, 1172. *See also* Saint Ignatius Loyola
Jesus Christ and Christology, 332, 357,
383, 396, 420, 435, 444, 481, 499,
520, 535, 559, 566, 574, 591, 624,
625, 676, 677, 697, 700, 702, 703,
705, 707, 787, 796, 843, 856, 894,
904, 934, 944, 951, 964, 965, 970,
985, 1075, 1077, 1087, 1088, 1090,
1091, 1101, 1106, 1112, 1117, 1119,
1129, 1137, 1149, 1159, 1161, 1164,
1176, 1177, 1178
John Inglesant, 252, 260
John of the Cross, Saint, 435, 469, 508,
700, 860, 945, 1016, 1181
Johnson, Lionel, 409
Johnson, Samuel, 186, 189, 430, 437,
457, 512, 590, 723, 732, 756, 940,
1040, 1073, 1115
Jonson, Ben (Jonsonian), 32, 379, 438,
619, 631, 668, 710, 714, 889, 908,
938, 939, 962, 1011, 1023, 1101,
1135, 1173
Joyce, James, 652
Julian of Norwich, 549, 594

Kant, Immanuel, 1091
Keats, John, 190, 194, 218, 272, 305,
317, 327, 334, 372, 414, 467, 483,
498, 503, 549, 551, 580, 584, 589,
697, 718, 803, 998, 1054
Keble, John, 171, 242
Keightly, Thomas, 1059
Keightly, William, 1059
Ken, Thomas, 242, 472

Kierkegaard, Sören, 1057
Kilmer, Joyce, 558
King, Henry, 417, 472, 549, 854, 866, 898, 1023

La Ceppède, Jean de, 754, 870, 937, 1024
Laforgue, Jules, 733
Lamb, Charles, 168
Laney, Benjamin, 374, 1088
Lanfranco, Giovanni, 1018
Laudian Movement (Laudianism), 479, 522, 575, 619, 700, 761, 907, 1088, 1139, 1154, 1163
Leavis, F. R., 691
Lee, Nathaniel, 553
Leishman, J. B., 570
Lessius, Leonard of Louvain, 405, 406, 407, 1025
Letter from Leyden, 14, 380, 470, 532, 997
Lever, Christopher, 766
Liber Memorialis (St. John's College, Cambridge), 282, 547
Lidyat, John, 404
Literature of tears tradition, 317, 764, 797, 956, 1104, 1130
Little Gidding, 101, 185, 248, 252, 291, 354, 380, 393, 396, 472, 479, 522, 575, 591, 598, 608, 700, 761, 766, 804, 821, 934, 1025, 1104, 1179
Little St. Mary's Church (Cambridge), 66, 74, 246, 288, 577
Liturgy (Liturgical), 237, 385, 452, 493, 499, 559, 619, 689, 754, 766, 788, 793, 958, 965, 968, 1001, 1005, 1074, 1088, 1101, 1137, 1139, 1154, 1164, 1170, 1176, 1177, 1181
Lloyd, David, 470
Lodge, Thomas, 304
Longfellow, Henry Wadsworth, 327
Lorrain, Claude, 735
Lorrain, Jean, 584
Lovelace, Richard, 309, 342, 527, 710, 898, 1013, 1022, 1041
Lowell, Robert, 704, 983
Loyola, Saint Ignatius (Ignatian), 508, 619, 645, 978, 986, 1005, 1034, 1104, 1116. *See also* Jesuits; Meditation
Lubrano, Jacopo, 833
Luyken, Jan, 823, 870
Lysons, Samuel, 100, 177

Mabbott, Maureen Cobb, 1141

Macauley, Thomas Babington, 259
Macdonald, George, 327, 351
MacLeish, Archibald, 494, 747
Malapert, Charles, 598
Malherbe, François de, 937
Mannerism (Mannerist), 780, 795, 832, 833, 886, 900, 902, 909, 1010, 1096, 1097, 1139, 1162, 1175
Manning, Stephen, 1026
Mapletoft, Robert, 608
Marcellini, Valerio, 716
Marenzio, Luca, 716
Marino, Gianbattista (Marinism), 19, 63, 95, 98, 99, 107, 122, 123, 131, 139, 147, 148, 154, 160, 183, 193, 213, 217, 224, 257, 279, 281, 300, 303, 304, 306, 307, 315, 321, 327, 341, 349, 350, 368, 373, 386, 398, 416, 420, 428, 430, 435, 438, 449, 459, 463, 483, 485, 489, 512, 520, 522, 527, 533, 541, 551, 552, 553, 575, 584, 591, 599, 605, 619, 627, 631, 647, 655, 661, 668, 672, 679, 681, 683, 688, 696, 708, 721, 739, 781, 786, 788, 796, 803, 811, 833, 850, 861, 865, 867, 870, 871, 872, 882, 883, 884, 890, 894, 895, 902, 911, 919, 957, 966, 980, 987, 989, 994, 1005, 1006, 1008, 1018, 1023, 1024, 1040, 1043, 1058, 1064, 1066, 1067, 1068, 1071, 1097, 1100, 1107, 1115, 1116, 1132
Markham, Gervase, 555
Marlowe, Christopher, 555, 864
Marshall, William, 4
Marston, John, 208
Martial, 712, 894, 908, 1173
Martin, L. C., 475, 483, 486, 487, 494, 540, 593, 725, 805, 810, 821, 913
Martz, Louis L., 829, 941, 1053
Marvell, Andrew, 163, 208, 299, 340, 413, 417, 479, 516, 545, 581, 604, 607, 662, 671, 691, 710, 729, 741, 752, 759, 764, 786, 789, 798, 815, 840, 850, 854, 859, 866, 870, 875, 895, 900, 911, 919, 922, 936, 967, 982, 984, 991, 1013, 1016, 1022, 1023, 1044, 1060, 1067, 1068, 1118, 1121, 1130, 1133, 1135, 1139, 1140
Mary (the Mother of Christ) (Mariology), 125, 383, 459, 474, 520, 535, 549, 578, 580, 600, 633, 700, 703, 787, 856, 944, 951, 1013, 1077, 1087, 1088, 1104, 1106, 1110, 1172, 1177

Mary Magdalene, Saint, 401, 435, 455, 456, 462, 520, 531, 545, 553, 563, 566, 595, 619, 700, 707, 712, 721, 730, 777, 787, 796, 797, 849, 882, 883, 914, 948, 952, 956, 964, 1086, 1090, 1107, 1127, 1129, 1159
Masque, 788
Mauburnus, Joannes (Jean Mombaer), 764
Maynard, Theodore, 558
Mazzeo, Joseph, 829
Meditation (meditative tradition, discursive meditation), 591, 764, 798, 807, 825, 838, 853, 889, 938, 941, 964, 968, 984, 1005, 1024, 1026, 1034, 1053, 1125, 1129, 1139, 1140, 1150, 1165, 1176. _See also_ Devotional Tradition
Meredith, George, 455
Merton, Thomas, 667
Metaphysical poetry (metaphysical tradition), 87, 417, 419, 420, 430, 463, 464, 503, 506, 516, 546, 552, 556, 561, 562, 563, 591, 598, 599, 617, 627, 630, 642, 651, 659, 666, 678, 704, 708, 710, 723, 730, 737, 741, 746, 747, 749, 751, 752, 753, 754, 756, 765, 787, 801, 803, 807, 808, 823, 827, 829, 831, 832, 840, 854, 870, 880, 881, 889, 895, 900, 918, 922, 929, 938, 940, 954, 958, 959, 967, 980, 982, 984, 991, 1000, 1006, 1013, 1017, 1020, 1023, 1024, 1033, 1036, 1040, 1042, 1044, 1051, 1058, 1071, 1080, 1085, 1100, 1115, 1134, 1140, 1167, 1168, 1179. _See also individual metaphysical poets_
Meynell, Alice, 437, 550, 589
Milton, John, 76, 90, 91, 92, 93, 94, 95, 97, 102, 107, 108, 112, 118, 122, 123, 127, 135, 139, 147, 158, 163, 165, 171, 173, 189, 200, 204, 213, 219, 254, 272, 275, 281, 284, 302, 304, 317, 327, 329, 333, 340, 342, 347, 355, 363, 369, 378, 379, 400, 409, 417, 425, 428, 440, 444, 466, 490, 493, 512, 515, 541, 549, 558, 560, 561, 567, 578, 595, 607, 618, 631, 634, 644, 658, 661, 662, 674, 676, 691, 697, 701, 721, 723, 724, 758, 764, 766, 772, 774, 780, 786, 805, 873, 880, 902, 904, 919, 930, 939, 954, 980, 990, 994, 1020, 1029, 1032, 1036, 1044, 1054, 1064, 1085,

1087, 1101, 1103, 1104, 1120, 1151, 1168, 1170, 1175
Minozzi, Pierfrancesco, 459, 753
Mīrām Bāī, 1074
Montagu, Edward, Second Earl of Manchester, 64
Montaigne, Michel Eyquem de, 499
Monteverdi, Claudio, 882, 1162
Montgomery, James, 171
Moore, Tom, 582
Moravians, 80, 892, 910
More, Henry, 701
Moseley, Humphrey, 24, 38, 502
Motin, Peter, 1024
Mourgues, Odette de, 827, 929, 1062
Mozart, Wolfgang Amadeus, 620
Murillo, Bartolomé Esteban, 459, 522, 598, 735, 880, 989, 1096, 1175
Music, 626, 631, 644, 724, 736, 818, 857, 876, 909, 950, 1034, 1063, 1162
Musical settings, 80, 436, 446, 482, 660, 685, 771, 806, 842, 867, 892, 910, 926, 946, 973, 1045, 1071, 1138, 1169
Mysticism, 388, 424, 427, 428, 433, 435, 438, 439, 452, 461, 469, 489, 490, 499, 517, 525, 541, 548, 591, 594, 595, 619, 625, 653, 684, 700, 775, 840, 915, 916, 945, 971, 988, 1034, 1078, 1104, 1114, 1119, 1126, 1150, 1161, 1165, 1181
Myth (mythological), 781, 1012, 1037, 1077, 1100

Nakao, Setsuko, 1136
Neill, Kerby, 812
Neri, Saint Philip, 549
Newman, John Henry Cardinal, 237, 242, 284, 379, 665, 666, 677
Nicols, Richard, 943
Normanton, Thomas, 30, 1059
Norris, John, 585
Nowell, John, 1163
Numerology 1112, 1177

Oldham, John, 609, 1121
Ovid (Ovidian), 19, 575, 712, 1082
Owen, John, 459, 621, 661
Oxford Movement, 587

Palestrina, Giovanni Pierluigi da, 1034
Palgrave, Francis Turner, 327, 372
Palotta, Giovanni Evangelista Cardinal, 21, 37, 227, 1039

Parnell, Thomas, 585
Pascal, Blaise, 140
Pastoralism, 693, 735, 781, 984, 1032, 1054
Patmore, Coventry, 308, 369, 388, 409, 415, 424, 530, 549, 601, 622, 657, 709, 884
Payne, John, 2, 593, 596
Peckard, Peter, 185
Pellegrini, Matteo, 753
Percivale, Sir John, 35
Peter, John, 1026
Peterhouse (Cambridge), 21, 26, 40, 64, 78, 352, 374, 380, 381, 392, 448, 470, 524, 532, 540, 577, 681, 907, 1163, 1171
Petrarch (Petrarchism), 63, 131, 138, 600, 746, 1107, 1137
Phillips, Ambrose, 438, 551, 564
Phillips, Edward, 450, 1085
Phillips, Peregrine, 90, 91, 92, 94, 96, 99, 119, 136, 189, 512
Pierrepont, Francis, 34, 50
Pilgrim Book (English College, Rome), 943, 1039
Pindar, 19, 631
Plato (Platonism), 332, 424, 469, 603, 978, 1057
Playters, Thomas, 1059
Plotinus, 1057
Poe, Edgar Allen, 582, 584
Pomfret, John, 939
Pope, Alexander, 77, 82, 85, 89, 90, 91, 92, 93, 94, 96, 97, 102, 104, 106, 107, 110, 114, 119, 121, 128, 131, 135, 136, 148, 149, 152, 154, 155, 158, 159, 162, 171, 172, 189, 214, 216, 241, 250, 253, 254, 257, 262, 270, 272, 279, 281, 302, 307, 317, 327, 330, 333, 342, 369, 372, 378, 379, 397, 400, 424, 463, 493, 512, 520, 560, 580, 582, 588, 590, 609, 649, 707, 709, 718, 721, 817, 940, 1020, 1021, 1085, 1174
Pound, Ezra, 600, 1036
Poussin, Nicolas, 735
Pozzo, Andrea, 735, 1175
Praz, Mario, 454, 483, 486, 589, 672, 746, 803, 812, 822, 932, 1060, 1131
Précieux poetry, 754
"Preface to the Reader, The" (1646, 1648), 16, 606, 610
Prior, Matthew, 939, 1029
Procter, Bryan W. 171

Prosody, 308, 361, 411, 600, 618, 619, 621, 631, 787, 789, 865, 917, 1022, 1071, 1135, 1169
Protestants (Protestantism), 125, 128, 162, 397, 479, 499, 525, 627, 681, 698, 758, 761, 766, 929, 998, 1024, 1027, 1032, 1102, 1112, 1137, 1146, 1147, 1165. *See also* Anglicans; Puritans
Prynne, William, 450
Puritans (Puritanism, Presbyterianism, and Nonconformism), 56, 401, 423, 425, 444, 452, 509, 523, 558, 559, 587, 713, 715, 761, 764, 766, 783, 816, 824, 907, 1026, 1113, 1120, 1154

Quarles, Francis, 97, 102, 119, 137, 163, 171, 173, 179, 186, 208, 293, 337, 379, 450, 457, 479, 518, 579, 585, 661, 698, 701, 710, 776, 786, 850, 866, 939, 963
Quevedo y Villegas, Francisco Gómez, 322, 1024

R., T. (translator of Marino, 1675), 95, 97, 184, 213, 215, 217
Racine, Jean Baptiste, 565
Rainbow, Edward, 187
Raleigh, Walter A., 954
Ramism, 746, 801, 824, 1080
Randolph, Thomas, 32
Ransom, John Crowe, 563, 652, 747, 1036
Reformation views and theology, 640, 870, 1104, 1146
Remi de Beauvais, 1159
Rémond, François, 459, 598, 1023
Reputation and critical reception, 272, 305, 327, 342, 372, 450, 457, 458, 470, 541, 560, 589, 619, 709, 751, 812, 831, 910, 927, 969, 1004, 1021, 1026, 1052, 1114, 1136
Retrospective Review, The (1820–1828), 1052
Revius, Jacobus, 870
Richards, I. A., 563, 1036
Richardson, John, 118
Robinson, Thomas, 401
Rochester, Earl of. *See* Wilmot, John
Rococo, 273, 620, 836
Rölker, Bernard, 210
Rolle, Richard, 379, 517, 622
Roman Breviary, 435, 1001, 1039

Romantic poets and poetry (Romanticism), 379, 457, 515, 551, 561, 563, 585, 589, 737, 767, 823, 1036
Roscommon, Wentworth Dillon, 4th Earl of, 82, 107, 171, 174, 199, 211, 259, 272
Rossetti, Christina, 417, 419, 471, 622
Rossetti, Dante Gabriel, 242, 284, 341, 584
Rous, Francis, 761
Routh, Helen, 380
Routh, John, 380
Rubens, Peter Paul, 459, 522, 549, 570, 598, 735, 880, 989, 1018, 1175

Sackville, Thomas, 98
Sacramentalism (Sacraments), 499, 559, 619, 657, 713, 966, 968, 1005, 1037, 1112, 1137, 1164
Sacred parody, 825, 966, 984, 1024
St. John's College (Cambridge), 282, 325, 547, 802
Saint-Amant, Marc-Antoine de, 754, 796, 1024
Saints and martyrs (hagiography), 358, 401, 420, 459, 499, 509, 549, 559, 578, 580, 619, 624, 700, 754, 982, 1088, 1177. *See also individual saints*
Saintsbury, George, 342
Saltmarsh, John, 621
Samaha, Edward J., 976
Sancroft, Archbishop William, 69, 70, 185, 810
Sandaeus, Maximilianus (van der Sandt), 357
Sanderson, T., 810
Sandys, George, 97, 107, 337, 479, 609, 939
Sarbiewski, Casimire, 783
Sassoferrato, Giovanni Battista, 780
Scheffler, Johann, 678, 687, 870
Schirmer, David, 870
Schöne, Albrecht, 1155
Science (New Science, New Philosophy), 726, 870, 897, 1128
Sedley, Charles, 1121
Seghers, Gerhard, 982
Selden, John, 99, 119, 136, 153, 189, 222
Senhouse, Roger, 686
Sforza-Pallavicino, Pietro, Cardinal, 753
Shakespeare, William, 32, 108, 158, 272, 286, 327, 342, 418, 541, 549,

558, 572, 676, 691, 718, 747, 850, 1175
Shaw, George Bernard, 676
Sheils, Robert, 1124
Shelford, Robert, 1088
Shelley, Percy Bysshe, 186, 190, 193, 194, 195, 198, 218, 254, 257, 272, 273, 277, 281, 284, 286, 290, 293, 300, 305, 307, 326, 327, 334, 337, 341, 342, 347, 349, 369, 372, 379, 387, 391, 396, 402, 409, 415, 420, 434, 438, 449, 459, 463, 479, 483, 485, 493, 507, 522, 541, 543, 551, 575, 582, 588, 589, 598, 626, 631, 647, 648, 658, 674, 683, 697, 718, 744, 793, 803, 884
Shibue, Tamotsu, 1136
Shirley, James, 1013
Sidney, Sir Philip, 32, 1170
Sitwell, Edith, 664, 704, 1115, 1145
Smart, Christopher, 975
Smethe, Symon, 381
Smith, Lady Margaret, 226
Songs (songbooks, song mode), 600, 750, 1014, 1139, 1169. *See also* Music
Southern, Henry, 135
Southey, Charles Cuthbert, 109
Southwell, Robert, 239, 242, 250, 304, 341, 369, 420, 435, 462, 469, 497, 499, 514, 517, 555, 565, 578, 579, 582, 598, 619, 627, 634, 661, 663, 671, 700, 702, 754, 764, 766, 786, 835, 839, 850, 860, 894, 902, 941, 982, 1054, 1071, 1174
Southwell, Sir Robert, 366
Spanish mystics, 533, 552, 553, 578, 647, 655, 663, 674, 702, 1005, 1066, 1078, 1116. *See also* Saint John of the Cross; Saint Teresa of Avila
Spee, Friedrich von, 257, 870
Spence, Joseph, 156, 940
Spenser, Edmund (Spenserians, Spenserianism), 19, 108, 154, 200, 272, 305, 379, 467, 575, 631, 668, 689, 691, 739, 776, 871, 909, 1012, 1023, 1042, 1067, 1115, 1170
Sponde, Jean de, 870
Sprat, Bishop Thomas, 86
Stanley, Arthur P., 259
Stanley, Thomas, 631
Sternhold, Thomas, 927
Stevens, Wallace, 704
Stewart, Richard, 538

Stillingfleet, Edward, 47
Strada, Famianus, 62, 76, 117, 148,
   156, 163, 167, 244, 279, 303, 438,
   533, 605, 631, 672, 736, 818, 857,
   867, 950
Strode, William, 1048
Suarez, Francesco, 1147
Suckling, Sir John, 208, 361, 527, 898,
   1014, 1023
Swinburne, Algernon Charles, 257, 277,
   279, 281, 293, 307, 334, 342, 351,
   372, 379, 387, 396, 409, 415, 420,
   459, 463, 467, 485, 495, 516, 522,
   527, 549, 551, 575, 582, 584, 589,
   598, 679, 709, 793
Sylvester, Joshua, 259, 902
Symbolists, 449, 747, 803, 808
The Synagogue. See Christopher Harvey
Sypher, Wylie, 709

Targa, Peter, 227
Tasso, Torquato, 19, 865
Tate, Allen, 563, 747, 1036
Taylor, Edward, 597, 1019, 1165
Temple, Sir William, 1089
Tennyson, Alfred Lord, 145, 277, 409,
   495, 691
Teresa of Avila, Saint, 99, 114, 115, 123,
   124, 152, 160, 165, 237, 242, 257,
   300, 317, 341, 368, 379, 383, 388,
   389, 394, 416, 435, 438, 456, 460,
   463, 469, 481, 500, 508, 511, 521,
   522, 539, 548, 549, 552, 553, 575,
   576, 591, 600, 612, 619, 628, 634,
   645, 646, 650, 653, 672, 683, 684,
   697, 700, 712, 731, 763, 775, 787,
   789, 796, 834, 849, 855, 860, 864,
   871, 883, 894, 911, 924, 934, 945,
   957, 970, 971, 980, 982, 1013, 1017,
   1030, 1056, 1077, 1097, 1114, 1117,
   1150, 1157, 1179
Tertullian, 246, 248
Tesauro, Emmanuele, 459, 746, 749,
   753, 1127
Testi, Fulvius, 420, 430
Theocritus, 19
Thérèse of Lisieux, Saint, 520
Thimelby, Edward, 121, 874, 943, 1059
Thomas, Dylan, 770, 813
Thomas of Celano, 591
Thompson, Francis, 295, 296, 297, 305,
   327, 358, 369, 388, 389, 391, 400,
   409, 415, 416, 417, 424, 428, 438,
439, 461, 464, 466, 474, 493, 527,
   530, 541, 549, 558, 587, 589, 631,
   657, 664, 697, 700, 709, 728, 776,
   788, 793, 830, 831, 855, 884, 951,
   957, 1093, 1141
Tintoretto, Jacopo, 1096
Tixall Poetry, 568, 874, 1059
Tourney, John, 6, 374, 1088
Townsend, Mrs. Richard, 173
Townshend, Aurelian, 866
Traherne, Thomas, 339, 349, 419, 427,
   439, 463, 465, 469, 485, 490, 527,
   541, 550, 591, 603, 662, 678, 700,
   710, 722, 724, 742, 764, 798, 823,
   866, 898, 925, 984, 990, 1005, 1016,
   1118, 1133, 1139, 1140, 1165
Trench, Richard Chenevix, 772
Tristan L'Hermite, François, 754
Turnbull, William B., 188, 194
Tutin, John Ramsden, 344, 348
Tuve, Rosemond, 749, 801, 824, 1080,
   1152
Tynan, Katharine, 558
Typology and typological, 818, 1106,
   1137, 1164, 1165, 1176
Typotius, Jacob, 616
Typus Mundi, 616

Urban VIII, Pope, 29, 435

Vaughan, Henry, 22, 171, 201, 253,
   293, 299, 321, 326, 334, 339, 342,
   345, 349, 350, 379, 383, 409, 416,
   417, 420, 427, 428, 439, 450, 457,
   463, 465, 469, 472, 477, 478, 479,
   485, 491, 507, 510, 514, 516, 523,
   527, 535, 541, 542, 549, 550, 552,
   553, 562, 565, 573, 579, 587, 591,
   599, 603, 604, 607, 609, 611, 622,
   628, 630, 655, 659, 661, 681, 691,
   700, 701, 707, 710, 722, 724, 734,
   742, 747, 756, 764, 766, 776, 779,
   785, 786, 788, 805, 815, 823, 826,
   835, 840, 850, 852, 853, 854, 860,
   866, 870, 877, 895, 898, 916, 917,
   919, 922, 925, 927, 930, 939, 984,
   990, 991, 1005, 1013, 1016, 1022,
   1023, 1094, 1101, 1118, 1133, 1139,
   1140, 1165
Vaughan, Thomas, 700
Vega Carpio, Lope Felix de, 797, 1024
Velásquez, Diego Rodriguez de, 982
Viau, Théophile de, 206, 754, 796, 870,

1024
Vida, Marco Girolamo, 180
Villon, François, 394, 565
Virgil, 19, 315, 396, 676
Virginia Company, 354
Vondel, Joost van den, 350, 420, 499, 700, 724, 870, 1067, 1107

Waller, A. R., 333, 334, 339, 344
Waller, Edmund, 204, 208, 272, 898, 917, 1013, 1029
Wallerstein, Ruth C., 770, 812, 963, 1085, 1155
Walpole, Horace, 177
Walton, Izaak, 472
Warnke, Frank, 929
Warren, Austin, 620, 627, 753, 812, 816, 822, 963, 1085, 1123
Warren, Robert Penn, 563, 747
Warton, Thomas, 86, 119, 162
Watson, Richard, 51, 524
Watt, Robert, 54
Watts, Isaac, 585, 676, 718, 783, 1063
Webster, John, 455
Wesley, Charles, 419, 601, 676, 718
West, Gilbert, 88
White, Helen C., 963
Whitlock, John, 34

Willey, Basil, 812
Williams, Archbishop John, 547
Williamson, George, 589, 627, 829
Willmott, Robert Aris, 158
Wilmot, John, Earl of Rochester, 898, 1121
Wilson, John, 867, 1169
Winstanley, William, 153, 450
Winters, Yvor, 709
Wither, George, 163, 419, 479, 1052
Wogan, Jo., 810
Wood, Anthony à, 153, 470
Woodoffe, Paul, 376
Wordsworth, William, 168, 173, 372, 561, 563, 826
Worthington, John, 38, 41, 486, 821
Wotton, Henry, 272, 327, 342, 472
Wriothesley, Henry, Earl of Southampton, 282, 325, 802
Wycherly, William, 128
Wylie, Elinor, 494, 704, 747

Yeats, William Butler, 563
Yelverton, Sir Henry, 263
Young, David, 327
Young, Edward, 93, 254, 302, 400

Zacharie of Lisieux, 1159

Index of Crashaw's Poems Mentioned in Annotations

Act. 8. On the baptized Aethiopian, 25
Ad Reginam, 3
Adoro Te, 39, 254, 411, 420, 424, 427, 491, 514, 583, 640, 685, 698, 775, 838, 930, 952, 968, 1010, 1055, 1108, 1179
Alexias, 96, 401, 484, 497, 575, 699, 1055
An Apologie for the fore-going Hymne, 115, 360, 576, 646, 653, 690, 745, 763, 970. See also Teresian poems (general)
The Authors Motto, 496, 690

Bulla, 15, 209, 274, 278, 459, 554, 772, 863, 1110, 1111

Charitas Nimia, 94, 342, 344, 411, 414, 437, 527, 535, 541, 619, 696, 702, 760, 865, 885, 922, 1024, 1034, 1055, 1114, 1164, 1179

Death's Lecture, 134, 402, 501, 1031, 1108, 1157, 1167
Description of a Religious House and Condition of Life, 65, 96, 252, 253, 354, 495, 1025, 1055
Dies Irae Dies Illa, 49, 61, 63, 82, 107, 141, 142, 161, 162, 171, 174, 175, 176, 199, 209, 211, 216, 220, 238, 249, 254, 259, 289, 313, 383, 389, 435, 460, 465, 497, 504, 509, 583, 611, 838, 1055, 1095, 1139, 1157, 1179

Easter day, 218, 390, 965, 1031, 1034, 1049, 1061
An Elegie on the death of Dr. Porter, 497
Elegies on Mr. Herrys (general), 200, 318, 396, 497, 521, 1167. See also Upon the Death of the most desired Mr. Herrys
An Elegy upon the death of Mr. Stanninow, 497, 863, 961, 1048
An Epitaph upon a Young Married Couple, 72, 111, 232, 338, 397, 447, 496, 633, 663, 667, 696, 800, 862, 866, 891, 983, 1013
An Epitaph Upon Mr. Ashton, 63, 71, 77, 92, 107, 171, 262, 285

Epithalamium, 441, 487, 614, 990, 1012, 1046, 1112, 1117, 1143, 1179

Fides quae sola justificat, non est sine Spe & Dilectione, 1163
The Flaming Heart, 115, 124, 250, 253, 277, 301, 307, 310, 311, 314, 323, 326, 337, 344, 351, 355, 372, 378, 379, 386, 397, 409, 411, 412, 427, 428, 433, 434, 449, 459, 460, 461, 463, 472, 480, 485, 487, 491, 496, 506, 511, 515, 516, 526, 527, 541, 545, 552, 553, 569, 585, 603, 626, 632, 634, 646, 647, 653, 657, 661, 672, 674, 676, 679, 683, 690, 695, 696, 702, 711, 715, 718, 720, 724, 730, 735, 760, 767, 784, 785, 793, 817, 837, 844, 849, 851, 858, 862, 864, 866, 871, 872, 886, 891, 919, 920, 921, 927, 934, 945, 966, 970, 980, 982, 987, 989, 990, 1013, 1023, 1028, 1031, 1034, 1046, 1070, 1091, 1098, 1108, 1115, 1117, 1136, 1140, 1147, 1150, 1157, 1170. See also Teresian poems (general)

Hymn for New Year's Day, 141, 329, 505, 911, 990, 1001, 1055, 1075, 1091, 1101, 1143, 1149, 1179
Hymn in the Assumption, 163, 254, 316, 350, 355, 411, 424, 468, 530, 544, 578, 583, 663, 699, 775, 909, 944, 965, 968, 1011, 1031, 1055, 1067, 1106, 1179
Hymn in the Glorious Epiphanie, 115, 116, 254, 267, 329, 332, 411, 460, 491, 505, 527, 541, 575, 619, 656, 712, 717, 718, 806, 842, 844, 894, 944, 951, 958, 961, 978, 982, 985, 1001, 1055, 1078, 1091, 1094, 1101, 1114, 1119, 1139, 1149, 1152, 1157, 1161, 1164, 1179, 1181
Hymn in the Holy Nativity, 154, 158, 163, 171, 174, 175, 207, 216, 218, 236, 254, 267, 283, 284, 304, 310, 311, 312, 316, 326, 329, 344, 355, 363, 364, 365, 367, 371, 372, 375, 376, 378, 382, 383, 410, 416, 420, 428, 435, 439, 440, 444, 446, 456, 465, 467, 468, 480, 482, 484, 487,

496, 505, 510, 515, 527, 537, 541,
558, 567, 575, 604, 615, 618, 623,
624, 631, 632, 647, 655, 661, 663,
664, 672, 676, 693, 695, 697, 702,
703, 724, 775, 814, 842, 847, 872,
886, 904, 930, 951, 961, 962, 968,
982, 984, 1001, 1010, 1013, 1023,
1032, 1045, 1054, 1055, 1061, 1087,
1091, 1097, 1101, 1103, 1104, 1119,
1120, 1136, 1149, 1152, 1170, 1179
A Hymn to Sainte Teresa, 109, 115, 116,
133, 143, 150, 256, 273, 277, 284,
309, 311, 314, 323, 331, 338, 339,
344, 349, 351, 356, 359, 361, 368,
369, 373, 378, 388, 400, 401, 409,
410, 416, 417, 419, 420, 424, 427,
435, 438, 456, 460, 463, 487, 489,
490, 506, 509, 511, 516, 520, 526,
541, 545, 552, 569, 618, 619, 631,
632, 646, 653, 655, 661, 674, 702,
717, 730, 745, 760, 767, 775, 788,
789, 833, 837, 839, 854, 855, 862,
865, 866, 871, 875, 878, 906, 916,
920, 921, 922, 924, 925, 934, 945,
949, 957, 959, 961, 962, 970, 982,
984, 988, 1015, 1016, 1017, 1018,
1024, 1028, 1030, 1046, 1051, 1056,
1057, 1058, 1067, 1073, 1091, 1097,
1104, 1108, 1119, 1147, 1157, 1164,
1166, 1175. See also Teresian poems
(general)
Hymn to the Name of Jesus, 68, 142,
154, 161, 163, 165, 175, 193, 235,
254, 293, 329, 344, 351, 355, 411,
416, 435, 436, 451, 460, 466, 480,
495, 506, 527, 541, 575, 597, 616,
618, 626, 631, 661, 676, 693, 698,
702, 718, 764, 771, 865, 876, 886,
889, 911, 938, 961, 968, 984, 990,
998, 1001, 1018, 1034, 1055, 1056,
1094, 1114, 1139, 1145, 1152, 1154,
1157, 1164, 1169, 1173, 1177, 1179
Hymnus Veneri. dum in illius tutelam
Transëunt virgines, 621

I am the Doore, 1137
In amorem divinum, 1173
In faciem Augustiss. Regis à morbillis integram, 1
In Picturam Reverendissimi Episcopi, D. Andrews, 36
In Pigmaliona, 1082, 1111
In praise of Lessius, 7, 63, 107, 130, 133,
165, 171, 178, 179, 185, 192, 193,
285, 405, 406, 407, 581, 725, 927,
1117

In Reginam, Et sibi & Academiae semper parturientem, 12, 586
In resurrectionem Domini, 965
In Serenissimae Reginae partum hyemalem, 8, 94
In spinas demtas à Christi capite cruentatas, 1173
In vulnera Dei pendentis, 1129

Joann. 2. Aquae in vinum versae, 114,
152, 156, 180, 182, 205, 214, 221,
225, 232, 262, 264, 275, 280, 287,
293, 319, 333, 357, 360, 621, 635,
666, 713, 936, 1089, 1173
Joann. 5. Ad Bethesdae piscinam positus,
936
Joann. 16:33. Ego vici mundum, 621
Joann. 20. Christus ad Thomam, 621
Joh. 10. Ego sum ostium, 1137

Lauda Sion Salvatorem, 39, 289, 514,
685, 838, 968, 1179
Lectori, 6, 237
Letter to the Countess of Denbigh, 27,
28, 243, 335, 408, 420, 427, 487,
503, 510, 516, 607, 616, 673, 679,
705, 767, 775, 786, 850, 865, 866,
872, 922, 923, 927, 949, 961, 997,
998, 1006, 1009, 1024, 1046, 1049,
1055, 1056, 1094, 1146, 1157, 1171,
1175, 1179
Loves Horoscope, 111, 257, 261, 284,
309, 310, 311, 316, 318, 369, 400,
420, 619, 697, 854, 961, 1009, 1046,
1121, 1179
Luc. 1:18. Zacharias minùs credens, 25
Luc. 2. Quaerit Jesum suum beata Virgo,
389
Luke 2. Quaerit Jesum suum Maria, 456,
480
Luke 11. Blessed be the paps which Thou
hast sucked, 488, 509, 856, 963, 1010,
1056, 1159, 1166

Marc. 10. The blind cured by the word of
our Saviour, 1034
Marc. 10: 52. Ad verbum Dei sanatur
caecus, 25
Marke 4. Why are yee afraid, O yee of
little faith?, 962
Marke 12. (Give to Caesar—) (And to
God—), 179, 235
Mat. 28. Come see the place where the
Lord lay, 390

Matthew. 27. And he answered them nothing, 891, 923

Musicks Duell, 38, 62, 74, 76, 117, 125, 127, 129, 130, 134, 138, 148, 149, 153, 156, 163, 165; 167, 168, 171, 181, 186, 190, 200, 212, 216, 234, 235, 237, 244, 254, 255, 257, 260, 273, 279, 285, 293, 295, 302, 303, 307, 310, 311, 317, 318, 326, 338, 344, 351, 355, 369, 429, 438, 449, 459, 495, 498, 506, 527, 534, 541, 545, 551, 554, 564, 575, 580, 581, 605, 619, 628, 644, 661, 672, 693, 697, 721, 724, 730, 736, 776, 795, 818, 857, 861, 867, 882, 950, 980, 989, 1023, 1034, 1046, 1070, 1152, 1160, 1162, 1178, 1179

Ode on a Prayer-book, 116, 133, 153, 161, 171, 172, 175, 192, 200, 223, 291, 310, 354, 370, 411, 427, 489, 534, 613, 631, 636, 684, 717, 718, 735, 775, 780, 865, 944, 961, 971, 982, 1006, 1026, 1046, 1064, 1091, 1119, 1139, 1143, 1152, 1179

Office of the Holy Crosse, 535, 575, 926, 946, 962, 1055, 1061, 1139, 1164, 1179

O Gloriosa Domina, 153, 567, 575, 838, 951, 968, 1055, 1179

On a foule Morning, being then to take a journey, 254, 318, 496, 1061

On Hope, 143, 150, 285, 521, 692, 767, 786, 891, 903, 961, 999, 1023, 1055, 1171, 1179

On Mr. G. Herberts booke, The Temple, 22, 44, 201, 310, 496, 837, 961, 982

On Nanus mounted upon an Ant, 52, 170

On our crucified Lord Naked, and bloody, 535, 663, 692, 776, 791, 866, 881, 891, 923, 926, 990, 1010, 1070, 1139, 1173

On St. Peter cutting of Malchus his eare, 437

On the Blessed Virgins bashfulnesse, 214, 232

On the Frontispiece of Isaacsons Chronologie explained, 4, 187

On the still surviving markes of our Saviours wounds, 361, 926, 1122

On the wounds of our crucified Lord, 535, 619, 718, 819, 850, 866, 872, 891, 966, 1013, 1026, 1093, 1117, 1119, 1122, 1129, 1139

Ornatissimo viro Praeceptori sue colendissimo, Magistro Brook (Dedication of 1634 to Brooke), 6

Our Lord in his Circumcision to his Father, 520, 567, 699, 1139

Out of Catullus, 107, 111, 144, 453, 484, 614, 1072

Out of Grotius his Tragedy of Christes sufferinges, 274, 280, 575

Out of the Greeke Cupid's Cryer, 107

Out of the Italian. A Song, 192, 233, 303, 314, 438, 600, 1034, 1169

Out of the Italian. ('Love now no fire hath left him'), 233, 303, 867, 1169

Out of the Italian. ('Would any one the true cause find'), 233, 303, 716

Out of Virgil: In the praise of the Spring, 1023

A Panegyricke (Upon the Royal Family), 12, 115, 484, 586

Phaenicis Genethliacon & Epicedion, 1061

Principi recèns natae omen maternae indolis, 10, 89

Psalme 23, 63, 107, 154, 166, 283, 289, 383, 459, 600, 609, 735, 764, 928, 962, 1053

Psalme 137, 120, 134, 289, 338, 459, 609, 764, 866, 1053

Reverendo Admodùm viro Benjamin Lany SS. Theologiae Professori, Aulae Pembrochianae Custodi dignissimo, ex suorum minimis minimus R. C. custodiam coelestem P. (Dedication of 1634 to Laney), 6, 237

Rex Redux, 5, 755

Sampson to his Dalilah, 25

Sancta Maria Dolorum, 344, 355, 389, 411, 527, 535, 575, 690, 693, 764, 780, 838, 888, 968, 1010, 1026, 1055, 1056, 1114, 1164, 1179

A Song ('Lord, when the sense of thy sweet grace'), 283, 316, 451, 526, 632, 660, 696, 702, 722, 750, 867, 925, 973, 1013, 1071, 1138, 1143, 1169

Song upon the Bleeding Crucifix, 467, 535, 575, 587, 663, 696, 699, 706, 775, 800, 843, 851, 865, 891, 951, 1055, 1064, 1108

Sospetto d'Herode, 38, 90, 91, 92, 94, 95, 97, 98, 99, 102, 107, 108, 112, 115, 122, 123, 126, 127, 130, 133,

134, 139, 147, 148, 149, 152, 153, 154, 156, 158, 160, 165, 171, 183, 184, 193, 204, 213, 214, 215, 216, 217, 224, 235, 237, 241, 253, 254, 279, 281, 285, 300, 302, 303, 307, 315, 317, 344, 349, 355, 361, 398, 435, 459, 512, 519, 521, 541, 560, 575, 578, 581, 619, 661, 672, 725, 781, 811, 883, 884, 890, 962, 977, 984, 994, 996, 1043, 1050, 1068, 1097, 1100, 1101, 1122, 1157, 1178, 1179

The Teare, 144, 340, 344, 453, 459, 463, 507, 543, 575, 604, 614, 693, 725, 850, 933, 968, 982, 1034, 1080, 1115, 1172

Teresian poems (general), 114, 130, 254, 286, 290, 358, 370, 383, 428, 459, 461, 472, 495, 575, 578, 583, 612, 645, 646, 650, 653, 672, 676, 693, 711, 836, 847, 906, 915, 930, 938, 970, 1005, 1006, 1023, 1054, 1055, 1070, 1139, 1143, 1179. *See also* An Apologie for the fore-going Hymne, The Flaming Heart, and A Hymn to Sainte Teresa

To [Mrs. M. R.] Councel Concerning her Choise, 291, 370, 411, 437, 616, 1091, 1179

To our Lord, upon the Water made Wine, 223, 280, 1034

To Pontius washing his hands, 232

To Pontius washing his blood-stained hands, 278, 936, 984, 1031

To the Infant Martyrs, 99

To the Morning. Satisfaction for sleepe, 91, 158, 163, 254, 285, 292, 309, 310, 318, 628, 1018

To the Queen's Majesty, 329, 505

Two went up into the Temple to pray, 25, 214, 241, 302

Upon Bishop Andrewes his Picture before his Sermons, 2, 36, 593, 596

Upon Ford's two Tragedyes, 285, 318

Upon Lazarus his Teares, 432, 1034

Upon our Saviours Tombe wherein never man was laid, 965, 1041, 1070

Upon the birth of the Princesse Elizabeth, 586

Upon the Death of a Gentleman [Mr. Chambers], 171, 311, 326, 497, 954, 961, 1049

Upon the Death of the most desired Mr. Herrys, 34, 50, 178, 235, 386. *See also* Elegies on Mr. Herrys (general)

Upon the ensuing Treatises [of Mr. Shelford], 9, 115, 133, 191, 194, 961, 1034, 1088

Upon the Infant Martyrs, 1070

Upon the Kings coronation, 586

Upon the Sepulchre of our Lord, 1034

Upon the Thornes taken downe from our Lords head bloody, 535, 1173

Upon two greene Apricockes sent to Cowley by Sir Crashaw, 464, 521, 866, 961, 1023

Upon Venus putting on Mars his Armes, 1023

Venerabili viro Magistro Tournay, Tutori suo summè observando (Dedication of 1634 to Tourney), 6

Vexilla Regis, 338, 462, 698, 838, 944, 1055, 1137, 1164, 1179

Votiva Domus Petrensis Pro Domo Dei, 246, 1163

The Weeper, 63, 130, 144, 194, 195, 196, 197, 198, 218, 257, 277, 278, 284, 285, 302, 305, 307, 309, 311, 314, 323, 326, 330, 342, 344, 369, 372, 389, 401, 410, 412, 420, 432, 435, 438, 440, 448, 449, 455, 456, 459, 460, 463, 465, 479, 499, 506, 507, 516, 517, 518, 527, 541, 545, 551, 552, 554, 555, 563, 566, 572, 575, 580, 582, 585, 599, 611, 619, 624, 625, 626, 631, 633, 652, 655, 659, 661, 667, 671, 672, 693, 695, 711, 717, 718, 721, 730, 741, 757, 760, 764, 770, 775, 777, 797, 813, 814, 815, 822, 833, 844, 849, 850, 851, 859, 862, 864, 865, 878, 882, 884, 886, 890, 894, 911, 914, 922, 923, 930, 933, 942, 945, 948, 952, 956, 961, 962, 964, 968, 980, 982, 984, 986, 1006, 1010, 1024, 1026, 1046, 1054, 1055, 1056, 1058, 1062, 1064, 1070, 1073, 1075, 1086, 1090, 1097, 1107, 1108, 1116, 1119, 1127, 1128, 1129, 1130, 1131, 1136, 1139, 1140, 1143, 1152, 1159, 1166, 1170, 1172, 1173, 1178, 1179

Wishes. To his (supposed) Mistresse, 13, 22, 63, 107, 115, 203, 210, 214, 223, 247, 250, 253, 254, 257, 258, 273,

284, 285, 307, 310, 311, 316, 318, 326, 332, 337, 338, 345, 351, 355, 360, 361, 369, 370, 373, 378, 379, 400, 420, 428, 438, 449, 463, 467, 468, 487, 495, 503, 506, 515, 516, 530, 543, 580, 603, 611, 619, 628, 639, 645, 647, 655, 672, 679, 689, 693, 697, 707, 711, 721, 727, 785, 805, 837, 851, 858, 862, 866, 891, 908, 949, 961, 962, 966, 990, 1023, 1033, 1046, 1047, 1054, 1071, 1097, 1136, 1160, 1178, 1179

With Some Poems sent to a Gentlewoman. I, 274, 278

With Some Poems sent to a Gentlewoman. II, 274, 278